# The Administrative Manager

# The Administrative Manager

HAROLD T. SMITH, C.A.M.
WILLIAM H. BAKER
Brigham Young University

SRA®

SCIENCE RESEARCH ASSOCIATES, INC.
Chicago, Henley-on-Thames, Sydney, Toronto
A Subsidiary of IBM

| | |
|---|---|
| COMPOSITOR | Graphic Typesetting Service |
| ILLUSTRATOR | Boardworks |
| DESIGNER | Rick Chafian |
| ACQUISITION EDITOR | Robert Walczak |
| PROJECT EDITOR | Mary McVey Gill |

ILLUSTRATION CREDITS

We would like to thank the following for photographs they provided:

Patrick Christian, p. 4 top
General Mills, Inc., p. 12, 166
Nile C. Greenhalgh, pp. 4 (top left and bottom), 9, 14, 88, 89, 98, 99, 100, 132, 266, 267, 434, 436, 438, 450, 456, 459, 473, 485
John Larsen, p. 407
Wide World Photos, p. 67

Cover photo by John Larsen



**Library of Congress Cataloging in Publication Data**

Smith, Harold T. 1932–
The administrative manager.

Includes index.
1. Office management. I. Baker, William H., 1944– joint author, II. Title.
HF5547.S577 651 78-6085
ISBN 0-574-20030-4

654

# Contents

# Preface

*The Administrative Manager* was written to help you gain an understanding of the work of an administrative manager and develop some managerial techniques to become more effective in working with people. It should also help you to better understand how offices operate and various functions people in offices perform.

People are the focal point of this book. Regardless of what you do in life, you will be interacting with people. As a leader or manager of any type, you will be attempting to get results through others. Other administrative- and office-management textbooks emphasize machines, equipment, and procedures. While these things are important, they are only tools and should receive less attention than the number-one resource of managers: *people.*

If you apply the principles you study in this book, you will become more effective as a manager and as a person. You will find yourself doing such things as setting objectives, organizing your time, actively listening to people, comparing all the alternatives while making various decisions, and turning over more responsibility to others.

Although the "office of the future" has become a very significant topic in current management literature and office technology is developing at a rapid rate, we must not overemphasize the technological side of office administration. Time and time again, recognized authorities in the field point out the importance of not sacrificing the well-being of the individual in the race to develop an automated office.

We hope many of the principles of this book will ring true in your mind and that you will be stimulated to delve further into the subject of office management.

Many practical business examples are incorporated into this textbook. These examples are based on the experience of the authors in business and governmental organizations. Our hope is that these real experiences will give you insight into office operations and the role of the administrative manager.

The authors are grateful to many people for their help in making this book possible. Without the support of the authors' wives and families the work could not have been accomplished. Particular thanks go to G. Edward Nelson and Merrill Bateman of the Brigham Young University administration, who provided necessary resource support. We are thankful to the following individuals who made many helpful comments during the reviewing process: Helen Brown, Auburn University; Mildred Butterfield, Mount Hood Community College; Randy E. Cone, University of New Orleans; Richard D. Featheringham, Central Michigan University; Kenneth Harsha, Central Washington State College; V. Wayne Klemin, Utah State University; Robert Kusek, Southern Illinois University; Mark Langemo, University of North Dakota; Max McKitrick, Western Michigan University; William Mitchell, University of Wisconsin at Eau Claire; Dennis L. Mott, Oklahoma State University at Stillwater; Frank Nelson, Eastern Washington State College; Alice Nuttall, Kent State University; Dwayne Schramm, California State University at Fresno; Philip Semprevivo, State University of New York at Albany; Lovena Tucker, University of New Orleans; and Patricia A. Wells, Oregon State University at Corvallis.

H.T.S.

W.H.B.

# PART ONE

# The Concept of Administrative Management

In Part One, background on the role of the administrative manager is provided, and emphasis is placed on working with people and getting results through them.

Chapter 1 presents an overview of management, and the terms *management* and *manager* are defined. Resources, basic management functions, and objectives are discussed, and the *systems* concept is introduced. Duties and qualifications of the manager are explained. The various levels of management and profiles of typical managers are presented. This chapter also zeroes in on the specialized part of management known as *administrative management*. First, the role of the administrative manager is discussed. The basic objective of administrative management is to provide information to top management to help them make decisions. Second, the selection of a career in administrative management is discussed; the advantages and disadvantages are examined.

Chapter 2 compares effective and ineffective managers, and the difference between effectiveness and efficiency is explored. A leadership model is presented, and leadership styles are discussed.

Understanding yourself, understanding others, and developing interpersonal relationships are the major topics presented in Chapter 3.

# 1

# Overview of Management and Administrative Management

## MANAGEMENT AND THE MANAGER

What mental image do you get from the word *manager?* Depending upon your experience, that picture will vary, but many people will think of a person who doesn't do any physical work. Your image of the manager is likely to be a *man* with his feet on his desk or a man playing golf. You also may be wondering how management applies to you directly. Let's find out.

If you are not a manager now, the probability is that you will be one in the future. This prediction holds true even if you aren't a man, or don't prop your feet up on a desk, or don't play golf. Let's come to an agreement on what the terms *manager* and *management* mean:

> A *manager* is a person who has authority and responsibility for getting specific objectives or results accomplished through other people. *Management,* then, is an art and science performed by managers for some type of organization.

While the focus of this book is on business organizations, the principles and practices discussed may be applied to any kind of organization—formal or informal—and to any type of setting—business or nonbusiness.

Managers are found in all of the following areas: sales, administration, finance, production, farm, city, personnel, and accounting. Our definition also includes homemakers, teachers, recreational leaders, youth leaders, clergy, and many others. People in all of these areas are concerned with getting results through others (see Figure 1-1).

The basic objective for each of these areas will vary. For example, the sales manager is concerned with maximizing the amount of sales for the organization. The personnel manager is involved with selecting and maintaining an

*Figure 1-1.* Three Types of Managers—Farm, Home, and Sales

effective work force. The homemaker is concerned with the efficient operation of the home and the rearing of the children. Teachers are attempting to impart information, develop skills, and mold character. While their objectives are different, all these individuals may be considered managers because they are trying to get results through other people.

As the title reveals, the focus of this book is on the administrative manager, one who has the special objective of supplying information to top management for decision-making purposes. Administrative managers work with office personnel to provide administrative services—those office activities that aid communication and the flow of information and ideas. Data processing, telephone communication, and mail services are examples of administrative services. You'll learn more about the administrative manager in the latter part of this chapter.

### Resources Available to the Manager

Managers have certain resources available to them to help accomplish their objectives, and their primary resource, of course, is people. Other important resources include materials and supplies, machinery and equipment, capital or money, and procedures or methods. An easy way to remember these resources is to think of them as the five m's: men and women, materials, machinery, money, and methods. The manager's task is to accomplish specified objectives through the use of these resources. Figure 1-2 shows a management model that illustrates how resources relate to basic functions and objectives.

### Management's Basic Functions

Managers perform four basic functions:

1. Planning
2. Organizing
3. Controlling
4. Leading

*Planning* involves setting goals and developing action plans to accomplish these goals. Planning can be divided into three essential stages—long range,

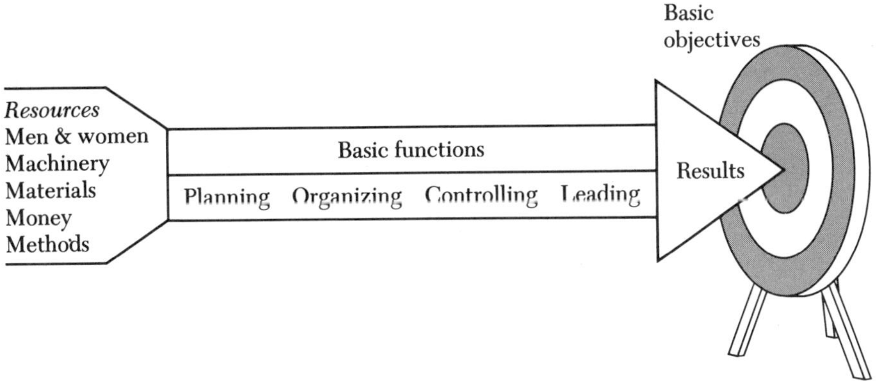


*Figure 1-2.* Model of the Management Process

intermediate range, and short range. To engage in effective long-range planning means visualizing what the future will be like five, ten, or twenty years from now. For every long-term goal, a number of intermediate and short-term goals are needed; their accomplishment will insure reaching the long-range goals if proper planning has taken place.

*Organizing* means arranging or forming resources into a complete and functioning whole. Our focus is still on people, with other resources such as materials and machinery available to help accomplish the work. People must be given specific assignments so they know what they are expected to accomplish. Authority and responsibility must be spelled out.

*Controlling* is a regulating action that is concerned with monitoring action plans to make sure that goals are accomplished. An organization's budget is an example of a control device that is very familiar to most managers. Any significant deviations from the approved budget must be explained, and action must be taken to reduce expenditures or to gain approval for increases.

*Leading* is the function that refers to getting people to want to achieve specified objectives. While this function is primarily concerned with motivating, coordinating, and directing, in its broadest sense it also refers to determining personnel policies, selecting, orienting, and training. *Actuating* is another term that is sometimes used to convey the same meaning as leading.

We can illustrate these four basic management functions in an example of a small movie-theater manager, John Havir. John is responsible for the profitable and successful operation of a theater in a small midwestern college community. He must make sure that the movies shown adhere to local decency standards and appeal to young college students. He is responsible for ticket sales, ushering, film projection, snack bar sales, advertising and sales promotion, theater and ground maintenance, finance and accounting, and personnel management. John does a great amount of *planning*—both on a long-term and a short-term basis. He schedules movies for a year in advance. He schedules the theater for use by community groups that need a large meeting facility. He plans special promotional events such as the annual children's Christmas party and the community talent contest. Also, he plans maintenance activities, advertising, office systems, and budgets.

Because John can't do everything himself, *organizing* is also an important function for him. He makes specific assignments to people in the following jobs: ticket clerks, ushers, projectionists, snack bar clerks, and maintenance persons. John uses *controlling* procedures to make sure that operations go according to plan. Expense records and ticket sales reports keep John informed and on top of what's happening. If ticket sales begin to drop, John examines the effectiveness of the advertising programs, the quality of films, and the quality of services. If expenses rise too quickly, John tries to find out why.

Finally, *leading* is the key function for John. He tries to be an example and to show personal interest in each employee by listening to each individual. If he can inspire his people to do their best, they will move on their own to try to make the theater a success.

## MANAGEMENT AS A SYSTEM

In our daily lives, we encounter many *systems*. Digestive systems, nervous systems, and computer systems are familiar examples. As shown in Figure 1-3, all systems consist basically of three parts: input, processing, and output. Also, feedback, or information about the quality of the output, is obtained; feedback may result in changes being made to the input or to the method of processing.

In the digestive system, the input is food and drink, processing involves chewing and the enzymatic action in the stomach, and finally the absorption process results in output of amino acids and glucose into the blood stream. Output also includes the waste products given off by the body.

In manufacturing, we can name many systems. For example, in the production system, raw materials are purchased as *input*. *Processing* involves the fabrication of the raw materials into a product. The product, which is distributed to wholesalers or retailers and ultimately to the consumer, is the *output* of the system.

Another example is an information system. Input involves data such as sales or expense figures. Processing includes arranging the data in proper form and making arithmetic calculations. Output from the system is produced in the form of printed reports.

Just as we may look at various phases of nature and of manufacturing as systems, we also may look at management as a system. The input to the system may be thought of as the resources that were discussed previously—men and women, money, materials, machinery, and methods. Processing in man-

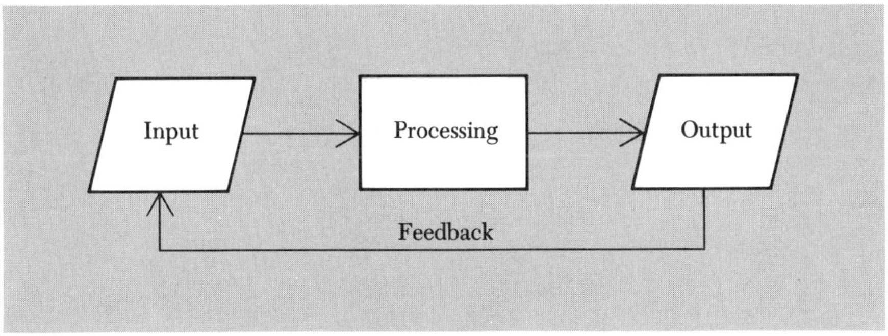


*Figure 1-3.* The Structure of a System

agement involves the basic functions—planning, organizing, controlling, and leading. Output in a management system consists of reports, decisions, and the effective operations of the organization. In other words, output is the result obtained.

### Duties of the Manager

Let's look at some of the major duties of the manager. Figure 1-4 illustrates the point that the major emphasis of a manager is people. All the duties on the inner circle relate to people. When managers are asked about the major duties or competencies that are critical to their effectiveness, they focus their responses on people-oriented activities. Managers tend to emphasize such

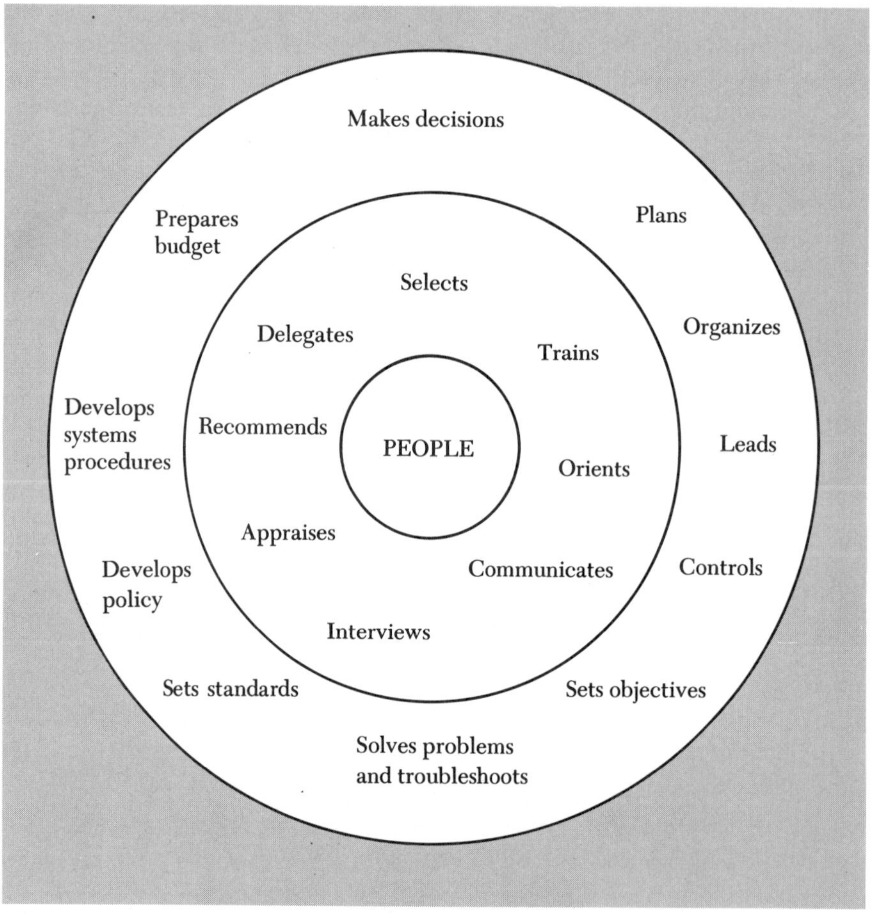


*Figure 1-4.* Duties of the Manager

people-oriented duties as selecting and training people, communicating with people, appraising them in relation to their work, and delegating specific tasks to them.

Duties found on the outer circle of Figure 1-4 tend to relate to things and ideas, although even here people are heavily involved. For example, the duty of setting standards is an abstract idea, but it has meaning only as standards are applied to the work of people.

The duties discussed in this section are not intended to be a complete listing, but they do present some of the major duties of managers. Also, the focus on people is emphasized.

### Qualifications of the Manager

What qualifications are to be considered in hiring a manager? Some of these qualifications are shown in the following list:

Gets along well with people and influences them to do what needs to be done

Communicates well with people, both orally and in writing

Conducts himself or herself well in face-to-face interviews

Has good eye contact—does not look away continually

Is honest and has good moral character

Is enthusiastic about life in general and certain things in particular

Is dependable and follows through

Has neat appearance

Has a positive attitude

Sets a good example

Thinks about the consequences of his or her actions, is able to define and solve problems, is able to prevent problems

Has good vision of the future and sees the big picture

Is committed to work and sticks with problems until they are solved

Anticipates questions the boss will have and has answers available

Is loyal to fellow employees

Engages in self-development

Is active in professional organizations

Believes in himself or herself, has a good self-image, believes in his or her ability to select good people and to help develop them into effective employees

Of course, not all managers have all of these qualifications, and those factors considered most vital to the manager's future success would be selected.

Many young high school and even college students expect to become presidents of large corporations or to become *consultants* to business when they graduate, but these opportunities just don't develop suddenly. Many business graduates recently out of college will be placed by their new employers into some kind of training program that may extend from one week to one year or more. Even after completing an extensive training program, they are likely to be placed in a staff position[1] or be assigned as an assistant section head or some similar position. Most business graduates will find themselves in sales or in administration. The chances are very good that someday they will find themselves in a middle-management position as some type of administrative manager.

### Levels of Management

Three basic levels of management exist in most large- and medium-size organizations, and even in many smaller organizations: middle managers report to top managers, and supervisory managers report to middle managers.

***Top management*** is primarily responsible for *policy* making and long-range planning. Policies are statements that outline the organization's general position pertaining to matters that affect the organization or the people relating to the organization. For example, the organization may have a policy that employees may use copy machines to make personal copies if they pay for the cost of the copies at a specific, designated rate. Another example of a policy is a statement issued by the organization indicating that employees may not hold a job with another organization for which any type of monetary compensation is given, unless special permission is obtained from the employee's supervisor. (Monetary compensation means wages, salary, or other benefits given for a person's services.)

Long-range planning refers to overall organizational plans that extend into the future for a year or longer. Occasionally, top management may be looking ahead 20 years or more. For example, if Janet Howard, the president of Vido Company, is now 45 years old, she may need to start thinking about developing a replacement who can take over when she reaches retirement at around age 65.

Let's examine the top management level by looking at an example of a top manager in action. Roger Carr is an executive vice-president for Sun International Corp. He is responsible for the successful operation of the corporation which owns 26 radio and television broadcasting stations across the country. Carr is a friendly man and gets along well with his employees, his boss, and his fellow managers. He requests that his employees call him "Rog."

Carr spends most of his time in meetings. He either meets with executives in the headquarters of the corporation or he travels and meets with representatives of each of the broadcasting units. Carr is primarily concerned

*Figure 1-5.* Conferences Are an Important Aspect of the Top Manager's Job

with making and implementing company policy and with developing long-range plans.

Carr is also concerned with developing relationships with influential people. These people include Sun's president, Edgar Martin; members of the board of directors; executives of other broadcasting companies; government officials, including legislators; and executives of other corporations which use Sun's facilities for advertising.

Carr enjoys his work. He gains a feeling of satisfaction from seeing the company grow and achieve new heights of success. He enjoys seeing his ideas become realities. However, not everything is good about Roger Carr's job. He usually works long hours and occasionally takes a briefcase full of work home in spite of advice to the contrary from "management experts." Also, being out of town so much causes disruption in Carr's family life. He enjoys being with his wife and their three children, but he doesn't seem to be able to spend as much time with them as he would like. He does try to make his time with them count.

*Figure 1-6.* The Middle Manager Is a Communications Link

Roger Carr is a success in the eyes of most people. He is an effective top manager. Many administrative managers work with a person like Roger Carr.

***Middle management*** serves as a buffer between top and supervisory management levels. Middle managers implement on a departmental level the policy that has been developed by top management. For example, Bob Kartchner (Figure 1-6), manager of the accounting department, may send a memo to all accounting department supervisors indicating the general statement of policy that employees are not allowed to hold outside jobs. An additional statement might be issued which states that preparing income tax statements for private individuals on a paid basis would be considered legitimate as long as this activity does not interfere with the employee's effectiveness on the job.

In this example, Bob Kartchner is a middle manager who is charged with implementing a policy developed by top management. The accounting department manager is primarily concerned with one department as contrasted with top management's concern for all departments. The accounting department manager works through the supervisors in the department to have policies placed into effect. One example illustrates the strategic position of middle management in causing the organization to move forward smoothly. In essence, the middle manager is a communications link who interprets for departmental supervisors the direction supplied by top management. On the other hand, the middle manager provides feedback to top management on daily operations supplied by the supervisors in the organization. The middle manager also coordinates with other middle managers to keep operations flowing smoothly.

In addition to implementing policy, middle managers develop intermediate range plans. The middle manager tends to plan and think in terms of this month, this year, and next year as contrasted with the top manager who tends to look further into the future. For example, the middle manager may be concerned with the quarterly departmental financial report or the yearly departmental progress report.

***Supervisory management*** persons are primarily concerned with daily operations and within their sections try to implement directives supplied by middle management. A good example is an individual who supervises a staff of order-entry clerks in a publishing company (Figure 1-7). The order-entry clerks process the daily orders for textbooks that are received by the company. To process these orders, the order-entry clerk must check on the credit rating of the purchaser, the availability of the product, the price, and other specifications. Because schools are generally interested in receiving their textbooks as soon as possible after ordering, middle management directs that orders need not be allowed to pile up on a day-to-day basis. So the goal for the department is to process all the orders that have been received in the previous 24-hour period. Since the spring and fall are busy times, frequently the supervisor must actually assist the clerks in the processing of orders. He or she must possess all of the skills of the clerks in addition to demonstrating the necessary leadership to get the job done, particularly in times of stress. Since accuracy is extremely important, the supervisor must be vigilant to be sure that correct prices are given, accurate shipping orders are transmitted to the warehouse, and all other details are attended to carefully.

Supervisors are in a delicate position because they must represent the interests of both management and employees. To illustrate this point, consider the case of Tim O'Connel, supervisor of administrative support services in the Redlands Insurance Company. Tim's boss, Ruby Schultz, says that the departmental executives need increased and improved administrative support. She thinks that the executives are having to do too many routine clerical tasks such as filing and errand running. Ruby also cautions Tim that he must operate within his budget. Tim feels that his people are doing a reasonably good job now and that he has only two alternatives to improve service: (1) hire more people or (2) find a better method for improving operations. As an effective supervisor, Tim must find a way of providing improved support to the executive without increasing costs and while maintaining good relations with his people.

*Figure 1-7.* Supervisory Management Persons Try to Implement Directives of Middle Management

## ADMINISTRATIVE MANAGEMENT

To this point, the discussion has centered on management in general; now we will focus on administrative management.

### Role of the Administrative Manager

A key idea to remember is that administrative managers are concerned with getting work done through people. All the principles of management discussed in the first section of this chapter apply to administrative managers.

Two aspects of working effectively with people are: (1) goal orientation and (2) employee development. Goals must be set so that work is accomplished properly and on time; for example, goals are important in assuring that reports are complete, accurate, and submitted by the due date. Employee development means that administrative managers must be concerned with their employees as people and accept the premise that all people have inherent worth as individuals. Effective administrative managers try to help their people grow and develop—to help them stretch to reach their potential. Managers find that one of the best ways to teach others is to be the model or the example of the point they are trying to teach. By being conscious of their own strengths and weaknesses and by constantly trying to improve, administrative managers have greater influence on their employees.

Like other managers, administrative managers must be effective communicators, since communication is the heart of all management practices. Effective communication results in understanding between people, in good morale, and in a strong desire on the part of the employees to want to do their best. When this understanding is lacking, management is ineffective.

Administrative managers are at all levels in the organization: top, middle, and supervisory. Of course, those at the top level are concerned primarily with making decisions that will affect the entire organization. For example, they may be in charge of developing an information system that affects all persons in the company. At the top level, they are supervising middle managers and working with other top-level managers. To illustrate, a typical top-level administrative manager in an insurance company might supervise the administrative services manager, data processing manager, and policy services manager (policy services involve handling and keeping policies up to date). This administrative manager might also work with the director of marketing, the director of claims, and the director of finance and accounting.

Relatively few administrative managers reach the top ranks of management because administration has not been recognized as one of the traditional, major functions of an organization. However, this view of administration is in transition, and some major corporations have vice-presidents for administration (or some similar title). The trend appears to be that more and more organizations will have administrative managers at the top level.

Currently, most administrative managers tend to be at the middle level of management. They coordinate and supervise the work of the supervisors and work with other middle managers. Commonly, administrative managers at this middle level report to the controller or vice-president of finance and accounting. These administrative managers carry out policy and plans that have been made by top management; for example, they may work with computer personnel to set up a new accounting system.

At the supervisory level, managers work directly with office employees who are doing the work. Examples of the type of work being done are typing letters, memos, and reports; filing documents; running small computers; finding information on microfilm; and operating copy or duplicating machines.

Administrative supervisors are responsible for the office work being accomplished and, therefore, must be familiar with all daily operations. They operate under the direction of middle managers.

### Administrative Management Objectives

As you read earlier, the basic objective of administrative management is to provide information to top management that will serve as the basis for decisions. This information must be in the proper form and be timely, accurate, and concise. Without proper information, the president or general manager would be unable to make the decisions that determine the course of the organization.

A secondary objective is to provide this information at the lowest possible cost. Administrative costs have a major impact on the profit picture of an organization. For example, a company averaging 6 percent net profit on gross sales of $10,000,000 would earn $600,000 profit in a year. Fifty office employees averaging $12,000 salary per year would earn $600,000 per year. Cutting the staff by five employees would have the same impact on profits as increasing sales by $1,000,000 ($5 \times \$12,000 = \$60,000$ salaries per year; $0.06 \times \$1,000,000 = \$60,000$ profit on sales).

Upon recognizing how much impact reducing office costs can have, some top managers try to cut the office force to a bare minimum and thereby increase their profits even more. However, if the office force is doing its job effectively, any such drastic reductions are disastrous to the company because of the interference with the flow of information in the organization. A business soon loses effectiveness when necessary information is not available. This example should point out to the administrative manager both the importance of controlling costs and of being as efficient and effective as possible.

### Administrative Services

Five areas of major concern to administrative managers include records management, systems analysis, data processing, word processing, and communication services. (Other managers may not become directly involved in these administrative areas.) These five areas of *administrative services* help to achieve the basic objective of getting the proper information to top management to aid in the decision-making process. One way of determining if a manager is an administrative manager is by checking to see if he or she is involved with any or all of these administrative services.

### Other Titles for Administrative Managers

Administrative managers may have many titles; consequently, difficulty may be encountered in attempting to classify the type of manager being considered. Some other names for the administrative manager used in business and other organizations include manager of administrative or office services, administrative assistant, vice-president, personnel manager, director of administration, administrative office manager, and office manager. Sometimes the only way to determine if the person is really an administrative manager is to look at the specific duties he or she performs.

### Duties of the Administrative Manager

Table 1-1 shows major activities performed by administrative managers and the percentage of managers who perform these duties frequently or infrequently. Most of these activities center around working with people, providing administrative services, and developing systems and procedures for accomplishing the objective of providing information to top management. Administrative managers become very heavily involved with personnel management and communication activities.

Many administrative managers may also have responsibility for building maintenance and security, cafeteria and vending machine operations, and automobile fleets and pools. All of these services can be vital to the efficient operation of a business.

As part of their systems work, administrative managers spend much time evaluating new equipment that is available—a time-consuming but necessary aspect since office technology is moving very rapidly. John B. Dykeman, executive editor of *Modern Office Procedures,* reported in June, 1976, that the number of significant office products introduced during the previous four months was perhaps more than for any similar previous period in industry history. Administrative managers must be familiar with these new products and must be able to determine which products would be most helpful in solving office problems and increasing worker productivity.

Keeping updated on office technology developments is a major task. Four major sources of product information include: (1) current periodicals, (2) vendors, (3) equipment shows, and (4) seminars. Periodicals with which every administrative manager should be familiar are *The Office, Administrative Management, Modern Office Procedures, Word Processing World, Word Processing, Words, Information and Records Management,* and *Infosystems.* Vendors of office equipment are eager to have their salespeople demonstrate their equipment and provide current information. Equipment shows bring together many vendors with their equipment to provide administrative managers a convenient means of comparing products. Seminars conducted by experts present unbiased information about products and current office equipment trends.

Armed with all of this information and with stimulating new ideas on technology, administrative managers are the logical choices to become the agents who will introduce change into their organizations. They may often face obstacles when attempting to get people to do things differently, but change is vital if the office is to keep pace with the increasing demand for information.

**Table 1-1. Activities of Administrative Managers**

| *Type of activity* | *Number of administrative managers performing* | *Often* | *Seldom* |
|---|---|---|---|
| 1. Personnel hiring and relations | 22 | 90.9 | 9.1 |
| 2. Written communication (letters and reports) | 22 | 86.3 | 13.7 |
| 3. Job analysis | 22 | 77.2 | 22.8 |
| 4. Oral communications (public and employees) | 21 | 90.4 | 9.6 |
| 5. Forms design and control | 21 | 52.3 | 47.7 |
| 6. Purchase and control of office machines, supplies, and furnishings | 20 | 65.0 | 35.0 |
| 7. Systems and procedures analysis and design | 20 | 65.0 | 35.0 |
| 8. Office design, layout, and other building responsibilities | 20 | 60.0 | 40.0 |
| 9. Records management | 19 | 68.4 | 31.6 |
| 10. Procedures writing | 19 | 57.8 | 42.2 |
| 11. Organization analysis and development | 19 | 57.8 | 42.2 |
| 12. Planning (with others) | 18 | 88.8 | 11.2 |
| 13. Planning (alone) | 18 | 83.8 | 16.2 |
| 14. Staff meetings | 18 | 83.8 | 16.7 |
| 15. Work measurement, standards, and cost of output | 18 | 72.2 | 27.8 |
| 16. Budget planning | 17 | 64.7 | 35.3 |
| 17. Mailing services | 17 | 52.9 | 47.1 |
| 18. Punched cards | 16 | 56.2 | 43.7 |
| 19. Reproductive services | 16 | 66.6 | 33.4 |
| 20. Cost study | 15 | 66.6 | 33.4 |
| 21. Compensation plans and fringe benefits | 13 | 38.5 | 61.5 |

*Source:* Gene W. Schmidt and William C. Lappe, "Analysis of the Role of the Office Manager," *The Delta Pi Epsilon Journal*, November, 1973, p. 27.

### Selection of a Career in Administrative Management

***Advantages.*** The work of administrative managers is challenging. They are constantly faced with problems to be solved—the problems of people and those of a rapidly expanding technology. They are in the mainstream of business operations because office operations serve as the nerve center for each organization.

***Disadvantages.*** However, some people do not enjoy the challenge and the heavy responsibility associated with administrative management. Discouragement may set in when people on an office staff don't come through as they are expected to and when plans don't materialize. Frequently, while in the process of developing problem solutions, administrative managers come face to face with the realities of organizational life. For example, some people with power don't want to see things changed; these people are likely to be defensive and fearful that change would disturb their area of self-interest. Also, administrative managers may have long hours at work and extra work to take home if they don't plan and organize properly.

### Preparation for the Administrative Manager

What is the best preparation for becoming an administrative manager? Surveys of administrative managers have been conducted to try to answer this question, and the following information is based on these studies.[2,3]

Students and others who have administrative management as their career objective should obtain a bachelor's degree in administrative management or a closely related field such as business management or accounting. For those who aspire to reach the top levels of management, master's degrees in business administration are appropriate.

Four major types of qualifications include: (1) reasoning ability, (2) communication ability, (3) mathematical ability, (4) interpersonal relations ability.

Administrative managers need to be able to think clearly and to apply knowledge and thought processes to practical organizational problems. They need to be able to solve practical problems and to deal with many variables in situations where limited standardization exists; for example, they may need to reduce excessive absenteeism or to select a specific item of office equipment.

In the area of communication, they should be able to converse easily with superiors and subordinates concerning routine daily activities. They should have the ability to use the English language correctly in a variety of communication situations; they should be able to write reports, give oral presentations, interview, counsel, and advise both superiors and subordinates.

An intermediate level of mathematical development is also required of administrative managers. At this level, candidates should be able to perform ordinary arithmetic and higher mathematical procedures in standard, practical situations. Advanced background levels are desirable as bases for rational thinking, but candidates will not necessarily need to apply their advanced mathematical and statistical knowledge to work situations.

Ability to develop effective interpersonal relationships and to get results is also a primary qualification for administrative managers. Interviews with administrative managers continually reinforce the importance of this ability to get results through people. Technical aspects of the work are secondary to human aspects in the minds of most administrative managers. In one research study, administrative managers were asked to rank and to rate various knowledges and skills as either required, desired, or not required. The results of this survey are reported in Table 1-2; note the emphasis given to people-related qualifications.

In Table 1-2, we see that the seven top-ranking skills or knowledge—human relations, written communications, oral communications, supervision, office organization and planning, personnel management, and accounting—are considered to be "required." Knowledge and skills that are considered "desirable" are finance, procedures and systems analysis, data processing, economics, business law, industrial organization, work simplification, business mathematics, records management, business statistics, purchasing, marketing, forms design and control, duplicating equipment, time and motion studies, and office machines.

### Career Ladder

A career ladder is the progression of jobs through which individual employees can expect to progress. Many college graduates hoping to build a career in administrative management can anticipate going into an on-the-job or formal company training program. The training period may last from a week or two up to a full year or more.

Other individuals in the company who have not received a college education come into business at the lower levels and work themselves up through the ranks. When a high rate of unemployment exists and demand for college graduates is low, many college graduates have been forced to take low-level positions and compete on that level for promotions. Those people who show the most promise are likely also to receive some company-sponsored supervisory training.

Whether the prospective administrative managers are college graduates or not, they are likely to start out in management as supervisors or assistant supervisors. Most likely, they will be responsible for one of the administrative services.

Effective supervisors have the opportunity of being promoted to middle management, which is the level at which administrative managers are classified. Some highly qualified individual may eventually move to the ranks of top management. In large information-processing service organizations such as insurance companies, administrative managers may be classified as top management and may hold the title of vice-president.

### Professional Activity

***Professional organizations.*** The Administrative Management Society (A.M.S.) is a professional organization intended specifically for administrative managers. Over 13,000 members are organized into 150 chapters located

**Table 1-2. How Administrative Managers Ranked and Rated Importance of Knowledge and Skills Required of Them**

| *Rank* | *Skill and/or knowledge* | *Percentage rating item as:* *Required* | *Desired* | *Not required* |
|---|---|---|---|---|
| 1 | Human relations | 84 | 16 | — |
| 2 | Written communication | 85 | 14 | 1 |
| 3 | Oral communication | 87 | 12 | 1 |
| 4 | Supervision | 85 | 13 | 2 |
| 5 | Office organization and planning | 68 | 28 | 4 |
| 6 | Personnel management | 61 | 37 | 2 |
| 7 | Accounting | 54 | 41 | 5 |
| 8 | Finance | 35 | 51 | 14 |
| 9 | Procedures and systems analysis | 40 | 51 | 9 |
| 10 | Data processing | 26 | 61 | 13 |
| 11 | Economics | 25 | 62 | 13 |
| 12 | Business law | 17 | 67 | 16 |
| 13 | Industrial organization | 23 | 48 | 29 |
| 14 | Work simplification | 35 | 55 | 10 |
| 15 | Business math | 32 | 56 | 12 |
| 15 | Records management | 37 | 50 | 13 |
| 16 | Business statistics | 15 | 70 | 15 |
| 17 | Investments | 10 | 36 | 54 |
| 17 | Purchasing | 28 | 44 | 28 |
| 17 | Marketing | 11 | 55 | 34 |
| 18 | Forms design and control | 24 | 58 | 18 |
| 18 | Duplicating equipment | 33 | 43 | 24 |
| 18 | Time and motion studies | 16 | 45 | 39 |
| 19 | Office machines | 34 | 47 | 19 |
| 19 | Credit and collection | 16 | 28 | 56 |

*Source:* Harold T. Smith and S. ElVon Warner, *Administrative Office Management Preparation*, Brigham Young University Press, 1971.

throughout the United States, Canada, and the world. The following services are provided by the society: publications, survey reports, management information service, conferences and seminars, educational programs, and a professional accreditation program (Certified Administrative Management).

One of the primary A.M.S. benefits is associating and sharing ideas with other managers who are in similar positions.

Other professional organizations that administrative managers may elect to join include the American Management Association, Records Management Association, Data Processing Management Association, Association for Systems Management, and International Word Processing Association.

***Certified Administrative Management (C.A.M.).*** C.A.M. is a professional designation that is similar to the Certified Public Accountant (C.P.A.) title (see Figure 1-8). In this program, sponsored by A.M.S., candidates must pass a series of five examinations and meet other requirements of experience, leadership ability, and character. Further details on this program can be obtained by writing to: The Director of Professionalization, Administration Management Society, Maryland Road, Willow Grove, Pennsylvania 19090.

## *Summary*

Managers are people who have authority and are responsible for getting results accomplished through other people. The principles and techniques of management are applicable in any type of organization, not just in business. Managers may be concerned with a variety of areas, but if they are trying to get specific results through other people, we classify them as administrative managers.

Managers have the following resources available to them: men and women, machinery, materials, money, and methods. They perform the basic management functions of planning, organizing, controlling, and leading in order to achieve designated results. Management may also be looked upon as a system, with input, processing, and output as the basic components of the system. Resources, functions, and decision making coincide with each of the components of the system. Managers perform a variety of specific duties, most of which relate to people as the key source. Qualifications for managers center

*Figure 1-8.* Official Logo for the Certified Administrative Manager (C.A.M.). Used by permission of the Administrative Management Society.

around qualities which are admirable in any person. To be an effective manager or leader, the individual must first be an effective person.

College graduates starting on their business careers will begin in some type of management training program or at the employee level. They will work their way up through the ranks of supervisory and middle management; a few will eventually find themselves in positions of top management.

Top management is primarily concerned with decision and policy making and long-range planning. Middle management serves as a buffer between the other two levels and is primarily concerned with implementing top-level decisions and with intermediate-level planning. The supervisor is mainly concerned with daily operations.

Administrative management is a demanding, challenging field. Administrative managers at the middle management level are key members of the management team, and their primary objective is to provide information to top management for decision-making purposes. To accomplish this objective, they involve themselves with administrative services: records management, systems analysis, data processing, word processing, and communication services. Administrative managers may be known by a variety of titles. Most of their time is spent in managing team members, developing systems and procedures, and providing administrative services.

People desiring to prepare for the position of administrative manager should graduate from college with a major in administrative management, business management, or accounting. Reasoning, communication, and mathematical abilities are important areas of qualification, although advanced or technical levels are not normally required. Training in the following areas is important: human relations, written and oral communications, supervision, office organization and planning, personnel management, and accounting.

College graduates going into the field of administrative management can expect to receive further training and supervisory experience before going on to the middle-management level. Most administrative managers are at this level, and a few will move into the ranks of top management.

Now that you have had a brief exposure to management and the job of the administrative manager, look next at the effective leader. What does the effective leader do? What does the ineffective leader do? What styles of management are there? How can you decide what style would be most effective for you? The next chapter will help you find the answers to these and other questions.

## *Review and Discussion Questions*

1. Do the terms *manager* and *leader* have the same meaning?
2. Do you think that you can properly make the statement that *all* people are managers? Why or why not?

3. Briefly explain why the four basic functions of management are essential.
4. Which of the basic functions is most important? Justify your answer.
5. Why can management be considered a system? How do resources, functions, and results relate to the management systems concept?
6. If you were required to select someone to fill the position of manager, what qualifications do you think would be most critical? Why?
7. What opportunities in management does the typical college graduate have? Does the noncollege graduate who is working full time in business have good prospects for a career in management?
8. How does the staff person get his ideas implemented in business?
9. Compare and contrast the roles of top, middle, and supervisory managers. Does the size of the company affect the nature of the duties that a top manager will perform?
10. Why would an organization have a difficult time in functioning if the administrative management function were absent?
11. The title "administrative manager" has to a large degree replaced the title "office manager." Why do you think this has happened?
12. Considering the advantages and disadvantages of the job of administrative manager, do you think a career in this field would be attractive to you?
13. Why has technology had a major impact on the field of administrative management?
14. Do you think the administrative manager must be technically competent to operate all equipment in the office, including the computer? Why? If this statement were made about an administrative supervisor would your answer be the same? Explain.
15. Why must the administrative manager balance concern for production with concern for development and welfare of the individual employee?
16. Explain why communication is at the heart of all management practices.
17. Would an administrative manager be wise to reduce administrative costs to the lowest possible amount? Why?
18. Why are administrative services important to an organization?

## *Application Exercises*

For each of the following exercises consult with your instructor to determine how he or she would like you to report your findings.

1. Search in your newspaper, news magazine, or television newscast for examples of managers who are performing management duties or functions. Your examples may come from any organization. For example, the president of the United States is a powerful manager of one of the largest organizations on earth—the government.

2. Interview a manager at each level of management. Try to find out what they do as managers and what their thinking is on current management practices and procedures. Include at least one administrative manager in your interview schedule and compare his or her duties with the other managers that you interview.
3. Conduct a debate in class (with permission of your instructor) on the issue of why women deserve equal opportunity to fill managerial positions.
4. Scan several business periodicals such as *The Wall Street Journal*, *Fortune*, *Harvard Business Review*, and *Business Week* to get a feel for topics that are important to business executives. Read one or more articles on general management topics to gain further insight. Learn how to use the *Business Periodicals Index* in your library to locate current information.
5. Invite an administrative manager to speak to your class about a relevant management topic. (Be sure to get permission from your instructor.)
6. Take a tour of an office to see how the office functions. Try to observe several types of offices so that you can obtain a representative picture.
7. Read an article from *Administrative Management*, *The Office*, or *Modern Office Procedures* that describes the work of an administrative manager.
8. Do a primary report (one based on first-hand observation) or a library research report on administrative management. See your instructor to clear a specific topic.
9. Look in the classified ad section of a large city newspaper such as the *New York Times*, *Los Angeles Times*, or *Washington Post* to determine what job openings are available for administrative managers and similar positions.

## *Case Studies*

1. *Lora Snarzyk*, an administrative manager at Central Co., has decided that she needs to create a new position of assistant administrative manager. The assistant will report directly to Lora. Don Haskins, vice-president for the information services division, is 55 years old and will be ready for retirement in about ten years. Lora feels that someone should be groomed to move into her position in the event that the opportunity opens up for her to become vice-president. Also, the work volume for administrative services is expected to double in the next year with the anticipated merger of Central with White Associates. She hopes to have her assistant assume responsibility for the communication services and take over as much administrative detail as possible.

Lora plans personally to investigate the feasibility of installing an automatic information retrieval system. She anticipates that preparing the annual budget will be an extra heavy burden this year because of the merger plans. Also, she plans to implement a system of objectives for the department this year.

Lora has presented her request for an assistant to Don, who has given tentative approval. Lora has thought about what she might include in a job description for this new position, but she has not yet written down her thoughts; she decides the next step is to make a list of qualifications she will look for in her assistant.

Assume the role of Lora Snarzyk, and prepare this list of qualifications for an assistant administrative manager. Be selective in choosing those qualifications that fit this particular situation. Select three or four qualifications from your list that you think are most important or critical to success in this position and explain your choices.

2. *Myron Kaufman* is the office manager in a small branch office of a major national insurance company. Myron is ambitious to get ahead in his profession. He looks forward in two or three years to either going to the home office in Kansas City as a supervisor in the administrative services department or being promoted to branch manager when his boss is promoted to a management position in company headquarters.

Myron has been searching for ways to develop himself as a manager. Recently he has joined the Administrative Management Society (A.M.S.) and has become active in the local chapter. He is considering working toward becoming a C.A.M. and attending seminar sessions at the A.M.S. international conference. Myron wonders if he should make the commitment of time and effort to be successful in these programs.

What advice would you give Myron as he makes decisions about a professional development program? What factors should he consider? What specific steps in planning a professional development program should Myron take? Can you recommend other activities with which he should become involved?

## Reference Notes

1. A *staff* position is one which is not in the direct line of authority. Staff personnel advise line managers, but have no authority to enforce their recommendations. Since they are specialists in their field, any authority that they have comes from their ability to persuade the line manager to accept their recommendations. Their persuasive power tends to rest in the strength of the ideas presented.
2. Gene W. Schmidt and William C. Lappe, "Analysis of Role of Officer Manager," *Delta Pi Epsilon Journal*, November 1973, pp. 24–32.
3. See also:

   Harold T. Smith and S. ElVon Warner, *Administrative Office Management Preparation*, a research report (Provo, Utah: Brigham Young University Press, 1971).

   "Duties of the Office Administrator," Dartnell Institute of Business Research, about 1970.

   Rick Minicucci, "What's Happening to the Administrative Manager's Job Description," *Administrative Management*, March 1975, pp. 20–22.

   Charles M. Ray, "The Functions of Administrative Office Managers with Implications for Collegiate Programs of Study," *Journal of Business Education*, February 1970, pp. 195–96.

   Donald C. Swedmark, "A Study of Office Management Executive In-Service Training Programs in Selected Insurance Companies with Implications for Improvement in the Collegiate Office Management Training Program," *Business Education Forum*, October 1971, p. 52.

# 2

# Effective Leaders: Style

## THE EFFECTIVE LEADER

Let's look at two department supervisors and the effects of their management. Ruby Schnell is effective in getting the typists she supervises to produce large quantities of high-quality work. The typists succeed in finding and correcting all errors, and as a group they are proud of their ability to achieve *turnaround time* (time required to complete a given amount of work) of three hours or less. Ruby doesn't have to strain to achieve these results with her department. She always appears to be calm and relaxed, even when the pressure is great.

Joe Kimoto, on the other hand, always seems to have difficulty in meeting his production quotas. Joe's typing operation, which is in another department in the same company, is similar to Ruby's. Workloads are comparable, but Joe's section is very pushed even though it has one more worker than Ruby's section has. Mistakes in Joe's section are common. Department managers often complain to Joe that the finished work they receive is not satisfactory. People in Joe's section remain after hours to get the job done, and turnaround time averages 24 hours or more. Joe frequently has to give personal help to get a rush job completed on time. The pressure is starting to get to Joe, and he appears to be nervous and run down.

What is the difference between these two operations? The different results can be accounted for in the leadership styles of the two supervisors. Why one leader is successful and another is not is the subject of this chapter. First, a definition of the term *leader* is needed.

A *leader* is anyone who inspires you to be a better person, causes you to complete a task, and inspires you to do more and better things because you want to.

When you are with a leader, you are inspired to do and be your best—to develop your potential. A leader is a developer, a teacher, an exemplar. But most important—a leader gets results.

Ruby Schnell is a good example of an effective leader. She works with her typists to help them develop their skills and derive satisfaction from their work. If any typist doesn't know how to solve a particular production problem, Ruby works with that person until competence is developed. Ruby goes beyond telling people what to do; she also shows them, lets them ask questions, and allows them to try tasks on their own. She always tries to provide a good example and to keep people informed on how they are doing.

### Balanced Concern for People and Production

Not long ago, a large life insurance company conducted an experiment to provide an answer to the question: "What happens when the nucleus of a group remains substantially the same and only the quality of leadership changes?" The company switched leaders of the highest producing departments to the lowest producing departments and vice versa. One year later, the production situation had reversed itself—the former low-production units were now the top producers, and the high-production units became the low producers. When workers in these units were asked to comment on their supervisors, two predominant points were made:

1. Leaders of highest producing units were interested in people and helped the employees to learn how to work more effectively.
2. Leaders of lowest producing units were primarily interested in production. They either did the work themselves or tried to drive the group members into greater production.[1]

Of course, production is also important; obtaining high production or good results is the major purpose of the organization. Without a high rate of production, the organization may soon cease to exist. The point is, however, that managers or leaders need to show balanced concern for both people and production; neglecting either part will surely spell disaster for most organizations. Effective leaders are "people builders" *and* "result getters."

### Effectiveness versus Efficiency

A clear understanding of the word *effectiveness* is necessary before considering the area of effective leadership. Effectiveness refers to the achievement of desired results or objectives; for example, an administrative manager who cuts costs by 25 percent while improving administrative services is an effective manager. The manager who increases profit by 38 percent in a year is also effective. Effectiveness involves setting priorities or making decisions about what is most important. Objectives and activities that have the greatest worth or value are given priority over other items of lesser value. The effective person gets things of real worth accomplished—which, of course, may be other than making money or increasing material wealth.

*Efficiency* is a word which is similar in meaning to effectiveness but which will have a particular meaning in this book. As used here, efficiency refers to getting things accomplished well or in a fast manner. There's a story that will illustrate this point; it's about an explorer in the Arctic who found himself getting farther and farther away from his goal of reaching the North Pole. He drove the team of dogs pulling his sled at a faster pace each day. In spite of his best efforts, however, he continually lost ground. He finally discovered he was on a huge iceberg that was floating southward at a rate faster than his dogs could go. This explorer was very efficient, but he was also very ineffective because he was making negative progress toward obtaining the results he wanted. He was moving away from his goal rather than toward it.

Perhaps an example from business would help in applying this concept. If a business person writes a necessary report that contains vital information and turns the report in by its due date, that person is acting effectively. But the person may have been inefficient in preparing the report; perhaps the report writer had to seek out data that should have been readily available. Or possibly the report had to be typed several times because insufficient attention was given to word selection and proofreading. This person was effective, but not very efficient.

*Efficiency* relates to the means or method of accomplishing an end result or objective while *effectiveness* refers to the value of the result or objective.

Effective managers tend to focus on results or the output of the system. They allow personnel who perform the work to determine their own methods and input to the system. The manager expects the worker to use an efficient method, but the primary concern is on making sure those things are done that make the greatest contribution to the organization. Thus, effectiveness is a more important concern than efficiency.

One word of caution is in order. Placing emphasis on the result does not mean that you should not be concerned at all with the means or the methods. For example, you might be able to force a group of typists to type more letters each day, and for a few days or weeks the group's effectiveness would be increased. Over several months, however, effectiveness might be decreased as employees quit their jobs or waited to be told what to do rather than moving on their own.

Ideally, the manager is both efficient and effective. The best methods are used to accomplish the most important objectives. For example, in preparing reports, only vital information is contained in the reports, and a well-organized, systematic approach is used to gather that information without undue effort.

### Effective versus Ineffective Leaders

What do effective managers and leaders do to increase their effectiveness? Are the activities that they engage in different from those of the ineffective manager? What should you do if you want to be effective as a manager or leader?

To answer these questions, consider a study conducted by the Life Insurance Agency Management Association. Agents were asked what they liked and disliked about their managers. The researchers found that ". . . good managers (1) are competent, (2) get along with others, and (3) are deeply interested in helping others. Conversely, poor managers (1) are incompetent, (2) push other people around, and (3) are self-centered."[2]

To be an effective leader, you must offer *challenge* to the people you are managing (see Table 2-1). At times, you may expect more from them than they expect from themselves, but don't be unrealistic in your demands. Give your employees the *authority* they need to get the job done. Let those who are working for you know that you will support them if they have problems. *Explain why* they need to follow policies and procedures (such as calling in by 8:00 A.M. if they are ill). If they have the necessary background for and understanding of their jobs, they will be able to work more intelligently. You will need to *delegate* effectively, *show trust and confidence* in your employees, but don't abdicate your responsibility to them. Remember that you are still ac-

**Table 2-1. Comparison of Effective and Ineffective Managers**

| *Effective managers . . .* | *Ineffective managers . . .* |
|---|---|
| 1. Challenge | 1. Allow motivation to work against them |
| 2. Give authority | 2. Are insensitive |
| 3. Explain why | 3. Don't keep promises |
| 4. Delegate | 4. Mistrust |
| 5. Show trust and confidence | 5. Fail to challenge |
| 6. Explain expectations | 6. Avoid constructive criticism |
| 7. Develop objectives | 7. Are self-centered |
| 8. Look for the positive | 8. Look for the negative |
| 9. Give rewards | 9. Emphasize either development of employees or work production |
| 10. Are patient | |
| 11. Set a good example | |
| 12. Think of employees as individuals | |
| 13. Listen | |

countable for your part. *Explain what you expect* at the time of delegation; don't wait until the work is completed. *Develop objectives* with them jointly.

You should learn to look for positive behavior on the part of your employees and then reinforce them with compliments or other *rewards*. Look for opportunities to praise them for accomplishment, but make sure that your praise is sincere; don't softsoap. *Be patient* with them and don't lose your self-control and composure when things go wrong. In order to *be an example* of what you expect from your employees, you must set the work pace yourself. Also, *individualize* your thinking about your workers and remember that they have emotions and feelings just as you do. Treat them as team members rather than hired hands. Lastly, and as important as any other managerial behavior, *listen* to them; by listening to them, you are telling your team members that they really are important. Moreover, you will find that you will learn from them. If you are able to follow these guidelines, you are likely to be an effective manager.

On the other hand, ineffective leaders usually act in ways you should try to avoid. They tend to allow employee job motivation, which is inherent in most people, to be depleted through discouragement and dissatisfaction. The employee reporting to a new job is generally highly motivated, but this motivation lasts only as long as the person finds satisfaction in his or her work. Ineffective leaders are insensitive to the problems and feelings of their employees; for instance, a secretary wants her boss to think of her as an individual, not just as another item of equipment. Ineffective leaders break their word and make promises that they can't or don't keep. Other problems are listed in Table 2-1.

Think about these areas of weakness. Are any of them characteristic of your managerial approach? If so, you should start making changes in that approach to improve your effectiveness as a leader.

### Leadership Effectiveness

Behavioral scientists (psychologists, sociologists, and people from similar areas) have studied leadership extensively. For years, the traditional point of view about leadership emphasized traits and focused on the question, "What kind of people make good leaders?" Recently, this point of view has changed, and the concept of effective leadership now is seen to depend on what the manager or leader does rather than on what set of traits he or she has. The question being asked has changed to "What do effective leaders do?" The primary reason for this shift in emphasis is that no specific sets of traits have been found to correlate with effective leadership. In addition, admitting that leadership effectiveness is dependent upon some set of inherent traits in an individual does not allow for the possibility that training and development will result in good leaders.

On the other hand, experience suggests that the correlation of leadership behavior with leadership effectiveness is not perfect; for example, two leaders may take the same leadership steps and get different results. How much of this difference can be accounted for by variations in the group of followers and how much by situational factors is unknown. If an experiment is conducted in which all factors (including leadership actions) are held constant with only the difference in leaders themselves varying, it is likely we would find a difference in leadership effectiveness. Those differences would have to be accounted for by something about the leaders themselves.

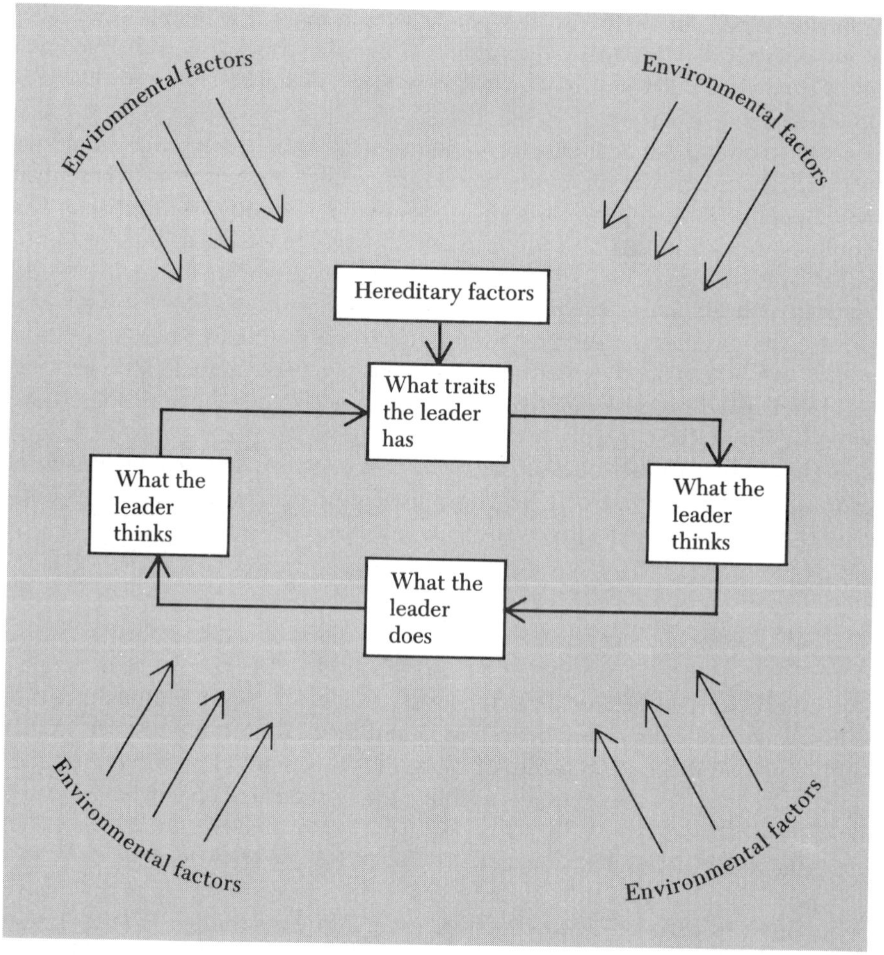


*Figure 2-1.* Leadership Effectiveness Model

Looking deeper into this question, we may ask, "What causes a person to behave in a certain manner?" William James, a famous psychologist and philosopher, answered this question years ago by saying that every voluntary act is preceded by a thought. In other words, thinking determines behavior. What you think is based upon the experiences you have had and also on your character or the kind of person you are. What you are is determined by *hereditary* factors (characteristics passed on by your parents) and environmental factors (characteristics influenced by your surroundings and other people) as well as by what you think. The full circle of these relationships is illustrated in Figure 2-1. Notice the impact of environmental factors on all phases of the leadership process. Effectiveness in leadership is dependent upon what you do as a leader, what characteristics you have, and upon what environmental or situational factors are involved.

Not only is effective leadership dependent upon these three factors, but *congruence* or harmony among these factors must exist before effective leadership will result. What you do as a leader must reflect what you are (your characteristics). Your behavior can't be phony; you must be genuine. If you distrust your assistant, it will be difficult for you to delegate important areas of responsibility to that person. In addition, what you do must be congruent with the situation and the people who surround you; you must be basically in harmony with the group and the situation. While variances or deviations can be expected at any one time, long-term differences eventually must be brought into basic agreement in order to achieve optimum leadership effectiveness.

## LEADERSHIP STYLE

When you assume a leadership role, you are likely to ask yourself the question, "What is the best way to approach my people?" "How can I relate to them and interact with them to get the job done in the best way possible?" "What model or example of other leaders I have known should I try to follow to get the best results?" The central issue is how *democratic* or *autocratic* you should be in dealing with your group. The democratic leader allows his or her subordinates to help make decisions, while the autocratic leader makes all major decisions.

### Four Basic Styles

In a classical work of 1958, Tannenbaum and Schmidt tried to answer these questions; Figure 2-2 presents their view of leadership as a continuum of behavior.[3] (A simplified version of this chart was used in the Roundtable film, *Styles of Leadership.*[4]) The four styles of leadership presented in the film can be pinpointed on Tannenbaum and Schmidt's continuum.

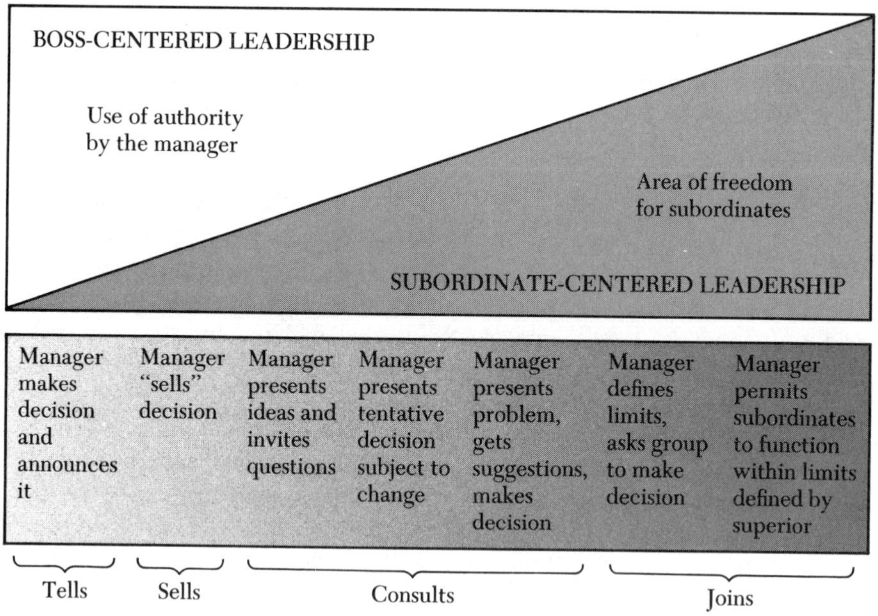


*Figure 2-2.* Leadership Behavior Continuum and Styles of Leadership
The style of leadership moves from boss-centered (on the left) toward subordinate-centered (on the right)—or from "Tells" to "Joins."

The *autocratic* type of leader, or one who *tells* group members what to do, usually has wide experience. He or she knows exactly what is wanted and how to get it. This leader does not want or need the participation of the group in decision making. This type of leader gets the job done quickly, and people know exactly what role they should play in their job performance.

The leader who *sells* decisions to the group tries to involve the group to a greater extent than the leader who merely tells. The seller, however, retains full control and retains the right to make all important decisions. This leader is likely to bargain with his or her followers to achieve the desired results. At times, this leader may even resort to use of unfair tactics to achieve his or her goals.

The leader who *consults* makes the decisions but allows the group to participate. The group members understand that the leader will make the decisions, but they know that they will have an influence on the outcome. The leader may have personal opinions but does not have his or her opinions "set in concrete" before consulting with the group. Groups that have the opportunity for greater input of ideas into the decision process tend to have members that contribute more possibilities for decision making than groups that have little or no input to the decision-making process. Also, when group members are involved in the process, they are more likely to support the decision and actively work to implement it.

The role of the leader who *joins* the group in making the decision is one of a discussion leader who explains the problem and then turns over the decision-making responsibility to the group. The leader joins the group to participate in this process. If the leader has opinions about how the decision should go, he or she is free to express his or her thoughts, but the group is not bound by these ideas. In fact, the leader is obligated to accept the decision of the group. With this style of leadership, group members have greater responsibility than with any other style. They become fully involved in the *democratic* process, and many benefits can result. On the other hand, the group process is slow and the leader may feel a loss of control.

Which of these four basic styles of leadership would be best for you depends on you, your group members, and the situation. Before we consider selection of a leadership style further, other dimensions of leadership style should be reviewed.

### Other Dimensions

Tannenbaum and Schmidt emphasized the boss-subordinate relationship and the degree to which employees participate in making decisions. Other research on leadership style has recognized second and third dimensions of leadership style.[5] First, the work or task and people considerations were identified at Ohio State University in classical leadership studies initiated in 1945. Robert R. Blake and Jane S. Mouton popularized these concepts in their managerial grid, which presented a graphic picture of various leadership styles. Later, the effectiveness factor was considered by William Reddin.

The work or task dimension of leadership focuses on efforts of managers to increase production. Managers who are highly task-oriented either try to drive their subordinates into getting the job done or try to structure and organize operations for their subordinates to insure that production will be increased. Some managers use both techniques. The highly structured or bureaucratic organization gives much attention to such things as the formal organization, communication channels, well-defined job specialities, and standardized methods and procedures.

The people dimension of leadership focuses on developing employees. Managers who are highly people-oriented stress training and professional development activities; building trust levels and developing interpersonal relationships are seen as critical, and employees are encouraged to participate in the decision-making process. Managers vary in the amount of emphasis they

(*a*)

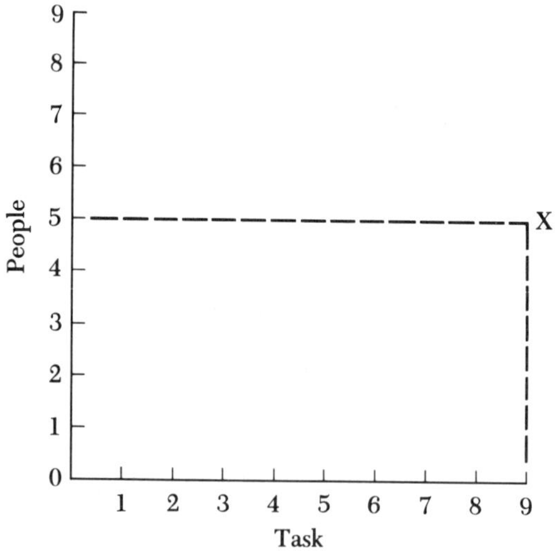


*Figure 2-3.* Leadership Styles
(*a*) Leadership style showing a high concern for task and a moderate concern for people (X)

place on getting the job done and on professional development, and emphasis given these two factors determines the style of leadership.

The two dimensions of leadership, task and people, are graphically presented in Figure 2-3, where one axis represents the emphasis on people and the other axis represents weight given to the task. A manager's leadership style may be plotted on the graph by finding a point on each scale that represents the amount of emphasis he or she places on each factor—people and task. In Figure 2-3(a) an X is shown on the graph for a manager who has moderate (5) concern for people and high (9) concern for production. Other managers emphasize each factor in varying degrees. For example, manager Y in Figure 2-3(b) is highly concerned about developing people and also about getting the job done; manager Z has low concern in both areas.

In considering leadership styles, we also need to consider how effective each style is. Effectiveness concerns whether the amount of emphasis placed on production and people is appropriate for the particular situation in order to achieve results. Looking back at Figure 2-3(b), you probably think that style Y is the most effective leadership style and that style Z is the least effective. But what if the manager were working with a highly trained group of professionals such as a group of programmer analysts or tax accounting specialists? Perhaps

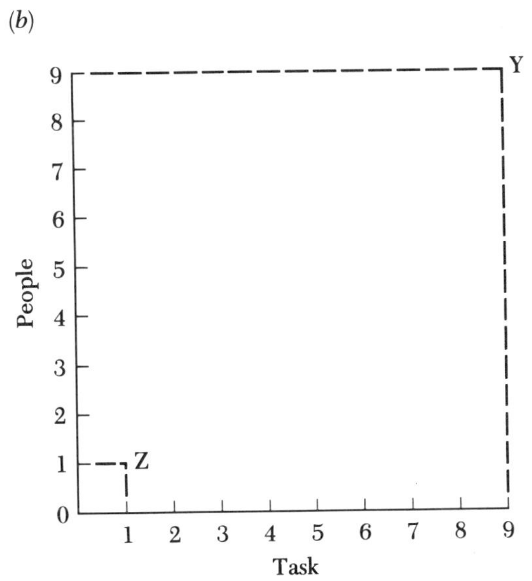


*Figure 2-3, continued* (*b*) Leadership style showing two situations: a high concern for people and a high concern for task (Y) and a low concern for both people and task (Z)

the best approach might be to stay out of the group members' way and let them do their jobs. Use of style Y might tend to inhibit operations, and in this case style Z might be the most effective.

One or two more illustrations should reinforce the point that the most effective leadership style to use is dependent upon the situation. If you are responsible for conducting training programs in your organization, you are likely to be highly oriented toward developing people and have very little concern for getting work accomplished. On the other hand, if you supervise a group of part-time workers on a one-time distribution of a million telephone books, you are likely to be very production-oriented.

Figure 2-4 illustrates how this third dimension of effectiveness relates to the other two dimensions of production and people. The box represents leadership style in a three-dimensional form, and this third dimension of effectiveness considers how effective the manager is for a given situation in emphasizing people and production. In this figure, we can show the effectiveness of managers Y and Z in a situation where they are supervising technical specialists; Z is shown as very effective and Y as very ineffective. Of course, in another situation, their effectiveness ratings might be very different.

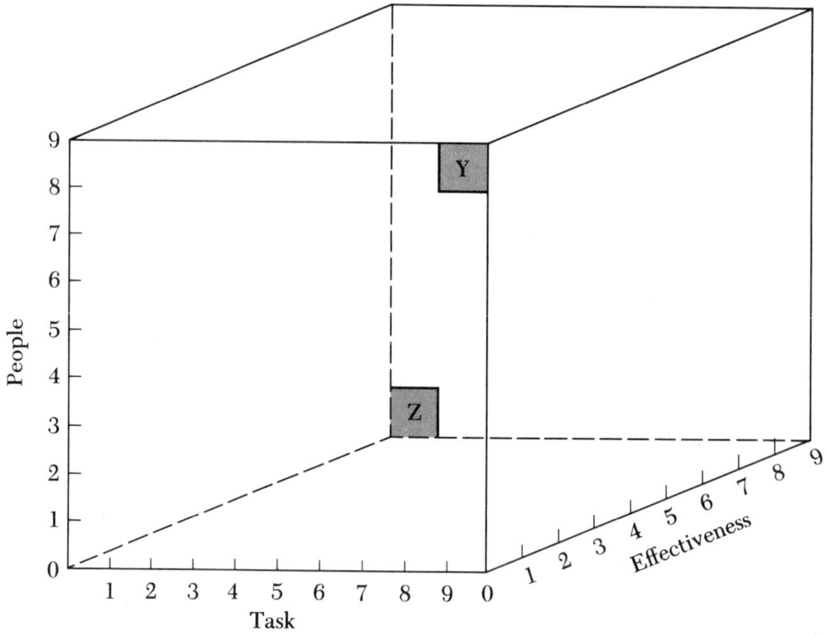


*Figure 2-4.* Three-Dimensional Model of Leadership Style

### Leadership Style Selection

If you were to choose a style of leadership from among those discussed, which one would you select? How would you know which would be best? Before these questions can be answered, you should realize that you are not restricted to one style of leadership. You may find yourself consulting most of the time, but at other times you may need to tell, sell, or join the group. In some circumstances, you will be concerned greatly about developing an adequate amount of structure for your people and getting the task accomplished. In other situations, you will have a high degree of concern about relationships with your group. In still other instances, you may decide to get out of the way and let them "run with the ball" on their own. The three variables that you must consider in making a decision about which leadership style to choose are (1) the group, (2) the situation, and (3) yourself as the leader.

Just as each individual has his or her own personality, each group also has its own personality. Group personality can be viewed as the result of the combination of individual personalities to form a composite or unique group character. The group personality will, in large measures, determine what style of leadership the leader will select. Some groups are much more willing than others to assume responsibility. Groups also vary significantly in their ability and status levels—knowledge and experience of the group influence this level. For example, a group of research chemists have a high level of education and status while a group of keypunch operators or file clerks do not enjoy these same advantages. The level and personality of the group will dictate the group's need for independence and the group's expectations of the leader. Development needs of the group will also have a bearing on leadership style decisions.

The situation itself will have a great bearing on the style of leadership selected. For example, the military platoon leader facing an enemy five hundred yards away will not stop to consult with his troops to ask them what they think ought to be done. He is likely to be very direct in his style of leadership and to tell them exactly what to do. In a business context, you would handle a crash project requested by the company president differently than you would a routine job of processing sales invoices. Factors that relate to the situation variable include (1) time pressure, (2) nature of the problem, (3) available information, and (4) organizational climate (trust level).

Finally, the group leader has an individual leadership personality that grows out of his or her values, life style, personal sense of security, and perception of the role of a leader. One leader might feel very uncomfortable in telling other people what to do, while a second leader might feel just as uncomfortable with any other style than telling. Other factors related to the leader that will have a bearing on choosing a leadership style include the experience and knowledge of the leader, trust in the group, and the need to involve the group to achieve motivation.

The *contingency approach* to management suggests that leaders should vary their leadership styles according to the situation. For example, in handling the crash project for the president, you might assume a telling style of leadership with a very high task orientation and very little concern for developing your group. You do what you need to do to get the job completed. When the task is planning the office Christmas party, you might turn over the whole project to an employee committee and request only a progress report from the committee. While the use of the contingency approach seems logical, in actual practice many managers are not able to make the shift that easily. Their personalities are basically set, and even though they might desire to use another style, they may not be capable of making the shift.

## *Summary*

Effective leaders need to balance their concern for production with a concern for people. In other words, they get the job done through other people who, of course, must be considered. In the process, employees are given room for professional development and are more highly motivated because of their association with their leader. Leaders should be more concerned with doing right things than with doing things right.

Leaders should offer challenging work situations to their people, give authority, delegate effectively, develop objectives, reward effective performance, show patience, provide a good example, and individualize their thinking about their employees. Ineffective leaders are more concerned about themselves and fail to develop their employees. Effective leadership is dependent upon what must be congruent with respect to task and the work group as well as with situational factors.

A leader relates to a group in four basic ways: tells, sells, consults, and joins. Recent research in leadership style suggests that concern for production, concern for people, and effectiveness of the leader are three major style variables. The selection of a leadership style is based upon consideration of the group, the situation, and the personality of the leader.

## *Review and Discussion Questions*

1. Consider leaders you have worked with and compare and contrast those who were effective with those who were ineffective. What are the critical differences between the two groups?
2. Someone once said, "Leaders are made, not born." In your opinion, is this statement true or false? Justify your answer.
3. Why is it important for you to draw a distinction in your own mind between effectiveness and efficiency?
4. Why do effective leaders try to balance their attention to production and to the development of people?
5. Why is congruence between the leader's characteristics and what he or she does important?
6. Explain what style of leadership is generally best for you and why.
7. Identify and evaluate three primary factors you should consider in choosing a leadership style.

## *Application Exercises*

1. Interview various people in leadership positions in order to gain insight into their leadership philosophies. Determine what they consider to be their most prevalent and their most difficult problems. Find out what leadership practices they think are most effective.
2. Ask your instructor to help you make arrangements to take one of the following leadership style tests or some similar test: Reddin's Management Style Diagnosis Test, Hersey and Blanchard's Leader Adaptability and Style Inventory, Atkins-Katcher's LIFO Strength Management and Strength Development Test. If you are in a leadership position, ask a person who reports to you to take one of these leadership tests. Have the

person complete the test from the viewpoint of how he or she thinks you would respond to the situations posed in the test. Compare your results.

3. Be alert to various styles of leadership used by leaders to whom you report and by other leaders with whom you come in contact. The leader could be your work supervisor, class instructor, or club president, for example. Report on your observations to the class.
4. Prepare a list of effective and ineffective leadership practices that you observe in your daily life. Be prepared to explain why practices were effective and what could be done to improve ineffective actions.

## *Mini-Cases*

For each of the following mini-case situations, decide which style of leadership you would be most likely to select. Be prepared to explain why.

1. You have had vast experience with your company, having served as an accountant, office manager, and administrative manager for 20 years. You need to get an important but routine report duplicated and distributed by the following day. The supervisor who will be responsible for the actual work is relatively new and has not prepared the report before.
2. As a relatively new manager of administrative services, you are faced with making a major decision on new computer equipment. You have had extensive experience with computers, but you lack the technical knowledge that some of your technical staff personnel have. You must make a decision by the end of the next quarter.
3. Your boss has asked you to recommend a course of action for implementing a new salary program. You have had experience with several salary systems in previous companies. Both of your assistants have formal training in salary administration, but no practical experience. Your report must be prepared within the next two weeks.

## *Reference Notes*

1. *Human Relations in Management* (Hartford, Conn.: Life Insurance Marketing and Research Association, 1975), p. 7. Reprinted with permission.
2. *Human Relations in Management,* p. 6.
3. Robert Tannenbaum and Warren H. Schmidt, "How to Choose a Leadership Pattern," *Harvard Business Review,* March-April 1958, Vol. 36, No. 2, p. 2.
4. *Styles of Leadership: Discussion Leader's Guide* (Beverly Hills, Calif.: Roundtable Films, 1961), p. 4.
5. For further information on research related to leadership style, refer to Robert R. Blake and Jane S. Mouton, *The Managerial Grid* (Houston, Texas: Gulf Publishing, 1964); Paul Hersey and Kenneth H. Blanchard, *Management of Organizational Behavior* (Englewood Cliffs, N.J.: Prentice-Hall, 2nd edition, 1972), p. 73; and William J. Reddin, *Managerial Effectiveness* (New York: McGraw-Hill, 1970).

# 3

# Effective Leaders: Development

Rarely do people come equipped to be effective leaders; most people have to work to develop their leadership capabilities. In order to make changes in your leadership style and become the most effective leader possible, you must accomplish three goals: (1) understand yourself, (2) understand others, and (3) develop effective interpersonal relationships.

## UNDERSTANDING YOURSELF

Three essential steps in understanding yourself include taking a personal inventory, determining the amount of self-acceptance that you have, and initiating a plan of self-change.

### Personal Inventory

Taking a personal inventory to see exactly where you stand is the first step toward self-understanding. A useful tool to express information about yourself is the self-awareness chart shown in Figure 3-1. At a given time, the chart shows one individual's self-information in relation to the information another person has about that individual. The chart is divided into four parts forming a two-by-two matrix: Column 1 refers to information about yourself that is known to you, Column 2 depicts information that is not known to you, Row A refers to things that other people know about you, and Row B pertains to items not known by other people about you. Four cells or boxes are formed by combining the two columns with the two rows, and the contents of the boxes can be explained as follows.

A1. *Open* information is known to yourself and to others. You are likely not to be threatened by anyone who knows information in this area. For example, you may be willing to share information about your job with anyone who is interested in listening.

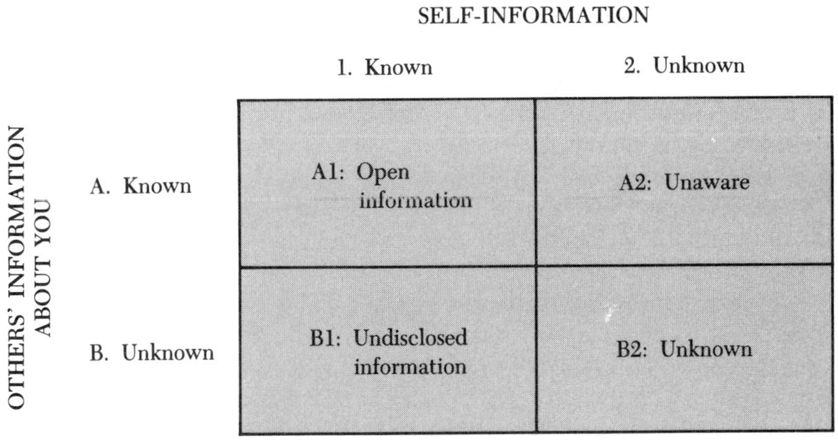


*Figure 3-1.* Self-Awareness Chart

A2. The *unaware* area indicates information about yourself that other people know but that you do not. Other people might feel threatened if they give you these data; they may be afraid of offending you, or they may be unaware that you are unaware of something. For example, they may know the real reasons why you were bypassed for promotion but are unwilling to inform you of them.

B1. *Undisclosed* information is information that you are aware of but that you have kept hidden from other people. You keep this information hidden because it might be threatening to you if others knew it too. Perhaps you are thinking of quitting your job; you don't feel safe in disclosing this information to any other person.

B2. Finally, the *unknown* area is one which is not known to you or to other people. This area of unawareness may come from lack of experience. Perhaps you have talents which have not yet been discovered.

George Zobell considers himself to be an effective manager, so when he heard about the self-awareness chart, he decided to use it as a tool to gain greater self-understanding. George decided to do three things to learn more about himself: (1) share information about himself with others in his office, (2) look inward in a self-examination process, and (3) ask others in the office to share information they have about him. As George became more open with others in sharing personal information about himself, he found that they became more open with him. From this process, George learned that his secretary resented his asking her to run personal errands downtown, such as buying a birthday gift for his wife. He learned that his administrative assistants saw him as being quite pushy in telling them how to do things they could easily decide for themselves. He also found that he had some hidden fears about his own inadequacies and that, as a result, he covered up his own problems by being pushy and quite critical of others. When George understood these things about himself, he was able to start to make some changes that he hoped would improve his relations with others.

Zelda Sorenson, on the other hand, heard about the self-awareness chart and did nothing about it. She rationalized in her own mind that she was doing the best she could with other people. When her employees at the office failed to make a new information system work, Zelda said they were incompetent and that if they had only listened to her the system would be working effectively. Zelda is brilliant, but she turns people off with her blunt mannerisms. The real problem is that Zelda doesn't recognize that she has any problems and she doesn't do anything to better understand herself.

Think of how this concept might apply to you. These four categories of information about the self apply to everyone. The size of each cell varies for different people depending upon how much is known about the self and how willing the person is to share information about himself or herself with others. The important point to remember is that if you maximize self-knowledge, the greater your effectiveness will be as an individual and as a leader. Also, sharing information of a personal nature about yourself will help you build rich, open relationships with other people.

(*a*) The basic model

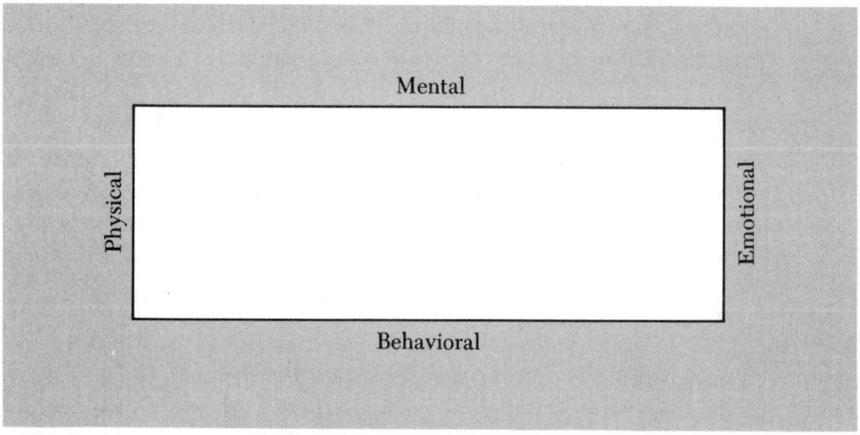


*Figure 3-2.* A Model Illustrating Self-Dimensions

(*a*) The basic model and (*b*) some variations showing an extended mental and emotional dimension, a short behavioral dimension, and an emphasized physical side.

What are your strengths and weaknesses with regard to physical and psychological aspects of your life? These are two major areas that you will want to include in your personal inventory. Figure 3-2 graphically depicts the self as a four-sided figure; the length of each side varies from one individual to another depending upon stages of development and time spent in each area.

***Physical.*** Physical status includes a knowledge of your health condition, fitness program, and available energy level. Eating, sleeping, and exercising habits should be assessed. If you are able to care for and discipline your body properly, you are likely also to be psychologically healthy.

(*b*) Some variations

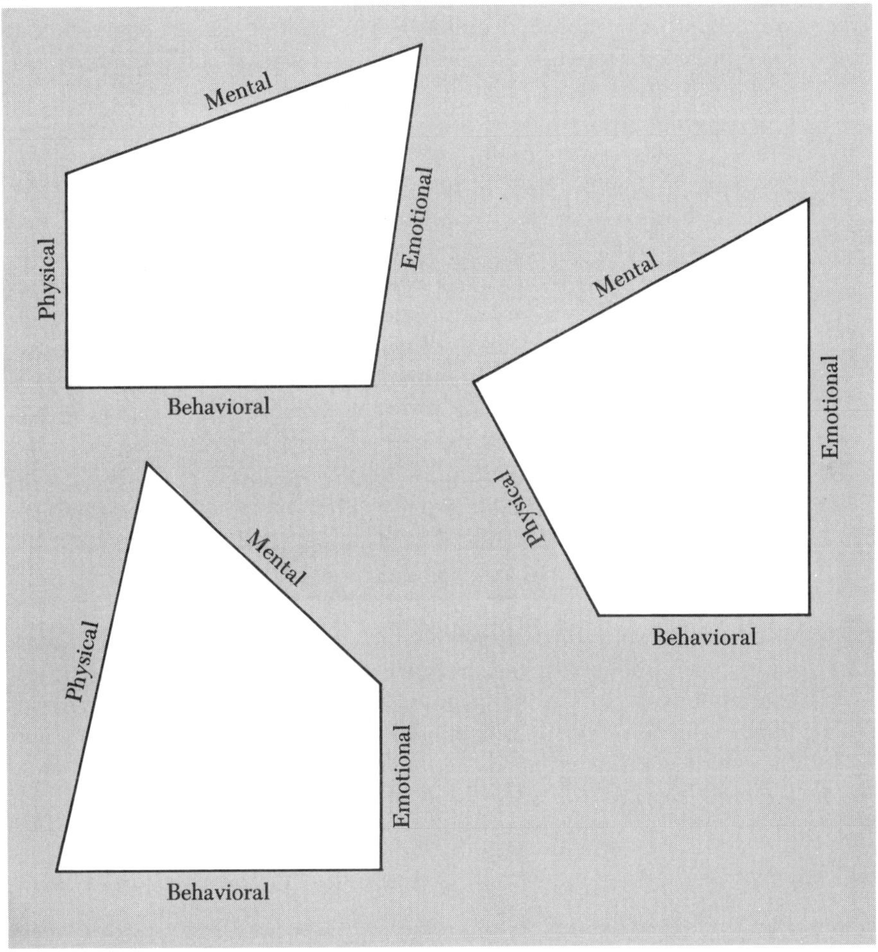


*Figure 3-2, continued*

***Psychological.*** The three psychological areas—mental, emotional, and behavioral—form a second phase of your self-examination.

1. Good leaders need sharp analytical and decision-making abilities. The ability to think through problems and make logical, effective decisions is important. Your level of knowledge must be adequate to support your leadership aspirations.
2. Effective leaders need to be emotionally healthy, and a good attitude is an important part of emotional health. People who are not defensive and who maintain a positive mental attitude are able to accomplish much. Those who gear themselves toward success are likely to be more successful than people who program themselves for failure. An enthusiastic attitude toward life and work will carry anyone a long way. An article published by the Royal Bank of Canada suggests that "people are defeated in life not because of want of ability but for lack of wholehearted effort."[1]

   Self-confidence, which is really a reflection of a positive mental attitude, is another important part of emotional health. Persons who lack faith in themselves will have a difficult time becoming effective leaders. For example, the young lady who expressed the thought in a public speech that she thought of herself as a "peeled zero," or a nothing, has a very low level of self-esteem. As Evel Knievel, the famous motorcycle trick rider, said as he was preparing to jump his cycle over 13 Mack trucks, "I must first sell *myself* on the idea that I *can* do it." The self-image controls the mind. Someone once said, "Sow a thought, reap an act; sow an act, reap a habit; sow a habit, reap a character; sow a character, reap a destiny." In other words, the thoughts you think will determine what you become.
3. The third part of psychological makeup is the behavioral area. Behavior tends to be an outward display of mental and emotional processes. Several aspects of behavior should be considered in your self-inventory. Effective leaders have good social skills: they tend to be oriented outward toward people rather than inward toward themselves, they show trust and are open with others, and they communicate effectively with other people. Also, they show a high degree of independence rather than dependence upon a group for support, and they understand what needs and wants motivate their behavior. They are creative and find better ways of getting things done.

### Self-Acceptance

In addition to completing the self-inventory, an examination of your level of *self-acceptance* or self-esteem is important. Have you ever thought about what you expect of yourself and to what degree you are reaching your *aspirations?* As your self-expectations tend to line up with your achievements, your acceptance of self will tend to increase. High levels of aspiration are fine, but the level must not be so high as to be unattainable or unrealistic. Taking time to think about what you expect of yourself is a useful exercise. Have you examined lately what you expect of yourself? Do you have real purpose in your life? A typical list of self-expectations is given here.

1. Do my best to achieve
2. Find peace and happiness
3. Interact effectively with others
   (a) Communication
   (b) Emotional support
4. Show progress
5. Stand up for what's right
6. Solve problems
7. Make good decisions
8. Do what my manager and others expect
9. Set realistic aspiration levels
10. Always find new mountains to climb
11. Accept myself for what I am
12. Develop employees to reach their potential

To determine how much you accept yourself, consider two circles in your life in which you will frequently find yourself—the circle of confidence and the circle of inferiority, a concept developed by Joseph C. Bentley.[2] In the *circle of confidence,* shown in Figure 3-3, if you feel good about yourself, you are able to turn outward and express concern for other people. As you do these things, other people see you as someone who cares about them. This perception leads them to respond to you with expressions of concern, which brings you back full circle to the point where your basic feelings of self-worth are reinforced by their positive responses.

The second circle in which you may find yourself entangled is shown in Figure 3-4, the *circle of inferiority.* When your own self-concept is down, you are likely to turn inward and express only concern about yourself and your problems. Others then see you as being selfish and uninterested in them; they, in turn, exhibit negative reactions toward you, reinforcing your basic feelings of inferiority that were evident in the first place. Have you ever found yourself caught in this circle of inferiority? Ways of breaking this circle and getting back into the circle of confidence will be considered in the next section on self-change.

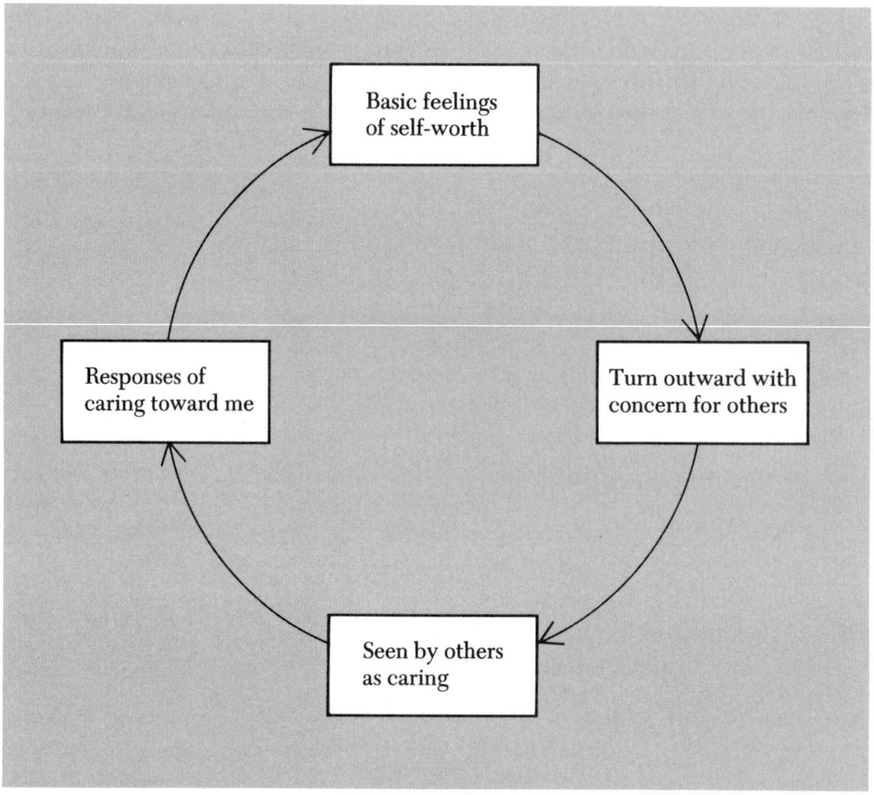


*Figure 3-3.* The Circle of Confidence

**Self-Change**

Assuming that there are things in your life that you would like to change—things about yourself which you find unacceptable—you might consider the following approach for initiating these changes. First, review your personal inventory. Find out where you stand, then determine areas you would like to change. Second, set objectives. Determine exactly where you want to be six months from now, a year from now, or five years in the future. For example, you may decide that within five years, you would like to become branch manager for your company. As a stepping-stone toward this goal, you think you have a chance of being appointed to the job of office manager for your branch by next year. To prepare yourself for the job, you have enrolled in an administrative office management course; you have been working hard in the course and expect to earn an "A" grade. Third, once you know where you are headed, you can develop an action plan that will get you where you want to go. Be as

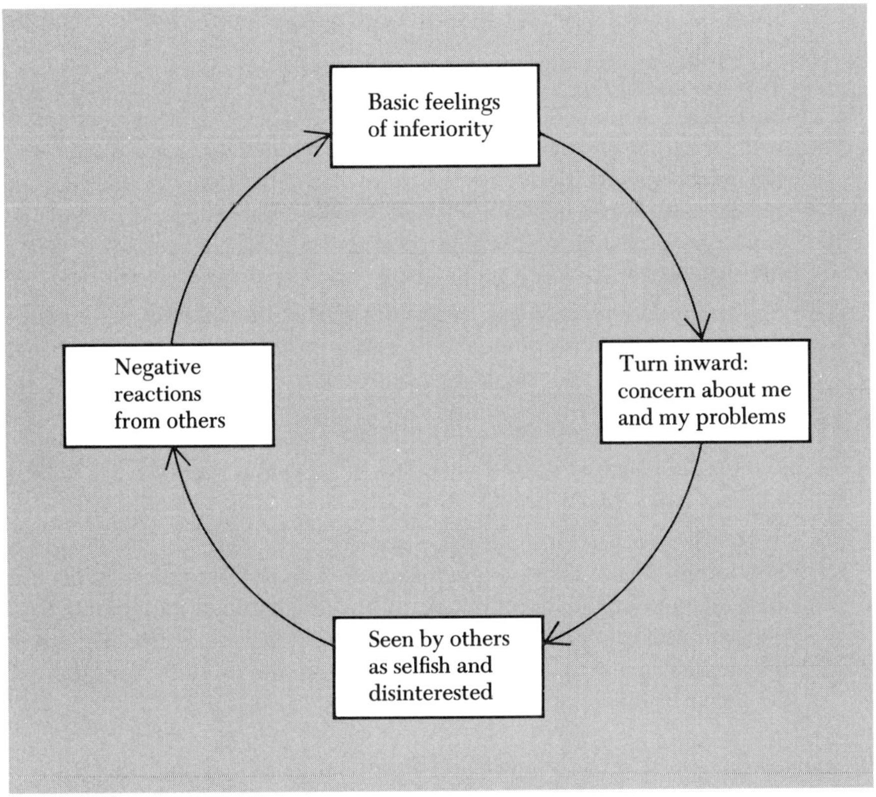


*Figure 3-4.* The Circle of Inferiority

specific as possible in setting forth the steps that will take you to your goals. Also, set time targets to help you to discipline yourself toward achieving progress.

***Guidelines.*** Several guidelines that should help you to attain your goals are listed below:

1. Build on your strengths; minimize your weaknesses. For example, Joe Fitzgerald, administrative manager, was good in communicating and working with people to get them to do what he wanted done. He capitalized on that strength. He spent most of his time talking with people and helping them to develop their abilities. Joe tried to be competent in all parts of his job, but he recognized some weaknesses such as a lack of mathematical skills. Joe made sure that he had assistants who were strong in his areas of weakness. Rather than concen-

trating on eliminating his weaknesses, he tried to use and build on his strengths.

2. A second guideline to remember is that you need to be yourself. Learn to be happy with what you are—and make the most of what you are. Don't always try to change yourself to fit the model of someone else who appears to be better than you. Strive for excellence and make needed changes that will make you a more effective leader, but don't try to change yourself just for the sake of change. Most likely, you are basically a very good person.
3. Another guideline is to use *feedback* to help you make improvements. Don't get defensive if someone is critical of what you have done. Turn the comments to your advantage by using them to help you recognize needed areas of improvement. Another point to remember is that if you are positive in your *attitude* toward other people, they are more likely to be positive toward you. Thus, the amount of critical feedback you receive is likely to be reduced—what you do get can be used to help you.
4. The last guideline is to be unafraid to seek help from others in making changes in your life. Seek out people who have information and skills that you need. Learn from other people who have already faced problems that you are facing. Weigh their comments carefully, and then do your own thinking and make your own decisions.

***Recommendations.*** As the last consideration under self-initiated change, let's examine how you can break the circle of inferiority and get back to the circle of confidence. Here are five suggestions:

1. Write down all the positive points about yourself. For example, you might be well organized, good at following through on assignments, and punctual. Ask a friend or relative to help you list these good points, if necessary.
2. Strive to make necessary changes in your life. Try to give up bad habits and change things about yourself that are making you unhappy.
3. Maintain a positive mental attitude. Look for the good in situations and in people to help balance out the negative. For example, if your boss is critical of a report you have prepared, do you become discouraged and think of yourself as a failure or do you remember that he praised the last report you prepared and that you have just received a $75 per month raise in salary? Everyone becomes discouraged at times, but usually these periods are only temporary.
4. Use music as a way of changing your moods. If you can't seem to get moving, try playing a rousing recording for stimulation.

5. Perhaps the most important point is to show concern for others. Perform acts of kindness toward other people. Do something nice for someone even if you don't feel like doing it at the time. (This is a good way to break into the circle of confidence.)

## UNDERSTANDING OTHERS

When you feel as though you have gained greater self-understanding, you are then in a good position to try to understand other people. Many of the ideas that are true for you will hold true for others, and the initial basis for understanding others is to understand yourself. Of course, no two people are exactly the same, so you must seek to identify their similarities and differences and to compare and to contrast these characteristics with your own and with those of others.

As we will discuss to a greater extent later in Chapter 8, the basic purpose of communication is to achieve understanding. It follows, then, that if you want to understand other people, communicating effectively with them is essential. If you succeed in gaining an understanding of a person, your communication with that person has been effective. Going below the surface, beyond the facade, to a depth that helps you really understand a person is important. For example, when you meet a quiet person, you may first assume that the person is snobbish because he or she fails to carry on a conversation with you; in reality, the person may be very shy or involved in his or her own thoughts.

Just as you have *expectations* for yourself, so will every other person have his or her own self-expectations; in the sense we are using the word, an expectation is a feeling about how someone should behave in specific situations. Other people will have expectations of you as their manager or leader; you will be expected to:

1. Look after the welfare of each of them as members of the team
2. Be fair and not show favorites
3. Keep everyone informed about events and policies that will affect them
4. Allow participation on important decisions that affect them
5. Give praise when earned
6. Give feedback on performance
7. Provide adequate resources
8. Provide explanations for decisions that result in a "no" answer
9. Be available for consultation
10. Be what you say you are

On the other hand, as a leader, you can expect your group to behave in certain ways. Some typical expectations you may have of them are to:

1. Do the assigned job
2. Meet certain quality standards
3. Follow the rules—the intent, not just the letter, of the "law"
4. Be loyal to the organization and to you as their manager
5. Report problems and develop recommended solutions
6. Meet objectives
7. Discuss grievances with you
8. Make recommendations for direction and new ideas
9. Support decisions of the group and the manager
10. Attend staff meetings
11. Follow the chain of command (designated line of authority)

Job-related expectations are an important aspect of understanding and working with people and should have certain characteristics that enable them to be attained. They should be:

*Explicit*

*Understood*

*Shared* (mutually agreeable)

*Negotiable* and fully discussed (depending upon how critical they are to the individual formulating them)

*Consistent*

*High* but obtainable—expecting more from individuals than they expect from themselves is really a compliment

Quite often, a wide variation exists in what the manager expects and what the employee thinks the manager expects. For example, Beth, the manager, may feel that Ron should recommend new types of printing machines for the duplicating department. Ron, on the other hand, may think that Beth is expecting him to "make do" with the old equipment in order to save money. When interviews are conducted to determine objectives for organizations, wide variations are frequently found between what the employees do and what the supervisors think the employees do.

To a great extent, how much employees produce depends on how much they are expected to produce. For example, if Andrea expects her secretary to type five dictated letters with no errors before 5:00 P.M., the work is likely to be accomplished; or, if she expects that only part of the letters will be ready and that they will include errors, she will probably also be right. *Managers are likely to get exactly what they expect from their employees.* Managers do have to communicate their expectations, and this communication process is accomplished more by how managers treat their people than by what they say. The actions of managers speak louder than their words.[3]

Research comparing what employees value most highly about their work shows a very low relationship with what supervisors think that their employees want. Items rated highest by the employees were frequently rated lowest by their supervisors. These studies point out the need for leaders and managers to gain a greater understanding of their people.

## INTERPERSONAL RELATIONSHIPS

Once you have a good understanding of yourself and a fairly good understanding of others, you can begin to develop more effective relationships. The beginning point is to accept people as they are, and a fundamental belief in the worth of the individual is essential for this acceptance. If your philosophy is that people are basically good, then you are able to show fundamental trust in their goodness and worth. When you communicate your unconditional concern and regard to others, they soon realize that you have a high regard for them as individuals.

In order to develop effective relationships, a person needs to show empathy for other people. Placing yourself in another person's shoes and seeing life through his or her eyes will help you to be more empathetic. Empathy and concern for your fellow man can distort your judgment, however. Many times, hard decisions result in actions that people don't like, but that are really in their best interests.

One excellent method of building effective relationships is to go out of your way to help others in any way that you can. People who try to help others normally have effective *interpersonal relationships* and are able to accomplish their own objectives with little difficulty. For example, Sharon Stromberg, a Civil Service Commission executive in Washington, D.C., helps people get jobs and get their projects accomplished. She knows many influential people, has cultivated good relationships, and has few problems working through other people to get her own goals accomplished.

One of the key principles in understanding others is to listen carefully to what they say and to what they intend to say. Receiving feedback from others will help you check your understanding of what they are trying to communicate. When people really listen, they start to see things from the other person's point of view. Listening lets other people know that you think they are important. You momentarily forget about your own desires and start to gain real understanding. One research study shows that listening is one of the key attributes of an effective manager. (Part III will deal in greater detail with how to improve your communication with other people.)

Another excellent principle for dealing with people effectively is that of *acting* rather than *reacting*. If someone says something that bothers you, losing control and taking drastic action without thinking will only make things worse. Calmly doing what you know to be right, based on decisions you have made when the pressure is not on you, is the best course of action. The following story illustrates this point. A man and his friend left their office one evening to have an evening out. On the way, the two stopped by the bank to deposit some money. The man was very polite and cheerful, in contrast to the bank teller who was very impolite and grouchy. As the two drove away, the friend asked if the teller was always that way. The man replied that he went there every day to deposit money and always found the teller to be disagreeable. "Then why was your reply so polite?" asked the friend. "Why should I let *him* determine how *I* act?" replied the man. This man had learned the principle that he would be more effective in his life if he acted instead of reacted, if he didn't let other people determine his behavior.

Managers need to get out of their offices frequently and visit with members of the staff on their own home ground. Some managers find that they need to schedule regular meetings with each staff member. Also, *staff meetings* held every week or every other week help to facilitate communication and build relationships.

Giving recognition and praise are also useful methods of building relationships. Of course, whatever you say or do should be sincerely given and deserved. Many people, when given an oral note of praise, react by being embarrassed, but anyone would appreciate a sincere note of gratitude for a job well done. (See Chapter 7 for more information on giving rewards.)

## *Summary*

In order to change your style of leadership and to develop as a leader, you must understand yourself, understand others, and develop your interpersonal relationship abilities. The self-awareness chart is an effective technique of self-analysis. In order to understand yourself, you will need to take an inventory of your strengths and weaknesses in physical and psychological areas. You will also need to determine your level of self-acceptance; determining if you are in the circle of inferiority will be helpful. Making changes in your characteristics involves following specific guidelines.

Understanding others involves drawing comparisons between others and yourself and attempting to understand them through the knowledge you have gained about yourself. Communicating effectively with others means getting to know them; an examination of your expectations of others and their expectations of you should prove useful in your approach to effective communication.

Believing in the basic worth of the individual is essential in developing effective interpersonal relationships. Showing empathy, going out of your way to help people, listening carefully, acting rather than reacting toward others, meeting frequently with your group, and being liberal in giving recognition and praise are essential principles to follow.

## *Review and Discussion Questions*

1. What procedure could you use in gaining greater self-understanding? How would the self-awareness chart help you in this process?
2. Do you consider analytical thinking ability to be of greater, equal, or lesser importance than attitude? Why?
3. What is meant by the statement, "The self-image controls the mind"?
4. Explain why you think that the *circle of confidence* and the *circle of inferiority* apply to your life at one time or another. How can you break the circle of inferiority and get into the circle of confidence?
5. What guidelines should you follow in attaining goals and making changes in your life?
6. What are *expectations*, as used here? List the characteristics of expectations that would contribute to a greater understanding among people.
7. What steps can you take to help you develop more effective interpersonal relationships?

## *Application Exercises*

1. Draw a self-awareness chart that represents the way you see yourself at this time. Try to show spatially the approximate relationships between each of the four cells.
2. While in a group situation at school or at work, observe the interactions of various members of the group. What actions were effective in contributing to group goals and what actions were counterproductive? Analyze your own group processes.
3. In the process of answering the following questions, think about your life and the things that really matter to you: Who am I? Where did I come from? Where am I going? Summarize your thoughts in an oral or written report.

## *Mini-Cases*

1. As a supervisor of a mail room, you have seven people reporting to you—three men and four women. Four out of the seven are new to the section within the last six months. You are concerned because there seems to be much conflict in the office, particularly between the men and the women. Your expectations in terms of time for getting the mail out have not been met. You know you have clearly communicated what you expect because you gave everyone a memo on the subject of delivery deadlines. You are considering the need to write another memo to try to clear the air and get everything straightened out. What action would you now take?

2. Your secretary has been doing an excellent job until just recently. Last month he was late twelve times and left work early seven times. You have also noted an increase in the number of uncorrected typing errors on correspondence. You mentioned the problems to him but got no results. You think now you are going to have to get tough about the matter. What action should you take?
3. Most of the people in your office do a good job, with the exception of two people. Nat and Ralph are just "goof-offs." You knew from the moment you first saw them three months ago, when they applied for transfers from the accounting department, that you were in for trouble. You didn't think they would meet production standards, and so far they haven't. Twice you have caught them engaging in horseplay and disrupting the office. You gave them "the word" in no uncertain terms. You are not sure what to do next, since Nat and Ralph have more seniority with the company than any of your other employees. How do you recommend proceeding?

## *Reference Notes*

1. "About Being Business-like," *The Royal Bank of Canada Monthly Letter,* Vol. 54, No. 10, October 1973, p. 2.
2. Joseph C. Bentley, "A Powerful Circle," *The Instructor,* November 1969, pp. 398–99.
3. For an interesting discussion of how managerial expectations affect employee production, read J. Sterling Livingston's "Pygmalion in Management," *Harvard Business Review,* July–August 1969. This is an extremely significant article which should be read by all prospective managers.

## *Administrative Manager Profile*

Meet Richard W. Pope, C.A.M., underwriting manager at Farm Bureau Insurance Company.

*Background and Experience.* Dick graduated from Drake University in 1959 with a B.S. degree, after his education was interrupted by a four-year hitch in the U.S. Navy. During his last year in college, he began his insurance career as a rate clerk with the Insurance Company of North America (INA). He worked for INA in various underwriting and managerial positions for fourteen years at several locations. In 1972, he returned to Des Moines to join Farm Bureau Mutual.

*Company.* Farm Bureau Insurance is actually two companies: Farm Bureau Life Insurance Co. and Farm Bureau Mutual Insurance Co. Both companies market in Iowa and Minnesota, and the life insurance company also markets in Nebraska and North Dakota. Assets for the two companies exceed $375 million, and new business premiums have been growing rapidly. In August, 1974, the companies moved into the new 180,000-square foot building located in West Des Moines.

*Job.* Dick, as underwriting manager, has four major responsibilities: (1) manages underwriting for automobile and personal lines of insurance, (2) develops and implements company training programs, (3) participates in corporate planning activities, and (4) represents the company before the state insurance commissions.

Making certain that $35 million worth of insurance policies are properly underwritten and issued in accordance with prescribed standards is Dick's primary responsibility. Naturally, he must understand the basics of insurance underwriting, but his primary task is to manage technical employees who get the job done. As a manager, he performs the basic management functions of planning, leading, organizing, and controlling.

Providing training for agents and agency managers has become an important and interesting secondary responsibility for Dick. Some of the training is conducted at the home office, but he travels frequently to scattered Farm Bureau agencies to conduct field seminars.

Dick's position on overall corporate planning councils reflects the amount of respect and trust higher management has placed in his judgment, and this responsibility is a particularly challenging part of his job.

Finally, Dick appears at hearings and other proceedings of state insurance commissions to represent the company. All of these responsibilities create an enriched job that he finds highly motivating.

*Observations.* Dick Pope is a professional manager. He earned his C.A.M. as a way of attaining professional recognition, but more than that, he pursued the C.A.M. as a means of managerial development. He wanted practical management training from a generalist approach. Through the C.A.M. program, he obtained functional management skills and knowledge necessary to improve his total administrative management potential.

Dick believes that his job is to make his employees successful. In order to do this, he tries to remove obstacles from the paths of his people. Employees who work for Dick participate in the decision-making process. By becoming involved in this process, they feel greater responsibility for departmental operations, contribute their experience to formulate better decisions, and are able to grow and to develop professionally.

Sound planning is another important part of Dick's work. He says, "If you can't plan it, you can't do it." In other words, you must be able to think through an operation in your mind before carrying it out. Also, he firmly believes in the value of delegation as a means of helping employees grow and helping the manager do the job.

The C.A.M. program fits well with Dick's interest in building people, delegation, and long-range planning. After preparing himself to be a C.A.M., Dick has worked to help build the program by serving as a member of the board of directors of the Academy of Certified Administrative Managers, by giving talks on the C.A.M. program, and by encouraging his employees to work for the C.A.M. designation.

# PART TWO

# The Administrative Manager Motivates

Getting people to move on their own — to be self-starters — is one of the major challenges all managers face. The theme of Part Two is how to get people to do things because they want to, not because they are forced to.

The first chapter in this part, Chapter 4, discusses conditions in business and industry prior to World War II and in the next two decades. You will learn about the Hawthorne studies, which were enlightening and instrumental in initiating the human relations movement. Also, you will become acquainted with Douglas McGregor's Theory *X* and Theory *Y*, which have had a great impact on shaping management behavior. McGregor will prod you to examine your viewpoints about people; in reality, how do you look upon other human beings?

Chapter 5 presents a motivational model that provides a framework for discussing motivation. You will learn about Maslow's hierarchy of needs and Herzberg's theory of motivation. Herzberg emphasizes the need to give people more responsibility in order to help them obtain satisfaction on the job. A simple, four-step procedure for developing motivation is discussed.

Job enrichment, a natural outgrowth of Herzberg's ideas on motivation, is presented next in Chapter 6. This chapter also focuses on the building of teams.

Chapter 7, the last chapter in this part, discusses positive reinforcement as another way of influencing people's behavior. Being positive and looking for the good in your employees rather than seeking their negative qualities is conducive to forming more satisfactory work attitudes. Providing rewards when they perform in an effective manner reinforces their positive behavior. The concept of the self-fulfilling prophecy is also examined in this chapter.

The principles discussed in Part Two should guide you in helping people move on their own initiative because they want to.

4

# Early Research and Thought on Motivation

Prior to the middle of this century, workers were treated as just another element of production. Working conditions were dreadful, and health and safety hazards were abundant. Employees were expected to work twelve to sixteen hours a day, six days a week; wages were low and fringe benefits, if given at all, were meager. Even though workers were exploited, they were grateful to have employment, particularly during times of recession or depression.

During the latter part of the 1800s, Frederick W. Taylor, the father of *scientific management*, introduced the scientific method to the business and industrial world as an organized or systematic approach to solving problems. Originating in science, the method is equally applicable to solving management problems. Five basic steps are involved in Taylor's interpretation: (1) define the problem, (2) gather facts, (3) develop a tentative solution or hypothesis, (4) implement the solution and try others if necessary, and (5) do the follow-up work to make certain that the solution is viable.

Frank and Lillian Gilbreth, well-known from the book and movie *Cheaper by the Dozen*, developed *time and motion studies* that broke down work into small, basic parts and involved the stopwatch to determine how much time is needed to complete basic operations. These studies are the basis for *work simplification*, *work standards*, and *incentive wage plans*. Work simplification is the study of work operations to develop the most efficient methods. For example, in processing a mail order for blankets, a work simplification study would attempt to eliminate unnecessary steps, cut down on the distance the order traveled from desk to desk, and make the order form as simple and as clear as possible. Work standards are indications of time that should be taken to complete various units of work. For example, the standard time to process an order might be 10 minutes. Incentive wage plans are bonuses paid for work completed in excess of a standard amount. If an order clerk had a standard of 50 orders to process in one day, incentive pay might be given for each order processed in excess of 50 in any one day. The Gilbreths also developed the *process chart* and the *flow diagram.* (See Chapter 19 for further explanation of the process chart and flow diagram.)

Employees were studied by *efficiency experts* who gave them new, faster methods of accomplishing work. "There's always a better way" and "Work smarter, not harder" are favorite slogans for this efficiency movement. With the simplification of work, assembly lines were introduced. People found themselves turning nuts onto bolts hour after hour or soldering a particular wire into place on products. Each person had one specific task to do for each car, radio, or other product that he or she worked on. People became cogs in the wheels of production and, in the process, lost the satisfaction that comes from a job well done. Workers felt unimportant, dissatisfied, and unmotivated by their routine, repetitive jobs. This brief background provides the setting for the Hawthorne studies that are discussed in the following section.

## HAWTHORNE STUDIES

One of the most important series of studies ever conducted in business has come to be known as the *Hawthorne studies.*[1] These studies changed the thinking of business authorities insofar as human motivation is concerned. Before the Hawthorne studies were conducted, managers commonly thought (and many still do) that workers could be manipulated simply by paying higher wages or by changing the physical conditions and surroundings in which the work was produced. Because of these studies, managers have come to realize that human beings are extremely complex and that numerous psychological factors enter into human behavioral patterns.

The Hawthorne studies were conducted at the Hawthorne plant of the Western Electric Company in Chicago. Elton Mayo was leader of the research team. The first experiment began in 1924, and the studies were continued for 15 years. Throughout the experiments, both workers and managers were kept informed about the research procedures. In other words, the participants knew that they were involved in the experiments.

The plant in which the studies were conducted engaged primarily in producing telephone equipment. Most of the workers had relatively highly specialized duties such as inspecting small parts, assembling relays, or winding coils. The first phase of the studies dealt with changing the lighting where the employees worked. The assumption behind these experiments was that output would be greatest under the most favorable lighting conditions.

To determine which level of lighting was best, the researchers altered the level of illumination while at the same time recording the change in worker production. They observed that when lighting was increased, production increased; moreover, additional increases in the illumination level also resulted in increased production. When the lighting was subsequently decreased, however, *production continued to increase.* At one point, workers were operating under almost moonlight conditions, yet their production was still increasing. The researchers realized something was happening that they did not understand and that brought unpredictable results. In later studies, they tried new research methods, but these studies were equally inconclusive. In most of the studies, worker production increased regardless of the different lighting variables introduced into the work environment.

### Analyzing the Factors

The researchers' frustration caused them to examine other factors in an attempt to determine what really caused the increased productivity. One of the subsequent experimental phases examined the effect of an incentive system on worker production. One group of workers was put on a production incentive system—for above-standard production, they received extra compensation. The group, called the "experimental group" because experiments were being carried out on the incentive system, increased its production as expected. But a second group that had no incentive system or other changes introduced also increased its production. From this phase of the studies, the researchers concluded that the incentive system could not be considered in isolation and that psychological and social factors also affected employee production and morale. (Psychological factors refer to those mental, emotional, and behavioral characteristics of a person that are not part of his or her physical characteristics. Social factors refer to relationships with other persons.) In other words, the attitudes of employees and their relationships with other employees were important factors.

### How Psychological and Social Factors Affect Response

In another phase of the study, workers and supervisors were interviewed to determine their feelings about such things as working conditions, supervision, and job preferences. The researchers frequently found that responses differed among individuals working on the same job in nearly identical environments. This finding suggested that workers were bringing many personal factors with them as they performed their work. The interviewers also found that employees' complaints were more often *symptoms* of problems rather than *causes* of problems; for example, when Joan complains of headache and fever, she is bringing out the symptoms of a disease and the doctor must determine whether a virus or bacterial infection is the cause. Similarly, Joan may complain about low wages (symptom) when her real problem might be a feeling of lack of recognition (cause) because she has found out that Barbara, who works at the next desk, is making more money than she is. The complaints were usually related to the employee's social position or relationship to other people. The researchers concluded that various job factors carried significant social values. This conclusion was further complicated by the realization that a specific job factor might be more important to one worker than to another.

Another experimental phase involved a group of men who performed the very repetitive task of wiring electrical "banks." These men were specifically selected and isolated for closer observation to see what effect social groups had on production. This group soon established a set of self-imposed rules that each group member was expected to observe. Among other things, the group set their own production quota: for example, to wire two units in a day. They might have easily produced six or eight units, but they enforced their own standard and restricted output. Violations of these rules and quotas resulted in social punishment from the other group members. One form of group punishment that was used is known as *binging*—a violator of group norms was punched on the muscle of the arm. Another form of punishment was excluding the offender from group participation. These group standards were effective in holding down production rates even though management was giving monetary incentive to produce more. The threat of losing status in the social group was more important to the workers than earning more money.

The Hawthorne studies showed that although people do work for money, how they work for their money is determined to a large degree by their attitude and by social values. Work serves not only as a source of monetary satisfaction, but also as a source of psychological satisfaction. Consequently, managers cannot assume that simply increasing pay will produce increased production and satisfaction. Humans are very complex creatures with psychological and social needs, and the more successful manager will work to satisfy both kinds of needs.

### The "Hawthorne Effect"

The researchers learned that the fact that research was being conducted was an influence on the behavior of the employees. The employees interpreted the research as attention or recognition from management. When the employees received this recognition, they increased their productivity. *The influence of the research itself on the results of a research study is known as the "Hawthorne effect"* and is something that modern researchers have come to recognize and have tried to overcome in their experiments.

Several major conclusions can be drawn from the Hawthorne studies. The Hawthorne studies:

1. Demonstrated the importance of employees' attitudes and human relations
2. Showed the importance of group relations in regulating production

3. Pointed out that complaints are often symptoms rather than actual causes
4. Showed that wages, hours, and working conditions are important as status symbols
5. Demonstrated the importance of informal social organization
6. Pointed out that increased recognition has more influence on production than changes in the incentive system or work methods

In short, the Hawthorne studies were influential in starting the human relations movement in business and industry. Another outgrowth of the Hawthorne studies is that effective administrative managers see the need for giving their attention to developing good relations with their group.

While interpersonal relations is probably the most important factor in management, the scientific approach to management still has its place. Scientific management tools such as systems analysis, work measurement, work standards, and incentive pay plans are still important.

## McGREGOR'S THEORY X AND THEORY Y

The Hawthorne studies set the stage for further exploration into the human side of the organization. Douglas McGregor, a pioneer in advanced management thinking, wrote *The Human Side of the Enterprise* in 1960.[2] He developed two contrasting theories about the nature of man that have been extremely influential in shaping management thinking—Theory *X* and Theory *Y*.

People can be divided into two groups according to the assumptions they make about others. In the first group are people who tend to feel that (1) most people will try to get by with as little effort as possible and (2) other people don't come through when needed. This first group is usually disappointed with the performance of other people and feels that most people are "selfish" (Theory *X*).

On the other hand, there is a second group that usually makes these kinds of assumptions about other people: (1) other people are basically good, (2) other people try to do the right things, (3) other people are helpful and cooperative. If people from this second group are assigned to team leader positions, they expect that their team members will cooperate fully. Sometimes team members disappoint them, but normally people come through (Theory *Y*).

McGregor, in the fifties, formalized these two contrasting viewpoints about the nature of human beings into what he called *Theory X* and *Theory Y* (see Table 4-1). These theories can be thought of as being placed on opposite ends of a continuum or as a series of variations from one extreme to another. In both theories, McGregor begins with the unstated assumption that management is responsible for using organizational resources to make a profit.

**Table 4-1. McGregor's Theory X and Theory Y**

| *Theory X—traditional assumptions about people* | *Theory Y—emerging viewpoint about people* |
|---|---|
| 1. "The average human being has an inherent dislike of work and will avoid it if he can." | 1. "The expenditure of physical and mental effort in work is as natural as play or rest . . . . Work may be a source of satisfaction . . . or a source of punishment. . . ." |
| 2. "Because of this human characteristic of dislike of work, most people must be coerced, controlled, directed, or threatened with punishment to get them to put forth adequate effort toward the achievement of organizational objectives." | 2. "External control and the threat of punishment are not the only means for bringing about effort toward organizational objectives. Man will exercise self-direction and self-control in the service of objectives to which he is committed." |
| 3. "The average human being prefers to be directed, wishes to avoid responsibility, has relatively little ambition, wants security above all." | 3. "Commitment to objectives is a function of the rewards associated with their achievement. The most significant of such rewards, e.g., the satisfaction of *ego* and *self-actualization needs*, can be direct products of effort directed toward organizational objectives." |
| | 4. "The average human being learns, under proper conditions, not only to accept but to seek responsibility. Avoidance of responsibility, lack of ambition, and emphasis on security are generally consequences of experience, not inherent human characteristics." |
| | 5. "The capacity to exercise a relatively high degree of imagination, ingenuity, and creativity in the solution of organizational problems is widely, not narrowly, distributed in the population." |
| | 6. "Under the conditions of modern industrial life, the intellectual potentialities of the average human being are only partially utilized." |

*Source:* Douglas M. McGregor, *The Human Side of the Enterprise* (New York: McGraw-Hill, 1960), pp. 33–34, 47–48. Also, McGregor, *Management Review,* November 1957, Vol. 46, No. 11, pp. 22–28.

*Figure 4-1.* In the past, management has treated workers as an element of production; these workers of the 1930s are in crowded conditions in a room with dim light and no ventilation.

### Theory *X*

Theory *X* is the traditional viewpoint about people that many managers still hold. In essence, McGregor is saying that many people have negative feelings about others and thus feel compelled to try to force them to work. For example, Mike McGuire grew up feeling that he had to fight for everything he got. He believed in "doing unto others before they could do it unto him." Mike was a loner. He found that he could never depend on anyone, so if he wanted something done right, he did it himself. Now Mike is an office supervisor and he feels that he must drive people to make them work. As long as they know who is boss, everything usually turns out okay. Mike's employees generally enjoy working for him. They always know where they stand, and they don't have to think too much about what they are doing.

### Theory *Y*

Theory *Y* is a concept that shows people as being basically good; this theory suggests that people generally will try to do the right thing and that the task of the manager is to set up the proper work conditions to encourage individuals to do their best. As an example, let's look at Maria Sanchez, an office supervisor who sees people quite differently than Mike McGuire does. Maria grew up in an atmosphere of trust and love. She likes most people and people tend to respond well to her. When Maria was promoted to a supervisor, she instinctively built good relationships and shared decision-making authority with her employees in the office. Maria concentrates on developing her people, and they respond by generally giving their best to their work.

Many people see themselves as being Theory *Y* oriented. They see other people, such as their boss, being the ones who are still Theory *X* oriented. For example, a supervisor named John attended a management seminar in which a young professor explained Theory *X* and Theory *Y*. John walked out of the seminar behind his boss, Elmer Stewart, who was three levels up in the organization. Elmer was a man of great autocratic power, a man who made all major decisions by himself. John overheard Elmer say, "By golly, that was great. My people sure needed that lecture." The boss had failed to see the relevance to his own life.

## Application

Seeing the wisdom in a theory and making lasting changes in your attitude toward human beings are two entirely different things. For example, Roger Merritt, administrative services manager, attended a seminar in which he learned about Theory *Y*. He became excited as he thought about its potential effect on his employees. Roger thought about some changes he could make in his own management style. He gave his accounting clerks more freedom to make decisions about the reports they prepare. He authorized the mail room supervisor to make her own decision on the new addressing machines. In general, he loosened the controls on his people and allowed them to make more of their own decisions. Roger felt good about the progress he was beginning to see in the way his employees were starting to use their own initiative. Everything was going along smoothly until three weeks after the seminar when a problem was revealed. Roger learned that in his absence his assistant, Mike Lamoto, had gone directly to the director of administration, Roger's boss, with a report on inventory discrepancies. Roger was furious! The inventory problems were minor and could be easily corrected. But now both he and the department looked as if they were ineffective. Mike tried to explain that he was just trying to do his job. Roger responded by saying that he just couldn't trust anyone else in the office to handle even a small problem. From then on, Roger decided to tighten the controls again, and that was the end of his short-lived Theory *Y* approach. Why did Theory *Y* not work in this case? The reason is that Roger had not made necessary changes in his life and thinking processes to accommodate the change. When the going got rough, he had very little real trust in his people.

Let us briefly compare and contrast how managers holding Theory *X* assumptions or managers with Theory *Y* viewpoints might approach various leadership problems or situations. Evelyn Bendiken is an administrative manager who holds Theory *X* assumptions. Evelyn controls her subordinates closely: everyone in the office must punch a time clock, coffee breaks are scheduled at 10:00 A.M. and 2:00 P.M. for everyone, and Evelyn personally checks to make sure everyone is back 15 minutes after the break. She personally checks all work that leaves the office and is quick to call attention to any errors. Most decisions about routine office problems are made personally by Evelyn. She relies on money and verbal tongue lashings as primary motivators to get work accomplished. For Evelyn, *performance appraisal* is a time to sit in judgment over her group. She doesn't mind telling them exactly what they have done wrong during the year. Evelyn feels that she must keep on top of everything so that her office will run smoothly and her employees won't take advantage of her.

In contrast to Evelyn, Tim O'Toole is an administrative manager who holds Theory *Y* assumptions. One of Tim's primary goals is to develop a *climate of trust* in his office. He believes in delegating broadly. When he delegates, he explains exactly what objectives he has in mind and then he leaves the person alone to develop his or her own methods for obtaining the results. Tim believes in motivating employees by giving them more responsibility and by *enriching* their *jobs* or making the work more meaningful. Tim consults his people on all key decisions and attempts to communicate openly with them on a two-way basis. He allows his people to prepare *self-evaluations* and to make their own suggestions for self-improvement. He tries to build teams of *self-starting*, self-directed individuals who attempt to do their best and reach their *potential*. Tim sees himself as a *resource person* and his personnel as members of a *team*. He doesn't see himself as a superior and his employees as subordinates.

Because of McGregor's important work, he was influential in getting managers to think about their assumptions with regard to people and in setting the stage for later motivational research which will be discussed in the next chapter.

## *Summary*

Prior to World War II and particularly in the nineteenth century, workers were treated as an element of production. They were shown little respect, and working conditions were poor.

The Hawthorne studies, which were started in 1924, revealed the importance of employee attitude and of social factors in employee work motivation. Employees generally responded favorably to the attention received from management as a result of the studies. Social pressure was shown to be a powerful force in regulating production. Employee complaints often were found to reveal symptoms rather than causes of problems. For example, an employee who complained about his or her salary may really have been concerned that someone else was making more money; the money was an important status symbol.

During the 1950s, Douglas M. McGregor developed Theory *X* and Theory *Y*. These theories present two contrasting sets of assumptions or viewpoints about the nature of man. Theory *X* assumes that man is not ambitious and dislikes work; management's task is to force employees to produce. On the other hand, Theory *Y* assumes that people want to do their best; lack of motivation on their part results from poor experiences in the organization.

The Hawthorne studies and Theory *X* and Theory *Y* have been influential in setting the stage for later motivational research.

## *Review and Discussion Questions*

1. In what ways does employee attitude affect work performance? Give examples.
2. How important is the peer group in regulating group behavior, enforcing adherence to group norms, and directing production performance? Can you think of examples from your own experience that indicate how you or other people have been affected by the group?
3. Status symbols are commonly used as motivators. Give some examples of status symbols you have encountered.
4. In your own words, explain why you think the Hawthorne studies are important. What were the major findings resulting from these studies?
5. What are the major premises of Theory *X*? Do you agree with Theory *X*? Why or why not?
6. What are the major points of Theory *Y*? Do you agree with it? Why or why not?
7. Can you give examples of people you have worked for who typify either Theory *X* or Theory *Y* managers? How did you feel about their leadership?

## *Application Exercises*

1. Interview one or more administrative managers or leaders in order to get their viewpoints about Theory *X* and Theory *Y* approaches to management. Explain the theories to them, in your own words, if they are not already familiar with McGregor's theories. (Report on your findings as directed by your instructor.)

2. Examine your own set of assumptions about people. Discuss your thoughts with a friend or a member of your family, and then make a list of the key assumptions you have made about human beings. Consider your own leadership behavior to see if your actions are consistent with your assumptions.
3. Observe groups in action to determine how important group pressure is in modifying the behavior of group members. Record specific incidents to confirm any conclusions you may draw.
4. Write a short research report on the life and/or the accomplishments of one of the following individuals: Frederick W. Taylor, Frank and Lillian Gilbreth, Elton Mayo, Douglas M. McGregor.

## *Reference Notes*

1. F. J. Roethlisberger and William J. Dickson, *Management and the Worker* (Cambridge, Mass.: Harvard University Press, 1939).
2. Douglas M. McGregor, "The Human Side of the Enterprise," *Management Review,* Vol. 46, No. 11 (November, 1957), pp. 22–28. Also, Douglas M. McGregor, *The Human Side of the Enterprise* (New York: McGraw-Hill, 1960).

# 5

# Development of Motivation

"Give me someone who is motivated—a self-starter. I want someone who will move on his own without my having to tell him everything to do."

These words could have been uttered by anyone who has ever attempted to manage. Most managers are looking for people who are motivated to do excellent work. They are looking especially for employees who do not only what the boss said but also what the boss intended to say.

*Motivation* is an internal process that causes people to take some particular action because they want to. For example, Betty is excited about the new dictation equipment that will be used in the office. She has read books, magazine articles, and reports in her spare time at home to help her become better informed. She even spent several lunch hours visiting other offices to see various types of equipment in operation. Betty has enjoyed this project and has moved ahead on her own because she wanted to. This desire to work results from an anticipation that rewards and satisfaction will result from an action. Frequently, reward and satisfaction will come from the doing itself rather than from the attainment of a particular end.

How to get people motivated, or in other words giving them something to work for, is the subject of this chapter. A model of motivation, or a diagram that shows a basic motivational plan, will be discussed to demonstrate how motivation functions. Then, two theories that explain what will motivate people will be discussed. The first of these theories is *Maslow's hierarchy of needs;* the second is *Herzberg's theory of motivation*. Finally, these ideas will be integrated. But first, let's look at the model.

## MOTIVATIONAL MODEL

Our model, Figure 5-1, is a systems model composed of the same four basic parts shown earlier in Figure 1-3. These parts are (1) input, (2) processing, (3) output, and (4) feedback. *Input* consists of an external *stimulus*, or something

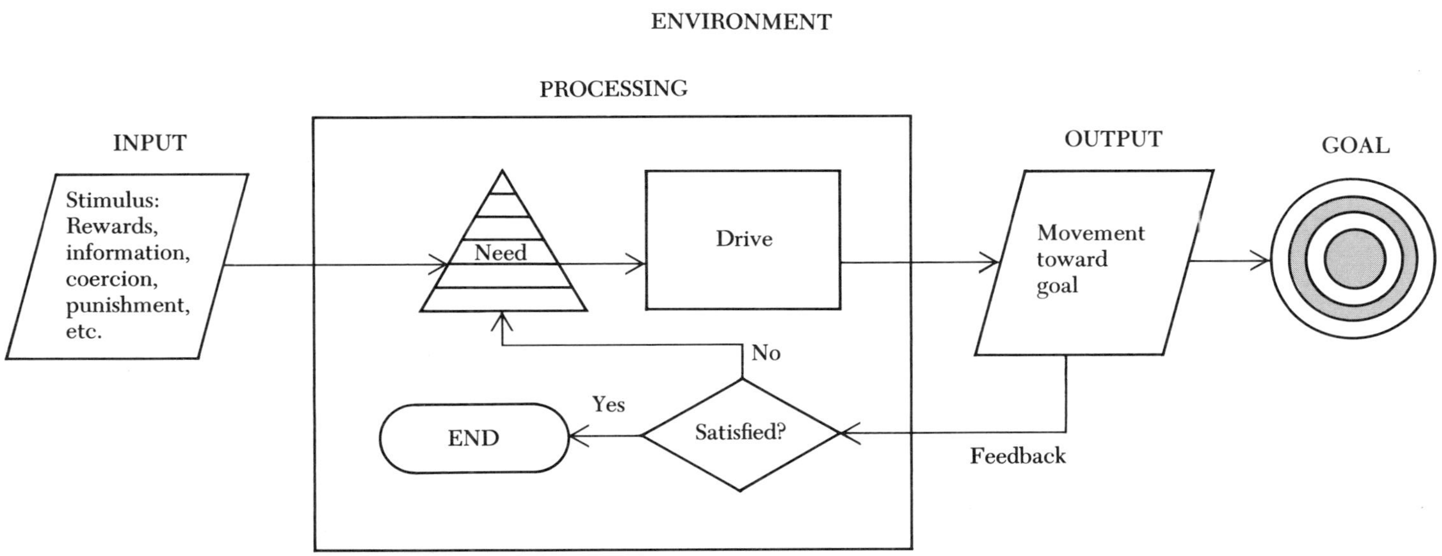
ENVIRONMENT
PROCESSING
INPUT
Stimulus: Rewards, information, coercion, punishment, etc.
Need
Drive
No
Yes
END
Satisfied?
OUTPUT
Movement toward goal
Feedback
GOAL

that causes action, such as anticipated rewards or information that is received by the individual.

*Processing* takes place in the mind of the person. Everyone has many needs, wants, and impulses that can be grouped together under the term *needs* for convenience of discussion. Examples of needs include a desire to have your boss tell you that you have done a good job in getting out a special report, a need for a pay raise so that you can buy a new car, and a feeling of being accepted by other people in your office. Needs trigger a drive within the person to accomplish a certain goal that will presumably satisfy the need. *Drive* is an intense desire or commitment to action that will result in *movement* of the individual toward the goal. Normally, the motivational process, which starts with the desire to have a need satisfied, will be triggered either directly or indirectly by some outside stimulus. For example, Geri, a file clerk, has a need for esteem or recognition (which is generated entirely internally), but her desire to satisfy that need in some particular way (e.g., always making the fewest filing errors) is influenced by outside stimuli such as comments from her supervisor. *Output* results from internal motivational processes and takes the form of movement toward the goal.

The fourth part of this system is *feedback*. Whether the individual is successful in attaining the goal or not, the results are reported back to the brain of the person. This process of checking up on how well one is doing in terms of goal achievement is known as feedback. For example, if you are successful in reaching your goal of reducing costs of office operations to their lowest level ever, you will have feelings of *satisfaction*. If you fail to achieve your goal, your feelings will be that of *frustration* and *dissatisfaction*. Positive feedback showing progress toward a goal tends to increase drive. On the other hand, feedback showing attainment of the goal results in fulfillment of the need, and drive is drastically reduced or eliminated. For example, after your boss compliments you on achieving your goal of reducing office costs, you will tend to think about other needs and goals. Frustration of progress toward the goal will either intensify, diminish, or eliminate drive for that particular goal. If feedback is eliminated, the previously motivated individual will tend to reduce his or her progress in moving toward the goal until feedback is received or until attainment of the goal appears to be imminent. In terms of the example of reducing office costs, if your boss fails to give you feedback on how he or she feels about your progress toward your goals, you will probably discontinue your progress toward the goal.

Hersey and Blanchard discuss the difference between *goal-directed activity* and *goal activity*.[1] Goal-directed activity is behavior that leads the person toward the attainment of a goal. For example, if your goal is to buy a new dictation machine, reading advertisements for equipment, driving to the office equipment distributor's showroom, and trying out the dictation equipment are all goal-directed activities. Actually making the purchase of the equipment is a goal activity. Goal activity, then, is the actual achievement of the goal, whereas goal-directed activities are actions leading toward that achievement. Goal-directed activities produce more intense drives than goal activities. Most of the motivation appears to come in the process of reaching goals. Once the goal is reached, the drive is either eliminated or diminished. As Maslow has said, unsatisfied needs are motivators; once a need is satisfied, it is no longer a motivator.[2] The need may become a motivator again in the future when the present satisfaction wears off. For example, after you have eaten a large meal, additional food is not motivating and the thought of more food may be sickening. But after a few hours, when you become hungry again, food again becomes motivating.

Figure 5-2 illustrates the process of goal attainment. (1) An individual moving toward goal A encounters an obstacle. The individual may have feelings of frustration, dissatisfaction, and motivation all at the same time. (2) The person may then take a second approach that is essentially the same or that is

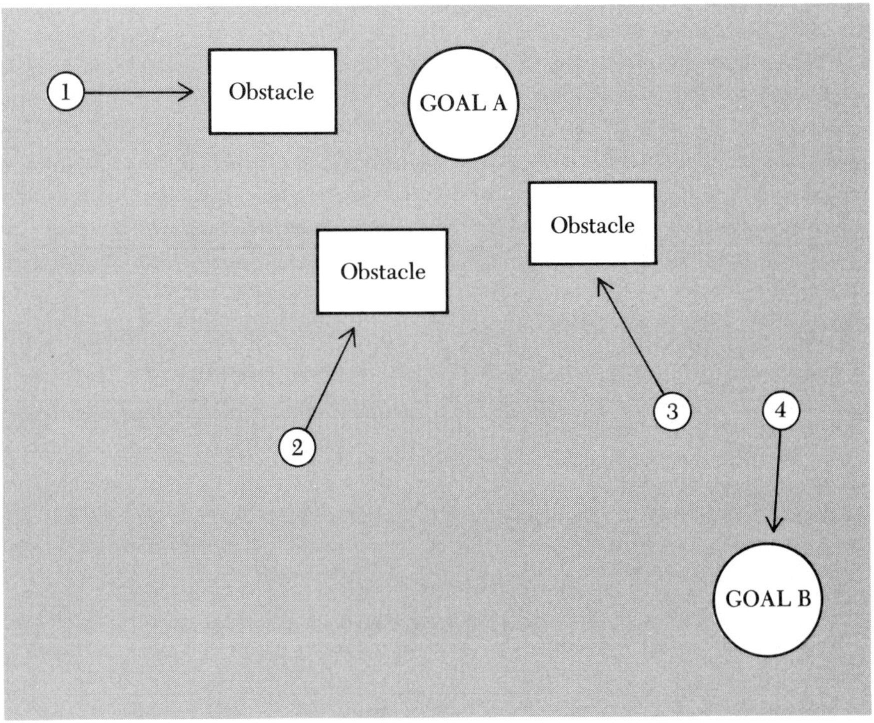


*Figure 5-2.* Goal Attainment

The process of attaining a goal is shown after several trials that resulted in frustration. Goal A was not attained and Goal B was substituted.

different from his or her first trial. Assume that an obstacle is again confronted. At this point, frustration and dissatisfaction are likely to increase. Motivation may weaken, increase, or remain the same, depending on the individual circumstances. (3) If additional trials present an obstacle, the individual is likely to abandon the goal and (4) move toward a new goal (B) which may promise more success. Progress in reaching the new goal will decrease frustration and, probably, dissatisfaction. Motivation will increase.

Now let's consider needs. Maslow's hierarchy of needs is helpful in gaining an understanding of this concept.

## HIERARCHY OF NEEDS

In 1943, Abraham H. Maslow developed a *hierarchy of human needs* in which he attempted to classify these needs according to five basic categories: physiological, safety, love, esteem, and self-actualization.[3] The scheme can be shown in the form of a pyramid (see Figure 5-3). The first level of needs is *physiological* or body needs, which include such things as air, food, water, clothing, and shelter.

This type of need is listed at the base of the pyramid because this need, when unsatisfied, is of primary importance and is of the greatest intensity. If you are hungry, the search for food is your main interest until that need is satisfied. Administrative managers need to think about the physiological needs of their employees and work hard to make sure that their employees have adequate incomes and comfortable office environments.

The second level is *safety*. Next in order of priority, safety needs include such things as job security, old-age security, and freedom from danger. Obviously, safety is very important to you if your life is threatened or if you see the possibility of losing your job. When physiological needs have been somewhat satisfied, safety needs come into play.

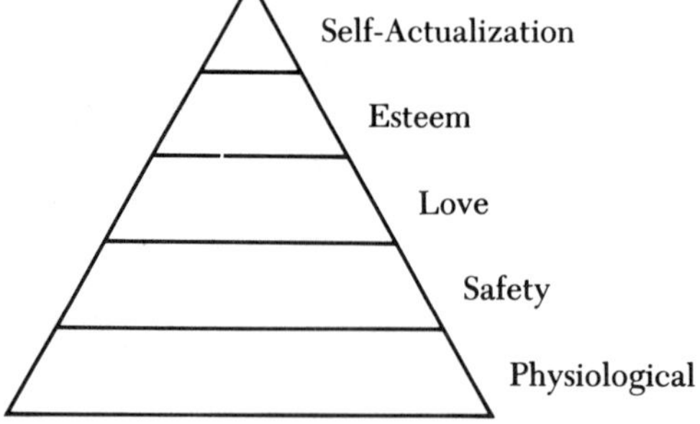


*Figure 5-3.* Maslow's Hierarchy of Human Needs

Of course, there are some exceptions to the pattern in which needs are satisfied in our lives. If someone is holding a gun on you, you are not likely to be too concerned about food unless you are literally starving. For the most part, however, people attempt to satisfy, at least partially, one level of needs before becoming concerned about the next level. The diminishing size of the area on the pyramid reflects its position of lesser attention and lower intensity than the physiological area.

The third level of needs is *love,* and examples of this area are to love, to be loved, and to belong. Love is the subject of poems, books, songs, and gossip, and it is something we all need. Love, as opposed to the first two levels of needs, is psychological rather than physiological. Psychological (mental, emotional) needs are very powerful determiners of our actions. Safety may be both physiological and psychological.

The next level of needs is *esteem;* examples of the need for esteem include self-esteem or self-respect, recognition (esteem of others), and prestige. Maslow said:

> Satisfaction of the self-esteem need leads to feelings of self-confidence, worth, strength, capability and adequacy; of being useful and necessary in the world. But thwarting of these needs produces feelings of inferiority, of weakness, and of helplessness.[4]

Thus, the esteem need is extremely important, and the manager or leader must be sensitive to this category of needs.

The last level of needs is *self-actualization.* These needs include reaching one's potential and self-fulfillment or self-realization. Maslow says that very few people become self-actualized, since most of us operate at a level far below our potential. Some people reach their potential in some areas while falling short in others. Can you think of anyone who has become self-actualized or at least is well along in the process? Answers to this question vary widely. Some will say Einstein, Abraham Lincoln, Thomas Edison, or other famous people.

Look at Figure 5-3 again; obviously, not everyone will have this same *pattern* of needs; for some people, the pyramid might be inverted with self-actualization being the most potent need and physiological the least. Someone else might be primarily concerned about love and have varying degrees of concern about other levels.

Maslow suggests that the way to motivate workers is to help them meet their needs. As a manager, you will need to get to know your employees in order to determine what needs are important to each of them and to see how each person's needs can be met through participation in the organization.

Table 5-1 suggests actions a leader might use to satisfy each level of needs. (Can you add to the list given in the table?) Let's look at a few of the items that may be less familiar to you—management by objectives, availability of resources, and catalytic leadership. *Management by objectives* is a goal-setting system that we will discuss in detail later in this chapter (and also in Chapter 15). *Availability of resources* means that the supervisor makes sure that resources are made available to his or her employees in order to accomplish their work objectives. *Catalytic leadership* refers to the concept of the supervisor or manager acting as a catalyst or change agent to help his or her employees get things done. For example, as a catalyst you might make a suggestion to one of your employees about what might be done to improve or increase production. If the employee reacts to your suggestion by taking positive action, you have served as a catalyst.

Most managers tend to provide for needs on levels 1 and 2 shown in Table 5-1, but they do not know how to work with self-motivated people who are reaching toward their potential. Managers who are able to delegate effectively, provide challenging work, manage by objectives, give freedom to their team members, provide adequate resources, and be catalysts are likely to be effective leaders. Let's turn now to Herzberg's theory of motivation.

**Table 5-1. List of Supervisory Actions Categorized by Maslow's Levels of Needs**

| *Level* | *Need* | *Supervisory Action* |
|---|---|---|
| 5 | Self-actualization | Challenging work<br>Management by objectives<br>Freedom<br>Availability of resources<br>Delegation<br>Catalytic leadership |
| 4 | Esteem | Recognition<br>Status symbols<br>Authority<br>Emphasis on positive |
| 3 | Love | Group identification<br>Appreciation<br>Climate of trust and approval |
| 2 | Safety | Pension plan<br>Safe environment |
| 1 | Physiological | Good salary<br>Good working conditions |

## HERZBERG'S THEORY

Rather than focusing on needs, Herzberg concentrated on what employees do on the job. He conducted research with engineers and accountants to determine what causes employees to be motivated on the job and what causes them to be dissatisfied.[5] He found that factors that lead to satisfaction or motivation are generally different and distinct from those factors that lead to dissatisfaction. The motivators are:

Achievement

Recognition

Work itself

Responsibility

Growth and advancement

All of these factors relate to the job as opposed to the work situation.

Factors that lead to dissatisfaction are:

Company policy and administration

Supervision

Interpersonal relationships

Working conditions

Salaries

All of these factors relate to things about the job situation rather than the work. Herzberg called these factors dissatisfiers or *hygiene factors*.

Herzberg suggested that motivators and dissatisfiers are not the opposites of each other. For example, increasing salary will eliminate dissatisfaction with the salary level; the increase will not provide motivation, however. The fact that decreasing responsibility does not cause dissatisfaction but causes a person not to be motivated is another example of Herzberg's theory.

Herzberg found that there is some overlap between the factors. For example, Wally Cordova, who operates an offset duplicator at English Products, works hard and expects to receive periodic wage increases. For most people, money is simply a source of dissatisfaction if the salary level is not adequate, but other people, like Wally, find money to be motivating to a certain degree. While this overlap does exist, the factors are generally separate and distinct.

Herzberg repeated his research with many different types of work groups and found basically the same results in all groups. He advocated trying to eliminate dissatisfiers as an initial step. Such things could be done as (1) increasing salary to a level slightly above the local prevailing wage, (2) cleaning up the working conditions, and (3) training supervisors to be more effective. Remember that eliminating dissatisfaction is a continual process, because employees forget such things as salary increases and soon become dissatisfied again.

After the work situation has been improved, Herzberg said something then should be done to provide increased motivation. Increasing responsibility and restructuring the job so that the employee gains greater satisfaction from the work itself can provide motivation to the employee. Motivation, however, is an internal process, and although the manager can manipulate the work and other external factors, the employee must supply his or her own motivation.

## EMPLOYEE MOTIVATION

In an attempt to integrate the theories of Maslow and Herzberg with our motivational model, let's discuss a procedure that could be used in helping your employees to be more highly motivated than they would be otherwise. Our concern is to help them install their own generators to keep themselves recharged and attempting to do their best. Essentially, responsibility is placed on the individual for his or her own accomplishment and contribution to the organization. Try to give the employee something to work for.

### The Four-Step Procedure

***1. Let the employee participate in setting his or her goals.***[6] These goals should be meaningful and challenging to the employee as well as make an important contribution to the organization. For example, your secretary, Jill, decides to set up a new filing system that will make important papers more readily available. She plans to purge the files (destroy unnecessary papers), investigate a new system for locating materials, set up a records center (low cost storage area away from the office), and prepare a filing manual (a book that explains the new system).

As a supervisor, you should know your employees well enough to understand each employee's needs. Keep these needs in mind as you make suggestions about the employee's goals. Also, another very important point is that allowing the employee to participate in the goal-setting procedure will help the employee to achieve self-actualization and esteem needs. The employee will reach toward his or her potential and will feel more important. Goals that the individual sets or participates in setting will give additional responsibility and more likely will be accomplished because the individual has had input in the goal-setting process.

*Management by objectives* (MBO) is a goal-setting program that involves persons at all levels of the organization in setting goals for their areas of responsibility. In the example used previously, Jill set up a goal to develop a new filing system. As the administrative manager, you decide that Jill's idea was excellent. You are pleased with the results in your office and you decide that the filing systems for your whole company should be reviewed. You ask your records manager, Barbara Merrill, to think about developing an appropriate objective. Together, you and Barbara study the problem and finally agree that about 45 percent of all of your current records could be destroyed or sent to a records center. You estimate that this action will save your company a minimum of $52,000 during the first year. Later you explain to Jill what has happened as a result of her idea. Jill, Barbara, and you are all excited about this project.

This example illustrates the motivating power of objectives. Notice, too, how the objectives worked their way up from the lowest level of the organization and were integrated into an objectives program for the entire organization. The goals were cooperatively set rather than imposed by the manager.

Accomplishment in an MBO setting is evaluated in terms of the objectives. In fact, all management functions can be related to objectives, and MBO ties in individual goals with the rest of the organization. (More information on this topic can be found in Chapter 15.)

***2. Provide resources that help your employees to accomplish the goals that have been set.*** Resources such as time, money, materials, equipment, assistance from other people, and technological knowledge are important factors in getting a job done. As a supervisor, you become a *resource person* who helps to provide these resources.

***3. Give the employee responsibility and authority.*** Then hold him or her *accountable* for accomplishing the goals which have been established. Allowance can be made for unusual circumstances, but the employee knows that results based on his or her own goals are expected. Frequent reports on progress made on the goals will be required.

***4. Do your best to improve the working conditions that cause dissatisfaction on the job.*** These factors, which are external to the employee, tend to center around things that are given to or done for the employee. It seems to be a truism that "the more people get, the more they expect," and there appears to be no way of avoiding this spiral of increasing fringe benefits.

This simple, four-step procedure integrates the best of Maslow, Herzberg, and the management by objectives program to provide a workable employee incentive plan. Maslow's higher needs have been provided for, and Herzberg's emphasis on providing responsibility and improving hygiene factors have been incorporated into our procedure. In addition, employees will be involved in setting their own goals and evaluating their own progress based on these goals.

Herzberg is correct in suggesting that responsibility tends to motivate. Responsibility will not always be a motivator, however. Only if individuals perceive the increased responsibility as an aid in helping them to move toward their own goals will the individuals be motivated by the additional responsibility. Responsibility perceived as an obstacle to goal attainment may actually be a demotivator. Because of the importance of the individual's perception of the responsibility, the individual should be involved in the goal-setting process that will determine what responsibility the person will assume.

Motivation is a feeling of desire for and an expectancy of success in accomplishing goals. Motivators result from what the employees do for themselves rather than what someone else does for them. Motivation results in job satisfaction if a person's goals are actually accomplished.

### Factors Limiting Motivation

Finally, let's see what causes people *not* to be motivated. The following factors tend to limit an individual's motivation. As a supervisor, you should attempt to neutralize as many of these factors as possible in order to improve the motivation of your group.

Job-related:

Highly structured work
Repetitive, routine tasks
Low level of responsibility
Confining duties
No creative opportunity
Limited resources

Supervisor-related:

Lack of confidence in employee
Low expectations of employee
Unacceptable goals imposed on employee
Unrecognized accomplishment of employee
Disregarded employee communication

Employee-related:

Limited ability
Limited training and education in comparison with job
Undefined goals
Little or no accomplishment
No new horizons

The typical file clerk's job is an example of a job that inherently lacks motivational opportunity. Bill Whiting recently took a job as file clerk in the central filing department of Atlanta Mutual Life Insurance Co. Bill codes letters and documents according to a prescribed pattern and files the papers away. He also locates materials in the file. Day after day, Bill finds that he is doing the same things in the same way. After only a month, he is getting bored with the work and wishes he could do something else.

Bill tries talking with his supervisor, Mrs. Nettie Jones, but receives no satisfaction. All Mrs. Jones says is that the work has to be done and that Bill better get back to work or she'll have to find someone new to take his place.

Bill dropped out of high school after one year and has floated from one job to another. He can't seem to get ahead and doesn't seem to know what he wants to do. Bill decides to stay on the job because he needs the money and work is hard to find.

In this case, the supervisor has quite a challenge to try to help Bill become motivated. Moreover, this supervisor appears to be completely unprepared to meet that challenge. Perhaps the real problem can be traced back to the relationship between Mrs. Jones and her supervisor, Mr. Moriority. Has Mr. Moriority been effective in helping Mrs. Jones to become motivated and in helping her to develop the incentives of her own staff? The motivational problem involving low-level work, unmotivated people, and poor supervisors is a real and challenging puzzle for the administrative manager to solve. The manager who has faith in his or her group, who is willing to work hard to develop them, and who provides more challenging work is likely to solve this problem of motivation.

(Chapter 6 will give attention to applying motivational theories and techniques to practical office situations.)

## *Summary*

Managers and leaders want motivated people who are willing to go the extra mile. Motivated people have something to work for; they work because they want to.

A motivational model presented in the chapter discusses motivation in terms of a *system*. The input to the system is an outside stimulus. The processing phase takes place when a need and drive within the individual are triggered. The drive then leads to movement toward a goal, which is the output of the system. Feedback informs the person of achievement or frustration of goal attainment, which results in feelings of satisfaction or dissatisfaction.

The difference between goal-directed activity and goal activity is discussed: goal-directed activity leads the person toward attainment of a goal; goal activity accomplishes the goal. Unsatisfied needs are motivators; once a need is satisfied, it is no longer a motivator.

Maslow suggested that the five basic needs (physiological, safety, love, esteem, and self-actualization) are arranged in a hierarchy. Lower physiological needs tend to demand at least partial satisfaction before higher psychological needs are attended to. There are many variations to this pattern, however.

The manager needs to understand the needs of his people, in order to help them to work toward satisfaction of their needs.

Herzberg suggested that motivators tend to center around the work itself. The motivators tend to bring satisfaction. A separate, distinct set of hygiene factors, or factors related to the work situation, tend to bring dissatisfaction. In order to motivate employees, hygiene factors should be improved as much as possible, and the job should be restructured in order to give the employee greater responsibility.

A basic, four-step procedure for developing motivation within employees is to:

1. Allow the employee to help set goals
2. Provide resources to your employee
3. Hold your employee accountable for results
4. Improve working conditions as much as possible

The employee who has something to work for will actively work toward goal achievement. As a supervisor, you will be helping in that process.

## *Review and Discussion Questions*

1. What is *motivation?* Is it an internal or an external process?
2. In your own words, explain how the motivational model in Figure 5-1 operates.
3. What is the difference between the terms *goal-directed activity* and *goal activity?* Why is this difference important?
4. Do you believe that the statement, "Satisfied needs are not motivators," is true or false? Defend your answer.
5. Name the five levels of needs on Maslow's hierarchy. Give examples for each type of needs.
6. Explain in your own words what Maslow is attempting to say in his hierarchy of needs.
7. Why should the administrative manager be aware of Maslow's theory? What steps could be taken to help an individual reach his or her potential?
8. Explain in your own words what Herzberg's theory of motivation is. Do you agree with his theory? Why or why not?
9. What are the motivators and the hygiene factors which Herzberg proposes? What do the motivators have in common? What do the hygiene factors have in common?

10. Compare and contrast the four-step motivational procedure suggested in this chapter with Herzberg's theory of motivation.
11. What causes people not to be motivated?

## *Application Exercises*

1. Discuss with your classmates (or associates in your office, if you are working) what things motivate them and what things dissatisfy them. Think about your own experience, particularly in business. Attempt to identify the motivators and dissatisfiers in your own life.
2. In a small group setting in one of your classes or in your office, apply the principles of motivation you have learned about in this chapter.
3. Observe your supervisor or interview an administrative manager to determine what motivational procedures are used. Determine how closely the manager has followed principles that you have learned from this chapter.
4. Conduct a survey in an office to determine what needs people have and what motivators and hygiene factors are most influential on them. Ask your instructor for suggestions on how to proceed with this survey. (Perhaps you could use this assignment to satisfy a requirement to complete a primary research report for a report-writing, business communications, or English class.)

## *Mini-Cases*

1. *Jane* used to be one of your most productive employees when she was first assigned to your section. She could outwork most of the employees. Lately, she has seemed to slack off. She doesn't seem to care about anything. As her supervisor, you have talked with her and feel that she feels good about your treatment of her. She has received average pay increases, and the working conditions are excellent. You wonder what you can do to motivate Jane.
2. *Paul* is a constant complainer. He periodically tells you that his salary is too low. Paul's salary is above average for the office, and the wage level for your company is above average for your city and state. He complains about being too cold and then about being too hot. Even though Paul frequently complains, he is a good worker. The problem is that Paul's comments cause the other employees under your direction to feel discontented. Beth, Paul's supervisor, has tried to satisfy Paul, but the more she does for him the more he seems to find to complain about. What action do you recommend that Beth take?

## *Reference Notes*


1. Paul Hersey and Kenneth H. Blanchard, *Management of Organizational Behavior: Utilizing Human Resources,* 2nd edition (Englewood Cliffs, N.J.: Prentice-Hall, 1972), p. 16. Reprinted by permission of Prentice-Hall, Inc., Englewood Cliffs, New Jersey.
2. A. H. Maslow, "A Theory of Human Motivation," *Psychological Review,* Vol. 50, 1943, pp. 370–396.
3. *Ibid.*
4. A. H. Maslow, "Dominance, Personality and Social Behavior in Women," *Journal (Soc.) of Psychology,* Vol. 10, 1939.
5. Frederick Herzberg, "One More Time: How Do You Motivate Employees?" *Harvard Business Review,* (January–February 1968), pp. 53–62.
6. Step 1 is discussed in more detail than the other three steps because a full discussion of MBO will not be presented until Chapter 15. The other three steps relate to concepts that have been discussed previously.

# 6

# Job Enrichment and Team Building

How can you apply the motivational theories you learned in the previous chapter? The concepts of *job enrichment* and *team building* will help you answer this question.

## JOB ENRICHMENT

### Introduction

Mass production and work simplification are made possible because of the specialization of work effort. Specialization means that employees have a limited number of minor responsibilities to perform. The total job is broken down into a number of small tasks. For example, to produce and duplicate a brochure, the first person composes the text, a second person prepares illustrations, a third person types the originals, a fourth person photographs plates from the originals, a fifth person runs the plates on the offset machine, and a sixth person collates, staples, and binds. None of the employees is involved with the total process; no one has the satisfaction of overseeing the product as it moves from its beginnings to completion. These *specialists* may even feel that their work is meaningless and that they are powerless to control the outcome; if so, a lack of job satisfaction will usually follow (Figure 6-1). On the other hand, specialists become proficient in their duties and are likely to be highly efficient (Figure 6-2).

Through structuring or restructuring jobs, employees are given broader responsibilities that are intended to be meaningful, challenging, interesting, and rewarding. The basic objective is to tap the potential talent and ability of each individual employee. An enriched job:

*Figure 6-1.* The Hazard of Specialization

Specialized work may seem meaningless to the worker when he or she is not involved in the total outcome.

1. Provides increased responsibility and as much decision-making authority as possible
2. Is usually a complete unit of work
3. Provides frequent, direct feedback to the employee

In our example of preparing a brochure, you could enrich the job of the typist by making him or her completely responsible for preparation of the

*Figure 6-2.* The Advantage of Specialization—Greater Job Efficiency and Productivity

manuscript. The offset machine operator's job could be enriched by adding the responsibility for production of the final copy; he or she could also prepare the plates, collate, staple, and bind the brochure as well as run off the masters. Both jobs would have increased decision-making responsibility and would probably then meet our three criteria for an enriched job. The jobs have more responsibility, greater decision-making authority, more complete units of work, and more effective feedback than they did before restructuring took place.

***Comparison of Job Enrichment to Job Enlargement*** *Job enlargement* is similar to job enrichment in that it increases the scope of the job by adding duties and responsibilities of the same or a similar type. For example, the offset operator's job could be enlarged by having him or her collate and staple duplicated material as well as run it on the duplicator.

Job enlargement involves *horizontal job loading*, which refers to reassigning duties from one job to another at the same organizational level of responsibility. For example, if worker A types and worker B proofreads, a horizontal shift might be made so that both A and B type and proofread their own work. Organizationally, this is a horizontal redistribution of work (see Figure 6-3).

*Job enrichment* is similar to job enlargement in that both usually involve making the job larger. This enlargement process is usually necessary in order to satisfy our second criterion of involving a complete unit of work. At the same time, in job enrichment, the job may be narrowed down on other dimensions in order to keep it at a manageable size. For example, in enriching the job of an order clerk, the supervisor may give the clerk additional duties such as checking credit and filing orders, so that one person has complete responsibility for one order. Then, instead of handling all orders, the clerk may be assigned to handle only those orders coming from a certain territory such as the western part of the United States.

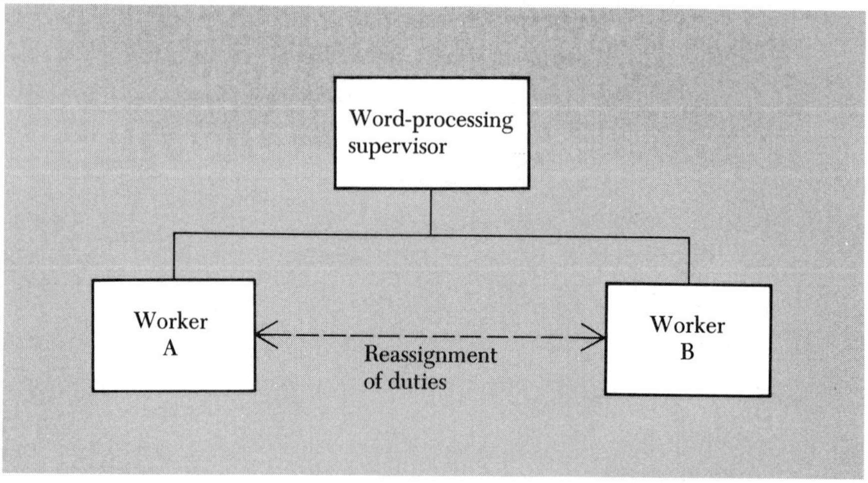


*Figure 6-3.* Horizontal Job Loading—A Feature of Job Enlargement

Duties are reassigned at the *same* level of responsibility.

Job enrichment really goes beyond job enlargement when the step is taken to give the employee more authority or decision-making responsibility. This process, known as *vertical job loading,* was developed by Frederick Herzberg. Vertical job loading means reassigning responsibility and authority from a manager, a supervisor, or a technical person to an employee lower in the organization whose job is being enriched (see Table 6-1). In the example of the order clerk, he or she might be given authority formerly held by the supervisor to make decisions about granting credit to customers; depending upon circumstances, this authority might be complete or restricted. Also, the clerk might be given authority to check his or her own work without having to consult with the supervisor. From Figure 6-4, you can see readily the vertical nature of the work being shifted. In the process, the employee is given greater control over what takes place on the job.

Adding these kinds of responsibilities results in job enrichment and in increased motivation. With job enlargement, no clear evidence of increased productivity has been demonstrated.[1] However, Herzberg found that job enrichment did increase performance and improved workers' attitudes about their jobs.[2]

***Benefits*** Job enrichment produces major benefits. Employees find greater motivation and job satisfaction in their jobs, productivity increases, and the quality of work improves. Employees find their work challenging, and the work becomes a way of satisfying higher psychological needs. Supervisors and managers find that they spend less time controlling activities, and more time

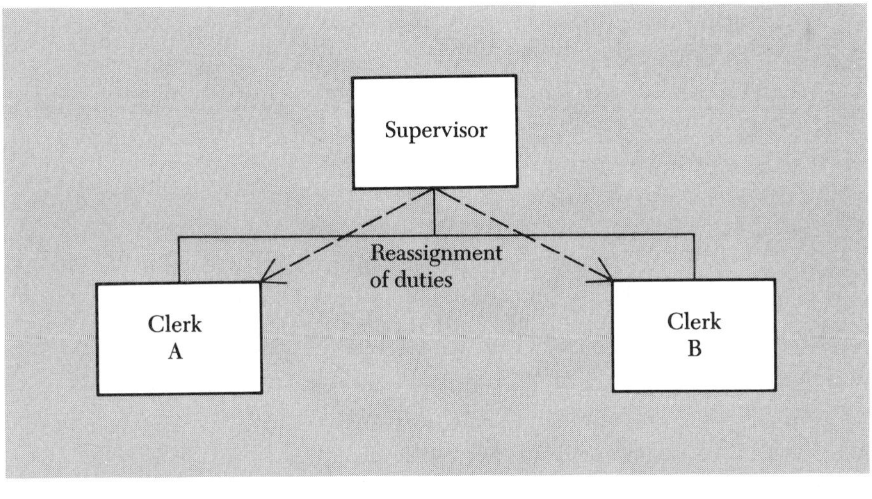


*Figure 6-4.* Vertical Job Loading—Characteristic of Job Enrichment
An employee is given more authority or responsibility.

**Table 6-1. Principles of Vertical Job Loading**

| *Principle* | *Motivators involved* |
|---|---|
| Removing some controls while retaining accountability | Responsibility and personal achievement |
| Increasing the accountability of individuals for own work | Responsibility and recognition |
| Giving a person a complete natural unit of work (module division, areas, etc.) | Responsibility, achievement, and recognition |
| Granting additional authority to an employee in his activity, job freedom | Responsibility, achievement, and recognition |
| Making periodic reports directly available to the worker himself rather than to the supervisor | Internal recognition |
| Introducing new and more difficult tasks not previously handled | Growth and learning |
| Assigning individuals specific or specialized tasks, enabling them to become experts | Responsibility, growth, and advancement |

*Source:* Frederick Herzberg, "One More Time: How Do You Motivate Employees?" *Harvard Business Review,* January–February 1968, p. 59.

is then available for long-range planning, policy making, and other managerial activities. While this decreased need for control should be an advantage, many supervisors see it as a threat and allow their resistance to change to impede progress. However, *Administrative Management* magazine reports that the use of job enrichment is on the increase.[3]

### Job Enrichment Procedure

The following suggestions indicate steps to be taken to implement job enrichment.

***1. Select the job to be enriched.*** Essentially, these are jobs where motivation is lacking and where increased motivation would result in greater productivity. Ask yourself why employees are currently unhappy:

Does the job provide challenge?

Is it primarily nonrepetitive in nature?

Does it require skill?

Is the work primarily planned by the employee?

Would *you* enjoy doing the work for eight hours per day, every day?

Suppose that you select the job of typist in the word-processing section of the engineering department as the one to be enriched. You ask each of the questions just mentioned about this job and come up with a "no" reply on each. You definitely couldn't see yourself typing eight hours per day, every day.

2. ***Study the job to determine how it is currently set up.*** All jobs involve the work itself, the organizational setting, the methods, the people on the job, the job environment, and the reward system. Study all aspects of the job to determine what parts of the job are sterile and unrewarding. Consult with the employees to determine what they like and dislike about the work. If you study the job of typist, you may find that this is a specialized position in the center; all each person in the typing pool does is type. You find that the main feature the typists dislike is the routine nature of the work. The procedure is as follows: each typist (1) takes the next work request from the in-basket or on the dictation system, (2) transcribes the document in rough draft or final form, (3) makes revisions as necessary and plays out the final copy on an automatic typewriter, and (4) gives the copy to the proofreader for review. Most of the typist's time is spent keyboarding or punching typewriter keys and waiting while the automatic typewriter types out data recorded on magnetic media such as cards or disks. The typists feel isolated from other people in the department, and they tend to feel that their work is not very important.

3. ***Brainstorm to develop suggestions for enriching the job.*** Brainstorming is a process of involving a group in creative thinking to bring out original ideas to solve a problem. During the first stage of brainstorming, the objective is to identify all ideas, no matter how unusual or impractical. No judgments about the ideas are allowed and hitchhiking on other people's ideas is encouraged. In the second stage, critical thinking takes place, and the long list is narrowed to those ideas which are most suitable.

In applying the brainstorming technique to our problem of enriching the job of the word processing typist in engineering, you might come up with ideas similar to these:

Have typists do their own proofreading.

Have typists work directly with engineers in solving problems about typing projects.

Have typists give completed projects to engineers.

Assign typists to administrative support team to work with engineers.

Organize teams of engineers with typists and administrative specialists assigned to team.

Have typists and other administrative support personnel trained to handle each others' duties and exchange places periodically.

Train typists in engineering terminology.

Train typists to handle routine work currently handled by engineers; examples: originating memos and reports, making copies, and filing drawings.

Some of these ideas might prove to be useful in enriching the typist's job. Suggestions for improvement should be requested from employees because they are so close to the job and will be more committed to making the changes work if they have been involved in developing them.

***4. Critically review the suggestions for enriching the job.*** Think carefully about the changes and their impact on all phases of the total work environment. Build a job that has real meaning, one that you would find challenging if *you* were performing it. In this critical review, as applied to the redesign of the typist's job, one of the central issues will be how much specialization versus how much breadth should be built into the job. The person who specializes in typing will become very proficient at that task. Some people might enjoy straight typing for a full work day, but most people would prefer having some variety in their assignments of work. Variety makes the work more interesting and provides a motivating factor that fights boredom. Thus, a trade-off between specialization and variety of work assignment is encountered. You want your typist to be typing as much as possible, but you also want that person to be motivated. A combination of (1) carefully designed work assignments, (2) carefully selected personnel, and (3) effective supervision will help in developing motivation.

***5. Introduce the changes and follow up.*** Meet with all people who will be concerned about the proposed changes. Using the example of the typists again, make sure that they understand what changes are being made and why. Have them try out their new job. Work out any "bugs" by checking back frequently to see how the job is going; see if there are any unexpected considerations. Keep records on typing performance to see if real productivity increases are occurring. (Real productivity increases refer to actual increases in number of units of production such as lines of typing or number of pages typed from one period to another.)

### Guidelines

Keep these five guidelines in mind as you implement a job enrichment program.

1. A properly designed job should include a good feedback system that will show employees any problems or errors and why they

occurred. The employees can then correct their own errors. The typist, in our example, should receive regular reports on his or her performance. This report would show lines or pages typed over the period of a week or a month. The typist would be able to compare his or her own performance over a period of time and also compare performance with others in the center. If the person needs help, the word-processing supervisor would be available for counseling.

2. Don't panic if employees make an error or two. When workers are allowed to check their own work, an increase in error rate does not usually occur.[4] For example, if you as a word-processing supervisor find an error, don't take back the authority you have given to your typists to check their own work; that action would tell them that you don't really trust them with the authority.
3. Realize that the new system will require a period of time to produce results. The typists, for example, will require time to learn their new jobs and to get used to increased responsibility. Production is likely to decrease initially, but once the initial learning period is over productivity should start to increase.
4. Realize that employee attitude toward work is dependent upon factors other than job content and technology. Supervision, general economic conditions, and hygiene factors are a few factors that have a major impact on the employee. To return to our example, don't be too discouraged if you don't reach all typists. A few are likely to remain unmotivated regardless of what you do.
5. Develop an adequate control system that holds employees accountable for meeting specified standards of production. Employees need to know exactly what standards they will be expected to meet. For example, on typing from dictation media such as magnetic belts or tape with no replay, you may expect at least six hundred lines per day from an experienced word-processing operator. Also, they need to realize that their efforts will be suitably rewarded. Successful applications of the job enrichment concept usually result in jobs that are more meaningful, have well-defined accountability, and have rewards related to employee performance.

**Application**

To show how job enrichment can be applied, let's look at how a secretarial job can be enriched. Improving the secretary's job gives the boss increased time for creative activities. Here is an analysis of the duties of a secretary and a manager.

| | |
|---|---|
| Secretary: | Receives and opens mail<br>Reads mail<br>Sorts mail by priority |
| Manager: | Reads mail<br>Requests files and other information from secretary for letters requiring an answer<br>Composes and dictates reply<br>Performs other action on mail not requiring a reply, e.g., underlines key points to be remembered, makes notes, marks materials for file, and so forth |
| Secretary: | Takes replies in shorthand and types letters or transcribes letters from machine dictation<br>Performs other action as directed by manager<br>Files material not involved with reply |
| Manager: | Reads reply, proofreads, and otherwise checks accuracy<br>Signs letters and returns them to secretary or requests corrections |
| Secretary: | Makes corrections as necessary<br>Mails letters<br>Files copies |

If you analyze this procedure carefully in terms of possibilities for job enrichment, you will note that the secretary's job may be rather dull and unrewarding. Also, the manager is doing some work that is quite routine and overlaps with the secretary's. This executive needs more time for creative activities that only a manager can do.

Giving the secretary greater responsibility for answering correspondence will make that job richer and will release the manager's time for more important activities. The following revised list of responsibilities shows how job enrichment principles can be applied.

| | |
|---|---|
| Secretary: | Receives and opens mail<br>Reads mail<br>Sorts mail by priority<br>Obtains files and necessary information<br>Composes and types replies to all letters except those that secretary knows should be answered personally by the manager<br>Proofreads letters<br>Signs routine letters personally, gives other letters to manager for signature<br>Reviews reference materials as time permits and summarizes key points on note cards |

| | |
|---|---|
| Manager: | Reviews and signs letters needing signature. Requests necessary corrections<br>Reviews note cards for information. Looks at references in more detail as necessary<br>Dictates answers to the few letters which require personal replies. Uses information supplied by secretary |
| Secretary: | Prepares dictated replies for manager's signature. Proofreads<br>Mails out other letters<br>Files letters and other materials |
| Manager: | Reads and signs letters that have been prepared for the manager's signature or requests corrections |
| Secretary: | Makes corrections as necessary<br>Mails letters<br>Files copies |

With this new procedure, the secretary has much greater responsibility. The manager answers only critical or very sensitive letters. The secretary answers most of the correspondence, does most of the research to obtain information, and does all of the proofreading.

The manager could not expect a new, untrained secretary to take on this much responsibility initially. The secretary must be trained carefully and gradually allowed to assume greater responsibility according to his or her ability. In this revised situation, the secretary should be highly motivated. The manager also should be greatly relieved of unnecessary work and be more productive.

Managers need to examine their own areas of responsibility to determine if the concept of job enrichment can be applied. Application of job enrichment is likely to help managers be more effective and to offer job incentive to those they supervise.

### Acceptance of Job Enrichment

While pointing out a rapid growth rate for job enrichment, *Administrative Management* magazine reported a high rate of dissatisfaction with job enrichment because of difficulty in measuring results.[5] Acceptance of this or any new program is related to the degree of skill with which the program is implemented. Specific criteria (such as number of lines typed or number of copies duplicated) must be identified. Involving employees in changes that affect them and communicating with them fully about what you are doing and why you are doing it will help to break down resistance to change. Following the principles and guidelines outlined in this chapter should help you to successfully implement job enrichment. To be most effective, job enrichment requires a Theory Y climate. As a manager, you must realize that a difficult but important phase in introducing progress is to bring about a change in attitudes and philosophy.

## TEAM BUILDING

Anyone who has played on a basketball or football team, served in an armed services combat unit, competed on a debate team, or had some similar experience knows how effective a team can be (Figure 6-5). Team members tend

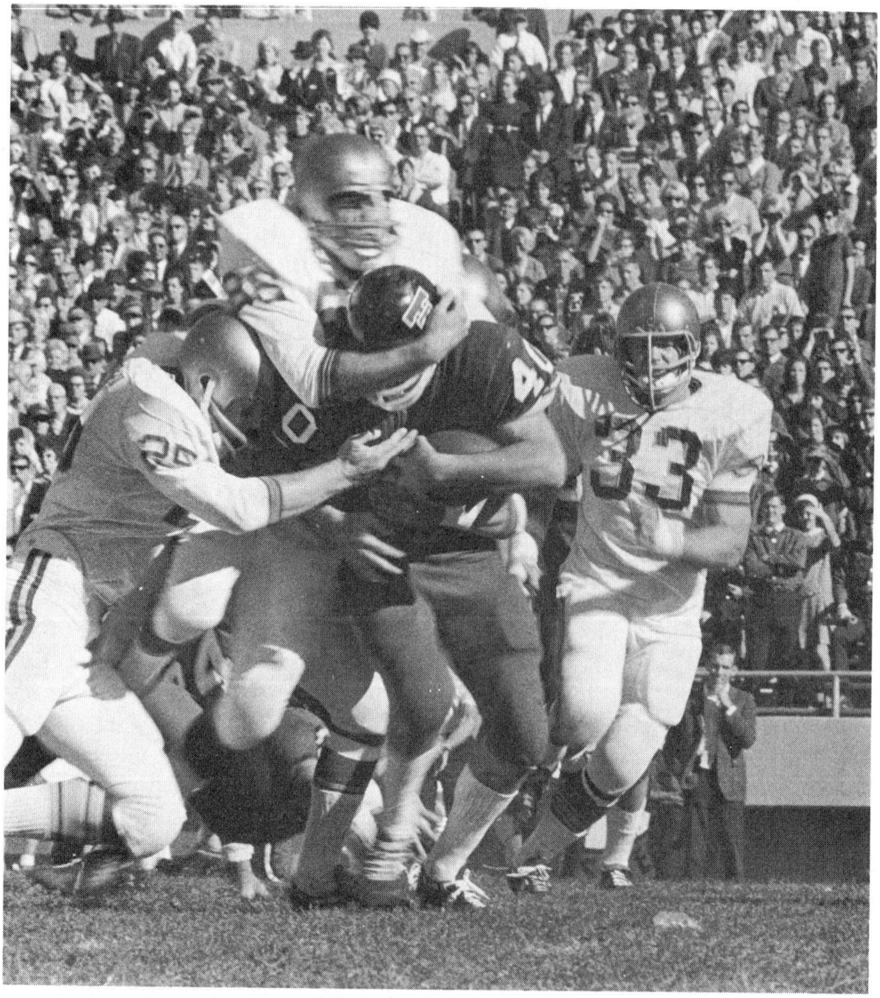

*Figure 6-5.* Teamwork Relies on the Effectiveness of Each Team Member

to understand their assignments and know that the success of the team depends upon the effectiveness of each team member.

Teams are used successfully in business, industry, and many other areas as well. For example, plane crews and ground crews operate harminously to keep giant airlines operating safely and smoothly. Another example is medical teams in which doctors, nurses, and paramedics work together to save lives. Business regularly uses project teams to solve special problems. Experts from various fields or disciplines are organized into teams for the purpose of solving specific problems. One national chain of hamburger drive-ins operates with the most efficient methods possible, and it was *time and motion studies* along with technological advances that made a three-minute food order a reality; this superspeed order is possible only when the employees function as a team and take pride in their accomplishment (Figure 6-6).

**Relation to Motivation**

Teams have also been used as a motivational tool when responsibility is shifted from a supervisor to a team. A team organizes and operates itself without

*Figure 6-6.* A Team Can Produce Faster Service

formal control from supervisors. The team has complete responsibility for the total process or a complete unit of work (Figure 6-7).

*Team building* is defined as the reorganization of individual workers, now doing only a small part of a total process or unit of work, into a team that is responsible for completing that total process or unit of work.

*Figure 6-7.* The Team Has the Responsibility for an Entire Unit of Work

A team is self-directed and makes all of its own operational decisions. The supervisor is available as a *resource person.* If a team determines that help is needed, the supervisor is called upon to provide assistance. A team sets its own *production quotas* and *quality standards.* Discipline is enforced by the team itself. If someone is seriously hampering the operation of a team, a recommendation may go to management to discharge the individual.

Limited experience with team building shows that a team can help to improve production and quality. Employees are more highly motivated and tend to accept responsibility well. Turnover and absenteeism are reduced. Although team building is still in its infancy, it holds great promise for the future.

We will use several examples to show how team building operates. General Foods' Gaines dog food plant reorganized office and production jobs on a team basis, and as a result motivation improved, absenteeism was reduced, and personnel turnover became negligible.[6] Kuriloff reported on a successful application of team building in an electronics company. He found the following results were obtained from the use of team building: (1) a 30 percent increase in productivity was obtained, (2) quality was improved, and (3) motivation was improved (as evidenced by the fact that many employees took electronic theory classes on their own time).[7] Rice reported an increase of efficiency and a decrease in damage rate in a textile mill after adopting team building.[8] Trist reported a major increase in productivity and the ability to remain on schedule or to move ahead of schedule in a coal mining operation where the team approach was used.[9]

### The Office Team

To help you understand how this team concept can be applied to the office, we will look at an example based on a real office situation. The scene is the headquarters building of a major corporation located in Minneapolis. You will be looking at the administrative support team in systems development, which is a part of systems and data processing and is under the consumer foods division. Systems and data processing occupies most of one level of the east wing of the large, sprawling building located in the suburbs.

Systems development is responsible for all computer systems and programs used in the division. The word *systems,* as used here, refers to a series of interrelated elements that perform business operations; one of those elements is normally the computer. *Programs* are detailed instructions that tell the computer how to operate. (Refer to Chapter 25 for more detail.)

Most of the systems development work is accomplished by programmer analysts who are organized into project teams; these analysts develop systems and write programs. Project team leaders direct the efforts of analysts assigned to them during the life of a project, which can last up to nine months.

Lora Oliver, formerly a programmer analyst, is responsible for the administrative support team—a group that supplies typing and other administrative services to the managers and technical staff. Lora reports to Larry Beam, who is a programming manager and who in turn reports to Darwin Heath, director of systems development. Darwin and Larry are both very supportive of Lora's efforts to develop an effective administrative support team.

Susan, LuAnn, Judy, and Darlene all are members of that support team. Susan is a bright young woman who serves as team leader and types on the Linolex word processor (automatic typewriter). LuAnn answers the phone, runs the copy machine, and runs errands. Judy and Darlene are both part-time employees who have been trained to operate the Linolex word processor. Judy works the midday period between 10:00 A.M. and 2:00 P.M., while Darlene comes in at night between 4:00 P.M. and 8:00 P.M.

The team operates on their own, for the most part, without much direct supervision from Lora; but they know that they can call on her if they need help. Lora handles the budget and purchases new equipment for the team as needed. The group is consulted and makes recommendations about major decisions that affect it such as equipment changes, reporting requirements, and work organization.

Susan takes the lead in keeping work moving and coordinating the efforts of the team. The team leader handles all supplies, prepares reports, and handles special work requests for the managers, that is, travel arrangements and scheduling meetings. All members of the team work with all programmer analysts, project team leaders, and managers in handling typing and other administrative work requests.

The managers and other systems personnel have very little correspondence activity; they prepare few memos and reports but many systems proposals and other documents that provide records of the work that is being accomplished. Currently, all of the material is drafted in longhand. However, next month a new computerized dictation system will be installed on a test basis.

The team has done an excellent job. But Lora and the team members are constantly searching for new methods and new equipment that will make the job easier and allow them to serve systems development more effectively. The team is able to meet requested deadlines for work requests about 90 percent of the time. Because the team is small and is normally extremely busy, some systems analysts are forced to do their own routine administrative work.

Lora has considered enlarging the size of the team, but is currently not able to do so because systems development has reached their "head count" ceiling (limitation on total members of authorized personnel). If someone leaves the organization, a new person could be hired. Lora hopes to someday have people on the team who could provide some of the writing involved with documentation and some of the flowcharts (charts used to show an overall picture of the systems). This type of support would be greatly welcomed by the programmer analysts.

Darwin, Larry, Lora, and the other systems personnel all feel good about the administrative team concept and the way it has supported the organization. The members of the team feel that they are making an important contribution to the systems development effort. They all enjoy their work and are highly motivated. Turnover (people leaving the company) and absenteeism among team members are very low. Job satisfaction and morale are high. This team is an effective one because it is providing good administrative support to personnel in systems development. The members of the team are highly motivated and move ahead individually and collectively as a team to get the job done.

Team building holds great promise for the future. Much is yet unknown about how to work most effectively in teams, but rewards for building successful teams are high. Here is a challenging area the enterprising administrative manager could use in applying motivational theory to build the will to work.

## *Summary*

Job enrichment provides a solution to the problem of lack of job satisfaction resulting from highly specialized, monotonous work that lacks meaning. By structuring or restructuring the job to build in more responsibility and decision making, the job provides greater challenge and more meaning. The enriched job also involves a complete unit of work and should provide frequent, direct feedback to the employee.

The primary benefits of job enrichment are greater employee motivation, increased production, and reduced errors.

Enriching a job involves the following steps:

1. Select the job to be enriched.
2. Study the job.
3. Develop enrichment ideas by brainstorming.
4. Think critically about the suggestions.
5. Introduce changes and follow up.

Vertical job loading principles expand the job to include responsibility previously held by supervision or management. Vertical job loading taps various motivators to give the work increased meaning.

Job enlargement is similar to job enrichment in that both attempt to restructure the job by reassigning duties. Job enlargement, however, uses horizontal job loading, which is shuffling duties from one job to another at the same organizational level.

A successful job enrichment program is generally based on Theory *Y* philosophies. The program should be thought through and strategy should be planned carefully.

Team building is a relatively new concept that gives a group of individual workers responsibility for completing a total process or unit of work. The team is given freedom to make its own decisions, including decisions about production quotas, methods and procedures and control methods. The supervisor becomes a resource person to the team. Many organizations have successfully used the team-building concept to develop increased motivation, to increase production, and to reduce errors.

## *Review and Discussion Questions*

1. Why have mass production and work simplification had an impact on job satisfaction?
2. Define *job enrichment.*
3. What characteristics does an enriched job have?
4. Compare and contrast job enrichment and job enlargement.
5. From your own experience, give an example of what changes can be made in a routine job to enrich it.
6. What benefits can a manager expect to obtain from job enrichment?
7. Discuss the procedure that you recommend following in order to enrich a job.
8. Define *vertical job loading.* List and explain the principles of vertical job loading developed by Herzberg.
9. Assume that a supervisor assigns an employee to proofread his/her own work as a means of job enrichment. How should the supervisor respond if he or she detects an error that was overlooked by the employee?
10. How well has job enrichment been accepted in business and other organizations?
11. Describe the concept of *team building* in your own words. How does a team function?
12. Explain what benefits may be obtained from team building?
13. If you have ever had experience with a team, explain how the team operated.

## *Application Exercises*

Report your findings from the following exercises as directed by your instructor.

1. Select an office job and apply the five-step job enrichment procedure. (Report on the results to your class.)
2. Consult the *Business Periodicals Index* for articles written about job enrichment. Read two articles and report on your findings.
3. Think about jobs that you have held or now hold. Were any motivators built into these jobs? What steps could have been taken to apply principles of vertical loading to your work?

4. If you are or have been a member of an athletic team or some similar group, think about how the team operates and prepare a report on how the team uses or fails to use sound motivational principles. If you have not had experiences with a team, interview someone who has to gather information about the team and principles of motivation.

## *Case Study*

*Joan Means* is assigned the responsibility of producing the six-page monthly newspaper for her company, J. C. Nickels, Inc. Nickels is a large department store located in Burning Tree Shopping Mall. To accomplish this job, she has a staff of four people who also fill in with other responsibilities in the communications department.

Sandy and Maurine write news and feature articles based on interviews with employees located throughout the store. Sandy dictates her articles on a dictation machine, while Maurine writes hers out in longhand. Roberto types all of the articles in rough draft form and on masters. As supervisor, Joan carefully edits and proofreads the articles and then has corrections made by Roberto. George is responsible for duplicating the newsletter and getting it to the mailroom for distribution.

Joan has a rather high turnover and absentee rate in her department. Sandy, Maurine, and Roberto have all been on the job for less than six months. Roberto came to the department as one of the employees hired by the personnel department to fill its quota of minority people hired. At first, Joan thought he would work out fine, but now she is not sure. She thinks that Roberto's attitude is poor. He doesn't seem to be motivated. Lately, Roberto has been making more errors and seems to have generally slowed down. Sandy and Maurine are good to work with, but they seem to lack initiative; Joan has to tell them everything to do. George is her best employee and seems to do well.

You have tried some human relations techniques lately, but the response has been generally poor.

1. What is likely to be the real problem in this newsletter operation?
2. What specific steps can you take to improve motivation in the supervisor's area of responsibility?
3. What benefits do you see accruing from your recommended improvements?

## *Reference Notes*

1. Edwin B. Flippo, *Principles of Personnel Management*, 3rd ed. (New York: McGraw-Hill, 1971), p. 51.
2. Frederick Herzberg, "One More Time: How Do You Motivate Employees?" *Harvard Business Review*, January–February 1968, p. 60.

3. "EDP Leads the Thirteen 'Most Popular' Management Techniques," *Administrative Management,* June 1973, p. 64.
4. Roy W. Walters, "Job Enrichment Isn't Easy," *Personnel Administration/Public Personnel Review,* September–October 1972.
5. *Administrative Management,* June, 1973, pp. 28–29, 64.
6. Paul A. King, "Personnel Trends '73: Will the Office Go AWOL?" *Administrative Management,* January 1973, p. 22.
7. A. Kuriloff, "An Experiment in Management: Putting Theory Y to the Test," *Personnel,* November–December 1963, pp. 8–17.
8. A. K. Rice, "Productivity and Social Organization in an Indian Weaving Shed," *Human Relations,* Vol. 6, No. 4, 1954.
9. E. Trist, "Organizational Choice," London: Tavistock, 1963, as reported by John Censor in "The Coal Mine," Managing Human Resources for Administrative Management Society, 1971.

# 7

# Modifying Employee Behavior

## INTRODUCTION

As an administrative manager, your real goal is to bring about results through other people. In order to accomplish that goal, you want to eliminate nonproductive behavior and errors. In essence, you want to achieve maximum efficiency and effectiveness with the people, machines, materials, and money available to you. Of those resources, the human element is the most difficult to control. The administrative manager's problems can nearly always be traced to human beings.

Every organization faces the same difficulties, whether the organization comprises family groups, political groups, social service groups, religious groups, recreation groups, or any other kind of groups where the leaders continually wrestle with the problem of getting the members to do the right things or to stop doing the wrong things. Such efforts are met with various degrees of success, depending on the effectiveness of the leaders in dealing with human behavior. Similarly, every day you try to get your associates to perform the actions you want them to do, and they try to get you to do certain things for them. Some people seem to be very effective at manipulating others, while some seemingly cannot even control their own actions. In addition, some persons can be easily directed by certain individuals and yet refuse to accept the direction of others.

How effective are you in working with others? Can you get them to do what you want them to do? This chapter will examine procedures that are helpful in identifying and solving behavior problems.

## PROBLEM IDENTIFICATION

Before you can solve a problem, you must first determine exactly what the problem is. In a sense, you perform a diagnosis somewhat like that performed by medical doctors. When a sick patient is taken to a doctor for diagnosis, the doctor checks for symptoms. Does the patient have a fever or nausea? Does the patient have pain? After all the symptoms have been examined, the doctor tries to determine the cause of the patient's problem. In other words, the doctor knows that the fever, nausea, or pain is not the *cause* of the problem; it is merely the *symptom*.

Such is also the case in employee performance problems. If Clara, an administrative assistant, begins to show a decrease in production, the problem is not simply a lack of output. The lack of output is a symptom of the problem. A closer look might reveal that Clara's work decrease began just after Bonnie was selected as the new supervisor of the administrative services department. The close timing of both of these events suggests a possible cause-and-effect relationship between them. Further investigation might show that Clara and Bonnie did not get along well when they were "equals" and that Clara has limited her productivity as a method of protesting the selection of Bonnie as the supervisor.

The problem that exists between Clara and Bonnie can still be classified as a symptom. (In fact, it can be argued that a manager can never determine the "basic cause" of a problem, because human characteristics grow out of family and cultural developments occurring over many years.) Consequently, you should attempt to determine the major cause of the symptoms so that by curing that cause you will eliminate most of the symptoms.

Problems occur in organizations because of three major reasons: (1) people *cannot* perform correctly because of physiological (physical or mental) limitations, (2) people *don't know how* to perform correctly, or (3) people *do not have sufficient motivation* to perform the way they know they should. In other words, most problems are caused by physiological limitations, lack of knowledge, or lack of motivation.

### Three Cases

Consider the following three cases which represent examples of these types of problems.

***Case A.*** Marvin was always an awkward, uncoordinated boy and had difficulties in any activity that involved eye-hand coordination. In spite of this problem, Marvin enrolled in typewriting in high school in hopes of obtaining a clerical position. After two years of typing instruction, Marvin developed enough speed and accuracy to enable him to reach the minimum level of typing proficiency (50 words a minute with 97 percent accuracy) required by Anderson Co. Marvin was hired with the assumption that his typing skills would increase substantially on the job. After six months' employment, Marvin's speed had not improved at all.

***Case B.*** Al Perez, purchasing agent for Marsden Manufacturing, Inc., attended a seminar on improving business communications. At the seminar he learned about a new business letter format called "AMS Simplified." This format eliminates the traditional salutation ("Dear Mr. Allen" or "Gentlemen") and replaces it with a subject line. This format also eliminates the complimentary close ("Yours truly" or "Sincerely"). Convinced that this style would make letter writing to women less awkward by eliminating the salutation, Al decided to try the simplified format in his correspondence. Accordingly, he stated in his next dictation, "Type this letter in simplified style." When the typewritten letter was delivered to him, it was in the traditional format.

***Case C.*** Rita worked as a typist in a word-processing center. At the conclusion of each job she completed she was to record on a production form the type of job, the time required, and the department for which the job was completed. Rita had been trained to complete the form properly and she had been diligent in recording all the required information during her first three months on the job. After that time, however, she would fail occasionally to make appropriate entries. As a result, Rita's supervisor would be unable to make accurate charges to the departments who submitted the work.

It is apparent that Marvin has a physiological problem, Al's secretary has a knowledge problem, and Rita has a motivational problem. If a problem you encounter is caused by physiological inability, you need to fire or reassign the present worker and to select a new worker who can perform properly. If the problem is caused by lack of knowledge, the employee has a training problem and you need to provide more information. If the problem is caused by a lack of motivation, however, you need to implement appropriate motivation or behavior modification (behavioral change) methods. Compared to training, behavior modification is much more difficult to accomplish. From the previous examples, you can see that only a few moments of explanation would be required to teach Al's secretary the simplified letter style. Rita, on the other hand, knows what is expected of her; yet occasionally she chooses to ignore her job duties. Such a problem may take weeks to solve if Rita simply doesn't want to cooperate. Motivational problems, therefore, are much more serious and can be much more costly than training problems. Consequently, behavioral changes must be dealt with in a most skillful manner.

To determine whether the employee has a physiological limitation, a training problem, or a motivational problem, the performance of the employee needs to be diagnosed. First, determine whether the employee has ever performed the desired action correctly. If he or she has, you are probably faced with a motivation problem; you need to determine further whether it might be caused by other events such as personnel changes, equipment changes, or policy changes. If the employee has never performed the desired action correctly, you may have a training problem or a physiological problem. If the worker could perform properly if properly educated, the problem is obviously training-oriented. If training would not enable the worker to perform correctly, he or she has a physiological difficulty. (See Figure 7-1 for a

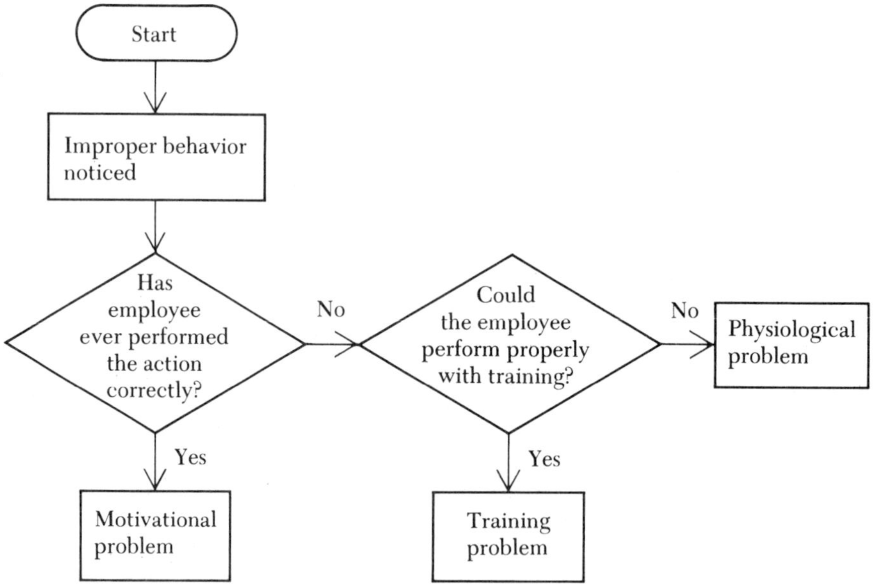


*Figure 7-1.* Problem Determination Process

simplified diagram of this process.) After you feel that you have accurately determined the cause of the problem, you must then determine a solution to the problem. (Solutions to training and physiological problems will be given in Chapter 13.)

Two of the more successful methods of solving motivation problems are *positive reinforcement* and *self-fulfilling prophecy.* These behavior modification techniques generally have a more limited focus than do job enrichment and MBO (management by objectives) programs. Positive reinforcement and self-fulfilling prophecy may be used alone or in connection with other motivation techniques. Thus, they are flexible in application yet influential and effective.

## POSITIVE REINFORCEMENT

Positive reinforcement is based on a very simple concept: *wait for the desired behavior to occur and then reinforce it with some kind of reward.* If you want your typists to learn to proofread effectively, you reward them when they make progress toward the goal. They are rewarded *only* when they make progress toward the goal. If they move in the wrong direction, they receive no reward. When they again move further toward the goal than they did on the last rewarded attempt, you reward them again.

This same basic concept will apply in many situations where you are working with people. For example, if you are trying to have your office force eliminate tardiness, you can use positive reinforcement. When Chris shows improvement by coming in at 8:05 rather than 8:10, you reward her by praising her for her effort to improve. If she comes later one morning, no reward is given; only when the desired behavior occurred would you reinforce it with a reward.

In the meantime, you may decide that the lateness is an intolerable situation. You may decide that you have to reprimand Chris or even fire her if this problem continues after giving her repeated warnings. Only you can make this decision. Reproval and punishment have their place, and they can be used effectively, but positive reinforcement usually results in longer-lasting change.[1]

After a person has learned and is performing to your expectations, how do you handle the rewards? If you were to reward your employees every time they did something right, the rewards would become commonplace and would soon lose their incentive value. For example, if you were a new executive assistant at Ajax Corp. and someone were to give you a $25 bonus, you would probably feel very good about it. If you received another $25 bonus the second week, you would still feel good. But how would you react if week after week you received the $25 bonus? You would soon come to expect it. It would be a routine, commonplace thing.

On the other hand, if you received a $25 bonus and then didn't get another one for three weeks and still another one for five more weeks, the bonus could be very enticing to you. This principle also applies to rewarding workers in the office who have learned to do some particular task. After they have mastered the task, reward them on an irregular or intermittent basis. This procedure will help to maintain a high level of performance.

Consider Rita from the previous Case C. To use positive reinforcement to change her behavior, the supervisor, Dennis, should initially provide reinforcement each day Rita records all the required information. Then following these several regular reinforcements, Dennis should make his reinforcement with decreasing frequency until the desired action becomes more or less automatic.

Summarizing the three basic positive reinforcement steps:

1. Identify the precise employee behaviors that you would like to see changed.
2. Ignore inappropriate behavior and reward the desired behaviors soon after they occur.
3. When a new behavior is being developed, reinforce it every time it occurs until it is firmly established. Thereafter, reinforce it on a more infrequent basis until occasional mention of it will still maintain it at a high rate.[2]

### Rewards

As an administrative manager, what different kinds of rewards can you give to your employees? Several possibilities are listed for discussion:

*Intrinsic rewards*[3]—relate to internalized factors:

Attention, praise, and recognition
Responsibility and promotions
Participation in decision making

*Extrinsic rewards*—relate to external factors:

Status symbols
Time off
Gifts and benefits (paid vacations, stock plans, and so forth)
Financial rewards

Attention, praise, and recognition are mentioned first because they are very powerful tools in the hands of a good leader. They satisfy one of the most basic *psychological* needs of man—being accepted and recognized by other people. In addition, they cost nothing except a little effort on your part. Look for the good in your workers and then say something specific about it. In an office setting, for example, you might praise a new records clerk for improving his or her file retrieval speed. Or you might recognize specific qualities in the report-writing skills of a new administrative assistant.

Responsibility and promotions are another type of reward. As discussed in previous chapters, many individuals enjoy the challenge that comes with increased responsibility, and they enjoy the sense of accomplishment that comes from a job well done. The highest form of motivation comes when people are working on tasks that they feel are truly significant. They lose themselves in a cause that they feel really matters. As a manager, you might give your secretary the responsibility of answering all routine correspondence or of developing a new office form. Or you might help an employee prepare for and achieve a promotion to administrative services supervisor or to senior word-processing operator.

Participation in the decision-making process can also be used as a reward. Those people who participate in determining policy and procedures will be looked up to by other members of the organization. Therefore, as an administrative manager, look for opportunities to consult with your employees. For example, involve all word-processing workers in major decisions affecting the word-processing department. Also, consult your mail center personnel in decisions that affect the flow and handling of mail.

Status symbols also could be used as rewards. A status symbol can be anything that makes a person feel more important because he or she is engaged in an activity or possesses a commodity that is socially desirable. Some people are more concerned about status symbols than they are about receiving more pay. Status symbols are really a means of gaining attention, praise, and recognition. All the rewards that have been discussed in the preceding paragraphs plus many other kinds of things may be used as status symbols. When one person earns more money than his or her peer, money may become a status symbol. Time off or vacations may also be status symbols. Titles are also frequently used as status symbols. For example, you might refer to the janitor as a custodial engineer, to the typist as a secretary, and to the secretary as an executive assistant. Finally, environmental factors may be used as status symbols. When you become a manager you might be given a private office with carpets, drapes, outside windows, and a private secretary.

Time off is an important incentive for many people. Try giving two people the same task of producing a list of five hundred names and addresses. Tell one person that as soon as the job is completed correctly to come back and you will give another assignment. Tell the second person that as soon as the task is finished correctly, time off will be given for the rest of the day. Most people will tend to improve their performance in the second situation. Time off can be overworked, though; if employees who do a good job are all rewarded in this way, they are removed from the job for a period of time. This type of a reward can be a disadvantage to the company since it pulls the employee away from the job and hence from higher production—the reason for the original incentive.

Gifts and benefits are another form of extrinsic reward. In a management position, you might be offered a two-week paid vacation to London for you and your spouse if your department achieves a 10 percent cut in operating costs, or perhaps stock in the company, a new company car for your use, or some other material item that might be rewarding to you.

Financial rewards are also powerful incentives. Although some motivational authorities might not agree, we are of the opinion that these monetary rewards should be directly related to job performance effectiveness. If people do a good job, they should receive a monetary reward because of their excellent job performance. The person using this type of reward should be sure that employee performance is truly benefiting the organization in terms of increased production. Otherwise, substandard work will be rewarded and fostered. As an administrative manager, you might notice that Jane, a word-processing operator, consistently produces 10 to 20 percent more output than anyone else in her department. To maintain her high level of motivation, it would be helpful if you increased her pay in proportion to her greater output.

### Guidelines for Applying Positive Reinforcement

Here are some well-established guidelines that will help in applying positive reinforcement to your leadership situation:

***Identify specific rather than general accomplishments.*** Rather than saying "You did a good job in preparing that report," say, "Your comparison of Andy's and Julie's performance on page 11 of the Monthly Performance Report was outstanding. You went even beyond what I had hoped for."

***Develop a positive approach—always look for the good and frequently give praise.*** Most people who criticize the work of others are looking for what is wrong, rather than what is right. Try being positive—for example, try complimenting a new typist on finding 95 percent of the errors in a manuscript rather than complaining about the 5 percent that were not found. You will find yourself with a new frame of reference if you are looking constantly for the good in other people's work. Once you find something good, be liberal in your praise.

***Use adverse criticism or punishment only when necessary.*** When you are constantly looking for the good and giving praise, you will usually find that it is not necessary to be negative. Individuals often will supply their own correction. In a positive climate, even an occasional negative critical comment will be well received as a means of improvement. If negative criticism is necessary, criticize the act and not the person; for example, talk about the typing errors made rather than about the "poor typist." Another key point to remember about criticism is that if you find that a sharp reproof is necessary, be sure to follow up with an increased amount of concern and support.

***Allow individuals to develop their own corrective feedback.*** Develop a climate in which the individual is not afraid to make mistakes and to fail. Provide constructive feedback and information to persons as they request it so they can assess their own behavior and make their own adjustments in behavior.

***Develop faith in positive reinforcement by putting the principle into action; start with noncritical areas.*** If you want to know the truthfulness of some principle, apply that principle in your life. Try living it. If you want to find out if positive reinforcement will work, give it a try. Start out on a small scale; for example, compliment your secretary on the effective job he or she does in screening telephone calls. As you start with areas of performance that are not critical to your organization, you will soon be able to work on more critical areas.

***Select rewards that best suit the individual.*** Because each worker is an individual with varying needs and drives, different workers will find that rewards provide varying degrees of incentive and satisfaction. While additional responsibility may be highly motivating to one person it may be very frightening and frustrating to someone else. After you have gotten to know the employee, select the form of reward that will obtain the best results.

***Be sincere in the praise that you give.*** Most people can detect a phony, insincere comment. If you were to praise a secretary for being an accurate typist when, in fact, he or she is very careless, your compliment would probably prompt a thought like "who does he think he's kidding?" If you can't find something that you can honestly praise, wait; keep looking until you feel good about your comment.

***Assign work that is challenging, but not so difficult that the individual loses self-confidence and has no opportunity for success.*** You need to find a reasonable, middle ground. For example, assume that you have a relatively new secretary, Amy, and you want to offer her challenging work. You first consider giving her responsibility for composing most of your correspondence. Then you realize that because Amy is still new in her job, she might not be ready to handle much of the correspondence; she might become discouraged rather than challenged. Therefore, you decide that you will initially let her compose some of the routine correspondence, because she can refer to previously written routine letters and use them as models or samples. Then you can add more advanced types of letter problems as she proves ready. Your success in achieving an appropriate level of challenge in the work for your employees will have a strong influence on their happiness and productivity.

***Set up information reporting on a positive basis.*** When positive rather than negative information is reported, individuals will develop a tendency to use the information for self-guidance in an effort to achieve goals that are higher than expectations of the organization. For example, your secretary could report the percentage of pieces of correspondence filed correctly rather than the percentage of pieces misfiled.

***Be cautious in comparing noncomparable groups or individuals.*** One group may have many new employees with many problem situations; another group may have all well-seasoned veteran employees with primarily routine problems to solve. Individuals, likewise, are not easily compared. Individuals or groups should be compared with their *own* past performance to determine what progress is being made. As a supervisor or manager, maintain accurate and detailed records of your workers so you can notice both the areas that merit compliments and the areas that need improvement.

The supervisor who follows these guidelines should find success in implementing a program of positive reinforcement.

## BENEFITS

Some of the benefits of positive reinforcement are that it:

1. Takes less supervisory time in the long run
2. Provides satisfaction for the employee
3. Reduces costly turnover

4. Reduces defensive behavior
5. Provides for self-directed, self-motivated employees
6. Provides for greater commitment to organizational goals

Behavior can be changed by several methods. Methods involving punishment, coercion, and chastisement will bring about change, but usually for just a short period of time; then the manager who uses this method will have to chastise again and again. In the process of repeated chastisement, the employee becomes further removed from the organization and becomes increasingly defensive. This employee will soon begin working against the organization rather than for it.

As a manager, you can avoid these problems by using positive reinforcement when you want to change behavior. As you use positive reinforcement, you'll find that behavioral change is more long lasting, you'll enhance your employees' self-esteem, and you'll help to create and maintain an overall positive feeling within your organization.

## SELF-FULFILLING PROPHECY

### Definition

Another aspect of human behavior that needs to be considered is called *self-fulfilling prophecy*—the tendency for people to become what they think others expect them to become. For example, you may act differently around different people because of the way you think they expect you to act. Most of what people do in life is prompted, to a very large degree, by somebody's expectations of them. In short, what others think about you influences what you think about yourself.

Self-fulfilling prophecy has both negative and positive aspects. If you treat employees as though they are better than they are, your expectations will tend to encourage positive growth in the employees. On the other hand, if you treat your employees as though they are less capable than they really are, they will tend to diminish in their performance.

Consider the following example. Each month Dee, the mail room supervisor, was required to give a brief oral report of the mail room activities. Dee did not particularly enjoy this experience; but he realized it was standard operating procedure, so he did it willingly. One month his manager told him "Dee, yours is my very favorite report. I enjoy your optimism and always look forward to meeting with you." Dee had not consciously been trying to be unusually optimistic and pleasant, yet he was proud to receive such a compliment. From that time on, he made an extra special effort to be pleasant and optimistic in his associations with his manager. His personality became even more positive because he felt his manager *expected* him to be that way. The influence of the self-fulfilling prophecy literally changed his behavior.

### Impact on Roles

Self-fulfilling prophecy is a primary determiner of the roles workers assume in business. One worker may cease to be productive several years before retirement because he is referred to as "the old man." Another worker may improve her productivity significantly because her supervisor repeatedly compliments her on being one of the most dedicated workers. Individuals change their behavior to fit the "mold" created for them by others. Throughout each day, you play a number of different roles depending upon the people you are with. At home you play one role; in each of your classes at school you play another role; at work you play still a different role. All of these role changes are caused by what others expect you to do. To a great extent, you are likely to become what you think others expect you to be.

Perhaps you can remember a time or two in your own life when someone has said to you, "You're always such a good worker" or "You're always so energetic." For those people, you probably made a definite effort to be just the kind of person they expected you to be. By nature, human beings have a desire to be esteemed by others, and because of this characteristic they place great importance on the comments made about them. The impact of a manager's comment becomes even more powerful if the worker has positive feelings toward him or her.

One note of warning is needed in this discussion of the self-fulfilling prophecy. The expectations of a manager must be seen by the subordinate as being realistic and attainable. If expectations are thought to be too high, a decrease rather than an improvement may be the result.[4]

### Applying the Self-Fulfilling Prophecy

Self-fulfilling prophecy goes hand in hand with positive reinforcement. The steps to follow in using the self-fulfilling prophecy technique in business are as follows:

1. Identify the specific behavior you want the person to emphasize.
2. Sincerely compliment the person on the way he or she portrays the quality you want to emphasize.
3. Apply positive reinforcement techniques and compliment the person's increased portrayal of the desired behavior.
4. Continue to treat the person as though he or she fully exemplifies the characteristic you want emphasized.

Consider the following example. Carla had worked for two years as an administrative assistant. Since she had performed so well, she was offered the opportunity to work as an analyst for the administrative services department. As an analyst Carla would conduct efficiency studies to determine how the administrative services departments could improve its service to the company.

Carla's new supervisor, Dan, had only one hesitation about Carla—she was always so positive that he feared she might not be able to develop the critical attitude that is essential for a systems analyst. Dan did not want to dampen Carla's optimistic attitude, but he did want her to be able to dig out all the relevant details in an analysis. Therefore, he occasionally referred to Carla as "the girl with the analytical eye."

As Carla began her work as an analyst, Dan complimented her each time he felt she had probed in depth in her analysis. A comment like "there's the girl with the analytical eye coming through again" would serve both to provide positive reinforcement and to accent the self-fulfilling prophecy.

Probably the most important ingredients necessary in implementing a self-fulfilling prophecy are honesty and sincere concern. Any employee can spot a phony compliment, and if employees feel that you are just buttering them up with "management psychology," you'll do more harm than good.

Perhaps the following statement will effectively help you remember the self-fulfilling concept: "Treat people as if they were what they ought to be and you help them to become what they are capable of being" (Goethe).

## *Summary*

Positive reinforcement is very effective as a behavior modification technique. It is based on the concept that human beings perform those actions that bring them satisfaction and that they avoid doing those things that bring no satisfaction or dissatisfaction. Positive reinforcement consists of waiting for the desired behavior to occur and then reinforcing it with some kind of reward. Research shows that praising brings better and more lasting results than reproving or ignoring.

Three basic steps are involved in effectively using positive reinforcement:

1. Identify the behavior you want to see improved.
2. Reward the desired behavior soon after it occurs.
3. Reinforce the desired behavior regularly during early stages of development. After the behavior becomes somewhat automatic, reinforce it on an irregular basis.

The same kinds of rewards will not be equally motivating to all employees. The successful manager will select a reward that is appropriate for each individual. There are a number of possibilities: attention, praise, and recognition; responsibility and promotions; participation in decision making; status symbols; time off; gifts and benefits; and financial rewards.

A set of guidelines should be followed to provide direction in applying positive reinforcement. Several specific benefits can be expected to accrue as a result of effective positive reinforcement.

Self-fulfilling prophecy was explained as a behavior modification technique. Self-fulfilling prophecy is the tendency of human beings to become what they think others expect them to be. Most of what people do in life is prompted by others' expectations of them. Self-fulfilling prophecy goes hand-in-hand with positive reinforcement; together these techniques will equip the manager with two of the most powerful behavior modification means available.

## *Review and Discussion Questions*

1. Why is it desirable to wait for the desired behavior to occur rather than to correct improper behavior and suggest a change?
2. Why do you think the improved performance of reproved individuals does not remain satisfactory for as long as the performance of positively reinforced individuals?
3. Why does ignoring bad behavior tend to diminish that behavior?
4. What are the three basic positive reinforcement steps? Give a specific example of how you could use these steps.
5. Why are the same types of rewards not equally effective with everyone?
6. Why is giving time off as a reward for good performance frequently not advisable?
7. Why is it best to identify specific rather than general accomplishments?
8. How do positive reinforcement and self-fulfilling prophecy relate to each other?

## *Application Exercises*

1. Psychologists suggest that many children misbehave just to get the attention of their parents. Children are conditioned in this way because most parents communicate with their children much more frequently during periods of misbehavior than during periods of good behavior. Observe parents and their children together. Note how frequently the parents commend their children for good behavior, and observe how frequently the children are reproved for doing something wrong. Discuss your findings with the class.
2. Think of a close associate whose behavior you would like to change. Follow the steps of positive reinforcement during the next few weeks and keep a record of the positive changes you see in that person's behavior. Prepare to report your findings in class.
3. Carry a note pad with you during the next 24 hours. Record the names of everyone you associate with during that time. Write a brief report explaining the different roles you assumed during that period because of others' expectations of you. How do your findings fit in with self-fulfilling prophecy?

## *Case Studies*

1. Look at the following data on copies that have come to you from your reprographics department. Assuming that the department has a backlog of requests that would enable it to accomplish additional work, identify the dates when you should have given positive reinforcement. How could you apply the self-fulfilling prophecy technique to this situation?

| *Date* | *Rate per day* | *Date* | *Rate per day* | *Date* | *Rate per day* |
|---|---|---|---|---|---|
| June 1 | 10,000 | June 11 | 14,800 | June 22 | 20,900 |
| June 2 | 10,900 | June 12 | 13,900 | June 23 | 20,600 |
| June 3 | 10,200 | June 15 | 15,100 | June 24 | 21,000 |
| June 4 | 8,400 | June 16 | 15,125 | June 25 | 20,880 |
| June 5 | 14,600 | June 17 | 11,300 | June 26 | 20,900 |
| June 8 | 11,200 | June 18 | 15,200 | June 29 | 19,900 |
| June 9 | 11,300 | June 19 | 20,650 | June 30 | 20,700 |
| June 10 | 14,700 | | | | |

2. Your secretary, Barbara Woodbury, has been very efficient and effective until recently. Lately she has been coming in late to work about three out of five times. Her lunch hours have extended well beyond the 45 minutes allotted. Coffee breaks which are scheduled for 15 minutes have been running 30 to 40 minutes. During the day, Barbara has been receiving personal phone calls which last 10 to 15 minutes each. On occasion, Barbara has had visitors come to the office to talk with her about personal matters. She is usually the first one out of the office at night.

Barbara's error rate is up. Recently, she has submitted several letters which were unmailable. Most of her work is good, but there are times when she has made costly mistakes and has prevented you from meeting important deadlines. You have asked for information which is on file, but Barbara was unable to produce it when you needed it.

You are concerned because you know Barbara is not working up to her capabilities. For several weeks now, you have talked with her at least once or twice each week. At times your criticism has been very severe. Each time you talk with her she promises to do better. She realizes that her actions are not justified. You have honestly felt that after each talk there will be improvement, but after a day or two of good performance, Barbara slips back into her sloppy performance pattern. You are not sure what to do, other than fire her. You have threatened her openly with this possibility, but you are reluctant to do so because she has been an excellent employee in the past.

Assume that you are Barbara's boss. Develop a specific, step-by-step approach to solve this performance problem.

## *Reference Notes*

1. Ralph W. Dent, "Commercial Management Training—Improving and Maintaining the Performance of Subordinates," *Operant Management Film Series*, p. 44.
2. Grant E. Barton and Harold T. Smith, "Managing a Reward Structure," excerpted from *Administrative Management*, Geyer-McAllister Publications, Inc., New York, February 1972, p. 87.
3. Extrinsic rewards are "external" in that they are rewards controlled by forces outside a worker. Intrinsic rewards, on the other hand, are "internal" because they arise from within the worker. No tangible gifts are associated with intrinsic rewards; instead, workers receive motivation because they "feel" good about the work.
4. J. Sterling Livingston, "Pygmalion in Management," *Harvard Business Review*, July–August 1969, p. 85.

## *Administrative Manager Profile*

Meet James P. Downey, Jr., general manager at the western home office of the Prudential Insurance Company of America.

*Background and Experience.* Jim graduated from Harvard University in 1951 with a major in economics. He was offered a career opportunity with Prudential as an auditor in the comptroller's department. In this position for a period of ten years, he gained experience in all facets of Prudential's operations. These included individual insurance, underwriting and transaction processing, group and pension insurance, investments, data processing, and field marketing. In 1961, Jim joined the management ranks of the company and was responsible for auditing and accounting, first at Boston and later at the Los Angeles regional home office. In 1967, he was reassigned to administrative operational executive responsibility. In this position, he was directly responsible for eleven managers who in turn supervised 650 employees.

*Company.* The Prudential Insurance Company of America is currently the largest insurer and the largest financial institution in the United States. In 1976, individual life-insurance sales were almost $20 billion, with about $136 billion in force. During this same year, group life-insurance sales exceeded $14 billion, with $125 billion in force. Other types of insurance sold include: health, pension, property and casualty, and aviation.

*Job.* Jim assumed his present position as general manager of the western home office in 1971. This position is primarily an executive staff assignment involving three major departments: personnel, data processing, and buildings. As head of the administrative services department, Jim has four executives, ten managers, and a staff of 600 reporting to him.

His major responsibilities in providing leadership have been: (1) to provide support services, (2) to seek out new ideas and to implement change when desirable throughout the entire regional home office, (3) to install new computer applications, (4) to recruit and train new management for Prudential, (5) to advise the administrative marketing department in strengthening its organization, and (6) to assist in long-range planning and expense management for the entire organization. An example of a specific project accomplished under Jim's supervision was planning for the recently built Woodland Hills office near Los Angeles.

*Management Philosophy.* Here are some of Jim's comments about his own management philosophy and style of leadership:

> "Throughout my career, I have always been anxious to provide a contribution to Prudential by recognizing the need for change and by effectively implementing new ideas."
>
> "Training and development of people, especially the future managers of the company, is a vital activity."
>
> "I have spent many hours in discussions with individuals encouraging them to plan and manage their own careers."
>
> "Each person can best control his own growth and development with minimum assistance and direction from others."
>
> "I continually refer to the following outline of executive requirements and try to balance my performance in each area. I hope this outline will be of benefit to you, the reader."

*Executive Requirements*

I. Planning
   a. Relates to total company
   b. Thinks long-range
   c. Identifies problems quickly
   d. Provides imaginative solutions

II. Organization
   a. Evaluates people accurately
   b. Develops people well
   c. Develops effective personnel strategy
   d. Builds organizations

III. Motivation
   a. Listens actively
   b. Counsels effectively
   c. Delegates well
   d. Expresses himself thoughtfully

IV. Control
   a. Builds effective controls
   b. Uses controls to insure good performance

V. Personal characteristics
  a. Intelligent
  b. Healthy
  c. Emotionally stable
  d. Good appearance
  e. Conscientious and ambitious
  f. Loyal
  g. Confident
  h. Non-defensive
  i. Well-organized
  j. Effective counselor to superiors
  k. Accepted by all groups
  l. Change initiator
  m. Capable of strong personal relationships

# PART THREE

# Communication

In Part Three you will have a detailed look at communication and the part it plays in business. Chapter 8 focuses on the communication process: transmission of thoughts via verbal and nonverbal means is examined, and feedback is explained. A communication model is also presented in this chapter.

Chapter 9 takes a look at the problems you face when you try to communicate with someone else. The impact of your individual point of view is examined, and the filters of the mind are explored.

In Chapter 10 you are exposed to a number of techniques that will assist you in improving the quality of your communication within an organization. Although communication problems will always be present to some degree, the application of effective management techniques can greatly improve organizational communication.

Effective interviewing is the topic of Chapter 11. Administrative managers must rely on interviews to accomplish many of their purposes, so interviewing skills are very important.

# 8

# The Communication Process

Communication—is it the sharing of ideas, the transfer of feelings, the tool of persuasion, or the process of understanding? What is communication and why is it such an integral part of our human organizations? Why is it such an important part of interpersonal business relations?

## FUNCTION AND OBJECTIVES OF COMMUNICATION

### Function of Communication

The primary function of communication in business is to achieve understanding between yourself and other people. Communication is successful if understanding is achieved, unsuccessful if it is not achieved. When communication is successful you feel satisfied, but unsuccessful communication makes you dissatisfied and sometimes very disturbed and angry.

### Objectives of Communication

***1. To help others.*** Frequently, in a business organization you will receive information that you feel might be useful to someone else. As a result, you will pass the information along simply for informational purposes. You expect nothing in return; you are just trying to be of assistance. For example, you might hear that a computer equipment show is being held in the near future. Therefore, you mention this information to the computer department manager.

***2. To persuade others to accept an idea or to perform some action that you desire.*** If the other person accepts your idea or performs the desired action, you consider your communication to be a success. For example, if you make a suggestion to Kathy, your receptionist, to be more pleasant with clients that come to your office, you will feel that your communication has been successful if she responds to your suggestion.

***3. To fulfill an innate need to communicate.*** Lord Byron said, "All who joy would win must share it. Happiness was born a twin." This statement suggests that when you gain joy, your emotions are running so high that you have a great internal need to tell others about your excitement. Heightened emotions of all types prompt the need to communicate with others because people have an inborn need to do so, and the greater the emotion, the greater the felt need to communicate. When an employee comes to you with a special problem or with a success story, you can safely assume that person has a strong feeling about the communication. Assume that a fellow worker comes into your office with a big smile on his face. He says, "Hey, did you hear the good news? I've been promoted to the assistant manager position in the midwest division." The information in this message is not something that you particularly *need* to know, but your associate is so excited about the information that he feels a strong need to tell others about it.

***4. To enhance yourself in the eyes of others.*** Frequently, in informal office conversations, you will note that the talk seems to be a case of "an I for an I"; you talk about yourself and the other persons talk about themselves. People are extremely gregarious, and they use communication as a tool to gain social acceptance and advancement in organizations. Most communication is prompted by self-interest. Consider the following statement made by a worker who has just bought a new suit. "Man, I can't believe the price they're getting for a new suit these days." More than anything else, this employee probably wants to draw attention to his new suit rather than to complain about the price he had to pay.

***5. To fill time.*** Most people experience a degree of anxiety when they are in the close presence of others with no one talking. Conversations based on this time-filling purpose usually meander aimlessly from one topic to another, and the participants are satisfied just to keep the conversation going. If you sit beside someone in the company cafeteria, for example, you will probably feel a need to exchange some type of conversation with that person simply because you feel uncomfortable with the silence. Comments like "Well, how's it going?" "I'm sure glad it's Friday," and "What department do you work in?" can usually be classified as time fillers.

Whenever you receive messages from leaders or subordinates, you should identify the real purpose of the message. By doing so, you will be in a better position to decide how you are expected to react to the message and to the message sender.

## PROCESS OF COMMUNICATION

On the surface, communication might seem to be a rather simple process of message transmission and reception. In reality, however, it is a very complex process with numerous chances for communication failure. (The message transmitted may not be received as intended.) As has been mentioned in earlier chapters, the major cause of problems in organizations is people; similarly, the major cause of communication problems is the interpretation of messages by human beings. In communication study, the primary focus must be on the human mind, because the minds of the individuals involved in the communication process will determine whether a communication attempt succeeds or fails.

### Input

Input comes to the conscious part of your brain from two major sources: (1) *Internal messages* retrieved from memory, and (2) *external messages* received from the outside, including the messages sent by other people (Figure 8-1).

***Internal Messages.*** Our brain is constantly processing information, and since the memory is filled with much information that is readily available, a large percentage of all input comes from memory. Some examples might help to illustrate the types of input that frequently come from memory. As you ride or drive to work, you are probably pondering the day that is ahead of you, and you might think of the following items: there is a problem with a recent purchase order that needs to be solved; Rosemary mentioned yesterday that she will be quitting work in a month; Brandt has seemed to be a bit slack in his work the last couple of days; and Denise requested that we pursue a proposed change in our office design. As you can see, the brain is a rich storehouse of information, and this memory tool plays a major part in the input process.

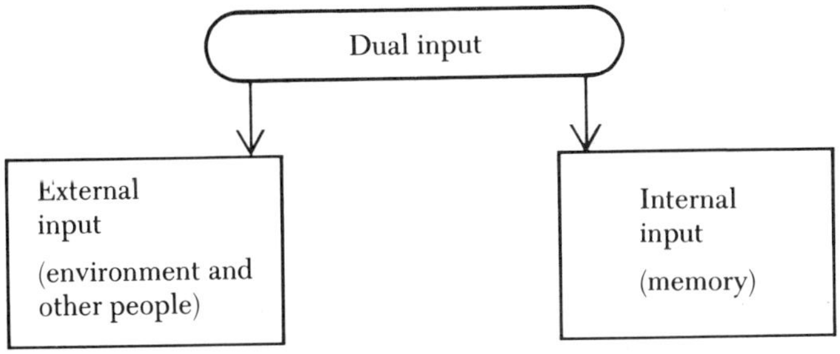


*Figure 8-1.* Sources of Information Input

***External Messages.*** The other major area is the external world. Since all communication occurs within some type of environment, the environmental messages are constantly competing with verbal messages as input information. For example, the administrative manager works in an environment of office furniture, business letters and reports, business forms, computers, typewriters, calculators, telephones, windows, walls, pictures, and files. All of these items are sources of input for the worker who takes notice of them.

Probably the most important type of external input comes from other people. Since the administrative manager must rely so heavily on people to accomplish the office objectives, he or she should understand completely the kinds of input that come from other people. Messages from people are transmitted either as verbal or nonverbal input.

*Verbal Communication.* The word *verbal* had its roots in the Latin word *verbum,* which refers to words or messages consisting of words. Verbal communication, therefore, refers to messages that are sent as spoken or written words. Oral communication in business usually consists of face-to-face or telephone communications. Written communication, on the other hand, consists of handwritten, typewritten, or duplicated notes, letters, and reports; and these may be received by a variety of manual, mechanical, or electronic means.

Verbal messages are an extremely important part of office communication, and you should take advantage of every opportunity to polish your verbal communication skills. Classes in report and letter writing and in oral communication should be a part of every business student's curriculum. (Since most students will spend a significant part of their educational preparation in verbal communication activities, further coverage of verbal communication will not be given here.)

*Nonverbal Communication.* Nonverbal communication pertains to all nonword aspects of input and is perhaps more critical than the verbal information it accompanies. Verbal messages are generally quite consciously planned and transmitted; therefore, if a person wants to misrepresent the truth, the distortion most frequently occurs in the verbal part of the message. Nonverbal messages, on the other hand, usually leak out without a conscious intention to send them. Consequently, nonverbal communication is usually unrehearsed and is generally more believable than its verbal counterpart.

Nonverbal communication includes far more than just gestures, facial expressions, and voice fluctuations. People communicate in the following nine nonverbal realms:

1. Body language: information sent by parts of the body
2. Space: messages communicated by the use of space
3. Touch: messages transmitted by touching
4. Object language: meaning communicated by different objects

5. Time: information transmitted by how time is used
6. Sound: meaning sent by manipulation of voice and other sounds
7. Color: messages transmitted by different colors
8. Smell: information communicated as odors
9. Taste: meaning transmitted to the taste buds

*Body language,* also known as *kinesics,* pertains to all nonverbal communication sent via the body. Two areas of the body that are associated with the majority of nonverbal communication are (a) the face and (b) the arms and hands. By watching a person's facial expressions and his or her arm and hand gestures, you can obtain a much richer message than if you just listen to the spoken message. In an employment interview, for example, you will want to pay close attention to the body messages of your interviewee. Watch for such clues as slumping in the chair, avoidance of eye contact, ducking of the head, and nervous mannerisms with the hands. These actions suggest that the person being interviewed might lack social tact, honesty, and self-confidence, and you should consider these connotations along with the verbal part of the message.

*Spacial communication,* or *proxemics,* deals with the way people use the space that surrounds them. Because of cultural conditioning, you probably have learned to guard closely the space immediately surrounding your body. If you live in the United States, it is as though you carry with you an invisible bubble that extends approximately two feet on all sides of you. When a stranger steps inside your personal bubble, you may become uncomfortable and move away so that your personal bubble can regain its original space.

Researchers have determined that the distance maintained between two persons communicates their feelings about each other.[1] In most cases, the more positive the relationship between two people, the shorter the distance will be between them. In other words, closeness *tends* to indicate positive feelings.

The space awarded to you by others will frequently indicate something about your importance in the organization; the more important you are, the more personal space you are given. For example, the president of an organization usually has a large, private office. The lowest level of workers, on the other hand, are generally grouped together with little privacy and very little personal space (see Figure 8-2). More important officers will be located closer to the chief executive's office than will officers of lesser importance.

*Tactile communication* refers to communication by touch. As an infant, you received nearly all your communication by touch. You were rubbed, powdered, bathed, cuddled, and patted. As you grew older and gained more ability to communicate with words, however, touch became a less important form of communication.

American business people use touch communication to a rather limited extent. For example, when you meet someone for the first time, you might

*Figure 8-2.* Lower-Level Workers Are Often Given Little Floor Space and Little Privacy

shake hands, or the manager may pat his subordinates on the back and at the same time tell them they're doing a good job. These examples suggest that touch is usually used to convey positive feelings to others.

*Object language* pertains to the way you use objects to communicate. In a typical office setting, you are likely to see such objects as family photographs, marriage rings, organization pins worn on the lapel of a coat, unusual objects displayed on desks, uniforms worn by workers, and unique letterhead stationery. Objects are used to communicate status, wealth, organizational memberships, professions, and life styles. As a manager, you can learn much about workers simply by "reading" their object language.

*Time* is an important nonverbal realm; however, the importance of time varies from one culture to another. To Americans, time is so important that wristwatches are worn to keep track of every precious minute. In many other cultures, time is less important. You use time to communicate in two major ways. First, by spending time with someone you communicate positive regard for that person; for example, when you sit down and write a letter to a business customer, you communicate not only the content of the letter but also your willingness to invest some of your time in his or her behalf.

Second, the time *when* you perform some action also communicates; for example, arriving early for an appointment communicates something completely different from arriving late. You are usually concerned much more about arriving on time for an appointment with your superior than you are about arriving on time for a meeting with a peer or a subordinate. If you arrive late for appointments, you communicate to other persons that you do not consider them important enough to require your arriving on time. Also, the time when a meeting is held, when a telephone call is made, or when a project is expected to be completed can frequently tell others something about the events.

*Sound* plays a very important part in nonverbal communication. First, the way you talk adds greatly to the words you speak. Talking can be varied in terms of pitch, speed, and volume, all of which modify the basic meaning of the words used. Highly emotional messages, for example, tend to be spoken at a higher pitch, a faster rate, and a louder volume than do less emotional messages. Along with a person's facial expression, the voice is probably the most reliable indicator of emotion and feeling.

Second, nonvoice sounds bombard you constantly. While you tend to ignore most sounds, you notice those that either help to fill your needs or contrast significantly from their competing sounds. For example, you may notice a buzzing business telephone both because it fills your needs and because it differs significantly from all other competing sounds.

Third, the duration, frequency, intensity, and quality of sounds carry rich communication cues. Think of the different kinds of messages you could make by varying knocks on a door. You could vary the number, frequency, intensity, and rhythm; and each of these variations could communicate much more than just "I'm here to see you; please let me in."

Fourth, the absence of sound, silence, is a very important communicator. With silence employees express many messages including hostility, reverence, boredom, meditation, politeness, and fear. As with all nonverbal messages, silence must be interpreted in context to be properly understood. Assume, for example, that Andria, a supervisor, has just severely chastised her subordinate, Daniel. For the next two or three weeks Andria might be given the "silent treatment." Daniel will be communicating that he is upset and that he does not want to associate with Andria. He feels that to remain silent places him in a power position and lets Andria know that he does not have to bow to her wishes if he doesn't want to.

*Color* is another realm of nonverbal communication. With color, people portray mood, boldness, submissiveness, and formality or informality. They also use color to attract attention or to conceal. Contrast is the key to color communication; if a color is different from what is expected or is in great contrast to its surroundings, it will be noticed. Colors that are too different might arouse negative human reactions, however.

Color is usually one of the more subtle nonverbal communication forms. Thus, it is usually perceived as being a less significant communicator than such dynamic forms as sound, object language, and kinesics. But it can be used very effectively with company letterhead, office decor, sales letters, filing systems, and employee notices; for example, an office manager might select office partitions in the yellow, orange, brown, and tan range to create a warm atmosphere for the workers. An administrative manager might also use a buff color for stationery and envelopes to set them apart from competitors' correspondence.

*Smell* plays a significant role in some communication settings, but it is rather unimportant in others. Smells such as perfumes and colognes will tend to enhance intimate acquaintances. Body odors, on the other hand, are undesirable in the American culture, and their presence will tend to thwart interpersonal progress.

*Taste* is probably the least important form of nonverbal communication. You can receive taste messages from others when food or drink is involved in the relationship; but beyond that, taste communication is rather limited in importance.

***Subjective Content: Feelings.*** So far, the emphasis on input has been in the area of the content of the message. Another important aspect of the input is in the emotion or feeling area. Both verbal and nonverbal messages can suggest emotion, but nonverbal input usually is a better indicator of this aspect of a message. Since people are usually guided more by their emotions than by their logical thoughts, the feeling input must be carefully considered. Therefore, when considering input from other individuals, pay attention to the "how" and "why" as well as the "what."

Consider a hypothetical situation in which a subordinate, Joan, has come to you to submit a report she has written. After you read the report, you suggest to Joan that she omit three paragraphs and submit new ones that you have written. You ask her, "Now, doesn't that seem a lot better to you?" She answers, "It is different, all right." To be agreeable, Joan tries to make her message as positive as possible without committing herself; but she still feels that her message is better and that you should have left it the way it was.

### Processing

Input received from the environment must be processed. First, it is desymbolized (changed from words, objects, movements, and colors to mental images). Second, this input, along with input from memory, is interpreted in light of a mental filter called a *frame of reference*. The frame of reference is built of every experience you have had in life, and each new experience you have changes the filter again. Thus, your office worker, Andrew, is not exactly the same today as he was yesterday; and he will be a bit different tomorrow than he is today. Granted, changes occur slowly, but changes do occur in everyone. Figure 8-3 further illustrates the communication input process.

Three dimensions have been identified in the interpretation phase of communication processing.[2] The first dimension involves *evaluation*, or the tendency of people to classify a message on a like-dislike, good-bad scale. The second dimension considers *power*, the tendency of people to assume either a superior or subordinate role in human encounters. The third dimension of nonverbal communication is the degree of *responsiveness* to a message; the impact of a message can be determined, to a large degree, by the degree of behavior change resulting from perception of a message.

To learn how to use the three dimensions in organizational communication, consider the following example. Suppose that you are a supervisor in Samson Business Forms Co. Assume that you have just completed and submitted to your subordinates a department personnel report. As you are working at your desk, Dan Wong, one of your subordinates, bursts into your office, slams a copy of the departmental report on your desk, and shouts, "I quit." Then he turns and storms out of your office, slamming the door behind him.

As the event is occurring, you are busy gathering facts in all the realms of nonverbal communication. You notice Dan's body language (angered facial expression, bursting into your office, slamming the book down, and leaving promptly), space usage (coming into your office uninvited and without knock-

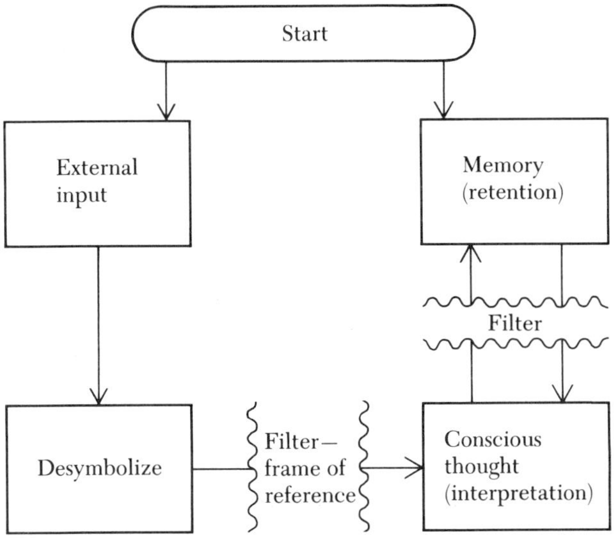


*Figure 8-3.* Information Received Is Processed by the Brain

ing), object language (the departmental report), time usage (entering and leaving hurriedly—without an appointment), and sound communication (shouting, slamming the book and the door).

Now, using the three dimensions of message interpretation, analyze the Dan Wong experience. As Dan's supervisor you will probably give a low rating on the *evaluation* scale (Dan should not have acted the way he did), a high rating on the *power* scale (Dan placed himself in a superior position when he entered your office uninvited), and a high rating on the *responsiveness* scale (Dan's receiving the report caused a significant behavioral reaction).

Conversely, if Dan had not taken time even to read the report, you would probably have given a low rating on the *evaluation* scale (he should have read the report), a neutral rating on the *power* scale (Dan neither elevated himself above you nor placed himself in submission to you), and a low rating on the *responsiveness* scale (Dan did not change his behavior at all when he received your report).

When analyzing messages that you receive, be certain to consider both nonverbal and verbal communications to achieve a more complete and accurate assessment of the sender's message. The importance of this point can be better appreciated as you consider the significance of "I quit" in the Dan Wong episode. This verbal statement must be considered before the nonverbal cues can be put in proper perspective, and the nonverbal cues must be considered before the verbal message can be properly interpreted.

The third phase of processing involves a decision either to respond or not to respond to the message. In this decision process, you consider whether you want to send information to aid someone else, to persuade someone to take some action, to fulfill an innate need to communicate, to enhance yourself in the eyes of someone else, or to fill time. If you want to achieve one of these objectives, you send a message. If you have no desire to communicate, however, you make no attempt to transmit a message.

### Output

In most cases, output is produced after the processing phase, even though output may not be conscious—it might be a look of surprise, happiness, anger, or frustration; or it might be transmitted via other nonverbal realms. The alert manager will be sensitive to these more subtle forms of output even when the sender is unaware of the message transmission. Figure 8-4 represents the communication process from the input phase to the output phase; the information input is received from the environment and from the memory and the decision of whether to transmit the message is made. The message may be intentional or unintentional. Since we can never "not communicate" (even saying nothing is communicating something), unintentional messages are transmitted.

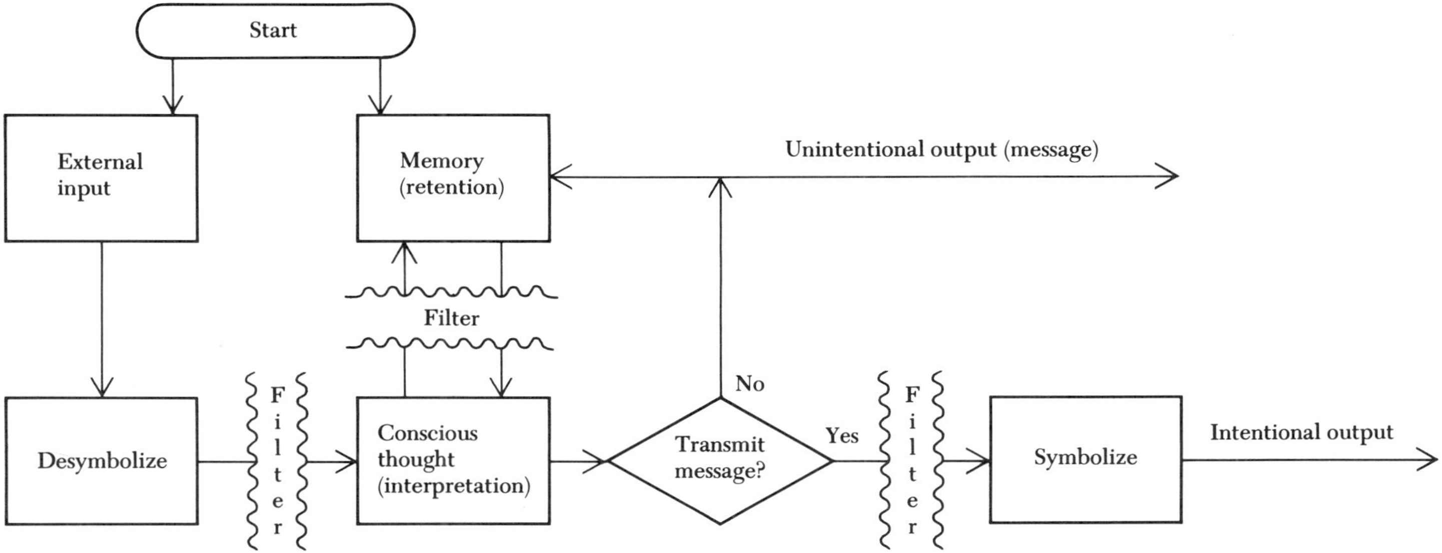


*Figure 8-4.* Information Input and Output

The diamond-shaped box is a major decision step, and the result of the decision determines the direction of the information flow. The rectangular figures are straight processing steps where the information goes the same direction every time.

Consider the case of Leonard Lopez, a supervisor in a regional office of the Internal Revenue Service. Leonard made it known to his subordinates that he was going to select an assistant who would be trained to take his place after his pending transfer. Two subordinates, Marcia and Elizabeth, applied for the position. Leonard considered both applications and subsequently chose Marcia for the promotion, even though he felt Elizabeth could have performed equally well. After informing Marcia of his choice, he invited Elizabeth to his office for an interview. He told Elizabeth of his choice, and mentioned that he hoped she would get a chance at the position when it opened up again. Elizabeth thanked Leonard and said she felt all right about the decision. Then she left the office. Leonard watched her closely and could tell that she was very disappointed, in spite of her verbal approval of the decision. During Leonard's remaining weeks on the job, he made a special point to show concern and appreciation for Elizabeth so she would know that he really was concerned about her and wanted her to be happy with her job.

The output sent by other people as they react to your messages is *feedback*. By analyzing the feedback you receive, you can determine whether others have understood your message and how they feel about the message. Figure 8-5 shows a complete communication cycle with a sender transmitting information and a receiver giving feedback to the sender.

The importance of feedback cannot be overemphasized, because without feedback you cannot determine whether you have achieved your communication objective. Therefore, be alert to feedback that is either intentionally given or unintentionally given. Remember that no reaction is, nevertheless, feedback. As you remain alert to feedback sent from others, you will be a much more effective communicator than the all-too-frequent manager who is "deaf" to these important messages.

## *Summary*

The major function of communication is to achieve understanding between two or more persons. The major objectives of communication are to give information for the aid of others, to persuade others to accept an idea or to perform some action, to fulfill an innate need to communicate, to enhance yourself in the eyes of others, and to fill time.

Study of communication must focus primarily on the human mind because most of the communication process is a mental process. Input comes into the conscious part of the brain from memory and from external sources—the environment and other people. Messages are received in either verbal or nonverbal form. Verbal messages are those that use words as communication symbols. Verbal messages consist of written and spoken communication. Nonverbal communication pertains to all messages sent without the use of words. Nonverbal communication is transmitted in at least nine realms: body language, space, touch, object, time, sound, color, smell, and taste. Messages

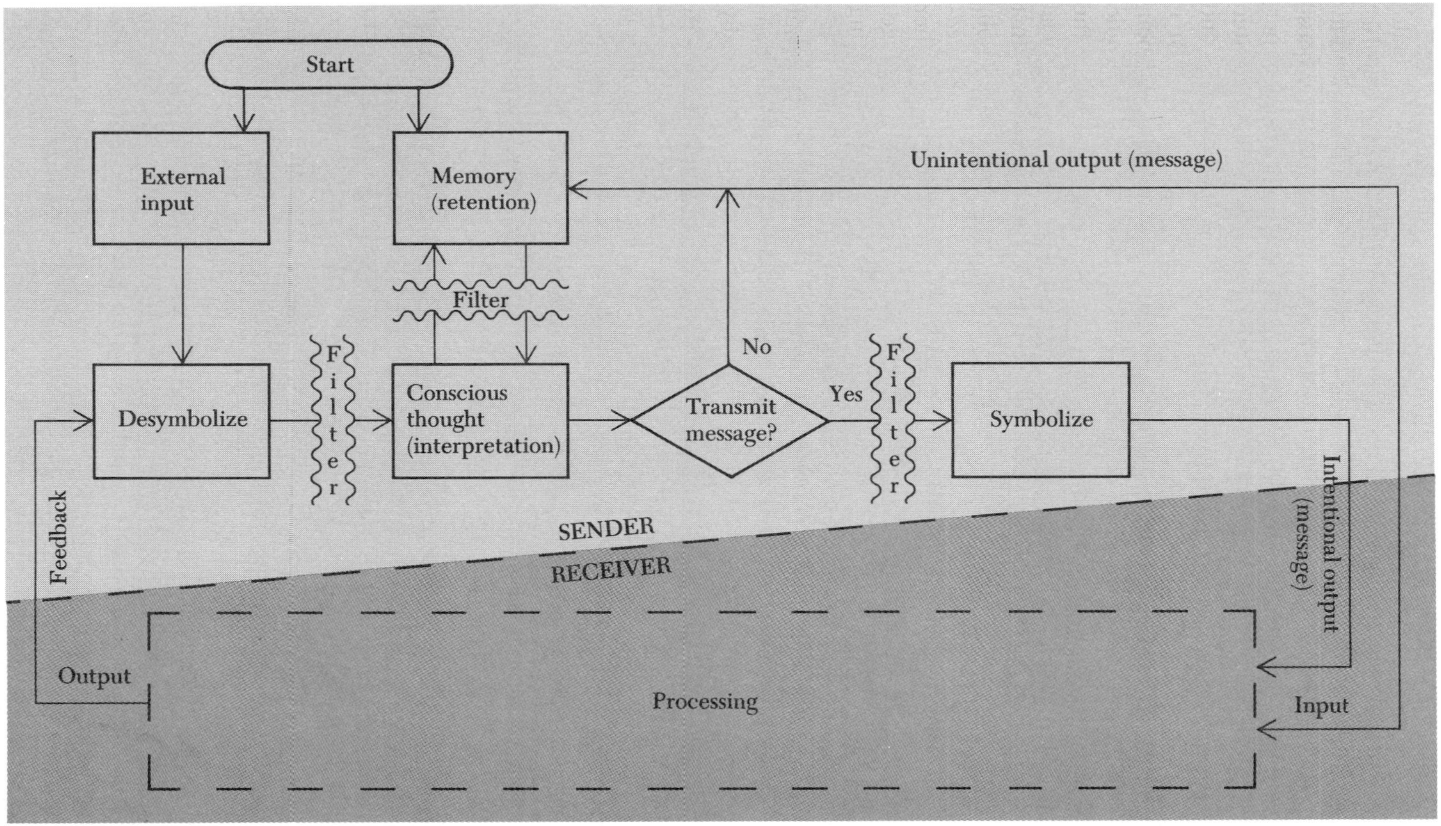


*Figure* 8-5. The Complete Communication Cycle

are analyzed in three dimensions: (1) evaluation, (2) power, and (3) responsiveness.

The mental position from which you interpret mental input is your *frame of reference*. Conscious thought is stored and/or transmitted either intentionally or unintentionally. Messages sent from a message receiver to the original message sender are *feedback*.

## *Review and Discussion Questions*

1. What is the major function of communication?
2. What are the major purposes of communication?
3. Why do people tend to communicate more at high emotional levels?
4. What is the meaning of *frame of reference*? Why is a person's frame of reference continually changing?
5. Why is memory input so important in the communication process?
6. Of the nine realms of nonverbal communication, which ones are the most important in the life of a manager? Which are least important? Defend your answers.
7. How do the nine realms of nonverbal communication relate to the three dimensions of communication interpretation?
8. What is the relationship between the distance between people and their feelings about each other?
9. What parts of the body are used most frequently to communicate nonverbally?
10. If verbal messages are contradicted by nonverbal messages, which is usually more truthful? Why?
11. Why is feedback so important in communication?

## *Application Exercises*

1. Go to a business office and observe people as they talk to each other. Notice the distance between these people during the conversations. As a result of your observation, determine what seems to be the "ideal" distance in a business communication situation.
2. Go to an office and observe an interaction between two of the workers. Using the three dimensions of communication interpretation, analyze this observation.
3. Watch a television show. Make a list of the nonverbal communications you notice in each of the nine realms discussed in this chapter.
4. Assume that your co-worker comes into your office and says, "I thought Hans went to Jim's meeting." Now repeat the sentence seven times, the first time emphasizing the word "I," the second time emphasizing the word

"thought," etc. Discuss the impact of voice fluctuation on message meaning.

## *Case Studies*

1. *Verna Olsen.* One week ago Verna Olsen, administrative manager for Bellwest, held a performance appraisal interview with Frederick, the supervisor of training and development. During the interview, Frederick inquired about the prospects of a salary increase in addition to the standard annual increment. Verna replied that she would be happy to consider the request at the next appraisal interview, but that at present she just didn't think Frederick was adequately aggressive in helping his subordinates set and achieve objectives. Verna suggested that Frederick reconsider his objectives for the coming evaluation period and come back in a few days for another visit.

Since that first interview, Frederick has been unusually sullen and somewhat defensive. On several occasions, Verna has passed him in the hall and Frederick has looked away without saying "hi" or giving some other greeting. Two days after the interview, Verna overheard Frederick mention to an associate, "I guess they expect you to be perfect in this outfit."

Yesterday, Verna saw Frederick in the hall and, in passing, said, "When are we going to get together on those objectives again?" Frederick snapped back, "I turned those in to you last week!" and walked on his way.

After reading this case, list all the nonverbal messages you have noticed. Then, using the three dimensions of communication interpretation, analyze the messages sent by Frederick.

2. *Edward Wilson.* Edward was an administrative management major in Southwestern State College. Edward was proud of the 3.62 grade point average he had earned in college, and he felt confident as he prepared his vita for employment interviews. Finally, the big day came when he was to have his first interview.

The interview was scheduled at 2 P.M. at Voltek, Inc. Edward left for the interview on time, but he got delayed by some unusually heavy traffic. Consequently, he arrived at 2:10 P.M. for the interview. Being late, he was nervous and somewhat "wilted" from perspiration. Sure enough, Mr. Andrews had been waiting for him. Edward decided not to apologize for being late; instead, he thought he would be able to make up for the problem with his good academic record.

The interview seemed to proceed well enough although Edward occasionally had to wipe the perspiration from his forehead with his hand, and his voice was a bit shaky from the anxiety of being late. At the conclusion of the interview, Edward stood up and offered his hand to Mr. Andrews. Mr. Andrews ignored Edward's hand and thanked him for coming. On his way out of the office Edward asked, "Shall I call you later on this week to see if you have made a decision?" Mr. Andrews responded, "We'll let you know if we need to talk with you again."

Evaluate this interview from a communication standpoint. Identify all the nonverbal communications that occurred and interpret them by using the three dimensions of message interpretation.

## *References*

1. Edward T. Hall, *The Silent Language* (New York: Doubleday, 1959), pp. 163–164.
2. Albert Mehrabian, *Silent Messages* (Belmont, Calif.: Wadsworth, 1971), pp. 111–118.

# 9

# Communication Barriers

A basic understanding of the communication process discussed in Chapter 8 does not guarantee perfect business communication. In fact, since human beings are so complex and unpredictable, it is unrealistic to strive for perfect communication—effective communication is a more realistic goal. An awareness of the major barriers of communication can provide a basis for reducing problems and for enhancing effective communication. Communication barriers arise from three majors areas—psychological, physiological, and environmental. This chapter will focus on these three problem areas.

## PSYCHOLOGICAL BARRIERS

### Development of Your Frame of Reference

Frame of reference is defined as the mental position from which the human mind perceives and interprets sensory input. Although your frame of reference is critical in your existence, it also is the root of most communication problems because it is composed of a complex system of relationships that you have learned throughout your life. The more experiences you have, the more complex your frame of reference becomes. Figure 9-1 illustrates a theoretical arrangement of a person's concept of a business office.

Your frame of reference is the base from which you interpret everything with which you come into contact. As Figure 9-1 suggests, the frame of reference is a mental judgment system complete with positive, neutral, and negative feelings. The main idea to remember about the frame of reference is that it is different for each individual, because no two individuals have had the same experiences and learning. Because all frames of reference are completely unique, it is impossible for two persons to see things from the same perspective. Consider the following office situation involving two secretaries, Phil and

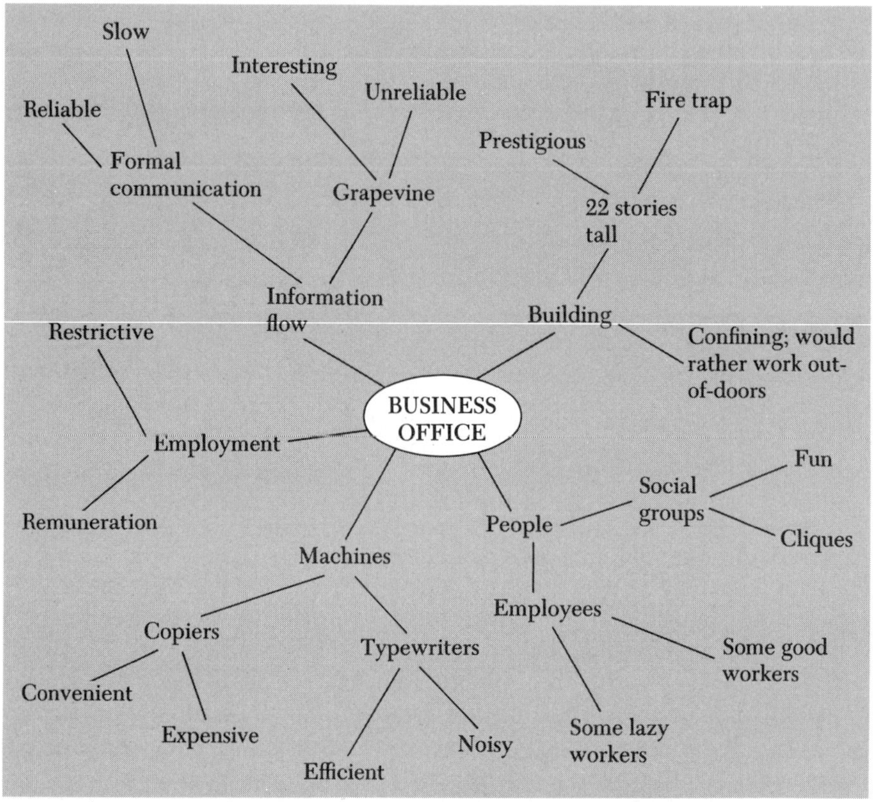


*Figure 9-1.* Theoretical Frame of Reference of a Business Office

Nita, and their supervisor, Carol Lee. Carol Lee has worked for the company for four years, three years as an administrative assistant and one year as supervisor of administrative services. Phil has worked for the company a year and a half and has his eye on becoming a supervisor. In fact, he wondered if he would be promoted to supervisor of administrative services when Carol Lee was chosen. Now he looks upon her as a hindrance to his progression in the organization. He is constantly saying to himself, "What can she do that I can't?"

Nita, on the other hand, joined the team after Carol Lee was made supervisor. Nita was just out of high school and lacked office experience. Carol Lee was very helpful to her, and Nita has the highest respect for her supervisor. Because of the very different frames of reference of Phil and Nita, they see Carol Lee from completely different vantage points. Consequently, whenever Carol Lee gives suggestions to her subordinates, Phil resists them and Nita accepts them readily.

As a communicator and manager, you should understand that the frame of reference is a mental filtering system involving at least the following three important processes: selective perception, selective retention, and selective transmission. All communication is greatly affected by these filtering processes.

### Selective Perception

Your five senses are constantly bombarded by literally thousands of stimuli, or communication cues, which your brain is physically incapable of handling simultaneously. Basically, your mind focuses on one thing at a time. Therefore, your brain is constantly involved in assigning priorities to the many stimuli that are available to be perceived. This process is performed somewhat subconsciously and is based upon current physical and mental needs. A few major factors affect the assignment of priorities in your perception:

1. You notice those things that lead to fulfillment of your needs. If you are a manager looking for a new and better computer, for example, you will be inclined to notice computer advertisements more than usual. If you have a subordinate who is anxious to advance in your organization, you'll be able to attract that individual's attention with information about how he or she can advance.
2. In familiar surroundings, you notice the unfamiliar, unusual things. Capitalizing on this tendency, you would use unusual attention getters in correspondence and in intracompany communication.
3. In unfamiliar surroundings, you notice familiar things because your mind tries to understand the unusual surroundings in light of the familiar matter it already understands. Thus, when you are explaining a new concept to an associate, you will be more successful if you show how the new concept relates to concepts your associate already understands.

Don Spotten was a purchasing agent for Armco Financial Corp. and had frequent contact with the sales representatives of numerous companies. Because he had had good success with JCN office products in the past, he was well acquainted with Connie Perry, the JCN sales representative.

Don read one day of an office equipment show to be held in San Francisco, so he made plans to attend. He wanted to look at several of the latest pieces of office equipment he had read about. On the day of the show, Don traveled to San Francisco and went to the hotel where the show was being held. As he entered the equipment show room, he was momentarily surprised by all the different displays. Suddenly he caught sight of the familiar JCN sign, and he began walking toward it. At the JCN display he hoped to see Connie Perry, but she wasn't there.

Don quickly glanced at the JCN equipment with which he had become so familiar. Immediately he noticed a new item, a new model of word-processing typewriter, and he examined it carefully.

In the preceding example, you can see that Don noticed the equipment show announcement because it would help fill his needs as a purchasing agent. At the equipment show (unfamiliar surroundings) he noticed the familiar JCN sign, and at the JCN display (familiar equipment) he noticed the new word-processing typewriter.

### Selective Retention

Retention pertains to the brain's ability to store mental records of messages it has perceived. Selective retention refers to the assignment of priorities in this mental filing system. The study of selective retention in connection with communication barriers is important because memory has a great impact on how you interpret and use information that comes into the brain.

The mind stores all information that makes up the frame of reference. In fact, many believe that the mind stores everything that it perceives. The important issue, however, is how readily that information can be recalled for use. Some information can be retrieved instantly, some with a bit of concentration, and some not at all. People remember things that filled their needs, that were significantly different from usual, and that were overlearned or repeatedly observed. Memories that qualify under these categories will be remembered readily and will have an impact on a person's perception and behavior, while those memories that are not readily retained will have little effect on a person's perception, behavior, and frame of reference.

When information comes into the conscious part of your brain, your mind searches its storage for past learnings that relate to the new information. In effect, the mind says, "In the past, this message cue has usually been accompanied by such and such. Therefore, it must mean ____ ." In your mind's diligent attempts to arrange input logically, it frequently considers perceptions as facts when they are really inferences or educated guesses. This act of making judgment before gathering enough information causes many problems because the probability of error is so high.

An example may help to illustrate the brain's function better. Assume that you are the supervisor of the reprographics department for JKL Co. You notice Janet Maughn walking briskly along the hall toward your office. You also notice that she is carrying what appears to be about five hundred sheets of paper. You immediately begin searching your mind for information that relates to this observation. In your mental files, you find that your department just completed a duplication job for Janet. You also recall that the only times that people have brought large piles of paper to you have been times when mistakes had been made by your department. Also, you remember that people usually walk more briskly when they are upset than when they are not.

On the basis of your mental search, you make a temporary conclusion that your department must have made an error in completing Janet's job, that she is bringing the job back to be redone, and that she is upset. Therefore, you begin to get emotionally uneasy and prepare for a confrontation with Janet.

This premature conclusion points out one of the most serious communication problems; that is, you perceive information that seems very much like something you have known in the past. Therefore, you jump to the conclusion that the observation *is* what you think it is; *inference* is interpreted as *fact.* Since subsequent decisions will be based upon these inference-fact discrepancies, the faulty-based decisions can cause devastating problems.

Just as Janet is approaching your office, she turns into the mail room. You breathe a sign of relief and resume your work. The preceding observation is replaced in your conscious mind by something else, but it is not forgotten. The experience has added to your frame of reference in the following ways: the assumption that problems accompany people who carry large amounts of papers toward your office is weakened; the thought that your department made an error on Janet's job is proven false, and your confidence in your employees is restored; but the assumption that people who are upset walk briskly remains unchanged, since you don't know whether Janet was upset or not in dealing with the mail department.

**Selective Transmission**

Output from the conscious part of the mind takes three basic forms: (1) all processed information is retained in the memory, (2) some information unconsciously leaks out via verbal and/or nonverbal means, and (3) some information is consciously transmitted via the verbal and/or nonverbal means. The information that is transmitted in the second and third forms makes up only a small portion of all mental output, because people can think faster than they can talk or write and they do not feel a great need to transmit most of their thinking. Assume, for example, that you are a supervisor and that you have received a call from Nile, one of your workers. Nile explains that he is feeling ill and will be missing work for the day. You thank Nile for calling and tell him you hope he feels better soon. In selecting his message, Nile did not feel it necessary to go into all the detail about his sore throat, his aching muscles and head, his upset stomach, and his restless night. He felt that all you needed to know was that he was sick and wouldn't be to work.

Because thoughts and ideas always exceed the actual transmitted message, you must remember that most of what others think is known only to them and that it is impossible to understand completely their feelings and ideas. Information that is transmitted unconsciously may occur through nonverbal means when there is no verbal accompaniment, or it may occur in conjunction with verbal messages. As mentioned in Chapter 8, because this type of information is transmitted unconsciously, it is generally a true reflection of feelings. Thus, it has high believability. Since much nonverbal communication falls into this category, nonverbal cues are usually valid indicators of real feelings. Albert Mehrabian and other researchers have found that if verbal and nonverbal communication contradict each other, the nonverbal message will usually be believed.[1]

Before messages are sent consciously, they must pass a thorough screening test. First, you must ask whether you should even send the message at all. Major reasons for not sending a particular message are as follows:

1. The message is not considered to be sufficiently important. For example, Phyllis, a microfilm clerk, receives a compliment from her fellow worker on her new dress; she doesn't tell anyone else about it, because she feels it is insignificant for others to know.
2. Negative repercussions are feared. For example, Phyllis would like to tell her supervisor about the supervisor's lack of communication with the individual workers, but she is afraid that her supervisor would get upset at that message. Therefore, she doesn't say anything about it.

The first reason for not sending messages is usually quite defensible. The second reason, however, is one of the most serious communication barriers that exists in organizations. The reason it is so serious is that this fear frequently stifles communication that *should be* transmitted. As you have communicated with other people you have, no doubt, noticed that many of your transmissions are not received as well as you would like. Consequently, you become very careful about what you communicate. You become conditioned to communicate by fear.

***Fear.*** Some examples of the fears you might feel as you anticipate communication are:

Others will not be interested and won't listen.

Others will condemn you for what you say.

Others might be offended by your message.

Others won't understand the message.

Others will pass information along to a person who shouldn't know about it.

The message might not be totally correct and you will expose your ignorance.

Because of anticipated repercussions, you usually try to send "safe" messages—messages that others will be interested in, messages with which others will agree, messages that are simple enough to understand, and messages that seem logical.

This attempt to create safe messages is a major communication barrier. In your attempt to tailor these ideal messages, you distort the real picture as it exists in your mind. Thus, the message receiver can't fully understand you because you have sent an incomplete message or misrepresentations. For example, Phyllis's supervisor, David, has prepared a proposal for management regarding the purchase of some new items of microfilm equipment. David asks Phyllis to read the proposal and to react to it. After she reads the proposal, she is convinced that it is weak in several spots. Because she thinks David wants only a compliment, however, she tells him it "looks good." Constant attempts to create messages that will seem appropriate for other people result in a perpetual guessing game—you try to guess what they are thinking, and they try to guess what you're really trying to say.

***Symbols.*** Another barrier results from the need to use symbols to transmit your messages. These symbols, in verbal and nonverbal form, have different meanings to everyone. So even though you might use words that you think accurately reflect your thoughts, the persons receiving your messages have a different interpretation of your words because of their unique frames of reference. This semantic problem is frequently overlooked; and people fail to realize that meaning occurs in the mind, not in the words themselves. The following example illustrates how verbal descriptions usually oversimplify real mental images and frequently result in serious message distortion.

1. Sender's original idea:

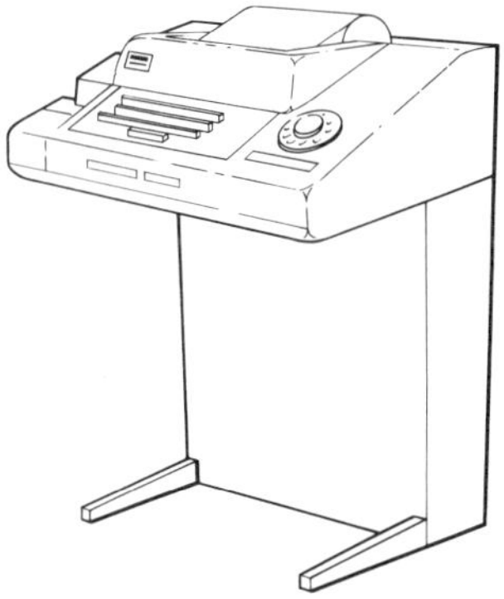

2. Symbolized by words: Telex, a telecommunication machine used for sending information
3. Transmission: encoded words transmitted and received, with environment and personal factors playing a part in the context of the situation
4. Words desymbolized: receiver creates his or her own interpretation of the words *Telex, a telecommunication,* and *machine.*

5. Receiver's idea:

6. Remembered:

The presence of heightened emotions may also cause you to distort your transmissions. Your bias tends to be reflected much more whenever you become very emotionally involved. Thus, your positive feelings might cause a message to be reflected in a more positive light than is really true. Negative feelings, on the other hand, frequently cause you to verbally attack another person or to defend yourself to protect your mental balance. Nothing is quite so painful as to have your self-esteem destroyed. Therefore, your defenses are up when you perceive your self-esteem being threatened. Defensiveness affects your behavior; thus, others readily observe your negative emotion and they usually react in like manner toward you. The result is a very destructive self-perpetuating cycle.

Notice, in the following example, how emotions and defensiveness destroy communication and interpersonal effectiveness. Janice Ward, an executive of Midwestern Mutual Insurance Co., walks into the word-processing center with a letter in her hand. She talks with Nola Smith, the word-processing center supervisor: "Look at this letter I just received from your center—six typographical errors on just one page. That's got to be the worst job of typing I have ever seen." Nola looks at the reference initials at the bottom of the letter and determines that Angela Perez typed the letter. She calls Angela over and shows her the letter. Janice interrupts at this point and says, "So you're the one who typed this mess. I should have known. How you ever got hired in the first place is more than I can understand." Angela snaps back and says, "Well, I'd like to see you try to type from your dictation. You always sound as if your mouth is full of mush. You could stand to take some dictation lessons from some of the others around here." "All right, all right," interrupts Nola; "Ms. Ward, let me handle this and I'll make sure you get a perfect copy in a few moments." No doubt you noticed that both Janice and Angela said things that they wouldn't have said if emotions hadn't gotten out of control. Good communicators are those who let their brains, rather than their emotions, govern their comments.

All transmission faults, whether they are intentional or not, result in a certain amount of communication distortion. Technically, there cannot be perfect communication in which both communicators understand each other totally. In the first place, the sender transmits a message that is only symbolic of the real thought. In the second place, the receiver (if he or she perceives the message at all) interprets the already distorted message according to his or her own logic system. Therefore, every transmission attempt is certain to suffer a certain amount of communication failure.

***Serial Communication.*** This distortion is increased many times over when *serial* communication is involved. Serial communication is the passing of a given message through a series of individuals; i.e., A to B, B to C, C to D. In experiments involving serial communication, the authors have found that by the time messages are passed orally through four or five persons, very little of the original message remains intact. Organizational communication frequently involves serial communication such as the transmission of messages through several steps in the informal (grapevine) or formal organizational structure. As a result, organizations are constantly plagued by problems caused by severe message distortion.

To understand better how communication can be distorted when passing through the grapevine of an organization, consider the following example. Roger Stalling works in the research and development division of Eastern Paper Products. In this same company, Suzette Jacobsen is a clerk in the shipping department, Mark Alder is employed in the accounting department, Sandra Black is an administrative assistant for the president, and Juanita Lopez works in the data-processing center. According to the company organization chart, these people should receive company-related information from their supervisors. As with all organizations, however, this company has an informal organization through which all kinds of information pass. Roger, Suzette, Mark, Sandra, and Juanita are part of the grapevine.

One day, Sandra overheard the president ask one of the vice-presidents to "check out that new property in West Beach." Sandra carpools with Juanita and mentioned to her that the president was looking at some new property out in West Beach. Sandra said that she didn't know what it was all about. Later that night, Juanita, who was bowling with Suzette, mentioned that the president was considering buying some property in West Beach. The next day Suzette mentioned to Mark, her long-time friend from high school days, that the president was buying some new property in West Beach. And the next Saturday, Mark had his weekly golf game with Roger and told him that the company had bought a new plant site in West Beach. On Monday, Roger asked his supervisor about the new plant site. The supervisor remarked, "Why am I always the last to know about things around here?" By Wednesday, the story had made its way up the formal organizational line to the president. By then many other grapevines had carried the story and it seemed that nearly everyone in the company knew about it. The president wrote a special memorandum to let the workers know that the company was simply considering the purchase of a new warehouse in West Beach and several other sites and that few, if any, workers would be affected by transfer in the event a purchase was made.

For many corporate leaders, the biggest problem is trying to communicate with workers at the bottom of the organizational hierarchy. Communications must pass through so many organizational levels that the top level frequently does not know if messages are received intact.

## PHYSIOLOGICAL BARRIERS

Problems arising from physiological bases result from limited sensing abilities. Everyone's senses are limited to the extent that people can see only so far and can hear only certain kinds of sounds. Compared with the seeing ability of an eagle or the smelling ability of a bloodhound, for example, human beings are very limited.

If your senses are fairly normal, you are under no greater handicap than anyone else. If a person's senses are impaired severely, however, special considerations must be made when communicating with them. For example, writing to a blind person and talking to a deaf person are ineffective methods of communication.

Physiological barriers are not generally as serious or prevalent as the psychological barriers just discussed, but some problems do arise when messages are spoken too softly to be heard or when nonverbal cues are too unnoticeable to be seen.

## ENVIRONMENTAL BARRIERS

Several categories of environmental barriers work against effective communication in organizations. Some of these factors can be controlled, but others lie outside the realm of the communicator's control. One of the more serious barriers is audio interference, which consists of other sounds that are present in the communication setting and which compete with messages you transmit or perceive. These audio interferences may consist of such things as other persons talking, static on a telephone line, machine noise such as that produced by typewriters and computers, or any other sound that might distract the message sender and/or receiver.

In addition to audio interference, you are also bombarded by numerous visual distractors. In a typical office setting, for example, there are other people, plants, equipment, desks, chairs, carpet, draperies, lights, people's clothing, papers—the list could go on and on. All these visual distractors combine with the audio interference to make competition rather tough for the business communicator. Consider a situation where you, as an administrative manager, receive a telephone call from another person. You are deeply engrossed in reviewing last month's financial reports. As the phone call is in process, you are very likely to continue to read your financial report while listening to your caller. Since neither the caller nor the financial review is receiving your undivided attention, both the reading and the listening processes suffer. The human brain simply cannot effectively process simultaneously received competing messages.

The channel you use for communication also presents definite communication barriers. Several of the more common channels used are face-to-face oral communication, telephone calls, written memoranda and letters, and written reports. Face-to-face oral communication has the advantages of both audio and visual cues, but it lacks the advantage of permanency that a written message provides. On the other end of the scale, written messages provide a permanent record for the communicators; but they lack the advantages that face-to-face communication provides. Each communication channel has certain advantages but also definite disadvantages. Since no communication channel is without weaknesses, you must accept the disadvantages each one carries with it.

The business organization itself presents communication problems. First, since businesses usually have several organizational levels, the step-by-step process of sending communication through these levels results in serious filtering and message distortion. Second, persons within each level of the organization are constantly being observed and evaluated. At stake are their jobs, promotions, salary increases, status, and self-esteem. To protect themselves against loss in each of these areas, employees tend to filter out any message that might be injurious to them. Third, organizations become so complex that matching individual persons with the information each needs becomes a practical impossibility. For example, if you obtain employment in an organization with several hundred other workers, you will find a great deal of the information that comes to you through the formal organization line to be irrelevant to your personal or work situation. On the other hand, you will find on occasion that information that you should have received was not given to you. Fourth, communication is the lifeblood of an organization; therefore, there is rarely a dearth of information passing. Since persons in organizations come in contact with so much communication they can't use, they tend to discard many messages without examining them carefully.

Time is another factor that has an effect on communication. Since workers are constantly performing under time pressures, they frequently take insufficient time to read, transmit, and listen to messages properly.

Physical distance is another communication barrier. Unless you are working side by side with another individual, you will probably have some difficulty in communicating with that person when and where you would like. If a person is located in a distant city, for example, you are saddled with the disadvantages of the less immediate communication channels that you must use.

After reading this chapter, you may be wondering how people communicate as well as they do with all that is working against them. Somehow, most organizations usually manage to achieve enough communication success to stay in operation. Organizational communication can be greatly improved, however, and Chapter 10 will suggest some ideas for this improvement.

## *Summary*

Communication barriers arise from psychological, physiological, and environmental factors. The major psychological communication problem arises because each person has a unique frame of reference, created by past experiences. No two people can see things from exactly the same point of view.

Based on your frame of reference, several filtering functions occur in the mind: (1) selective perception—your mind perceives only a few of the phenomena that could be perceived; (2) selective retention—your mind assigns a priority to all phenomena it senses, and it can retrieve more effectively those phenomena that receive higher priority ratings; and (3) selective transmission—only a few of the many thoughts that are stored in your brain are transmitted to the outside world. These filtering functions performed by your brain are necessary to help you keep your mental balance, but they cause serious problems in achieving effective communication.

Because you have had negative experiences with some messages you have sent, the element of fear enters into the communication process. In essence, you tend to send safe messages—messages that will not cause any negative repercussions for you.

The necessity of using symbols to transmit your thoughts causes many problems. Words are only imitations of the ideas you have in your mind. Heightened emotions also cause problems, especially if the emotions are negative. Negative emotions cause you to distort your communication and to become defensive against those people you feel are attacking you.

Physiological barriers arise from the different sensing abilities of individuals. Persons with limited hearing or seeing ability are under a definite handicap when involved in communication.

Environmental barriers are those factors outside your mind that compete for your attention. Visual and audio distractors bombard you from all sides and at all times. The channel you use in message transmission also carries with it certain limitations with which you have to cope.

The complexity of the business organization causes logistic communication problems as well as psychological ones. Although some improvement can be made in organizational communication, problems will always occur. Time and physical distance are two additional communications factors that have an impact on the organizational communication barriers discussed.

## *Review and Discussion Questions*

1. From what three areas do communication barriers arise? Which area is most critical? Why?
2. What is a *frame of reference*? How does it affect communication?
3. How do the three filtering processes in the communication cycle affect your ability to communicate accurately?
4. What can you do to get others to notice and remember your written messages?
5. Why does fear play such an important part in determining what messages you transmit?
6. How do heightened emotions affect a person's communication behavior?
7. How does serial communication affect organizational communication?
8. What do you think are the most serious environmental barriers? Why?

## *Application Exercises*

1. Can you remember what happened on this day last year, six months ago, three months ago, last week? Can you remember what happened last Christmas? Last New Year's Eve? On your last birthday? Discuss the reasons for remembering special-event days more than regular days.
2. Visit with a person who works in a large business organization. Have this person discuss the organizational communication problems that he or she frequently encounters.
3. Think of a recent disagreement you have had with another person. Based on the concepts discussed in this chapter (frame of reference, filtering, and symbolizing), analyze the disagreement.
4. Assume that you are a personnel manager and have responsibility for interviewing and hiring activities. Explain how selective perception, retention, and transmission affect your job.
5. Based on what you have learned about selective transmission, explain why organizations have more downward than upward communication.

## *Case Studies*

1. *Locating the new distribution center.* Gary Laird and Rose Walker were assigned by their manager to select a new West Coast site from which National Mills could distribute its products. They considered a number of factors

and finally boiled down their choices to San Francisco and Los Angeles. At that point there was total disagreement. Rose remembered one experience she had had at the Los Angeles airport where she missed a plane flight because of poor directions given her by an airport worker. She argued for the site to be located in San Francisco, telling Gary it was impossible to get qualified workers in the Los Angeles area. Gary, on the other hand, had a number of close friends in Los Angeles and argued for that city, claiming that it had a better population base than San Francisco.

Give at least two types of communication barriers that are present in this situation.

2. *A meeting missed.* Shirley Erickson had been out of town for three days and returned to her office to find her desk piled high with work. She thumbed through all the papers to determine the content of each, and she made two piles—work needing immediate action and work that could wait. One of the items that was placed in the second pile was a memo from her division manager. She had scanned enough of the memo to learn that it dealt with reducing office costs, so she did not think that to be a matter of immediate concern.

For two days Shirley worked diligently to complete the urgent work. At the end of the second day she received a telephone call from the division manager who said somewhat impatiently, "Why weren't you at the meeting today?" "What meeting?" Shirley replied, "Nobody told me about any meeting." "Didn't you receive a memo from me?" asked the manager. "Well, yes, I did," stammered Shirley, "but I didn't notice anything about a meeting." "Well, perhaps we had better talk about it at nine o'clock in the morning," the manager said firmly.

Shirley hung up the phone and hurriedly searched through the pile of papers until she found the memo. Reading it carefully she discovered that not only was she to attend a meeting but also that she was to give a report on how her department would propose to cut administrative costs. The last line read: "Let me know if for any reason you cannot attend the meeting and make the presentation." Shirley was mortified.

Using Chapter 9 as a basis for your information, explain precisely what caused the communication problem in this case.

## *Reference Note*

1. Albert Mehrabian, *Silent Messages* (Belmont, Calif.: Wadsworth, 1971), p. iii.

# 10

# Improving Organizational Communication

In spite of the numerous barriers that were discussed in Chapter 9, managers can implement programs that will greatly improve organizational communications. As you become acquainted with different organizations during your lifetime, you will readily notice that the personalities of these groups will differ significantly. In some, you will observe very guarded, defensive communication in a climate of suspicion. In others, you will see the opposite—open, honest communication in a climate of trust.

The interesting factor in each of these situations is that communication climate is largely dependent upon management. In other words, management determines by its actions and attitudes whether communication will succeed or fail.

Probably the most critical communication objective is to create a climate in which all workers feel free to express themselves. This type of organizational climate is important because workers who can express themselves freely will be less likely to talk and work *against* the organization. Simply stated, effective communication improves morale and organizational effectiveness. Chapter 10 outlines a number of actions that you, as a manager, can take to enhance the communication climate of your organization.

## PERIODIC COMMUNICATION SESSIONS

Because the hustle and bustle of the typical office provides so little opportunity for undisturbed thoughtful communication, managers should establish a periodic personal communication schedule in their organization. At least every quarter, they should meet with each of their subordinates for personal, one-to-one communication. (This communication session ties in with management by objectives, discussed further in Chapter 15.) Basically, this periodic communication session focuses on the following topics: praise of employee for work well done, evaluation of objectives established during previous interview, establishment of new objectives, and unstructured time used at the discretion of the interviewer and the interviewee.

Consider the case of Roberta Blanchard, the manager of communication services in a midwestern office of the federal government. Roberta has responsibility for the supervisors of reprographic services, telecommunication services, office purchasing and inventory, and administrative services. A number of significant changes have been occurring in Roberta's office and she has been working overtime nearly every day for the past two months. Consequently, she has spent very little time with those whom she supervises. She realizes that three months have gone by since she had her last interview with Don Turner, supervisor of administrative services. Therefore, she asks Don to come in for an interview on Monday of next week.

Roberta prepares well for the interview and finds that her efforts pay off. During the interview Don hints that he has felt somewhat forgotten during the last busy period. Roberta assures him that she has not been intentionally ignoring him and that she will try to be more available in the future. Don also mentions that he has been having considerable difficulty in getting office supplies through Louis, supervisor of office purchasing and inventory. Don says he has talked with Louis a number of times about depleted inventories but that the problem still hasn't been solved. Roberta promises that she will check into the problem and get some action for Don. As Don leaves the interview he thanks Roberta for the chance to talk with her on a one-to-one basis. "There's nothing more frustrating than to feel that I have no one in management that I can talk with," says Don.

As illustrated by this example, the periodic communication session provides several benefits to an organization:

1. The interview forces the superior to take time to visit on a personal basis with each subordinate.
2. The subordinate has the chance to visit with the superior without his or her peers wondering "what's up."
3. The interview lets the subordinate know that management is interested in his or her feelings and opinions.
4. The interview fosters upward communication (communication from a worker to his or her superior officers).
5. The interview focuses on the establishment and accomplishment of objectives. Consequently, since the subordinate knows that objectives set at the previous interview will have to be accounted for, he or she will feel an increased desire to accomplish the objectives.

If used faithfully, the periodic, personal interview will be one of the most effective communication problem solvers you will find.

## ACTIVE LISTENING

A vital ingredient to interpersonal communication effectiveness is the ability to listen. No amount of one-to-one interviewing will be effective if the interviewer does not listen. Therefore, until managers master the art of listening, they are not prepared to communicate. As was discussed in Chapter 8, communication is a two-way process, not just one way.

The type of listening most needed by managers is active listening, and the process involved in this type of listening is illustrated in the flowchart shown in Figure 10-1. The only way communicators can determine whether their messages have been properly received is to obtain feedback. Thus, active listening focuses mainly on the feedback process.

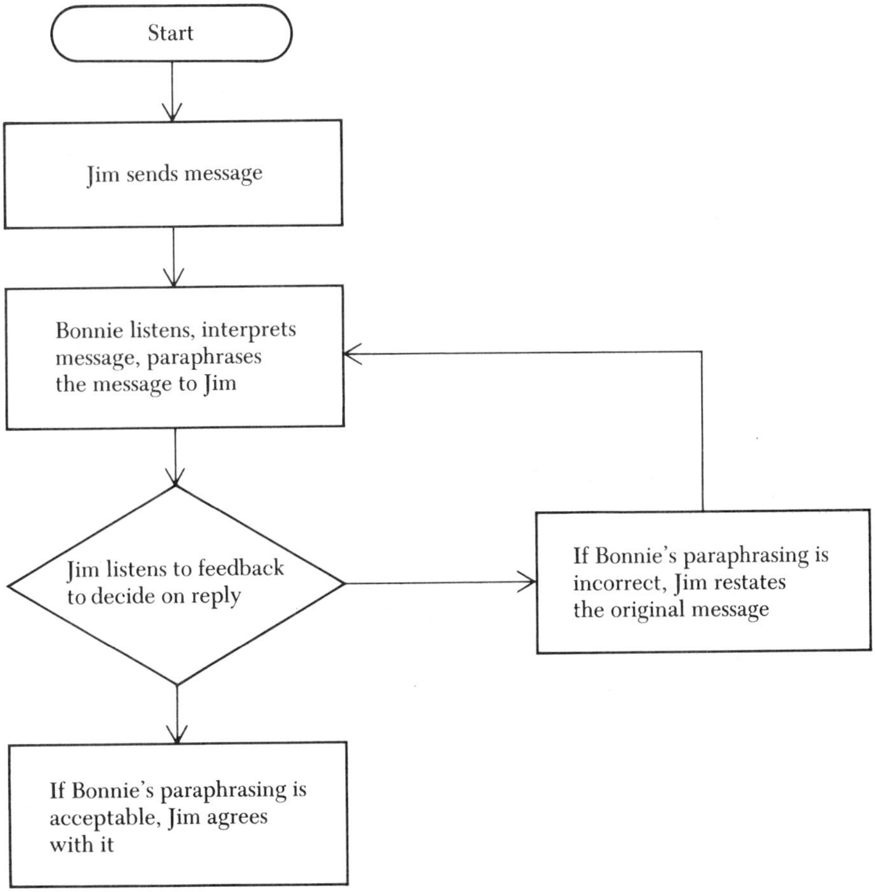


*Figure 10-1.* The Active Listening Process

Active listening should also involve two major parts of every message—the content and the feelings. Every message is, to a certain degree, tied to emotions; and if you fail to perceive and respond to the *feeling* part of the message, you are seeing only part of the picture.

The following conversation involves active listening. See how Jennifer uses active listening to understand Alison, her supervisor.

"You did quite a job on that letter, Jennifer."

"You liked it?"

"I didn't say that."

"There was a problem with the way I typed it?"

"Well, I did find a few errors that I thought should have been corrected. Here is a strikeover and here's a misspelled word. I also noticed that you forgot the comma after the closing."

"You'd like it retyped then."

"If you would, please, Jennifer."

In this series of responses, you saw Jennifer as a good listener because she continued to send back her perceptions until she completely understood the real message Alison was sending her. Even though Alison's first statement was somewhat ambiguous, Jennifer was able to determine what she really had on her mind.

The use of active listening seems to be most practical in oral, one-to-one situations, but it can also be used very effectively in small-group settings. Here, active listening can be accomplished in basically two ways. With the first way, one member of the group can act as an *informal moderator* for the entire group. Using this moderator approach, you would attempt to rephrase individual group members' messages (both content and feeling) until they affirm that you understand them.

Assume that Marie, Doug, and Ben are in a meeting in which the problem of tardiness is being discussed. Marie and Doug both have strong feelings about this topic and have engaged in a rather heated argument about the causes and cures of the problem. Ben notices that Marie and Doug are not listening to each other. They seem to be trying to shoot each other down rather than trying to understand one another. Therefore, Ben waits for a slight pause in the conversation and then says, "In other words, Marie, you feel that the real problem is caused by the congested traffic and parking problems around the company?" Marie agrees that this is the problem as she sees it. Then Doug jumps back in and says, "Even if we didn't have traffic and parking congestion, the same people would still be tardy." Again, Ben takes the opportunity to speak and says, "So you feel, Doug, that the problem arises more out of personal habits rather than out of traffic problems." Doug says, "Yes, that's exactly the way I feel."

At this point, both Marie and Doug are satisfied that at least someone in the group understands them. In addition, they have been "forced" to sit back and listen to the other person's point of view. Even though Ben is "just another member" of the group, he has been able to exert a significant influence on the communication of the group.

The second way to use active listening in small groups is to have each member *rephrase* the previous speaker's message before being allowed to make any new comments. For example, if Bernie has just spoken and Gina now wants to speak, Gina must rephrase to Bernie's satisfaction the content of his message. When he agrees that Gina understands his message, she may proceed with her comments.

Both methods of small-group active listening are extremely effective in keeping emotions in check and in achieving understanding. As you attend small-group meetings in the future, watch the communication patterns of the participants. You'll see that certain members will repeat themselves again and again simply because they don't think others have understood their message. In many cases, these same people will need to state their message only once if you will rephrase their message until they can say, "Yes, that's what I mean."

Use this same approach with angry group members and you'll see that in many cases they will immediately calm down. Although this practice is most effective when every member uses it, in most cases others either don't know about active listening or they become so emotionally involved that they forget to listen. In all cases you can add great stability to a group if you will faithfully practice active listening yourself.

## INVOLVEMENT OF SUBORDINATES IN DECISION MAKING

Along with many other researchers, we have found that group decisions are usually much better than individual decisions. When you involve your subordinates in making decisions that affect them, they will be much more willing to abide by those decisions. In essence, they are simply abiding by their own law; or, if they find that they dislike the decision, they at least feel that they had a voice in it. Also, subordinate involvement in decision making gives workers a chance to communicate their best ideas. With individual decisions, these ideas remain untapped, and subordinates will complain, "If they had asked me, I could have told them what to do." Subordinate involvement provides great satisfaction to your workers because it makes them feel a part of the management team.[1] Consequently, they work to maintain the trust shown in them.

Obviously, you cannot involve your subordinates in all the decisions you must make. As Chapter 2 indicates, different situations require different leadership styles. Before deciding to involve your workers, you must make certain that (1) they are qualified to make worthwhile contributions to the decision, (2) you have sufficient time to involve the group in the decision—group decision making is a slow process, and (3) the group members will cooperate sufficiently to make a unified decision. As you gain experience in management, you will become more skilled in deciding when to involve others in decision making.

Subordinate involvement in decision making provides an excellent way of stimulating upward communication in your organization. Since employees frequently complain that "nobody up there understands me," this practice is well worth using.

## FORMAL ORGANIZATIONAL COMMUNICATIONS

A communication practice that results in some of the same advantages as involvement of subordinates in decision making is that of keeping employees aware of organizational happenings. This open communication process involves the use of periodic bulletin board announcements, memoranda, reports, letters to employees, meetings, and house organs (periodic magazine-type publications issued by an organization to its employees or clients) to keep employees informed of organizational and individual concerns. This open communication practice is helpful for four reasons:

1. People work more diligently when they realize what they are working toward. If they understand how their work contributes to the objectives of the entire organization, they will be much more inclined to perform their share of the work.[2]
2. People will feel complimented if you consider them important enough to keep them informed of organizational concerns.
3. Open communication from the top down will tend to encourage more openness in communication from the bottom up. Since so many advantages accrue from increased upward communication, this point is extremely important.
4. Open communication tends to make all members of an organization feel that they are "members of the family." Employees who feel that they belong to the family will speak of the organization in "we" terms rather than in "they" terms. In addition to providing coverage of companywide concerns, these formal organizational communications provide excellent opportunities to reward and publicize outstanding service and performance by individuals and departments. Such publicity provides additional incentives for dedicated employee service. Although these media, the time, and the personal work involved in preparing the messages cost the organization a sizable outlay of cash, the resulting benefits will more than offset the expenses.

## COMMUNICATION AND WORKERS' SELF-IMAGES

Organizational communication research has shown that serial communication distortion correlates negatively with worker self-confidence and job security. In other words, if you feel insecure and unsure of yourself in a job, you will tend to distort communication to protect yourself and to cover up your inadequacies. Conversely, if you feel secure and sure of yourself, you will tend to transmit truthful messages because you do not feel threatened by them.

You can readily see that if you make decisions that are based on information you have received from very insecure subordinates, chances are great that your decisions are based on false information. The subordinates have probably passed to you only information that will be beneficial to them.

To combat this communication problem, you have at least two alternatives. First, you can double-check all communication that comes to you from insecure employees. Second, you can help those insecure employees develop a healthy self-image, so they will feel safe in transmitting any kind of information to you. The first alternative is obviously a poor choice because it will tend to perpetuate the problem. When employees discover that you are checking up on them more than usual, they will become even more fearful and their feelings of insecurity will increase. However, when you encounter a problem that seems to be more significant than the usual company concerns, you will be better off to double-check the message accuracy so that you will not react needlessly; when double-checking the accuracy of messages, be sure to go through proper organizational channels.

By choosing the second alternative, developing self-confidence in your employees, you will not only alleviate your communication distortion problem but also help develop human beings—the greatest resource any organization has. Throughout this textbook, you will read of management practices that will help to develop self-esteem in employees. Positive reinforcement, praise, management by objectives, team building, training and development, and other techniques will help give your employees a feeling of success that will, in turn, enhance communication in your organization.

## IMPROVEMENT OF MANAGEMENT CREDIBILITY

Managers would be among the first to admit that company policies, directives, and other communications do not guarantee that employees will believe in and conform to suggested management guidelines. Workers at even the lowest level in the organization still possess veto power over management directives. This veto power will always be available to workers, but it begins to be a serious problem in an organization when subordinates lose faith in their superiors. Once this basic faith in superiors is lost, the subordinates will question nearly every communication that comes from higher echelons within the organization. Management must continuously strive to retain or win basic respect from their subordinates.

Chad Pearson was an employee at a southern division office of a large national corporation. Chad's division manager, Mr. Davidson, circulated a memorandum to the office staff suggesting that they carpool as much as possible to conserve energy and to aid the fight against pollution. Chad read the memo and agreed that carpooling would be a good idea. Subsequently, he found that two other workers in his section lived close enough to him to make carpooling feasible. Chad talked with the two workers, Marion and Leon, and suggested that the three of them carpool. "Are you kidding?" replied Marion. "Haven't you ever noticed Mr. Davidson come to work? He drives his big car that guzzles more gas than mine ever could. And I don't see him sharing rides with any one else. Listen, when he starts carpooling, so will I." This example illustrates the veto power of even the lowest employee and shows the importance of developing trust between workers and management.

Generally, the more positive the feelings between two persons, the more persuasive power those two individuals will have with each other. Therefore, if you as an administrative manager want to have the power to persuade your employees to believe in you and to perform properly, you will find your persuasive ability will be greater with those who have the most trust in you.

Management credibility is established by following four basic actions:

1. Select competent leaders. Leaders who lack either sufficient technical knowledge or managerial abilities will find respect from subordinates very difficult to obtain.
2. Listen. Of all management information sources, listening is the most important.[3] As an administrative manager, you need to learn early when to talk and when to listen. It seems rather obvious that you learn more when you listen than when you talk. Therefore, if you want to keep learning, keep listening. By listening you'll be a better decision maker. In addition, you'll be appreciated for being considerate enough to listen to others' points of view.
3. Be dependable. Everyone likes a person whom they can depend on. If your employees know they can trust you and depend on you, they will feel comfortable around you. If you are unpredictable, however, they will feel uneasy about you and will not trust you.
4. Set a proper example. Managers should exemplify all the traits that they themselves desire in their very best employee. Since human beings are in a constant state of change, management should provide the very best model possible to encourage change in positive directions. Employees might not always emulate the good examples set by managers, but some employees frequently exploit to their advantage a bad example set by some unthinking manager.

By following these actions, you'll find that your organizational climate will become positive, uplifting, and success oriented. Managers and subordinates will begin working together toward organizational goals, and everyone will benefit.

## QUESTION/SUGGESTION BOXES

Since many employees frequently feel too threatened to communicate their true feelings, organizations usually have many employee dissatisfactions and problems that management knows nothing about. As a manager, you need to provide ways of tapping these reservoirs of discontent. One method that has been used with considerable success is the question/suggestion box method. Several guidelines should be remembered when implementing and operating such a system.

1. Place question/suggestion boxes in strategic locations that are noticeable to everyone.
2. Protect the identification of the participant. If confidentiality of the users of this system is not guaranteed, employees may not submit their questions and suggestions. One method that has proven effective involves the selection of a nonmanagement, middle person who receives all questions and suggestions in confidence and who finds answers and has suggestions evaluated. Another method uses perforated, numbered forms; the employee removes the receipt for the suggestion as it is placed in the box. Thus, no name needs to be written on the form at all. This method provides confidentiality and makes possible the recognition of worthy suggestions. A suggestion form is illustrated in Figure 10-2.
3. Provide prompt response to all questions and suggestions and give justification for all responses.
4. Give appropriate rewards for suggestions that result in significant improvement in organizational operations. Rewards of this type will improve employee morale and will foster additional helpful suggestions.

   For example, if you find yourself in an administrative management position working with people in word processing, records management, data processing, and systems analysis functions, you could persuade management to agree to reward employees who make money-saving suggestions in the organization. One employee, for example, might come up with a revised paper-flow system that would save your company $20,000 per year in paper costs. This employee might be given a percentage of the resulting savings for the first year the system is in operation.

General Mills

7278 GM-1 6/76

**EMPLOYEE SUGGESTION FORM**

SUGGESTION

Nº 89645

| Submitted by: | Date received ______ |
|---|---|
| Name ______ | Location ______ Code ______ Group ______ |
| Department ______ Title ______ | Action ______ Action Date ______ |
| Office/Plant ______ City ______ | Date suggester notified of action ______ |

Present only one (1) suggestion on each form - print or type **(DO NOT USE PENCIL)**

Date ______ I suggest that ______

DETACH AND KEEP THIS STUB Nº 89645

| Name ______<br>Department ______<br>Date ______<br>Suggestion ______ | If you need help in explaining your idea, ask your supervisor<br>Be clear. Diagrams or drawings may help sell your idea. Attach samples when your idea involves new or revised forms.<br>Be specific. What needs to be done? Why? How do you propose doing it? |
|---|---|

*Figure 10-2.* Sample Suggestion Form

5. Educate all employees about the workings of the question/suggestion box system, and constantly encourage its use.

If all managers, supervisors, and workers were perfect communicators, question/suggestion boxes would be unnecessary; subordinates would have no fear in communicating their problems and suggestions to their supervisors. Since all organizations are composed of imperfect communicators, however, the question/suggestion box can be an effective alternative.

## IMPLEMENTATION OF FORMAL COMMUNICATION TRAINING

Most workers in an organization have had rather limited communication training. Aside from traditional English and language classes, workers have had little exposure to many of the communication basics that can make such a difference in interpersonal communication. Persons in the management level usually have had greater exposure to additional communication training; but you have no doubt found that what you learned in classes you took several years ago has largely faded from your mind. Consequently, both management and employees can benefit greatly from ongoing communication training.

Several major sources of communication training are available:

Management consultants who specialized in presenting communication seminars

Company personnel who have had specialized training in communication

Correspondence courses in communication

Formal communication courses at community colleges and other colleges and universities

Special seminars focusing on organizational communication

Topics for in-house communication training (training offered within the organization) can be many and varied. Some that would prove to be both interesting and beneficial to most business persons are listed below:

The meaning is in the mind, not in the words

Is it inference or fact?

Letters versus telephone calls

Communication barriers

Serial communication: problems and solutions

The business interview

Writing better letters and reports

Nonverbal communication

Active listening

In-house communication training is employed with great success by numerous business organizations. This training has a positive effect on managers and employees individually and on the organization as a whole. Communication is truly the lifeblood of an organization, and a periodic transfusion will enrich this vital function.

## *Summary*

The communication climate of an organization is largely dependent upon the communication practices and attitudes of management. Consequently, management must do all within its power to foster open and supportive organizational communication.

Managers should have periodic one-to-one communication sessions with each of their immediate subordinates to enhance open communication. Active listening is a vital tool in letting employees know their ideas are important and that management is willing to listen. Active listening is useful both in one-to-one settings and in small-group settings.

Another technique used to obtain useful information from employees and to increase employees' feelings of belonging is to involve the workers in decision making. The use of formal organizational communications (bulletin board announcements, memoranda, reports, letters, meetings, and house organs) will also help employees to feel that they are an important part of the organization.

Managers must remember that insecure employees tend to distort their communication to protect themselves. Thus, managers should engage in development programs to increase workers' self-confidence, thereby improving the validity of employee communication. Management must constantly strive to earn the respect of workers; if workers do not respect management, managerial communication will frequently fall on deaf ears.

To aid organizational communication, some organizations have question/suggestion boxes for employees to use in communicating to management. This technique can be very effective.

Finally, managers and workers can benefit from ongoing communication training. This training is vital for those who have had little such instruction in the past and is an important review even for those who have had previous communication training.

## *Review and Discussion Questions*

1. Why is *serial communication* a major problem in large, complex organizations?
2. Why should the anonymity of suggestion-box users be protected?
3. How do periodic one-to-one communication sessions with employees benefit both employees and management?
4. What is *active listening*? Why is it so useful in achieving an understanding in communication?

5. Why do so few people practice active listening?
6. As a manager, would you involve your subordinates in making *all* your decisions? Why or why not?
7. What basic steps would you recommend for improving management credibility?
8. Why is in-house communication training important? What sources of communication training are available to you as a manager?

## *Application Exercises*

1. Examine the grapevine within an organization with which you are familiar. Identify who talks informally to whom and how frequently these conversations are held. Draw a chart that identifies these communication patterns.
2. For the next two or three days, make a dedicated effort to apply active listening in all your conversations. Write a report of your feelings about active listening, how effective it is, and how difficult it is to practice; then, discuss your report with your class.
3. Identify three persons whom you respect. Evaluate them on the basis of the four steps that establish management credibility. Determine whether these persons "fit" these four suggestions.
4. Have a discussion on a current controversial subject with several students in your class. During the discussion, employ active listening using the *moderator* approach. Then involve another group of classmates in the same situation. Have all members of this group use active listening before allowing them to speak.

## *Case Study*

In the following situation, Davis is trying to tell Hardman that errors Hardman committed in composing a report need to be corrected. After reading the report, complete the following exercises:

1. Discuss what went wrong in the conversation.
2. Rewrite the conversation to have Hardman use active listening.

DAVIS: This is quite a report you turned in, Hardman.

HARDMAN; Thanks, I really spent a long time on it, but it turned out to be 32 pages long.

DAVIS: Well, that wasn't really what I was meaning to say.

HARDMAN: Look, I know you like shorter reports, but when something has to be said, it has to be said. Don't you agree?

DAVIS: I'm not even talking about the length of the thing, Hardman; frankly, I don't care nearly as much about the length of a report as I do about the content and accuracy.

HARDMAN: Have I ever turned in a shoddy report? Well, have I?

DAVIS: *(How in the world can I get through to this guy?)* Look, Hardman, your analysis completely overlooks the population increases that had such a positive effect on sales in your area last year.

HARDMAN: Listen, do you think management would show any sympathy if sales had gone down because of a population decrease? Absolutely not. So why should I not get personal credit when luck just happens to break for me?

DAVIS: Perhaps we ought to talk about this at another time, all right?

## *Reference Notes*


1. *Dartnell Management Report,* April 15, 1977.
2. *Ibid.*
3. Phillip V. Lewis, *Organizational Communications: The Essence of Effective Management* (Columbus, Ohio: Grid, 1975), p. 91.

# 11

# Effective Interviewing Techniques

How would you feel if your instructor or supervisor said to you, "Say, will you come into my office, I need to talk with you for a few moments?" Would you look forward to the conversation or would you begin thinking, "What have I done now?" At least part of your initial reaction would probably be a bit defensive; you would be prepared for bad news. This tendency to react defensively is just one of many interview-related problems that you will face as a manager. The principles discussed in this chapter can assist you in breaking down barriers in all types of interviews, from personnel selection to problem solving and performance appraisal.

## PURPOSE OF THE INTERVIEW

As a manager, you will find numerous situations that will require your interviewing one or more persons. In general, interviews are conducted for four basic purposes: (1) to collect information, (2) to give information, (3) to shape attitudes, and (4) to solve problems. Interviews may frequently involve more than one of these general purposes, but all interviews are conducted to accomplish at least one of them. More specifically, there are several reasons to conduct interviews with other people in your organization.

- Selection—when deciding which of several applicants to fill a vacancy in your organization
- Orientation—when inducting a new employee into your organization
- Objective setting—when meeting with a subordinate to establish personal or organizational goals and objectives
- Appraisal—when evaluating employees' job performance or achievement of objectives
- Promotion—when considering an employee for advancement or when informing an employee of an advancement

- Personnel problem solving—when attempting to determine, analyze, or solve personnel problems
- Delegation or task assignment—when giving instruction concerning new assignments

## PLANNING THE INTERVIEW

Regardless of the specific or general purpose of the interview, you should approach the situation thoughtfully and carefully. Several specific steps should be taken to insure a successful interview.

***Determine your objectives.*** Before you even decide to hold an interview, you need to ask yourself, "What do I want to accomplish?" In answering this question, state your general as well as specific objectives. For example, in a personnel selection situation, your major objective will be to determine whether a person is qualified for the job. If you were preparing to interview a prospective secretary, Henry Jackson, your general objective might be to determine whether he is qualified to work in your secretarial services department. Specific objectives could be as follows: determine Henry's typing skill; determine his communication skill; find out how long he wants to stay with the company; assess his interpersonal and social skills; determine his mathematical abilities; evaluate his ability to follow directions. Determine whether one or more personal interviews will help you reach your objectives. If you feel that interviewing will be an effective tool, proceed to the second step.

***Collect information pertinent to the interview.*** Find out as much as you can about the persons you are going to interview. Depending on the type of interview, you might determine how long they have been with the company, how long they have held their present positions, how their performance has been, what their general attitudes are, and what problems or difficulties they have experienced. Also, research the situational factors that will affect those who will be interviewed. In short, learn all you can about the entire interview situation. This mental preparation will be a distinct advantage to you as you conduct the interview.

***Plan the approach.*** After you are armed with the information that you collected in the second step, you should determine the best way to approach the interview. In general, you have two styles of interviewing. In the first style you, the interviewer, take the lead and you direct what is said and done; this is a *directive* approach. Consider the following directive interview narration:

JOLENE: How did you like your previous supervisor?

HENRY: Oh, fine. He was very good to work for. In fact, I hated to have to quit work there.

JOLENE: Did you get along all right with the other workers?

HENRY: Well, all except one. And he was just a goof-off. No one in the department liked him. In fact, he got fired about a month before I moved.

JOLENE: Were you ever given any leadership positions in that job?

HENRY: No, not really.

In this narration, you can see that Jolene definitely is controlling the direction of the interview.

The second interview style is the extreme opposite of the first; the interviewee leads the conversation and the interviewer simply follows along. This style, involving heavy use of active listening, is the *nondirective* approach. Look at how Jolene would act in a nondirective interview.

JOLENE: You say you have previous work experience?

HENRY: Yes, I worked for R & R, Inc. Mr. Wilson was my supervisor there, and I really liked him.

JOLENE: He was a good supervisor, was he?

HENRY: Yes, he made it a point to get to know everyone personally. Everybody liked him; we were just like one big happy family.

JOLENE: You feel he got along well with all his workers?

HENRY: Better than any supervisor I've ever seen. Of course, there are always some workers that no one can get along with totally.

You will notice in this second narration that Jolene more or less follows the direction of the interview as it is directed by Henry, the interviewee.

Directive and nondirective interviewing are effective in the following situations:

- Giving and collecting information—*directive*
- Drawing out information—*nondirective*
- Shaping attitudes and solving problems—combination of *nondirective* and *directive*.

After you decide which interviewing style will be most appropriate, determine the general outline that you think the interview should follow. For example, if you will be conducting a goal-setting interview, you might make a general outline something like the following one.

1. Discuss the person's work in general. Engage in some small talk. "What did you think about the hockey game last night?" "How do you feel about the new insurance benefits announced last week?"
2. Talk about the company's or department's general objectives. "Let's see, the company really wants us to push for that 10 percent decrease

in order-filling time. How do you feel about that?" "We've been trying to cut back on the time required to retrieve records from the files. This would help make things go a lot smoother, don't you think?"

3. Discuss the importance of setting objectives. Management experts have determined that one of the major differences between successful and unsuccessful employees is that successful workers set goals and then strive hard to accomplish them.
4. Examine employee's proposed objectives for next evaluation period and discuss any necessary adjustments in the objectives. "Are you sure that a 20 percent increase in your typing output is reasonable?" "Do you think it would be a good idea to have an objective related to accuracy?"
5. Express appreciation to employee and close the interview. "Thanks for coming in. I really appreciate your positive attitude." "I'm pleased with your objectives. Let me know whenever I can help you with them."

Of course, the general outline will vary from interview to interview, but the main point to remember is that a general outline will give the interview a sense of purpose and direction that will be lacking otherwise.

***Prepare specific questions.*** Following the preparation of your general outline, you might decide to prepare a number of specific questions that will help you achieve more effectively the objectives of the interview. If you are conducting an employment interview, for example, you will undoubtedly want to know very specific items of information. Therefore, you will want to have a list of questions that will elicit the information that you need. If you are conducting an appraisal interview, you might want to prepare a specific question that will introduce a potentially explosive topic in an unemphatic way. In nondirective interviews, on the other hand, you will have to develop your questions spontaneously as the interview progresses.

***Gather materials.*** Depending on the purpose of the interview, certain kinds of materials will be needed. In an interview with a job candidate, for example, you would want the applicant's letter of application, vita (data sheet), and letters of recommendation. For performance appraisal interviews, you would want a list of employees' personal objectives, the organizational objectives, and any record of employee accomplishments during the evaluation period. For each interview, you should prepare a file which contains all the materials and information you need. Nothing is more unimpressive than to be interviewed by a manager who needs to stop periodically to retrieve certain records or information that should have been obtained beforehand.

***Arrange the environment.*** The environment in which the interview is held can make or break the interview. Arrangement of furniture, provision for privacy, and scheduling of sufficient time are all important environmental concerns. As you consider the arrangement of furniture, you should realize the impact that a desk can make. If you want to retain a power or authority position during the interview, leave the desk between you and the other person. If you want the interview to be more intimate or relaxed, or if you want to appear as more of an equal to the interviewee, move from behind the desk.

People usually feel somewhat uncomfortable sitting too close (usually closer than 36 inches) in a face-to-face setting. To ease this anxiety you can place the chairs at a slight angle rather than at a straight face-to-face arrangement. A side-by-side arrangement beside a table also allows for closeness without discomfort. Figure 11-1 illustrates an informal seating arrangement with a desk, without a desk, and with a table.

Arrangement for privacy is a must in preparing for an interview. Interviewees must feel that their conversation is being held in strictest confidence and that no one will observe them during the interview. Therefore, you should close all doors and arrange for all telephone calls and visitors to be stopped during the interview. The confidence and openness that are essential for interview success cannot be established if you are constantly being interrupted.

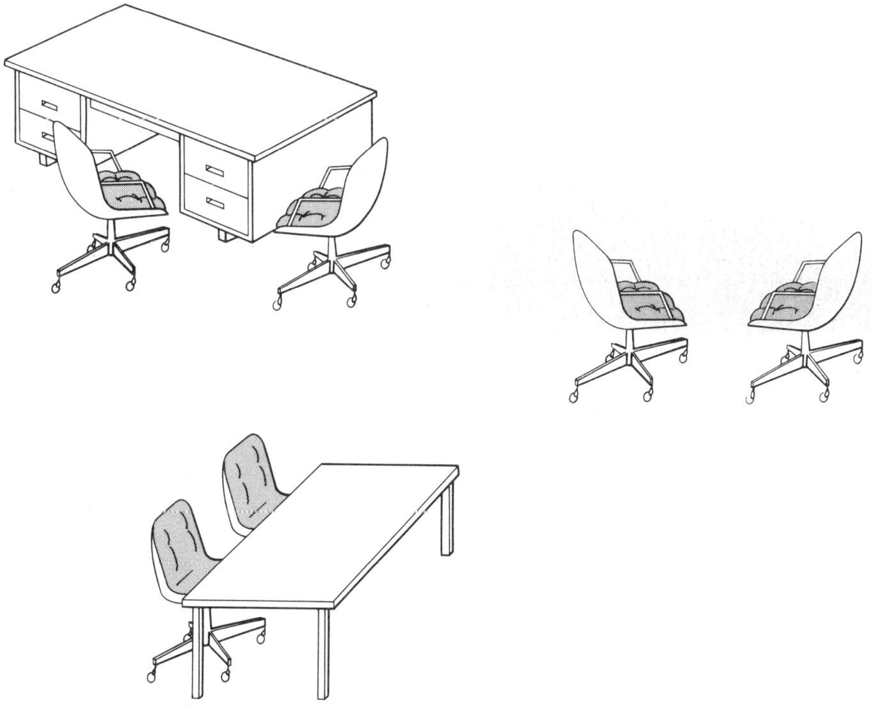

*Figure 11-1.* Arrangements of Chairs in Informal Interview Situations

Insufficient time can also keep a person from confiding in you; since genuine communication is so essential in an interview, adequate time must be allowed to establish the trust that will bring about open communication. In addition, do not have several persons waiting to see you. The person you are interviewing may feel rushed to finish so that the others can see you. In summary, the environment for an interview should be created to encourage a feeling of privacy, confidence, and trust. Within such an environment, you will have the peace of mind that is essential in communicating effectively with the interviewee.

## CONDUCTING THE INTERVIEW

### Preliminary Discussion

Because many people have a tendency to be somewhat on edge as they approach an interview, it might be necessary for you to engage in a few moments of small talk for relaxation. The warm-up period is especially important for prospective and new employees who tend to feel more unsure of themselves than more seasoned employees. This warm-up period also serves to get an interviewee talking, an important accomplishment by itself. The warm-up may not be necessary if the person is in the frame of mind you desire. But if you think the interviewee is already in an appropriate frame of mind, you can proceed directly to the major objectives of the interview. In corrective interviews designed to "shape" attitudes, people may be so nervous or defensive that your best efforts to relax them will fail. In such cases, you may have to proceed with the interview and just do the best you can.

### Questioning Techniques

Whenever you need to obtain information, you also need to know how to encourage people to talk. The best way to stimulate talk is to establish a climate of trust. Such a climate is not always possible to achieve, and it is even more difficult to measure. Therefore, you need to be armed with some specific kinds of questions that will encourage interviewee communication. Questions that help encourage the employee to talk more freely are those that: (1) cannot be answered by a simple yes or no response, (2) do not disclose your attitudes and biases, and (3) do not lead interviewees to answer the way you would like them to. Questions that possess these characteristics are termed *open questions*. First, let's look at a few questions and statements that are *not* open and see why they violate our guidelines:

1. "Do you think you can support this company policy?" (Can be answered by a simple yes or no.)
2. "You can understand why this cutback is necessary, I am sure." (Reveals your bias.)

3. "Can you imagine someone doing a job as sloppy as that?" (Reveals your bias and leads the interviewee to answer the way you want. Also, could be answered by a yes/no response.)
4. "What do you think of that new nitwit in your department?" (Reveals your bias.)

Very little thought or explanation would be required in an interviewee's responses to these types of questions. Rather, the interviewee would give a brief answer, and you would be thinking of a new question again. Now consider these next few questions, and think how people would answer them.

1. "What do you think is the major problem?"
2. "How do you feel about your performance during the past three months?"
3. "Which person do you think is best qualified for the job?"

These three questions cannot be answered by simple yes/no responses, do not disclose bias, and do not lead interviewees to answer the way you would like. Questions of this type are very effective in encouraging interviewees to express themselves more completely. In addition, since these questions do not reveal your bias and do not lead, respondents will be more inclined to give honest responses. Open questions are useful in both directive and nondirective interviews. In directive interviews, a series of open questions may be used. In nondirective interviews, an open question may be used to get people talking, then a series of active listening responses would be used to encourage them to go where they want to go in the conversation.

In many interviews, there will be a need to use a type of question that is more definitive than the open question. This type of question is called a *closed question* since it does not seek enlargement or expansion of a topic or issue. Instead, it seeks specific information not generally open to disagreement. Examples of closed questions are:

1. "How long did you work for RST Company?"
2. "When do you plan to retire?"
3. "Have you submitted your monthly sales report?"
4. "What is our present inventory of letterhead stationery?"

After reading these questions, you can see that the responses desired are of a quantifiable or yes/no variety. Closed questions are very direct and effective and should be used when the information desired is of a precise, nondiscussion variety.

### Nonverbal Encouragement

Another proven method of eliciting additional information is to encourage them nonverbally. The following nonverbal cues will tend to communicate, "Tell me more."

1. Nodding your head (indicates that you are listening, that you understand, or that you agree)
2. Saying "Mmm-hmm" (indicates that you are listening, that you understand, or that you agree)
3. Eye contact (used without accompanying verbal communication, it creates anxiety; interviewee will keep talking to release anxiety)
4. Silence (indicates that you want further clarification and elaboration or that you simply have no comment)
5. Eyebrow movement (shows such ideas as, "I don't understand; tell me more," or "I am a bit surprised at that; are you sure?")

On the average, responses encouraged by nonverbal cues will be significantly longer than those not encouraged by nonverbal cues. Nonverbal communication, therefore, can be used as a communication regulator in personal interviews.

### Responding Techniques

Because interviewees might tend to skip over something that is negative, and because interviews represent such a golden opportunity for in-depth, honest communication, active listening is useful in the majority of interviews conducted. In fact, it is the key to nondirective interviewing. Active listening tends to draw truth, depth, and openness from others. It indicates to the interviewees that you are honestly interested in what they have to say, and it lets them know when you really understand what they are trying to say. Listening is the key to understanding, and active listening is the highest form of listening.

Active listening is not just a gimmick that can be turned on and off at will; it is an extension of the genuine feeling of the listener. Thus, if you employ active listening without really being concerned about the feelings of others, they will sense your inconsistency, and your active listening attempt will fail.

Active listening is nonjudgmental in nature in that you do not judge, condemn, ridicule, or tear apart; you listen for the purpose of understanding from others' points of view. You listen not only to the words spoken but also to the feelings that accompany those words as well. After all, since people's feelings are frequently more powerful than their logic, their feelings often constitute the major part of the message they transmit.

As indicated in Chapter 10, in active listening the listener summarizes the speaker's message (both content and feeling) until the speaker agrees that the listener understands the message. The following statements and responses serve as examples of how *not* to listen.

SUSAN: I just can't seem to get Maria to increase her typing output.

LAURA: Have you talked with her about it in private?

SUSAN: Well, not directly.

LAURA: Well, it seems obvious to me that if you want a person to change, you should let them know exactly what you expect of them. Don't you agree?

SUSAN: I suppose so.

LAURA: All right then, pull Maria aside this week and talk with her. Don't let her pull the wool over your eyes either. Let her know in no uncertain terms what you expect of her. She'll come through if you do.

SUSAN: I'll see what I can do.

In the preceding example, you saw Susan mention a problem that she was having with one of her subordinates. She did not go into detail; all she exposed was the small tip of the much larger iceberg. Laura asked one question to get another small bit of information, then she charged headlong into giving one of her pet cures for solving the problem. Had she practiced active listening and held back her judgment until she knew all the facts, she would have been in a much stronger position to make judgment.

You might have noticed, too, that during the discussion Susan took a smaller and smaller part in the conversation. Since Laura was so dominant and headstrong, she caused Susan to draw into a shell and to remain quiet rather than to volunteer additional information. Examine the following conversation and see if you can see differences between it and the previous discussion.

SUSAN: I just can't seem to get Maria to increase her typing output.

LAURA: You feel that she isn't producing up to her capacity.

SUSAN: I'm sure of it. She's a talented girl with a lot of ability, but she's just not using it on the job.

LAURA: She's making only a halfhearted effort.

SUSAN: Yes, I just don't know what to do.

LAURA: You're not sure what will solve the problem.

SUSAN: No, I'm not. That's why I came to see you.

LAURA: You want me to help solve the problem. *Laura has been paraphrasing Susan's comments to insure understanding. Nondirective approach.*

SUSAN: Yes, I do. *Susan wants to get an immediate solution from Laura; she wants to stop talking.*

LAURA: I'm not sure I fully understand the total situation yet; why don't you give me more facts. *Laura asks an open question to get Susan talking again, to get more information.*

SUSAN: Well, Maria is producing only about 70 percent as much typewritten work as Devon, who has been on the job only about four weeks. Maria has been with us for three months.

LAURA: And you think she should be ahead of Devon.

SUSAN: I think so, yes. Devon is no faster than any other new person we have hired; I think she's about average. There's just no good reason why such a difference should exist in their output.

LAURA: Then you think it's something other than ability that is causing the problem.

SUSAN: Well, that's what *I* think. I think it's just a matter of attitude. Maria is quite a talker, and she visits with other workers more than she should. I do manage to keep that somewhat in check, but it still occurs more frequently than I would like. Another thing she does is take too long to get back to work after a coffee break. It seems like she takes 10 minutes or so to get back into the swing of things.

LAURA: So she's dividing her attention and time between work and socializing. *Laura has been paraphrasing (nondirective interviewing).*

SUSAN: Yes, that's right. What do you think I should do? *Susan wants to stop talking again; wants advice.*

LAURA: What are our alternatives? *Laura asks another open question to get the best of Susan's thinking regarding possible solutions.*

No doubt you can see a drastic difference between this interview and the earlier one. In the latter conversation, you saw Laura taking a nondirective approach. She simply practiced active listening. You'll notice that Susan talked much more in this conversation than in the earlier one. She volunteered more emotion, gave more honest input, and showed more trust in Laura. As a result of the active listening, Laura gleaned far more information than she did in the prior interview. Active listening can, on occasion, be an end in and of itself. At times people just need someone who will listen to them; they need to feel that someone understands them. In such situations, active listening provides the therapy that is needed.

In most interview situations, however, active listening is a means to an end. That end may be to solve a problem or to establish an employee objective. Thus, as exhibited in the preceding narration, when you feel that you have obtained all the appropriate information that the interviewee has to offer, you should switch to a more directive interview approach using open and closed questions and giving information as needed. Active listening is a tool, and like all tools it can be misused in the hands of unskilled interviewers.

## CONCLUDING THE INTERVIEW

Interviews should be concluded when either of the *two* following conditions has been met: (1) when the objectives of the interview have been achieved, or (2) when you feel that as much as possible has been accomplished in the present interview and that another session will be necessary to achieve your objectives. Interviews can be closed by briefly summarizing the major points of the interview, by expressing encouragement or support to the interviewee, by thanking the interviewee for the chance to visit, by establishing a time for a return appointment, or by giving an invitation to return for further discussion if it seems necessary.

Engaging your interviewees in additional small talk is discouraged because it wastes time and tends to detract from the interview. Numerous verbal and nonverbal cues can be used to indicate to others that you're ready to terminate the conversation:

1. Push your chair back and stand up.
2. Move toward the door and open it for them.
3. Glance quickly at your watch.
4. Shake hands and say, "Thanks for coming in."
5. Say, "Let me walk with you to your desk, I've got to see someone in the accounting department."
6. Say, "Well, I'd better let you get back to work."

For the insensitive person who doesn't seem to get the hint, you'll have to be more direct with something like, "Well, I've got another appointment I need to prepare for. Perhaps we can visit at another time." Talk might be cheap, but time is expensive. Therefore, spend *enough* time to accomplish your communication objectives, but avoid excessive, meaningless small talk.

The interview frequently does not end when the interviewee leaves your office. Many times you'll need to make notations on records, dictate results of the interview to others, or perform some other action as an outgrowth of the interview. Immediately following the interview is the time when you have the sharpest memory of the visit; therefore, take all necessary post-interview action as soon after the interview as possible.

## *Summary*

Interviews are conducted for four general purposes: (1) to collect information, (2) to give information, (3) to shape attitudes, and (4) to solve problems. No matter what your purposes are, you should follow several steps in planning for the interview. First, determine your objectives; second, collect information pertinent to the interview; third, plan your approach; fourth, prepare specific questions; fifth, gather necessary materials; and sixth, arrange the environment.

Two general approaches are followed in most interviews: First, the directive approach involves the interviewer's guiding the interview. Second, the nondirective approach allows the interviewee to guide the direction of the interview while the interviewer follows. Different interviewing situations will require varied use of these approaches.

At the beginning of an interview, you might occasionally need to engage in a bit of small talk to relax the interviewee and to get him or her to talk. Open questions that cannot be answered by a simple yes or no response, that do not disclose your attitudes and biases, and that do not lead interviewees to answer the way you would like them to are effective in getting interviewees to talk more freely. Nonverbal encouragement also tends to encourage longer responses from an interviewee.

The overall best response to an interviewee is an active listening statement. Active listening builds trust, encourages openness, and provides more depth in interviews.

Interviews should be concluded when the interview objectives have been achieved or when you feel another appointment is necessary to accomplish the objectives. Close interviews without unnecessary small talk, then take any postinterview action that is necessary.

## *Review and Discussion Questions*

1. Why do you think many people have defensive reactions when they are called in to visit their supervisors?
2. What are the four general purposes of interviews?
3. What are the six steps in planning for an interview?
4. Why is the nondirective approach generally inappropriate in an information-giving interview?
5. If you were conducting a performance appraisal, what materials would you need for the interview?
6. When should you keep a desk between you and the interviewee?
7. What steps should be taken to arrange for privacy in an interview?
8. How does time affect the success of an interview?
9. When is a preliminary warm-up conversation necessary in an interview?
10. Why should bias be eliminated from your interview questions?
11. How can you encourage more responsiveness from an interviewee?
12. What part does active listening play in interviewing?
13. Why are closed questions effective in certain parts of personnel selection interviews?

## *Application Exercises*

1. Write 10 open questions that conform to the three guidelines mentioned in the questioning techniques discussed in this chapter.

2. Write 10 closed questions that you might use in a personnel selection interview.
3. Engage in a conversation with someone you know quite well. During the conversation, avoid giving any kind of nonverbal encouragement to this person. Notice any changes in his or her behavior after you eliminate your nonverbal cues.
4. Engage in a conversation with a person whom you do not know very well. Employ an active listening approach in this conversation. See how soon you can get that person to open up and confide in you.
5. Observe others when they are trying to terminate conversations. Notice the nonverbal and verbal cues that are sent to say, "I need to go now."
6. Role play a personnel selection, problem-solving, or decision-making interview with a classmate. Prepare several open and closed questions and use them in the interview. Also, use active listening as much as possible during the interview.

## *Case Studies*

1. *Gretchen deHaan* serves as assistant personnel manager for Bis-tek Forms, Inc. As assistant personnel manager, she frequently conducts screening interviews to try to discern those job applicants who will be best suited for work with Bis-tek. On February 13, she conducted an interview with Wally Williams, a young man who was seeking employment as a filing clerk. Here is how the interview went.

RECEPTIONIST: Ms. deHaan, Mr. Williams is here to see you.

GRETCHEN: Oh, is he here already? Well, send him in.

GRETCHEN: Hello, Mr. Williams; it's so nice to see you. Have a chair, please. Now tell me, what can I do for you this morning.

WALLY: Well, I came to talk with you about that job opening you have in your records department.

GRETCHEN: Oh, that one. Excuse me just a minute while I visit with the records supervisor about that job. *Gretchen disappears for 10 minutes and then returns.* Listen, Mr. Williams, Mr. Sharma says he just needs someone who is good in spelling and reading. How do you fit in those categories?

WALLY: I have done pretty well in English in high school and I think I . . .

GRETCHEN: What do you mean "pretty well"? Do you mean A, B, C, or what?

WALLY: I've gotten A's and B's in most of my English classes.

GRETCHEN: That sounds fine. Can you tell me something about any previous jobs you have had?

WALLY: Well, I had a paper route when I was younger and I have mowed lawns for the last few summers. I also worked as a bagger in a small grocery store near my home during my last two years in high school.

GRETCHEN: Have you done anything that is related to this job you are seeking?

WALLY: Well, I guess not directly; but I think that the jobs I have held have . . . *The telephone rings and Gretchen answers. She talks on the telephone for about three minutes.*

GRETCHEN: Let's see, where were we?

WALLY: I'm not sure, I think we were talking about my qualifications for the job.

GRETCHEN: Oh yes; well, go on.

WALLY: Well, I think I could do the job; I think I'm qualified.

GRETCHEN: You think you could do the job, do you? Tell me, how long would you plan to work if you were hired?

WALLY: At least for a year. I've just graduated from high school and I'd like to attend Valley Community College when I save enough money. And even then I would probably go to school in the evening. I could probably work for two or three years.

GRETCHEN: Did you fill out an employment application?

WALLY: Not yet. I planned to do that while I'm here this morning.

GRETCHEN: Yes, be sure to do that before you leave. Well, do you have any questions for me?

WALLY: Yes, I wonder if you could tell me how much you pay beginning employees.

GRETCHEN: The minimum wage. Anything else?

WALLY: No, I guess that's all.

GRETCHEN: Fine, we'll let you know if we can use you.

Based on your reading of Chapter 11, evaluate this interview. Following your evaluation, rewrite the interview conversation as you think it should have gone.

2. *Martin Miller* is an administrative manager in the municipal offices of a large northeastern city. The city manager has implemented a policy that each employee who quits his or her job be interviewed to determine the cause of termination. This following dialogue is such an exit interview between Martin

and Lola Daggett, supervisor of the word-processing center and administrative services department.

MARTIN: Lola, could I talk with you for a minute? *They walk to Martin's office.*

MARTIN: Company policy says that I have to have an exit interview with all employees that quit their jobs to determine why they are quitting. Would you care to tell me why you are leaving this job? Is it for more money?

LOLA: Well, not really.

MARTIN: You mean you're not going to get paid as much in your new job?

LOLA: I didn't say that.

MARTIN: Well, are you?

LOLA: That's confidential information.

MARTIN: All right, all right. Why don't you tell me straight out why you're leaving this job. Don't you like it here?

LOLA: It's all right most of the time.

MARTIN: Did they promise you a bed of roses at your new job?

LOLA: No, not really. But I think I will like it there.

MARTIN: Better than here?

LOLA: Well, I don't know. I'll have to wait until I've been working there for a few weeks before I can answer that.

MARTIN: We're going to have to spend a great deal of time training your replacement, I guess you know.

LOLA: That shouldn't be too tough; I didn't receive any training when I got the job.

MARTIN: Sure you did; you had worked in the department for three years before you were made supervisor. This new supervisor is coming to us from the outside, and she doesn't know our company or our people or anything.

LOLA: She'll probably get along okay.

MARTIN: Well, I don't know about that; if you weren't leaving we wouldn't even have to worry about it. *Slight pause.* Do you have anything else you'd like to say?

LOLA: No, I guess not.

MARTIN: Well, thanks for coming in, and good luck in your new job.

Based on your reading of Chapter 11, evaluate this interview. Following your evaluation, rewrite the interview conversation as you think it should have gone.

## *Administrative Manager Profile*

Meet Martin A. Scholz, field systems officer at Kemper Insurance Companies.

*Background and Experience.* Martin Scholz entered the insurance business in 1955 when he became an underwriter trainee with Great American Indemnity. In 1956 he joined the Kemper organization and has been in a variety of supervisory and management positions. Martin earned the C.P.C.U. (Chartered Property and Casualty Underwriter) certification in 1972 and an associate degree in management from Insurance Institute of America in 1977.

*Company.* The Kemper Insurance and Financial Companies were started by James S. Kemper in 1912 and since then have grown to a $2 billion organization of multiline insurance and financial companies with over 10,000 employees. Kemper provides insurance for about three million policyholders throughout the United States, Canada, Europe, Australia, and South America.

Kemper offers many types of insurance to both businesses and individuals: automobile, homeowners, travel-accident, life, burglary, robbery, theft, fire, liability, health, and workers' compensation insurance.

Kemper is one of the largest insurance organizations in the country; they are ranked twelfth in size among property-casualty insurers in the United States. Over 7,000 independent agents sell Kemper insurance throughout the country.

*Job.* Originally, Martin was called to the home office as project manager to head a feasibility study in on-line technology and its applications to the organization's computer systems. Martin's responsibility has recently been broadened to include current systems coordination and enhancements. Roughly forty managers, systems analysts, coordinators, and clerical staff are currently employed by the field systems group.

Martin is a manager in a largely technical area with a great variety of projects and assignments. His background provides him with the viewpoint of the generalist helpful in dealing with people within and across defined functional lines. His time is divided between meetings, travel, seminars, and a never-ending reading assignment to keep up with developments in the various fields of office automation and systems development. Frequent contact with counterparts in other insurance companies and with vendors of software, hardware, and office equipment, is another time-consuming but educational and profitable part of his working day.

*Management Philosophy.* "The role of the manager," says Martin, "is to create the environment that fosters all those essential elements an individual or a group of people needs to be productive. The manager must communicate, provide the means to do the job, set objectives and standards, acknowledge performance, and control the forward motion much like a conductor leads an orchestra.

"Essential in a professional or technical group is individual initiative, the ability to motivate oneself, to think independently. It also requires being able to be part of the team. This is a different individual, consequently a different group of people when compared to a group in a strict production environment. In management, however, some universally applicable 'basics' hold true. I maintain that . . .

clear, concise, and frank communication, objectives, and plans

high standards of performance and appropriately 'above-board' appraisals

interest in an individual's development

accessibility—not just the 'open-door' policy

rewards commensurate with performance (this can be negative too)

'above-board' administrative practices—employment, promotion, salaries

and a 'common-sense' approach to human relations go a long way toward success."

# PART FOUR

# Personnel Management

As an administrative manager, effective personnel management must always be a prime concern to you, because the success of your management is measured by the performance of your employees.

Chapter 12 explains the benefits that result from careful personnel selection. Selection procedures are discussed, and the impact of the Equal Employment Opportunity Commission is explained. The importance of properly orienting new employees is next highlighted, and guidelines for effective orientation are given.

Chapter 13 first discusses different types of employee training that are frequently used and the advantages and disadvantages of each type. The importance of having ongoing personnel development programs is mentioned and methods of developing personnel are presented. Next, promotion and its impact on personnel morale are discussed, including the decision to promote from within or to hire from outside the organization and different types of promotions. Then, the three types of termination are pointed out, and the impact of governmental legislation regarding retirement is explained.

Chapter 14 focuses on people problems, problems that keep workers from producing the best work they can. The reasons for employee turnover and the problems that are associated with high turnover rates are treated. Also, the importance of controlling absenteeism is stressed, as is employee abuse of time (breaks, etc.); in this regard, the disastrous effects of drug and alcohol abuse are presented. Finally, safety and accident prevention are explained; like hiring procedures, the areas of safety and health are governed by federal legislation.

# 12

# Personnel Selection and Orientation

Behind the scenes of an efficient office is a system of personnel movement—getting the right person in the right job. Much of this movement is concerned with moving employees from one job to another *within* the organization. But there is also the need to bring new people *into* the organization from the outside; business expansion, retirement, and turnover all contribute to the need for new employees.

A methodical decision-making process should be followed closely in selecting new employees even though thorough selection procedures are costly in both time and money. If an inappropriate selection is made, the organization will end up paying far more for that mistake than it would have spent in making a more thorough search and a better selection.

## BENEFITS OF CAREFUL SELECTION

At least four major benefits result from appropriate personnel selection. First, you can expect fewer workers to resign or be fired because of mismatches between job and employee. New employees will be more likely to find their jobs stimulating and satisfying; consequently, they will be far less likely to look for a new position because of job dissatisfaction. Since employee turnover is very costly in both time and money, turnover reduction through careful selection is certainly well worth seeking.

One example of job-employee mismatch occurred when a businessman in a small organization hired a typist—or so he thought. He asked the job candidate if she could type, and she replied, "Yes, I had a year of typing in high school." This individual was hired; but when she produced her first letter on the job, her manager was shocked to discover that her typing was substandard. He had only himself to blame, though, because he had not bothered to obtain a sample of her typewritten work.

The second major benefit of appropriate selection is a reduction of personnel problems. Managers spend so much time solving people problems that they are less effective managers than they really could be.

The third benefit is a natural outgrowth of the second—proper personnel selection results in increased effectiveness. When properly trained and qualified individuals are working effectively in an organization, their major focus is on organizational objectives. When people begin working as a team, when they begin pulling in the same direction rather than in different ones, they can be extremely effective workers and all the more valuable to the company.

A fourth benefit is that fair selection will prevent costly legal battles that can arise from discriminatory hiring practices. After a two-year court battle, American Telephone and Telegraph was fined approximately $15 million in a personnel discrimination lawsuit. A number of other companies have been ordered to pay hundreds of thousands of dollars to their employees who have suffered from discrimination. This constant threat of discrimination lawsuits demands that companies be as careful as possible in their employment and personnel practices. The following section discusses governmental regulations that you must understand as you become involved in business organizations.

## GOVERNMENTAL REGULATIONS

A major problem in many organizations is making sure that people have equal employment opportunities regardless of their race, color, sex, age, religion, national origin, or some other arbitrary criterion. Traditionally, minority groups and women have been at a disadvantage when it came to competition for advancement to and within management.

As is frequently the case when abuse of power or social privilege takes place, the government has developed regulations to correct the problems. Most of these regulations date from the early 1960s when President Kennedy backed legislation for equal rights in regard to employment. In 1961, the President's Committee on Equal Employment Opportunity was established, and it had the responsibility for achieving that equality in government and in governmental contracts. The committee enforced compliance of its regulations by canceling the governmental contracts of those who maintained discriminatory employment practices. The Equal Pay Act of 1963 was then passed to ensure that employers provide equal pay for men and women performing similar work. The next year, the comprehensive Civil Rights Act of 1964 was passed. Title VII of that Act forbids discrimination on the basis of race, color, national origin, sex, or religion, with respect to compensation and employment privileges. It also prohibits the use of screening tests that do not prove or disprove a job candidate's ability to perform a job he or she is seeking. In 1965, the president issued Executive Order 11246. This order, amended by Executive Order 11375, requires federal contractors to develop and implement written *affirmative action* programs—organizational plans to improve the hiring, training, and promotion of minorities and women. The Age Discrimination in Employment Act of 1967 was later passed to prohibit employers from using age as an employment factor for persons in the 40 to 65 age category.

The Equal Employment Opportunity Commission (EEOC), established by the Civil Rights Act of 1964, was given enforcement power in the Equal Employment Opportunity Act of 1972. Prior to 1972, this body did not have the power to enforce its regulations; now the Commission can file charges in court against employers who are suspected of unlawful discriminatory practices and can give advice and assistance to groups and individuals who file charges against employers.[1]

Initially, most of these federal acts were binding only on employers that had federal contracts or that were over a certain size (i.e., fifty or more employees). Now, however, many companies are bound by the regulations. Many employers appoint an affirmative action officer with adequate authority to effectively implement the program and with the skill and ability to represent all groups. In order to have adequate influence, this officer should report to upper-level management.[2] Also, he or she should develop opportunities for minorities within the organization and should keep informed on legislation, court rulings, and EEOC rulings at all times.

Management needs to be alert to their responsibility to treat all employees fairly and equally. The entire company stands to gain when individuals with good potential are identified and advanced within the organization. The administrative manager should cooperate with the affirmative action officer or personnel department to inventory employees such as women, blacks, Hispanics, American Indians, and orientals to see if their training and skills are appropriately used. Studies should be conducted to determine if they are progressing as well as white, male Americans at the various job levels in the organization. The entire organization should actively recruit minority people for managerial and professional level jobs and should develop real opportunities to match talents and abilities of potentially well-qualified people.

## PERSONNEL SELECTION PROCEDURES

When the need for a new employee is determined, the supervisor or manager responsible for the open position should advise the personnel department or the person in charge of recruiting and should provide a description of the job. (Figure 12-1 is an example of a secretarial job description.)

### Sources of Applicants

The employer has a number of excellent sources from which qualified workers can be chosen. For example, the following individuals obtained their present employment in the Apex Manufacturing Co. secretarial services department

**NONEXEMPT POSITION DESCRIPTION**

| POSITION TITLE | | | | POSITION NUMBER |
|---|---|---|---|---|
| SECRETARY | | | | 2612 |
| | | | | APPROVAL<br>RHS |
| DIVISION OR STAFF DEPARTMENT<br>All | LOCATION<br>All | REPORTS TO | | EFFECTIVE DATE<br>July 1979 |
| DEPARTMENT OR ACTIVITY | SECTION | POINTS<br>121 | GRADE<br>4 | REVISES<br>Nov. 1978 |

JOB SUMMARY

Performs clerical, stenographic, and some relatively simple administrative duties for one or more professional, technical, or administrative employees.

NATURE OF WORK

Performs a wide variety of office duties, including most of the following:

1. Typing acceptable correspondence, reports, manuscripts, graphs, charts, etc., from shorthand notes, dictating machine tapes, and/or handwritten drafts.
2. Assembling and organizing data and performing relatively structured and elementary processing functions.
3. Receiving telephone calls, visitors, and incoming mail.
4. Establishing and maintaining department files and records.
5. Scheduling appointments and meetings; making reservations.
6. Performing administrative duties as directed, such as collecting and compiling statistical data, general reference materials and information pertaining to company, division, or department practices and procedures.
7. Performing related duties such as duplicating, supply ordering, and mail sorting.

Works somewhat independently, receiving a minimum of detailed supervision and guidance on established office procedures. Most work is checked. Usually spends less than 30 percent of time on administrative duties.

QUALIFICATIONS

High school education or its equivalent plus one year of business-related experience and a typing skill of at least 50 words per minute. Must be developing proficiency in English grammar, punctuation, spelling, and proper word usage and skills in business and public contacts. Must have the ability to acquire a working knowledge of the organization's practices and procedures. A shorthand skill of at least 80 words per munute is necessary if required in a specific position.

*Figure 12-1.* Secretarial Job Description

in a number of different ways. Dianne is a graduate of a technical school, Patrice graduated from high school, Art completed a secretarial course in a nearby community college, and Madeline earned a degree in secretarial studies at a state university. These workers were hired shortly after they completed their respective educational training programs, and their training has helped them become effective workers.

Darwin was referred to Apex by a public employment agency, and Dorothy learned of her present job through a private employment agency. The service provided by the public agency was free of charge, but the private agency assessed a charge to Dorothy for its placement services, which resulted in both time and money savings for the personnel manager of Apex.

Linda learned of her job through the classified ad section of the local newspaper. Because the newspaper has so many readers, it frequently attracts numerous applicants for advertised job openings. Such was the case when Linda applied for her job. Nearly 50 people applied for that particular job; consequently, the personnel department was kept extremely busy interviewing candidates until Linda was hired.

Roselyn is one of the people who was interviewed for the job Linda was eventually given. Like Linda, Roselyn was well qualified; so the personnel department kept her application form in a special file. Four weeks later another job became vacant, so the personnel department searched their files for qualified applicants who previously had been denied employment. As a result of this file search they called Roselyn—she came in for additional interviewing and was given the job.

JoAnne first heard about her job through a friend who worked for Apex. The personnel department posts notices of job openings on the company bulletin boards, and it was such an action that got the word to JoAnne. Other intracompany communications can also be used to notify all employees of new job openings.

Harry secured his position after working for the company in a cooperative education program. In these programs, businesses give part-time employment to students during the latter part of the students' training. During the working experience, a student's supervisor can determine whether the student should be considered for full-time employment after the program concludes. Hence, the company provides the school a service by providing experience for the student, and the school provides a service to the company—an opportunity to observe the student on the job without first making a commitment to hire that person.

Two other people in the department—Kelly and MaryAnn—work for Apex only temporarily. Actually, they are employed by a temporary-help agency and they fill in for workers who are on vacation, who are ill, or who have been terminated and not yet replaced. Also, they occasionally handle seasonal work so that permanent workers do not need to be hired.

### Preliminary Screening Procedures

Generally speaking, the more critical the responsibilities of the job being filled, the more careful and thorough the selection procedures must be.

Some organizations spend literally thousands of dollars researching the background of their more important job applicants.

Numerous screening devices have been used to determine the best qualified job candidates. Four of the more common screening tools and techniques that you might use in screening persons for jobs are the application blank review, reference checks, tests, and interviews with applicants.

*1. Application blank review.* When all job seekers have completed an application form, the personnel department can examine all candidates' applications to determine those who clearly do not meet minimum job requirements. Although most applicants are relatively honest in reporting about themselves in their applications, some may falsify answers that would decrease their chance of employment. Therefore, verify all information that is of consequence in the selection procedure. Figure 12-2 illustrates an application form that generally adheres to EEOC guidelines.

*2. Reference checks.* All persons listed on the job candidates' applications may be contacted for further information. In checking these references, remember that only persons who will give positive recommendations typically are listed as references. Referents' comments, therefore, must be weighed very cautiously.

Former supervisors or managers are frequently good sources of information about the applicants' behavior and productivity in other jobs. Telephoning an applicant's former supervisor is fast and inexpensive—and a person is usually more likely to be frank in a spontaneous phone call than in a well-planned letter.

Joe Sethmore was a personnel manager in an insurance firm in Texas. He advertised a secretarial job opening and had nine people apply for the position. After studying their application forms carefully, Joe narrowed the choice to three: Jane, Rick, and Nettie. He then called the companies where each had worked previously and talked with the supervisors of the three people. Jane's prior supervisors stated that she was pleasant to work with and was quite a good producer. Rick's previous supervisors indicated that he had great capacity for production but that he had occasional problems getting along with fellow workers. The supervisors who had previous acquaintance with Nettie indicated that she was not an extremely fast typist but that her work, once it was finished, was usually flawless. She had experienced no problems with other workers.

*3. Tests.* Various forms of testing are used occasionally as screening tools in the selection process:

a. Motor skills tests measure applicants' physical abilities to perform certain kinds of manipulative functions. A typing test to determine how fast a person can type is an example of a motor skills test.

## APPLICATION FOR EMPLOYMENT

**PERSONAL INFORMATION**

| | | |
|---|---|---|
| NAME (LAST—FIRST—MIDDLE) | | SOCIAL SECURITY NUMBER |
| ADDRESS (STREET—CITY—STATE—ZIP) | | PHONE AREA CODE: NO: |
| BIRTH DATE (MO.—DAY—YR.) * | CITIZEN OF U.S.? ☐ YES ☐ NO | DID YOU LOSE ANY TIME FROM WORK OR SCHOOL IN THE LAST TWO YEARS? ☐ YES (Explain) ☐ NO |

**GENERAL INFORMATION**

| | | |
|---|---|---|
| POSITION APPLYING FOR | | ☐ FULL TIME ☐ PART TIME FOR ________ HOURS PER WEEK |
| STARTING SALARY EXPECTED $ | WOULD YOU BE WILLING TO RELOCATE? ☐ YES ☐ NO | HAVE YOU PREVIOUSLY APPLIED FOR A POSITION WITH OR BEEN EMPLOYED BY THIS COMPANY? ☐ YES ☐ NO |
| WHAT PROMPTED YOU TO SEEK EMPLOYMENT WITH US? | | |

**EDUCATION**

Circle highest grade completed: ELEMENTARY 1 2 3 4 5 6 7 8; HIGH 1 2 3 4; COLLEGE 1 2 3 4 5 6 7;

| SCHOOL | NAME AND CITY—STATE SHOW DAY (D) OR NIGHT (N) CLASSES | D OR N | DATES ATTENDED FROM MO.—YEAR | TO MO.—YEAR | MAJOR | TYPE OF DEGREE OR DIPLOMA |
|---|---|---|---|---|---|---|
| HIGH | | | | | | |
| COLLEGE | | | | | | |
| COLLEGE | | | | | | |
| BUSINESS, SECRETARIAL OR TRADE | | | | | | |

| | |
|---|---|
| SUBJECTS YOU LIKED MOST | SUBJECTS YOU LIKED LEAST |

WHAT SCHOOL ACTIVITIES DID YOU PARTICIPATE IN AND WHAT OFFICES HELD (OTHER THAN THOSE WHICH INDICATE RACE, COLOR, RELIGION, SEX OR NATIONAL ORIGIN)?

WHAT OFFICE SKILLS CAN YOU PERFORM AND WHAT BUSINESS MACHINES CAN YOU OPERATE?

PROFESSIONAL OR CIVIC ORGANIZATIONS IN WHICH YOU ARE AN ACTIVE MEMBER (OTHER THAN THOSE WHICH INDICATE RACE, COLOR, RELIGION, SEX OR NATIONAL ORIGIN)

**UNITED STATES MILITARY SERVICE**

| | |
|---|---|
| Have you served? ☐ YES ☐ NO If "YES" which branch? | Rank? |
| Are you in a reserve unit? ☐ YES ☐ NO | If "YES," what is the termination date of your current obligation? |

* The New York Human Rights Law prohibits discrimination because of age.
The Age Discrimination in Employment Act of 1967 prohibits discrimination on the basis of age with respect to individuals who are at least 40 but less than 65 years of age.

*Figure 12-2.* Employment Application Following EEOC Guidelines

b. Mental ability (achievement) tests measure mental maturity, or the degree to which individuals can use their minds to solve problems. These tests frequently have items such as: "If Andy can ride his bicycle 18 miles in an hour, how far can he ride in 45 minutes?" or "Town Q is northwest of Town P. Town Q is east of Town O. Is Town Q north of Town P?"

**EMPLOYMENT RECORD**
**(LIST MOST RECENT EMPLOYMENT FIRST)**

| COMPANY | POSITIONS YOU HELD AND SUPERVISOR'S NAME | DATES OF EMPLOYMENT | STARTING & ENDING SALARY | REASONS FOR LEAVING |
|---|---|---|---|---|
| NAME | POSITION | FROM (MO.—YR.) | STARTING | |
| ADDRESS | SUPERVISOR | TO (MO.—YR.) | ENDING | |
| NAME | POSITION | FROM (MO.—YR.) | STARTING | |
| ADDRESS | SUPERVISOR | TO (MO.—YR.) | ENDING | |
| NAME | POSITION | FROM (MO.—YR.) | STARTING | |
| ADDRESS | SUPERVISOR | TO (MO.—YR.) | ENDING | |
| NAME | POSITION | FROM (MO.—YR.) | STARTING | |
| ADDRESS | SUPERVISOR | TO (MO.—YR.) | ENDING | |
| NAME | POSITION | FROM (MO.—YR.) | STARTING | |
| ADDRESS | SUPERVISOR | TO (MO.—YR.) | ENDING | |

HAVE YOU EVER WORKED UNDER A DIFFERENT NAME FOR ANY OF THE ABOVE COMPANIES? ☐ YES ☐ NO

NOTICE: This is to inform you that as part of the normal procedure for processing your employment application, an investigative consumer report may be prepared whereby information is obtained through personal interviews with your neighbors, friends, or others with whom you are acquainted. This inquiry includes information as to your character, general reputation, personal characteristics and mode of living. You have the right to make a written request within a reasonable period of time to receive additional, detailed information about the nature and scope of this investigation. I acknowledge receipt of a copy of this information.

It is a requirement of employment that you be bonded (at the expense of the employer) and therefore this application is subject to your acceptance by the bonding company.

I understand that any deliberate misstatement of fact or omission from this application can, in the event that I am hired, subject me to immediate dismissal.

APPLICANT'S SIGNATURE ______________________ DATE __________

**FOR COMPANY USE**

| STARTING DATE | SALARY $ ☐ 4 WEEK ☐ PER HOUR | JOB CLASSIFICATION | | JOB CODE |
|---|---|---|---|---|
| COMPANY | FUNCTION | DEPARTMENT | LOCATION | DIVISION |
| ☐ FULL TIME ☐ PART TIME—HOURLY ☐ PART TIME—4 WEEK—TOTAL HOURS PER WEEK | | ☐ PERMANENT ☐ TEMPORARY OR SUMMER ONLY ☐ SCHOLAR | ☐ ADDITION ☐ REPLACEMENT FOR | |
| APPROVALS: DEPT. | DATE | PERSONNEL | DATE | |

*Figure 12-2, continued*

c. Personality tests measure applicants' major personality variables such as aggression and cheerfulness. These tests commonly have items such as:

| | | |
|---|---|---|
| "I feel nervous around large groups of people." | T | F |
| "I enjoy working with new and different people." | T | F |
| "I usually feel tired and seem to lack initiative." | T | F |

d. Aptitude tests measure potential. They are used to predict people's future performances. Two samples of aptitude test questions follow: "Underline the two symbols that are alike: As ss SA AS SS sA aa SA aS AA."
"Three of the following numbers are alike in a particular way. Circle the number that is different from the other three: 6453 8675 9768 4231."

e. Interest tests seek to determine occupational areas in which people have some interest. An example of an interest test item would be, "Which would you prefer to do, write a sales letter for a new product or give a sales presentation to a new client?"

Because of recent EEOC guidelines, a test may be used as a screening tool only if the skill or characteristic being measured is a bona fide occupational qualification (BFOQ) and if the test is valid. A test is considered to be valid when it really does measure what it purports to measure. If you want to measure typewriting ability, for example, you would not use a personality test, because personality gives no indication of typing ability. Instead, you would administer some form of test that samples the person's actual typing ability.

Because of EEOC guidelines, testing has become significantly less important as a screening device. Motor skills tests are still used frequently since they are relatively easy to validate, but personality and achievement tests are not easily validated. Their use demands much more knowledge, time, and effort, and management is frequently not willing to expend the resources required for such an undertaking. In addition, since personality factors are difficult to establish as BFOQs, they should not usually be considered in the screening process.

***4. Interviews with applicants.*** The oldest and still very popular form of screening job applicants is the personal interview with the applicant. Although the personal interview does not seem to reveal candidates' future potential as accurately as would be desired, most personnel managers still prefer to meet job applicants in a face-to-face setting where open exchange of information can be accommodated. The interview offers several benefits:

a. Information that is not revealed in questionnaires, application blanks, and tests can be determined in an oral interview.
b. The interviewer has an opportunity to observe the applicants' communicative skills.
c. The interviewer can observe the applicants' social sensitivity, that is, how well they relate to others.
d. The interviewees can ask questions about the organization, and they can get immediate clarification on any concerns they have about the company.

To the job applicant, the interview may seem like a very spontaneous, unplanned interaction. Good interviewers, however, know what they are looking for in their interviews, and the applicants are usually unaware that they are revealing so much about themselves.

To be consistent with EEOC rulings, interviewers must be constantly on guard against asking questions that would infringe on applicants' rights to equal consideration (e.g., age, marital status, national origin, race, religion, sex, and physical disabilities that do not impair the individual's ability to perform the job being sought).

### Final Screening Procedures

After the personnel department completes the initial screening, the several most qualified candidates are recommended to their potential managers or supervisors for final screening. These supervisors and managers usually will take the information gleaned by the personnel department, examine the information, interview the candidates, and make final determinations based on the information and conclusions provided by the personnel department and the final interview.

From the previous example involving Joe Sethmore, personnel manager, three individuals were cleared through the initial screening process. These

*Figure 12-3.* The Personal Interview

people, Jane, Rick, and Nettie, were recommended for final consideration and interviews by their potential supervisor, Nelda Patterson. Nelda examined the employment applications, the results of the reference checks, the typing test results, and the results of the interviews conducted by Joe Sethmore. Finally, Nelda conducted a thorough interview with each of the candidates and considered these interviews with the information previously analyzed. She found that all three applicants were well-qualified typists, but she was a bit concerned about Rick's tendency to have interpersonal conflicts with his fellow workers. She finally decided that Jane and Nettie were essentially equally qualified. In the interviews Nelda observed that Jane was white and that Nettie was black; therefore, because Nelda's firm had been trying to increase the proportion of minorities in the company, she hired Nettie.

When a final candidate selection is made, all applicants should be notified of the decision. The files of the candidates who were not selected must be retained for at least a year in the event any decide to file suit against the company for discriminatory hiring practices.

If the selection process has been effective, the chosen candidate will prove to be a profitable employee; and the time and money expended in the selection process will prove to be well spent.

## ORIENTATION PROCESS

In most cases, there is an air of excitement and anticipation when a person obtains a new job. For all too many people, however, this excitement turns to frustration when the person reports for work. Most companies do not pay adequate attention to the proper orientation of new employees; consequently, employees experience disappointment instead of satisfaction during their first few days on the job.

A well-planned orientation program offers the following six advantages:

1. Mistakes caused by lack of knowledge, especially prevalent during the earlier periods of employment, will be reduced.
2. Adjustment to the social aspect of the organization will be more quickly accomplished.
3. The workers will have specific objectives to work for because they will understand what is expected of them in relation to the organization's objectives.
4. The new workers will realize the importance of their position and contribution in relation to the total organization picture.
5. The new employees' self-confidence will be enhanced because they will possess much of the same important information held by their fellow workers.
6. The workers will be able to benefit from available fringe benefits, thus increasing their job satisfaction.

These advantages clearly show that an organization cannot afford to be without a well-planned orientation procedure.

### Guidelines for Effective Orientation

The following list of general guidelines can help managers develop an effective orientation plan for their organizations.

1. Establish a list of specific learning objectives to be met during the orientation. Frequently, the topics important in the orientation process will be included in an employee handbook or an orientation handbook. The general contents of one such handbook are as follows:

   *History*
   History of company
   Company purpose
   Organizational chart

   *Policies and Procedures*
   Equal employment opportunity
   Hours of work/overtime
   Attendance
   Wages and salaries
   Promotions and transfers
   Time card requirements
   Your paycheck
   Termination of employment
   Employee entrances and exits
   Personnel record changes
   On-the-job injury
   Dress standards
   Telephone
   Visitors/security
   Confidential business
   Office solicitations
   Housekeeping
   Fire escape plan
   Complaint procedure
   Conflict of interest
   Lost and found

   *Employee benefits*
   Group health care coverage
   Group life insurance
   Retirement program
   Bank time
   Paid holidays
   Vacation
   Liability insurance—workers' compensation
   Unemployment insurance
   Leave of absence
   Sick leave
   Employee education plan
   Service pins

   *Services/facilities*
   Parking
   Cafeteria
   Blood bank
   First aid
   Bulletin board
   Employee publications
   Recreational activities
   Employees' association
   Credit union

   In addition to knowing about general company information, new employees need to understand their job responsibilities, reporting requirements, and obligations to other employees; to know their supervisor, peers, and subordinates; and to be familiar with the work area and other areas important for properly carrying out the job.

2. Select a well-qualified person to coordinate the orientation process. Although many individuals can assist in orientation, one individual needs to be responsible for seeing that the objectives of orientation are met. Frequently, the orientation coordinator will use an *induction checklist*, which is a list of the objectives, steps, or topics included in the orientation program. This type of checklist provides the control that is necessary in ensuring effective orientation.
3. Build effective timing into the orientation plan. Give only absolutely essential information for the first few days of employment. Then follow this initial orientation session with other well-timed sessions that both give additional information and reinforce previous learnings. The timing in a sample checklist is shown in Table 12-1.
4. Evaluate the employees' learning and performance that result from the orientation. Since employees are generally evaluated more frequently during their first few months of employment, these periodic appraisals provide a natural opportunity for checking on the employee's acquaintance with orientation topics. During these appraisal interviews, the supervisor should review the orientation topics and ensure that the employee fully understands them.

**Table 12-1. Orientation Program with Recommended Time Indicated**

| *Procedure* | *Department* | *Time* |
|---|---|---|
| 1. New employee receives employee packet | Personnel | At time of hire |
| 2. Employee meets with supervisor for introduction to department procedures and to find out where he or she fits in | Individual | First day of work |
| 3. Host is assigned to new employee to help integrate and to provide fellowship | Individual | First day of work |
| 4. Employee attends new employee orientation | Personnel | Within first week of employment |
| 5. Brief tour of building (optional) | Personnel | Following orientation session |
| 6. Employee meets with supervisor for a feedback session as a check for problems or questions that might have come up | Individual | 4–7 days following orientation |
| 7. Employee attends personnel development resource seminar to become acquainted with resources for individual development | Individual and personnel | 1–2 weeks after orientation |

*Source:* Corporation of the President, The Church of Jesus Christ of Latter-day Saints.

A carefully planned orientation process can be very effective in easing the anxiety and frustration usually experienced when starting a new job. Such a plan must be implemented if an organization is to benefit fully from the talents of its new workers, for even the best new employees can become discouraged and dissatisfied quickly if they are improperly oriented to their job and work situation.

## *Summary*

Selecting effective personnel is a critical part of building and maintaining an effective organization. When new personnel are selected wisely, a company will experience fewer job-employee mismatches, management problems will be reduced, organizational effectiveness will increase, and employment-related court claims will be reduced.

Recent governmental actions have resulted in the passage of laws that prohibit the use of nonjob-related factors in hiring and promoting. Age, sex, race, color, religion, and national origin have been singled out as the most critical problems of discriminatory hiring practices. All factors, however, that are not bona fide occupational qualifications must be eliminated as hiring and promotional considerations. Affirmative action plans should be implemented in every business to assist minorities and women in finding employment and in advancing within organizations.

Good sources of job applicants are educational institutions, employment agencies, mass media, company files, word of mouth, cooperative education programs, and temporary employment agencies. Job candidates generally pass through a preliminary screening process involving an application blank review, reference checks, and interviews. Tests may be used only if they are valid measurements of bona fide occupational qualifications. The major part of the final screening process is another interview, this time with the individual who will supervise the new employee.

## *Review and Discussion Questions*

1. Why was the Equal Employment Opportunity Commission established? What is its primary function?
2. Why should the personnel office be notified as soon as the need for a new employee is determined?
3. Why should the applications of persons who are not successful in gaining employment in an organization be kept?
4. Why has the use of employment tests declined in recent years?
5. Do you agree with the following statement: An employer may use any test for screening purposes as long as it is a valid test. Why?
6. Why is an effective orientation process essential to an employee?
7. What is the meaning of *affirmative action*? An affirmative action plan?

8. Why must a personnel department eliminate from its application form requests for age, sex, marital status, race, religion, and national origin?

## *Application Exercises*

1. Under the direction of your instructor, ask a personnel manager of a large firm to visit your class and discuss hiring practices and procedures. Allow for questions from class members regarding interviewing techniques and the EEOC guidelines explained in this chapter.
2. Obtain several job application blanks and see how many comply with EEOC guidelines. Recommend changes for those that might be considered discriminatory.
3. Look at the "Help Wanted" section of your local newspaper. Examine the job listings to see the types of jobs that are typically advertised in this medium. Discuss how effective you think the newspaper is as a recruiting medium.

## *Mini-Case*

*Toni Tremonti* is personnel manager of Jantell Corp. Toni is aware of EEOC guidelines and regulations, but she still feels that such factors as age, sex, marital status, race, and national origin play a significant part in workers' success in her company.

Toni has eliminated all mention of these factors from the company job application blanks, so on the outside it appears that she is in full compliance with EEOC guidelines. In screening job applicants, however, Toni has developed a system that still enables her to gather these data and to use them in employee selection. The system works like this:

1. When the applicant first comes into Toni's office for a personal interview, Toni marks on a separate slip of paper F or M to denote the person's sex and C, N, or O to denote race.
2. As Toni interviews the applicant, she asks questions that indirectly obtain additional information. To determine marital status, she asks, "If we found it necessary to ask you to travel for the company, how would your family feel?" To determine age she says, "Since 65 is the usual retirement age, could you tell me when you would retire if we should hire you."
3. Unknown to the applicants, Toni manages to get most of the information she wants. She considers sex, age, marital status, and other such factors in deciding which candidates to recommend to company supervisors and managers; and then she destroys the slips of paper on which she has recorded her information.

How do you feel about Toni's "compliance" with EEOC guidelines?

## *Reference Notes*


1. For additional information on EEOC guidelines, consult *Equal Employment and Affirmative Action: Guidebook for Employers* (Vol. 1), Equal Employment Opportunity Commission, Washington, D.C. 20506.
2. Rosaline Loring and Theodora Wells, *Breakthrough: Women into Management* (New York: Van Nostrand Reinhold, 1972), pp. 42–43.

The office pictured above is shown in color at the top of the next page after it was rearranged and redecorated.

*Source:* Steelcase, Inc.

*Sources of color photos:* p. 1 top, courtesy of Steelcase, Inc.; p. 1 bottom, courtesy of Haworth, Inc.; p. 2, PlanScape Screens by Vogel-Peterson Co., Elmhurst, Illinois; pp. 3 and 7, courtesy of Haworth, Inc.; pp. 4, 5, 6, and 8 reprinted from *Modern Office Procedures* and copyrighted by Penton/IPC, subsidiary of Pittway Corporation: p. 4 is from the January 1978 issue of *Modern Office Procedures;* p. 5 top, 6 bottom, and 8 bottom left and right from the October 1977 issue; p. 5 bottom, March 1978 issue; p. 6 top, December 1977 issue; p. 8 top, July 1977 issue, *Modern Office Procedures.*

3 3

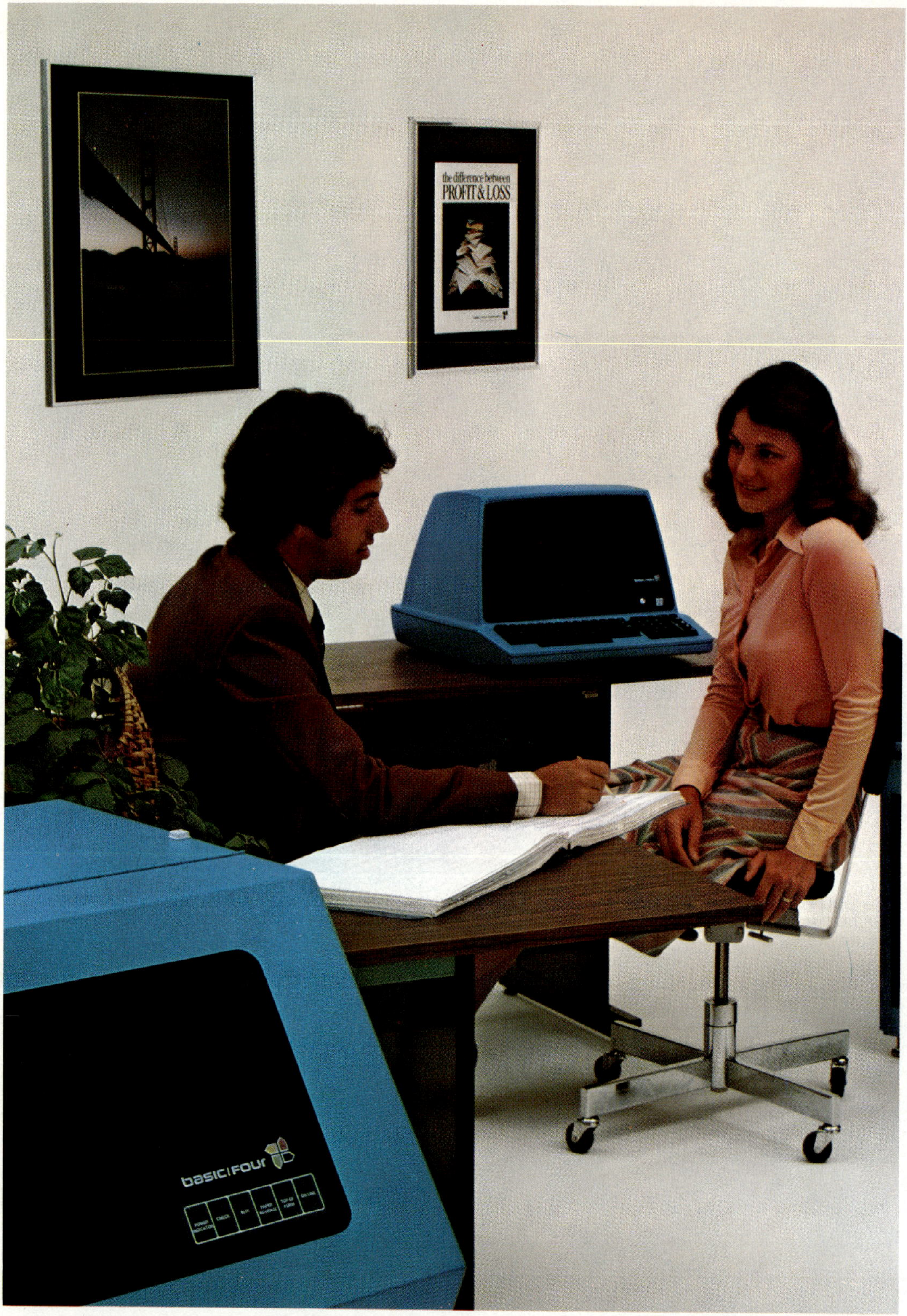
the difference between
PROFIT & LOSS
basic/four

# 13

# Training, Development, Promotion, and Termination

While the objective of orientation is to teach the new employee about the company and the job, the goal of training is to teach the new employee how to actually perform the job. The more effective the training program, the sooner the organization will be able to reap the benefits of the new employee's talents and skills. Also, the more effective the selection process (discussed in Chapter 12), the easier it will be to train the employee.

## FACTORS AFFECTING TRAINING

To be effective, a training program must incorporate characteristics that enhance learning. The following list provides a good basis on which to build a training program:

***1. Use of a skilled teacher.*** The use of a person who is both knowledgeable about office skills and effective in teaching techniques is a must in developing a good training program. Renee, the supervisor of records management at Atlantic Mutual Insurance Corp., worked with the personnel department to select the best possible trainer for her new employees. Renee reviewed the applications of thirteen prospective trainers, interviewed the best five applicants, and then contacted the references of these five applicants. After she narrowed her choice to three, she had each of them teach a half-hour microlesson in the company's learning resource center. After these presentations, Renee selected Ruth Brady because she felt Ruth possessed the teaching qualifications needed for the job. Since hiring Ruth, Renee has kept close contact with the training program to ensure correlation between the training and the positions for which the training is conducted.

***2. Similarity between training and the actual job task.*** The more the training simulates the job, the greater the transfer of training will be. Brad Harding, a recent high school graduate, sought employment with Atlantic Mutual and was hired as a records clerk. To function effectively on the job, Brad needed to learn about filing systems, indexing rules, cross-referencing, sorting, transferring files, and checking out records. Brad's supervisor, Renee Keller, had examined a number of filing books as potential training aids but found that none of them was exactly what was needed at Atlantic Mutual; therefore, she had special materials prepared that were suited to the situation. As a result, when Brad came on the job, he was trained with materials that were representative of the actual tasks he would perform on the job. The training was conducted in a special learning resource classroom designed by the company.

***3. Individualization of instruction.*** Since different individuals learn in different ways and at different speeds, the need for at least some individualized instruction is essential. When Brad Harding joined Atlantic Mutual, he was accompanied by four other young people who also were hired as file clerks. The training materials included periodic tests to determine the learners' levels of competency. As soon as a new employee passed one of the examinations, he or she could proceed to a new training unit. Brad had been a good student in high school and mastered the learning materials very rapidly. Other new workers, however, took longer, and one had to have special one-to-one tutoring sessions to understand some of the concepts. With individualized instruction, all the new employees had successfully mastered the training materials within a two-week period.

***4. Use of examples, demonstrations, and models.*** Learning is enhanced when the student can see as well as hear about the behavior or task that he or she is trying to learn. In addition, the chance to see good examples and poor examples will sharpen the learner's ability to discriminate between the two. Because new records clerks were hired so frequently at Atlantic Mutual, Ruth Brady, a former high school business teacher, was hired as a special records clerk trainer.

To enhance the training of new file clerks, Ruth showed both correct and incorrect file arrangements in her training materials. In addition, she showed her trainees a number of the company filing cabinets and explained how each was organized. She also arranged for the trainees to watch experienced workers perform sorting and other filing functions to enable them to visualize the work they would be doing at the conclusion of their training.

***5. Instruction based on measurable objectives.*** Both the instructor and the student should understand in advance the objectives that are being sought. These objectives should also be the basis for the post-training evaluation.

Part of Ruth's training materials was a list of objectives that let the trainees know what was expected of them at the conclusion of their training. During the training sessions, Ruth specified the indexing rules that had to be properly applied, the cross-referencing forms that had to be correctly completed, the methods that should be used in sorting papers for filing, the proper methods for transferring files to inactive storage, and the general principles of filing systems that had to be understood. In addition, she indicated the maximum time that should be taken to file and find records in the company files.

***6. Provision for meaningful practice.*** Nearly all office tasks require practice before proficiency can be expected. Such practice should be timed and should focus on efficiency and effectiveness of movement.

Ruth had developed a "practice set," a packet of actual letters and other documents that the new workers used to practice filing. With these materials, the trainees applied their learning in such areas as indexing, cross-referencing, coding, sorting, and signing out files to users. With each of these activities, the new workers could time themselves to determine whether they were measuring up to the standards established for the department.

## A Four-Step Method in Training

In training new employees, Ruth uses four basic steps to achieve maximum effectiveness. First, the trainees have explained to them the specific who, what, why, when, where, and how of the job. This thorough background enables them to see their work in proper organizational perspective. Second, the trainees have the work demonstrated for them and see step-by-step how the job is to be accomplished. Third, the trainees imitate the trainer's performance. They actually perform the job themselves and are carefully observed by the trainer. Fourth, the trainer gives feedback to the trainees. This feedback consists of positive feedback for those phases of the job performed correctly and of appropriate corrective information and demonstration for those phases performed incorrectly.

This trial and evaluation procedure is repeated until the trainees perform the job correctly. Following this point in the training process, the trainees are left more and more on their own, although quality checks are made occasionally and positive reinforcement is given to support correct job performance.

This four-step process can be easily understood by watching how Ruth worked with Brad in his sorting instruction. The purpose of sorting is to arrange papers for rapid filing. Brad first read about this process in the training materials, then Ruth demonstrated it with a number of letters and other business documents. Following the demonstration, Brad arranged 30 letters and business documents in the order he thought was correct. Ruth complimented

Brad on 28 correct decisions; then she explained very carefully the rules that had been violated in the two improper decisions.

In general, employee training follows one of two types—on-the-job and vestibule training. A brief discussion of each type is given in the following section, along with a listing of the advantages and disadvantages of each.

## TYPES OF TRAINING

### On-the-Job Training

The most frequently used method of teaching a new responsibility or task is on-the-job training under the direction of an experienced worker. This training is accomplished on the site; that is, the worker learns the new job by actually performing the job.

For example, assume that Charlene has recently been employed as a word-processing operator (typist using electronic typewriters). Charlene has good typing skills, but she has not had direct experience working the IBM word-processing equipment used by the company. To assure that Charlene is trained properly, Floyd, the supervisor, assigns one of his better operators to work with Charlene for a two-week period. Initially, Sam, the trainer, teaches Charlene a few basic skills so she can type several of the more simple jobs handled by the operators. After Charlene masters these skills, Sam teaches her several more and gives her several of the more complex jobs to complete. This process is repeated during the two-week period, at the end of which Charlene can handle any job she is given.

A major advantage of on-the-job training is that it places the primary responsibility for training on the new employee's supervisor, even though the supervisor might have another group member perform the actual training. Consequently, the supervisor feels a greater responsibility for the new employee than he or she would if someone else were ultimately in charge of training.

Another advantage is that the workers are trained at the same job they will be performing for the company, so that no transfer of training to another job is required. As trainees, they experience the same kinds of problems, concerns, and satisfactions that they will after the training program is completed.

On-the-job training does not require the employment of additional training staff or the purchase of extra equipment; consequently, it may be seen as an economical training method. This economy may be offset, however, if the supervisor or the designated trainer is an ineffective teacher, does not spend sufficient time training, or does not appreciate the importance of effective training.

In many organizations, a new employee will be hired one or two weeks before the actual termination date of the person who is leaving. An obvious disadvantage of this practice is that the company suddenly has two people on the payroll doing the work of one. Also, production will decrease and errors will increase during this time. These disadvantages can be largely offset, however, if the person who is terminating does a good job of training the replacement. This training can be enhanced by having the trainer become adequately prepared in advance and by incorporating into the training the factors and guidelines suggested in this chapter. Training of the new employee by the terminating employee is the most common on-the-job training method used in business.

On-the-job training is effective if the job to be learned can be mastered within a week or two and if the number of trainees is very small. If the training is a long process or if the number of trainees exceeds two or three at a time, the supervisor simply will not have sufficient time to keep up his or her regular work *and* the training. If either of these conditions exists in an office situation, the organization may choose to implement a vestibule training program.

### Vestibule Training

Vestibule training is characterized by a single trainer instructing a group of trainees simultaneously—typically in a classroom setting. The training situation for a file clerk discussed previously in this chapter, which involved Brad Harding and Ruth Brady and showed Brad receiving training in a special classroom, can serve as an example of the vestibule method. Vestibule training usually permits more emphasis on effective teaching techniques, because training is the major job responsibility of the teacher—not a sideline responsibility as it is in the case of the supervisor. In a vestibule training situation, the trainee is freed from the pressures of the real job and is thus able to concentrate more on rapid learning. In addition, any mistakes made during the training session are "free" in the sense that they have no effect on the company's actual product or service.

Several negative factors must also be considered with the vestibule training method. Cost may be a limiting factor if additional office equipment must be purchased for the training. Also, the trainees are not contributing directly to the company's immediate output as they would be in on-the-job training. Splitting the responsibility for training between the supervisor and trainer sometimes results in "passing the buck" if the trainee does poorly on the job after training. The supervisor may say the trainer is at fault, and the trainer may say the supervisor is at fault—a buck-passing episode that results in strained relations between them over the problem employee as well as over any future training.

When you become involved in a situation where training is required, you will need to examine the situation closely to determine whether on-the-job training, vestibule training, or some variation of the two offers the most advantages.

## DEVELOPMENT

After new employees are properly trained and are performing their assigned duties, the organization needs to consider appropriate methods of developing the employee's abilities even further. Employee development has two main objectives:

1. To increase workers' ability to fulfill their present job duties. This objective focuses on providing *refresher* experiences and on encouraging employees to continue their efforts to seek for new and better methods of accomplishing their work.
2. To prepare individuals for increased responsibility and advancement. This objective pertains to the development of individuals who appear to possess aptitude and desire for leadership within the organization. Managerial development is especially critical if the organization usually promotes from within the organization rather than hiring most of its managers from the outside.

Selecting the types of training needed to increase workers' ability to fulfill their present job duties is usually determined simply by being alert to weaknesses frequently noticed among employees. For example, in a secretarial services department, Floyd, the supervisor, might notice frequent proofreading errors in typewritten letters, frequent mathematical errors in budget analyses, and poor telephone etiquette. Following the determination of the most critical problems in the department, the supervisor then provides special instruction to help the employees improve. Floyd provides a proofreading training session to improve proofreading accuracy, a refresher math course to improve mathematical accuracy, and a special telephone company film to improve telephone etiquette. Following each development session, he works closely with his people to ensure that the training is implemented on the job.

### Employee Evaluation

Although in many cases nearly all employees in an office receive some type of professional development to fulfill their present jobs, only selected individuals are given really intensive training to prepare them for supervisory or managerial assignments. To determine the individuals who show the most promise of becoming good managers, an organization relies heavily on the judgment of supervisory and middle management levels. As the middle managers and supervisors meet periodically with each of their subordinates, they should be watchful for people who possess leadership characteristics. For example, they might be on the lookout for people who are leaders of informal groups, effective and efficient in their work, sensitive to the needs and feelings of others, and well educated relative to the functions and objectives of the company. In addition, supervisors and managers must look for every good opportunity to move members of minority groups into development programs. Figure 13-1 illustrates a form that may be used in evaluating and selecting employees for leadership development.

After prospective management candidates are identified, some companies subject them to a screening process in an *assessment center.* In a typical assessment center, the candidates engage in activities that simulate the kinds of work that are required of supervisors and managers; the candidates are observed and evaluated by several qualified assessors—managers trained in assessment techniques. Typical assessment center activities include:

1. Management games: games that simulate production and selling situations and that test a person's ability to plan, organize, and control. Example: Given a situation involving a CB radio manufacturing company, the candidate would make decisions about the price of the product and the amount of money devoted to research and development, capital equipment, and marketing.
2. In-basket exercises: situations that require the candidate to read, evaluate, and take action on a variety of memos, letters, and reports, in a hypothetical manager's in-basket. Example: Given a situation where the candidate is filling in for an office manager who is absent, decisions are made on a number of in-basket items such as personnel action, equipment purchases, customer relations, and policy making. The candidate may postpone or take action on any of the items.
3. Case studies and problem-solving exercises: problem settings that exhibit a person's analytical and problem-solving abilities. Example: Given a situation involving an equipment-shortage problem in a secretarial services department, the candidate isolates the root of the problem, analyzes several methods of solving the problem, and makes appropriate recommendations. Since case studies are frequently written, the candidate demonstrates his or her writing ability along with the ability to solve problems and make decisions.
4. Communication activities: situations that require the candidate to demonstrate writing, oral, and interpersonal communication abilities. Example: Given the case study presented in the preceding paragraph, the candidate gives a written or oral presentation of the solution he or she thinks is best. In a group setting, the person may also show his or her ability to function effectively in a group.

Many of the characteristics important to a manager can be observed in an assessment center setting. Dimensions frequently assessed with this screening method include creativity, interpersonal sensitivity, tolerance, risk taking,

## PERFORMANCE ASSESSMENT FOR NONEXEMPT EMPLOYEE

| NAME | JOB TITLE | GRADE | DATE |
|---|---|---|---|
| LOCATION | SECTION | DEPARTMENT | DIVISION |
| APPRAISING SUPERVISOR | REVIEWING SUPERVISOR | DATE EMP. PRES. POS. | DATE OF LAST REVIEW |

| CHECK ONE | Annual | New Emp | Termin. | OTHER (Explain) |
|---|---|---|---|---|
| | | | | |

CHECK ONE BELOW: O E G F U

A. PERFORMANCE CHARACTERISTICS:

| | O | E | G | F | U |
|---|---|---|---|---|---|
| KNOWLEDGE OF JOB – A clear understanding of the facts or factors pertinent to the job<br>Comments: | ☐ | ☐ | ☐ | ☐ | ☐ |
| QUALITY OF WORK – Thoroughness, accuracy and neatness of work . . . , . . . . . . . . . . .<br>Comments: | ☐ | ☐ | ☐ | ☐ | ☐ |
| PRODUCTIVITY – Demonstrated accomplishments, volume of work . . . . . . . . . . . . . . . .<br>Comments: | ☐ | ☐ | ☐ | ☐ | ☐ |
| DEPENDABILITY – Conscientious, responsible, reliable with respect to attendence, work completion<br>Comments: | ☐ | ☐ | ☐ | ☐ | ☐ |
| COOPERATION – Ability and willingness to work with associates, supervisors, and others<br>Comments: | ☐ | ☐ | ☐ | ☐ | ☐ |

OVERALL RATING BASED ON ABOVE ☐ OUTSTANDING ☐ EXCELLENT (Above Standard) ☐ GOOD (Standard) ☐ FAIR (Below Standard) ☐ UNSATISFACTORY

Comments:

B. POTENTIAL FORECAST:
1. Positions for which READY NOW:
2. Positions to consider IN THE FUTURE (indicate timing):
3. The reasons for these estimates of potential are:

C. DEVELOPMENT PLAN:

| Appraising Supervisor | Date | Reviewing Supervisor | Date |
|---|---|---|---|

*Figure 13-1.* Form Used for Leadership Development Selection

*Source:* Reprinted from *Modern Personnel Forms*, Copyright 1976, Warren, Gorham, and Lamont, Inc., 210 South Street, Boston, Mass. All Rights Reserved.

communication ability, assertiveness, judgment, initiative, independence, flexibility, tenacity, motivation, analytical ability, and decision-making ability.

Stress interviewing may also be used to determine managerial potential. In a stress interview, one person is subjected to intensive questioning by a panel of interviewers. Stress tolerance, communication ability, interpersonal sensitivity, judgment, tenacity, analytical ability, and independence can all be assessed to a certain degree in a stress interview. Interaction with peers and performance in a simulated setting are missing in a stress interview, however.

### Development Program Approaches

The formal development of employees can be accomplished in three different ways: (1) employees go to sources outside the company, (2) outside consultants come into the organizational setting to assist in the development of employees, or (3) the organization prepares and administers its own in-house development program.

#### *Sources outside the Company*

*Professional organizations.* Employees can increase their knowledge, leadership abilities, and professional acquaintances through active membership in professional organizations. Such special interest organizations are frequently on the forefront of their particular interest areas and they keep their members well aware of current developments in such areas. Several such organizations are the Administrative Management Society, International Word Processing Association, Association of Records Managers and Administrators, and National Micrographics Association. The Certified Administrative Manager program of the Administrative Management Society is probably the best all-around professional development program for administrative managers.

*Special workshops and conventions.* Intensive sessions dealing with a wide variety of topics are readily available and provide an excellent opportunity for training. Word processing, micrography, and computers are just three of the many topics covered at office-related workshops and conventions.

*Correspondence courses.* Technical education, in particular, is offered via correspondence courses. Executive development packages are also available, however, and offer excellent materials for development. Among other courses offered through the Administrative Management Society is a correspondence course entitled "Systems and Information Management for the Administrative Manager." In this course, the student studies the following areas: information systems, system study and design, forms and the system, file systems, information output techniques, and computer-based information systems.

*Formal education classes.* Courses offered by public and private educational institutions are becoming more and more available as the need for lifelong education is recognized. Community colleges, especially, are making an effort to accommodate the educational needs of people who are working full time.

In addition, for those located away from the institution, a number of educational institutions provide special off-campus programs for special training or for complete degree programs. For example, the University of Oklahoma offers a Bachelor of Liberal Studies degree that is largely earned by independent study away from the campus.

***Consultants.*** Consultants may be used both to analyze and solve particular development problems within the organization and to conduct special sessions of interest to those involved in development programs. Consultants from professional consulting firms, from higher education institutions, or from special service industries often introduce fresh ideas that were not apparent or known to persons inside the organization.

Outside consultants should be hired when it is deemed that such an action would produce the best development program for the organization. Specific objectives should be outlined for the consultants and their performances should be evaluated in light of those objectives. Topics such as leadership style, communication, delegation, management by objectives, decision making, organizational development, governmental regulations, motivation, and performance appraisal are typical of the special sessions conducted by special consultants.

***In-House Development Programs.*** Development programs administered by the organization itself can take a variety of forms and can use a number of different methods. A selected list of development methods is given here.

*Job rotation.* Workers are trained to perform jobs other than just their own. For example, a word-processing operator and an administrative secretary could rotate positions for a six-month period. Employee flexibility, sensitivity and empathy, and a better overall understanding of other workers' roles in the organization are among the benefits that accrue from job rotation.

*Understudy.* The worker assumes the position of an apprentice and learns a particular job by working as an assistant to the person who actually holds that job. In a data-processing department, for example, a person could gain excellent experience by working as an assistant to the data-processing supervisor.

*Role playing.* In a group setting, the learners have hypothetical persons and problems described to them; they then assume the point of view of those persons and in those roles interact with each other. This "let's pretend" activity helps group members to empathize with others, to see other points of view, and to understand why people act differently.

*Management games.* Games that simulate business problems and situations are available for both groups and individuals. Game guidelines frequently will point out alternatives not previously thought of by the learner.

*Classroom lecture.* An instructor orally presents information about a topic important to the development of the employees. The lecture is the oldest form of teaching and is particularly useful in disseminating information of a factual nature to a large number of people.

*Modeling.* Desirable behavior traits are displayed before those individuals whose behavior you wish to change. (Because modeling is such an effective development technique and because most managers are relatively unskilled in its use, modeling is given greater coverage here than previous development methods.) The word *model* is used to describe the person being used as the good example; *observer* refers to the person who is emulating the example of the model; and *modeling effect* is the amount of change observed in the observer after the modeling process. Since workers can emulate both positive and negative characteristics, both negative and positive modeling effects can result.

When implementing modeling in the development of workers, you should remember the following considerations:

1. Modeling, or demonstration, is essential for behavioral change.
2. Modeling is effective only insofar as the desired traits are observable.
3. Modeling plus reinforcement are required for a maximum modeling effect.[1]
4. Proximity and frequency of contact should be provided during the modeling process.
5. The observer must have at least some respect for the model before any positive modeling effect will occur.
6. A maximum modeling effect cannot be achieved through coercion.

Implementing the modeling process in a development program is a five-step procedure:

1. Identify the specific behavior the observer should acquire.
2. Select (or help the observer select) one or more models who have the desired behavior.
3. Have the observer watch the model closely and emulate the desired behavior.
4. Evaluate the observer's new behavior. Give appropriate positive reinforcement.
5. Have the observer make appropriate adjustments in his or her behavior patterns until the desired behavior is acquired.

In a climate of trust and unity, modeling can be used very effectively. In such a climate, employees are generally not afraid to admit weaknesses or to look to their leaders and peers for development assistance.

The implementation of development programs must be carefully planned.

Remember that not all individuals have the same interests and desires for development, people learn at different rates, the same teaching method is not equally effective with everyone, and all individuals are not equally prepared for particular learning experiences.

## PROMOTION

As was pointed out in Chapters 5 and 6, promotion is a great motivating factor for human beings. People have an innate desire to climb the ladder of success, and if they feel that they are standing too long on the same rung of the ladder, they will become dissatisfied. Promotion not only helps the individual employee, but it also produces company returns in the form of increased productivity through increased motivation and dedication to the organization. Therefore, effective promotion practices are in the best interest of both the employee and the organization.

Analyses of employees' records determine readiness for promotion, and therefore, these records should be designed to accumulate the information that is necessary for promotional consideration. Data should be entered on the record each time employees are appraised or interviewed by their supervisors. In addition, other information of significance that occurs between sessions with the supervisor should be recorded. For example, job performance, demonstrated abilities, education and development activities, and significant contributions to the company should be included in the employee's file. Employees might be given the opportunity of reviewing their records on a periodic basis to determine the accuracy and completeness of the information. Figures 13-2 and 13-3 illustrate two forms that can be used to accumulate promotional information.

### Hiring versus Promotion

Whenever positions within the organization need to be filled, management must decide whether to hire someone from outside the organization's ranks or to promote someone from within the company organization. Bringing in someone from the outside has two distinct advantages: (1) the individual brings in fresh ideas from the outside, and (2) the person comes in with a "clean" record. The major disadvantage of this practice is that employees within the organization frequently resent an outsider coming in to assume positions that they may have been working toward.

Conversely, promoting from within the organization has the advantage of building employee morale but the disadvantage of promoting persons without fresh ideas. Also, as new supervisors begin exerting direct influence over those individuals who were just yesterday their peers, the comment "Who does she think she is?" is likely to be heard. Hiring from within the organization creates a kind of "domino" vacancy effect, that is, the promoted person

**Management by Objectives Form**

Name ______________________ Date ______________________

Position ______________________ Department ______________________

| Objectives | Results |
|---|---|
| | |

*Figure 13-2.* Example of a Form Used by Management to Record Information about an Employee

leaves a vacancy that must be filled. If it is filled by a present employee, that in turn creates another vacancy; of course, this domino effect has the advantage of providing advancement opportunities for individuals on several levels within the organization. Most organizations will adopt a combination approach to promoting—they hire from within whenever the present employees are qualified to fill vacancies, but they hire from outside whenever it is advantageous to do so. Hence, they maintain a good balance between the two promotion alternatives.

### Types of Promotions

There are three general types of promotions—*rank promotions, job promotions,* and *horizontal promotions. Rank promotions* are given when there are several levels for each job performed. In other words, three persons performing the same task may hold three different ranks. For example, a company may reward outstanding secretaries with a promotion to "senior secretary." In spite of the two different titles, the job duties are the same. Rank promotions are given for outstanding service to the organization, but they do not result immediately in increased responsibility. When employees are promoted to a higher rank, they normally also receive an increase in pay as well as an increase in status.

**Promotion Assessment Form**

| Name: | | Date: |
|---|---|---|
| Position: | Department: | |

Use the following rating scale to evaluate a worker's promotion readiness: 5 = excellent, 4 = good, 3 = average, 2 = fair, 1 = poor.

| | |
|---|---|
| Job performance . . . . . . . . . . . . . . . . . . . . . . . . . . . . . . . . . . . . . . . . | ________ |
| Significant development activities. . . . . . . . . . . . . . . . . . . . . . . . . . . | ________ |
| Communication . . . . . . . . . . . . . . . . . . . . . . . . . . . . . . . . . . . . . . . . | ________ |
| Organization . . . . . . . . . . . . . . . . . . . . . . . . . . . . . . . . . . . . . . . . | ________ |
| Decision making . . . . . . . . . . . . . . . . . . . . . . . . . . . . . . . . . . . . . . | ________ |
| Self-direction . . . . . . . . . . . . . . . . . . . . . . . . . . . . . . . . . . . . . . . | ________ |
| Delegation . . . . . . . . . . . . . . . . . . . . . . . . . . . . . . . . . . . . . . . . . | ________ |
| Total | ________ |

*Overall rating:* ☐ Promotable ☐ Promotable with additional development
☐ Not promotable in the foreseeable future

*Additional comments:*

*Figure 13-3.* Another Type of Form That Can Be Used to Assess Employee Performance

*Job promotions* result in actual changes in work responsibilities. For example, an assistant supervisor could be promoted to the position of supervisor. These promotions are usually accompanied by title changes, increases in pay, and increases in job status. Like rank promotions, job promotions are given as rewards for outstanding job performance. Before job promotions are given, management must make certain that the person being promoted is qualified to assume the different job requirements. Otherwise, the performance of the promoted person may decline rather than increase or even stay the same. Careful examination of the job requirements and the employee's qualifications and desires will help ensure a good match of person and position.

Another form of job promotion is *horizontal promotion*. This type of promotion may not result in increased pay or in a more responsible or prestigious job. The horizontal promotion may be thought of as a transfer to a position which offers more possibilities for professional advancement to persons being moved. The horizontal move is thought of as a promotion since it signals to employees that the company is giving them the "go ahead" in this assignment.

For example, assume that Christine is a top producer in the word-processing center of Business Systems, Inc. There is little chance of promotion for her, however, because the current supervisor will likely remain in his position for at least two years. In the administrative service center, the supervisor is scheduled to quit her job in four months. Consequently, the administrative manager asks Christine to consider moving from word processing to administrative services with the possibility of assuming the present supervisor's position in four months. Christine realizes that she is not being offered an immediate promotion but that in the long run she will have better chances of advancement. Therefore, she decides to make the move to administrative services.

The techniques for selecting candidates for promotion resemble very closely the techniques used in selecting new employees. One major difference with promotion, however, is that the company has had an opportunity to observe candidates' performance within its own organization. Consequently, the selection decision can be based on the employees' performance appraisals, the accomplishment of their objectives, and the judgment of company managers who have had the opportunity to observe their work. As in the new employee selection process, the job promotion process must take the approach of matching the job and the employee. Seniority, experience, and EEOC considerations play an important part in this process, but the major question should be: Will the person do the job that needs to be done?

## TERMINATION

Sooner or later in the life of all employees comes the time for termination. Employees leave an organization for one of three reasons: self-initiated termination, dismissal, or retirement. Since all three types of termination have significant effects on the organization, careful attention must be given to all individuals involved in such actions.

### Self-initiated Termination

Self-initiated termination results from a variety of reasons, among which are to accept other employment, to get married, to have a baby, and to relocate with spouse. Whatever the reason for leaving, a personnel officer or other appropriate person should have an *exit interview* with the departing worker. The major purposes of this action are (1) to determine the real cause of separation, (2) to obtain suggestions for improving the organization, (3) to express appreciation for the worker's service to the organization, and (4) to ensure that all papers and clerical tasks associated with the separation have been completed. As management accumulates and analyzes the exit interview data, it can improve organizational effectiveness by focusing on solving problems and implementing worthwhile suggestions that are given in the interviews. Figure 13-4 shows one form that can be used to summarize the causes of separation.

### Dismissal

Every company is eventually faced with the unpleasant task of giving involuntary separation to certain employees. Workers are dismissed from an organization for two main reasons: poor performance on the job and employee layoffs caused by insufficient funding or work.

An employee of Atco Corp. can serve as an example of a poor performer. Jared has recently been released from his job as a general clerk in the purchasing office. He enjoyed his work but could not produce as well as the other employees could. Compared with the others, he was slow and frequently his work contained errors. Consequently, his supervisor could not trust him and had to check on his work constantly. The supervisor had talked with Jared on a number of occasions about obtaining additional training, but Jared didn't avail himself of the opportunities. Therefore, after repeated warnings about the quality of his work, Jared was dismissed from his job.

When managers or supervisors notice that certain employees are not performing at company expectations, appropriate steps should be taken to help the employee improve. The focus should be on training and keeping employees rather than on firing and replacing them. If the employees will not respond to training, however, either a transfer or termination should be considered. Before dismissing workers, the supervisor should give appropriate advance notice so that the employees have time to make other employment provisions. Even though such action may cause negative feelings at the time, the long-range effects are usually beneficial to both company and dismissed employees. If employees are not performing well, they cannot fully enjoy their employment, and they are better off seeking another job to which they are better suited. Likewise, the company will benefit from the dismissal because the dismissed individuals can be replaced by employees who are likely to give better performances.

Sheila, a young black woman from Chicago, has recently been released from her job because of a technological change. Sheila was hired by the firm as a secretary in the personnel department. She enjoyed her work and performed well on the job. After being employed for just three months, she received notice that she would be released from employment in two weeks. The reason for the action was that the company was implementing a word-

**SUMMARY OF SEPARATIONS BY REASON**

| | 19.... | 19.... | 19.... |
|---|---|---|---|
| *Action of the Company* | | | |
| Irregular attendance | | | |
| Poor conduct | | | |
| Neglect of duty | | | |
| Not adapted for work | | | |
| Work unsatisfactory | | | |
| Total | | | |
| *Action of employee* | | | |
| Another position | | | |
| Did not like work | | | |
| Needed at home | | | |
| Health | | | |
| School | | | |
| Failed to return from LOA | | | |
| Failed to report to work | | | |
| Left city | | | |
| Pregnancy | | | |
| Marriage | | | |
| Enter military service | | | |
| Retirement | | | |
| Personality problems | | | |
| Death | | | |
| Other—unaccounted for | | | |
| Too far to travel | | | |
| More money | | | |
| Completed exchange visitor program | | | |
| Total | | | |
| Grand Total | | | |

*Figure 13-4.* A Form Showing a Summary of Causes of Employee Separation from a Company

*Source:* Hospital Authority of Gwinnett County, Ga. Reprinted from *Modern Personnel Forms*, Copyright 1976, Warren, Gorham, and Lamont, Inc., 210 South Street, Boston, Mass. All Rights Reserved.

processing center and that three of the company secretaries would no longer be needed. Because Sheila was next to the last secretary hired, she was one of the three to be released.

When employees are dismissed because of general employee layoff demands, efforts should be made to assist the employees in finding other employment or in reinstating them in the organization at the earliest possible date. Some organizations have warded off employee layoffs during difficult times by getting all company personnel to agree to a temporary salary cutback. Although this action has a negative effect on all workers, it has the advantage of uniting all personnel in a common cause and of saving some employees the negative effects of the dismissal.

A serious concern faced by many companies during economic setbacks is caused by their use of seniority rule. Such a rule causes the last hired to be the first laid off, as in Sheila's case in the previous example. In recent years, since many of the last hired have been minority groups, the organization soon faces the same minority imbalance it had before implementing its affirmative action plan. Companies that face such a possibility might consider rewriting their layoff policies and union contracts so seniority is not the only factor considered when layoffs are required. In May, 1977, the Supreme Court upheld the seniority rule, however, thus indicating that a seniority system is legal in worker layoff situations.

### Retirement

During the last several decades, increased emphasis has been given to providing for the financial needs of retired persons. This emphasis has been prompted by the high percentage of people who retire only to face a life of poverty and welfare. Retirement benefits come from two major sources—social security and business retirement plans (pension plans). Since social security benefits rarely provide sufficient retirement income, business retirement plans attempt to make up the difference.

In developing retirement plans, managers need to place a great amount of emphasis on accurate wording for easy comprehension and thorough analysis of all available data. The following factors are generally considered in creating an employee retirement plan: age of employee, salary level, years of service, retirement age and options, contributions of employee and employer, transferability of plan, retirement benefits and options, and death benefits. A number of insurance firms and financial institutions are usually anxious to make bids on retirement plans, and several such offers should be analyzed thoroughly to determine the one that offers the best possible coverage available. Within a company, someone well versed in retirement-related legislation should play a major part in the development of a retirement plan.

***ERISA.*** The Employee Retirement Income Security Act of 1974 (ERISA) was enacted to require organizations to communicate clearly their retirement plans and to provide the opportunity for individuals not covered by group pension plans to establish their own individual retirement accounts. Basically, ERISA provides that individuals can contribute up to 15 percent of their annual income (not to exceed $1,500 annually) for the establishment of an individual retirement account. These contributions are not taxable until the money and earned dividends are actually withdrawn, usually at retirement age when most people are in a much lower tax bracket. As a result, the tax paid on ERISA accounts is usually much lower than it would have been if it had been paid when the individuals earned it. Individual retirement accounts may be established at banks, savings and loan associations, and credit unions. (For additional information on individual retirement accounts, consult Internal Revenue Service Publication 590; see also "Summary of Employee Income Security Act of 1974," prepared by A. S. Hansen, actuaries and consultants, a special Dartnell Office Administration Service Guide, 4660 Ravenswood Avenue, Chicago, IL 60604.)

***Maintaining a Retirement Program.*** This process is primarily one of keeping employees informed and of maintaining accurate and up-to-date records. When an employee begins service with a company, he or she should be informed of the retirement options that are available. The advantages and disadvantages should be explained in full during the employee's orientation, so that the worker will have the best information base available to make a decision.

After the decision is made, the office personnel in charge of the retirement records should make certain that the new worker is properly instated. Subsequently, the office staff must make certain that proper contributions and entries are made to the participants' accounts.

As employees near retirement age, they should be informed about the options for retirement. Generally, when employees elect to retire early, they must also realize that their monthly retirement payments will be less than if they retired at an older age. This reduction is necessary because of the additional years during which the pension will be paid.

An organization has both a legal and a moral responsibility to communicate very clearly to all employees the benefits they will receive at retirement—including the early retirement options. An attitude of open and clear communication about retirement will save the organization legal problems and will help employees anticipate and prepare properly for retirement. Income restrictions and tax laws should also be understood by persons who are anticipating retirement in the near future.

## *Summary*

New employees are usually trained for their new position by either on-the-job training or by vestibule training. Both types of training offer unique advantages and disadvantages. In addition to training, an organization should provide an ongoing employee development program via outside sources, consultants, or in-house programs.

Employee promotion is the step that logically follows employee development. Well-kept employee records are essential for effective decisions regarding promotion. Promotions are of three types: rank promotions, job promotions, and horizontal promotions. Selecting individuals for promotion resembles the process of selecting new employees, except that the organization has the chance to actually observe the individual who is to be promoted. Promoting from within the organization has definite advantages (employee incentive), but its disadvantages should not be overlooked (antagonism from former peers, etc.).

Employees leave an organization for any of three reasons:

1. Self-initiated termination—exit interviews should be held to determine why an employee wants to leave an organization.
2. Dismissal—reserved primarily for those who will not respond to training or motivational efforts.
3. Retirement—retirement plans should be properly administered to provide the best possible pension for retirees.

## *Review and Discussion Questions*

1. What is *on-the-job training?* How does it differ from *vestibule training?*
2. Why is employee development important?
3. Under what conditions is modeling most effective?
4. What is meant by *job rotation, in-basket exercises, case studies, role playing,* and *management games?*
5. If you were a manager, would you hire from outside or promote from within your company? Why?
6. Why might an organization want to give a promotion without an accompanying increase in responsibility?
7. If an employee is eligible for social security benefits, why would he or she want additional coverage from a company or private pension plan?

## *Application Exercises*

1. Teach someone a new skill by following the four training steps discussed in this chapter. For example, teach someone to operate a copy machine or perform some other office-related function that you already know how to do.
2. Determine at least one behavior trait that you would like to incorporate into your own life. Select that trait from a person who seems to portray it, and use that person as your model. During the next few weeks, watch the

person frequently and try to emulate his or her behavior. Be diligent in trying to acquire the trait you seek. Evaluate your progress periodically and make any changes that you determine are necessary.

3. Survey several large and small offices in your city and determine the typical training practices used in these offices. Analyze your findings to see if significant differences exist between different sizes of offices. Suggest improvements for offices of both sizes.
4. Obtain a copy of the retirement plan offered by your school or business to its employees. Read it carefully and make sure you understand all the terminology it uses.

## *Mini-Cases*

1. *Cynthia* had been encouraged to pursue a professional development program in an effort to prepare for management as soon as an appropriate opening presents itself. Lil Mortimer was Cynthia's immediate manager, and Lil was anxious to help Cynthia as much as possible.

During many conversations with Cynthia, Lil noticed that Cynthia was a poor listener—she would cut in frequently when Lil was only halfway through a sentence. The result was that many times Cynthia thought she knew what Lil was going to say when in reality Lil never really got a chance to express her complete feelings.

Lil was an advocate of active listening, and she wished she could get Cynthia to learn how to be an active listener. Not only would this achievement improve the relationship between Cynthia and Lil but it would help Cynthia throughout her future management career.

If you were Lil, what would you have done?

2. *Jana* was hired as a file clerk at Middleton Insurance Co. When going to work her first day, she was excited and felt that she wanted to do her very best. After receiving a brief orientation to the company, she was directed to her work station and was introduced to her supervisor, Russell Lunceford. Russell showed Jana a stack of letters and said, "I've got to go to a meeting in a minute. While I'm gone, why don't you go through this pile of papers and arrange them alphabetically?" Jana had that task completed in ten minutes, but Russell didn't return for two hours.

When Russell did return, he said to Jana, "Listen, I'm going to have you just follow Cecil around today and kinda' watch what he does." After following Cecil around for the rest of the day, Jana was discouraged and frustrated.

What should the supervisor have done that he didn't do?

3. *Martha* is the administrative manager for General Supplies, Inc. and has been notified that the mail room supervisor is going to be quitting soon. Carl Boyer has worked in the mail room for two years and has been a good worker.

He has mentioned to the present supervisor that he would like to "move up" in the organization, but the company has not provided any development opportunities for him yet.

Martha is aware of Carl's aspirations, but she also knows a mail room supervisor in a nearby business, and she thinks she could entice that supervisor, Gordon, to come to General. Gordon has supervisory experience, which she thinks is important, but he is unacquainted with the workings of General.

What factors should Martha consider in making her decision?

## *Reference Note*

1. Robert H. Woody, *Behavioral Problem Children in the Schools: Recognition, Diagnosis, and Behavioral Modification*, © 1969, p. 196. By permission of Prentice-Hall, Inc., Englewood Cliffs, N.J.

# 14

# Common Administrative Personnel Problems

Management means getting specific results accomplished through people. Although that point has already been made frequently in previous chapters, it is especially significant in this chapter on personnel problems. Personnel are the major source of problems for the administrative manager, because any employee behavior that reduces potential results may become a problem. Specific problem areas that will be considered here include turnover, absenteeism, and abuses of time, drugs, and alcohol. Development of employee self-discipline will be discussed, and some consideration will be given to office safety.

If management were completely effective in its motivation, communication, MBO, delegation, selection, orientation, training, and leadership techniques, concern for personnel problems would be reduced. But because people are human, interpersonal problems will always be common. In this chapter, we examine a few of the major interpersonal problems in a business setting and suggest some possible approaches for handling them.

## TURNOVER

*Personnel turnover* is defined as the rate during a given period at which employees leave an organization and are replaced by newly hired people.

Organizations that are able to reduce turnover to a low level—where five or ten people out of a hundred are replaced in a year—are considered to be effective in eliminating high turnover. These organizations will profit from not having to spend thousands of dollars unnecessarily to select and to train new people.

### Causes of Excessive Turnover

Some effective management practices that help to reduce turnover are explained in Table 14-1. One major corporation that has a very low turnover rate makes a determined effort to follow the seven practices listed in this table; present and former employees speak highly of the company and readily point out the advantages of working there.

Several factors may cause high turnover; among them are *ineffective management* and an *organizational policy* that purposely builds in high turnover rates. For example, an organization may use a large number of part-time students in connection with a policy to provide student employment or in an effort to reduce the cost of wages to the company. Turnover rates of 30 to 50

**Table 14-1. Effective Practices That Reduce Personnel Turnover**

| *Practices* | *Explanation* |
| --- | --- |
| 1. Effective selection procedures | 1. Care is taken during the hiring process to choose people who will be well qualified (not overly qualified) and happy in their positions. |
| 2. Proper orientation and training | 2. New personnel are systematically and thoroughly oriented to their new organizations and positions. They are thoroughly trained to perform their jobs so that they will have confidence in their ability to work. |
| 3. Effective supervision | 3. Supervisors will help to develop employees under their direction and will develop a climate of trust, open communication, and helpfulness. |
| 4. Desirable personnel policies | 4. The organization follows personnel policies that that create a favorable image of the company in the minds of the employees. People feel that they are treated fairly. |
| 5. Good salaries and benefits | 5. Salaries and benefits should be a bit higher than the prevailing rates for the industry and the geographical area. |
| 6. Challenging jobs | 6. Employees feel that they are making a meaningful contribution in their jobs and that they are continually developing. |
| 7. Satisfactory interpersonal relations | 7. Unity of purpose, team spirit, and commonality of interest are developed among employees in an office. |

percent and even higher are not uncommon, and because people die, retire, move, or become disabled, some turnover will always be occurring.

The formula for turnover rate given as a percentage is

$$\text{Turnover} = \frac{\text{Total number of terminations}}{\text{Average annual employment}} \times 100$$

Annual turnover rates for businesses average about 25 percent. According to the Administrative Management Society, the turnover rate for office personnel in 1975 was 14 percent.[1]

According to the Women's Bureau of the U.S. Department of Labor,[2] *turnover rates for women* tend to run higher than those for men. The bureau states the reason for this tendency is the work life pattern of women. After working for a few years after graduation, many women get married and have children and then return to the labor force when their children are grown or reach school age. However, an increasing proportion of young married women with and without children are remaining in the personnel force. The bureau suggests that labor turnover rates are influenced more by the skill level of the job, by the age of the worker, by the worker's record of job stability, by the worker's length of service with the employer, and by the level of pay for the job or occupation than by sex.

Personnel turnover statistics published by the Women's Bureau reflect different pictures on the turnover rate for women as compared with men depending upon the particular data considered. In comparing the quit rate in manufacturing (number of people quitting their jobs) for men and women in 1968 (the last year such information was collected by sex), the rate for women was 2.6 percent, compared with 2.2 percent for men.

Another measure of employee turnover is *job tenure*, which is length of time an employee has been with his present employer. As of January 1973, 33 percent of the men as compared with 43 percent of the women had been on their jobs less than two years. At the other extreme, 30 percent of the men, but only 18 percent of the women had ten or more years of service with their current employer. Overall, employed men averaged 4.6 years of continuous service with the same employer, compared with 2.8 years for women. The number of years on the job for women clerical workers averaged 2.7 years as of January, 1973.[3]

Emphasis has been given to personnel turnover for women because about 78 percent of all clerical workers are women. About 35 percent of all women in the labor force in 1975 were in this category as compared with only 7 percent of all males.[4] "Clerical" is the largest single occupation category with 22 percent of the total U.S. labor force in 1973. During this same year, it is estimated that the expense (salary, fringe benefits, overhead, space, etc.) for these personnel was $350 billion.[5]

Turnover can be traced to three primary reasons in 80 percent of all terminations, according to a former vice-president for personnel of a New York insurance firm: (1) management attitude and competence, (2) static jobs, and (3) salary.[6] Specific reasons why office personnel terminate are found in Table 14-2.

### Cures for Excessive Turnover

Flowers and Hughes conducted research on the turnover problem to determine why employees stayed on the job.[7] Their findings correlate well with Herzberg's motivational theory discussed in Chapter 5. People stay on the job for three basic reasons: (1) motivational factors, (2) maintenance factors in the company environment (Herzberg's dissatisfiers), and (3) factors in the external environment such as family ties, friendships, and other job opportunities. Managers and professional personnel stay on the job primarily for reasons related to their work and work environment. Clerical personnel show similar patterns. On the other hand, Flowers and Hughes found that low-skill manufacturing workers stay mainly for maintenance or environmental reasons with many reasons relating to the external environment.

**Table 14-2. Percentage of Total Separation, by Reason**

| | *Exempt** | *Nonexempt* | *Total* |
|---|---|---|---|
| Another job | 36% | 28% | 30% |
| Pregnancy | 1 | 6 | 5 |
| Marriage | 2 | 2 | 2 |
| Return to school | 3 | 8 | 7 |
| Health | 4 | 3 | 3 |
| Stay home | 2 | 8 | 8 |
| Leave city | 8 | 12 | 10 |
| Dismissal | 11 | 16 | 15 |
| Reduction in staff | 12 | 10 | 10 |
| Retirement | 18 | 5 | 8 |
| Military service | 0 | 1 | 1 |
| Death | 3 | 1 | 1 |

*Source: Management World,* September 1976, p. 5. The total number of terminations studied was 91,305, of which 21,852 terminations related to exempt positions and 69,453 terminations related to nonexempt positions.

*"Exempt" refers to those executives and administrative personnel who are exempt from the minimum wage, equal pay, and overtime pay requirements of the Fair Labor Standards Act, commonly known as the Federal Wage and Hour Law. "Nonexempt" employees are subject to these federal regulations.

Administrative managers seeking to formulate personnel policies that will reduce turnover should consider the implications of this research. For them, it is safe to follow the "golden rule"—treat their office employees the same as they as managers would want to be treated. To encourage the office staff to stay in their positions, administrative managers should concentrate on enriching the jobs and improving the work environment.

Turnover is extremely costly. Depending upon the level of the job, turnover costs range from a few hundred dollars for nonskilled workers to several thousand dollars for middle managers. If we use an average cost of $750 and an average turnover rate of 25 percent, we can estimate that the annual turnover cost for a firm of 400 employees is $75,000.

Controlling turnover begins with determining the real reasons why employees are leaving and staying. An exit interview or questionnaire can be helpful in gathering information from former employees, if you are sure that the responses are honest. Responses will be honest if the exiting employees feel assured that their candid comments will in no way harm them in the future. Opinion surveys will help you to determine why employees stay and how satisfied they are with their jobs. Administrative managers normally should turn to the personnel department for help in conducting these surveys or interviews.

As you analyze turnover statistics and interview data, you may discover certain trends. A certain amount of selection error can always be expected, and it is likely that the selection and placement processes in your organization have not always been effective. To some extent, turnover is healthy, in that it indicates that you are replacing dissatisfied or incompetent workers and that you are bringing in new blood. On the other hand, if you are losing the most qualified employees or if you are forcing dissatisfied employees to stay, there is cause for concern.

To illustrate these points, consider some examples. If Marti, who is a constant complainer and trouble maker, leaves her job, her office manager, Yvonne, will probably breathe a sigh of relief. However, if Yvonne's very able assistant Lois leaves, think of the problem and expense of replacing her. But, if Lois is dissatisfied and forced to stay with the company because of forthcoming pension funds or stock payments, consider the potential problems. Lois could change from an effective employee to a disrupter in the department.

In summary, careful attention should be given to selection, placement, orientation, training practices, salary, and other personnel policies in order to reduce the turnover problem.

## ABSENTEEISM

The second people problem to be considered is absenteeism, and its most common cause is illness or accident. The common cold is the most prevalent of all causes of absenteeism, and transportation difficulties, care of children, and personal problems are other typical problems.

Traditionally, women have been thought to have more absence from work than men. The reason given is that women are less likely to be building careers and, therefore, are more prone to place family responsibilities ahead of their jobs. However, a recent Public Health Service survey shows little difference between men and women in their absence rate due to illness or injury: 5.2 days a year for men compared with 5.6 for women.[8] Overall, when the absenteeism rate for men and women within the same occupational group are compared, little difference is noted according to Esther Espenshade of the Illinois Department of Labor.[9] Those women who are dependent upon their job to make a living on a continuing basis tend to have about the same rate of absence as men. Also, the Department of Labor reports that ". . . the total financial loss caused by women's absences was about the same as that caused by men."[10]

Ashell reports that in the United States the cost of absenteeism caused by sickness alone is about $25 billion per year. He also suggests that the annual rate of absenteeism is on the increase despite the fact that the general health of people has improved.[11] Clark suggests that absenteeism costs a typical firm with 400 employees who average 8 days' absence per year about $200,000 annually.[12]

The best approach to controlling absenteeism is to first gather information about absenteeism in your organization. Classify your data by department and by various categories of employees. Look for trends such as increased absences on Fridays, Mondays, and before and after holidays or special events. For example, Glenn Potter is the administrative manager in an insurance company in Wichita. When Glenn analyzed absentee statistics in his department, he was surprised. He found that the absence rate was nearly twice as high on those days just mentioned as on payday. Glenn decided something had to be done to reduce this rate of absenteeism.

First, he found that 80 percent of the absences were caused by 20 percent of the employees. Second, he found that most of the absences were occurring in two or three of the ten sections under his supervision. Next, Glenn called his supervisors together to discuss the problem. He explained that absenteeism was costing the company $25,000 annually in this department alone; about 625 man days were lost at an average rate of $40 per day. He said that he was going to hold them accountable for their own sections. He counseled his supervisors to be firm in administering personnel policies. Glenn has found over the years that if a few people are allowed to violate the rules, others may soon follow their example. He cautioned them that their employees may think of the supervisors as "nice people" but also "soft touches."

Finally, Glenn made some suggestions to the personnel department about the company's absenteeism policy. For instance, he suggested that the policy should spell out specifically that any employee who is unexpectedly absent must always notify his or her supervisor before 9:00 A.M. on the day of the absence. Also, anyone needing to be absent for personal reasons, such as handling personal business affairs or going on a personal trip, must discuss the situation with his supervisor before the absence.

The following procedure is recommended to the administrative manager or supervisor in working with employees who have an excessive rate of absenteeism:

1. Point out the number of absences over a given period of time.
2. Explain why you are concerned about the problem.
3. Ask for an explanation and actively listen to the response.
4. Tell the employee that the number of absences must be drastically reduced.
5. Ask for and discuss possible solutions with the employee.
6. Offer your help.
7. Develop a mutually agreeable specific action plan with the employee and set a specific date for follow-up.

The following conversation between Glenn Potter, administrative manager, and Nancy Kosley, an employee who has been absent excessively, illustrates this recommended procedure:

GLENN: Nancy, thank you for coming to my office. How are you coming along on the computer program for our automated purchasing system?

NANCY: I am coming along fine, Mr. Potter. It has been a real challenge.

GLENN: Challenge?

NANCY: Yes. I had hoped to have it done by now, but it really has been slow. I have been gone so much lately that when I am here I can't seem to find time from my regular duties to work on the program.

GLENN: My records show that you have been gone five days during the past two weeks. You said these absences were personal problems and that you weren't really sick. Is that right?

NANCY: Yes.

GLENN: Nancy, I am concerned about your absence. That program is a part of one of the department's key objectives. It really should be in operation now. Besides, absenteeism is very expensive. Absenteeism cost our department $25,000 this past year. What's the problem, Nancy?

NANCY: Like I told you before, Mr. Potter, my car has been acting up and I have been staying up late trying to get ready to move.

GLENN: I know what you mean, Nancy. But we all have those kinds of problems. We just can't let them keep us from getting the job done. I think there's something else bothering you. Is there anything else that you want to tell me about?

NANCY: Well . . . (Pause) I've been wondering . . . but I didn't want to mention it. (Long pause)

GLENN: What is it, Nancy?

NANCY: Well, I was wondering if maybe you could get someone else to do the program.

GLENN: Someone else?

NANCY: Yeah, someone else. I just don't seem to know how to go ahead on it.

Glenn is finally getting to the real problem. The absence has really been only a symptom of some real problems Nancy has been experiencing lately. As Glenn goes deeper, he finds that Nancy has been having some self-identity problems. Writing the program has been a source of frustration to her because she hasn't felt adequate to do the job. Some other incidents happened in the office that added to her difficulties, and when the going got rough Nancy escaped by being absent from the job. Glenn can help her to see that she must face her problems, and together they may be able to work out a solution.

## ABUSES OF TIME

A third area of people problems is related to abuses of time in addition to absenteeism. A common problem is abuse of the coffee break. While coffee breaks do have advantages—they help employees become better acquainted, help them learn what others are doing, and help develop team work—they also can result in disadvantages. Abuse of this time may mean that coffee breaks extend to unreasonable lengths, disrupt work and leave telephones unattended if everyone in a section goes for coffee at one time, and disturb other workers who are located near the cafeteria or area where coffee is served.

Tardiness and leaving work early are also very serious problems. Some supervisors jokingly say that some employees arrive late and then leave early to make up for their tardiness. Johnnys- or Janes-come-lately and clockwatchers usually do not give their employer a *fair day's work* and are disruptive to others who are trying to do their own work properly. The same can be said for employees who use company time for personal phone calls and personal visits of friends and who take extended lunch hours. All of these time abuses can cause workers to be less effective than they might otherwise be.

An organization should develop specific policies on time abuse problems and then have supervisors enforce these policies. An office policy on coffee breaks might state that personnel will take their fifteen-minute breaks at the same time (10:00 A.M. and 2:00 P.M.). Another policy might specify that no personal phone calls can be made or received in the office except for emergencies. Supervisors and managers should set the example and also should communicate openly with employees who are abusers of allotted time to determine what reasons they have for their behavior.

The procedure recommended for handling absentee problems is readily adaptable to time abuse problems. If an employee had been stretching a one-hour lunch period to ninety minutes, you would point out the problem, explain your concern, and ask for an explanation; then you would tell the employee that lunch periods must not exceed sixty minutes. If some problem exists, you would work with the employee to develop a solution.

## DRUGS AND ALCOHOL ABUSE

A fourth area of personnel problems pertains to improper use of drugs and untimely or excessive use of alcohol—major social diseases that have spread to the office. Employees involved with drug and alcohol abuse tend to produce less and to be involved with problems of turnover, absenteeism, time abuse, and interpersonal conflict.

Drug abuse is found in businesses of all sizes and types. Many administrative managers have had the experience of having drug addicts employed in their offices. The addicts are discovered when someone informs on them or when the manager observes unusual work habits. A Dartnell survey shows that most companies prefer to ignore the drug problem because management is not ready to work with the problem on a positive basis.[13]

How would you recognize a person who is on drugs? The symptoms of drug abuse are many and varied. In fact, two different types of drugs may have opposite effects. To illustrate what to look for in drug abuse cases, let's look at a person who smokes marijuana. A marijuana user may display any of the following characteristics: be sleepy or talkative, have enlarged pupils, lack good coordination, lose memory, display erratic behavior, or have "high feeling." Other drugs produce different symptoms.[14]

Excessive use of alcohol has been an age-old problem among male employees, but according to Wilbert E. Scheer, the number of female alcoholics has been increasing recently.[15] This increase is certain to have major impact on administrative managers and supervisors because of the large number of women clerical workers.

A relatively large number of progressive companies are formulating personnel policies and programs to educate supervisors and managers about alcoholism and to rehabilitate the alcoholic. As with drug abuse, blood and urine tests can be used to screen out potential problem employees. But employees may increase their use of alcohol after joining the company and may later have difficult problems.

A number of signs are evident about the person who is becoming an alcoholic. The individual drinks greater quantity, more frequently, more rapidly. Cover-up techniques and lies are typical of alcoholic behavior. Temporary amnesia; loss of control; and loss of family, friends, and job are typical results.

Organizations using therapy programs have had good success in rehabilitating drug addicts and alcoholics. One company reported a 70 percent rehabilitation rate as a result of its therapy program.

The following methods in dealing with these drug and alcohol abuse problems are recommended:

1. Include appropriate blood and urine tests as part of a preemployment physical examination to screen out potential problem employees.
2. Identify employees who have poor achievement, high accident, and chronic absenteeism records. Have these employees take complete medical examinations. Refer individuals who have drug and alcohol abuse problems to proper social agencies or in-company sources for therapy. Dismiss those who refuse therapy.
3. Keep informed on current developments and seek help of appropriate agencies dedicated to combatting these social problems.

## DISCIPLINE

All of these problems point to the need for employees to become self-disciplined, responsible people. Supervisors are in reality teachers and developers of individuals. They need to be models and to develop programs of positive reinforcement to help people develop a sense of responsibility and maturity. Supervisors should know their people and know how to work most effectively with them.

When employees violate organizational rules, some form of disciplinary or corrective action must be taken. The action to be taken should be in line with the seriousness of the violation and should be based on accurate and complete facts. Minor infractions of rules do not warrant application of severe punishment. For example, if a normally conscientious employee is fifteen minutes late returning from a coffee break for the first time, a five-day suspension would seem overly severe corrective action. A mild verbal warning might be necessary. Notice that the phrase "might be necessary" was used. If one of your better employees is a few minutes late returning from a coffee break, there may be a very good reason. Don't be critical until you have had an opportunity to fully investigate. The procedure shown in the following list will help you administer proper corrective action when rules are violated.

1. Define the problem. Determine exactly what rule has been broken.
2. Gather the facts. Talk with the employee to find out his or her side of the story; make sure that you have a complete picture.
3. Analyze the facts. Make sure that you have a proper perspective.
4. Develop a plan for corrective action. Involve the employee in providing input with regard to a proper solution.

5. Apply the corrective action. Seek opinions of all persons involved with regard to the advisability of action to be taken.
6. Give positive reinforcement to the employee being corrected when he or she makes positive improvement.

To illustrate the procedure, consider this situation: Marilyn Barlow, administrative manager, just learned that Judy Wang has returned from lunch today in a drunken condition. Marilyn talks with Judy and determines that the report is correct. Marilyn requests that Jodi Silvers call a cab and make sure that Judy gets home safely. Marilyn tells Judy to report to Marilyn's office at 8:00 A.M. the next morning. Marilyn talks with two other people who went to lunch with Judy and finds that Judy is not in the habit of drinking. She had a few drinks to celebrate one of the girls' birthdays and soon was unable to control her actions and her voice. The next day, Judy tells her story and apologizes to Marilyn. Marilyn decides to give Judy only a verbal warning. Marilyn clearly explains to Judy that being drunk on the job is against company policy and any further infraction of the rules will be handled by suspension or dismissal. Judy promises that she will never let this problem happen again. Marilyn checks with Judy periodically and finds that she has had no further problem.

Remember that the purpose of disciplinary action is to correct behavior that violates company rules. Some dos and don'ts that should prove helpful in handling your discipline problems are given here.

DO:

Talk with employees in private to avoid embarrassing them

Allow employees to participate in making rules that affect them

Keep records on all pertinent circumstances and actions taken

Base all decisions on facts rather than hearsay

Be firm but fair

Gather all available facts before taking action

Listen to all sides of the story

Consider the employee's previous record

Operate in accordance with disciplinary clauses in your union contract, if one exists

Be consistent but flexible

DON'T:

Lose your temper or use profanity

Be too hasty in taking corrective action

Procrastinate in making a decision

Make idle threats

Administer punishment that is out of line with the offense

Discriminate against any employee because of race, religion, sex, age, nationality, or other external criteria

You are attempting to get your employees to act in accordance with the rules (on their own) because they want to do the right thing. If they do the right thing because of fear of punishment or force, they may willfully violate rules when the element of fear is removed. To a large degree, your approach to the disciplinary question will be determined by how you view people—whether you hold Theory *X* or Theory *Y* assumptions.

Managers or supervisors may need to counsel employees on problems. Personal problems of employees are of little concern to the supervisor unless they affect the employees' work performance. Anything that influences the individual's performance on the job, either personal or work-related factors, should be a legitimate concern of the manager or the supervisor. While managers cannot act as psychologists, they can listen to their employees, make helpful suggestions, help individuals to solve their own problems, and refer employees to proper sources of help. Chapter 11, which discusses interviewing, is a helpful resource in conducting counseling interviews.

## OFFICE SAFETY

Offices tend to provide a safe environment, but enough hazards exist for the administrative manager to be concerned. This problem has been called even more forcefully to the attention of management since 1970, when the Occupational Safety and Health Act (OSHA) was enacted.

OSHA's purpose is to eliminate safety hazards and improve working conditions. All employees working for companies engaged in interstate commerce are covered by the Act. Health and safety standards that employers are expected to comply with have been set and cover conditions of safety and health such as providing first-aid kits and fire extinguishers and keeping fire exits open. Compliance officers make unannounced visits to organizations to make inspections. If violations are found, citations are issued, and the employer has fifteen days to comply or appeal. Penalties of up to $1,000 for each violation may be assessed. In the event of continued noncompliance, additional penalties of up to $1,000 per day may be levied.

OSHA stipulates that organizations must keep accurate records on work-related deaths, major injuries, and illnesses. Three records are required: (1) a log of cases, (2) a supplementary record, and (3) an annual summary. A sample "Supervisor's Report of Accident" form is found in Figure 14-1.

Some of the most common violations cited by OSHA inspectors include:

1. Overloaded and faulty electrical circuits and wiring
2. Inadequate and unposted safety records

**SUPERVISOR'S REPORT OF ACCIDENT**

EMPLOYER ______________________________

Supervisors must report all incidents involving an injury to an employee. This form must be completed and forwarded to management immediately.

Employee ______________________________ Age ______ Sex ______
Occupation ______________________________ Clock ______ Length of service ______
Incident date ______________ Time ______ A.M. ______ P.M. Dept ______________
Location of incident ______________________________
Who advised you of incident? ______________________________ When ______________
Description of incident ______________________________

Nature of injury and part of body involved ______________________________

What protective equipment was being used? ______________________________

What job was employee doing, including tools, machine and materials used? ______________________________

What events occurred immediately before incident? ______________________________

What did employee do unsafely? ______________________________

What safety rules were violated? ______________________________

What was defective, in unsafe condition or wrong with method? ______________________________

What safeguards should be used? ______________________________

What steps were taken to prevent similar incidents? ______________________________

What steps should be taken to prevent a recurrence? ______________________________

Was there any property, product or equipment damage?—If yes, describe. ______________________________

Who provided medical care? ______________________________ When? ______________
Doctor ______________________ Hospital ______________________
Did employee report to work the next scheduled work day? Yes ______________ No ______________
Names of witnesses to incident ______________________________

I HAVE READ THIS REPORT AND IT IS CORRECT.
SIGNED: ______________________
Employee

Signed ______________________ DATE ______________ DATE ______________
Supervisor

*Figure 14-1.* Supervisor's Report of Accident

*Source:* Lovell-Safety Management Co., Inc., New York, N.Y. Reprinted from *Modern Personnel Forms,* 

3. Inadequate fire control measures
4. Hazardous floor conditions
5. Inadequate or blocked aisles

As an effective administrative manager, you must be on the alert to make the office a safe and healthful place in which to work. Review information on OSHA standards available from your local OSHA office. Office management journals also are good sources of information. Then, inspect the office and take necessary preventive steps to insure compliance with standards.

Here are some typical examples of safety hazards found in the office:

If a file clerk pulls out the top two drawers of a file cabinet he or she may find that the cabinet topples over.

A file or desk drawer left open may be tripped over.

Someone leaning back in a swivel desk chair may fall backwards.

A loose scatter rug on a tile floor may cause someone to go flying.

Bookshelf brackets insecurely fastened may cause a heavy load of books to fall.

Avoiding these types of safety hazards requires good communication between supervisors and employees and the application of common sense.

### *Summary*

Whenever you get two or more persons together, you are likely to have people problems. Some of the most common problems that administrative managers face are (1) turnover, (2) absenteeism, (3) time abuse, and (4) drug and alcohol abuse.

Turnover rates vary greatly from one organization to another. When searching for a cause for turnover, many different factors should be considered, and the sex of an individual may not be as important as other factors when causes of turnover are being sought. Turnover is very costly and needs to be controlled; exit interviews and questionnaires help to determine causes of turnover. Careful attention should be directed to personnel procedures: selection, placement, orientation, and training.

Absenteeism has many causes, and two of the most important are illness and accident. Historically, women have been thought to have much higher rates of absence than men. Further analysis reveals that rates for men and women are not extremely different when financial loss to the company is considered. Like turnover, absenteeism is very costly and should be controlled; absenteeism data should be analyzed for causes and trends and supervisors should be held accountable for absenteeism in their departments.

Abuse of time includes extended coffee breaks, tardiness, and leaving work early. Again supervisors should be accountable for these abuses and should work toward improving communication between themselves and employees in order to offset these abuses.

Drug and alcohol abuse are prevalent problems that managers prefer to wink at rather than develop positive programs to combat. Therapy programs tend to be effective remedies. Complete physical examinations will reveal these problems and are useful employment requirements.

Employees should develop self-discipline as much as possible. Managers need to make certain that they have gathered all necessary information and have treated employees fairly, firmly, and impartially.

The Occupational Safety and Health Act (OSHA) has had dramatic impact on business and industrial efforts to improve working conditions and eliminate safety hazards. Strict enforcement procedures and the threat of heavy fines have forcefully induced compliance with standards. Administrative managers need to be alert to office safety hazards and take prompt corrective action.

## *Review and Discussion Questions*

1. Define the term *personnel turnover.* Why does turnover occur? How can it be reduced? Why is it costly? Is there any reason why turnover would be healthy?
2. What are the major causes for absenteeism? What can be done to control it?
3. Do you feel that coffee breaks are good or bad? Why? How can they be controlled?
4. How can other abuses of time such as tardiness, leaving work early, and using office time excessively for personal business be controlled?
5. Why do you think drug and alcohol abuse is on the increase in business offices? How do you recommend handling these types of problems?
6. How do you recommend handling the difficult task of disciplining an employee who requires it?
7. What is OSHA? Why is OSHA important to administrative managers? What can administrative managers do to promote office safety?
8. What institutions outside of business have major impact on administrative managers? What action should administrative managers take to stay on top of their organization and be aware of these outside influences?

## *Application Exercises*

1. Interview one or more administrative managers or other office employees to get their views on people problems in the office.
2. Prepare a case study on one or more employee problems that you know about or that you have been involved with personally. Discuss these problems in class under the direction of your instructor.

3. Search out information (newspapers, magazines, TV newscasts) on governmental regulation that affects the administrative manager. Also, be alert to this issue in other college business courses you may take.
4. Survey office and business periodicals to determine what office personnel problems appear to be most prevalent and of most concern.

## *Mini-Cases*

1. *Barry Ellis*, supervisor of a computer room, found that his personnel costs had been skyrocketing over the past few years; last year, his personnel costs were over $500,000. The number of persons on his payroll has averaged 28. He has had 11 people terminate during the past year for various reasons; of the 11, 8 were technical computer persons and 3 were clerical people. Trained replacements have been impossible to find. The average length of absenteeism last year was two weeks.

How should Mr. Ellis proceed to investigate this problem?

2. *Phil Sikora* arrived back in his office after having returned from an extended 35-minute coffee break. Whenever he spent this much time on a break, he felt a few pangs of guilt because the authorized time for morning and afternoon coffee breaks is 10 minutes. Phil doesn't feel too bad, however, because there are a few days when he is unable to take both of his breaks. Also Phil comes to work 5 minutes early every day and sometimes he doesn't get away in the evening until 5 or 10 minutes after the appointed quitting time of 5:00 P.M.

If you were Mr. Sikora's supervisor, what would you do about his extended coffee breaks?

3. *Ray Johnson*, an accounting clerk in the accounts receivable section, is normally one of your best workers. During the past two months, his absenteeism rate has gone up considerably and he has made many more errors than usual. You have talked with him four times, and each time you have felt good about the interview. After each interview, Ray responded well in changing his behavior. Then, a short while later he would slip and the problems would recur. During your last interview with Ray, you warned him that any further recurrence of these problems would result in severe disciplinary action.

Your assistant has just reported to you that Ray is in his office drunk. He is creating a disturbance and you are needed immediately. You talk with Ray about leaving and ask him to report to you tomorrow when he is sober. Ray refuses to leave.

As Ray's supervisor how would you handle this situation?

4. *Larry Williams'* accident. One Wednesday afternoon you are busy at your desk writing a progress report on a special project. You hear a commotion in

another office and you check to see what the problem is. Doug tells you that Larry Williams was leaning back in his swivel chair when all of a sudden he toppled over backwards hitting his head on the file cabinet as he went down. Larry appears to be dazed and is bleeding from the head. He complains of a headache and he has a lump on his head.

As Larry's supervisor how would you handle this accident?

## *Reference Notes*

1. "1975 AMS Office Turnover Survey," *Management World,* September 1976, p. 3.
2. *1975 Handbook on Women Workers,* U.S. Department of Labor, Employee Standards Administration, Women's Bureau, Bulletin 297, 1975, p. 60.
3. *1975 Handbook on Women Workers,* pp. 60–63.
4. *Women Workers Today,* U.S. Department of Labor, Employee Standards Administration, Women's Bureau, 1976, p. 7.
5. Paul A. Strassmann, "Managing the Costs of Information," *Harvard Business Review,* September–October 1976, p. 134.
6. Ronald R. Webber, "How Companies Curb Employee Turnover," *Administrative Management,* September 1974, p. 23.
7. Vincent S. Flowers and Charles L. Hughes, "Why Employees Stay," *Harvard Business Review,* July–August 1973, pp. 49–60.
8. *The Myth and the Reality,* U.S. Department of Labor, Employee Standards Administration, Women's Bureau, 1975, p. 1.
9. "Do Women Miss Work More Than Men?" *The Better-Work Supervisor Bulletin,* Clemprint, 1976, p. 4.
10. *1975 Handbook on Women Workers,* p. 1.
11. Ben Ashell, *Controlling Absenteeism* (Chicago: Dartnell Office Administration Service, no date), p. 1.
12. William Clark, "How to Cut Absenteeism and Turnover," *Administrative Management,* March 1971, p. 65.
13. *Survey Indicates Drug/Alcohol Use Is Business Problem* (Chicago: Dartnell Office Administration Service, September 1972), p. 1.
14. It is beyond the scope of this text to treat this topic in detail. People interested in learning more about the symptoms of drug abuse should consult with local social service agencies or write for further information to the National Drug Abuse Education Program, Inc., P.O. Box 12644, Dallas, Texas 75225.
15. Wilbert E. Scheer, *Alcoholism—A Problem at Work and at Home* (Chicago: Dartnell Institute of Business Research, no date), p. 2.

## *Administrative Manager Profile*

Meet Jo Anne Moslemi, supervisor of word processing at American National Bank and Trust Company.

*Background and Experience.* Jo Anne received a B.S. in education from Southern Illinois University at Carbondale in 1972. After joining American National that year, Jo Anne worked as an accounting clerk within the international banking operations department. After one year she transferred to general force (an operations support division), where for three years she received various levels of training in several operations departments (wire transfer, teller operations, safe deposit vault, and so forth). During the last year Jo Anne was promoted to supervisor; in October 1976, she became the supervisor of word processing.

*The Bank.* American National Bank opened for business in 1933 at LaSalle and Washington in Chicago; by 1950, it was one of the nation's 100 largest. A decade later the bank had become the fifth largest in Illinois and established a record growth in Chicago banking. Today it is one of the nation's major banks, offering all of the domestic and international services available in the banking industry.

*Job.* In her present position, Jo Anne is responsible for all word-processing services within American National. There are three word-processing divisions, with three division supervisors, five senior word-processing specialists, and twelve word-processing specialists servicing approximately 190 originators from the commercial banking, trust administration, and retail departments.

Jo Anne's primary responsibilities consist of dealing with the work originators, coordinating work and personnel through the word-processing department, determining short- and long-term objectives for all centers, staying abreast of the word-processing market, and performing all aspects of personnel management for her department. While all of these responsibilities are very important, Jo Anne feels the area of personnel management (in particular, developing people) has the greatest impact on her other responsibilities and is one of the most time-consuming.

Selecting the right people to fill the various positions within word processing is the first step toward personnel development. Each job opening is analyzed carefully by the division supervisor and Jo Anne to determine exactly what skills an individual would require to meet the needs of the division. Placing an individual in the wrong position would hurt not only the individual, but the division and the bank as well. Working closely with the personnel department has been very helpful to Jo Anne in selecting the best candidates. Since she has found that prior experience with word-processing equipment has not been a major factor in the overall success of an individual, a training program within the division has been established. Jo Anne has found that the gradual acquisition of knowledge and skills brings about greater retention and self-confidence in a new employee. However, the training program should be responsive to the trainees, letting them progress at a faster rate if they can. This seems to increase motivation and enthusiasm for moving into the next phase of training and alleviate some of the boredom often associated with training programs.

Communication between the supervisor and the trainee is very important, so Jo Anne often tries to offer encouragement and suggestions to new employees. She emphasizes that timely positive and negative feedback is crucial.

Jo Anne has also found that it is important that employees feel their jobs are challenging and can lead to advancement. Again, she uses the personnel department in assisting her when seeking promotions for qualified candidates from word processing—whether within word processing or into other areas of the bank. Jo Anne feels advancement of an individual or his (her) co-workers is a highly motivating influence for all members of the staff.

As individuals reach higher positions within the word-processing department, Jo Anne assumes more responsibility for their training. One of the most effective methods she uses is to enroll individuals in the bank's seminars and workshops. The interaction in these activities gives subordinates a greater sense of involvement in the organization, an opportunity to meet their peers, and a chance to find that they are not alone in the problems they face.

*Management Philosophy.* In addition to leading subordinates, Jo Anne finds it is just as important for her staff to know she is supportive of their interests and goals. She strives to maintain a leadership style that combines the "team" and "individual" approaches. Subordinates want to be an important part of the organization and yet still be recognized and treated as individuals.

"Maximum output can only be achieved if there is a strong team effort in processing work, solving problems, and improving the present system," says Jo Anne. "Staff meetings are held frequently to discuss problems and ask for recommendations. If a recommendation is implemented, we make sure to recognize the individual or division as soon as possible. I submit monthly reports on the division's performance and hold supervisory meetings at least weekly to discuss whatever is uppermost in the supervisor's mind, in addition to points which I feel are important. I stress the importance of cooperation, communication, and teamwork with everyone in word processing.

"Some of the methods I use to motivate and recognize individuals are to:

1. actively seek suggestions and advice from the staff
2. listen carefully to their problems and suggestions
3. implement improvements and solve problems quickly
4. give personal recognition to an individual for a job well done
5. hold counseling sessions semi-annually to discuss performance and the goals of the individual."

PART
FIVE

# The Use of Effective Management Techniques

The major responsibility of administrative managers is to manage — that is, to get results through management relationships with other people. As you have learned so far in this book, administrative managers apply principles of leadership, motivation, communication, and personnel management to secure the results they need. Administrative managers also have management techniques available to them, and some of these techniques are the subject of Part Five.

Chapter 15 focuses on how to get more done, and the two main topics of discussion there are management by objectives and time management. You will learn how to develop objectives and how to get the employees you manage to develop objectives that will assist them as individuals and that will also help the organization. You will find in this chapter some valuable suggestions on how to use your time effectively, and the three-step procedure of planning, doing, and evaluating is discussed; the importance of priorities is emphasized.

Chapter 16 delves into the critical delegation process. Effective administrative managers are effective delegators. Delegation maximizes the manager's time and provides developmental opportunities for individual employees. Suggestions are given here to help you to delegate more effectively.

The appraisal process is discussed in Chapter 17. The objective of appraisal is to help employees realistically understand their strengths and weaknesses and develop a plan for making needed changes.

Chapter 18 focuses on the key task of decision making. Here you will gain a sure-fire technique for making good decisions. You will also learn about the various types of decisions and the common weaknesses of decision makers.

# 15

# Getting More Done

## MANAGEMENT BY OBJECTIVES (MBO)

If you had only five years to live, what would you like to accomplish? What if this five-year period were shortened to one year, or six months, or one month, or even one week? If you knew you were going to live only for a short period, would you change drastically the things you are now doing and your lifestyle? How do you know that you don't have five years or less to live?

Reflections on these questions soon points up the need to have goals and objectives in your life. Goals and objectives are similar in that they both refer to results to be achieved.

*Objectives* are usually considered to be short-range, specific, definite, and precise. They are usually set on a daily, weekly, or monthly basis. One or more objectives must be completed in order to achieve one goal. Here are some examples of objectives:

Complete monthly progress report by June 20.

Install new dictation system by March 1.

Write draft of supply requisition procedure by October 10.

*Goals*, on the other hand, are long-range, general areas of accomplishment that include much uncertainty. They are usually set for a one-year period or longer. Goals should be stated as specifically as possible. The following are examples of goals:

Reduce total administrative costs by 15 percent before the end of fiscal year 1982.

Develop new automated accounts receivable system by the end of next year.

Design new office layout and furnishings to improve communication and facilitate change. Submit plans for approval by September 1, 19__ .

The basic purpose in setting goals and objectives is to encourage individuals and organizations to decide exactly what results are wanted. In an organizational setting, supervisor and employee must communicate and must reach agreement on what goals are important for the individual. The employee needs to understand how his or her goals relate to organizational goals and objectives.

An analogy will be useful in explaining the importance of agreement on goals. Assume that you have come to a point in your life when you must make a career decision. You have thought about going into medicine, law, accounting, or business management. You have taken all of the general courses required for a bachelor's degree, and now you must begin to specialize—otherwise you will not be able to graduate on schedule. You have taken a basic course or two in each career field and you have enjoyed all of your studies in these fields.

Your parents feel that you should prepare for a career as a medical doctor. They have pointed out to you the material advantages and the satisfaction that you can obtain from helping people to attain good health. Your older brother also advises you to attend medical school and to specialize in an area such as brain surgery. You feel that you could be very happy as a medical doctor.

On the other hand, you have been thinking seriously about becoming an accountant. You enjoy working with figures and feel a great amount of intellectual stimulation from achieving concrete solutions to problems. Even though you enjoyed your general business and exploratory law courses, you have ruled these career fields out of further consideration. Your aptitude and interests tests reveal a bright picture of potential success in either medicine or accounting.

Obviously, these two careers are not compatible, and pursuing one would interfere with attainment of the other. You must come to agreement on what direction you should take. Likewise, organizations must be in agreement on direction for movement of the organization. For example, an office machine manufacturing company must decide whether they will continue to produce conventional automatic typewriter systems or move to terminals linked to minicomputers; organizational objectives must supply this directional focus.

Management by objectives (MBO) is a method of management using objectives as focal points. MBO will help give any organization direction and is *results oriented*—the focus is primarily on "what" rather than "how" (on what is to be attained rather than the means of attaining it). MBO can be defined as a system of determining where an organization is going, deciding how it can get there, and measuring what has been accomplished. Determining where an organization is going implies that decisions will be made to determine what key result areas are most critical. Deciding how an organization can achieve the goals and objectives means that action plans must be developed. Measuring what has been done suggests that the goals and objectives must be quantified or stated in a manner that allows counting or measuring the degree of their completion.

As important as it is to set specific, measurable goals and objectives, the real value of MBO lies in the ability of the manager to *involve the individual in the process of setting goals.* If MBO is in fact only a formalized reporting system in which individuals are compelled to achieve objectives and goals set by other people, the real power of the system will not be realized. When individuals participate in making their own decisions about goals and objectives, they are committed to achieving results; individual decision making and achievement are highly motivating.

To further clarify what MBO is, let's turn to an example of how it can be used in an office. In Lennis Knudsen's office, daily operations seemed to be disorganized and hectic. The office workers seemed to be confused and lacked direction. Lennis spent most of his time "putting out fires"—rarely did he spend time in training and advanced planning. Then Lennis decided to go to a seminar on management by objectives and results. Afterwards, with the help of another manager, Georgia Bettger, Lennis implemented an MBO program in his office and found surprising results. It took much hard work, soul searching, and guidance from Georgia, but the people in Lennis's office have become involved and excited about MBO. They have a sense of direction; they know what they are doing because they are involved in deciding what they will do and how they will do it. They look forward to performance checks with Lennis because they enjoy seeing their accomplishments. Lennis is available to help with problems, but most of his time now is spent in developing future plans.

## MBO in Operation

***General Procedure for Implementing MBO.*** Eight steps necessary for implementing an MBO program in an organization are shown in the flowchart in Figure 15-1. We explain these steps and give an example for each of them in the following list.

*Step 1. Determine the organizational level on which MBO will be implemented.* Either one department, one section, or the entire organization will be involved. To be most effective, MBO should have *top management support;* however, a department manager can install the program in his or her own department without this support.

*Example:* Lucy O'Conner, an enterprising administrative manager with Globe Insurance Co., learned about MBO in a special company course presented by Globe's training department. Many Globe managers were in attendance at these sessions. The president and executive vice-president attended the first session and spoke about the importance of MBO. Because of other involvements, they were unable to attend further sessions. Since the end of the training program six months ago, nothing has been done in the company on MBO. Lucy decides that the program has great merit and should be implemented in her department. She feels that if the program is successful in her department, other departments may decide to adopt the program.

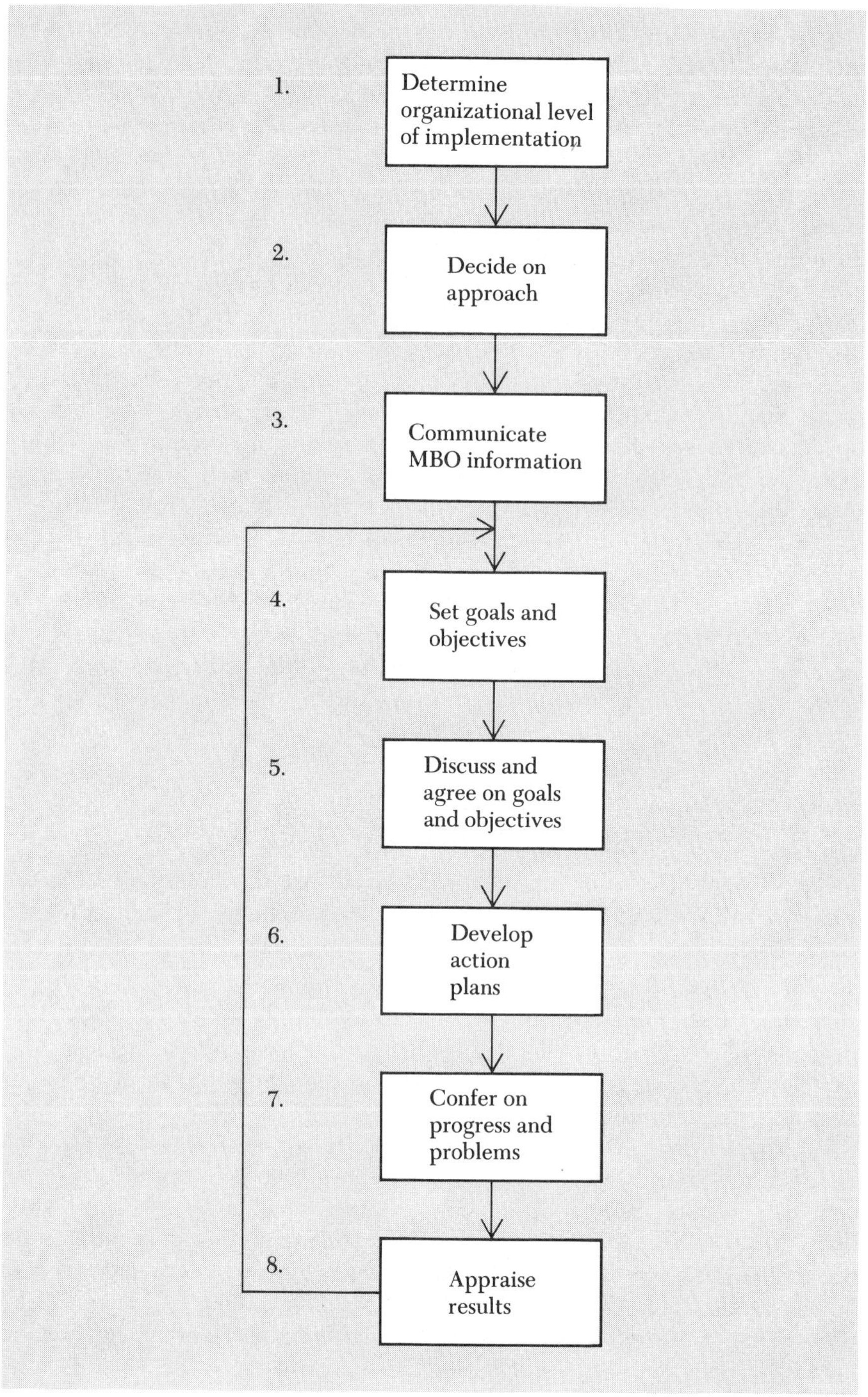


*Figure 15-1.* MBO System Flowchart

*Step 2. Decide on the approach that will be used.* The two basic approaches are *top-down* and *bottom-up*. In the top-down approach, goals and objectives for the entire organization are set by top management and communicated through middle management to the rest of the organization. At each of the lower levels within the organization, objectives are set to support and carry out objectives handed down from the top. Figure 15-2(a) illustrates this process by means of an organization chart for Globe Insurance.

Using the bottom-up approach reverses the direction of this process, as shown in Figure 15-2(b). Objectives are the cumulative result of individual goals and objectives. Company goals are the sum total of department goals.

*Example:* Lucy considered the merits of the two approaches. The top-down approach has the advantages of lending weight to the program from her level on down and of emphasizing objectives that are particularly important for the department. On the other hand, the bottom-up approach tends to have better motivational effect because people are enthusiastic about working toward goals and objectives that they originate themselves.

Lucy decides that the bottom-up approach is best for her particular department and will complement her consulting style of leadership. Lucy's Theory *Y* assumptions also create a good climate for this approach.

*Step 3. Communicate essential MBO information to all involved.* Meetings and training sessions are held to communicate and educate the staff. All personnel who will be involved in the program will need to know what MBO is, how it operates, and what is expected of them. If a top-down approach is being used, organizational and departmental goals and objectives will be presented.

*Example:* After thoroughly preparing herself, Lucy calls a meeting of all members of the administrative management department to explain what MBO is, why she thinks it is important, and how the program will operate within the department. Lucy explains that her four supervisors will be trained in MBO by the training department. The supervisors will be expected to train their employees in the details of MBO. The meeting is opened to questions and discussion; during the session, several employees seem very enthusiastic about the program, but two people seem to be quite negative. The two say they have a difficult time in writing goals, and they are concerned about the added paperwork. Lucy acknowledges their comments and summarizes the benefits. She says she feels that when people try the program they will feel that any drawbacks are outweighed by the advantages. The two people who were opposed to the program finally agree to try it out.

*Step 4. Have individuals set goals and objectives.* This step is the heart of the program. Guidelines presented later in this chapter should be followed in developing these goals and objectives. Supervisors should write goals and objectives for themselves as well as for their employees.

*Example:* All those in Lucy's department are requested to think carefully about their own responsibilities and set three to five objectives and one or two

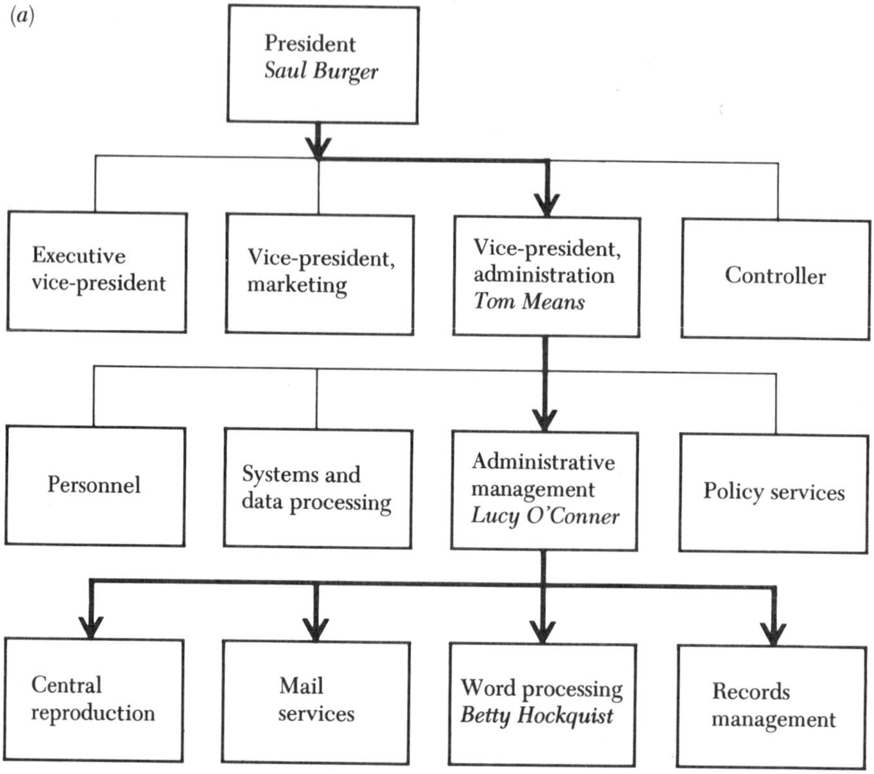


*Figure 15-2.* Globe Insurance Co. Organization Charts (Partial) *(a)* Emphasizes the administrative channel and illustrates the top-down approach to MBO. *(b)* Emphasizes the word-processing channel and illustrates the bottom-up approach to MBO.

long-term goals. They are asked to think about how their job relates to the department and to the company. Then they are asked to be prepared to present suggestions about desirable future directions for departmental goals and objectives. To begin with, Lucy sets an objective of organizing all form letters and standard paragraphs used by the department into a looseleaf binder with an index.

*Step 5. Discuss and come to agreement on goals and objectives.* This step is the key to the success of the program. Supervisor and employee sit down together and frankly discuss what each sees that the employee should be doing. The supervisor shares his or her thinking with the employee about where the organization is heading and how the employee should be involved.

(b)

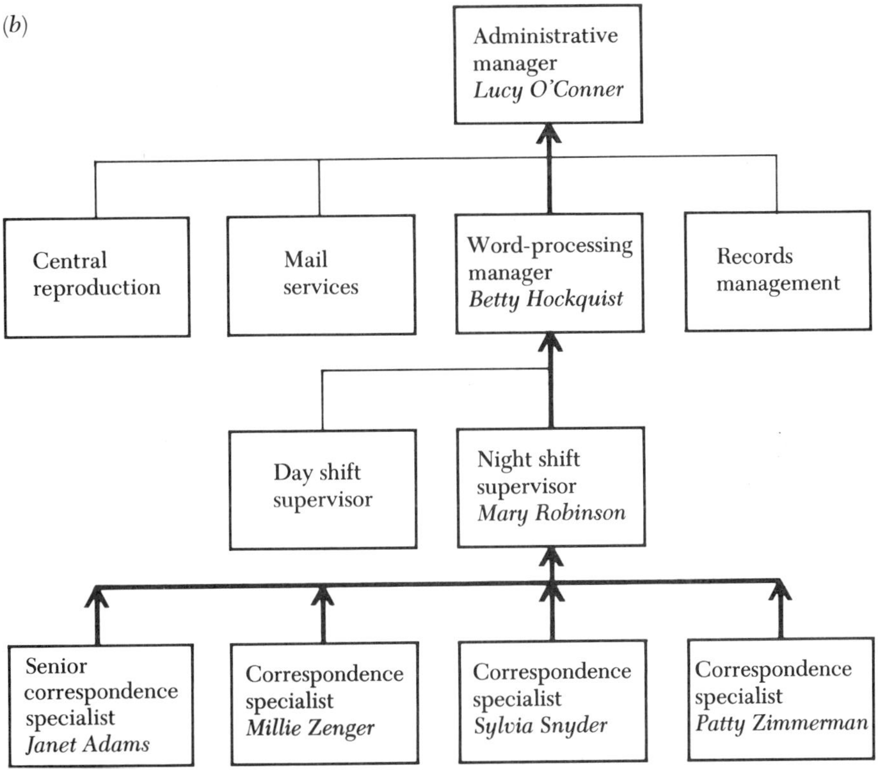


*Figure 15-2, continued*

Likewise, the employee's thoughts are influential in molding direction for the department.

*Example:* In several cases, this is the first time that this type of dialogue has ever occurred in Lucy's department. In about one-fourth of the goals and objectives set by employees, supervisors and employees have entirely different concepts about what is important for the employees to do. This is a two-way communication opportunity. To a larger extent, mutual understanding starts to grow out of these goal-setting sessions.

Mary Robinson, a supervisor, is extremely pleased with Patty's goal as a correspondent to organize the form letters and paragraphs—one of the department objectives that will benefit everyone in word processing.

In working with Sylvia and Millie, Mary had to help them see the need for changing one of their goals. Sylvia wanted to test a new low-cost brand of mag cards (word-processing storage medium) in order to reduce costs. Mary explained to Sylvia that Betty Hockquist had mentioned the probability that new word-processing machines with a "floppy disk" storage medium to replace the mag card machines will be purchased.

Millie stated that for one of her objectives she wants to increase her production to 650 lines per day on new dictated material. This number seems low since Millie is currently averaging 600 lines per day and at times goes as high as 850 lines per day without much difficulty. Mary and Millie together decide that 700 lines per day is a realistic objective.

In working with Betty, Lucy finds that Betty tends to impose her objectives on her supervisors. Betty uses MBO as a method of reporting work accomplished. She discourages employees from setting their own objectives. Lucy reviews with Betty how the objectives should be set and demonstrates how the process should go by allowing Betty to set her own objectives.

*Step 6. Develop action plans.* Once agreement is achieved on end results to be obtained, employees should have the freedom to develop action plans to achieve the results. They should be able to work out their own methods. Later in this chapter, guidelines are suggested for preparing action plans.

*Example:* Personnel in Lucy's department accepts the challenge of becoming responsible for results and for working out their own methods. Most are enthusiastic; however, two people are defensive and unable to break from the traditional authoritative system. They request transfers. Patty Zimmerman develops a plan on her project which makes it easy for her to know exactly what she has to do.

*Step 7. Confer on progress and problems.* Supervisors and managers are resource persons to their personnel. Employees should seek help from their supervisors when needed. Supervisors should be available and should be willing and able to provide help as needed. Problems should be handled as they develop, not when it is too late to take action.

*Example:* The supervisors provide resources such as time, supplies, and equipment to accomplish goals the employees set. Patty Zimmerman picks out the supplies she needs and Mary Robinson submits the purchase request. Mary encourages Patty and compliments her on the progress. When Patty runs into some problems in setting up the index, Mary gives some suggestions that prove helpful.

*Step 8. Use goals and objectives as the basis for appraisal.* Appraisal sessions are conducted at least annually and in some cases more frequently. Rather than emphasize personality factors, the focus of the interview is on accomplishment of results. Goals are evaluated in terms of economic and other conditions encountered during the performance review period. (See Chapter 17 for further information on the appraisal process.)

*Example:* When Lucy holds an appraisal interview with Betty Heckquist and the other managers, the focus is on results achieved in the word-processing center. The new form letter system developed by Patty Zimmerman, the center's progress in achieving a four-hour turnaround time, and progress in reducing costs are three goals that are discussed. Betty and each of the employees express a sense of achievement with regard to completed goals. They also feel a sense of responsibility for goals and objectives not yet completed. They are accountable for achieving their own goals. In a sense, they are independent agents who move on their own. Each person has built-in feedback about his or her own progress. Problems that have been encountered are discussed, and Betty and Lucy both discuss some possible solutions. Also, decisions about future goals and objectives, training, development, and resource allocation are made.

***Benefits and Pitfalls of MBO.*** This remark, once displayed on a real estate office billboard, suggests the benefits of MBO: "Most people spend half their time wishing for things they could have if they didn't spend half of their time wishing for things." MBO puts an end to wishing and starts a person or an organization on the road to achievement.

MBO provides specific benefits:

1. Individuals and their supervisor meet to discuss *mutual expectations*. Individuals learn of the organizational goals, and their supervisor learns of the subordinates' personal objectives.
2. *Performance criteria* are stated specifically.
3. Evaluation is based on results rather than personality or some other intangible factor.
4. Individuals become *self-motivated* and determined to achieve their goals and objectives.
5. Not only does the organization function more effectively through these programs but the employee also benefits through individual development.

All of the benefits listed were evident in the example of the MBO program implemented in Lucy O'Conner's administrative management department at Globe Insurance Co.

Some of the potential pitfalls of MBO:

1. Some managers may give lip service to the system and not really involve themselves.
2. Resistance to change may be evident.
3. Managers may think that they are too busy to implement the system.
4. Individual objectives may not be in line with organizational goals.
5. Expectations for MBO may be too high.
6. Immediate benefits may not be forthcoming.
7. Employees may water down their goals to make sure the goal can be attained.

8. Managers may think of MBO primarily as a reporting system and not allow participation of employees.
9. Interest in MBO may waiver if appropriate positive reinforcement is not given for the goals achieved.

Notice that several of these pitfalls were evident at Globe Insurance. The president and vice-president were too busy to get involved with MBO, but they did give it lip service. You saw resistance to change on the part of the two employees who finally asked for transfers. Also, you saw some potential pitfalls averted as Mary worked with Sylvia and Millie in setting realistic goals in line with departmental objectives.

### Guidelines for MBO

***Individual Goal-Setting Guidelines.*** Here are some suggestions for setting goals:

*Think carefully about your goals.* Set those that really matter. Individual goals should be related to the goals of the organization and should be stimulating to you as an individual. Consult your supervisor and carefully consider his or her expectations and priorities. Your goals should be balanced; don't emphasize one or two areas to the exclusion of other important areas. Your goals should be at the *optimum level of difficulty.* They should be sufficiently difficult so that you will need to stretch to reach them, yet not so difficult that you constantly fail and become frustrated. They should be realistic, but not so easy that they offer no challenge.

*State your goals in writing.* Be specific. Use action verbs such as "develop," "install," "write," "implement"; follow with a statement of results, and include your target date. Keep your eye on the end, not the means; reserve discussion of methods for your action plan. An example of an effective individual goal is "Attain C.A.M. designation before June 12." The person using or reading this goal knows exactly what has to be done, when it must be completed, and when the task has been accomplished.

*Develop an action plan to accomplish your goals.* Will Rogers once said, "Even if you are on the right track, you'll get run over if you just sit there." Some people spend all of their time planning and never get around to doing. An action plan will help you get started because you will know exactly what you have to do to accomplish your goal. Think in detail about all necessary steps. Identify problems that might prevent your attainment of the goal; specify what must be done to overcome these problems. For example, what training do you need? What outside help is necessary? What resources are required? Consider emergencies and forecast all probable events; develop alternate plans. Seek the help of your supervisor if needed. The following action plan is an example of applying MBO principles to selecting an office copying machine:

1. Read the June issue of *Administrative Management* magazine to determine what copy machines are available and their key features; accomplish by October 1.
2. Select three makes and models of copy machines that appear to be most suitable; accomplish by October 8.
3. Interview salespeople from appropriate companies to gather further information and determine names and addresses of users of machines; accomplish by October 15.
4. Interview three users of each item of equipment and select the most promising make and model; accomplish by October 25.
5. Make an agreement with a supplier to test equipment for three months, after which a final decision will be made; accomplish by October 31.
6. Make a final decision or retest other equipment; accomplish by February 1.

*Imagine the goal being accomplished.* Picture the goal in as much detail as possible. This step will help you actually accomplish your goal *(self-fulfilling prophecy).*

***Overall Program Guidelines.*** Guidelines related to the overall MBO program are as follows:

*MBO should have a Theory* Y *setting* (flexible and open to discussion) rather than a Theory *X* setting (fixed and closed) to be effective. Managers should be able to place trust in the people reporting to them. Lucy O'Conner from the Globe Insurance Co., for example, held Theory *Y* assumptions and created a good climate for MBO.

*Goals should be set by individual employees* rather than be imposed on them from above. Goals should be "people centered"; they should focus on talents, aspirations, and values of employees as well as the needs of the organization. For instance, Lucy tried to follow this guideline by telling and showing her supervisors how to involve their people in the goal-setting process.

*Some goals should be developed on a team basis* whenever possible. Individual employees would be expected to cooperate in achieving group goals. In a situation such as a word-processing center, a cooperative team effort is essential in setting many goals. For example, in working toward a reduced turnaround time, all team members would need to cooperate.

*Objectives for management.* R. Alec MacKenzie and Glenn H. Varney suggest that MBO be tied into the management process by defining the management functions in terms of objectives:

*Plan* Predetermine a course of action to achieve intended objectives.

*Organize* Arrange and relate work for effective accomplishment of objectives.

*Staff* Select competent people for positions in the organization in order to achieve objectives.

*Direct* Bring about purposeful action toward desired objectives.

*Control* Ensure progress toward objectives according to plan.

*Make decisions* Arrive at conclusions and judgments necessary to accomplish objectives.

*Communicate* Ensure understanding of information relating to objectives, plan assignments, provide decisions and feedback.

Now that MBO has been examined, let's turn to the section on time management in which methods of becoming more effective in the use of time will be discussed.

## TIME MANAGEMENT

Perhaps the single most important asset an administrative manager can possess is skill in managing time. If the manager can effectively control his or her time, that person will be able to devote balanced attention to interpersonal relations and production.

Most people don't have enough time and money. Just as you must decide what items are more important than others for you to buy, so must you decide on what activities should occupy your time. Many of us seem to spend much of our time doing things that are not important. Montaigne said, "The things that matter most should not be at the mercy of the things that matter least."

A lifetime chart can help to illustrate the significance of time planning. This chart graphically portrays past, present, and expected future life. As you can see in Figure 15-3, a person at age 25 has already lived a major portion of his or her life. The remaining time available in life must be used wisely in order to accomplish everything that he or she would like to do.

Most managers can recognize the importance of managing their time well, but most managers find themselves dealing in trivia during a large part of their office time. Becky Schwartz, an administrative manager for Cassell's Department Store, finds herself continually performing insignificant activities such as making copies on the copy machine, finding letters in the file, and answering trivial questions. She can't ever seem to get around to doing important things such as planning a new management information system or studying the feasibility of adopting new word-processing equipment. At the end of a day, she wonders where the time has gone and why she hasn't been able to accomplish something important. People literally waste their lives away. How can you accomplish more in the office or with your life in general so that you truly make a contribution in both areas?

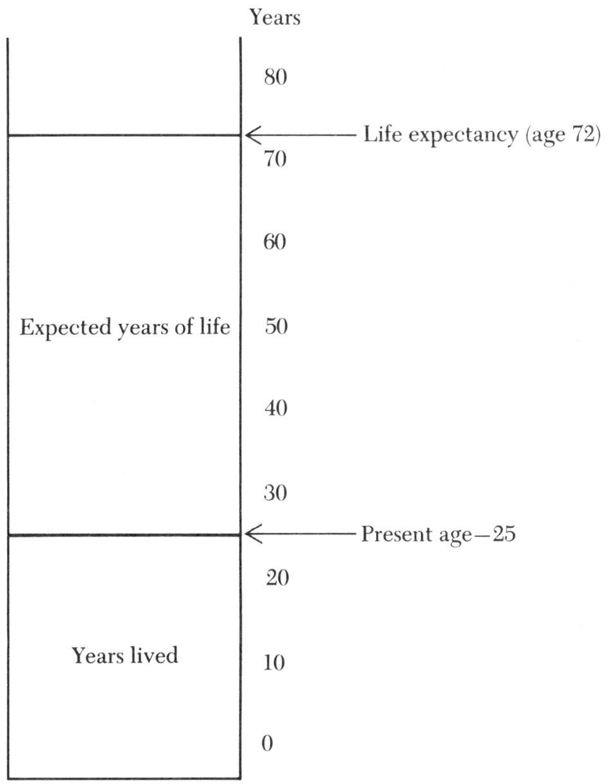


*Figure 15-3.* The Human Lifespan

A simple three-step procedure can help you to be effective in managing your time:

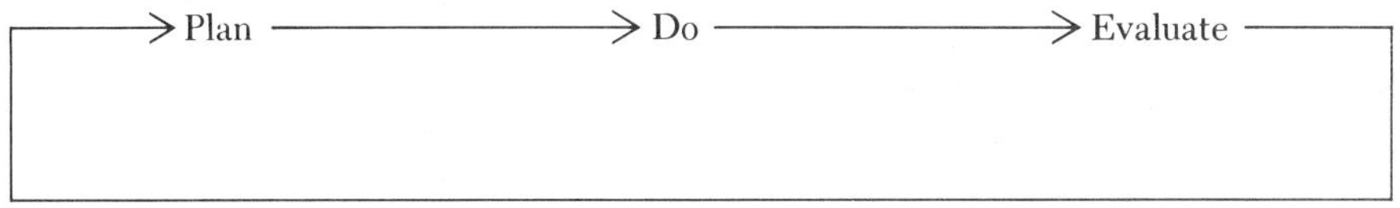


## Planning Time Usage

The starting point in any work operation should be planning. This statement sounds obvious, but how many times have you found yourself jumping into your activity without prior planning?

The planning period is a time when you *think* about the future, a time to set the goals and objectives talked about previously. This period is a good time to be creative and innovative in developing your strategy to achieve your goals. The planning period is the time when you develop *commitment* to your work, and it is a period of *meditation*—a time to think deeply about what is most important to you and what action you should take to achieve results. The time you spend in planning is among the most important times of your life.

To illustrate how this planning process should operate, consider again the case of Lucy O'Conner at Globe Insurance. Lucy decides that she just has to take some time to do some creative planning. She has been extremely busy lately, but she doesn't seem to be getting some important things done. While she feels really good about the way the MBO program has been operating, she has not had time—or has not *taken* time—to even think about some projects that are important to her and to the department. Lucy sets a Tuesday afternoon aside to plan. As a result of her thinking, she isolates the following three projects for further work: (1) preparing a talk on "the office of the future" for possible presentation at an AMS meeting, (2) preparing to take the C.A.M. examinations, and (3) planning a feasibility study on the use of a minicomputer in the office. She decides that during the coming year she will spend a block of four hours each week on these projects.

***Priorities.*** During the planning period, you should think about all of the things that you need to or could do. Assign priorities to each item by giving it a letter—A, B, or C—according to its importance. A—extreme importance to you; B—medium importance to you; C—little importance to you; will have minor impact on your life.

In assigning priorities, take time to determine why certain things are considered A and B category items. Are these things that *really* matter; are they really important to *you*? Or, is someone else imposing insignificant work on you? If your boss is the one that is the source of your problem, you may be hard pressed to make necessary changes. You may need to think through your position and determine if you are properly placed. Ideally your goals and those of your boss should be compatible. If they are not, you may need to talk it over and come to some agreement or even make a change in employment.

Priority activities, category A, have an impact on your life, either singly or when considered with other A items. Here are some reasons why Lucy assigned top priority ratings to her three projects:

| *Items* | *Reasons Why Important* |
|---|---|
| Prepare talk on office of the future for AMS meeting | Good learning experience<br>Chance to do research<br>Opportunity to develop speaking ability |
| Prepare to take C.A.M. exam | Professional development opportunity<br>Good learning experience<br>Chance to interact with other administrative managers<br>Professional recognition |

| | |
|---|---|
| Plan feasibility study on minicomputer | Potential cost savings<br>Increased capability to process office work<br>Potential man-hour savings |

All of these items have a potentially high value to Lucy, yet they are the kinds of activities that she could avoid if she overlooks their importance.

In addition to importance, a second consideration is time pressure. All activities can be classified as follows: (1) should be done immediately, (2) should be done as soon as possible, and (3) can be done when time permits. Assign a number or a letter to each of these categories and classify your activities according to time pressure. With this system, you consider both importance and time pressure as factors in determining priority. For example, an A1 item such as investigating the minicomputer is important and is pressing because Lucy's office costs are high and she needs to increase productivity. An A3 item is important, but delaying its completion will not be harmful.

An example of A3 item is the research and talk on the office of the future; this work is important, but the time element is not particularly critical. Lucy will have to be careful with an item such as this one, because the natural tendency is to delay this type of project and never get it accomplished.

C1 items are usually numerous. They are not important to you, but they clamor for your attention. For example, the safety office needs your report immediately or the personnel department needs a signature on some personnel action forms. All C items should be examined carefully; perhaps the best answer is to simply refuse to do them; perhaps you can delegate them. As a last resort, if they are pressing and you have no way of avoiding them, complete them as soon as possible and concentrate your attention on A items. Avoid the unimportant and insignificant like the plague.

***Time Planning System.*** Develop your own planning system that best meets your needs. Calendars and lists are usually essential parts of any system. A recommended system includes both. A small notebook with the following items can be used:

1. One page with long-range goals that are to be completed during the next five to ten years.
2. One page with objectives for the current year.
3. Twelve pages for things to be accomplished each month during the coming year.
4. One page for items to be done during current week. This page is referred to frequently.
5. Two pages for each day as shown in Figure 15-4. One page is marked off by time periods for appointments and scheduled events and one page is for writing action steps to be taken with priorities and notes; this is a working section that is referred to throughout the day.

6. Twelve double pages for monthly calendars of the type shown in Figure 15-5 where scheduled events are recorded.

This system provides a place to record all information that you need in managing your time.

Some people prefer a more simple system than the one described here. They simply have a 3 × 5 card in a pocket or purse on which they write what must be done that day. Whatever your system, choose one that is effective for you. Be sure that it is flexible enough to meet your needs.

***Planning Improvement.*** Reviewing your evaluation of previous plans and actions is the last phase of planning that requires discussion. The evaluation process tells how effective you were in accomplishing your plan. Lack of accomplishment or unforeseen circumstances create a need for more planning. You adjust old plans and make new plans in light of what has happened during

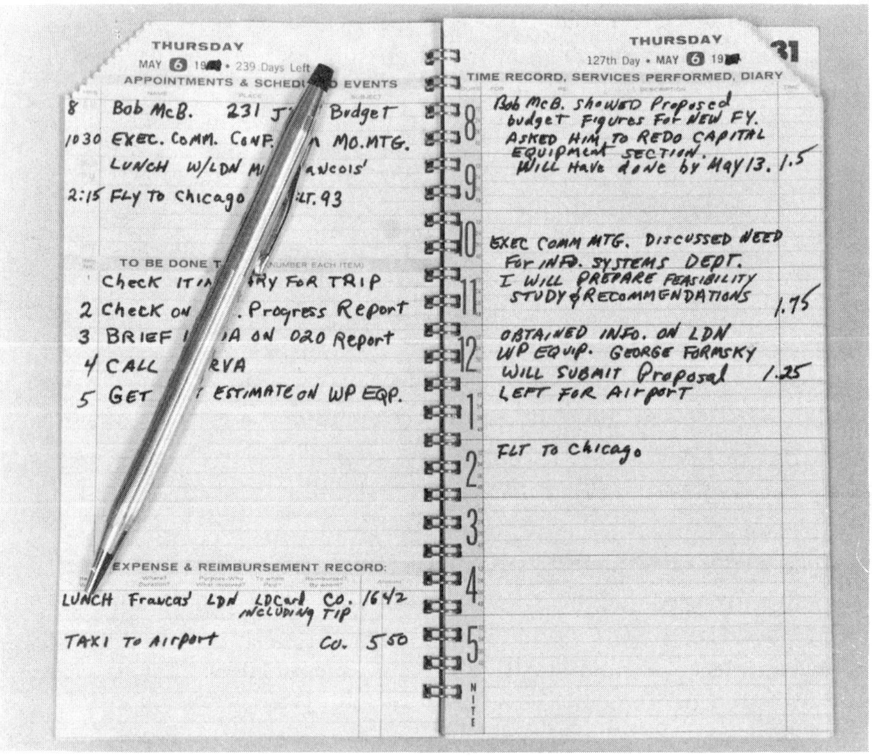


*Figure 15-4.* A Daily Time-Planning Calendar

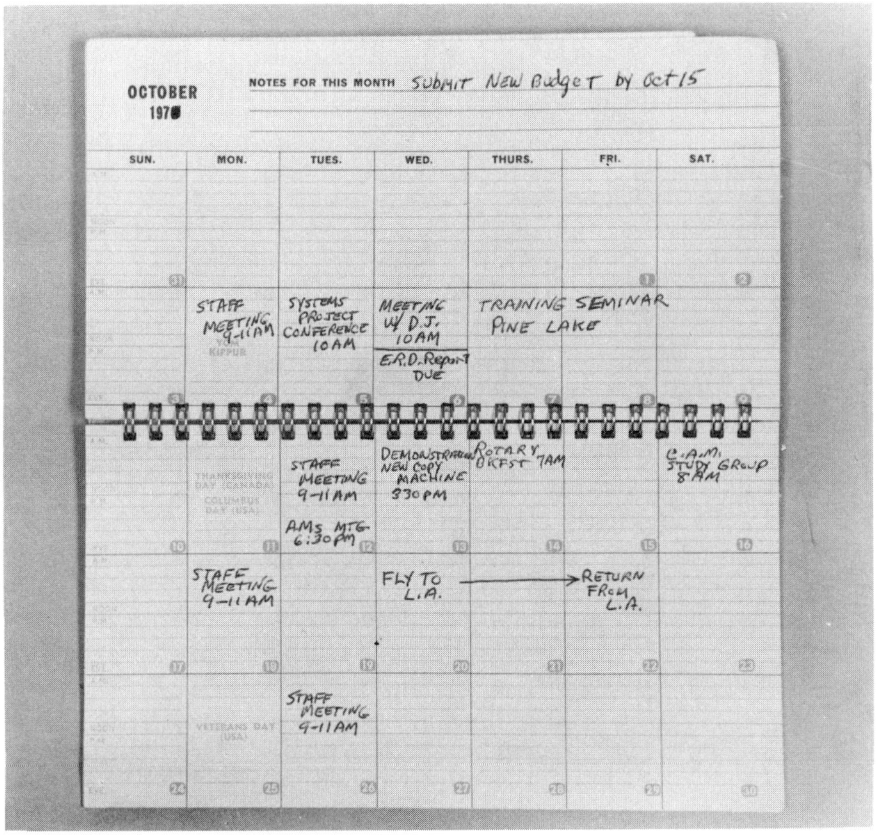


*Figure 15-5.* A Monthly Time-Planning Calendar

the *doing* phase of operations. (This concept will be discussed in greater detail in the next section on evaluating.)

***Planning Benefits.*** As you can well imagine, all of this planning takes much time, but it is a high priority stage that can help to improve your effectiveness. Most people spend their time like this:

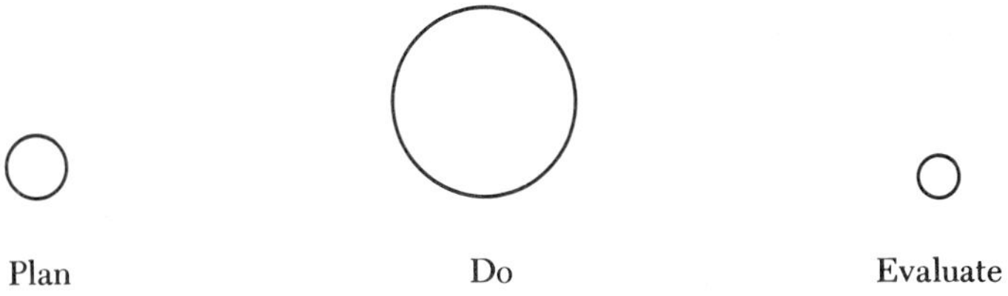

They should spend their time like this:

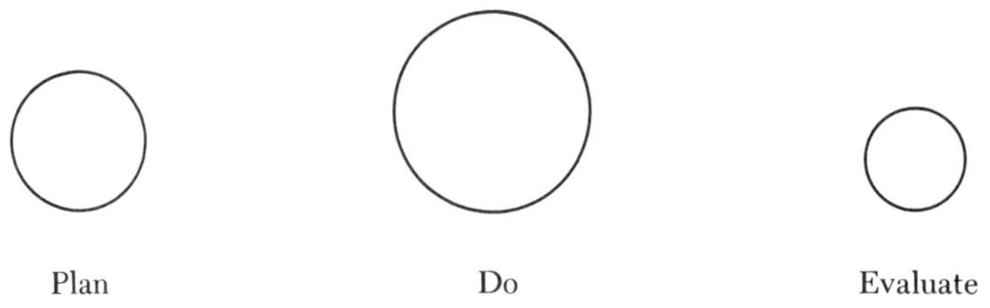


Spending adequate time on planning and evaluating as well as doing should help to insure adequate results.

## Using Time Wisely

The second phase of effective time management is *doing* or using time wisely. We emphasized the importance of planning, but the action or doing phase can't be neglected either. Some people get so involved in planning that they never do get around to putting their plans into action. Doing is oriented to the present, the time that is always with you, the time that you need to make the most of because it is so fleeting.

***Hard Work.*** In an attempt to emphasize the need for thoughtful planning, many management books and articles leave the mistaken impression that the manager is not a hard worker. The effective manager does attempt to avoid much of the routine operational work. Still, he or she must spend much time on such things as checking reports, writing letters and memos, and giving instructions to secretaries and assistants. Good hard work is essential for success in management as in any occupation; but still, the emphasis must be on results. You are really not interested in how hard a person works but rather in his or her results.

***Priorities.*** In the doing phase, you work on your list of activities one by one in order of priority. Generally, you work on A items before B items and B items before C items. Even if you don't get done, you are always doing the most important things. Lucy found that by paying attention to priorities she could get more of the important projects done. She enjoys scratching items off her list as she completes them.

***Time Savers.*** In the doing phase, you should try to find as many ways as possible to improve your effectiveness. Here are a few suggestions to help you prevent waste of time:

*Use the principle of controlled availability.* In other words, limit the numbers of people who visit with you in your office or talk with you over the phone by asking your secretary to screen visitors and phone calls. You will need to be available to some people at any time. For example, your boss and your spouse are privileged individuals with regard to your time. Other people will have limited access to you. Your subordinates, for example, may need to see you frequently, but not too frequently. If you are too freely available, they will not learn to move on their own. You may want to see salesmen only on a limited basis. Some people who only waste your time should be screened out completely. Following this principle will reduce distractions but may hamper communication and thereby reduce effectiveness. One solution to this problem is to set aside periods of time for receiving visitors, returning phone calls, and planning or engaging in other activities that require concentration.

*Let your secretary and assistant help save your time.* In addition to screening telephone calls and visitors, your secretary or assistant can help you terminate interviews by giving you a reminder of other pressing demands on your time or appointments. Your secretary can screen your mail, prepare answers to routine correspondence, gather needed information, and generally help you to be more effective. Your assistant can aid you by doing many routine things that you would have to do otherwise. Take time to teach your people how to handle these tasks properly.

*Delegate responsibilities to those who report to you.* (See Chapter 16 for a detailed discussion on delegation.)

*Limit the time you are involved in meetings.* Plan your meetings carefully and develop an *agenda.* Show the time periods to be allotted for each topic. Limit the attendance at meetings to only those people who need to be there and who can make a contribution. Designate priorities. Discuss most important items first and allow the most time for them.

*Block out adequate periods of time to work on major tasks.* Keep these times free of interruptions. Concentrate specifically on that item being considered.

*Learn to use dictation equipment and other labor-saving devices to your own advantage.* Portable, battery-powered dictation units allow you to dictate at any time or place. Use your machine to capture ideas, gather information, and give instructions. Listen to cassette recordings of management development topics while driving or doing other things to inform you and aid you in your management development program.

*Consider innovative approaches to reducing time wasting.* An article in *U.S. News & World Report* reported on some approaches used by managers.[2] One executive cut the temperature in his office by five degrees, one removed all of the extra chairs, another hung up in midconversation and pretended that the phone line was malfunctioning. Still another suggested that when drop-in visitors ask if you have time to talk to them, say "no." Another manager recommended holding stand-up meetings that start at odd times such as 10:37 A.M. and end at 11:48 A.M. Some of these measures are pretty drastic and even a shade dishonest. You are likely to feel uncomfortable with some of these ideas, but they do illustrate the possibilities of things you can do to help control the drastic waste of time most of us experience. Develop your own ideas for conserving time by using your imagination.

On the other hand, remember, as a manager, your major job is to get work accomplished through other people. If you are too effective in cutting other people out of your life, you may actually reduce your effectiveness.

### Evaluating Time Usage

After the doing phase, comes the time to evaluate. How effective have you been implementing your plans? Are you moving on target? Have you wasted too much time? Are you getting good results? The evaluation phase is a period in which you pause to look back and see how well you have done. You can profit from your experience and use it to improve the future. Don't spend too much time looking at the past, however, because you can do nothing to change it.

***Time Analysis.*** One profitable exercise is to analyze your time. Record by major activity the amount of time you spend during a one- or two-week period. Break the time down by categories. Major goals and objectives, functions, or some combination thereof are good possibilities for these categories. Analyze your time record to determine how much time you are spending on key objectives and how much time is being wasted.

Figure 15-6 is a time analysis form prepared by Lucy O'Conner. Activities are classified by priority (A, B, and C) and the form shows the amount of time and percentage of time for each priority. Note that Lucy spent 41 percent of her work week on A priority activities, 11 percent on B activities, and 48 percent on C priority items. Actually, this is a good proportion of time spent on high priority items. The analysis should be run for another week or two to see if this week is typical. This type of analysis reveals the activities on which the person's time is being spent and how the time is divided by priorities. The analysis provides very valuable information to use as a base for making improvements in time usage. Lucy used this analysis process and found ways of plugging the gaps and getting better control of her time so that she could be more effective.

## *Summary*

Both individuals and organizations need objectives and goals. Goals are long-term, general areas of accomplishment, while objectives are short-term, specific statements that lead toward goals. MBO is a management technique that formalizes this objective- and goal-setting procedure in an organization. MBO focuses on results, output, and the end to be achieved. Effective MBO programs involve all levels of the organization. Individuals gain

Time Analysis by Day and Priority

Week of November 14

Name Lucy O'Conner

| | Activities by priority | Monday | Tuesday | Wednesday | Thursday | Friday | Saturday | Sunday | Total |
|---|---|---|---|---|---|---|---|---|---|
| A | Staff meetings | 1.0 | | | | 1.0 | | | 2 |
| | Prepare annual report | 1.0 | 3.25 | 4.50 | 3.0 | 2.25 | 2.0 | | 16 |
| | Time spent and percentage | 2.0<br>25% | 3.25<br>38% | 4.50<br>53% | 3.0<br>37.5% | 3.25<br>38% | 2.0<br>100% | | 18<br>41% |
| B | Executive committee meeting | | | 2.50 | | | | | 2.5 |
| | Computer feasibility study | 2.0 | | | | | | | 2.0 |
| | Time spent and percentage | 2.0<br>25% | | 2.50<br>29% | | | | | 4.5<br>11% |
| C | Meeting with salespeople | | 1.0 | | | .75 | | | 1.75 |
| | United Fund Drive | 2.0 | | | 2.0 | | | | 4.0 |
| | Visitors | | | 1.0 | | | | | 1.0 |
| | School tour | | 3.0 | | | | | | 3.0 |
| | Company planning\|meeting | | | | 2.0 | | | | 2.0 |
| | Breaks | .50 | .75 | .50 | .25 | | | | 2.0 |
| | Routine correspondence | 1.50 | .50 | | .75 | 3.0 | | | 5.75 |
| | Prepare inventory report | | | | | 1.50 | | | 1.5 |
| | Time spent and percentage | 4.0<br>50% | 5.25<br>62% | 1.5<br>18% | 5.0<br>62.5% | 5.25<br>62% | | | 21.0<br>48% |
| | Total time and percentage | 8.0<br>100% | 8.5<br>100% | 8.5<br>100% | 8.0<br>100% | 8.5<br>100% | 2.0<br>100% | | 43.5<br>100% |

*Figure 15-6.* A Weekly Time Analysis Chart, Showing the Number of Hours or Minutes Spent Each Day for A, B, and C Types of Activities

an understanding of what is expected of them, where they are headed, and how they relate to the rest of the organization. Individuals and the organization both benefit from an effective MBO program. Potential pitfalls can be avoided by following the guidelines presented in this chapter.

Goals and objectives are the basis for developing action plans and appraising performance. Once MBO is implemented and people develop proper habits, MBO will become an organizational life style. Individuals will think in terms of results, and the organization will function more effectively because people in the organization will be more effective and more highly motivated by their recognized accomplishments.

Time is an important resource and should be used for accomplishing the most important things in life—the things that really matter. A three-step procedure that involves planning, doing, and evaluating can help people to use their time wisely. Planning is the key step in this cycle and provides a time for thinking through what people are going to do and for assigning priorities. Priorities help to get the most important things done first. Every person needs to develop a planning system that works effectively for him or her, and one system is suggested in the chapter. Spending time planning, doing, and evaluating brings a good payoff in results.

The doing phase involves following plans, working hard, and following priorities. Many time-saving ideas can be applied to improve effectiveness. Finally, evaluating is a phase that allows a person to look back to see how well he or she has done. Every person should analyze his or her own time to develop ways to improve.

## *Review and Discussion Questions*

1. In your own words, describe the management by objectives program.
2. How does an *objective* differ from a *goal*?
3. How can individuals be involved in setting their own goals and still have these goals tied in with organizational objectives?
4. Define the role of the supervisor in an MBO program.
5. What benefits do you see coming from MBO?
6. What are some of the potential dangers or pitfalls you might expect to encounter when implementing an MBO program?
7. What criteria do you suggest using to determine the effectiveness of your goals?
8. Why should goals be written out rather than just remembered? Why is it important to make your goals specific?
9. How does an action plan relate to goals and to objectives?
10. Why would imagining your goals being accomplished be an important practice?

11. What guidelines would you recommend following as an administrative manager to implement MBO into your organization?
12. What relationship do you see between objectives and management functions?
13. What are some of the problems that administrative managers face with regard to time management and getting things done?
14. Why is the planning phase of time management important?
15. How can the use of priorities be of value to an administrative manager in improving effectiveness?
16. What time planning systems are currently available?
17. Discuss steps that administrative managers could take that would help them to be more effective in the doing phase of their daily activities.
18. Explain how time analysis can be used to improve the use of time. Do you feel that time spent keeping track of time usage and analyzing how it was used is worthwhile?

## *Application Exercises*

1. Interview several administrative managers or other managers to determine to what extent they are using MBO. Find out how effective it has been for them and what problems they have encountered.
2. Using the *Business Periodicals Index*, find at least one article on MBO and read it. In small groups in class, discuss MBO from the viewpoints of the authors of the articles that your group members read.
3. Invite someone who has used MBO in his or her organization to speak to your class about it.
4. Implement an MBO program into your own life. Decide where you want to be ten years from now, and then develop short-range objectives and an action plan to allow you to achieve your long-range goals. Get going on your program and continually check your results to be certain that you are moving on target.
5. Observe your instructors, classmates, and work supervisor to see how they use their time. Note those who are most effective and those who are least effective in the use of time. Try to identify the differences.
6. Interview managers and other people whom you think are particularly effective in managing their time. Ask them to give you some suggestions.
7. Read articles on time management in magazines, newspapers, and books to help you gain greater insight about effective time management principles.
8. Develop your own system for managing time by applying the ideas you have learned so far and the sources listed in this chapter. Try out your system for two weeks to see if you are able to get more accomplished.

## *Case Studies*

1. *Minidress Corp.* Minidress is a small clothing manufacturing company that makes clothing for babies and young girls to age six. The corporation has only been in existence for four years, and during that period the company has grown rapidly. In fact, the company's major problem is growth; it cannot produce dresses rapidly enough to keep up with demand.

Ballard Wolf, general manager of Minidress, is extremely hard working and energetic. Ballard frequently arrives at work at 5:00 or 6:00 A.M. and stays until 7:00 or 8:00 P.M. He has developed the policy that the company will be completely self-sufficient by the end of next year. The only outside sources that the company will depend on in the future will be suppliers of such items as cloth, paper, and sewing equipment.

As head of all administrative functions for the company, you are trying to determine what you can do to make the office and administrative services as independent as possible. You also are interested in having your area make a contribution to profits by trimming excess administrative expenses and by improving the information flow within the company.

Currently, you contract with a computer service bureau for all accounting, inventory, and payroll computer processing. All printing work such as preparation of labels, advertising brochures, forms, and patterns are sent out to commercial printers. Sales volume reports and work measurement records, which are the basis for an incentive pay system, are maintained by a manual record-keeping system by the five persons who work in the office.

Current administrative costs are averaging 27 percent of total sales. You know that this figure is high because the industry average for companies of similar size and type is only 21 percent. You believe that a minicomputer installed in your office could reduce these costs by at least five percentage points. Also, the purchase of an offset press could allow your staff to do 90 percent of all printing work. You believe that the purchase of the minicomputer and the offset press would allow you to complete all administrative functions within your company and still be able to reduce the number of persons on the office staff by one.

You have read much about the management by objectives program and you wonder if it might be of value to you at Minidress.

What steps do you recommend taking to determine if MBO is appropriate for Minidress? If your study were to prove favorable, how would you proceed to implement an MBO program at the company?

2. *The Training Directors.* In this case, you will be introduced to two training directors in two different organizations. One is an effective time manager, the other is not. At the end of the case, you will be asked to compare these two managers and to point out the effective and ineffective time management practices.

*Ted Straughman.* Ted is the director of clerical training for a government agency in Washington, D.C. He has been a federal career employee for fourteen years and really enjoys his work. Unlike the stereotype of government employees, Ted is an effective, hard-working manager. He is conscious that the public generally has an unfavorable image of bureaucrats and works hard to dispel that image.

Before Ted leaves the office each night, he makes a list of four or five top-priority items that should be completed the following day. While commuting on the bus to and from his home in Springfield, Virginia, Ted is able to keep up with his current reading of reports and journals. He usually arrives in the office about an hour early each day, because he finds this is an excellent time to plan and to work; he can do more work in that hour than he can in three or four hours during the day when there are many interruptions.

Ted uses a variety of methods for increasing his effectiveness in the use of time. He works on important projects that require considerable thought and effort during his best morning hours. He is faithful in evaluating the priorities of work to be done; anything that is not essential for him to attend to personally is delegated to his secretary or to an assistant.

Many meetings must be attended, so Ted tries to handle those that he conducts as efficiently as possible. If he calls a meeting, he may schedule it before the lunch hour or quitting time to make sure it does not extend too long. An agenda is always used. Only those people who need to attend a meeting are invited. Weekly staff meetings and scheduled meetings with individual employees are held as a means of improving communication and reducing the need for unscheduled meetings and conversations. Mrs. Mardson, Ted's secretary, is very helpful in guarding his time; she screens visitors and phone calls. Because she has had much experience, she is able to answer many of the routine questions people ask; she also is able to answer much of his routine correspondence. Mrs. Mardson knows that one of the keys to being a good secretary is to be able to *anticipate* the needs of her boss.

Ted constantly searches for new ways to be more effective and more efficient. For example, to answer much of his correspondence, he writes a reply in the margin of the original letter or memo as an answer to specific questions or comments. A photocopy of the letter is placed on file and the original is returned to the sender. Also, he tries to handle a letter only once. Otherwise, each time the letter is handled means time used to become reacquainted with its contents.

*Roger Morton.* Roger is the training director for a large corporation that manufacturers toys. Roger started with the company twenty-six years ago as a personnel interviewer and has since held several different jobs in the personnel department.

Anyone who walks into Roger's office soon gains an impression of disorderliness. On his desk, six or seven stacks of papers, books, and magazines cover the surface. Several baskets of papers are stacked high. Cardboard boxes and file cabinets jam the room. Pictures and certificates covering the walls attest to Roger's achievements. A manual typewriter sits on the table behind Roger's desk. Any remaining space in the office is filled with training aids such as games and all sorts of objects.

When a person leaves Roger's office, he or she is sure to notice Roger's beautiful secretary, Paula. Paula is very attractive, particularly to the young men who flock around her at the office. She spends a major part of her day visiting with people, in person or on the phone. Paula has little office experience so she is not able to help her boss, Roger, in conserving his time.

Roger is a very friendly person and loves to visit. People stream in and out of his office all day long. Sometimes they come to pass the time of day or just to raid Roger's candy jar, which is always filled with goodies. Roger spends much time on the telephone in personal and business conversations.

Much of Roger's day is spent in attending meetings. These meetings usually last several hours and often do not pertain to the people in attendance. When agendas are used, they are not followed very closely.

In answering or initiating correspondence, Roger either types or writes his letters in longhand, and they are then typed by Paula. To find a particular letter, Roger usually has to dig through several piles of paper. Each item is usually handled several times before action is taken on it.

Roger learned long ago that if you want to get something done right, you should do it yourself. He tries to handle all key decisions and matters personally. When he delegates he usually tells the person he is delegating exactly how the job should be done.

Roger wonders why he doesn't get much of any consequence accomplished. He wonders if he doesn't need another assistant to help him get more accomplished.

1. Compare Ted and Roger in the way they manage time. List the effective techniques that Ted uses and the ineffective habits that Roger has acquired.
2. How would you go about helping Roger to be more effective in his use of time? Do you have any suggestions to help Ted become even more effective in his use of time?

## *Reference Notes*

1. R. Alec Mackenzie and Glenn H. Varney, *The Business Quarterly* (London and Ontario, Canada: The University of Western Ontario), August 1973.
2. R. Alec MacKenzie, "How to Make the Most of Your Time," *U.S. News & World Report*, December 3, 1973, pp. 45–48.

# 16

# Effective Delegation

## BENEFITS OF DELEGATION

The ability to delegate work effectively is crucial to the success of a manager. As we have discussed previously, the administrative manager is vitally concerned with giving balanced attention to production and to the development of those on his or her office team.

*Delegation* is a management technique that involves entrusting work to another person and gaining mutual understanding of expected results.

Effective delegation results in increased production and better qualified, more highly developed employees. As office team members take on additional responsibility, office production increases. They learn new skills and gain knowledge that contributes to their progression.

As a manager or supervisor, you will not be effective in obtaining desired results if you do not delegate; you are likely to get bogged down, and the worry and stress can cause serious health problems. Here's a specific situation. Pedro Juarez, supervisor of data processing, was overworked. He came to work early and quit late. As more reports in his company were required, his data-processing operation was taxed to the limit keeping up with information requests. Pedro was conscientious and wanted work produced on the computer to reflect a high standard of accuracy; he personally supervised all computer jobs and double-checked everything.

If errors in programs were discovered, Pedro worked with the programmer to make sure that corrections were properly made. Since Pedro had experience in programming, operations, and system work, he was highly qualified to keep operations running smoothly. He found that it was easier and quicker in the long run to do things himself than to train someone else in how to do something. Pedro tried delegating work to his people, but he was never satisfied with the results.

Just last week, the director of the computer center, Joyce Osoko, told Pedro that plans were underway to go to a more advanced computer system. Joyce asked Pedro to prepare a lengthy justification report.

Pedro replied, "I just don't have time to make that report. I am too busy with my regular work."

Joyce snapped back, "Why don't you turn some of that stuff over to someone else?"

Pedro carefully considered Joyce's question. He knew she was right; he had to learn to delegate.

If you are to be effective as a manager, you must learn quickly how to delegate. As a new member of the management team, you may be reluctant to give up duties that could be handled by someone else. But while you are involved with routine aspects of your work, you are likely to be neglecting the important job aspects that relate to managerial functions.

Delegation also provides increased job satisfaction to the employees who assume delegated responsibilities. People who are learning and progressing are likely to be happier and more highly motivated. As we learned earlier, increased responsibility is a primary motivating factor on the job. Pedro Juarez had not even considered the consequences for his employees when he had refused to delegate to them. They needed the opportunity for growth and development that comes with taking on greater responsibility. Given proper training and guidance, these employees would eventually be able to assume a major portion of Pedro's workload, thus freeing him to take on more supervisory work than he had been able to do previously.

## INEFFECTIVE DELEGATION

Two primary problems of delegation are that (1) managers fail to delegate as many responsibilities as they should and (2) they fail to delegate skillfully.

Like many managers, you may hesitate to delegate because of one reason or another. Or you may think that you are delegating when in reality you are merely assigning specific tasks to be accomplished. You may attempt to delegate, but you may not be effective. Delegation is easy to talk about and easy to understand, but it is not as easy to accomplish effectively. Four major reasons why managers fail to delegate effectively include:

1. Fear
2. Lack of time
3. Misconceptions about delegation
4. Lack of acceptance of delegated responsibility

Let's look in greater detail at these reasons for not delegating. Consider the case of Carol Bentley, office manager in the College of Social Sciences at New Jersey University. Carol has been in her present position for nine years. One full-time employee, Doris, and five part-time clerks who are students work for Carol. She is a very precise person who is not comfortable unless all of the work she produces is letter perfect. At times, her need for perfection has conflicted with the pressure to meet time deadlines. When Carol gets behind, she is forced to work late. This week is the final one in the semester and is a time when work always piles up. Carol has worked until 10:00 P.M. twice this week already, and it is only Wednesday; she is tired, nervous, and on edge. In addition, her ulcers have been causing problems. At one time or another, Carol has been bothered by most of the problems that cause people to fail to delegate:

1. The first reason for not delegating is fear. Fear shows up in a number of different forms. A person may be afraid of the loss of job satisfaction, of making mistakes, or of losing authority. From time to time, Carol has had all of these feelings. She enjoys office work and frequently runs the offset duplicator herself because she enjoys doing it. She could easily ask one of the student clerks to run the machine, but she likes to do it herself. Carol worries that the students won't do things right. She fears that Dean Farnsby, her boss, will blame her for their mistakes. Carol also worries that Doris, who is very intelligent and talented, may get too much credit from the dean if Carol gives important work to Doris to do. Carol has to support herself and can't afford to lose her job or take second place to Doris.
2. Lack of time may also be a reason why a manager fails to delegate work effectively. Carol feels that there is not adequate time to train and instruct the employees. The pressure of responsibilities calling for immediate attention lures her into thinking that adequate time is not available for delegation planning.
3. A manager may believe that his or her delegation practices are adequate. This belief, if false, may interfere with the person's recognition of the problem and of the need for improvement. Carol misses opportunities to delegate that are available because she thinks she is already doing a good job of delegating. She thinks she is delegating if she asks Doris to type a letter or asks one of the girls to take coffee to the dean.
4. Lack of acceptance of the delegated responsibility on the part of the employee is another reason why a manager may fail to delegate work effectively. Employees in the dean's office may find that it is easier to ask Carol for answers and solutions than it is to think the problem through on their own. The students are concerned that Carol may

criticize them if their work is not perfect. Sometimes lack of necessary information, resources, or skill hampers the employees in assuming responsibility. Two of the students lack the self-confidence to take on a new assignment, and the incentive to take on more responsibility is lacking—the extra work does not seem worthwhile to them. Finally, the employees feel that they are wasting time in moving on their own because Carol always gets her own way.

## EFFECTIVE DELEGATION PROCEDURE

### An Approach to Delegation

Table 16-1 gives an overview of how to delegate effectively, and studying it carefully will help you to learn the essentials of effective delegation. Notice that there are five basic steps to delegation:

1. Select the job carefully.
2. Select the person carefully.
3. Prepare and motivate the employee for his or her assignment.
4. Turn over an assignment skillfully.
5. Maintain adequate control.

A case study will illustrate how these steps should be carried out by following the guidelines given in the table. Ben Shapiro is an effective administrative manager in a regional telephone company office. Among other things, he is responsible for receiving payment of all bills, collecting delinquent accounts, keeping the telephone directory listing current, and publishing and distributing telephone directories. Four first-line supervisors (supervisors who work directly with operating personnel) and his secretary, Donna Atwood, report to Ben. He finds that he has to be moving constantly to keep on top of things.

Ben finds that the only way he can be effective in his job is to be a good *delegator.* He learned to become a good delegator by taking a special company course on delegation, by reading books and professional journals, and, most importantly, by applying delegation principles on the job.

In delegating, Ben tries to follow the five steps and as many as possible of the guidelines outlined in Table 16-1:

***1. Select the job carefully.*** Quarterly, Ben reviews how he is spending his time on his job. He is checking to make sure that he spends his time primarily on those activities only he can do and delegates as many other activities as possible. The first group he has designated as "S" for those duties he will handle by himself, the second group as "D" for those duties he will delegate, and a third group as "M" for those that are marginal—they could be delegated

**Table 16-1. Delegation Procedure and Recommended Guidelines**

| *Delegation procedure* | *Guidelines* JOBS AND ASSIGNMENTS | PEOPLE | MANAGEMENT |
|---|---|---|---|
| 1. Carefully select the job. | Assignments should be important, interesting, and challenging, without being overly difficult.<br>Areas where there is no delegation should be determined.<br>In selecting work for delegation, look for:<br>a. Heavy workloads<br>b. Tight deadlines<br>c. Frequent absence of person delegating<br>d. Distant location of person to whom work is delegated<br>List jobs you do and time taken to do them<br>Rank jobs in order of importance.<br>Classify activities:<br>a. Those only you should do<br>b. Those only your subordinates should handle<br>c. Marginal—either way is okay | | Establish boundaries of optimum delegation (which is delegating at the most effective level).<br>Assign important responsibilities with adequate authority, but don't try to unload everything. |

**Table 16-1 (continued). Delegation Procedure and Recommended Guidelines**

| *Delegation procedure* | *Guidelines*<br>JOBS AND ASSIGNMENTS | PEOPLE | MANAGEMENT |
|---|---|---|---|
| 2. Carefully select the person to whom work will be delegated. | | Base decision on capability and personal preferences, of the individual if possible.<br>Find someone who will benefit from learning the new assignment.<br>Find a "mover"—someone who is preparing for promotion.<br>Give employees minor responsibilities, if uncertain about their abilities. | Follow the "chain of command"—don't bypass people who need to be informed.<br>Gain conviction about a person's ability to do the job and then don't give up on him or her. |
| 3. Prepare and motivate the employee for his or her assignment. | Explain importance of assignment by showing how job relates to total work picture. | Explain what qualifications are needed and why employee was selected.<br>Compliment employee on previous work that has been well done.<br>Develop relationship of trust and mutual understanding. | Explain that the activity is something you have been doing yourself. |

| | | | |
|---|---|---|---|
| 4. Turn over assignment skillfully. | Explain what the job is.<br>Show the employee any tangible aspects of the job such as a report or a document.<br>Use written or visual aids if available.<br>Explain key points.<br>Establish priorities on what is to be done. | Get feedback by having employee ask questions and explain job in his or her own words.<br>Allow employee to select his or her own methods, as long as results and agreements made at time of delegation are met.<br>Encourage employees to further delegate.<br>Hold employee accountable. | Provide list of key results expected.<br>Ask employee to give you list of specific goals.<br>Offer help as needed, but explain employee's responsibility to carry the ball.<br>Agree on specific dates and contents of progress reviews.<br>Make expectations clear—in regard to quantity and quality and standards of performance.<br>Provide adequate resources such as supplies, people, and technical advice.<br>Give employee delegation model (your example) to follow.<br>Provide structure and instructions on such things as:<br>a. Background<br>b. Possible (not required) methods<br>c. Suggestions on problems and pitfalls<br>Seek optimum level of preparation—too much will take away initiative, too little will be frustrating.<br>Retain control over results. |

**Table 16-1 (continued). Delegation Procedure and Recommended Guidelines**

| *Delegation procedure* | *Guidelines* JOBS AND ASSIGNMENTS | PEOPLE | MANAGEMENT |
|---|---|---|---|
| | | | Retain broad control over results—expect frequent progress reports. |
| 5. Maintain adequate control. | | Bring recommended solutions for problems.<br>Allow people to fail if necessary, in order to learn.<br>Don't be overly critical, but provide constructive suggestions.<br>Provide recognition and rewards for successful results. | Remember that you still have the responsibility for results.<br>Use progress reviews and reports to keep informed and to maintain broad control over results.<br>Keep channels of communication open and encourage feedback.<br>Develop climate in which employees feel free to discuss problems and failures as well as successes.<br>Don't take back responsibility. |

or done by him personally. Some of the activities in each of these groups are shown here:

| S Group (Self) | D Group (Delegate) | M Group (Marginal) |
|---|---|---|
| Prepare budget | Initiate routine correspondence | Orient new employees |
| Plan future departmental activities | Coordinate Community Chest Drive | Develop job descriptions for new positions |
| Plan new systems projects | Maintain file on new office equipment | |
| Keep current on new office technology | Check on delinquent accounts | |
| | Schedule travel | |
| | Investigate new word-processing system to produce directory | |

Ben is a firm believer in carefully establishing the boundaries of optimum delegation (delegation at the most effective level). The person delegating assigns important responsibilities with adequate authority but doesn't try to unload everything on anyone who is willing to take the responsibility. Table 16-2 shows the various types of managers and their approaches to delegation. On one extreme is the manager who won't delegate anything, and at the other extreme is the manager who tries to delegate everything. In the middle are other managers who say that they are willing to delegate, but who are not really willing to let go; they make all of the mistakes listed in the second column of Table 16-2. The optimum delegator delegates at just the right level. Ben gives major portions of work with plenty of authority to get the job done, but he still retains general control. Qualities of the optimum delegator are listed in column 3 of the table. As an administrative manager, Ben needs to know what is happening because he is still responsible for making sure that the work gets done properly.

Ben recently became interested in the possibility of using new word-processing equipment to produce the telephone directory. By storing names, addresses, and phone numbers on magnetic media such as tape, card, or disks, this information would not require retyping. Changes and additions can also be accumulated on magnetic media and merged with the data not being changed. A photo composition unit, which is a machine that prepares printing plates, can use the magnetic media as input. This system promises to save up

**Table 16-2. Delegation Continuum**

| *"Do It Yourselfer"* | *Delegator—but . . .* | *Optimum Delegator . . .* | *"Dumper"* |
|---|---|---|---|
| Not really a delegator | 1. Takes back the work frequently<br>2. Splits up the work into small parts<br>3. Checks every detail<br>4. Keeps most desirable work for himself or herself<br>5. Punishes mistakes<br>6. Takes all the credit | 1. Establishes mutual trust<br>2. Uses open communication<br>3. Develops individuals<br>4. Gets results (high production)<br>5. Promotes high job satisfaction<br>6. Has low turnover<br>7. Shares decision-making authority<br>8. Develops self-motivation<br>9. Retains general control | Manager turns over responsibility to team member |

to one-half of the time the old method took to prepare the directories. Gathering information about this new system is an excellent project to delegate. It is important, interesting, and challenging.

**2.** ***Carefully select the person to whom work will be delegated.*** Ben considers all of the people to whom he could delegate this assignment. Of all his supervisors, Delores Burtelson, head of the word-processing section, is the most likely person to do it; however, she is extremely busy and probably could not do it now.

Several other people could probably conduct the investigation, but Ben finally decides to delegate the project to Lon Adams, who is very intelligent and anxious to learn more about the business. Lon is a college senior majoring in administrative management and administrative systems; he types during the afternoons in the word-processing department.

Ben's next step is to talk to Delores to explain the project and to tell her why he has selected Lon. Delores was fully aware that the project was coming and agrees that Lon is an ideal person for this assignment. She says that she wanted to see how Lon would respond to taking on increased responsibility, so she tried him out on a special assignment to update the word-processing instruction manual. She says he came through with flying colors.

***3. Prepare and motivate the employee for his or her assignment.*** Ben thought about how he might approach Lon in delegating this assignment. In Ben's mind he enacted the following two scenes:

*Scene 1*

BEN: Lon, I'm so busy that I can't possibly do everything. I want you to investigate a new word-processing system for producing the directories. Will you do it?

*Scene 2*

BEN: Lon, we have a need in the department to increase productivity and reduce costs. One way to do this is to develop a new system in word processing to produce the directories. I read in *Modern Office Procedures* about a new system that might help us in this regard. Why don't you read this article?

LON: I would be interested in reading it.

BEN: Good, I thought you would. I have carefully considered everyone in the department, and I think you are the best qualified to take on a special, important project. Delores Burtelson tells me that you are doing an excellent job for her. Also, I have been impressed by the work I've seen you do. I know you are thorough and have a keen mind. I understand you enjoy doing research and systems design work.

LON: Gee, thanks Mr. Shapiro, I'm trying to do my best. I really do enjoy doing research and I'm particularly interested in designing systems. I had one year's experience at it in the army."

BEN: Good. We appreciate you, Lon. I would do this project myself, but right now I am involved in several other key projects.

Ben quickly realizes that the second approach is far superior to the first one.

***4. Turn over the assignment skillfully.*** Ben explains to Lon exactly what is involved in the assignment. He starts by giving Lon a list of key results expected:

*Sample Key Results List*

(For a study to investigate a new word-processing system to produce a directory)

1. Basic goal: To develop a system for producing telephone directories on word-processing equipment to reduce current costs and production time while maintaining the present low rate of error (0.02 percent).
2. Review all articles in administrative management, word-processing, and office technology journals to determine what experience other companies have had in solving similar problems.

3. Prepare a written project proposal to outline methods that you will use to solve this problem. Include in the proposal the following information:
   a. Statement of the problem
   b. Background information and need for the study
   c. Anticipated benefits
   d. Methods of investigation
   e. Time schedule
   f. Investigation costs
4. Develop a list of vendors, equipment, and product information. Include copies of brochures, articles, and other written information about equipment and manufacturers.
5. Provide list of sources of information about products.
6. Prepare systems and procedures charts to provide a picture of how the system will operate.

Ben gives Lon sample copies of system project proposals, product brochures, and systems charts that he has collected. Together, they discuss a completion date, and Lon agrees to have the project proposal completed by April 10. Ben says that he will be available to answer any questions that Lon cannot answer for himself but that Lon should develop his own methods and move independently as much as possible. He further explains that he would like to have Lon report to him on problems and progress each Friday at 3:00 P.M. Finally, Ben asks Lon if he has any questions or comments. Lon responds by asking several questions and making the comment that he is very pleased to get involved with this project and will do his best.

***5. Maintain adequate control.*** Ben Shapiro knows that if Lon makes any major errors on this project that cost the company money or that cause problems, Ben's boss will come straight to him and not to Lon for accounting. Therefore, Ben keeps informed on exactly what is happening on the project by meeting with Lon each Friday and by requiring monthly written progress reports.

Later in the project, Lon finds that he can't get unbiased written information on an item of word-processing equipment. He comes to Ben and asks for a solution. Ben suggests that Lon think through the problem for himself and come back with a recommended solution. Lon decides that he will talk with administrative managers in companies that have the equipment installed. Ben knows that Lon won't get much objective information because the equipment is too new to have much history and mentions that to Lon, but Lon is insistent that this is the way to go. Ben decides to let Lon learn for himself without interfering; later, Lon reports that he didn't get the information he had hoped to obtain. Together they decide that the best approach is to obtain a bulletin on the subject from an independent testing bureau.

Each time Lon makes significant progress on the project, Ben compliments Lon. When Lon runs into problems, Ben reacts to Lon's ideas and gives helpful suggestions. Lon has learned to listen to Ben's ideas. In fact, Lon feels that he is having an excellent growth experience. Ben is pleased to see the project move forward and to anticipate the expected benefits.

### Analysis of an Approach to Delegation

Refer to Table 16-1 again, to review the delegation process. As you read it over, think about how Ben Shapiro applied many of the suggested guidelines as he delegated the project to Lon Adams.

Delegation is a very deceiving process. Initially, when a person thinks about delegating responsibility, it seems to be a very simple, straightforward process. But the more you try to delegate and the more people try to delegate to you, the more readily apparent it becomes that delegation requires great skill. Ben Shapiro was quite skillful in his approach: he was effective in selecting work to be delegated; he knew exactly how he was spending his time and what projects he wanted delegated to other people; he showed many of the qualities of the optimum delegator; and the project he selected to delegate—investigating a new word-processing system to produce the directory—was particularly challenging.

The selection of the proper person to handle this project was carefully done. Ben made an excellent choice in asking an enthusiastic employee to tackle this assignment. Lon will get the job done and will develop in the process.

Notice, too, that Ben was following the *chain of command* by keeping the supervisor informed about Lon's participation in the proposed project. Chain of command refers to that part of the organizational chart that presents the line of authority from an individual worker through the various levels up to the president or general manager of the organization. In Figure 16-1, you see a simplified chart for a typical, medium-sized manufacturing organization. The line of authority or chain of command from a worker to the president is indicated by a bold line. In Figure 16-2 you see one vertical slice cut from the organization chart which portrays a chain of command found in a typical administrative unit. If the administrative assistant had a problem, he or she shouldn't go directly to the vice-president for information or to the administrative manager but to the word-processing supervisor. If the line of authority were bypassed, the people with authority who were not consulted would, in effect, be released from their assigned responsibilities. As a manager, you should be alert to this potential problem.

Preparing and motivating Lon for his new assignment was also a crucial part of the delegating process. In the approach in Scene 2, Ben explained how the results of the research would increase productivity and reduce costs, so that Lon was sure to feel this assignment was important; also, to further point

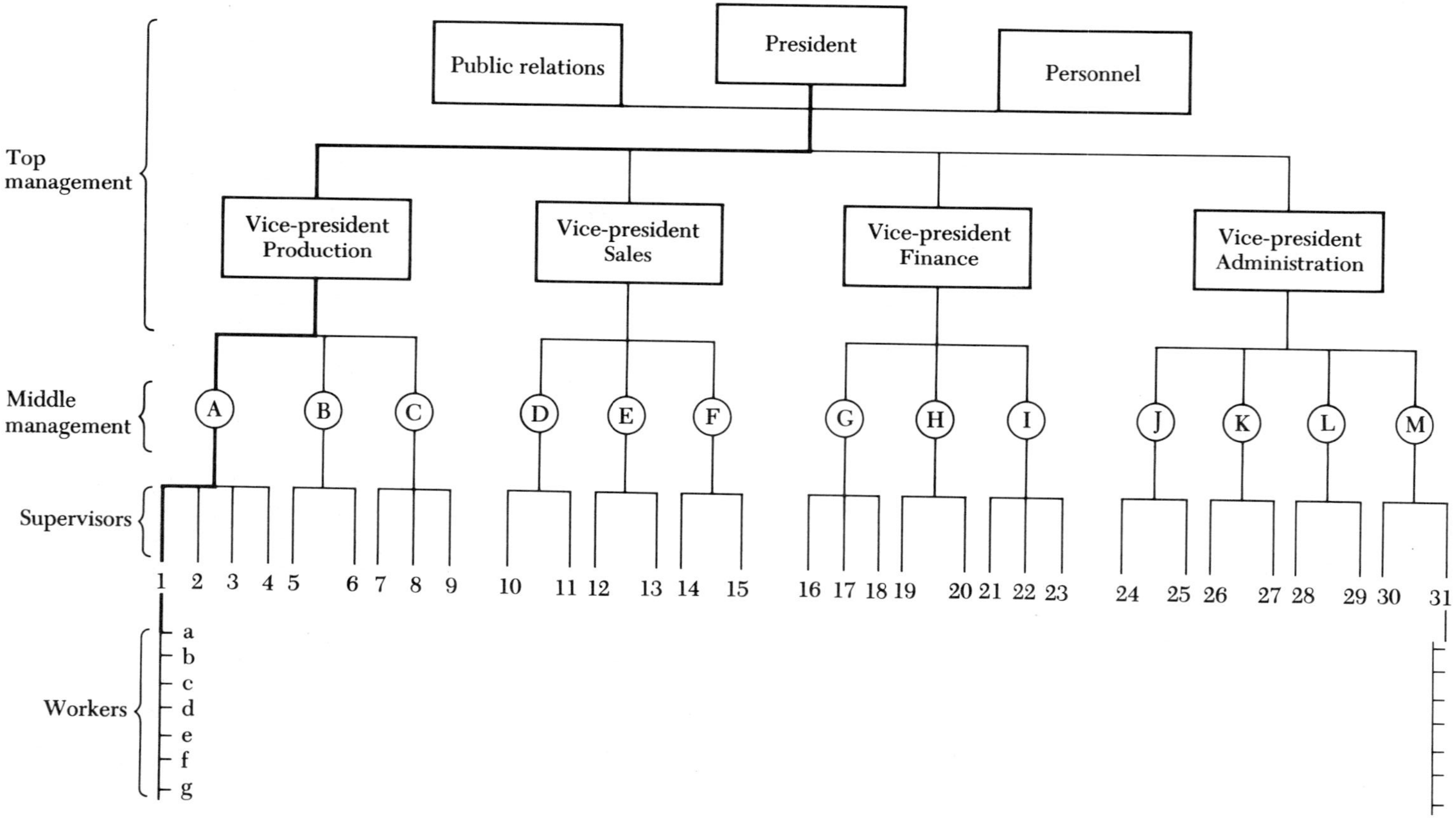


*Figure 16-1.* Simplified Chart Showing the Organization of a Medium-Sized Manufacturing Company or a Similar Firm

For simplicity, only workers reporting to Supervisor 1 have been shown on the chart. In actuality, each supervisor would have a similar group of employees reporting to him or her.

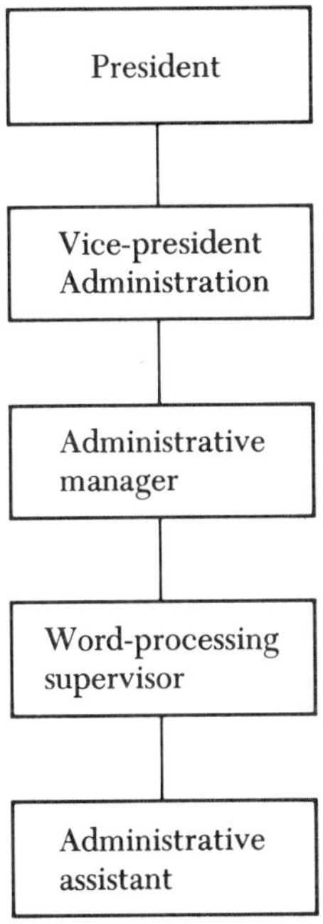


*Figure 16-2.* Chain of Command (Part of an Organization Chart)

out its importance, Ben mentioned that he would have handled the project himself if he were not involved in several other key projects. To give Lon confidence, Ben showed his awareness of Lon's qualifications and complimented him on the good work he was doing.

After this introduction, Lon should have been well prepared to look at the assignment in detail; but imagine how he might have felt if Ben had used the approach in Scene 1. Lon's impression might have been that Ben wanted to get rid of this assignment because he was too busy to do everything; the approach did not provide motivation.

As for turning over the assignment skillfully, again Ben did an excellent job. The list of key results thoroughly explained what Ben expected from Lon; the sample proposals and charts gave Lon something specific to go on. A specific deadline for the proposal was agreed upon, progress reviews were scheduled, and Lon was invited to move independently but was offered help if he needed it. Finally, feedback was requested in the weekly meetings and monthly reports. Ben recognized his responsibility to maintain adequate control. Through the regular reviews and written reports, Ben was kept informed on the problems and progress encountered in the project. Ben didn't allow Lon to bring problems back, but insisted on getting recommended solutions from Lon. Ben refrained from taking back responsibility from Lon when he could have told Lon how best to gather information. Ben was free to compliment and to make constructive suggestions when requested.

In short, Ben is an effective delegator. He has established a good *organizational climate* in which employees are free to develop and move on their own. Also, he has achieved the key to successful management—he is able to get results through other people.

## Summary

Delegation is a management technique that expands production and develops individual employees by sharing responsibility with them. Delegation relieves the work load of the manager, thereby allowing concentration on his or her more important duties. Delegation results in greater work satisfaction for all involved.

In spite of all of the benefits, most managers fail to delegate as much as they should, and those who do attempt to delegate frequently fail to do so skillfully. The four major reasons why managers fail to delegate effectively are (1) fear, (2) lack of time, (3) misconceptions about delegation, and (4) lack of acceptance of delegated responsibility.

Guidelines for effective delegation center around three major areas: jobs and assignments, people, and management. A five-step formula for effective delegation involves (1) selecting the job carefully, (2) selecting the person carefully, (3) preparing and motivating the employee for his or her assignment, (4) turning over the assignment skillfully, and (5) maintaining adequate control.

## Review and Discussion Questions

1. If you were seeking to delegate additional responsibility to an employee who reports to you, what justification could you give to persuade him or her to assume the added work?
2. Why do managers fail to delegate effectively? Under what conditions is a manager justified in not delegating to his or her subordinates?
3. In your own words, make a list of specific guidelines that you think are important to follow when you are attempting to delegate.
4. If you delegate to a person reporting to you, do you retain the responsibility yourself or do you relieve yourself of it by delegating?
5. What is *optimum delegation*?
6. What problems are frequently encountered that reveal less than optimum delegation?
7. What is the ultimate effect on delegated responsibility when people in the line of authority (chain of command) are bypassed?
8. Under what conditions would you expect to see delegation flourishing within an organization?

9. Explain what you could do as an administrative manager to develop an organizational climate that would be most supportive of effective delegation.

## Application Exercises

1. Accomplish the following exercises under the direction of your instructor. With your instructor's consent, arrange to have a panel of managers visit your classroom to discuss the realities of delegation. Do they themselves attempt to delegate? Why or why not? If they do delegate, what practices do they find most effective?
2. Critique a chapter or an article on delegation that you read in a management book or a current business or leadership periodical. Present your personal opinion, negative and/or positive, about statements made by the author. Report results to your class.
3. Following the guidelines presented in this chapter, delegate an appropriate assignment to someone who reports to you in any kind of an organizational capacity. Report the results. Be sure to include a statement that indicates what you might do in the future to improve your delegation effectiveness.
4. Observe how other people, such as your work supervisor, student body leader, or teachers, delegate to you. Have they followed the guidelines presented in this chapter? What could they do to improve their delegation performance?

## Case Studies

1. *The Product Information Report.* Office manager Tom Maper was disgusted with himself. He was overwhelmed with work and things were getting worse. It was all his own fault. He was taking too much on his own shoulders and not delegating properly.

The new product information report was a good example of delegation problems. This report reviewed the status of all new products under development in the company, and Tom personally gathered information regularly for this report. Meanwhile, he is expected to keep all of the other operations in the office going. Tom spent about four hours out of every week on the product report; it was an important project, but one that any of his assistants could be handling.

One morning, Tom decided it was time that he started to delegate responsibility. Looking over the departments' employee roster, he called Mark Haywood into his office. As an experienced employee and a reasonably intelligent person, Mark would be ideal for the assignment of handling the production report. Tom explained the requirements of the product information report as clearly as he could, but Mark wasn't overjoyed about the assignment. "I've got too much work already," he complained. Tom didn't take the complaint seriously—most employees think they have too much to do. "This job won't amount to too much," Tom assured him; "less than four hours a week."

Tom wrote the next report with Mark at his side, making sure that he understood what was required. The following week he let Mark complete the report on his own.

Total disaster! Mark spent seven hours preparing the report only to find that most of the information was incorrect. Tom had to spend another four hours straightening out the mess. The report went in two days late, to top off everything. Because of the extra time involved both Tom and Mark fell behind in their regular work. Needless to say, Tom was disillusioned with delegation as a management technique.

What went wrong? What should Tom have done differently? What should he do now?

2. *Charles Wantola Case.* Charles Wantola is administrative manager in the Power Electric Supply Co., a small company, owned and managed by Stan Wiley. Charles is responsible for personnel, purchasing, and accounting. Twelve people, including his secretary, report to Charles. Mr. Wiley regards the administrative department as the headquarters and service unit for the other two departments—sales and production.

The company has been rapidly expanding; consequently, the work load has been increasing for all departments. Regularly, Charles has been spending sixty hours per week in the office, and he realizes that he can't keep up this pace for long. Recently, he read that one group of executives estimated that they could relieve their work loads by 25 to 35 percent by simply delegating work to their secretaries and broadening responsibilities at that level.

Delegation sounds great to Charles, but he doesn't know how to begin. He can keep books and negotiate a good deal on wire cable, but he really doesn't know what to do to delegate effectively.

Assume that you are the sales manager in this company and that Charles has asked you to help him. He wants you to advise him on what to do in effectively delegating work to his secretary and assistants. He also posed the question to you, "If I delegate all of my work to my secretary, what will I find to do?"

# 17

# Performance Appraisal

Have you ever been in a situation where you wanted to know how well you were doing? Perhaps you have been in a class where you had no idea whether you would get an A, B, C, D, or failing grade. More than likely, you have worked on a job where your boss gave no indication of how well you were doing. Perhaps you had made an effort to improve your work performance by working harder and by trying new ideas. If your boss failed to give you feedback in response to your efforts, you probably became frustrated. People need to know how well they are doing in all phases of life. The purpose of this chapter is to explain how evaluation is accomplished in the office.

Some activities provide immediate, continual feedback on performance while others do not. If you prepare a copy on the copy machine, you know immediately if your copy is legible and properly centered. If an accountant makes an error in counting cash receipts, his or her books will not balance, and the error can be noticed immediately. On the other hand, activities that are more abstract or subjective will tend to provide less effective feedback. For example, if you make a decision about adopting a new training program, you may not really know whether the program is effective or not.

## EXPLAINING THE PROCESS

### Definition

*Performance appraisal* is an important management communication tool designed to provide feedback to employees about their job performances.

In a systematic manner, employees and managers learn together how well the employees have been doing on their job for a specific period of time. Special circumstances that might affect performance are also considered at this time (such as phasing out a position or the installation of a new machine).

The appraisal interview provides an opportunity for administrative managers to give positive reinforcement to their employees on good results obtained. The emphasis should be on positive accomplishments rather than on failures, on completion of objectives rather than personality traits.

Let's look at the case of Lucille Potter, supervisor, and Nancy McGuire, office clerk. Nancy's performance has been generally satisfactory, but she has some areas in which she needs to improve. Compare two approaches that Lucille takes in conducting a performance appraisal interview with Nancy. Keep in mind that, in each case, Nancy's performance is the same; the difference lies in Lucille's attitude and approach.

> "Nancy," Lucille said, "I'm proud of your performance this past quarter. You did an exceptional job in training Bob on the new equipment we just purchased. Also, your cost analysis report on copy machines was complete and well documented." "Thank you," said Nancy. Lucille continued, "As we mentioned earlier, the section on maintenance will require more work. I am pleased to see your progress in overcoming the problem on absenteeism that we discussed last quarter. Congratulations on your progress. How do you feel about your performance during this quarter?"
>
> "I've felt good about my progress," responded Nancy. "I am still working on several areas." (Interview continues.)
>
> Alternatively, Lucille might have taken a different approach. She might have said, "Nancy, it's time we have to fill out this performance rating form again. As you can see, I've rated you average on all factors except appearance, attitude, and initiative. Your appearance is excellent. But, your attitude leaves something to be desired, and I think you lack initiative."
>
> "Is that so? I think my attitude is above average. . . ," retorted Nancy angrily.

In the first instance, Lucille was positive. She pointed to specific accomplishments and rewarded in a positive manner Nancy's efforts to do the right thing. Lucille was honest and mentioned the areas of improvement that Nancy is working on. She opened the door to further discussion centered on performance and improvement. Nancy in turn responded positively and centered her comments on her progress and anticipated improvements.

The second approach was completely different. Nancy's performance, however, was the same. Lucille was in trouble as soon as she referred to the negative factors of attitude and initiative. Of course, Nancy reacted defensively. Little, if anything, of real value can be expected to result from this second appraisal interview.

### Purposes

Performance appraisal has the following purposes: (1) provide a communication tool, (2) build motivation, (3) serve as a basis for training and development, (4) provide a basis for salary determinations, and (5) supply information for promotion and transfer decisions. Let's look at each of these purposes.

*1. **Provide a communication tool.*** Supervisor and employee in an open, two-way communication setting discuss work performance and completion of objectives. The appraisal interview should yield no real surprises because it is merely one part of an on-going communication process. On a daily or weekly basis, the supervisor and employee have been discussing problems as they developed and work performance. The appraisal interview provides a target check to evaluate progress. As you learned in Part Two of this text, feedback is essential to good communication. Two-way feedback is the primary thrust of the appraisal interview. Supervisor and employee both learn what is going on and attempt to share mutual expectations and feelings about progress.

*2. **Build motivation.*** Motivation results from positive reinforcement given by the supervisor and from the employee's opportunity to focus on growth and achievement. For example, when a typist, Darlene, increases the average number of lines typed per day from 500 to 600, the supervisor should reinforce her behavior during the normal course of work and during the appraisal interview. This praise should help Darlene to become further motivated. The employee should leave the appraisal interview with renewed determination to continue to do a good job.

*3. **Serve as a basis for training and development.*** You, as an administrative manager, and your employees need to know how well they are doing in developing abilities and skills to accomplish job objectives. In the previous example, Darlene could see her progress at increasing typing production. Also, deficiencies can be identified at this time and become the focus of the training development processes. For example, Darlene may be overlooking an average of 10 errors per day and should be made aware of this problem. During the appraisal interview, Darlene and her supervisor could discuss the procedures for correcting this problem and could determine other training and development that she needs. (Review Chapter 13 for further details on this process.)

*4. **Provide a basis for salary determinations.*** Some management experts have suggested that salary determinations should be separated from performance appraisals. A time lapse between the two events is recommended. They reason that salary determinations are too threatening to be associated with training and development, which require a nonthreatening climate. Nevertheless, salary decisions require a base of performance information. The performance appraisal usually supplies this information need. Whether organizations admit to it or not, performance appraisal is commonly used as a basis for setting salaries and determining rates.

**5. *Supply information for promotion and transfer decisions.*** Ultimately, hard decisions need to be made about who should be promoted and who should be transferred. Information about strengths, weaknesses, and achievements is needed in order to make intelligent decisions. Each of these decisions is really only one step along the career path of the individual.

## PERFORMANCE CYCLE

Performance appraisal is an important part of the performance cycle. The *performance cycle* begins with planning that involves setting objectives and developing an action program (see Figure 17-1). Next, individual performance takes place that is expected to result in the completion of the work. An appraisal or evaluation of the performance in relationship to planning is the final step in the cycle. The appraisal process provides feedback that influences future planning. The basic criterion for determining the success of an employee's performance cycle is whether or not the objectives that were to be met have been achieved. Employees are continually receiving feedback on an informal basis as they perform the work; they also receive formal communication from their supervisor during the appraisal interview. In addition to objectives, other factors such as use of resources, long-term human relations, and similar factors are considered in the appraisal.

For example, one person with limited equipment or money available may complete a special business research project single-handed. Another person may require a great amount of help and a large expenditure of money to complete a similar project. One person may reduce office expenses by 15 percent at the expense of creating bad feelings with his or her employees, while another person may achieve a similar objective and maintain good relationships.

## APPRAISAL METHODS

The supervisor has primary responsibility for the appraisal process within his or her organization. The personnel department normally has responsibility to train the supervisor in appraisal methods. Two basic types of performance appraisal methods, traditional and behavioral, are available to administrative managers.

### Traditional Methods

So far, the discussion of performance appraisal has represented the ideal. The point has been made that appraisal should focus on employee behavior and

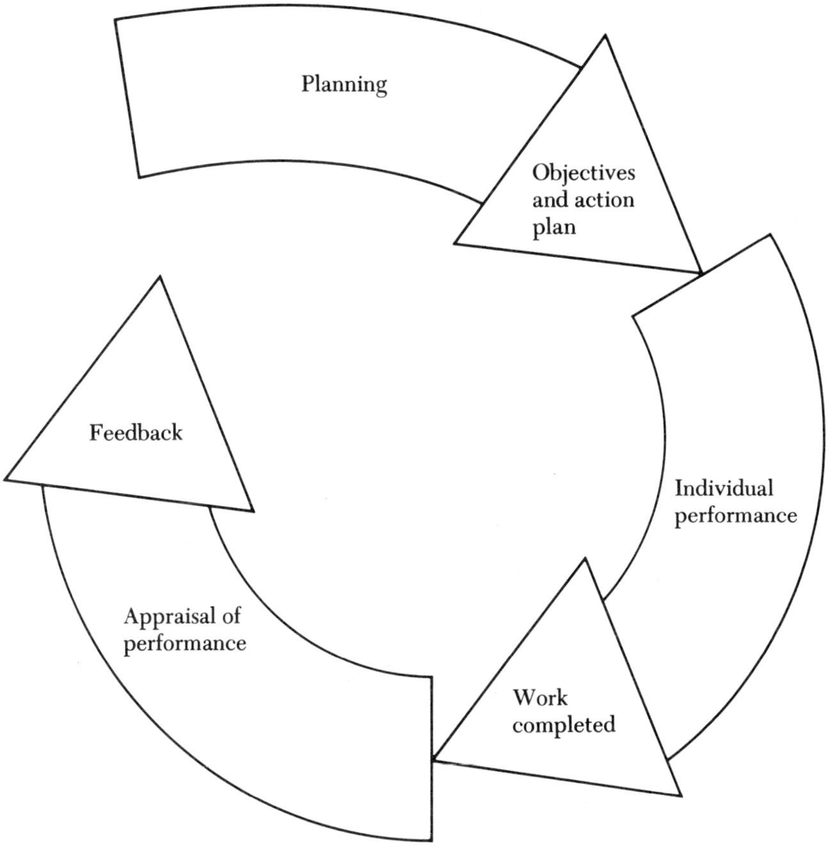


*Figure 17-1.* Performance Cycle

accomplishment of objectives. Also, the performance appraisal interview has been pictured as a part of the continuing communication process.

Realistically, this position is not an accurate representation of what is happening in most business organizations. According to Douglas McGregor, many managers tend to look upon the appraisal process as a threatening experience that they are forced to become involved with because of their managerial positions. Appraisal interviews are threatening to managers because they view this as a time when they must judge the workers reporting to them.[1] Notice that they are concerned about judging the workers, not the work performance of the workers. This judgmental process tends to be a negative, critical type of action. Employees have traditionally responded defensively to the whole business of appraisal. Managers know that they are going to have to live with their employees on the job and, consequently, tend to be quite apprehensive about the appraisal process. In an attempt to make appraisal less distasteful, the supervisor may rate employees all "average" or all "excellent." Also the "bologna sandwich" technique, in which a slice of criticism is slipped in between two pieces of praise, may be used.

In most organizations, some type of appraisal form has been developed, usually by the personnel department. Supervisors are expected to fill out these forms on an annual or semiannual basis. Supervisors may be asked to *rank* the employees on a scale from 1 to 3 or from "best" to "poorest," or, more commonly, they may be called upon to *rate* the employees on various factors.

A typical rating sheet is shown in Figure 17-2(a), and factors on which the employee is evaluated are listed on the form along with a rating scale (from "poor" to "outstanding"). These factors include quality of work, quantity of work, performance under stress, knowledge of work, adaptability, judgment, initiative, and appearance. An explanation of how these characteristics are evaluated is given in the accompanying list.

*Characteristics explanation*

1. Quality of work—dependability of results, neatness, and accuracy.
2. Quantity of work—productivity under normal daily requirements.
3. Performance under stress—ability to work under pressure and meet deadlines.
4. Knowledge of work—utilizing training and experience, understanding importance of job to organization, understanding of mechanics of work performed.
5. Initiative—alert to opportunities for improvement, getting started without having to be told.
6. Adaptability—flexibility, making adjustments to new or different conditions or types of work, versatility, ability to learn new responsibilities and/or adapt to new methods.
7. Judgment—soundness of conclusions, absence of guesswork and snap judgments in performance of duties.
8. Resourcefulness—ability to respond to problem situations without supervisory directions.
9. Cooperation—teamwork, willingness to cooperate with and assist both supervisors and coworkers, ability to deal with others.
10. Job presence—promptness, staying on the job, absenteeism.
11. Telephone manners—attitude toward customers and coworkers.
12. Typing ability—accuracy, production.
13. Administrative ability—work completed efficiently and on time; ability to organize work.
14. Shorthand ability—transcribes accurately.
15. Dictation ability—transcribes accurately.
16. Appearance—neat, makes good impression, careful of dress and personal care.

### JOB PERFORMANCE APPRAISAL

| | |
|---|---|
| NAME Marla Payson | DEPARTMENT Word Processing Center |
| JOB TITLE Correspondence Specialist | GRADE 3 |
| EMPLOYMENT DATA June 10, 19-- | DATE OF EVALUATION September 10, 19-- |

Carefully consider each of the job performance categories listed below and place an X or checkmark in the column that best describes the employee's performance.

Poor — consistently unsatisfactory performance

Fair — generally unsatisfactory but sometimes acceptable performance

Satisfactory — consistently acceptable performance

Very good — consistently better than satisfactory performance

Outstanding — consistently superior and excellent performance

| Job performance characteristics | Poor | Fair | Satis-factory | Very good | Out-standing |
|---|---|---|---|---|---|
| 1. Quality of work | | | | ✓ | |
| 2. Quantity of work | | | ✓ | | |
| 3. Performance under stress | | ✓ | | | |
| 4. Knowledge of work | | | ✓ | | |
| 5. Initiative | | | ✓ | | |
| 6. Adaptability | | | ✓ | | |
| 7. Judgment | | ✓ | | | |
| 8. Resourcefulness | | ✓ | | | |
| 9. Cooperation | | | ✓ | | |
| 10. Job presence | | | ✓ | | |
| 11. Telephone manners | | | | ✓ | |
| 12. Typing ability | | | ✓ | | |
| 13. Administrative ability | | | ✓ | | |
| 14. Shorthand ability N/A | | | | | |
| 15. Dictation ability | | | ✓ | | |
| 16. Appearance | | | | ✓ | |
| 17. Attitude | | | ✓ | | |

*Figure 17-2.* *(a)* Performance Appraisal Chart

17. Attitude—accepts authority, policy, and criticism without resentment; loyal to the department, company, and fellow workers; pleasant to everyone in general outlook.

**FURTHER EVALUATION OF JOB PERFORMANCE**

Averaged 600 lines per day on draft work for period June - August

This is Marla's first job and she is gaining good experience. Marla needs training in office procedures but so far she has been unable to find time to take such a course.

CROSS TRAINING COMPLETED Proofreader

| SIGNATURE OF EMPLOYEE APPRAISED | DATE |
|---|---|
| Marla Payson | 9/10 |

**COMMENTS AFTER DISCUSSION OF APPRAISAL WITH EMPLOYEE**

Marla's husband graduates from the University in June and she will probably be moving.

DOES EMPLOYEE HAVE FURTHER POTENTIAL? EXPLAIN

Has some interest and ability in office supervision

| SIGNATURE OF SUPERVISOR MAKING APPRAISAL | | DATE |
|---|---|---|
| George Morris | | 9/10 |
| REVIEWED BY Joyce Kindall | TITLE Director of Aministration | DATE 9/17 |

*Figure 17-2.* (b) Comments and Signatures on Performance Appraisal

Providing an explanation of factors for the supervisor helps to make the ratings more uniform from one rater to another. Factors should be as specific as possible; for example, "quality of work" is more specific than "good worker." On the form, notice that Marla was rated "very good" in the quality of work she produces, telephone manners, and appearance, "fair" in performance under stress, judgment, and resourcefulness, and "satisfactory" in the other categories. In Figure 17-2(b), the rater's comment that Marla should take a course in office procedures may indicate that some sort of problem is evident in her work. Marla's unwillingness to take the course may also suggest another problem.

There are many variations of this basic rating form that attempt to make ratings more consistent. Some forms substitute grades or numbers for subjective ratings of "outstanding" or "very good." Other forms substitute or add descriptive statements to further clarify the meaning of the ratings; an example developed by a bank is found in Figure 17-3.

Let's look now at the advantages and disadvantages of traditional performance appraisal techniques.

*Advantages*

1. Familiar to employees and supervisors alike.
2. Easily understood.
3. Simple.

*Disadvantages*

1. Disliked by many.
2. a. Low *validity.* Ratings may not measure what they are supposed to measure.
   b. Low *reliability.* Ratings may not be consistent from one rater to another.
   c. Low *objectivity.* Ratings rely on opinions rather than behavior that can be observed and verified.
   d. Factors and rating scales may be ambiguous. Different people reading the forms may form different impressions in their minds about meanings of factors and degrees of qualification.
3. Individual biases and rating errors influence ratings.
4. Supervisors may not be willing to put effort and time into doing a good job of preparing rating forms.

Disadvantages of rating forms tend to outweigh the advantages, but the forms tend to remain in common usage because managers are not prepared adequately and are not sufficiently knowledgeable to use more sophisticated means such as behavioral methods.

### Behavioral Methods

In an attempt to avoid the subjective process of measuring personality and character traits, behavioral scientists have suggested that performance appraisal be based on employee behavior that can be easily identified and measured. Five methods of measuring behavior are (1) forced-choice checklist, (2) critical incidents list, (3) speciman checklist, (4) management by objectives, and (5) self-evaluation.

EMPLOYEE JOB PERFORMANCE EVALUATION

Name__________________ Job Classification__________________ Dept.__________

Period Reviewed__________ 19__to__________ 19__Immediate Supervisor__________

Reason for Review:__End of Probationary Period__Annual__Transfer__Promotion__Probationary period for below Standard Job Performance__Other. Date of last review__________

Instructions for Rater:

Select from the following factors ONLY THOSE WHICH ARE RELEVANT TO THE EMPLOYEES WORK. The number of factors you select is far less important than the relevance of each choice. Indicate your evaluation of the employee's performance for each of the selected factors by: (a) checking the statement that most closely approximates your impression and as necessary line out wording of selected statement to make it more accurate (b) and as necessary, write your own statement in the space provided.

A (OUTSTANDING) B (HIGHLY SATISFACTORY) C(SATISFACTORY) D (MARGINAL) E (NOT ACCEPTABLE)

1. QUALITY OF WORK -- (Consider neatness and accuracy regardless of quantity of work)
   - A. Always outstanding; never has to be redone, very neat, errors rare. __A
   - B. Highly Satisfactory; seldom has to be redone, errors uncommon. __B
   - C. Satisfactory; makes occasional errors, may lack neatness. __C
   - D. Barely Passable; often must be redone, errors frequent. __D
   - E. Slipshod; must be redone many times, errors very frequent. __E
   - Additional Comment:__________________

2. QUANTITY OF WORK -- (How much work does employee produce?)
   - A. Works rapidly; completes exceptional amount of work consistently. __A
   - B. Better than average producer; volume more than satisfactory. __B
   - C. Completes average amount of work; works at a steady pace. __C
   - D. Works slowly; rather low production. __D
   - E. Excessively slow; output consistently below standard. __E
   - Additional Comment:__________________

3. KNOWLEDGE OF WORK -- (How well does employee know the elements of the job?)
   - A. Completely familiar with all phases of work; excellent knowledge of duties. __A
   - B. Well informed on most aspects of job; seldom requires assistance. __B
   - C. Satisfactory knowledge; requires moderate amount of supervision. __C
   - D. Slow to learn; responds poorly to training, needs supervision on routine tasks. __D
   - E. Cannot or will not learn job; needs constant supervision. __E
   - Additional Comment:__________________

4. INITIATIVE -- (Does employee assume responsibility?)
   - A. Has unusual degree of self-reliance; exercises independent thought and action. __A
   - B. Offers intelligent suggestions; does job on own, able to handle irregularities. __B
   - C. Routine worker; does what is required but rarely more. __C
   - D. Needs supervision; relies on others for ideas, not able to handle irregularities. __D
   - E. Has no initiative; needs detailed instruction, confused by irregularities. __E
   - Additional comment:__________________

5. RELIABILITY -- (Can employee be counted upon to carry out job duties conscientiously?)
   - A. Completely reliable; merits utmost confidence. __A
   - B. Reliable; almost always follows instructions carefully and correctly. __B
   - C. Usually dependable but must be checked on more important matters. __C
   - D. Somewhat unreliable; requires occasional checking on routine tasks. __D
   - E. Unreliable; requires constant checking even on routine tasks. __E
   - Additional Comment:__________________

6. PUBLIC CONTACT --(Does employee build good will or promote new business for the bank?)
   - A. Outstanding public relations; goes out of way to serve public and promote MNB __A
   - B. Highly satisfactory PR; creates favorable impression and attempts cross-selling. __B
   - C. Usually friendly and courteous; sometimes abrupt. __C
   - D. Frequently unfriendly; often curt or irritable. __D
   - E. Create a bad impression; almost always unwilling to go out of way to help. __E
   - Additional Comment:__________________

*Figure 17-3.* Performance Appraisal Form with Descriptive Ratings

***Forced-Choice Checklist.*** This list presents pairs of behavioral incidents, and the appraiser must select one from each pair that is most typical of the behavior of the person being evaluated. For example, the manager completing the

7. ATTITUDE -- (Is employee interested in and trying to improve job performance?)
A. Outstanding interest; welcomes criticism, exceedingly co-operative. __A
B. Highly satisfactory; co-operative, accepts policy and criticism without resentment. __B
C. Satisfactory interest; co-operates, occasionally becomes diffident or careless. __C
D. Shows little interest in job; frequently unco-operative or unpleasant. __D
E. No interest in job; co-operates when forced to, resents criticism or authority. __E
Additional Comment:____________

8. TECHNICAL PROFICIENCY --(Consider depth of technical knowledge and application)
A. Always meets or exceeds standards; has excellent work habits and sense of follow-through, has depth of technical knowledge in excess of that required for present job. __A
B. Seldom fails to meet standards; technically thorough, superior performance is reflected by an understanding of principles applied to work. __B
C. Normally meets required standards; is generally attentive to important details, occasionally requires guidance where procedure is unusual, understands nature of procedures and their importance in related activities. __C
D. Sometimes fails to meet technical standards; inconsistent in attending to details, has little understanding of processes or relationships involved. __D
E. Is unable to meet technical standards; often slip-shod with details, has no comprehension of underlying principles, does not appreciate how work affects others. __E
Additional Comment:____________

9. ATTENDANCE -- (Can you depend on employee to meet work schedule and hours?)
A. Extremely conscientious regarding attendance. __A
B. Very dependable; absent or late only when absolutely unavoidable. __B
C. Dependable; usually has legitimate excuse when absent or late. __C
D. Undependable; may be absent or late without good reason. __D
E. Undependable; often late or absent without good reason. __E
Additional Comment:____________

10. SUPERVISOR POTENTIAL -- (Consider future utilization in a supervisory capacity.)
A. Outstanding ability to plan and schedule work; consistently shows initiative, improves knowledge and position by outside study. __A
B. Highly satisfactory degree of progression; shows imagination and solves problems. __B
C. Shows average initiative and ability to make constructive suggestions. __C
D. Performs routine work if under supervision; lacks initiative or desire. __D
E. Requires constant supervision; not reliable, produces below what he can and should. __E
Additional Comment:____________

GENERAL COMMENTS

1. Can this employee more effectively contribute to MNB in some other work? If so, what?
____________
2. What are employees principal strengths?____________
3. What are employees principal weaknesses?____________
4. How can employee improve job performance?____________

Over-all Rating: Considering employee's overall performance check term which is applicable:
A__Outstanding
B__Highly Satisfactory
C__Satisfactory
D__Marginal
E__Not Acceptable

Rater
Signature__________ Position__________ Date__________
Employee
Signature__________ Position__________ Date__________
__Concur
__Do not concur Signature__________ Position__________ Date__________
Reviewer (If you do not concur in evaluation explain in remarks section)

REMARKS SECTION:

*Figure 17-3, continued*

checklist would have to choose one statement of behavior from each of the pairs shown in Figure 17-4 as being most representative of the behavior of Barbara, who was being appraised. Both statements in a pair are equally

**EMPLOYEE PERFORMANCE CHECKLIST**

Name Barbara Levinson Department Word Processing

Supervisor John Flannagan Date 11/5

*Instructions:* For each of these pairs of statements, check the item (A or B) that most nearly applies to the employee being evaluated.

| | | |
|---|---|---|
| Pair 1 | | |
| Makes decisions promptly | A. | ✓ |
| Follows work schedule closely | B. | |
| Pair 2 | | |
| Follows work schedule closely | A. | ✓ |
| Submits work on time | B. | |
| Pair 3 | | |
| Arrives at work early | A. | |
| Takes shorthand at 120 or more words per minute | B. | ✓ |

*Figure 17-4.* Sample Forced-Choice Checklist

favorable toward the employee (or equally unfavorable), but only one of the statements has been found to have a high degree of relationship with success on the job. This method was designed to reduce the error of leniency on the part of the supervisor or appraiser but there have been problems with it. Supervisors dislike the method because they find it difficult to choose between equally appealing alternative descriptions of behavior.

***Critical Incidents List.*** This evaluation is a list of outstandingly effective or outstandingly ineffective incidents recorded by the supervisor. For example, in Figure 17-5, the supervisor recorded critical incidents about the behavior of an employee, Ron Dennis, during the past three months. This method is quite objective, but it is limited by the infrequent occurrence of outstanding incidents and the supervisor's inattention to other incidents that are important but not outstanding.

***Specimen Checklist.*** G. H. Whitlock developed the specimen checklist in the late 1950s and early 1960s.[2] This method employs a specially developed list of 100–200 critical incidents pertaining to the job of the employee being appraised. The manager using this checklist simply has to recall incidents that have happened during the appraisal period. His or her memory is prompted

## CRITICAL INCIDENTS LIST

Name Ron Dennis

Supervisor Hal Gatza

Department Adm. Systems

| Date | Positive | Negative |
|---|---|---|
| 8/3 | Report submitted two days early | |
| 8/17 | Volunteered to develop written procedure on his own time | |
| 9/23 | | About 30 minutes late for work |
| 9/25 | Suggested new method of preparing performance reports that will save company $10,000 per year | |
| 9/30 | Recognized by company as outstanding employee of the month | |
| 10/5 | Developed new, improved order form | |

Comments:

*Figure 17-5.* Sample of Critical Incidents List

by the list of incidents that are likely to apply. Examples of incidents on the checklist are as follows:

Refused to follow instructions, even though they were clearly described.

Required prodding to get work in on time.

Made recommendations for improved departmental procedure.

Received suggestion award from the company.

Note that these are the same type of incidents used in the critical incidents list in Figure 17-5. The difference between the two methods is in how the incidents on the list are obtained. In the specimen checklist method *the incidents are obtained from research,* whereas the critical incidents list is developed by the supervisor. The specimen checklist method tends to be accurate, complete, and reliable. It does not provide for differences in value or relative importance of each incident nor does it consider the actual accomplishment of the worker.

***Management by Objectives.*** MBO, the fourth behavioral method to be considered here, evaluates employees in terms of their accomplishment of objectives. Effective employees get results. Logically, to evaluate how effective employees are, you should measure the contribution they make to the organization in terms of completed, mutually agreed upon objectives.

Tamara Kosley, office supervisor, praised George Christenson for his excellent work during the past six months as departmental secretary. Tamara evaluated George on the following MBO goals which they agreed upon at their last appraisal session:

1. By May 1, set up a new departmental filing system that would allow retrieval of any piece of correspondence or report within three minutes with 95 percent certainty of finding the materials.
2. By June 15, learn to use dictation equipment to prepare routine correspondence and reports.
3. By June 30, develop office procedures manual that explains in detailed, narrative form with accompanying graphic charts all the major office procedures.

Using these objectives as a focus, Tamara could readily tell that George had been effective because specific accomplishment was easily measured. Tamara and George identified additional objectives that George would work on during the next appraisal period, and they talked about the resources and help from Tamara that George would need in order to accomplish the objectives.

With MBO, all factors must be accounted for, but the output is the major criterion for judging effectiveness. MBO is an objective method, but even with this method some subjectivity is present when reasons for failure to complete objectives are analyzed. The specimen checklist possibly could be combined with MBO to treat both accomplishments and behavior.

When both the employee and the manager focus attention on objectives rather than personalities, the tendency to be defensive is reduced and the attainment of positive solutions is emphasized. The situation of April Anderson illustrates this point. April is curious about how her boss, Gerald Romney, is going to evaluate her work. April says to her friend, Nicea, "If he thinks he can shove me around, he's got another think coming. Last week he made a comment about my being 15 minutes late for work. I am fed up with hearing about the boss's opinions of my personality and dependability." April is pleasantly surprised during the interview to find that the focus is on objectives. Gerald works with her in setting up specific objectives pertaining to developing a new records system, eliminating unnecessary forms, and selecting new dictation equipment. They also discuss what April needs to do in order to qualify for promotion.

***Self-Appraisal.*** Self-appraisal can be handled entirely individually or in conjunction with the supervisor's evaluation. Self-appraisal shifts the responsibility to individual employees to assess how well they are doing on the job. Self-evaluation operates under the basic assumption that most of the time people know when they have done well and when they have done poorly. A Theory *Y* climate and an extreme amount of faith and trust in people are necessary for this method to be successful. Also, employees need to be well trained and experienced on the job.

Combining the supervisor's evaluation with the self-appraisal of the employee has several advantages: (1) an overall viewpoint is brought into the picture (employee's view plus supervisor's), (2) an outside viewpoint that tends to be more objective about some areas is included (supervisor's), and (3) a representative of management who has control over the resources and the destiny of the individual presents a picture of how the employee has met expectations of management (supervisor's view).

An example will help you to see more clearly how self-appraisal could operate. "John, think about your performance this past year and prepare a self-evaluation report for me. I want you to look at your progress on goals, your personal development, your contribution to departmental objectives, your use of resources, your future goals, and any other factors that seem important. If you'll get this report to me by July 7, I'll have time to meet with you and discuss your findings before you go on vacation. Does that date sound okay? Do you have any questions?"

### Comparison of Behavioral Methods

The five behavioral methods of evaluating employee performance are compared in Table 17-1. The specimen checklist, MBO, and self-appraisal methods are rated higher than the forced-choice and critical incidents methods. An excellent approach to appraising employee performance is to use a combination of specimen checklist, MBO, and self-appraisal methods to get as complete a picture as possible.

**Table 17-1. Comparison of Behavioral Methods of Evaluating Performance**

| *Factor* | *Forced choice* | *Critical incidents* | *Specimen checklist* | *MBO* | *Self-appraisal* |
|---|---|---|---|---|---|
| Objective | + | √ | + | √ | – |
| Thought requirement | √ | + | √ | + | + |
| Employee behavior focus | √ | + | + | + | + |
| Easy to develop | – | – | √ | √ | √ |
| Familiar to employees and supervisors | – | + | √ | + | √ |
| Easily understood | – | + | + | + | + |
| Simple | – | + | + | + | √ |
| Behavior range | √ | – | + | – | + |
| Employee involvement | – | – | – | + | + |
| Theory *Y* organizational climate | – | – | – | + | + |
| Uniformity of evaluation criteria | + | – | + | – | – |
| Reliable (consistent ratings) | + | – | + | – | √ |

Key: + = high, √ = medium, – = low rating.

## EFFECTIVE PERFORMANCE APPRAISAL

To show how the performance appraisal interview should be conducted, a case study of how one manager conducted the appraisal of one of his employees is presented. The manager of word processing at Merchants National Bank in Louisville, Kentucky, is Doug Toans. He is preparing to conduct an appraisal session with Joan Morantini, a correspondence specialist in the word-processing center. This is Joan's first job since graduating from high school. She has improved her typing speed very well during the past six months she has been at the bank. She still has a major problem in discovering errors that she makes, however. Her attitude is very good and she gets along well with the other operators.

### Gather Information about Employee's Performance

Doug's first step was to gather as much information as possible about Joan's performance. He has been observing her work since she first started, and when he finds something noteworthy about her performance, such as the time she volunteered to stay after hours to type an important report, he records the information. He has collected some critical incident information. Also, he reviews all pertinent, written performance reports and retains them in his file to show trends of progress or lack of it. All of this information is reviewed with each employee periodically. The other day, Doug reviewed Joan's list of objectives and mentally noted his perception of her results achieved. Before the interview, he will ask her to give him a report that compares results against her objectives. Another thing he will do is review circumstances that might have affected Joan's performance. An example is the two-week period when Joan's automatic typewriter was working improperly. Finally, he will ask her to evaluate her performance.

### Conduct Interview in Accordance with Recommended Procedures for Interviewing

(Refer to Chapter 11.) Doug decides to allow three hours for the interview. He plans also to apply the following accepted interview principles:

Conduct the interview in private.

First, put the employee at ease by some light conversation.

Use a positive approach by emphasizing accomplishment rather than negative factors.

Listen carefully to the employee and make the interview a two-way process by asking open-ended questions and by encouraging questions from the employee.

Doug's basic purpose for the interview is to exchange information about Joan's performance and to gain mutual understanding about how her performance can be improved.

### Develop Specific Approach for Interview to Appraise Employee's Performance

During the interview, Doug plans to review Joan's statement of results compared with objectives on a point-by-point basis. Together, they will compare her self-evaluation with his evaluation as her supervisor; Also, he will review his list of critical performance incidents with her.

Growing out of this preliminary review of information will come four specific targets: (1) identify progress made or lack of it, (2) identify problems encountered, (3) develop recommended solutions and give specific help, and (4) agree on specific goals and actions for the future. We can look at the middle portion of the interview with Joan and spot these targets in the key points made. (Some preliminary, warm-up conversation has already taken place.)

### *Portion of an Appraisal Interview*

| *One Approach* | *Key Point* |
|---|---|
| MGR.: Let's look at what you have done in relationship to improving your productivity. I have several accomplishments listed for you. How about you? Would you like to start? | A. Focuses attention on expected results and actual accomplishment. Start with area where you know there have been good results obtained. |
| JOAN: I feel good about this area. Every week for the past seven I have increased my line count production. I went from 500 last June to 625 per day now. | |
| MGR.: Gee, that's great, Joan. I really feel good about your progress here. You have improved your speed more than anyone else in the department. Do you have anything else listed? | B. Takes opportunity to provide positive reinforcement. |
| JOAN: That's all. | |
| MGR.: How about making deadlines? What percentage of the work requests you have typed have been completed on time? | C. Identifies another measure of results related to productivity. |
| JOAN: Oh, yes, I forget about that. About 95 percent of all work requests given to me were completed on time. | |
| MGR.: Again, that's excellent, Joan. Now how have you been doing on accuracy of your work? | D. Reinforces positively again, then shifts to another area where performance has not been so good. |
| JOAN: Well, I have been trying to improve. . . . | |
| MGR.: Do you know the average number of errors that the proofreader has been finding for your work per day? | |
| JOAN: I am not sure. It must be about twelve. | |
| MGR.: My reports indicate that it is currently ten. That's down from two | E. Has done his preparation and has facts at hand. |

months ago, but it is still well above our expected standard for the department.

JOAN: I know you are right; but sometimes the deadlines are so tight that if I took more time in proofreading my percentage of deadlines completed would go down.

MGR.: How much more time does it take to carefully proofread an average three-page document as opposed to skimming it lightly and then having the proofreader return it to you for correction?

F. This question helps to clarify the issue.

JOAN: No longer, really. In fact, it probably takes longer to make the corrections when a document is returned rather than when done right in the first place. I'm sure you are right but I have always had a difficult time in catching all of my errors even when I go over the material several times.

MGR.: Is that right? Did you know, Joan, that you can do some specific things to improve your proofreading? Let me show you two specific ideas: (1) Read the document over to make sure that all words make sense in context. On this reading, you should catch any errors where the wrong words were used. For example, in reading for context, you might catch these errors: "Please give me *you* report." (2) Read the document a second time, on a word for word basis (point to each word as you read). This approach will help you to catch the following types of errors: "Please give to me your report on *progres* made on *productivety.*"

G. Gives some specific help on proofreading.

| | |
|---|---|
| JOAN: Yes, I see what you mean. | |
| MGR.: Do you have any suggestions on what else you might do to solve this problem? | H. Turns responsibility to Joan to think about solutions. |
| JOAN: Well, maybe I could talk with Christy who proofreads full time and get some ideas from her. Also, I am going to have to commit myself to doing a better job of proofreading. In fact, Mr. Toans, I want you to know right now that I am going to do a better job of proofreading. I intend to find all of my errors—at least most of them anyway. | I. Comes up with some specific ideas and makes a commitment to improve on proofreading skill. |
| MGR.: Why don't you aim for the standard of not more than two errors per day. Perhaps one more thing might be helpful. After you feel comfortable with your progress in proofreading, perhaps you might cross-train on Christy's job as a proofreader. That experience could really be helpful to you. Also, we have a programmed instruction manual on proofreading available that might prove helpful. | J. Helps to establish realistic goals and also provides some additional specific help on proofreading. |
| JOAN: Thank you very much, Mr. Toans; I really appreciate your help. I'm almost excited about learning this new skill. | K. Hints at feelings of motivation. |
| MGR.: Are there other areas that we need to review? We might focus on any problems that you might be having that interfere with productivity. I'll try to help if I can. | L. Opens way for further discussion of problems. |

**Follow Up**

After the appraisal interview is completed, Doug will follow up to make certain that Joan's performance continues to improve. He will follow through on any promises that he has made during the interview. He will also check with her periodically to make sure that she is progressing as they anticipated during the interview. If Joan encounters any unforeseen problems, Doug will help her take immediate action to solve those problems.

## *Summary*

People need to know how well they are doing in any activity in which they are engaged. Performance appraisal is a systematic approach to helping both employees and their supervisors understand how effective the employees have been during a specific period of time such as three months, six months, or a year. From the appraisal interview, employees should have a good understanding of what is expected of them in the future in terms of objectives to be accomplished. Performance appraisal is used to improve communication, to build motivation, to provide a basis for training and development, and to arrive at salary, promotion, and transfer decisions.

The performance cycle begins with planning that results in development of objectives and action plans. Planning leads to performance of work and completion of objectives. This phase is followed by a performance appraisal that results in feedback being given to employees, which in turn affects the planning process for future work.

Traditional methods of appraisal that include ranking and rating tend to concentrate on evaluating individuals as persons rather than on their behavior and the results they achieve. Consequently, defensiveness and negative attitudes often result.

Behavioral methods of appraisal include: (1) forced-choice checklist, (2) critical incidents list, (3) specimen checklist, (4) management by objectives, and (5) self-evaluation. All of these methods tend to focus on the behavior of employees rather than on their personality traits. Each method has strengths and weaknesses, and a manager might well use several of these methods in combination in order to get the best results.

A recommended procedure for conducting an appraisal interview was presented. Used properly, appraisal is an effective management tool.

## *Review and Discussion Questions*

1. Define *performance appraisal* and explain its major purposes.
2. Explain why each step in the performance cycle is important.
3. Compare and contrast the *traditional* and *behavioral* methods of performance appraisal. Can you identify problems that an administrative manager might encounter in using either approach to performance appraisal?
4. Name the five behavioral methods of performance appraisal. Describe each method and discuss any advantage or disadvantages that you can see for each of them.

5. Explain the procedure you would recommend in conducting an appraisal interview.
6. What other management techniques and concepts is performance appraisal related to? Explain the relationships.
7. Why is performance appraisal an important management tool?

## *Application Exercises*

1. If you have had business experience, think back on a time when you were involved with your supervisor in an appraisal interview. How did you feel? What aspects of the interview were handled well? What aspects were handled poorly? What recommendations do you have for improvement of the appraisal interview? Report on these questions to your class.
2. If you are currently working in business and at least one employee reports to you, plan how you can conduct an effective appraisal of that person. Complete the appraisal and then report on the results to your class. If you are not working currently in business, simulate and evaluate an appraisal with another student.
3. Interview an administrative manager, personnel manager, or some other manager to determine what types of appraisal methods are used. Try to determine why certain techniques and tools are preferred over others. Report your findings.
4. Read the *Harvard Business Review* classic, "An Uneasy Look at Performance Appraisal," by Douglas McGregor in the May—June, 1957 or September–October, 1972 issues of the *Harvard Business Review.* Discuss in class whether this article is relevant to management problems today. How does this article relate to McGregor's Theory *X* and Theory *Y*?

## *Case Studies*

1. *Mary Johnson's Promotion Review.* Assume that you are a manager in an engineering office. Fourteen professional engineers and eight administrative/clerical personnel report to you. One of your responsibilities is to evaluate the performance of your employees and to make recommendations for promotion. Your company has recently developed a promotion policy that sets up strict criteria for professional promotions. In the past, promotions have come primarily as a result of seniority. Now the engineers are expected to do research and writing in professional journals, support professional organizations, and develop supervisory abilities in addition to their primary task of developing first-class engineering projects.

Mary Johnson has been in her present grade for the past seven years and has expressed rather vocally in the department her conviction that she should be promoted to senior engineer. Mary has published a number of articles and made numerous presentations to professional groups. You and several of the truly professionally oriented engineers in the department consider Mary's articles to be rather nonscholarly. Her presentations do an excellent job of entertaining the audience but there is really very little "meat" to them. Mary has done some research, but it is really not of the caliber that you think it should be; in fact, your definition and her definition of research are miles apart. Mary holds several important offices in professional organizations related to her specialized branch of engineering and is quite well-known nationally in her field. She has little supervisory experience, but her project work is generally satisfactory. However, you don't rate most of her projects more than "good" and certainly none is "outstanding."

A departmental evaluation committee composed of three members of the staff has met with four candidates for promotion. You sat in the committee's meeting with the candidates to form your own independent judgments. Only one candidate was considered ready for advancement by the committee. The recommendation for Mary was that she not be considered further for promotion at this time. You concur.

Your task now is to interview all four candidates for promotion and explain the decisions to them. Because of the committee's negative recommendations, you need to work with the individuals and help them to develop an improvement program that will qualify them for promotion later.

Prepare yourself to conduct this first interview with Mary. Simulate the interview with another student from the class, and then evaluate your effectiveness in handling the appraisal interview. If possible, have a third person observe the simulated interview and give you feedback.

2. *Ms. Mandini Case.* Assume that you are JoAnn Mandini who has recently been promoted to the position of team leader for a group of seven computer programmer and systems analysts. You feel that the five men on your team resent working for you, a woman supervisor. They have implied that you are not tough enough to supervise the team and maybe you were promoted because you are a woman.

You have scheduled a three-hour appraisal session with Bob Marx, who is one of the sharpest persons on the team and who was the favorite of the team members for your job as supervisor before you were promoted. Bob is one of your sharpest critics. You intend to give him the following ratings:

| | |
|---|---|
| Job knowledge: | Excellent |
| Attitude: | Fair |
| Relations with others: | Poor |
| Productivity: | Good |
| Enthusiasm: | Fair |
| Reliability: | Excellent |
| Overall rating: | Good |

Bob recognizes your ability as a systems analyst. He frankly thought that he would be promoted to the position of supervisor which you received. At first, Bob was disappointed that he was not promoted; in fact, he recognizes that his attitude and productivity suffered for awhile. He is not too worried, however, because he thinks he can "snow" you during the coming appraisal interview. He intends to push for an overall rating of excellent with no rating below good.

(a) As the team leader, JoAnn Mandini, determine how you will approach this interview. What basic objectives will you have?

(b) Role play this interview with another student, under the direction of your instructor.

## *Reference Notes*

1. Douglas McGregor, "An Uneasy Look at Performance Appraisal," *Harvard Business Review*, September–October 1972, pp. 133–34.

2. G. H. Whitlock, "Performance Evaluation Through Psychophysics," unpublished manuscript, University of Tennessee, 1956; and "Application of the Psychophysical Law to Performance Evaluation," *Journal of Applied Psychology*, 1963, Vol. 47, pp. 149–155. Copyright 1963 by the American Psychological Association. Reprinted by permission.

# 18

# Effective Decision Making

Of all the activities required of the administrative manager, probably none causes so much frustration and concern as the act of making decisions. In your own life, no doubt, you can remember having to make difficult decisions, and perhaps you wished at those times that someone would make your decision for you. Decision making is an important part of management and life in general, and the concepts presented in this chapter will be helpful in both your business and personal decisions. As you begin to apply these concepts, you'll notice immediate positive results: you'll begin to rely less upon emotion and snap judgments, and more upon firm-founded logic.

## IMPORTANT ASPECTS IN DECISION MAKING

Wise decision making is largely dependent upon an intelligent use of important facts. Simply stated, the more vital facts you have at your command, the better your judgments should be. Conversely, the fewer critical facts you have, the poorer your judgments likely will be. As you have already experienced in your own life, decision making frequently brings much mental discomfort because there is risk involved. Risk refers to the possibility of making an improper decision and having to suffer the consequences. And the greater the risk, the greater the discomfort.

Adam Alexander of Montex Co. experienced this discomfort as he was contemplating obtaining six new copy machines. Adam had decided to obtain Xerox copiers, but he was not sure whether to purchase or to lease the machines. From a cost standpoint, he would prefer a purchase arrangement; but he was fearful that he would have difficulty selling the machines when improved models came on the market. Because of this risk, Adam was very unsettled about his decision.

Scholars who have studied decision theory intensively have developed statistical methods for quantifying decision making. These theorists first determine the expected risk involved with each possible choice, and then they apply statistical techniques to determine which alternative carries the least risk and the greatest possible gain. Decision theory is especially useful with important decisions involving a great degree of uncertainty.

Another aspect that is always present in decision making is the importance of the decision. You should, of course, expend much more effort in making a decision that will have major impact on either you or your organization than you would on unimportant decisions; conversely, you should worry very little about decisions that have relatively little significance. Decisions that have great importance usually produce much greater anxiety in the decision maker than do those that have low importance; for example, a decision regarding the purchase of a million dollar computer is much more important than the purchase of a stapler, and the computer purchase would produce far more anxiety.

Feelings enter into decision making in various ways. They must be considered if other people are either involved in or affected by your decision. Moreover, people can be deeply emotional, and those emotions often take precedence over objective logic in their thoughts and actions. Feelings must play a rather important part in decisions involving very few facts; in such situations you have little more than your intuition to base your decision upon. In decisions involving many facts, subjective feeling should take a back seat to objective logic; unfortunately, emotions continue to rule in too many cases. As an example, you will probably encounter situations in which a company officer will order merchandise from a certain company simply because he has a close friend in that company. The merchandise is ordered from the friend's company even though other companies offer better prices or products.

## ORGANIZATIONAL DECISION LEVELS

Generally, you will find that the higher a person's position in an organization, the more important decisions he or she will make; conversely, workers occupying lower positions in an organization will usually make fewer important decisions. Consider the various levels of decisions in a company: top officers might decide whether to expand company operations to another city or region; a middle management officer might make a decision regarding the development of a streamlined mail-handling system; a lower-level employee in a record center might make a decision regarding which of several record requests to handle first.

If you plan to advance into the supervisory or managerial levels of an organization, you must learn to be a good decision maker. Since this skill rarely comes by accident, you must learn and practice proven decision-making techniques to gain proficiency. One of the best approaches to the process is explained in the paragraphs that follow.

## DECISION-MAKING PROCESS

Obviously, the prerequisite for making a decision is to sense that you have a problem; a problem can be simply a mental concern that something is not as you think it should be. As is mentioned in Chapter 7, make certain that your problem analysis focuses on the real problem, not just on the symptoms of the problem. Problems of an administrative manager may take many forms such as equipment failures, employee morale problems, inefficient work methods, ineffective supervisors, or communication failures. Whatever problem you might have, you must examine it thoroughly and objectively so that you understand completely the basis for the decision you will make. If the problem is somewhat complex and involved, you might even want to put the problem statement in writing to make certain that all who assist in the decision fully understand the problem they are trying to solve. When you feel that you fully understand the problem, you are ready to begin the decision-making process.

### Steps Involved

***1. Define Objectives.*** First, you should define the major objective that you desire to accomplish as a result of the decision. After you determine your major objective, you must determine the major factors that relate to the achievement of the objective.

*Factors*, in a decision-making situation, are problem-related concerns that should be considered in judging the adequacy of possible solutions.

For example, assume that you are an administrative manager in Rocky Mountain Systems and that your major objective is to install an updated dictation system in your word-processing center, a typing center with electronic dictation and typewriting equipment. After discussing dictation systems with your word-processing personnel, you might decide that the factors that should be considered are as follows: expense, capacity (number of authors who can dictate into the system), compatibility (technological fit with the other equipment in the word-processing center), service and maintenance (adequacy of the vendor's maintenance and repair agreement), time (average delay between dictation by the authors and transcription by the typist—caused by moving the dictation medium from the dictation machine to the transcriber), color (appropriate match with existing office color scheme), and other (features that are offered beyond the basic factors just mentioned).

For each factor you establish, you would also decide upon a certain standard of judgment that you would use to measure possible solutions to the problem. This standard of judgment is referred to as a *criterion*. For the factors mentioned in the previous paragraph, you might decide on the following criteria:

Expense: Must be within budget allowances for current period.

Capacity: Must accommodate the dictation of 60 authors.

Compatibility: Must use company's existing touch-tone telephone system for input.

Service and Maintenance: Must offer next-day service on faulty equipment.

Time: Must allow for dictation to be transcribed at least as soon as author is finished dictating.

Color: Should be compatible with present system's avocado color.

Other: Should offer additional extras that would make equipment more functional.

Since these factors are obviously not arranged in priority of importance, you would want to decide which factors are very important and which ones would just be nice to have. Based on your evaluation of the importance of each item, you might decide to arrange them in the following order of priority: capacity, compatibility, time, service and maintenance, expense, other, and color. Following your arrangement of the factors in order of importance, you are ready to proceed to the second step in the decision-making process.

***2. Gather and Evaluate Data.*** You should now begin to gather data that pertain to your factors. These data would be related to people, methods, equipment, materials, financial concerns, and other resources that could contribute to the achievement of your objectives.

As an administrative manager, you must be an effective fact finder. You are not expected to *know* all the facts pertaining to a particular problem, but you must have the know-how to *find* those facts. There are several sources that you will call on repeatedly in your management work:

*Your memory.* Usually you will be able to recall some facts that will provide leads to additional information. Frequently, these thoughts will provide at least a basis upon which you can build. In the dictating machine case, you would probably remember at least several companies that produce dictating equipment.

*Persons within the organization.* People in your organization who have had or who are having experience with factors relating to the decision you must make can be a source of very helpful information. As a manager, you will frequently involve your subordinates in the entire decision-making process, from determining the problem to making the final decision. The involvement of subordinates in managerial decision making is a concept referred to as *participative management,* where employees participate with management in decision making and other activities. This concept provides opportunities for achievement, recognition, and responsibility—powerful motivational tools.

For the selection of the dictating machine, you may find that your word-processing personnel can be very helpful in providing information about service and maintenance problems with the present dictating system. These people can also indicate the extra features that are very helpful to them.

*Consultants.* Numerous professional consulting firms are available as a source of expert advice. Although some of these consultants charge relatively high fees, the information gained is usually among the best available. Advice from the appropriate consultant can probably yield good data on nearly every dictating machine vendor available. These consultants can also indicate the systems that have proven to be most effective in situations like yours.

*Sales representatives.* If your decision involves the acquisition of goods and services from other organizations, representatives of these firms are usually very willing to provide you with data about their products or services. Although some degree of bias accompanies these presentations, they are excellent sources of helpful information. These people can give actual demonstrations of their equipment and can answer questions regarding cost, extra features, capacity, and compatibility.

*Company files.* If you or anyone in your organization has dealt with a decision of this type in the past, chances are good that files will still contain some very helpful information. You might find in your files some information about the reasons earlier dictation systems have proven inefficient or inadequate.

*Libraries.* Public, special, and educational libraries are sources of vast amounts of literature. Your own organization might have publications within its own collections that will provide information for your use. A search through your company library might yield a number of articles or professional publications pertaining to dictating systems.

*Business periodicals.* As an administrative manager, you should keep well informed of current writings in periodicals related to your particular field. *Management World, Administrative Management, The Office, Modern Office Procedures, Dartnell Office Administration Service Publications, Word Processing World, Information and Records Management, Infosystems,* as well as other periodical literature relating to specific administrative services areas, will become invaluable aids to you as you constantly face administrative management problems. Keep current in your reading of these materials and file them for future reference. You might find in your search that *Word Processing World* has a number of articles about other companies' dictation systems.

*Professional Affiliations and Contacts.* Personal contacts made at professional meetings, exhibits, trade fairs, and seminars frequently prove helpful. These personal acquaintances can share their own experiences and can refer you to other acquaintances for additional help. Regarding the dictation machine problem, you may find that one of your AMS chapter members has recently installed a new dictation system and that he or she will spend time discussing his or her new system with you.

Make certain that the data gathered from all these sources are related directly to your particular problem, that they are current, and that the reliability of their source is beyond question. When you are satisfied that you have accumulated enough information, you are ready for the next step.

***3. Develop Alternatives.*** After you have accumulated all the information you need for the second step, develop alternatives based on the data collected. These alternatives are simply different ways of achieving your objectives. At this stage in the decision-making process, you need an extra measure of resourcefulness and creativity. You need to be able to look at a mass of information and be able to see relationships among various parts of the mass. You need to be able to rearrange common patterns of doing things and to look at the ordinary and be able to see possibilities for positive change. The more involved the problem is, the more deep thought, analysis, and creativity that will be required. For example, if the processing of a certain type of form in your office has been resulting in a bottleneck at one worker's desk, you need to examine the entire process to see where the problem starts and to see where possible improvements can be made. In the dictating machine problem discussed in this chapter, your alternatives might be to purchase a dictation system from IBM, Lanier, Dictaphone, or Sony. After all possible alternatives have been identified and fully explained, proceed to step 4.

***4. Evaluate the Alternatives.*** In the alternative evaluation stage, you measure the alternatives by their objective-filling potential. Use the criteria that you established as a measuring stick. The alternatives that come closest to meeting the objectives are obviously the better choices.

To illustrate this process with numeric values, assume that you were to rate the alternatives on the degree to which they meet the established criteria. The factors previously mentioned in this chapter might receive the following point values:

| | |
|---|---|
| Capacity | 15 points |
| Compatibility | 15 points |
| Time | 12 points |
| Service and maintenance | 10 points |
| Expense | 9 points |
| Other | 4 points |
| Color | 1 point |

Table 18-1 illustrates a hypothetical analysis of the alternatives and the criteria. In Table 18-1 you will notice that the third alternative (Lanier) fully meets the criteria relating to capacity, compatibility, time, service and maintenance, other, and color; therefore, it receives full point value in these areas (65 out of a possible 66). Since it only partially meets the expense criterion, it receives only 8 points instead of 9 in that area.

**Table 18-1. Sample Evaluation of Alternatives: Analysis of Factors and Alternative Dictation Systems**

| | | *Systems (vendors)* | | | | |
|---|---|---|---|---|---|---|
| *Factors* | *Possible points* | *Dictaphone* | *IBM* | *Lanier* | *Lanier B* | *Sony* |
| Capacity | 15 | 15 | 15 | 15 | 15 | 15 |
| Compatibility | 15 | 15 | 10 | 15 | 10 | 15 |
| Time | 12 | 12 | 12 | 12 | 12 | 12 |
| Service and maintenance | 10 | 10 | 10 | 10 | 8 | 8 |
| Expense | 9 | 7 | 6 | 8 | 9 | 8 |
| Other | 4 | 3 | 3 | 4 | 2 | 2 |
| Color | 1 | 1 | 1 | 1 | 1 | 1 |
| Total | 66 | 63 | 57 | 65 | 57 | 61 |

Although you would not use numeric ratings in most decision-making situations, you would still be going through much the same process mentally. Step 5 follows logically after an in-depth evaluation of all your alternatives.

***5. Make the Decision and Implement It.*** The fifth step is to make your decision based on the evaluation of the alternatives. You choose the alternative that most closely meets your objectives—the one that gives the most return for the least expenditures of energy and resources. The third alternative in the preceding table would be the alternative to choose, since it meets the objectives best. If two alternatives had seemed to promise equal benefits at equal costs, you would probably rely upon feelings or a certain degree of intuition for your final decision.

Now that the decision has been made, you must implement it. Implementation involves the four basic functions of management: planning, organizing, controlling, and leading. If you have faithfully followed the first five basic steps given here, your decision stands an excellent chance of being successful.

***6. Follow Up.*** As decisions are implemented, you will frequently notice that the alternative selected is not completely solving the problem it was designed to solve. As a result, you need to refine the decision by repeating the basic decision-making process shown in Figure 18-1. You can see that decision making is really a continuous process. Although everyone makes a wrong choice

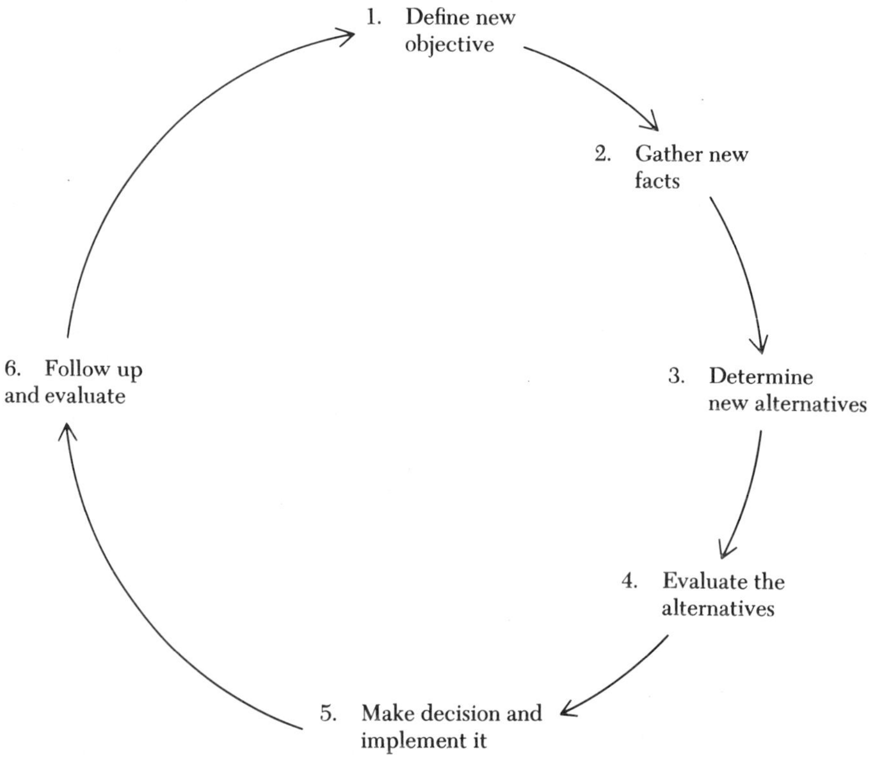


*Figure 18-1.* The Decision-Making Process

occasionally, those who follow the basic decision-making process make far fewer inappropriate decisions than those who do not.

Terms such as *problems, symptoms, objectives, factors, alternatives,* and *criteria* are common to effective administrative managers. These managers make a regular practice of making decisions and solving problems by the six-step method explained in this chapter. As you implement this process in your own life, you'll find that you, too, can become a very skillful decision maker.

## GROUP VERSUS INDIVIDUAL DECISION MAKING

Chapter 10 suggested that involving subordinates in decision making is an effective way to improve both organizational communication and employee motivation. In addition to providing these two benefits, the involvement of subordinates in decision making also improves the decisions themselves. When subordinates are involved in the decision-making process, there are definite advantages.

Decisions made by groups are on the average significantly better than decisions made by individuals.

The more total group involvement there is, the better the group decision will be. In other words, decisions made by all group members are superior to those made by just a portion of the group members.

In spite of these important advantages of group involvement, a major disadvantage is that group decisions take much more time than do individual decisions. Thus, if time is a crucial factor in a decision-making situation, you may not be able to involve your group in making the decision. This disadvantage arises from the time required to allow group members to give comments, receive feedback, discuss, refine, vote, and perform all functions that are necessary in helping a group achieve its objectives. Assume that you receive a phone call late one afternoon from a company that is printing some brochures for a department you supervise. The person calling you indicates that he is out of the type of paper requested for the brochure and he wonders what he should do. Since the two people in charge of developing the brochure are out of town for two days, you realize that you don't have time to wait for their advice. Therefore, you make the best decision you can by yourself.

Because the interaction that results from group communication seems to be far more effective in refining decisions than does one individual's thought process, extra time taken by group decision making usually pays for itself in effectiveness. Perhaps the general rule that should be followed is the more important and critical the decision is, the more a manager should consider involving the group.

## WEAKNESSES OF DECISION MAKERS

As an administrative manager, you will be required to make numerous decisions every day. Therefore, you should be aware of the major weaknesses that continuously tempt every decision maker.

***1. Requiring too many facts and procrastinating decision making.*** This type of temptation is particularly strong when any or all of the following conditions are present:

The emotions of many people are involved in the decision.

The decision is very important.

The decision carries a high-risk factor (few facts available).

The results of the decision are highly visible.

In selecting dictating equipment, for example, you might be inclined to procrastinate your decision because your subordinates disagree about the "best" system, the decision is very important to the success of the word-processing function, and the results of the decision are visible to many workers.

As a decision maker, you will have to develop both the talent to sense when you have analyzed the situation as well as you can and the courage to make the decision even though risk is high.

2. ***Drawing snap conclusions; not considering all the facts.*** This second temptation arises when you don't realize the importance of the decision or when you are simply unaware of the resources or implications associated with your choice. A weakness of this sort could enter into a decision about dictation equipment. You might visit with the sales representatives of just Sony and Dictaphone and then decide to purchase the Dictaphone system. By making this premature decision, you deprive yourself of the additional benefits offered by other systems.

It has been suggested that the most important thing you can learn in life is to place the proper priority on things. Such is certainly the case in decision making. You need to be able to discern between important and relatively unimportant decisions, and to have the self-discipline needed to devote appropriate amounts of energy to the different kinds of decisions.

3. ***Letting bias or emotion influence decision.*** Human beings are emotional creatures, and in many situations feelings play a major part in people's actions. In selecting dictating equipment, for example, you might select a certain type of equipment simply because it has many extra features. You realize that you don't need all the features, but you like to show off all the gadgetry to others when they visit your center.

In an administrative management capacity, this kind of biased decision making would get you into trouble. Businesses are in existence to make money; and if your decisions don't lead to increased economic productivity, your employment with the company won't last long. Therefore, begin making a practice of eliminating as much emotion as possible in your decisions. You'll find the self-discipline to be excellent training as you assume responsible duties in administrative management.

## *Summary*

The more important factors that affect decisions are availability of facts, importance of the decision, and feelings of people affected by the decision. During the decision-making process, six basic steps are involved. First, define your objective. Determine specifically what you want to accomplish and list the factors that are important to the objective. Assign priorities to these factors.

Second, gather and evaluate data. Get as much input as possible that relates to the decision. Check the input for validity and importance, and be realistic about what data you actually need and when you have enough. Sources of information are your own memory, persons within your organization, professional consultants, sales representatives, company files, libraries, and business periodicals.

Third, develop alternatives. From the data gathered in the second step, organize as many plausible alternatives as possible that will achieve your objective. Fourth, evaluate the alternatives. Examine the risk of each alternative, and see how effectively each alternative will meet your objective.

Fifth, make the decision and implement it; and sixth, follow up the decision and make appropriate corrections as needed.

Whenever appropriate, other persons should be involved in decision making, since decisions made by groups are usually superior to those made by individuals. Group decisions are more time consuming, but the extra time and effort expended seem to pay for themselves in terms of decision effectiveness.

Decision makers seem to suffer from three major weaknesses: (1) Requiring too many facts and procrastinating decisions, (2) drawing snap conclusions, and (3) letting bias or emotion influence decisions. The wise decision maker will constantly guard against these three temptations.

## *Review and Discussion Questions*

1. Why do an abundance of facts and the degree of risk have a negative correlation in decision making?
2. Why is it important to arrange your objectives in order of priority?
3. Why should an administrative manager keep up-to-date in reading administrative management periodicals?
4. Describe the difference between *factors* and *criteria.*
5. How does creativity relate to the establishment of alternatives?
6. Against what measuring stick should alternatives be compared?
7. Under what conditions would you use a group in making a decision?
8. Why should a manager follow an objective decision-making process instead of his or her natural intuition?

## *Application Exercises*

1. Assume that you are going to purchase a typewriter for a small travel agency. Follow the decision-making process discussed in the chapter and recommend a particular typewriter model.
2. Assume that you need to hire a shipping clerk for the summer. Determine the factors that are important to this objective and rank them in order of importance. Then interview three classmates to determine which one comes closest to meeting the criteria you feel are critical for the job. Make a decision after you analyze your three alternatives.
3. With several other members of your class, select a problem that you feel is of major concern to your school. As a group, follow the decision-making process and recommend your final decision to an appropriate person.

4. Analyze the process you followed in determining your life's work. Determine whether you followed the basic decision-making steps in making that decision.

## *Mini-Case*

Assume that you are supervisor of the records management department of the Apex Manufacturing Co. One of your file clerks has given notice that he is leaving your firm in two weeks. Therefore, you want to find a replacement for him as soon as possible. The position is full-time work involving occasional overtime. Good reading and alphabetic skills are required; therefore, a high school diploma is highly desirable. Above-average English grades have also proven to be good indicators of success on the job. Training time is not extensive, but someone who would stay with your firm for a longer period of time would be preferred. The following three persons have applied for the position.

Jana Wilson: Female, 19 years of age, single, completed all but one year of high school; B+ grades in English; previously employed as a waitress for six months; health, good; corrective contact lenses worn; no definite future plans.

Marva Williams: Female, 18 years of age, single, just graduated from high school; wants to go on to college when financially able; B grades in English; no prior employment; walks with a slight limp, but claims no other health problem; eyesight, 20-20.

Jerry Jackson: Male, 18 years of age, single, just graduated from high school; wants to earn money to enter college in three months; A grades in English, previously employed as a department store box boy; good health; wears contact lenses.

Use the decision-making process, and select one of the three candidates for your file clerk job. Write each step you would take in making this decision.

## *Administrative Manager Profile*

Meet Darwin John, director of systems development at General Mills in Minneapolis, Minnesota.

*Background and Experience.* Darwin received both a B.S. degree in production management in 1965 and an M.B.A. in 1971 from Utah State University. He worked for Thiokol Chemical Corp. and Honeywell (computers), prior to joining General Mills in 1973. One of his first positions at General Mills was manager of project management and planning.

*Company.* General Mills was formed in June, 1928, with the merger of a number of leading U.S. milling concerns. Gold Medal flour, Cheerios, Wheaties, and Betty Crocker cake mixes are a few of the well-known products produced by the Consumer Foods Group of General Mills. The company has grown rapidly with sales of $2.9 billion in fiscal year 1976—77 and has produced excellent earnings for its stockholders.

The company has become highly diversified through the acquisitions of leading subsidiaries. A few of these include: Parker Brothers (games), Kenner Products (toys), Lionel (trains), Red Lobster Inns of America (seafood restaurants), Kimberly Knitwear (women's knit clothing), Monet Jewelers, and Eddie Bauer (recreational clothing/equipment).

The general headquarters and executive offices for the company are located in Minneapolis. Manufacturing facilities, flour mills, regional sales offices, and subsidiaries are located throughout the U.S. and the world.

*Job.* In his present position, Darwin is responsible for all information systems development efforts in support of the Consumer Foods Group and the headquarters of General Mills. About one hundred managers, systems analysts, and clerical personnel are employed in systems development. Darwin sees himself as a manager, not as a technician, even though his organization is highly technical.

Two time-consuming activities for Darwin are meetings and travel. He averages thirty hours per week in meetings of all types. He meets with project team leaders to set up and review progress on systems development projects. He also meets with key corporate officials in solving problems and developing long-range plans. For example, Darwin may meet with a committee of executives to help make decisions about informational needs of the company. Travel is also a key activity; Darwin flies to New York, San Francisco, or Miami during a typical month to attend meetings with other systems development executives and to keep up to date on the latest developments in his field.

At least once each year, Darwin interviews each of his employees to appraise the individual's performance, discuss problems, and develop future goals. These interviews provide an opportunity for two-way communication. To further enhance communication, he has set up small communication groups that meet together frequently to discuss relevant information and concerns of group members.

Darwin also spends much time in meeting with representatives of equipment manufacturers. He evaluates their proposals and recommends what equipment should be purchased or leased.

*Management Philosophy.* Here are some of Darwin's comments about his own management philosophy and style of leadership:

"I expect a lot from myself, my subordinates, and others."

"I expect my people to be highly committed and able to achieve results on their own initiative."

"To help my personnel become responsible workers, I try to

1. Carefully place them in jobs with responsibilities that match individual abilities.
2. Set high standards of performance.
3. Provide needed information or feedback that will allow my personnel to control themselves.
4. Provide opportunities for participation in the decision-making process that will give my personnel managerial vision."*

"I try to be honest and straightforward with my people so that they can learn to help themselves."

"Allowing a person to stay in a low performance status is really a disservice to that person."

"Every day I stop to ask myself, 'Is what I'm going to do this day contributing to my objectives and those of the organization?' "

"In my position I am required to be a 'change agent.' By that, I mean that I cause change to happen within the organization. I try to recommend changes that will be beneficial to the organization."

*Darwin John's four-point program for helping personnel become responsible workers is suggested by Peter Drucker's *Management: Tasks, Responsibilities, Practices* (New York: Harper & Row, 1974).

# PART SIX

# Administrative Services

We will look at major areas of administrative services in the next seven chapters: "Administrative Systems Analysis" (Chapter 19), "Building and Office Environment" (Chapter 20), "Office Layout Analysis" (Chapter 21), "Records Management Services" (Chapter 22), "Communication Services" (Chapter 23), "Word Processing" (Chapter 24), and "Data Processing" (Chapter 25). Within the boundaries of these areas are the special administrative services established to assist management. These services are essential—every business organization must analyze its systems and environment, keep records, communicate, and process information and data in order to remain in existence for a long period of time.

The name "administrative services" indicates that the seven areas included in the broad category exist for the primary purpose of serving business administrators. We can think of these areas as staff or support functions, inasmuch as they exist to support the business in its effort to reach its objectives. If used properly, administrative services are tools that can help the organization become more effective.

As an administrative manager, your main purpose is to provide information to management for decision-making purposes. Of course, you will also use administrative services in your own office just as any other manager in the company would. These administrative tools aid in getting major functions accomplished more efficiently and effectively, and they must be cared for; never be too busy to select and maintain equipment and materials used in administrative services.

As we examine each of these areas more closely, you will learn about modern business offices using administrative services and the procedures and policies involved in administering them.

The last chapter in this book, Chapter 26, provides a glimpse into the office of the future and current expectations of how highly mechanized an office will be in order to increase production. You will also see, once again, the importance of people in a company and the need for effective management techniques to get the best results with employees.

# 19

# Administrative Systems Analysis

## ADMINISTRATIVE COSTS

### The Problem

A business magazine reported that "Costs in the office are running uncontrolled. . . . Where office costs used to be 20% to 30% of the total in a company, they have now grown to 40% to 50% of all costs."[1] This statement is rather startling to top managers. Until recently, top management has been largely unaware of the impact of office costs on the total profit picture of an organization. People in management have been concerned with *cost reduction* as a method of *maximizing profits*, but they have centered their attention on manufacturing and distribution costs. Office *administrative costs* have not been considered important until recently, and in many companies the impact of these costs—and interest in them—is still hidden.

One official from a major oil corporation indicated that a research project in this corporation revealed that interest in the administrative area and its costs varied inversely with the level of management. In other words, the higher you go in management in this corporation, the less interest there is in administration and its costs.

In a second giant corporation, an executive said, "Our administrative costs aren't high—we are in manufacturing, not in the insurance business." A few moments of discussion and a few rough calculations soon revealed that this company was spending over $21 million per year for salaries and benefits for its clerical and administrative personnel in its headquarters alone; imagine the total administrative costs for this organization. We can also imagine what the costs are in industries such as insurance and banking where the administrative arm of the business carries the most weight.

The information presented in these two examples is in line with information reported by Paul Strassman, Xerox's staff director for administration and information systems. In 1973, he estimated the cost of information processing in the U.S. at $418 billion. Only 6 percent of this total ($26 billion) went for data processing. About 10 percent ($42 billion) was spent on administrative processing equipment. About 84 percent, or $350 billion, was used for clerical and administrative personnel salaries and benefits (see Figure 19-1).[2] From these data, it is apparent that clerical personnel costs must be controlled.

Increases in office costs could be justified if office productivity increased correspondingly. According to Alan Purchase, senior industrial economist for Stanford Research Institute, during the period from 1960 to 1970, productivity for blue collar workers increased by 83 percent while productivity for white collar workers rose by only 4 percent.[3] No wonder management is starting to cry for greater productivity in the office.

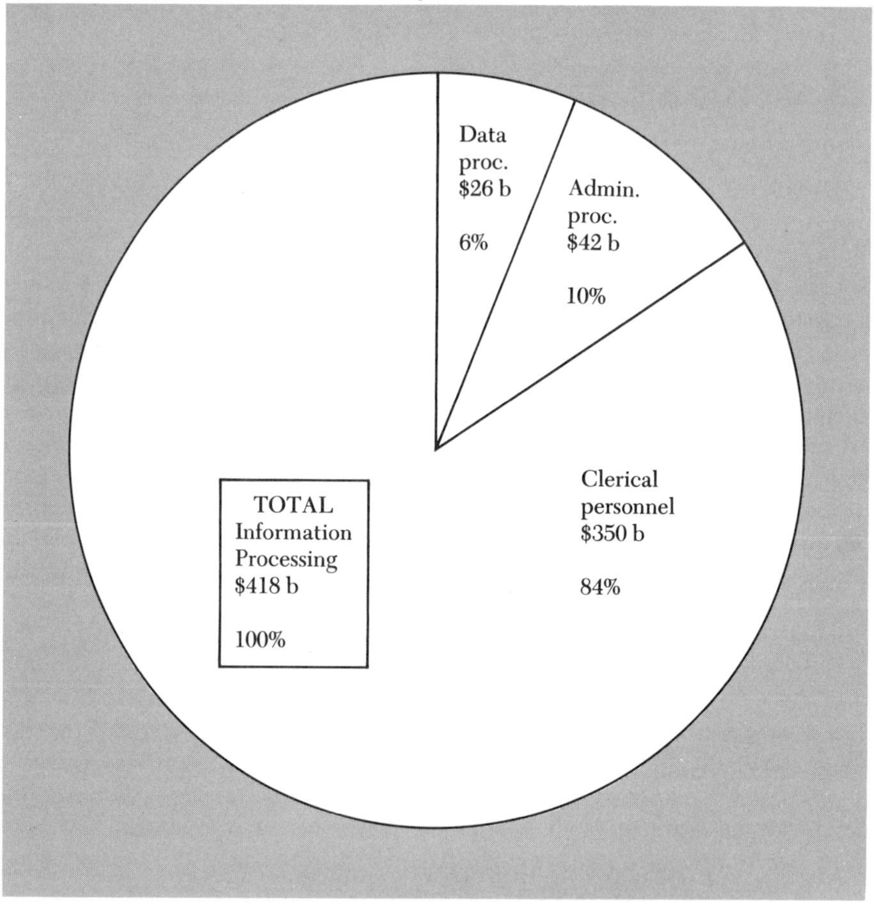


*Figure 19-1.* Pie Chart Illustrating the Amount of Money Spent on Information Processing during 1973 (in Billions of Dollars)

One might ask the question, "*Why* have office administrative costs been allowed to get out of control?" The primary reason has been discussed—top management's apathy and unawareness of the problem. Other reasons include:

1. Increased size of organizations and need for more communication
2. Imposed reporting requirements by government
3. Resistance to change
4. Inadequate technology
5. Established organizational customs and traditions (For example, each executive tends to have a private secretary whether one is needed or not. Also, because management tends to work closely with administrative support personnel, its objectivity about related costs tends to be reduced.)

Other questions that one might ask are, "What has been done to try to control administrative costs?" "Why have these approaches been ineffective?" "What can be done to correct the problem?"

In the past, many administrative managers have attacked office cost problems by using work simplification and work measurement tools such as those that will be described in this chapter. Their efforts were effective in their local offices but did not have major impact on the overall productivity picture. As the computer developed, a new field known as *systems analysis* was developed to plan cost-effective systems for processing data.[4] Systems analysis cut across organizational boundaries by looking at companywide systems. With some innovations, systems analysts have used the basic tools of work simplification effectively. Up to this point, however, systems analysis has concentrated on computerized data processing. With an attitude similar to that of top management, systems analysts have had little concern and little impact on administrative processing.

Efforts to control administrative costs have been largely ineffective so far for three reasons: administrative managers have not had adequate power to affect a large part of the organization in many cases; systems analysis has not spread beyond computerized data processing; top management support for improvement projects and capital expenditures has been lacking.

## Administrative Cost Control

In order to correct the runaway administrative cost problem, five steps need to be taken:

1. Top management must be oriented to the problem and its support must be gained. Overall and individual organizational cost figures should be presented to gain attention and to convince management that it must act.

2. A steering committee of high level administrative executives should be organized, with the controller or vice-president (or someone similar) as chairperson. This committee's function is to provide guidance and direction to a second group known as a *task force* (a working group that will study the problem and make recommendations). On the task force are persons who have good working knowledge about administrative systems.
3. The task force will likely develop a proposal to organize a department headed by a vice-president, to assume responsibility for all administration and information. This department might be called the administration department, the information processing department, or some similar title. All administrative services and processing would be grouped under this department; its organization would be similar to the one in Figure 19-2. All information processing costs would be charged to this one organizational segment as a major step forward in controlling these costs.
4. Systems analysts should be trained to solve administrative processing problems and to develop cost effective systems. Problems in working with the processing of "soft information" (qualitative verbal informa-

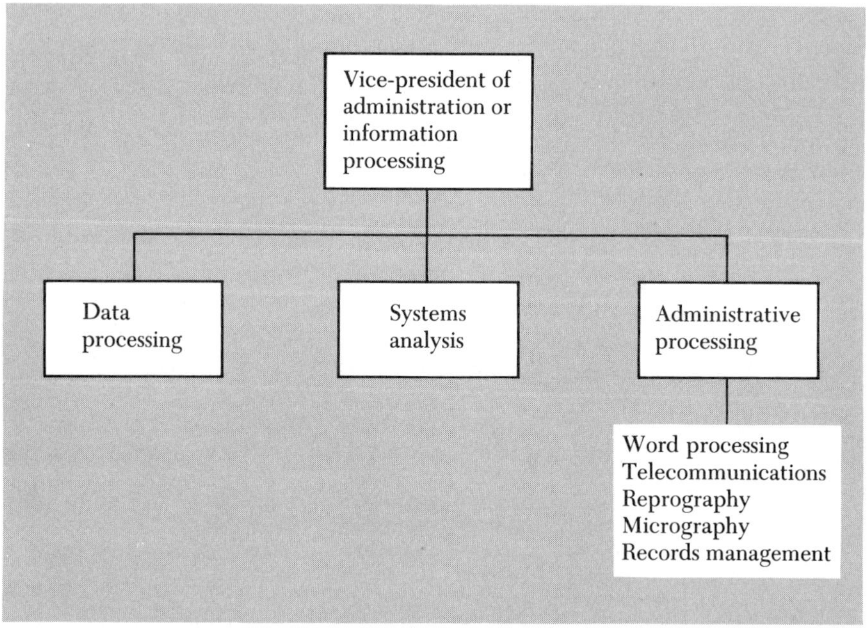


*Figure 19-2.* Organization Chart for an Administration or Information-Processing Department

tion) are different from those problems found in processing "hard data" in the data-processing area. Let's look at the difference between "soft information" and "hard data":

*Soft Information*

Reasons for buying brand A dictation machine versus brand B: sound quality, operational convenience, salesman's personality, machine company's ability to make an impression, and maintenance capability

Willingness and availability of an executive to attend a meeting

Feelings of concern about workability of a new system

Persuasive reasoning why Darwin rather than Robert should be promoted

Judgment about a new personnel policy

Information about a new government regulation on hiring minority persons

Performance appraisal information

*Hard Data*

Cost of preparing a letter in the word-processing center

Cost of various types of dictation equipment

Number of dictation machines sold

Number of hours machines in operation are down or unworkable

Number of orders received from Western territory

Sales figures for each sales person

Cost of inventory on hand

Amount of money owed company (accounts receivable)

Number of orders not shipped on time

Cost of shipping orders

Amount of money contributed to Community Chest, by department

Cost of products sold

5. Study new systems for administrative processing. Wherever possible, use technology to handle routine clerical work. One person with good equipment can perform at lower cost the work of several persons without the equipment. For the sake of comparison, we can point out that currently the capital investment for clerical workers is much lower than that for farmers or production workers, as shown in Figure 19-3.[5] However, this $2,000 investment for equipment per clerical worker could easily go to $10,000 during the next ten years and would have the overall effect of reducing information processing costs; greater expenditure on equipment that replaces employees has low-

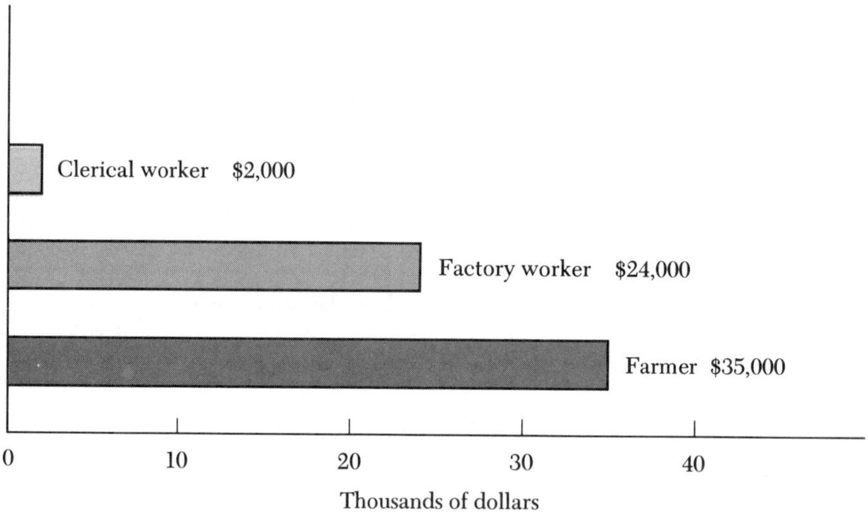


*Figure 19-3.* Average Investment in Capital Equipment for Various Types of Workers

ered costs in the past and can be expected to do so in the future. Remember that 84 percent of total information-processing costs go to pay salaries and benefits for clerical personnel.

## DEFINITIONS

In Chapter 1, the concept of systems was discussed; it centered on systems in general and on their application to management. Here the discussion will focus on systems to accomplish office work. George Terry, a noted author on management, said, "System includes a group of parts or elements interacting to achieve a particular goal. A system exists within an environment that supplies resources as inputs to the system and that accepts processed resources as outputs from the system. A system exists to achieve something."[6] That "something" in an administration department is providing services and management information.

The equipment, records, procedures, methods, and personnel involved in the completion of a major unit of work make up a *system*.

Through various systems, the organization meets its objectives. For example, an organization is likely to have the following systems: personnel, financial accounting, cost accounting, sales, and purchasing.

A system is composed of a number of *procedures*—sequences of operations by which recurring activities are performed.

The personnel system would be composed of procedures such as selection, orientation, training and development, appraisal, promotion, and salary and benefits. In turn, procedures are accomplished by certain methods.

*Methods* are step-by-step means by which work elements are performed.

For example, the personnel selection procedure involves specific methods such as preparing classified advertisements, conducting college recruitment campaigns, using employment agencies, and making announcements in the company. The concept of how a system, procedures, and methods fit together is illustrated in Figure 19-4. (To simplify the illustration, only methods for the selection procedure are shown.)

The major difference among methods, procedures, and systems is the level of detail that is considered. Methods charts can be very detailed, to the point where they indicate individual hand and body motions. Procedures explain exactly how to accomplish major units of work, but provide less detail than methods descriptions. A systems chart gives a very general picture of how a broad, major segment of an organizational mission is accomplished. A systems flowchart for an order system is shown in Figure 19-5.

Systems analysis is known by other names such as procedures analysis, methods improvement, work simplification, and efficiency studies. However, *systems analysis* is the preferred term because of its broader implications.

*Systems analysis* is either a detailed investigation of an existing system to develop improvements or a detailed planning process to define a new system. The objective is to accomplish designated results in an efficient and cost-effective manner. *Administrative systems analysis* is systems analysis applied to the administrative functions. It implies finding a better way of doing administrative work, thus leading to cost reduction. Systems, procedures, and methods efficiency can save an organization thousands of dollars each year.

Administrative managers have the major responsibility for administrative systems analysis, not only for their own organization, but for all administrative systems throughout the entire organization. Larger organizations have full-time systems analysts and even departments with whom administrative managers can work in systems development. Systems work is a continuous, ongoing function, because systems improvement is never totally accomplished. There will always be a "better way" to be discovered as long as wasted motion and materials cost organizations large amounts of money.

In the next section we will look at the five-step analysis procedure, which can help you in solving many basic office problems and in developing new or improved systems.

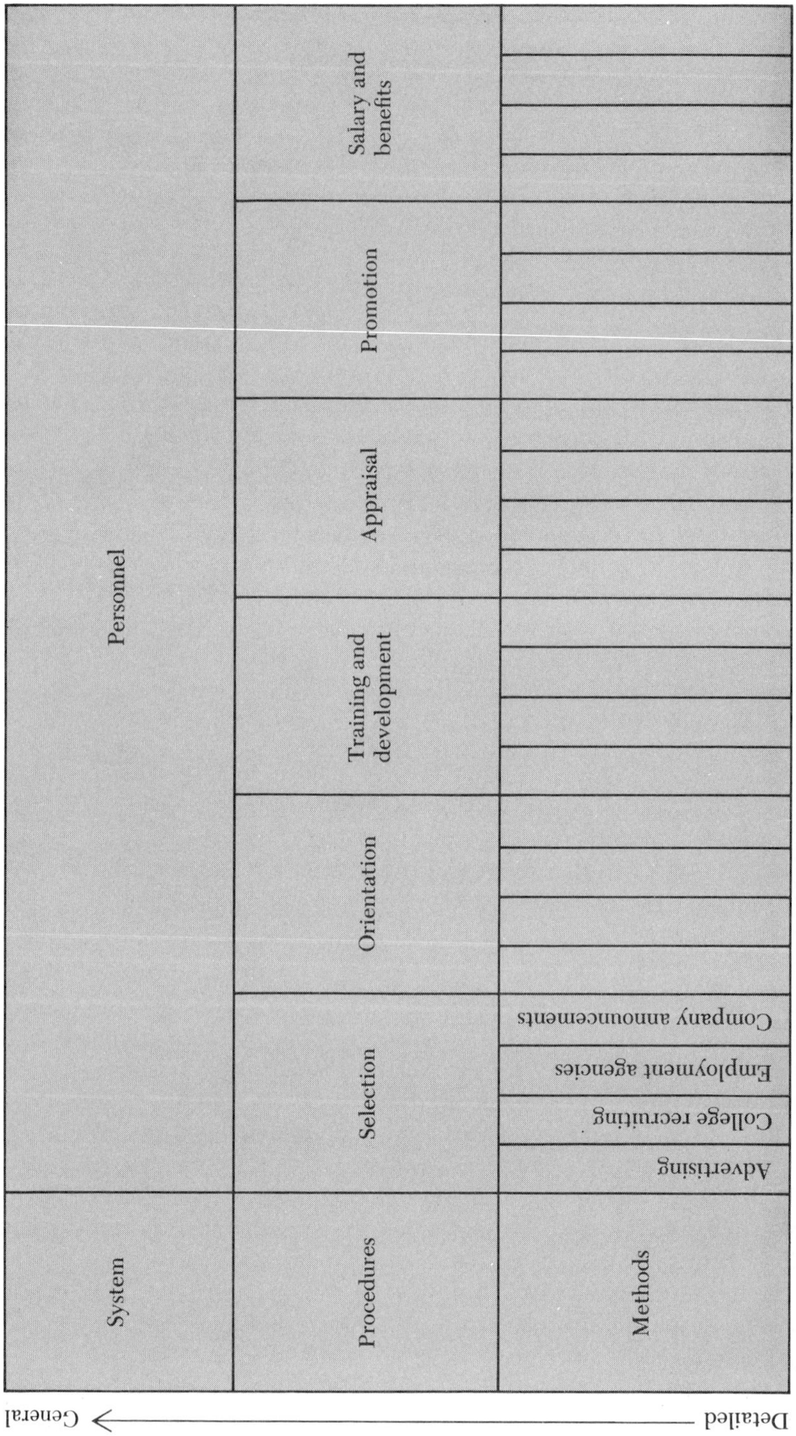


*Figure 19-4.* Diagram Showing Relationship of System, Procedures, and Methods, Using an Example of a Personnel System and Its Selection Methods

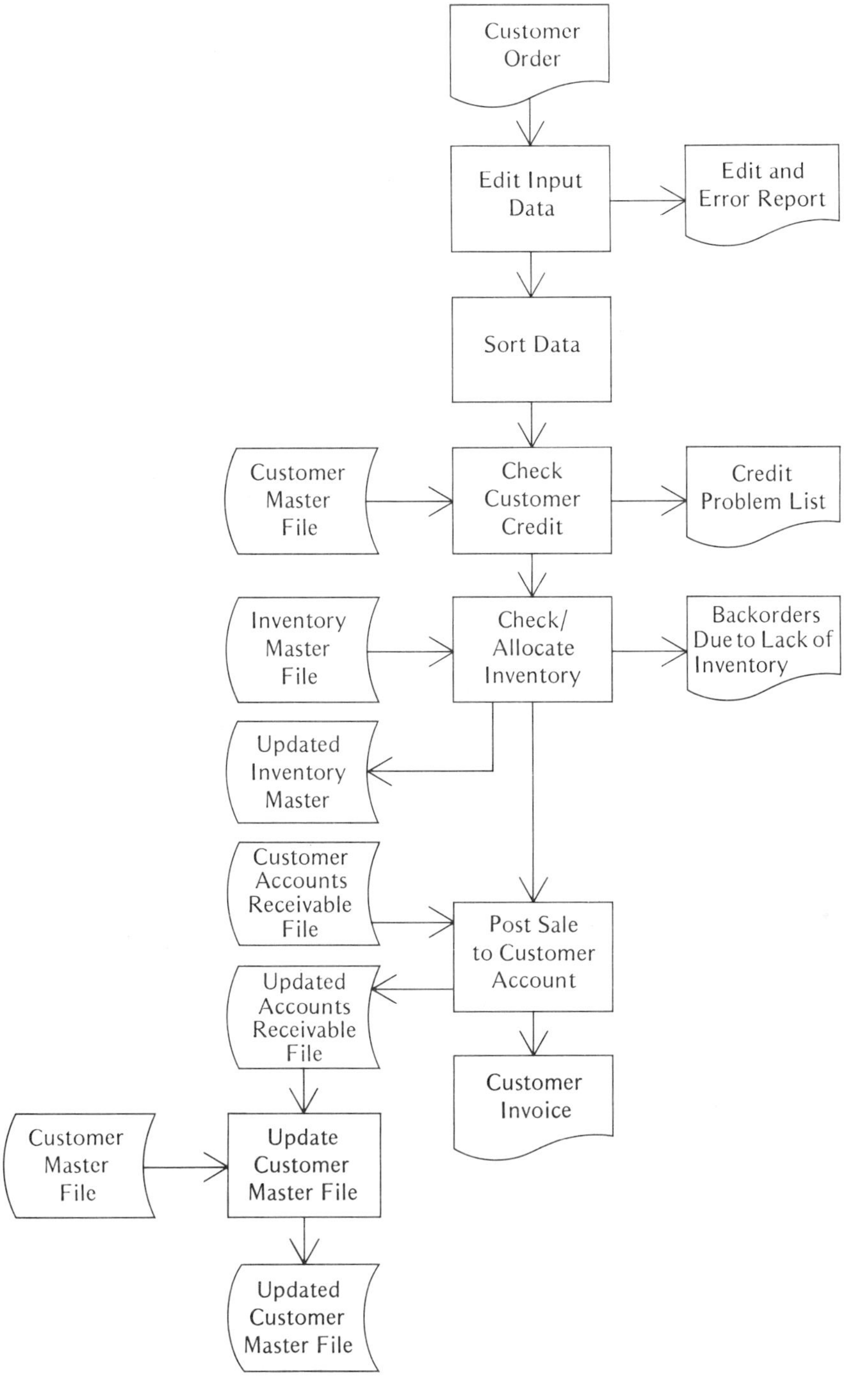


*Figure 19-5.* Example of a Systems Flowchart

*Source:* Philip C. Semprevivo, *Systems Analysis* (Chicago: Science Research Associates, 1976), p. 63.

## FIVE-STEP ANALYSIS PROCEDURE

The five basic steps of a recommended analysis procedure are:

1. Select an element of work to be improved.
2. Describe present methods and procedures.
3. Analyze the present method and design an improved method.
4. Sell and implement the improved method or procedure.
5. Maintain and audit the system.

1. *Select the element of work to be improved.*

Example: Ed Beame, administrative manager for a minicomputer company in Massachusetts, has been concerned about his department's ability to provide adequate secretarial support to marketing and engineering personnel, who write many letters, memos, reports, and technical papers. Preparing all of this paperwork is time consuming and costly. Because the documents are revised heavily and often, typists type the same document several times. From the time a document is composed until the final draft is completed takes about two days to two weeks.

Key points: Work was selected that (1) is costly, (2) is time-consuming, (3) involves a long turnaround time.

Other problem indicators are that (1) delay is caused, (2) bottleneck is created, (3) materials are wasted, and (4) employees or customers are dissatisfied.

Look for work that is repeated frequently.

2. *Describe present methods and procedures.*

Example: Ed gathered information about the present method by observing how documents were prepared and by interviewing people involved such as sales representatives, engineers, and secretaries. He asked questions to help him learn the system. Typical questions: What are you doing? Exactly how do you get information for that particular report? What happens to the letter next? To help him gather information, Ed used the flowchart, flow process chart, and movement diagram.

Later, Ed found that he needed to know more about how the work-

Key points: Information-gathering techniques (asterisk * indicates tools and techniques used by Ed in his study):

*Interviews
Questionnaires
*Observations

Analysis tools:

*Flow process chart
Management flow charts
*Movement diagram
*Productivity study chart
*Work distribution chart

load was divided and how much time individuals spent on various activities. To gather this information, he selected the productivity study chart and the work distribution chart.

As part of his information-gathering procedure, Ed obtained ideas and suggestions from the people involved in doing the work. He felt that they were in the best position to understand the problems involved in doing the work.

Narrative procedure description

(These tools will be described in detail later in this chapter.)

In the example, notice how tools were selected to accomplish specific purposes.

3. *Analyze the present method and design an improved method.*

Example: As Ed began to analyze his information, he took nothing for granted; he questioned everything. His first and most important question was "Why?" Why is this letter necessary? Do we really need this report? What if we discontinued preparing this description of how you developed this new computer; what would happen? If he was convinced that the document was necessary, he looked in detail at the method of preparing it. He questioned why each step of the procedure was necessary. Why does that statement have to be typed? Could it be left in handwritten form or could it remain on an orally recorded medium? Are copies of that report necessary? For steps determined to be essential, he questioned the method, person, place, and time with regard to each step. For example, could that information be phoned to purchasing rather than hand carried? Could Jill rather than her boss get that information?

As a result of asking these questions, Ed was able to take or recommend four action steps: (1) eliminate, (2) combine, (3) improve or

Key points: analysis questions:

*Why* is this work necessary?

*Why* is each step in the procedure necessary?

*What* is done? What isn't done? What problems are frequently encountered? What materials and equipment are involved?

*How* is the action performed? How many units are produced during a given period of time?

*Who* does the step? Who is affected by the action? Could someone else better accomplish this step?

*When* is the action performed? When do problems most frequently occur?

*Where* is the action performed? Where are the materials and information obtained from?

*Develop a questioning attitude.* Consider the relationship between the analysis quessimplify, and (4) mechanize or automate. In some cases, he found that preparing a report or letter was not necessary. No one really needed the information; in others, he found that while the information was needed, a handwritten note in the margin of the original memo was all that was necessary. He found that at times a secretary could request certain information over the phone rather than have her boss dictate a letter. Sometimes the secretary could compose a message rather than her boss or a form letter could be used in lieu of composing an original letter.

Once Ed was assured that the work was necessary and being accomplished in an efficient manner, he considered the possibility of using machines or a computer to do the job. He realized that he had to carefully examine the first three action steps before considering mechanization or automation. A method or procedure should be operating as effectively as possible before the technology is applied. Otherwise he felt that he would be simply speeding up an inefficient procedure or method. Ed had learned this lesson well when he had worked on improving a procedure to collect money owed to the company (accounts receivable). Unneeded information and extra steps to obtain that information were involved in the original procedure. Without making system improvements first, automating that procedure simply speeded up the inefficiencies built in.

Back to the task at hand, Ed felt good about his analysis and his application of the first three action tions and the basic improvement actions:

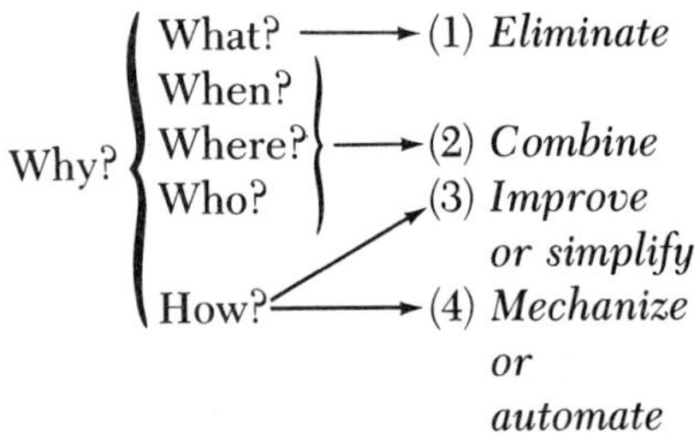


Follow the sequence shown in applying the action steps. This sequence eliminates unnecessary work, makes procedure efficient, and applies speed and the sophistication of technology.

Concentrate your attention on the *approach* to solving the problem.

steps. He was ready to recommend the use of automation to speed up the procedures. He carefully considered how word processing could be applied to this problem and concluded that the best solution was to adapt one of the minicomputers produced by his company to perform word-processing operations. He also decided that a new dictation system and a high-speed copy system were necessary.

4. *Sell and implement the improved method or procedure.*

Example: Because Ed's organization was oriented to helping other organizations accept change, he anticipated that he would not have much trouble with selling and implementing improvement. Even in this situation, Ed found at first that his people were uneasy when they learned about possible changes. They didn't know how these ideas would affect them. They wondered if cuts would be made in the number of people on the staff. They wondered if they could become accustomed to these new approaches.

Ed decided that he wouldn't rush into making changes. He decided to call a meeting in his department to inform everyone of all the changes he was thinking about. He called for questions and asked for suggestions. His personnel were free to express their ideas and some new ideas were brought out that Ed had not thought about before.

Also, he suggested to the managers of the engineering and marketing departments that they discuss the proposed changes with their people. Again, new ideas were brought out and final procedures

Key points: The introduction of change usually involves some resistance. As with many other personnel and management problems, poor communication is usually the source of the problem and effective communication is usually the answer. People need to understand how changes will affect them and how they will benefit. Also, they need to be involved in suggesting answers and in implementing change. If an idea is not accepted, the person making the suggestion needs to understand why his or her ideas were not accepted.

were agreed upon. Ed learned that most of the people involved felt good about the proposed changes. They understood what was happening and why. They felt that they had a voice in determining how the changes would be implemented.

5. *Maintain and audit the system.*

Example: When the new word origination system was installed, there were some problems initially. At first, the executives had difficulties getting accustomed to the new dictation system. Then as they learned the new system, they felt more comfortable with it and were much more efficient. One of the word-processing units didn't function properly at first. Maintenance persons from the equipment vendor worked closely with the word-processing personnel until all of the "bugs" were worked out.

Ed continued to check on the system and found that new ways of making improvements could be found. He found that the word-processing operators from time to time had suggestions on improvements. He also found that the vendor had new "software," or ways of giving instructions to the machines to increase the capabilities of the "hardware" (equipment).

After six months of operation under the new system, Ed sat back and looked at what had been accomplished. He felt good about the increase of productivity on the part of his clerical personnel as well as on the part of the engineers and sales representatives. They were also able to do more now than they had been able to do in the past.

Key points: Once a new system has been installed or improvements have been made in an old one, followup action must take place to make sure that the system is operating smoothly and that changes are made as new problems appear and new technology is developed.

The new system should be evaluated by comparing productivity measures for the old and new systems. Amount of time and cost are good examples of productivity measures.

## ANALYSIS TOOLS

To accomplish the process of analyzing and improving the systems and procedures of an organization, a number of analysis charts have been developed. With these charts, you can see in detail how a particular routine job is performed and detect areas of inefficiency. Once discovered, these areas can be eliminated by new and better ways of performing the task being studied. Several of the more widely used analysis charts are presented to illustrate the tools that can be used in systems work.

### Flow Process Chart

Probably the most popular chart used in the study of work processes is the flow process chart or work simplification chart. The flow process chart is used to symbolize step-by-step the various activities involved in office procedures. It enables you to get a detailed look at the particular process being studied.

The American Standards Association has developed a set of symbols that are quite widely used by systems personnel. The symbols make chart reading much more effective than verbal description alone. As shown in Table 19-1, work activities can be represented by five symbols; explanations and examples for the symbols are included.

**Table 19-1. Flow Process Chart Symbols**

| *Symbol* | *Name* | *Explanation* | *Examples* |
|---|---|---|---|
|  | Operation | "Doing" or production step | Typing a letter<br>Dictating a letter<br>Sealing an envelope |
|  | Transportation | Movement of person or thing from one place to another | Walking to mail room<br>Sending form to purchasing |
|  | Inspection | Verification or check on quality or quantity | Proofreading a letter<br>Inspecting an offset master |
|  | Delay | Temporary hold-up in the process | Placing letter in an in-basket<br>Waiting to see boss |
|  | Storage | Long-term delay or deposit for future | Placing document in file<br>Putting microfilm in drawer |

| FLOW PROCESS CHART | | No. | Page No. | No. of Pages |
|---|---|---|---|---|
| Process: ANSWERING MAIL | | | | |
| [X] Man or [ ] Material | | | | |
| Chart Begins: P/U Mail Fr. In-Basket | Chart Ends: Sign Correspondence | | | |
| Charted By: G. Harding | Date | | | |
| Organization: Administrative Unit | | | | |

| SUMMARY | | | | | | |
|---|---|---|---|---|---|---|
| ACTIONS | Present | | Proposed | | Difference | |
| | No. | Time | No. | Time | No. | Time |
| ○ operations | 12 | | | | | |
| ⇨ transportations | 1 | | | | | |
| □ inspections | 5 | | | | | |
| D delays | 3 | 20 | | | | |
| ▽ storages | 0 | | | | | |
| Distance Traveled (Feet) | 30 | | | | | |

| Step No. | DETAILS OF METHOD [X] Present [ ] Proposed | operation / transportation / inspection / delay / storage | Distance (In Feet) | Quantity | Time | analysis (why?) what? | where? | when? | who? | how? | NOTES | analysis: eliminate | combine | chng: sequence | place | person | improve |
|---|---|---|---|---|---|---|---|---|---|---|---|---|---|---|---|---|---|
| 1 | Pick up mail from in-basket | ○ ⇨ □ D ▽ | | 25 | | | | | | | | | | | | | |
| 2 | Open envelope | ○ ⇨ □ D ▽ | | | | X | | X | | | Have secretary open mail, sort by priority | | | | | X | |
| 3 | Scan letter, memo, or other document | ○ ⇨ □ D ▽ | | | | X | | X | | | and place in the in-basket or on desk | | | | | X | |
| 4 | Sort into piles by priority | ○ ⇨ □ D ▽ | | | | X | | X | | | | | | | | X | |
| 5 | Read top priority correspondence | ○ ⇨ □ D ▽ | | | | | | | | | | | | | | | |
| 6 | Note action, etc. | ○ ⇨ □ D ▽ | | | | | | | | | | | | | | | |
| 7 | Ask secretary to retrieve reference materials from file | ○ ⇨ □ D ▽ | | | | X | X | X | | | Have secretary bring reference material with | | X | | | X | |
| 8 | Wait | ○ ⇨ □ D ▽ | | | 5 min | | | | | | mail | X | | | | | |
| 9 | Dictate reply to secretary | ○ ⇨ □ D ▽ | | | | | | | | X | Use dictation equipment | | | | | | X |
| 10 | Read 2nd priority correspondence | ○ ⇨ □ D ▽ | | | | | | | | | | | | | | | |
| 11 | Note action, etc. | ○ ⇨ □ D ▽ | | | | | | | | | | | | | | | |
| 12 | Ask secretary to retrieve reference material from file | ○ ⇨ □ D ▽ | | | | X | X | X | | | Bring with mail | | X | X | | X | |
| 13 | Wait | ○ ⇨ □ D ▽ | | | 5 min | | | | | | | X | | | | | |
| 14 | Dictate reply to secretary | ○ ⇨ □ D ▽ | | | | | X | | X | X | Use dictation equipment in word processing | | | | X | X | X |
| 15 | Pick up finished reply from in-basket | ○ ⇨ □ D ▽ | | | | | | | | | center (WPC) | | | | | | |
| 16 | Read reply | ○ ⇨ □ D ▽ | | | | | | | | | | | | | | | |
| 17 | Make necessary corrections | ○ ⇨ □ D ▽ | | | | | | | | | | | | | | | |
| 18 | Give to secretary | ○ ⇨ □ D ▽ | 30 | | | | X | | X | | To WPC | | | | X | X | |
| 19 | Wait | ○ ⇨ □ D ▽ | | | 10 min | | | | | | Do something else | | | | | | |
| 20 | Read corrected reply | ○ ⇨ □ D ▽ | | | | | | | | X | Read only corrections | | | | | | X |
| 21 | Sign correspondence | ○ ⇨ □ D ▽ | | | | | | | | | | | | | | | |

*Figure 19-6.* Sample Flow Process Chart for Present Process of Answering Mail

Flow process charts incorporating these symbols are prepared for use in the systems description and analysis process. A typical chart showing an

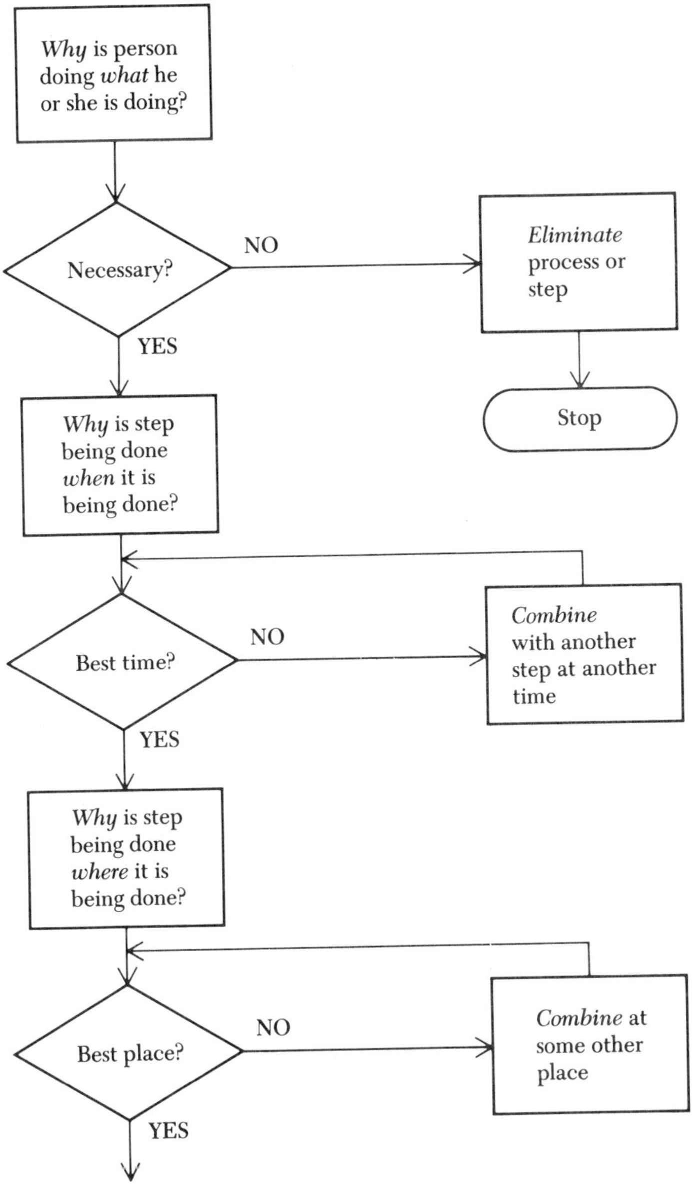


*Figure 19-7.* Analyzing a Procedure or a Method

example of a present method of answering mail is found in Figure 19-6. On each line of the chart, you describe a specific part of the process or step that you are studying; then you indicate which of the five symbols are involved in

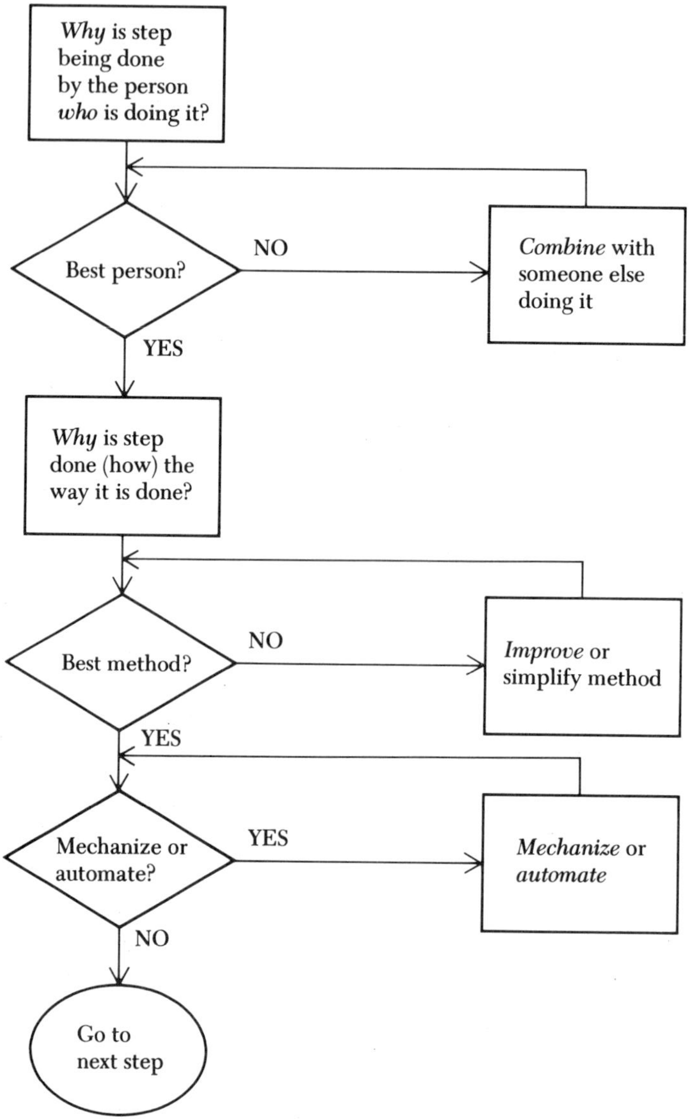


*Figure 19-7, continued*

that particular activity. After all steps included in the process are listed, you draw a line from the appropriate symbol on one line to the appropriate symbol on the next line, and so on until all of the steps in the process being studied are described by a line connecting a series of symbols (see Figure 19-6).

When the description of the present method has been completed, you begin the real "analysis" part of your work. You examine in detail all steps

**Table 19-2. Improvement Actions Taken in Developing Recommended Mail-Handling Procedure**

| *Improvement action* | *Steps involved (see Figure 19-7)* | *Comments* |
|---|---|---|
| Eliminate | 1 | Mail placed on desk; not necessary to go to in-basket |
| Eliminate | 2 | Secretary does this |
| Eliminate | 3 | Secretary does this |
| Eliminate | 4 | Secretary does this |
| Eliminate | 6 | No longer necessary; just take action |
| Eliminate | 7 | Secretary does this step automatically when reading mail |
| Eliminate | 8 | No longer necessary |
| Mechanize | 9 | Use central dictation system (word-processing center—WPC) |
| Eliminate | 11 | No longer necessary; just take action |
| Eliminate | 12 | Secretary brings reference material with mail |
| Eliminate | 13 | No longer necessary |
| Mechanize | 14 | Use central dictation system (WPC) |
| Eliminate | 15 | Finished replies placed on desk or handed to the executive |
| Mechanize | 17 | Corrections dictated directly to WPC |
| Eliminate | 18 | No longer necessary |
| Eliminate | 19 | No longer necessary |
| Improve | 20 | Read only corrected portions of documents |

involved in the total process. For each step, you ask the why, what, who, when, where, and how questions (see Figure 19-7). During this analysis process, keep detailed notes to later formulate your suggestions for improvement.

Your objective is to include the optimum number of operations (the "doing" steps) and to eliminate as many of the other symbols as possible. Figure 19-8 illustrates a proposed procedure for handling mail that resulted from analysis of the present method shown in Figure 19-7. Notice how steps have been eliminated, combined, simplified, and mechanized. Table 19-2 explains what improvement actions have been taken; the secretary and word processing center are used to save the executive's time. In developing your improvements, you will use all resources available to you—past experience, published information, other organizations with similar processes, and other persons who possess the needed skills and ability. As a result of your analysis, the total time involved in completing the process should be reduced as a result of eliminating steps, shortening distances, and making other improvements.

| FLOW PROCESS CHART | | No. | Page No. | No. of Pages |
|---|---|---|---|---|
| Process: ANSWERING MAIL | | | | |
| [X] Man or [ ] Material | | | | |
| Chart Begins: Read Top Priority Material | Chart Ends: Sign Correspondence | | | |
| Charted By: G. Harding | Date: | | | |
| Organization: Administrative Unit | | | | |

| SUMMARY ACTIONS | Present No. | Present Time | Proposed No. | Proposed Time | Difference No. | Difference Time |
|---|---|---|---|---|---|---|
| ○ operations | 12 | | 6 | | 6 | |
| ⇨ transportations | 1 | | 0 | | 1 | |
| □ inspections | 5 | | 6 | | (+1) | |
| D delays | 3 | 20 | 0 | 0 | 3 | 20 |
| ▽ storages | 0 | | 0 | | 0 | |
| Distance Traveled (Feet) | 30 | | 0 | | 30 | |

| Step No. | DETAILS OF METHOD [ ] Present [X] Proposed | operation / transportation / inspection / delay / storage | Distance (In Feet) | Quantity | Time | analysis (why?) what? where? when? who? how? | NOTES | analysis: eliminate / change: combine, sequence, place, person, improve |
|---|---|---|---|---|---|---|---|---|
| 1 | Read top priority documents and reference materials | ○ ⇨ □ D ▽ | | 2 | | | Mail is presorted by secretary and placed on desk in piles | |
| | | ○ ⇨ □ D ▽ | | | | | | |
| 2 | Dictate replies | ○ ⇨ □ D ▽ | | | | | Use central dictation system | |
| 3 | Read medium priority documents and reference material | ○ ⇨ □ D ▽ | | 5 | | | Low priority material–18 items–handled by secretary | |
| | | ○ ⇨ □ D ▽ | | | | | | |
| 4 | Dictate replies | ○ ⇨ □ D ▽ | | | | | Top priority work typed while executive had been working on medium priority work | |
| | | ○ ⇨ □ D ▽ | | | | | | |
| 5 | Read typed replies for top priority documents | ○ ⇨ □ D ▽ | | | | | Goes directly to WP operator | |
| 6 | Dictate necessary corrections | ○ ⇨ □ D ▽ | | | | | | |
| 7 | Read typed replies for medium priority documents | ○ ⇨ □ D ▽ | | | | | | |
| 8 | Dictate necessary corrections | ○ ⇨ □ D ▽ | | | | | | |
| 9 | Read corrected reply for priority documents | ○ ⇨ □ D ▽ | | | | | Read only corrected portion of document | |
| 10 | Sign correspondence | ○ ⇨ □ D ▽ | | | | | | |
| 11 | Read corrected reply for medium priority documents | ○ ⇨ □ D ▽ | | | | | | |
| 12 | Sign correspondence | ○ ⇨ □ D ▽ | | | | | | |
| 13 | | ○ ⇨ □ D ▽ | | | | | | |
| 14 | | ○ ⇨ □ D ▽ | | | | | | |
| 15 | | ○ ⇨ □ D ▽ | | | | | | |
| 16 | | ○ ⇨ □ D ▽ | | | | | | |
| 17 | | ○ ⇨ □ D ▽ | | | | | | |
| 18 | | ○ ⇨ □ D ▽ | | | | | | |

*Figure 19-8.* Sample Flow Process Chart for Proposed Process of Answering Mail

## Flowchart

Another useful tool is the flowchart, which depicts in visual form, with limited narrative description, all of the key steps in a work procedure. Figure 19-9 presents an example of a typical day in the life of an office worker (written

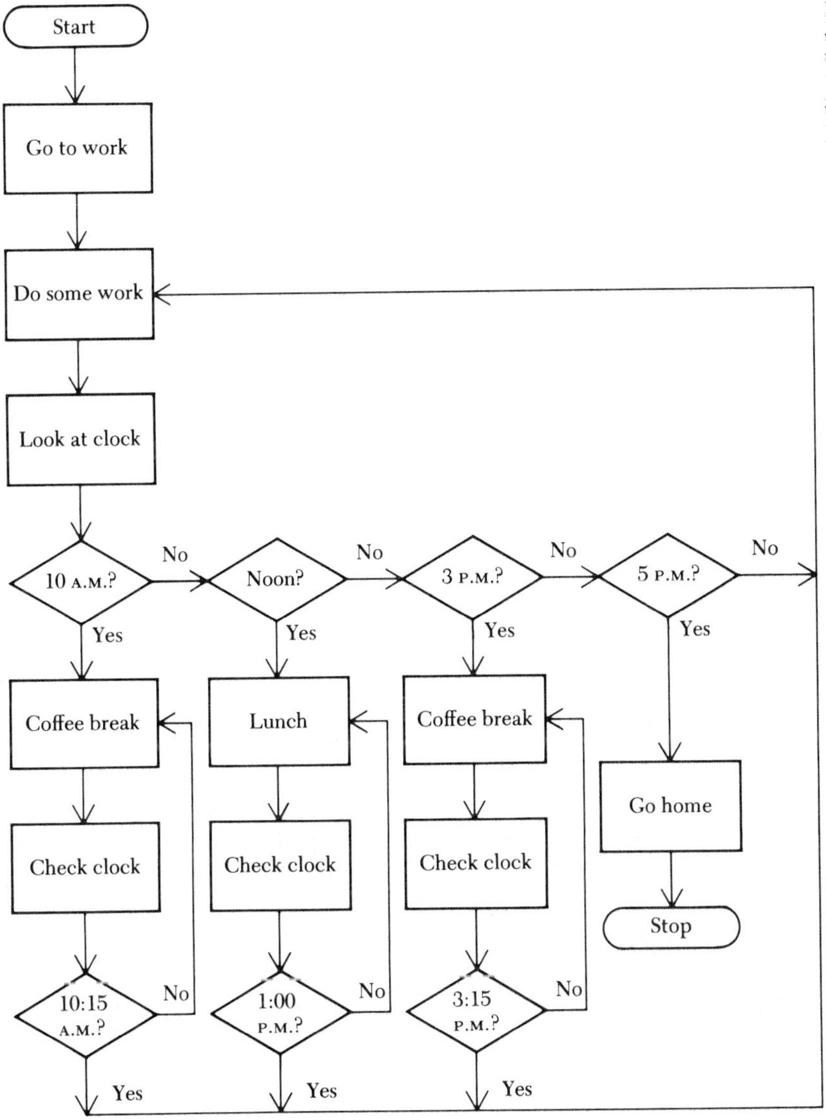


*Figure 19-9.* An Example of a Flowchart.
Start or Stop, Operation, and Decision

from a humorous viewpoint) and displays the three basic types of symbols used in flowcharts. The first symbol represents the start or stop of the procedure, the second represents an operation, the third represents a decision, and the fourth can be used to show multiple copies of a form (the movement of forms through an organization is often shown in flowcharts). Arrows can be used to show what happens to each copy of the form.

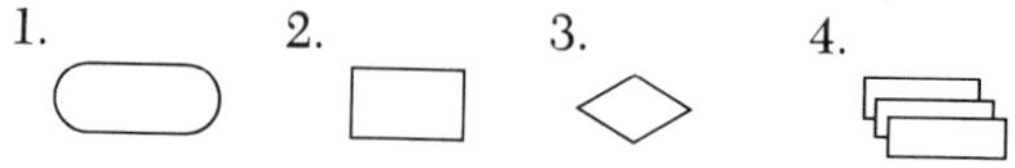


The important aspect of the flowchart (Figure 19-9) is that all basic actions and decision points have been accounted for; the entire work day has been programmed. Of course, the chart has been drastically simplified so that you can see how a flowchart operates. Notice the three small loops starting at 10:00 A.M., noon, and 3:00 P.M. There is also a large loop that starts and ends with "Do some work." An employee would go around the 10:00 A.M. loop until 10:15 A.M. when he or she would return to work. The key element in the chart is the step "Do some work." In order for this system to operate properly, it would be necessary to break this one step down into many specific operations and decision points. (Figure 19-5 showed an example of a real flowchart used for a business situation.) In Figure 19-10, standard flowcharting symbols are shown.

### Management Flowchart

Another frequently used type of chart is the management flowchart; basically, it is composed of rectangles in which short descriptions of operations are placed. No special symbols need to be learned to understand the management flowchart; although symbols or miniature drawings of specific types of equipment are often used in this type of chart, managers who are already familiar with office equipment readily recognize the pictorial representation. The ease of composing and understanding the management flowchart has helped to make it one of the more favored types of systems charting.

An example of a management flowchart is shown in Figure 19-11. Notice that this type of chart has no particular direction in its flow. Different operations could extend upward, downward, or to the left or right of preceding operations.

### Flow or Movement Diagram

A chart that allows you to portray movement of people or flow of documents through an office is the flow or movement diagram. The purpose of the chart is to reduce wasted movement. First, obtain or prepare a layout chart of the office showing desks and files and other equipment in the office. On this chart, draw an arrow for each move of the person or document you are charting. In many offices, much wasted movement is made evident with a flow diagram, as you can see in Figure 19-12. By rearranging the locations of the supervisor and the clerks, the travel can be reduced. Caution must be exercised to avoid disturbing some other major flow or movements in the office in the process of making changes.

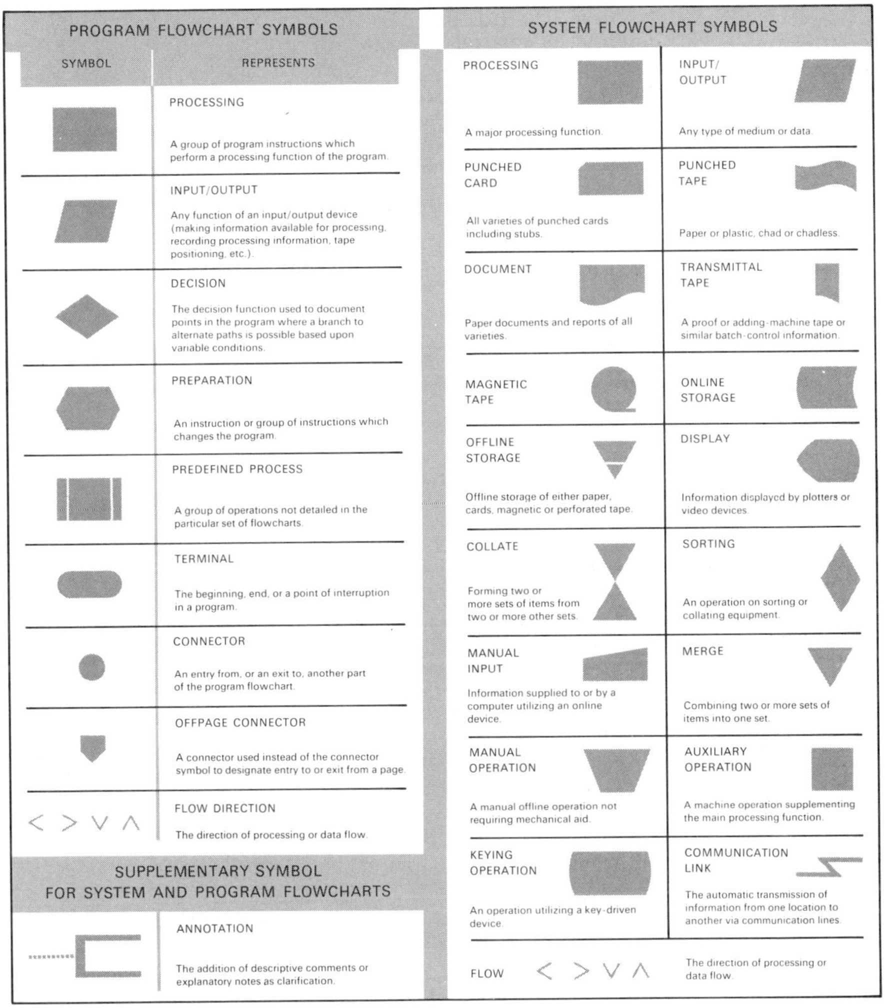


*Figure 19-10.* System and Program Flowcharting Symbols

*Source:* Marilyn Bohl, *Information Processing*, 2d ed. (Chicago: Science Research Associates, 1976), p. 146.

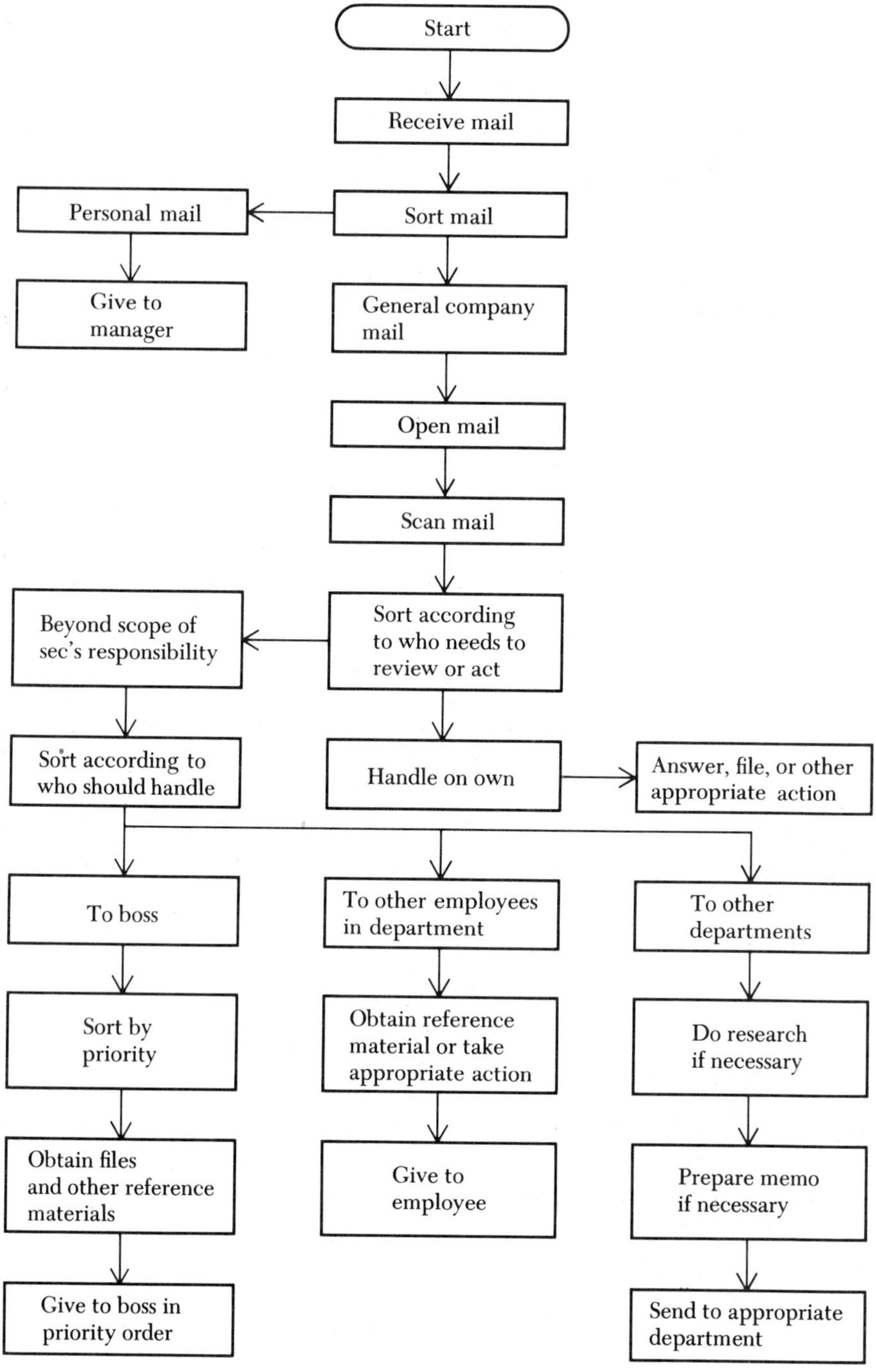


*Figure 19-11.* Management Flowchart of Secretarial Duties

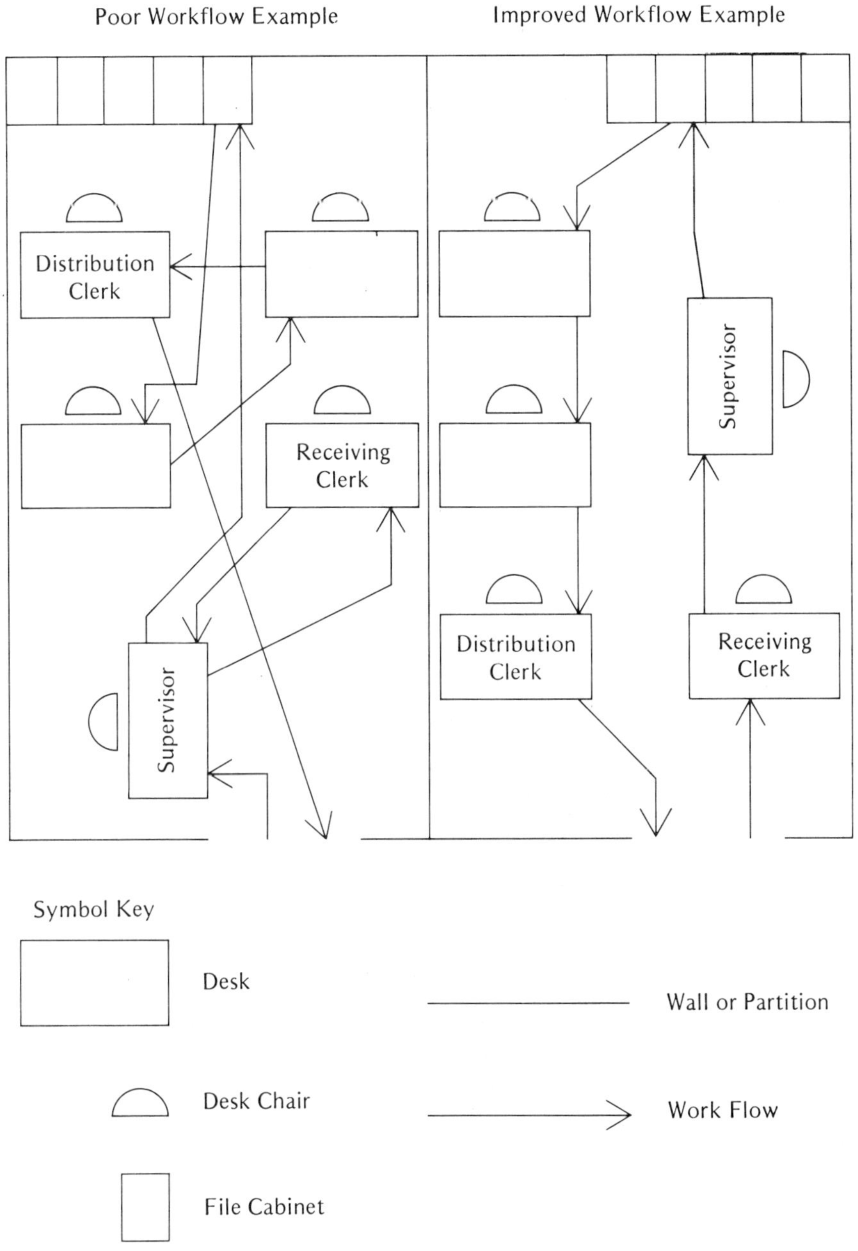


*Figure 19-12.* Flow or Movement Diagram

*Source:* Philip C. Semprevivo, *Systems Analysis* (Chicago: Science Research Associates, 1976), p. 126.

### Productivity Study Chart

The productivity study chart is used to determine the percentage of time individual employees spend in major activities. Either the employees, their supervisors, or an analyst record the time spent each day doing major activities such as typing, filing, duplicating, and telephoning. Figure 19-13 shows one productivity study chart kept by Barbara Jones, a stenographer. She will have nine more of these charts by the time the two-week study is completed. Barbara spends about two-thirds of her time on typing, taking dictation, and transcribing. This chart shows good time utilization for Barbara because her job is stenographer and she should be spending most of her time in preparing correspondence. The rest of her time is spent on a variety of functions. The one hour spent on personal time is probably realistic. The productivity study chart is an extremely useful tool, particularly when used in conjunction with a production count that gives the quantity of items produced such as letters typed, line items typed, or forms filed.

### Work Distribution Chart

Whereas the flow process chart and also the motion analysis chart (which will be discussed later in this section) provide microscopic views of work, the work distribution chart gives a telescopic view of the operation of a section or department. As you can see from the sample presented in Figure 19-14, one column is provided for major activities and one for each person working in the office.

By examining the amount of time spent in each major activity, you can determine if time is being spent on the most important functions. You can also spot duplication of effort, degree of specialization, evenness of work loads, and abuses of time.

### Narrative Procedure Description

A narrative procedure description basically tells who does what. As you can see in Figure 19-15, the job position title is listed in the left column. In the column to the right, a detailed description of what is done and how it is accomplished is presented. Information about forms that are used is included, as is any additional reference information that the employee involved with the procedure would need to know. The purpose of this tool is to put into writing information about procedures so that work can be accomplished in a uniform manner and disruptions will not occur if an employee is absent or terminated. The narrative procedure description is a very commonly used tool.

### Other Tools

Three other tools are available to the administrative manager for use in systems work: the layout chart (to be described in detail in Chapter 21), the motion analysis chart, and the person-machine chart. Because these charts are

## PRODUCTIVITY STUDY CHART

(Time Recorded in Minutes)

Date 7/9

Position Stenographer

Name Barbara Jones

| Time | Type (misc.) | Dictation | Trans-cription | Filing | Dupli-cating | Mail | Budget | Tele-phoning | Personal time | Misc. | Comments |
|---|---|---|---|---|---|---|---|---|---|---|---|
| 830 | | | | | | | | | | | |
| 925 | | 55 | | | | | | | | | |
| 1000 | | | 35 | | | | | | | | |
| 1020 | | | | | | | | | 20 | | Coffee break |
| 1030 | | | | | | | | | 10 | | Personal call |
| 1045 | | | | | | | | 15 | | | Business call |
| 1130 | | | 45 | | | | | | | | |
| 1200 | | | | | | 30 | | | | | |
| 100 | | | | | | | | | | | |
| 119 | | | | | | | | | | 19 | Coordinate with Mary |
| 130 | | | | 11 | | | | | | | |
| 230 | | | 60 | | | | | | | | |
| 255 | | | | | | | | | 25 | | Coffee break |
| 500 | 125 | | | | | | | | | | |
| 530 | | | | | 30 | | | | | | |
| Total | 125 | 55 | 140 | 11 | 30 | 30 | | 15 | 55 | 19 | 480 |
| Percent | 26 | 11.5 | 29.1 | 2.3 | 6.3 | 6.3 | | 3 | 11.5 | 4 | 100% |

*Figure 19-13.* Productivity Study Chart Showing Percentage of Time Spent in Various Activities

**WORK DISTRIBUTION CHART**
(Time Recorded in Hours)

Week 7/12 Section: Word Processing

| Activity | Time | Jill (Supv.) | | Marsha | | LaRae | | Joan | | Barbara | |
|---|---|---|---|---|---|---|---|---|---|---|---|
| Correspondence | 30 | Reviews | 5 | Types | 15 | Types | 10 | | | | |
| Handouts | 25 | | | Types and duplicates | 10 | Types and duplicates | 15 | | | | |
| Manuscripts | 30 | Types | 20 | Types | 10 | Types | 5 | | | | |
| Supervision | 20 | Instruction<br>Work count<br>Training | 10<br>1<br>4 | | | | | | | | |
| Telephone | 40 | | | | | | | Answers phone | 30 | Answers phone | 10 |
| Filing | 10 | | | | | Files correspondence | 5 | | | Files correspondence | 5 |
| Errands | 5 | | | | | | | Miscellaneous errands for department | 5 | | |
| Supplies | 5 | | | | | | | | | Purchases supplies | 5 |
| Miscellaneous | 15 | | | Production report | 5 | Personal time | 5 | Personal time | 5 | | |
| Total | 180 | | 40 | | 40 | | 40 | | 40 | | 20 |

*Figure 19-14.* Work Distribution Chart for a Word-Processing Section

SUBJECT: COPY AND DUPLICATION PROCEDURE
DATE: September 1, 19__

| Responsible position | Action to be taken |
|---|---|
| Manager or staff person | 1. Initiate request to have reproduction work accomplished by completing Form 1977, Request for Reproduction Work. Be certain that the following items are completed: name, date, office number, department, date needed, priority designation, number of copies required, desired method of reproduction, color of paper desired, and need to collate and staple.<br>2. Attach Form 1977 to originals to be duplicated. |
| Secretary | 3. Forward reproduction request to copy center. |
| Receiving clerk, copy center | 4. Date stamp request and check Form 1977 for completeness and accuracy.<br>5. Forward request to appropriate operator according to type of duplication or copy process requested.<br>Note: If more than 9 copies, send request to duplication section. If fewer than 9 copies, send to copy section. |
| Operator | 6. Detach Form 1977.<br>7. For duplication, prepare master on camera.<br>8. Run original or master. Check to make sure that copy is properly centered and legible, good quality copy.<br>9. Mark appropriate charges in log and on Form 1977.<br>10. Place copies in appropriate departmental box. |
| Secretary | 11. Pick up reproduction work and give to person who initiated request. |

*Figure 19-15.* Narrative Procedure Description

not frequently used, detailed explanation will not be given; however, you should be aware of these tools in the event that you have occasion to use them.

The *motion analysis chart,* like the flow process chart, shows in detail the movements of both the right and left hands of an operator as he or she performs an operation. This chart is usually used for repetitive types of operations where savings of even a few seconds, when multiplied by the hundreds or thousands of times the step is repeated, add up to large savings. The process of collating or bringing pages together in proper sequence is a good example. Incidentally, these repetitive types of jobs are the ones that lend themselves to mechanization.

The *person-machine chart* presents in a detailed manner the relationship between the work of a person (operator) and one or more machines. Through this analysis, you can determine the optimum number of machines one operator is able to handle.[7]

## WORK MEASUREMENT

### Purposes

In order to determine the effectiveness of your systems analysis efforts, you must be able to measure work produced to see if your efforts result in a payoff of increased production and quality. Employees need to know how much is expected of them and how long they should take to complete a specified unit of work. Separate standards of quality are also needed. Other uses of work measurement include: (1) estimating human resource requirements, (2) estimating length of time required to complete projects or units of work, (3) providing bases for wage incentive systems, (4) monitoring performance, and (5) estimating costs. Work measurement usually leads to a comparison of how long it should take to complete a unit of work with how long it actually takes.

### Essential Elements

Two basic ingredients for time standards used in work measurement are the *time* required to complete a unit of work and the *quantity* of work produced. For example, you observe that your secretary takes two hours to prepare four letters for your signature. You don't know if this performance is outstanding, adequate, or poor until you obtain further information. How many lines of typing were involved? At what pace or rate did the secretary type? What specific method was used? Finally, what outside factors beyond the control of your secretary were encountered? When you have answers to these questions, you can determine a *standard time* to complete each letter—or, in other words, the time that the operator *should* take to do a given amount of work.

Most of the emphasis in work measurement is on the time element. Relatively minor attention in textbooks and periodicals has been given to quality standards. Quality is essentially a subjective value judgment. Each manager has his or her own concept of quality standards, and these standards also are relative to the situation. For example, a letter going to the president of the company must be typed neatly, error free, and properly centered. A memo being directed to another employee in your department may be hand written or roughly typed with corrections made in ink.

### Extent of Use of Standards

Standards and work measurement have been used very effectively in industry but have had a difficult time gaining acceptance in the office. Most offices still do not have formal time standards for white collar employees. Administrative work is thought to be difficult to measure and the stopwatch is resented. Recently, with the event of automated data processing and word processing, standards and work measurement have received increased emphasis. For example, line counts in word-processing centers are very commonly reported and used by administrative managers.

Because of the number of problems caused by a lack of work measurement, management would be well advised to utilize office standards whenever and wherever possible. To qualify for meaningful work measurement, an office procedure must be (1) fairly routine, (2) performed rather frequently, and (3) capable of being measured in quantitative terms. Many activities in the records, communications, and data-processing areas qualify under these requirements. If anticipated increases in office automation materialize, work measurement will be increasingly more important in the office.

## Methods

Presenting detailed explanations for methods of developing time standards and measuring work is beyond the scope of this book. Most managers, if they are called upon to set time standards, would need to consult with an expert or do intensive study to prepare themselves. The following methods of measuring work and developing time standards are briefly described to acquaint you with the available techniques.

***Historical or Past Performance.*** Standards are determined from records of how much work over a given period has been completed. For instance, word-processing centers normally keep excellent production records that show the amount of time spent on projects and the units of work such as number of lines or pages typed. This information is basically all that is necessary to set a rough standard.

***Employee Log.*** Employees are asked to record their production count and the amount of time required to complete the work. An average or high figure is used as the standard. A sample of this log is shown in Figure 19-16.

**Employee Log**

Name Marilyn Stapleton     Date July 14

| Time | | | Task code | Number of units produced | Comments |
|---|---|---|---|---|---|
| Start | Finish | Total Minutes | | | |
| 0800 | 0845 | 45 | 19 | 24 | |
| 0846 | 1000 | 74 | 22 | 14 | |
| 1000 | 1015 | | | | Break |
| 1016 | 1155 | 99 | 15 | 108 | |
| 315 | 330 | 15 | 17 | 3 | |
| 331 | 431 | 60 | 32 | 7 | |

*Figure 19-16.* Sample Employee Log Recording Time Taken to Complete Work

***Work Sampling.*** Supervisors or analysts observe work performance on a random basis to determine how long it takes an employee to complete various units of work. Figure 19-17 shows an example of a work sampling form that was developed for a supervisor's use.

Observer LA Location WPC

Date 10/1

| Activity | Lois | Susan | Luann | Judy | Total |
|---|---|---|---|---|---|
| 1. Typing | 𝍸 𝍸 𝍸 𝍸 | 𝍸 𝍸 // | | | 32 |
| 2. Copying | // | /// | 𝍸 | 𝍸 // | 17 |
| 3. Duplicating | | | | 𝍸 // | 7 |
| 4. Collating * | | | // | //// | 6 |
| 5. Proofreading | /// | //// | | | 7 |
| 6. Running errands | | | // | | 2 |
| 7. Arranging conferences | | | / | | 1 |
| 8. Distributing documents | | | | 𝍸 | 5 |
| 9. Placing and answering phone calls | | | 𝍸 𝍸 𝍸 | | 15 |
| 10. Composing, writing | // | /// | | / | 6 |
| 11. Receiving visitors | | | // | | 2 |
| 12. Handling mail | | | / | /// | 4 |
| 13. Retrieving information | / | / | /// | / | 6 |
| 14. Maintaining files | | | | 𝍸 | 5 |
| 15. Preparing illustrations | | | // | | 2 |
| 16. Ordering supplies | // | | | | 2 |
| 17. Preparing reports | / | / | | | 2 |
| 18. Arranging travel | | | /// | | 3 |
| 19. Training | /// | | / | // | 6 |
| 20. Keeping time logs | / | / | / | / | 4 |
| 21. Idle | // | 𝍸 | 𝍸 / | /// | 16 |
| 22. Personal time | /// | //// | //// | // | 13 |
| 23. Away | | // | | 𝍸 | 7 |
| 24. Miscellaneous | ///* | | | | 3 |
| *Special project for Mr. Brown | | | | | |

*Figure 19-17.* Example of Daily Observation Record for Work Sampling Showing Number of Observations of Employees Performing Various Activities

***Stopwatch.*** An analyst observes work operations, records step-by-step detailed descriptions of how work is performed, times each element, rates the pace at which the operator is performing, and accounts for nonproductive time such as fumbles, delays, and personal time. The standard time developed is an accurate estimate of how long the average operator should take to perform a given task. (See Figure 19-18 for a sample copy of a stopwatch recording form.) Most people tend to feel intimidated, however, by the stopwatch.

***Predetermined Time System.*** Standard times to complete basic hand and body motions derived from stopwatch studies previously made are summarized in terms of fractions of a minute or an hour. Analysts observe or simulate those work operations, record the motions required, and record standard times. A sample form is shown in Figure 19-19. This method requires highly trained analysts but eliminates the use of the stopwatch.

***Standard Data.*** Stopwatch and predetermined time data are summarized for major units of office work. Published tables of standard data are available to administrative managers. One good reference on standard data is *A Guide to Office Clerical Time Standards* published by the Systems and Procedures Association, 24587 Bagley Road, Cleveland, Ohio 77138. These data are easy and convenient to use.

## *Summary*

Administrative costs have been increasing rapidly and have gotten out of control. Administrative systems analysis is a means of gaining control by finding the best ways of performing administrative activities.

Systems, procedures, and methods are means of explaining how work is to be accomplished. Systems are general; procedures are more specific; and methods are very specific and detailed.

A five-step analysis procedure involves: (1) selecting an element of work to be improved, (2) describing the present methods and procedures, (3) analyzing the present method and designing an improved method, (4) selling and implementing the improved method or procedure, and (5) maintaining and auditing the system.

Analysis tools include: (1) flow process chart, (2) flowchart, (3) management flowchart, (4) flow or movement diagram, (5) productivity study chart, (6) work distribution chart, (7) narrative procedure description, (8) motion analysis chart, (9) person-machine chart, and (10) layout chart.

Work measurement is a tool that allows you to compare how much time is taken to complete a given unit of work with how much time should be taken. Time standards are the product of work measurement and indicate how long an employee should take to complete a given amount of work. Time and quantity are two basic ingredients of work measurement. Work measurement has

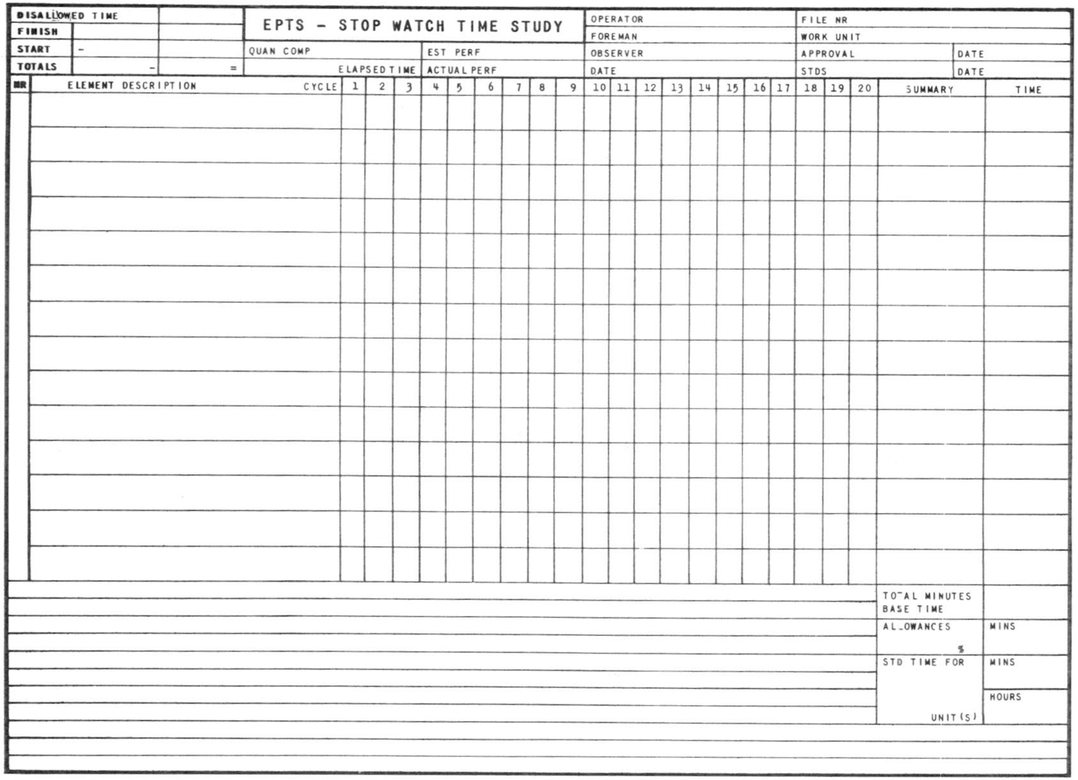


*Figure 19-18.* Sample Stopwatch Form

| EPTS - BASIC MOTION TIMESTUDY | | PAGE OF PAGES | FILE NR |
|---|---|---|---|
| ORGANIZATION | WORK UNIT | | DATE |
| OPERATION | FOREMAN | OPERATOR | OBSERVER |
| DATA | APPROVED | | DATE |
| | STDS SUPVR | | DATE |

| | LEFT HAND MOTION | SYMBOL | TIME | SYMBOL | RIGHT HAND MOTION | |
|---|---|---|---|---|---|---|
| 1 | | | | | | |
| 2 | | | | | | |
| 3 | | | | | | |
| 4 | | | | | | |
| 5 | | | | | | |
| 6 | | | | | | |
| 7 | | | | | | |
| 8 | | | | | | |
| 9 | | | | | | |
| 10 | | | | | | |
| 11 | | | | | | |
| 12 | | | | | | |
| 13 | | | | | | |
| 14 | | | | | | |
| 15 | | | | | | |
| 16 | | | | | | |
| 17 | | | | | | |
| 18 | | | | | | |
| 19 | | | | | | |
| 20 | | | | | | |
| 21 | | | | | | |
| 22 | | | | | | |
| 23 | | | | | | |
| 24 | | | | | | |
| 25 | | | | | | |
| 26 | | | | | | |
| 27 | | | | | | |
| 28 | | | | | | |
| 29 | | | | | | |
| 30 | | | | | | |
| 31 | | | | | | |
| 32 | | | | | | |
| 33 | | | | | | |
| 34 | | | | | | |
| 35 | | | | | | |
| 36 | | | | | | |
| 37 | | | | | | |
| 38 | | | | | | |
| 39 | | | | | | |
| 40 | | | | | | |
| 41 | | | | | | |
| 42 | | | | | | |
| 43 | | | | | | |
| 44 | | | | | | |
| 45 | | | | | | |
| 46 | | | | | | |
| 47 | | | | | | |

*Figure 19-19.* Sample Predetermined Time Form

not been widely used in the office but will be more widely used in the future as offices become more highly automated.

Six basic methods of setting standards are: (1) historical or past performance, (2) employee log, (3) work sampling, (4) stopwatch, (5) predetermined time system, and (6) standard data.

Work measurement and systems analysis are two means of keeping costs under control.

## *Review and Discussion Questions*

1. Why are administrative costs high and what can be done to control them?
2. What is *administrative systems analysis* and why is it important?
3. Distinguish the difference between system(s), methods, and procedures. Give an example of each.
4. Who has primary responsibility for administrative systems analysis and cost control?
5. List and describe the five steps in the analysis procedure for making administrative improvements.
6. How do the analysis questions—why, what, who, when, where, and how—relate to the four improvement actions—eliminate, combine, improve or simplify, and mechanize or automate?
7. How do you recommend getting employees to accept changes and improvements in office systems?
8. What analysis tool would you use for each of the following specific purposes?
   a. An overview of work accomplished to include a picture of who does what and how much time is spent on various tasks and activities.
   b. A detailed look at a particular method or process used to accomplish a given unit of work.
   c. A graphic picture of the flow of documents from one station to another within the office.
9. What are the five basic symbols used on the flow process chart? What specific questions would you use in analyzing this chart?
10. For what purposes is work measurement used?
11. What essential elements are involved in work measurement?
12. What is the difference between "work measurement" and "standard"?
13. How well has work measurement been received in the office in the past? Why? Do you see any major changes in the status of office work measurement in the future?
14. What methods can be used to set time standards? If you were an administrative manager, which method would you choose in setting office time standards? Why?

## *Application Exercises*

1. Select a specific, office-related project or task that you perform or that someone you can observe performs. Study the work performance using tools presented in this chapter. How efficiently was the work accom-

plished? Do you think a better way could have been found? What suggestions do you have for improvement? Be observant and think about other work processes that are taking place all around you. Can you draw any generalizations about levels of productivity and what can be done to make improvements?

2. Apply the five-step analysis procedure presented in this chapter to solve an office problem that you have observed or to increase the efficiency of an administrative procedure. Prepare a report of what you do and what you accomplish. Include copies of any tools you use in the study, such as flow process charts, work distribution charts, or movement diagrams.
3. Interview one or more office managers to determine their impressions of systems analysis and work measurement. Have them show you systems, procedures, and methods charts and other related materials that they use.

## *Case Studies*

1. *Camp's Administrative Problems.* You have recently been promoted to the position of manager of the Administrative Services Department for Camp Co., a manufacturer of camping equipment. For the past month, you have observed office operations and have concluded that there is much administrative inefficiency.

Here are some of the problems that you have observed:

a. Unequal distribution of work. Some employees appear to be overworked while others don't have enough to keep them busy.
b. In some cases, several people are doing the same tasks. In other instances, employees perform a number of unrelated tasks. Employee skills are not effectively used. Some workers have skills that are not being used, while others are doing tasks for which they have not been trained properly.
c. Turnaround time (the length of time required to complete a unit of work from start to finish) for preparation of correspondence is 24 hours or longer. You have observed that letters and memos sometimes sit in the in-baskets for several hours simply waiting to be checked or to have minor corrections made.
d. Most of your typewriters are at least five years old and in need of repair. In fact, you still have several manual typewriters in use. Very few executives have access to dictation equipment. A few older-type calculators are in use. You feel that equipment is generally inadequate.
e. You have observed clerks and secretaries walking back and forth to handle paperwork.
f. When a clerk or secretary is absent for a day or two, people who take over the work have difficulty in knowing how to proceed. They have to stop and ask many routine questions of the supervisor.

How would you proceed to attack these problems? What specific systems analysis tools would help you to solve these problems?

2. *The Payroll Office.* Boyden Mining Co. is a large open-pit copper mining corporation located near Reno, Nevada. Approximately 8,000 production employees work at the mine and various factories located within a 25-mile radius of Reno. In addition, about 750 white collar employees work downtown in a high-rise office building known as the Boyden Building.

The payroll office, which is an element of the accounting department, is responsible for the following:

a. Receiving and verifying the accuracy of 8,000 time cards prepared by the production employees and checked and initialed by their supervisors.
b. Determining correct pay and allowances for all employees based on regular and overtime work plus eligibility for special pay provisions and allowances.
c. Preparing computer input media (punched cards) to initiate computer processing of checks and supplementary records and reports.
d. Verifying accuracy of computer output by spot-checking printouts and checks.
e. Mailing checks and special records to employees or to their banks.
f. Keeping informed on changes in union contract provisions that affect employee pay status.
g. Maintaining information on pay transactions as a basis for settling claims which result from court action.

The payroll office consists of a supervisor and seven full-time employees. The supervisor, Karl Martin, reports directly to the assistant manager of the accounting department. Karl spends his time supervising and improving the payroll systems and procedures.

Each employee is specialized according to plant, mine, smelter, and refinery. Three employees check all time cards for the mine; two employees check those for the smelter and two check those for the refinery; one employee checks time cards for the plant.

The employees in the payroll office are generally satisfied with their work. They tend to be very busy during three out of four weeks every month in getting payrolls out according to the following schedule:

| *Week* | *Schedule* |
|---|---|
| 1 | Production workers pay period |
| 3 | Production workers pay period |
| 4 | White collar pay period |

Production workers receive wages for the number of hours worked. They are paid twice per month. White collar workers receive salaries, or an equal amount of earnings, regardless of the number of hours worked. They are paid at the beginning of each month. The second week of each month is a time when the payroll personnel are not busy because they do not have payrolls to get out. The office is staffed for the peak periods, which means that it has a sufficient number of employees to handle the work load during the period when the work is heavy. During the second week (and the fifth week if there is one), employees have much free time to visit with each other and to take extended coffee breaks.

Karl is concerned about these problems and feels that the office is "fat" by about one or two people, but he is also concerned about getting the checks out on time and preparing special reports when they are needed.

Every day, about 8,000 time cards are received in the office for the previous day. A standard 80-column IBM card is used to report starting time, stopping time, number of regular hours worked, overtime hours worked, and special pay status such as vacations or sick leave. Cards are checked for accuracy. Typical problems encountered are incorrect addition of hours, lack of signature of supervisor, and incorrect code numbers for work status. After the cards are checked, they are sent to the keypunch room where they are punched and sent on to the computer. The keypunch operation is organized under the administrative services department. Information is accumulated on magnetic tape to be used as input for the payroll check routine. Time cards are returned to the payroll office, which files the cards until they run out of space.

On the average, cards for a three-month period are stored in the office. Cards are then taken to the basement where they are stacked in cartons on metal shelves. After about a year or two, the cards are moved to a warehouse where storage space is leased from Acme Storage Co. The cards must be kept for three years by state law, but the accounting department has directed that the cards be retained for at least ten years because they are needed to settle claims filed by employees or to arbitrate disputes with the unions. Karl feels that something needs to be done to reduce this card storage problem.

Karl also feels that something could be done to improve the check mailing procedure. The entire office force is involved when the time rolls around to type addresses on envelopes and mail checks. This is the top priority item for that day. The only items of equipment used for the mailing operation are a postage meter and a check signing machine.

Assume that you are assigned to work with Karl in improving operations of the payroll office.

1. What specific recommendations would you make?
2. What additional information would you need before proceeding to make improvements?

3. What approach would you use in solving these problems?
4. What people would you use as resource persons in helping you to solve these problems?

## *Reference Notes*

1. "The Office of the Future," *Business Week,* June 30, 1975, p. 49.
2. Paul A. Strassmann, "Managing the Costs of Information," *Harvard Business Review,* September–October 1976, pp. 133–42.
3. Alan Purchase and Carol F. Glover, "Office of the Future," from *Guidelines for Corporate Planning* (Menlo Park, Calif.: SRI International, 1976), No. 1001, p. 6.
4. "Cost-effective systems" refers to systems that can be proved to warrant the money spent on them and, in some cases, to pay for themselves.
5. Alan Purchase, "Office of the Future," p. 6.
6. George R. Terry, *Office Management and Control* (Homewood, Illinois: Richard D. Irwin, seventh edition, 1975), p. 27.
7. For more information on the motion analysis chart and the person (man)-machine chart, refer to George R. Terry, *Office Management and Control,* pp. 94–98 and 100–102. Dr. Terry refers to the motion analysis chart as the operator-machine activity chart.

# 20

# Building and Office Environment

Current environmental concern has had an impact on analyzing the office environment—the conditions in which employees work. Moreover, since working conditions are very much the business of the administrative manager, so is improving those conditions as they exist in the office. By *office environment,* we are simply referring to the surroundings in which you work—the amount of office space, area dividers, furniture, equipment, heating, ventilating, air conditioning, lighting, and sound control; in short, as we are treating it here, it includes all of your surroundings except people.

A good office environment provides surroundings that help individuals working alone or in teams to accomplish their organizational and personal goals. It should also encourage employees to work, think, and communicate productively. Moreover, they should enjoy their office surroundings and feel comfortable in them. Rather than bending systems and people to fit the environment, you should organize office furniture, equipment, and other parts of the environment to fit the office system and the employees. The office must be a place that is favorable for creative work and open communication.

The office did not change its appearance significantly during the one-hundred-year period from the Civil War to the early 1960s. However, during this period, typewriters were invented—the first of many office machines that would change the pace of doing business. Typewriters needed operators, and office staffs grew when many people—including women—started working as typists. The conventional office was set up so that desks and file cabinets were arranged in straight rows. The environment reflected the Theory *X* assumption about people that was prevalent at the time—the arrangement of the office emphasized autocratic supervisory practices.

The office has changed as much during the past ten years as it did in the previous one hundred. With the introduction of the computer to the office during the sixties, significant changes in business processes and office needs were introduced; then, more equipment—the electrostatic copy machine—was adopted on a wide scale. In the seventies, the concepts of word processing and a type of office floor plan, *office landscaping*, became extremely popular.[1]

## CHANGE

It now appears that the only constant we face is change itself, and we can expect it to continue at an increasing rate. Businesses are changing, expanding, and requiring new procedures and systems. Employees are developing greater independence. As you have learned throughout this book, management is developing new techniques such as team building, open communication, delegation, employee participation, and management by objectives. All of these techniques mean greater emphasis on communication and individual employee development—and change in the office environment. Also, an emphasis on administrative cost control has called for more effective use of space, adoption of new systems, and easy implementation of changes.

As one office equipment manufacturer put it, "The challenge then was (and is) to create an office environment which would facilitate and accommodate change—while at the same time enabling a company to continue to grow and to make more effective use of their people, their space and their existing changing systems and procedures."[2] Management must be sensitive to the need for initiating changes in the organization and in the office environment. Robert Propst, president of the Herman Miller Research Corp., said,

> . . . change initiation is never a consensus act of the majority. It is essentially initiated by a *change agent* minority who are then followed by the majority. The majority will rigorously stay as it is until it sees a demonstration of change by those they respect.
>
> For this reason, change imposed by leadership on others without signs of acceptance by themselves is doomed to failure.
>
> The degree of change and the rate at which it can be implemented is 90% dependent on adoption rate by those established as the change agents. The organization can stand as much as the leadership can.[3]

Two major considerations in creating a climate that is conducive to change and productivity are the building and the office itself. The discussion on the building will be divided into the topics of (1) location, (2) services, and (3) office conditions. The last part of the chapter will treat the topic of office planning concepts.

## BUILDING

### Location

Office buildings have been traditionally concentrated in cities, with many of the city buildings being the typical *high-rise* type. Some of the famous buildings in this category are the Sears Tower in Chicago (world's tallest building), the Empire State Building and World Trade Center in New York City, and the Bank of America Building in San Francisco. These types of buildings have the advantages of concentrating administrative activity in one central location and of saving valuable city space. Disadvantages include the high cost of construction and maintenance. Also, skyscrapers house numerous companies and bring many people into the city, contributing to transportation problems and congestion.

In many cities, large office buildings are still being constructed, but there is currently a trend to move offices to suburban areas. Many suburban offices are located in large sprawling buildings or in an office park. The decision of where to locate the office may involve input from the administrative manager. Important factors to consider in making the office location decision are the following: proximity to the operational part of the organization, proximity to other businesses and services, transportation, parking, cost, land availability, environmental impact, and labor supply. General Mills, IBM, Prudential Life Insurance, and Kemper Insurance are major corporations that have chosen to locate major office buildings in the suburbs.

### Services

Frequently, the administrative manager is responsible for providing building services. He or she may either administer the services directly or coordinate with outside vendors or agencies that provide the services. Some of the services that must be provided for an office building include housekeeping or janitorial, security, food and refreshments, and reception.

Housekeeping is a major function in a large office building. It is costly, time consuming, and extremely important to the well-being of all persons who occupy the building. This function also relates directly to the next factor that will be discussed—conditions. Decisions on air conditioning, carpeting, and lighting will certainly have a great influence on the housekeeping function. For example, carpeting may be installed primarily to reduce noise, but carpeting also reduces costs of maintaining floors. Of course, the purchase of cleaning equipment would be affected. Let's look at one more example to illustrate the magnitude of the housekeeping function in a major office building. A large building has thousands of windows to be kept clean. If the windows are properly hinged, the outside of the windows can be cleaned from the inside simply by rotating the window.

Security is an important concern of administrative managers. Currently, bomb threats and illegal entry are frequent occurrences. Data processing and records are vulnerable to individuals' stealing or destroying invaluable information. Recently, a computer sales representative told of a woman who became angry at her supervisor and quit. Before leaving, she destroyed all of the information stored in the computer.[4] Employees steal millions of dollars worth of office supplies each year. To combat these security problems, professional security personnel are employed, key cards with changeable lock combinations are issued, television monitoring devices are used, and buildings are built without windows. Also, duplicate records are stored on microfilm in underground vaults, and elaborate security checks on prospective employees are made. Many other control measures are taken to protect the office and its personnel from dishonesty and violence.

Food and refreshment services vitally affect the lives of office employees. Lunch and even breakfast and dinner are served in employee cafeterias and executive dining rooms. Coffee-break refreshments are served in dining areas, snack bars, or right in the office by means of rolling snack wagons. Frequently, food services are provided either by outside contract agencies or by vending machines with employee organizations gaining a share in the profits.

The last building service to be discussed is reception activities. Each organization normally has its own receptionist who frequently doubles as a telephone operator in small offices. In a large building, hosting and information services are required to answer questions and to provide building tours.

These services are among the most important ones that keep the modern office building and the personnel housed in it operating smoothly and efficiently.

## Office Conditions

Environmental conditions are extremely important because they affect the health, safety, and morale of employees. The productivity of employees may be increased by a good office environment. (On the other hand, motivated, competent employees also may work effectively under poor conditions.) Improving conditions may not cause unmotivated or incompetent personnel to increase production, but improving the condition of the environment is likely to cause employees to feel good and to do their best. At least when administrative managers improve the environment, employees will recognize that management is concerned about the welfare of the workers. Six areas of environmental office conditions will be discussed: (1) heating, ventilating, and cooling of air; (2) color; (3) lighting; (4) noise reduction; (5) music; and (6) furnishings.

Several factors are important in air conditioning an office: circulation, humidity, temperature, and purity all affect the health and comfort of office employees. While the effects of air conditioning on productivity are difficult to measure exactly, there is little doubt about the value of proper air conditioning in increasing productivity. Reports of productivity increases from 10 to 20 percent or higher because of air conditioning installation are common.

Many companies are attempting to save energy during the present energy crisis. In accordance with the request from the president of the United States, thermostats are set at 65 degrees to reduce fuel consumption needed to supply heat. For ventilating and air conditioning, two heat-producing elements must be considered: lights and large computers give off great amounts of heat. However, this heat can be captured in the winter and used to heat the building. In the summer, heat must be blown out of the building to reduce the air conditioning load; some companies such as Bell Telephone reduce lighting in halls and other nonwork areas to reduce the amount of heat in a building.

Color is used in the office for a variety of reasons. According to Littlefield, Rachel, and Carruth, the psychological climate of the organization is influenced by color. Strong, dynamic colors tend to stimulate the emotions. Red tends to produce feelings of warmth, excitement, and action; orange, yellow, and brown are warm colors; while blue and green are cool colors.[5] The particular type of work normally undertaken should be considered when the color for a room is selected, because color has a subtle impact on efficiency. Also, one's perception of size is influenced by color, and a room that is painted with dark colors appears to be smaller than one that has light colored walls. In recent years, bright colors for walls and equipment are used in the office much more frequently than in the past. Finally, color is used as a way of improving visibility for close work and reading; tints tend to reduce glare while glossy paints and surfaces tend to increase it.

Lighting in an office is extremely important because of the detailed nature of much of the work. Between 50 and 100 footcandles (a unit of measurement used to measure intensity of light) are generally recommended for office work such as reading, transcribing, filing, and sorting mail. For detailed drafting and design work, at least 200 footcandles of light are recommended.[6] Good lighting tends to improve the quality of work, to reduce eyestrain and mental fatigue, to improve employee morale, and to increase productivity. Indirect lighting, where light is reflected from the walls and ceilings, tends to be an excellent general lighting method. Most offices use fluorescent lights rather than incandescent lights, which have been predominant in the past. With recent emphasis on reducing energy consumption because of energy shortages, some offices have turned to greater use of direct lighting on individual work areas. The administrative manager should consult with lighting specialists when installing lighting systems or when lighting problems are encountered.

Noise reduction is a constant source of concern to the administrative manager. After conducting a controlled experiment on noise, one acoustical expert concluded that in a modern open plan office where there are few interior walls there are three primary factors for controlling noise:

1. Voice effort. Educating people to lower their voices and shielding noisy office machines are primary means of reducing annoying noise.
2. Distance. Noise-producing activities should be placed as far away as possible from areas where employees need to concentrate.
3. Masking noise. Masking or controlled background noise is electronically generated and played over a loudspeaker system. Another name for this device is *white sound.*

This study on acoustics also concluded that conventional control devices commonly thought to be effective for noise reduction may not be as valuable as most people think. Ceiling baffles, screens, and furniture make an almost negligible contribution to noise control. *Acoustic tile* ceiling and carpet were recommended because they provide a more subdued atmosphere and reduce specific annoying noises such as chair scraping and heel clicks.[7]

Music is popular in offices as means of improving the psychological climate. Independent research studies have been conducted to determine the effect of music on production. Increases up to 15 percent have been noted. Office employees generally favor having music in the office.[8]

Music in the office may be supplied in two ways—commercially or internally. Commercial groups such as MUZAK may wire in specially prepared programs or an organization may play recordings over its own system. Music should be specially selected to avoid distraction, played softly, and played at intervals during the day rather than continuously. The intervals selected will have an effect on productivity.

Finally, office furnishings such as desks, chairs, file cabinets, and miscellaneous equipment are an important environmental element. Currently, *modular desks* are quite popular because of their ability to provide maximum working space. Figure 20-1 compares a modular desk unit with a conventional desk to show that the use of space is maximized with a modular unit.

An innovative desk style (see Figure 20-2) has been introduced that departs from the conventional rectangular form. This desk provides greater usa-

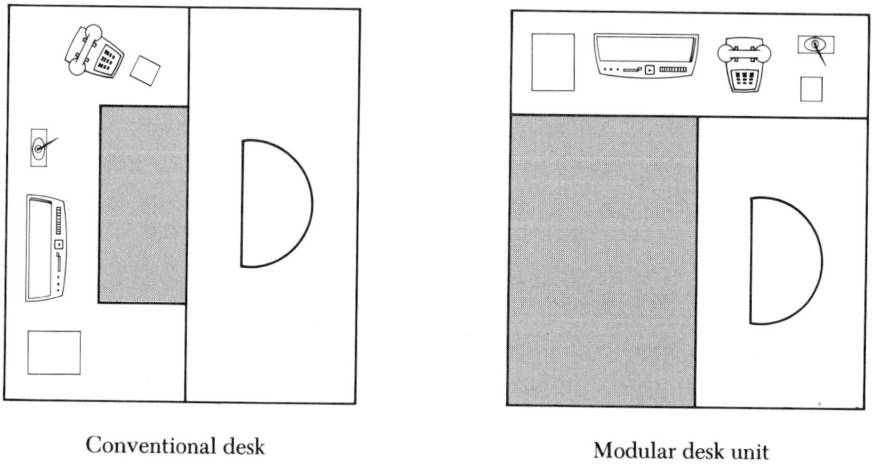


*Figure 20-1.* Comparison of Working Surface Available with Conventional Desk versus Modular Desk Unit in the Same Amount of Floor Space
(Shaded area indicates actual work space.)

ble work surface (95 percent) than the traditional desk (68 percent). As you can see from the figure, these desks can be grouped easily with other desks, file units, partitions, and equipment to form functional units.

Chairs are an important office furnishing because they affect the health of office employees. Office chairs tend to follow three types of designs: the executive desk chair, the secretarial or typist's chair, and the conference or

*Figure 20-2.* Innovative Desk Styles

*Source:* Oxford Pendaflex Corporation, Garden City, N.Y.

visitor's chair (see Figure 20-3). The primary considerations in chair selection are comfort and effect on posture. Figure 20-4 shows various postures that a person in the office may assume; notice that in each position the chair back still fully supports the model.

File cabinets can be integrated with desks and other items of office furniture to form a functional unit (described in more detail in Chapter 22). *Lateral file cabinets*, which open from the side rather than the end, have received considerable attention recently as part of modern office arrangements. In Figure 20-5, notice how laterals have been combined with desks to form efficient modular units.

One more remark about office conditions. Any environmental changes undertaken should have one primary objective: to make the work of people easier, more pleasant, and more productive.

## OFFICE PLANNING CONCEPTS

An administrative manager is faced with the challenge of planning the use of space within the office to achieve maximum production and to conserve the space used. While the cost of space is high, it is much less than the cost of personnel. Irene Place estimates that personnel costs are about 60 to 70 percent of total office costs while overhead, which includes space, is 15 to 20 percent.[9] George Terry suggests that office space runs from $.50 to $15 per square foot.[10] The wise administrative manager, while trying to conserve on the costs of space, will at the same time invest money in office furnishings to maximize the efficient use of personnel. For example, a new $400 desk or a $200 file cabinet could help an employee be more productive and would be a good investment.

Aside from increased productivity, the administrative manager stands to gain the following benefits from effective office planning: improved work quality, increased employee satisfaction, improved health and safety, better office appearance and increased public relations value, improved communication, better work flow, more effective space utilization, increased flexibility in adapting to change, and greater economy of operation. There are two basic approaches to office planning: traditional and modern.

### Traditional

Most people are very familiar with the traditional office, which is the product of conventional office planning. Table 20-1 compares the characteristics of the traditional approach with the modern approach to office planning. Most traditional offices have been set up on a very rigid, *rectilinear pattern* with straight rows of desks all facing the same direction (see Figure 20-6). The supervisor sits at the back of the room so that control can be maintained. Managers,

*Figure 20-3.* Three Basic Types of Office Chairs
*Source:* Herman Miller, Inc., Zeeland, Mich.

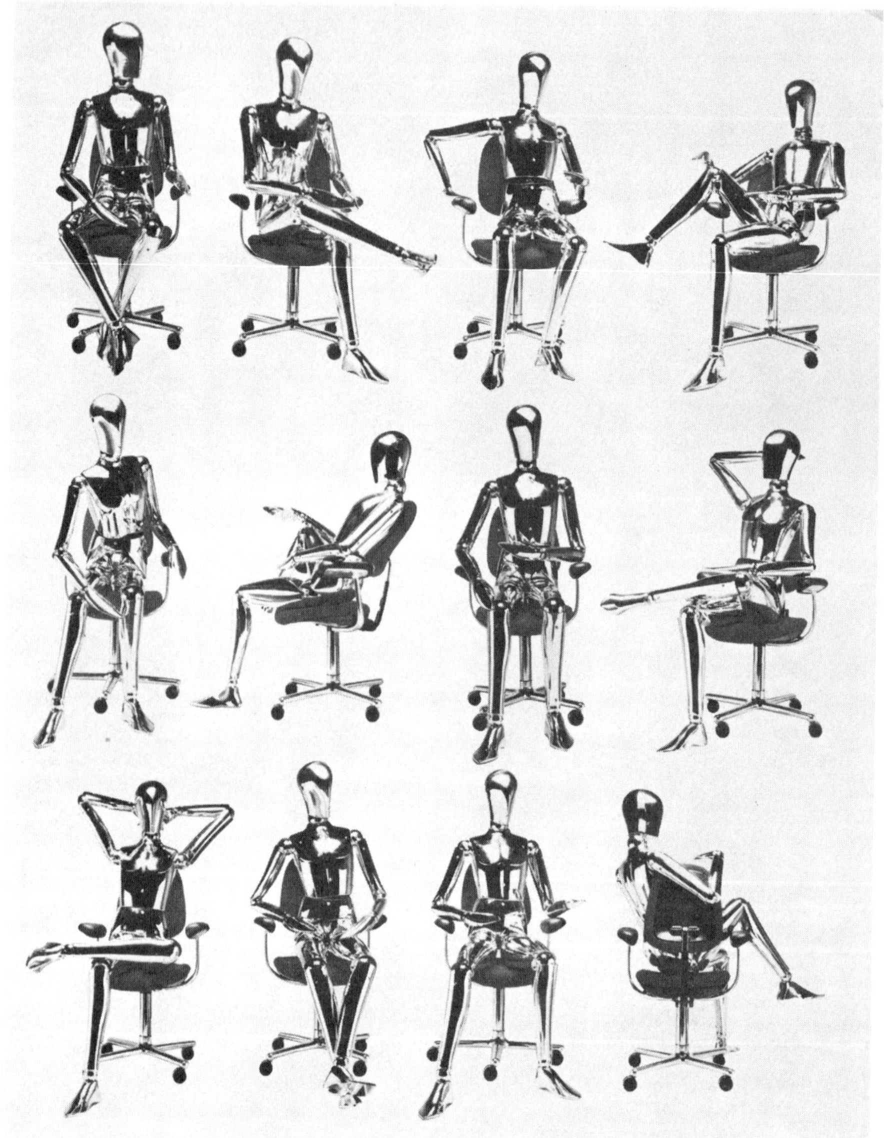

*Figure 20-4.* Typical Sitting Positions
*Source:* Herman Miller, Inc., Zeeland, Mich.

*Figure 20-5.* Typical Modern Office Scene Showing Combination of Lateral File Cabinets and Desks to Form Modular Work Units

*Source:* Steelcase, Inc., Grand Rapids, Mich.

particularly at the top level, are housed in private offices and usually occupy the four corners of each floor in the building. The most important executives have the larger offices and are located on the top floor. This traditional approach has both strengths and weaknesses, as shown in Table 20-1. The approach may fit best the autocratic leadership style of the manager and the organization.

### Modern

The modern approach to office planning was introduced during the 1960s when the office landscape concept was brought to the United States from Germany. Three basic concepts associated with the modern approach are (1) office landscape, (2) privacy panels, and (3) a flexigrated plan, which is a combination of traditional, privacy panel, and office landscape approaches.

***Office Landscape.*** An office landscape concept eliminates the inside walls, private offices, and rectilinear pattern of desks and file cabinets (see Figure 20-7). Individuals are grouped together according to their need to communicate. Office landscaping creates a network of integrated *work stations* rather than the traditional rows of individual desks. Aisles meander through areas rather than form the straight traditional pattern. Low movable screens, plan-

**Table 20-1. Traditional vs. Modern Approach to Office Planning**

| | *Traditional* | *Modern* |
|---|---|---|
| Characteristics | Tends to<br>Be *formal*<br>Emphasize *rules and standards*<br>Have *Theory X* focus<br>Seek *uniformity*<br>Dwell on *Control*<br>Follow formal *organization chart* | Tends to<br>Be *innovative*<br>Accommodate *change*<br>Emphasize *Flexibility*<br>Have *Theory Y* focus<br>Enhance productive *communication*<br>Emphasize *planning* and *doing*<br>*Follow functions* performed |
| Strengths | 1. People are comfortable with system<br>2. Removal of existing walls not necessary<br>3. Purchase of new, expensive<br>4. Confidential matters are protected<br>5. Concentration is aided by private offices | 1. Change is easy to make and less expensive<br>2. Environment is designed to improve productivity<br>3. Environment is pleasant<br>4. Communication and information flow are aided; office personnel who interact frequently are located near each other<br>5. Less space is required |
| Limitations | 1. System does not adapt to change readily and is not flexible<br>2. System may block communication and work flow<br>3. Employees may be less effective in this type of environment | 1. Number of distractions may be increased; noise and visual disturbances may disrupt concentration<br>2. Personnel may resist eliminating status symbols such as private offices or window locations<br>3. Employees may be dissatisfied if top management retains private offices<br>4. Too much communication, to the point of wasting time, may take place<br>5. Electrical and telephone connections cannot be in fixed floor positions; lighting, heating, and air conditioning must be available in all parts of the open area |

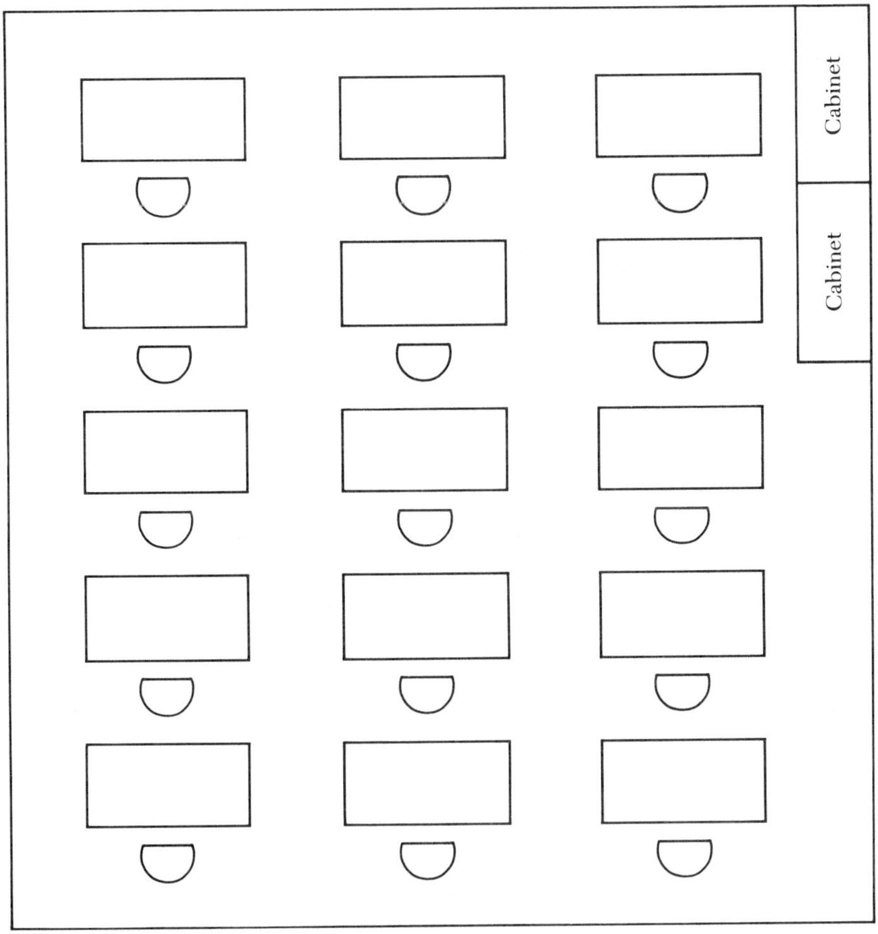


*Figure 20-6.* Characteristic Rectilinear Pattern of a Typical, Traditional Office

ters, and partitions replace standard walls as a means of dividing space. Page 2 of the color insert shows a typical landscaped office scene. Notice that the area is "open" in the sense that it has no fixed walls in the center part of the office area. Work areas are divided by low partitions, file cabinets, and plants. A conference area is shown in the right center part of the picture. Privacy is achieved by means of the panel that extends almost all the way around the conference area. Straight rows of desks and aisles are eliminated. The luminous ceiling provides good visibility. The use of color and green plants lends a warm atmosphere even though windows are not available. Figure 20-7 shows a floor plan for a landscape area.

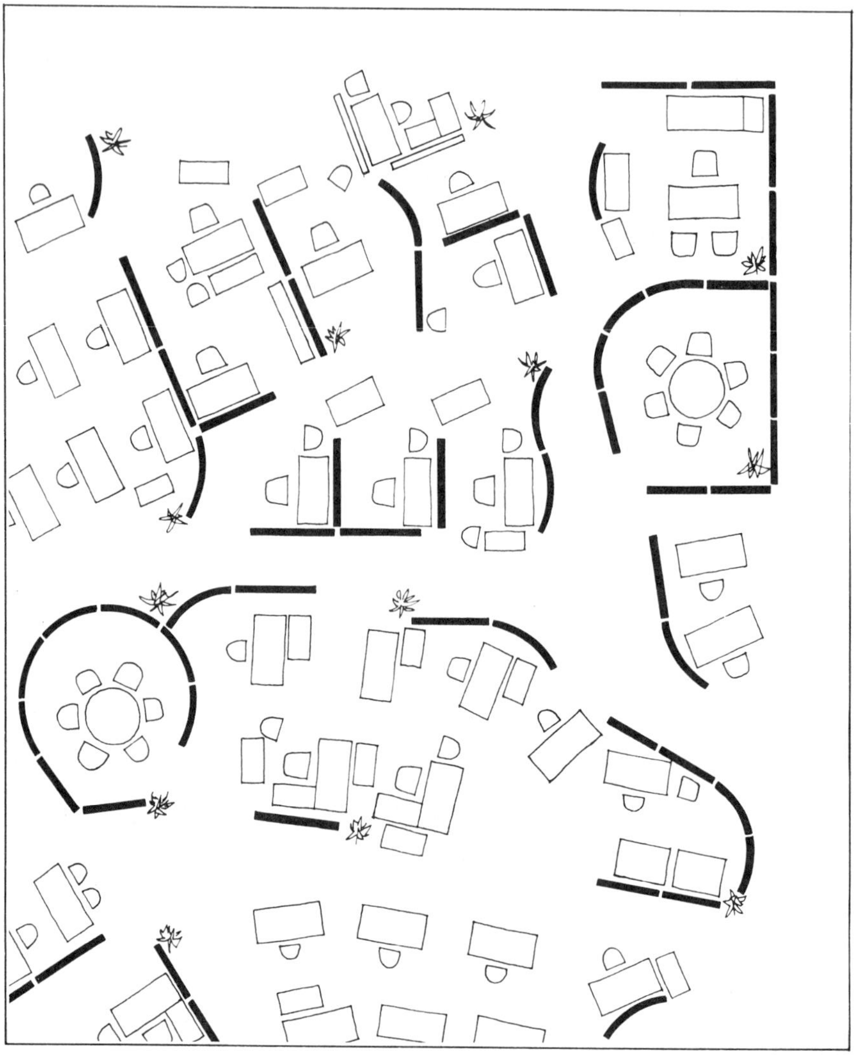

*Figure 20-7.* Typical Office Landscape Floor Plan
(Heavy lines indicate movable screens.)
*Source:* Vogel-Peterson Co., Elmhurst, Ill.

Office landscaping was intended to remove the walls and substitute a free-flowing climate to encourage productive communication and foster innovation. Advantages and disadvantages of the landscaped office are shown in Table 20-1 under the heading "Modern."

***Privacy Panels.*** A work area system can be designed to improve office work operations, to facilitate thought, and to improve communication.[11] Figure

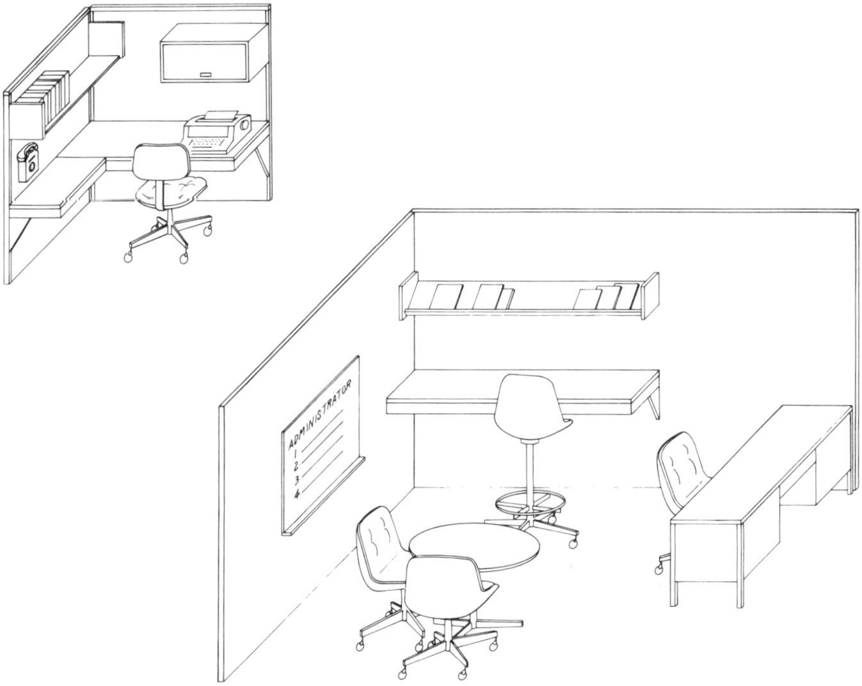


*Figure 20-8.* Privacy Panel

Two versions of the privacy panel, showing how work surfaces, storage areas, and panels can be combined.

20-8 shows placement of the panels in two different work areas and variations in panel height. The panel system is based on research that studied how office personnel actually operate within an office.

Herman Miller Research Corp., the research and development arm of a major office furnishing company, conducted an experiment to test the effectiveness of an experimental work station as compared with a conventional facility. *Time lapse movies*, which are a series of pictures taken at regular intervals a few seconds apart, were used to record all movements of a programmer in his office environment. Analysis of the data showed how the programmer interacted with his environment and with other people in the environment. The study also revealed how changing the environment influenced the effectiveness of the programmer. As a result of this research, the privacy panel concept was born.

This concept is based on the way three physical features—work surface, storage, and panels—are combined to design a functional work area. Work surfaces, storage shelves, and cabinets are hung from movable, free-standing panels (Figure 20-8 shows these types of work areas). A picture showing a work area is found on page 3 of the color insert.

The major features of the privacy panel concept are described in Table 20-2 in terms of function and location. The major function of a work surface is to provide an area on which work such as writing, drawing, calculating numbers, and obtaining reference information can be performed. Materials used to accomplish the work should be located on the work surface, and it should be kept free from inactive and nonessential materials.

Within the panel area, several work surfaces may be available to perform different types of work, and the height of the surface as well as its location in the enclosure may vary. For example, a programmer may have one work surface for doing routine paperwork duties and another work surface for preparing flowcharts, which may require an art table. Good use of the vertical as well as the horizontal dimensions of space is made from the standpoint of work surfaces and storage facilities. Materials that are in frequent use are readily available and papers are kept in bin files or in binders on shelves. Inasmuch as an adequate but limited amount of storage is provided, workers are encouraged by the physical facilities to get rid of unnecessary items. The vertical dimension of space is well used because cabinets and shelves are placed at convenient heights according to frequency of use. Vertical space on the panel also allows use of various display devices such as chalkboards and bulletin boards for highlighting important information.

Panels are free standing and can be placed together to form an enclosure. The number of panels used and the arrangement or configuration will vary depending upon the situation. While the panels provide privacy, the amount of privacy attained depends upon the height of the panel used. Most important, the panels are readily movable if the situation or individuals change, and this type of flexibility is simply not possible with fixed walls.

To the advantages for the privacy panel concept listed for the modern approach in Table 20-1, we can add the following: (1) work areas and storage devices have been scientifically designed to meet the needs of office employees, (2) all parts are interchangeable, (3) employees can design and modify their own work area, (4) vertical space is effectively used, and (5) employees can change positions and work surfaces within the work area depending upon the work to be accomplished at that time. (Disadvantages are similar to those of the office landscape concept, along with high cost.)

***Flexigrated Plan.*** Flexigrated is a coined word that combines the words "flexible" and "integrated." These are the key features of a combined or open-ended concept that allows the persons who plan the office to use any or all of the other three concepts (traditional, landscape, or privacy panel) according to the specific circumstances encountered. In some cases, private offices and traditional, rectilinear patterns may prove to be the best. In other situations, a landscape or privacy panel concept may prove to be best. There is no problem in using a combination of these patterns as long as they are integrated and seem to fit together.

**Table 20-2. Features of the Privacy Panel Concept**

| *Physical feature* | *Function* | *Location* | *Comments* |
|---|---|---|---|
| Work surface | Facilitates work by providing more work space | Variable locations, by type of work<br>Variable height, according to chair, stool, or stand-up positions | Hang from panels or freestanding<br>Good use of vertical and horizontal space |
| Storage | Easy retrieval<br>Free work surface<br>Allows display of important items | Nearby, according to use | Adequate but limited; panel hung or freestanding<br>Good use of vertical and horizontal space |
| Panels | Privacy<br>Limit distractions: visual and sound<br>Enhance private communication | Movable<br>Variable heights<br>Variable locations | Adapt to change<br>Freestanding<br>Variable arrangement |
| Combined effect of features | Facilitate work, thought, and communication | Variable, to provide functional system | Physical facilities adapted to person and job<br>Worker develops final design |

## *Summary*

Environmental concern has spread to the office, and on that level it is aimed at improving office surroundings in order to enhance the efforts of individuals as they perform work individually or in teams. Historically, the office environment changed little until the last decade or so when word processing and office landscaping made their impact. Now, businesses, other organizations, employees, and managers are all changing, and the office faces the challenge of adapting to this rapidly changing world.

The office building and the offices in it are undergoing change in order to provide an adequate physical environment. Three important areas for consideration are location, services, and office conditions. Traditionally, offices have been located in large cities, but the trend to move offices to suburban areas has developed; careful study should precede any decision to relocate the office. Important services provided in an office building include: housekeeping, security, food, and reception services. Six office conditions of great importance to the administrative manager are air, color, lighting, noise, music, and furnishings.

Four basic planning arrangements or concepts from which the administrative manager may choose when he or she develops the basic plan of the office are (1) traditional, (2) office landscape, (3) privacy panel, and (4) flexigrated. Each has advantages and disadvantages.

## *Review and Discussion Questions*

1. Why is environmental analysis important?
2. What events and inventions have had an impact historically on the office?
3. Who should be responsible for initiating and implementing environmental changes?
4. If you were responsible for making a recommendation to the president of your company on where to relocate your office building, what factors would you consider most important? Why?
5. What environmental conditions associated with an office building do you consider to be most important? Why?
6. Explain the traditional approach and the three basic modern concepts of office planning.

## *Application Exercises*

1. Visit several offices. Try to find an application of each of the four planning concepts (the traditional plus three modern) discussed in this chapter. Look for good planning principles that have been followed and those that have been violated. How effective are the office environments that you visit?
2. Interview one or more managers to determine their reactions to the new planning concepts such as office landscaping and/or privacy panels. Do you detect a relationship between management style and preference for office styles for each of the managers that you interview?
3. Visit one or more office buildings and observe physical conditions. Does the building have central air conditioning? Does it make effective use of color and music? What distracting noises do you hear? What devices have been used to control noises? How would you describe the total climate or "personality" of each building that you visit?
4. Examine your own work area at home, at work, or at college to determine if your work environment contributes to your own productivity and psychological welfare. What changes can you make to improve your surroundings?

## Case Study

*Administrative Research Corp.* George Bendiski is administrative manager for the Administrative Research Corp. (A.R.C.), a publishing firm located in New York City. The president of the company, Mary Norton, has asked Mr. Bendiski to serve as chairperson of a task force to select a new site for an office building. She is also interested in knowing what type of building—single-story rambler or multistory—would best serve the company.

A.R.C. currently has 412 employees working in the home office and 49 sales representatives who travel most of the time. Of the 412 office employees, 42 are either managers or supervisors and the rest are clerical employees. All services such as maintenance and housekeeping are presently supplied by owners of the building in which A.R.C. is currently housed. A.R.C. leases five floors of the 92-story Martin Building. Management is currently dissatisfied with the inconvenience of being located on several floors.

The primary functions performed in the main office are as follows: textbook development (from proposal to manuscript), editing, design and graphics, sales promotion, administrative services, order processing, book distribution, and management. The books are printed by a commercial printing firm located in Chicago.

Three sites for the new location that have been actively considered by management are South Bend, Indiana; Atlanta, Georgia; and Pomona, California.

You are to prepare a report for Ms. Norton that will provide recommendations on where to locate, what type of building is needed, and what type of services and facilities will be required. Use the decision-making process that you studied in Chapter 18 as a guide in making your study of the problem.

## Reference Notes

1. Refer to Chapter 24 for a full discussion of automated word processing in such forms as letters, reports, and memos.
2. *Planning Principles for Effective Office Interiors* (Grand Rapids, Mich.: Steelcase, 1975), p. 8.
3. Robert Propst, *The Office—A Facility Based on Change* (Ann Arbor, Mich.: Herman Miller, 1968), p. 70.
4. Kenneth W. Hart orally conveyed this information to the authors on March 16, 1977.
5. C. L. Littlefield, Frank M. Rachel, and Donald L. Carruth, *Office and Administrative Management*, 3d ed. (Englewood Cliffs, N.J.: Prentice Hall, 1970), p. 347.
6. Littlefield, Rachel, and Carruth, *Office and Administrative Management*, p. 345.
7. Ranger Farrell, "Sounds of the Open Plan," *Environment Planning and Design*, July–August 1970.
8. *MUZAK in Offices*, booklet published by the MUZAK Corp.
9. Irene Place, *Office Management*, 3d ed. (Boston: Allyn and Bacon, 1971), p. 461.
10. George R. Terry, *Office Management and Control* (Homewood, Ill.: Richard D. Irwin, seventh edition, 1975), p. 432.
11. "The Human Performer in the Machine-Related Office," *Environment Planning and Design*, 1969.

# 21

# Office Layout Analysis

Now that you have studied the overall environment of the office and had a chance to consider four concepts of office planning, you need to learn specifically how the office layout is planned. *Layout* refers to the floor plan diagram or model that shows exact locations of various office furnishings and equipment. A sample office layout that follows a traditional plan is found in Figure 21-1.

Most traditional offices use the organization chart as the basis for determining where personnel and their office equipment and furnishings will be positioned (see Figure 21-2). People in the most important positions get the largest offices in choice locations, such as the corners and the upper floors. The office can be an important status symbol. Unfortunately, the location that offers the most status will probably not be the best location to improve the flow of work and communications.

## BASIS FOR ANALYSIS

Rather than base the layout on status factors, the *work flow* and *communication patterns* should be analyzed to form the basis for layout decisions. Work flow refers to the movement of documents being processed in the office. For example, if an office processes incoming orders, the work flow for that office is the movement of order forms from the mail room to each desk where the order is processed and to the warehouse where goods are shipped. (Refer to Chapter 19 for a discussion of the movement or flow diagram.)

*Communication patterns* mean the network of communication lines or flow of communication from one person to another in the organization.

Here is an example:

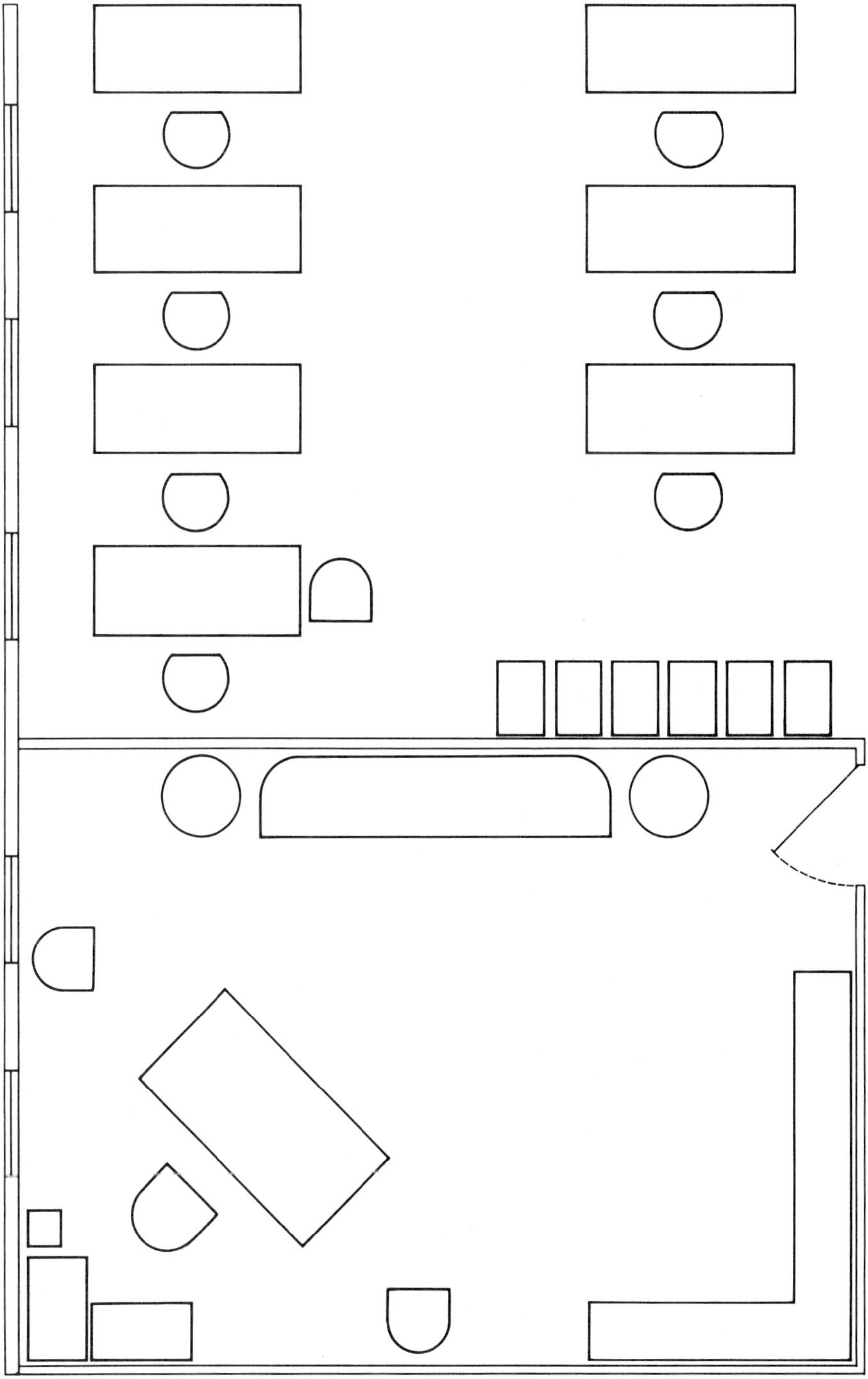

*Figure 21-1.* A Typical Plan Drawing of a Traditional Office

(a) Organization chart

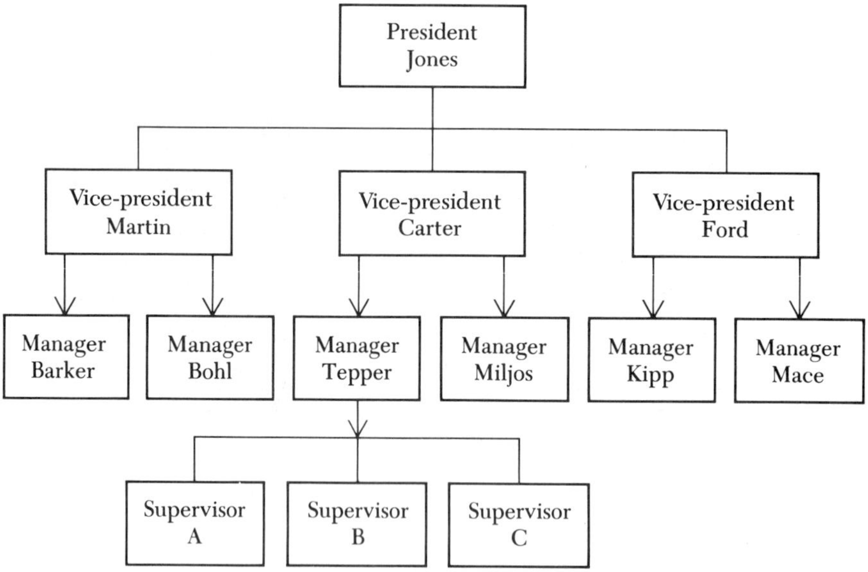


*Figure 21-2.* Comparison of Organization Chart *(a)* with Office Building Diagram *(b)* to Show Correlation

Planning an office layout involves the same five-step analysis procedure for making an administrative systems analysis that you studied in Chapter 19. We will consider the problems of office layout analysis in terms of these five steps:

1. Determine specific problems.
2. Gather information about present layout.
3. Analyze the present layout and design an improved one.
4. Sell and implement the improved layout.
5. Follow up on the new layout.

### Determine Specific Problems (Step 1)

You first need to determine exactly what the problem is. Through careful observation and questioning of your office employees, you are likely to find a number of symptoms that indicate problems in the layout of your office. Some of these symptoms are listed in Table 21-1.

Note that all of these symptoms potentially have a root cause in the office layout. As an example, look at the first symptom. Employees are having to walk excessive distances to copy machines and file cabinets. By moving the

(*b*) Location of offices in building

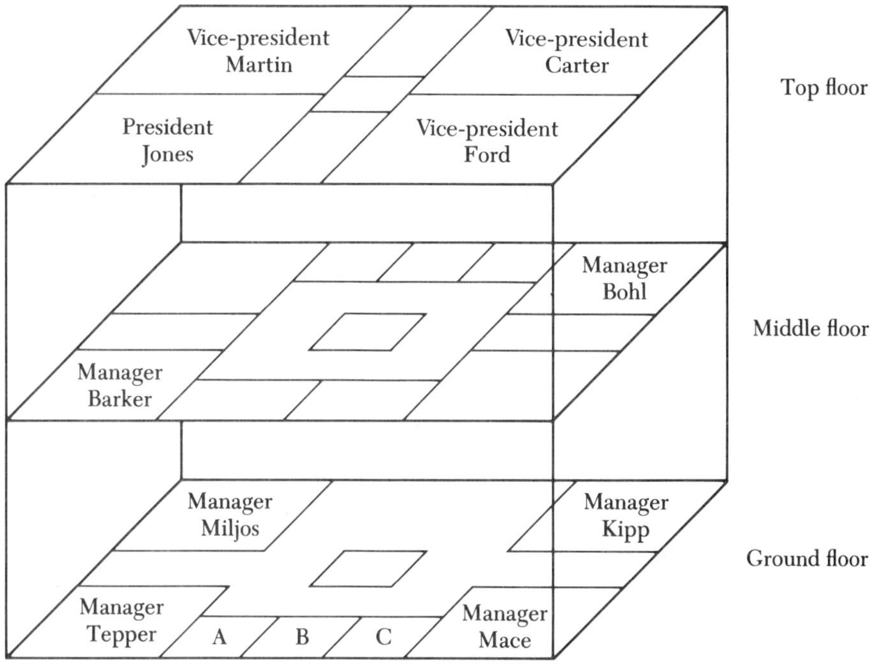


*Figure 21-2, continued.*

copy machines or file cabinets closer to the employees using them, the problem of excessive walking could be eliminated.

In making any layout decision, care should be taken to make certain that all aspects of the system are reviewed. In the previous example, you would need to make certain that the copies being made and the information being retrieved are necessary. Also, you would want to make sure that if the work is necessary, you are using the best methods. That is, in this case, perhaps copies could be made automatically from a magnetic medium, or information could be found or retrieved using a TV-type screen as a terminal.

## PREPARING DIAGRAMS FOR LAYOUT, WORK FLOW, AND COMMUNICATION PATTERNS

### Gather Information about Present Layout (Step 2)

Four basic types of information are required: (1) sketch of present layout, (2) lists of people and jobs, (3) diagram of work flow (movement diagram), and (4) diagram of communication patterns.

**Table 21-1. Symptoms of Layout Problems**

| *Problems* | *Symptoms* |
| --- | --- |
| Excessive office traffic | Employees walk excessive distances to equipment such as copy machines and file cabinets.<br><br>Employees who need to work together are in dispersed locations.<br><br>Nonemployees have to walk excessive distances to their point of contact in the building. Here are some specific examples:<br><br>*Public* — *Company destination*<br>Salespersons — Purchasing<br>Job applicants — Personnel<br>Delivery persons — Supply room<br>Mail persons — Mail room |
| Slow work flow | Documents being processed backtrack and crisscross.<br>Documents travel excessive distances from one work station to another. |
| Noise | Noisy equipment operation and loud talking make concentration difficult. |
| Crowded conditions | Aisles are narrow, so that it is difficult to move through the office.<br>Desks are close together, and it is difficult to move about. Office is cluttered because storage facilities are inadequate. |
| Poor lighting | People have difficulty reading and doing close work. |
| Poor positioning of utility connections | Electrical, telephone, and central dictation system connections are difficult to reach. |
| Inflexibility | Making changes in the office layout is difficult because of lack of flexibility. |

***Present Layout.*** Either use a scale drawing of the office, if one is available, or prepare a sketch yourself using a tape measure to get accurate measurements. Begin by drawing permanent outside walls and inside partitions. Indicate windows, doors (also whether door swings in or out), columns, and electrical outlets. Next, show locations of desks, files, tables, chairs, and heavy equipment. A standard scale of ¼ inch equals 1 foot or ⅛ inch equals 1 foot is commonly used. Figure 21-3 illustrates how your sketch might appear.

Or, you could use layout tools (described in the next section) for a more detailed sketch. These tools would be particularly appropriate for preparing a layout of a large office.

***People and Jobs.*** In the larger office, it may be necessary to get a list of personnel assigned to the office as well as their job titles. If you are not already familiar with the jobs, you would need also to learn about the work performed and the requirements for equipment and information to do the job. All of this information is necessary to plan adequate work stations.

The work itself should determine what the work station will be like. For example, a cost accountant who analyzes office costs will have need for access to many computer reports. If a microfilm system is not used, he or she will need to store these large bulky reports in suitable storage cabinets that provide easy access; in turn, these storage cabinets require adequate space. On the other hand, a traveling salesperson who is on the road 80 percent of the time may require only a small desk and a chair with very little other space needed.

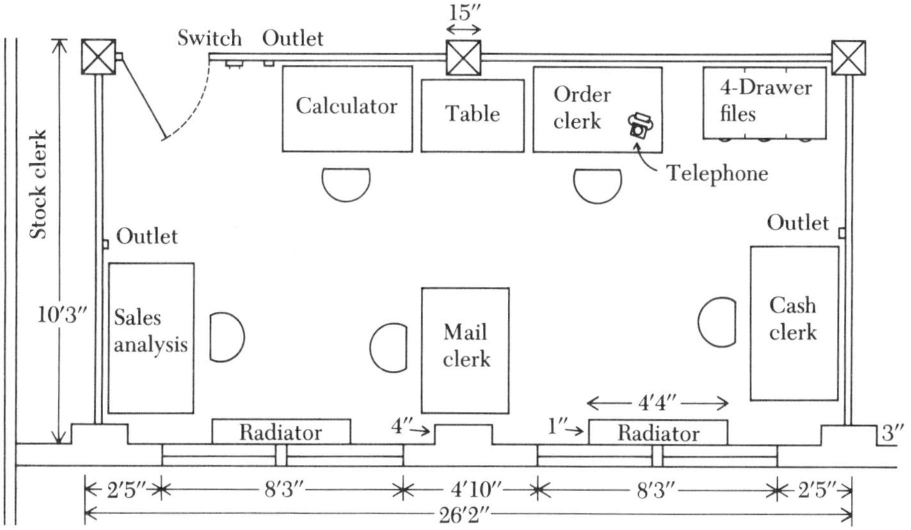


*Figure 21-3.* Sketch of Office Layout

*Source:* From a report, *How 278 Companies Plan Office Layout.* Copyright © 1962, The Dartnell Corporation, Chicago, Illinois.

***Work Flow.*** Most offices have only one record or a limited number of records that are the basis for the predominant procedure found in that office. Examples: customer order, insurance application, insurance claim, job application, and work request. You need to identify the major document and then track it through the office to develop a movement or work flow diagram (see Figure 21-4). Information about the flow of work may be obtained from written procedures, employees, and supervisors. After examining the most time consuming and the most important procedures, other minor procedures can be fitted in. Their impact on efficiency will not be as great as that of the predominant procedure, however.

***Communication Pattern.*** *Communication interaction analysis* is a technique designed to determine the communication patterns within the office. A sample communication interaction questionnaire is included here (see Figure 21-5). Each person fills out one questionnaire about every other member of the organization under study (excluding himself or herself). For a 10-person organization, 90 questionnaires would be completed. Because of the heavy volume of questionnaires and the extensive analysis process, the computer is normally used to do the processing. The computer product is a diagram that shows the interaction of every person in the office. Let's study a case example that illustrates how to prepare this analysis. Figure 21-6 shows the present

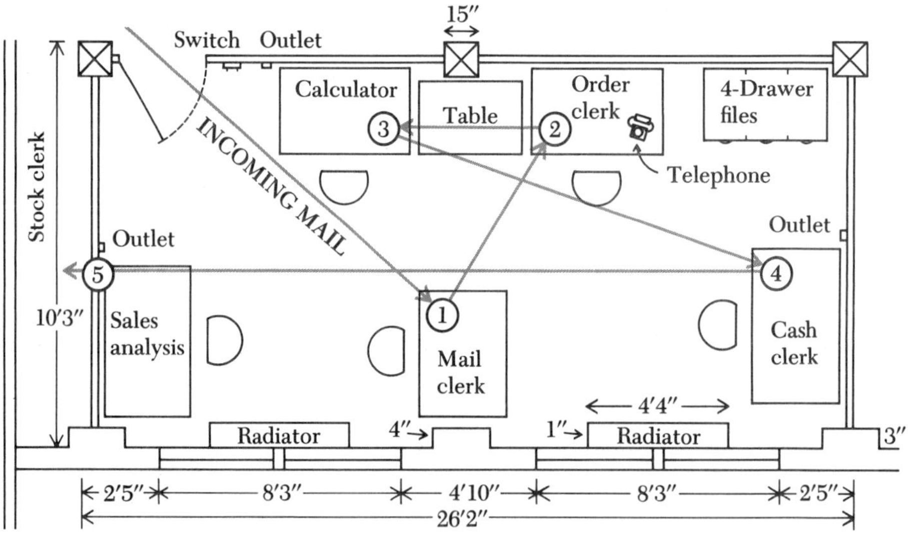


*Figure 21-4.* Movement or Work Flow Diagram

*Source: How 278 Companies Plan Office Layout.* Copyright © 1962, The Dartnell Corporation, Chicago, Illinois.

## COMMUNICATION INTERACTION ANALYSIS QUESTIONNAIRE

Your name________________________
Name of employee
considered________________________

*Instructions:* For each of the following questions, indicate your response by checking (✓) Column A, B, C, D, or E.

*Answer key:* A = almost always; B = often; C = no established pattern; D = seldom; E = almost never

| Questions | A | B | C | D | E |
|---|---|---|---|---|---|
| 1. Do you receive information from this individual which may eventually be applied to your area of responsibility? | __ | __ | __ | __ | __ |
| 2. Does this individual guide the conduct of your routine office activity? | __ | __ | __ | __ | __ |
| 3. Does the information received from this person provide you with alternative approaches and/or solutions to your particular task? | __ | __ | __ | __ | __ |
| 4. Do you retain the information received from this individual for future reference? | __ | __ | __ | __ | __ |
| 5. Does the information supplied by him/her outline the methods or procedures that you follow when performing your task? | __ | __ | __ | __ | __ |
| 6. Would you seek an opinion from this individual even though it may challenge your decision regarding a specific subject? | __ | __ | __ | __ | __ |
| 7. Do you discuss general ideas or concepts with this person that pertain to your work activity? | __ | __ | __ | __ | __ |
| 8. Do you receive announcements or directives from this individual that concern the total organizational activity? | __ | __ | __ | __ | __ |
| 9. Do you confer with this person on topics relative to your particular task prior to taking action on them? | __ | __ | __ | __ | __ |
| 10. Do you supply him/her with information for his/her activities? | __ | __ | __ | __ | __ |
| 11. Do you direct the course of this individual's administrative activity? | __ | __ | __ | __ | __ |
| 12. Do you advise him/her concerning decisions that he/she must take? | __ | __ | __ | __ | __ |
| 13. How would you rate the importance of communication contact with this individual in terms of your task activity? | __ | __ | __ | __ | __ |
| 14. How frequently do you communicate with this person when performing your task activity? | __ | __ | __ | __ | __ |

*Figure 21-5.* The Interaction Analysis Questionnaire Can Be Used to Study Patterns of Communication in an Office

*Source: The Administrative Officer,* available from the Communications Group, Herman Miller, Inc., Zeeland, Mich. Fourteen analysis questions, copyright 1977, Herman Miller, Inc. The term "*communication interaction analysis*" is a registered service mark of Herman Miller, Inc.

conventional office layout that follows the formal organization chart. Notice how corner offices are assigned to the most important officers according to the formal organization.

The interaction analysis questionnaire was administered to the 19 persons working in this office, including the general manager. The results of this

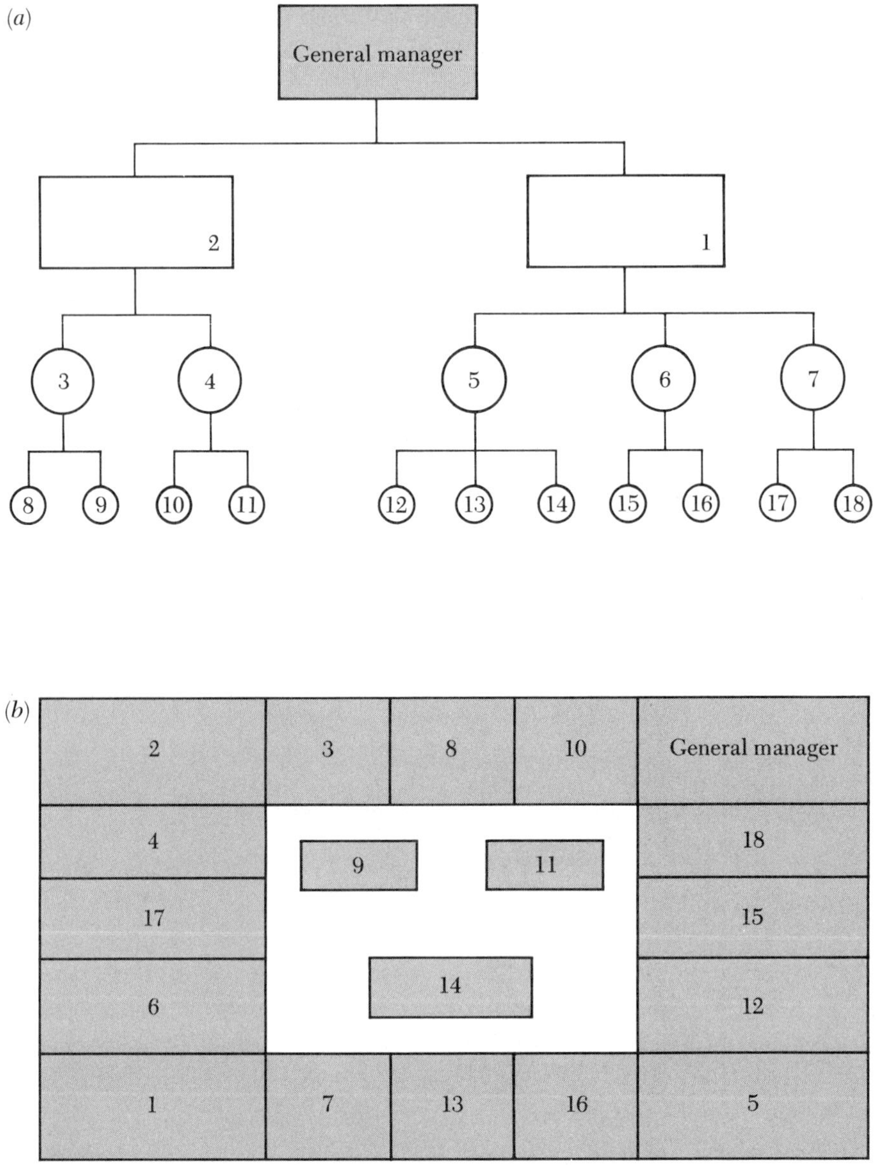


*Figure 21-6.* Comparison of an Organization Chart and an Office Layout
*(a)* Organization chart showing formal communication channels.
*(b)* Conventional office layout with private offices; no use is made of communication interaction analysis.

analysis are shown in Figure 21-7. Note that 1 and 2 are both supervisors who report to the general manager. Because of their positions, both supervisors have frequent interaction with the general manager, with each other, and with most of the members of their work groups—as shown in the figure. Numbers 1 and 12 have extensive communication, but communication between 1 and 16 and 18 is very light. Also notice the typical complexity of communication patterns for this relatively simple analysis of 19 persons in a company.

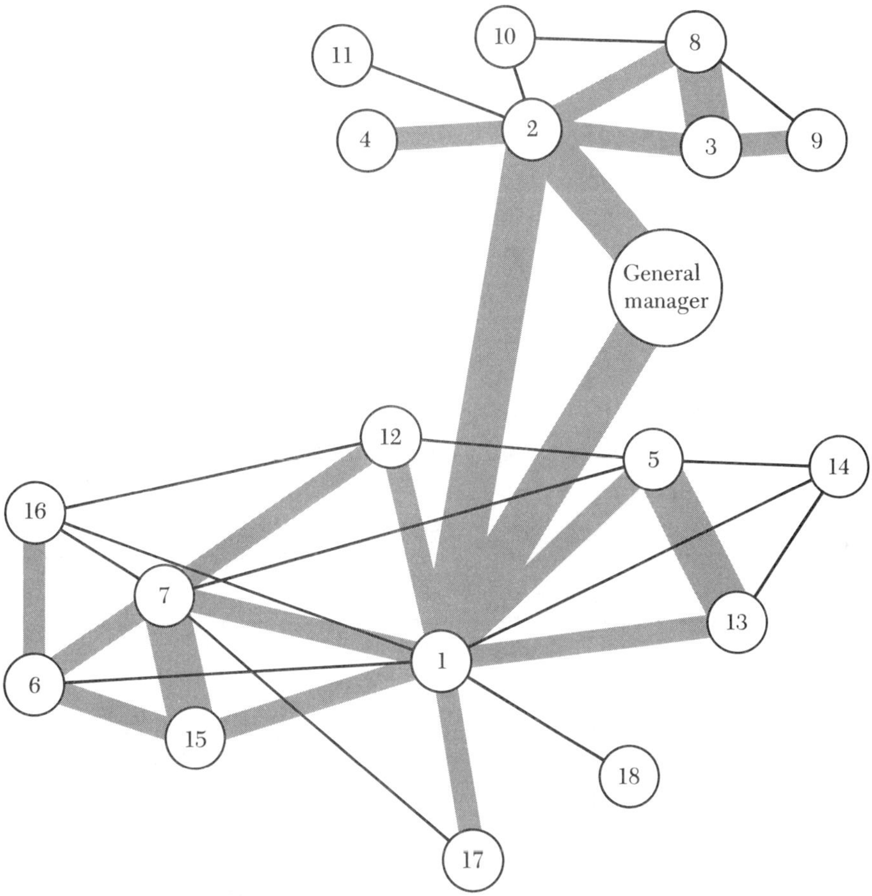


*Figure 21-7.* Communication Interaction Pattern in Department (Width of connecting lines shows frequency and intensity of interaction.)

## QUESTIONING AND IMPROVING THE OFFICE LAYOUT

### Analyze the Present Layout and Design an Improved One (Step 3)

***Analysis.*** Gather all information you have collected in step 2 and question everything about your present layout. The movement diagram may reveal backtracking and wasted movement occurring during the processing of work. The communication interaction diagram will reveal which people are communicating with each other and to what extent; it will also show which people are not communicating with each other. Use the Layout Analysis Questions to complete your analysis.

*Layout Analysis Questions*

1. *Have departments, teams, and service facilities been placed in locations that will facilitate operations?*

   Some teams and departments have frequent contacts with each other. Some operations have frequent contact with the public or agents of other organizations and should be placed near entrances or elevators. For example, the personnel department and purchasing office should be readily accessible to outsiders. Service facilities such as the word-processing center and reprographics should be centrally located.

2. *Have individual work stations been grouped according to the office communication pattern?*

   Some work involves very little communication with other people. These jobs are single-person type activities, and these people should be located away from the mainstreams of interaction. Other persons are dependent upon their communication with other empoyees to get the job done in an effective manner. These people should be clustered together in interaction groups according to their communication patterns.

3. *Have individual work stations been grouped according to the office work flow?*

   The basic flow of work in the office should flow smoothly and directly without backtracking and wasted movement. Conveniently placed work stations will reduce distance traveled and increase productivity. Ask yourself this question: If work station locations were rearranged, would the flow of work move more directly?

4. *Are equipment and storage facilities conveniently located?*

   For example, if you have frequent need to use a copy machine that is located a long distance away, much valuable time will be wasted. Perhaps using two smaller copy machines rather than one would improve efficiency.

5. *Should the workers who are communicating extensively with each other be doing so, or are they wasting time?*

   Perhaps the separation of certain individuals in the organization might prove to be beneficial.

6. *Are there any personnel who should be communicating with each other who are not doing so?*

   Possibly a change in location of personnel would facilitate communication.

Some basic principles of office layout will provide guidelines for making decisions with regard to designing the new layout.

*Office Layout Principles*

1. Departments, divisions, sections, and personnel that have similar and related functions should be placed near each other to reduce travel time.
2. Work should flow continuously as much as possible without undue backtracking and crisscrossing.
3. Central service units such as word-processing centers, central file areas, data-processing centers, reprographic centers (copy and duplicating machines) should be located centrally. Administrative support groups that provide secretarial and other support should be located near the executives and other personnel that are being served.
4. Furniture and equipment should be arranged in a manner that improves efficiency, promotes communication, and conserves space. At the same time, the office environment should be comfortable and should provide a feeling of security for employees.
5. Space allowances should be adequate for work needs and employee comfort. *Space standards* have traditionally been an important consideration in space planning. Some average space allocations are: clerks—65 square feet; interviewers—80 square feet; and supervisors—100 square feet. With innovative concepts of office planning, the emphasis has been on how much space is *needed* to accomplish a particular job rather than how much is wanted. Of course, as a matter of practicality, the administrative manager must consider the impact of space allotments on the morale of his or her employees. Consequently, consistency in giving the same amount of space to all personnel doing the same type of work is important.
6. Furnishings and panels or partitions should be standardized and modularized. *Standardized* means that the parts of the work station should be uniform in size as much as possible; *modularized* means that the parts should fit together to form larger units. For example, desks and lateral file cabinets (file cabinets that open to the side) can be grouped together in various combinations to form as many work stations as needed. The ad-

vantage of having equipment standardized and modularized is one of cost reduction, because fewer items of various sizes need to be kept in the store room for future expansion.

7. Aisles should be sufficiently wide to provide easy access to all personnel and equipment. Exits and fire escapes should have easy, unobstructed access for safety reasons.
8. Proper light and air conditioning should be provided for all employees.
9. Noisy machines such as typewriters, duplicators, and data processing equipment should be isolated as much as possible to eliminate distracting noise.
10. Private and partitioned offices or rooms should be provided for or made available to those individuals who perform work that requires privacy or concentration. For example, an administrative manager working on a confidential budget needs an area that is closed off from other people. Also, private offices serve as status symbols. An executive with a private office (and usually a personal secretary) gives signals to others of his or her importance to the organization. This is a major question, and the threat of losing status is the real reason why many innovative office layout systems have failed. Top management must take a stand on this issue. If the president of a company were to move into an office that was landscaped or had privacy panels, the rest of the organization would have little cause for complaint.
11. Provisions should be made to accommodate handicapped employees. For example, people in wheelchairs will need to have ramps and elevators available rather than stairs; also, they will need special restroom facilities and parking areas.

***Improved Layout.*** Develop an improved layout based on your analysis. Seek input from employees and other persons involved, and use your creative thinking ability in developing the new layout. Keep in mind that any solution that you develop will be a comprimise and that you cannot please everyone.

Based on your analysis of the movement diagram and communication interaction analysis diagram, the location of workers can be determined. Figure 21-8 shows how persons in our example finally were located, according to the communication patterns previously described in Figure 21-7. From this space location diagram, a final layout is prepared using layout tools.

***Layout Tools.*** Most people are familiar with the problems associated with changing furniture around in the average household. People have a difficult time in deciding how various pieces of furniture will fit and go together. Usually after a long time (and much back-breaking work) furniture is effectively arranged. If office employees had to use this trial and error method, particularly in a large office, much time would be wasted. Fortunately, there is a better way.

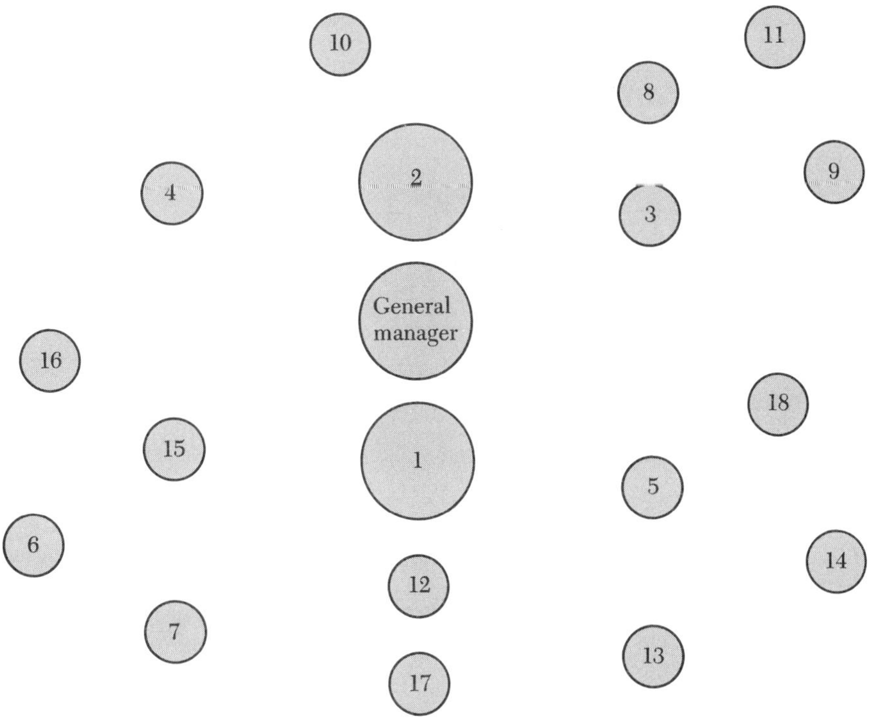


*Figure 21-8.* Space Location Diagram, Showing Areas within the Office Where Employees Will Be Placed as a Result of Communication Interaction Analysis

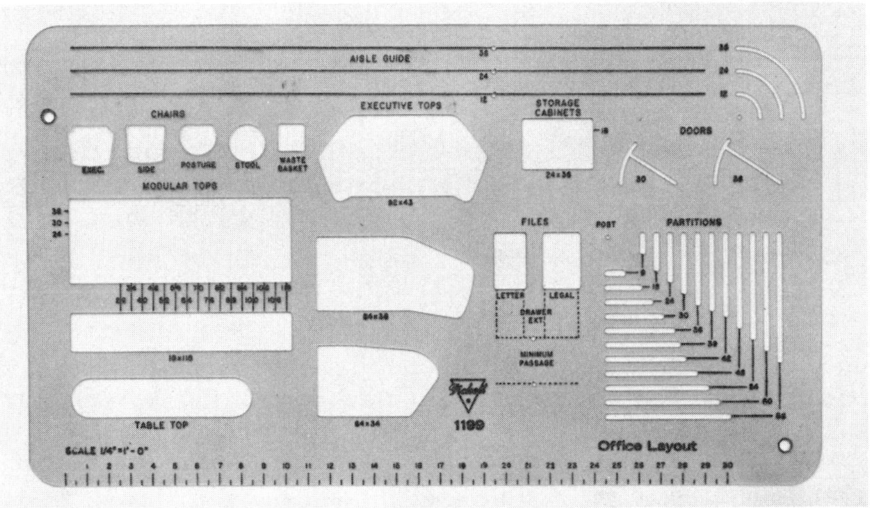


*Figure 21-9.* Office Layout Stencil

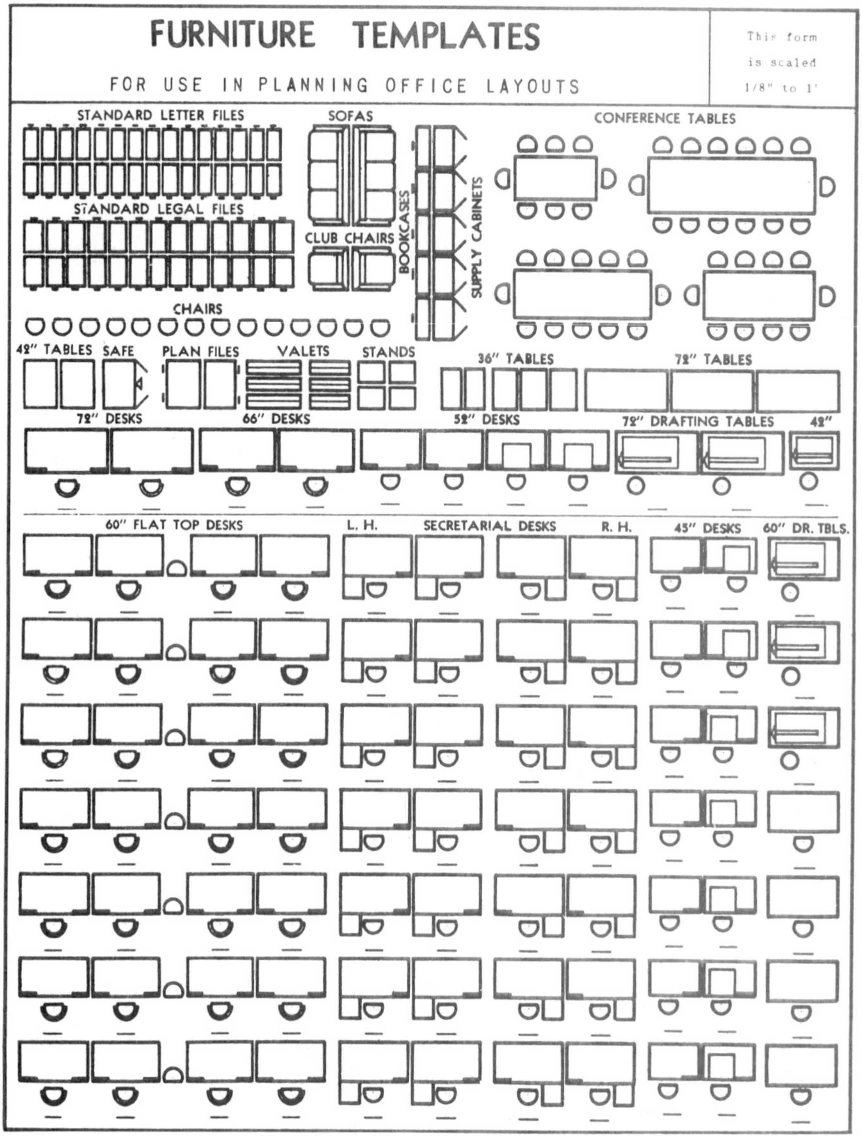


*Figure 21-10.* Sample Office Layout Templates

*Grid sheets* (or graph paper), *plastic tape, stencils, templates, models,* and *three-dimensional drawings* are convenient layout tools. Grid sheets are available in plastic, paper, cardboard, or metal. Plastic tape of various widths, instead of pencil lines, can be used to show walls and partitions. Copies of the office outline can be made on the copy machine and used to make various possible layouts.

layout is attained. When the final version is developed, the templates can be attached to the grid. These templates are also available in plastic or magnetized metal. The plastic template can be affixed to a plastic grid simply by pressing on the template. The magnetic version clings to a metal grid.

Plastic models provide yet another approach to preparing the layout. Samples of model office furnishings and partitions are shown in Figure 21-11. Models can be easily moved and provide three-dimensional, realistic detail. They are rather expensive to purchase, however. Finished layouts are prepared by photographing the models on the grid.

Finally, the three-dimensional drawing shown in Figure 21-12 can be made. This technique provides the detail and the three-dimensional effect of the plastic models without the expense. Instructions for using this procedure are found in Figure 21-13.

## FACTORS AFFECTING THE IMPROVED LAYOUT

### Selling and Implementing It (Step 4)

Involvement of employees in the process of developing an improved layout should gain their support. Keep them informed about proposed changes. When the time comes to implement your new system, involve your employees in making final plans. Let them develop their own refinements to the system such as location of files and which types of shelf unit to use.

Call on vendors of office furnishings or work through your purchasing department to make contacts. Get written proposals and bids from each vendor. Check with other administrative managers who have redesigned their office layouts to get further information.

Finally, after thorough analysis of all the alternatives, go ahead and have the new furnishings installed. The office landscape and privacy panel furnishings can be completely installed within a day or two.

### Follow Up on the New Layout (Step 5)

The last step is to check to make certain that the new office layout is working out smoothly. If things are not going as planned, make necessary changes. Again involve the employees in making minor changes in their own work station. Review your layout periodically to make certain it is keeping pace with a dynamic organization.

Using an office layout stencil, such as that found in Figure 21-9, possible layouts can be drawn from which a final selection can be made. An alternate procedure is to use templates such as those shown in Figure 21-10. These templates can be cut out and moved around on the grid until an optimum

*Figure 21-11.* Office Layout Models
*Source:* A'D'S Co., Indianola, Pa.

One of the major advantages of the office landscape and privacy panel concepts is that changes can be readily made as changes are made within the organization. For example, assume that an office is assigned to take on a new function such as handling records for a new region of the company. With mod-

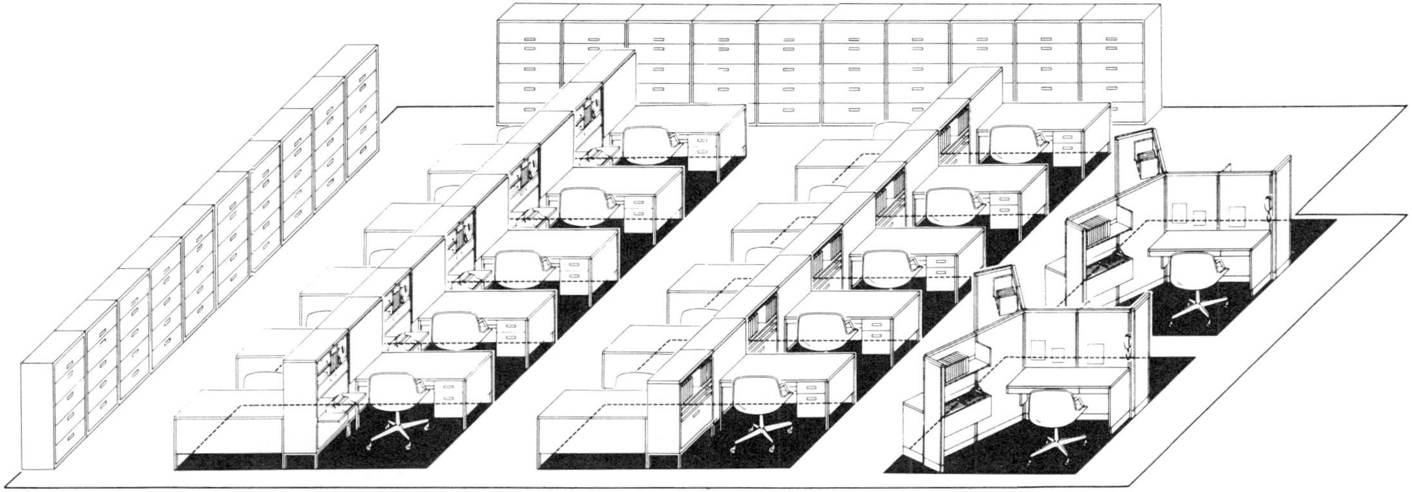

*Figure 21-12.* Part of a Typical Three-Dimensional Drawing of an Office
*Source: Steelcase Mobiles* (Grand Rapids, Mich.: Steelcase, Inc., 1974), p. 83.

**How to Plan Three-Dimensional Drawings**

"What will my space look like?" "Can you give me a quick drawing showing the new work stations?"

You've planned the space. Now you need to communicate the answers to these two questions to other people. Here's a new easy way to do it. Remember: You're working on a 45° angle—literally with parallelograms rather than rectangles. You'll find the first one strange to do. But after the first one, it's easy. Follow these steps:

1. Plan the entire space using plan views provided. Most of the 28 ideas have plan views in 1/8″ scale. All scales are clearly marked.

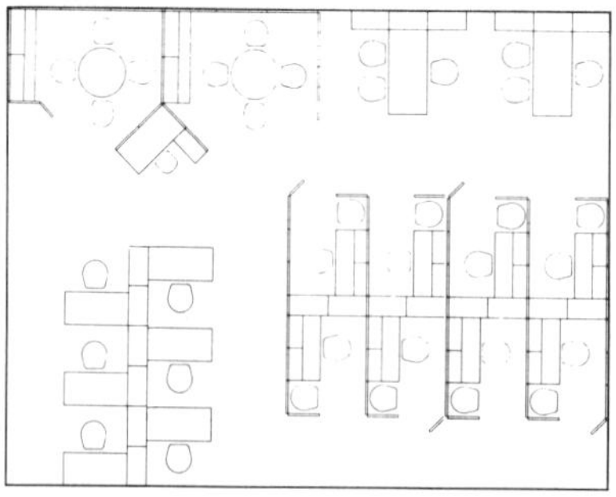

2. All 28 ideas are executed in 45° 3-dimensional—a drawing method that allows you to experience the work station. All scale drawings are in 1/4″ scale.

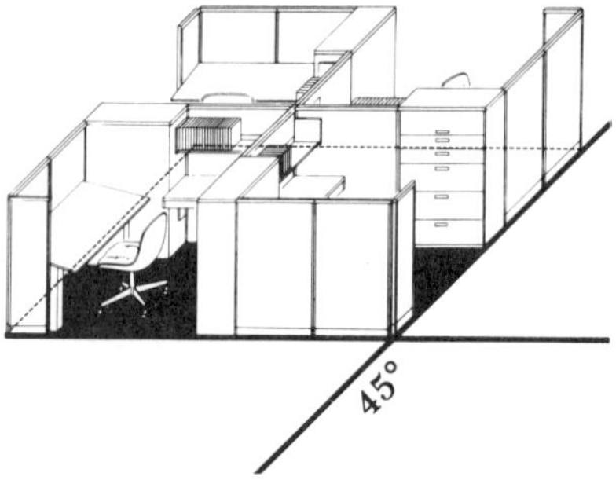


3. Take the blank grid page. On a copy machine, make as many copies as you'll need. The grid has a heavy rule every 10 units. It too is executed in 1/4″ scale.

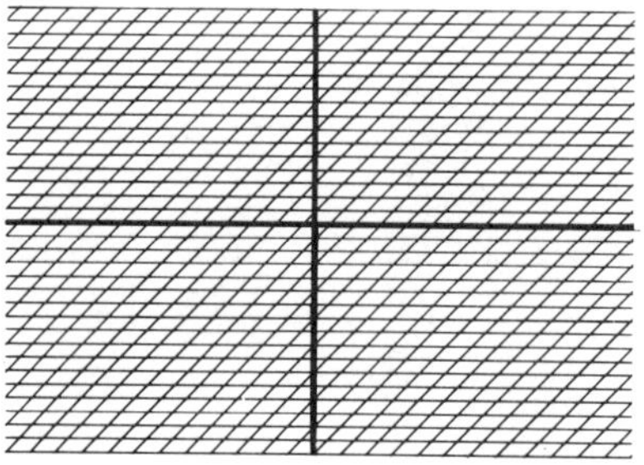

4. On a copy machine, make sufficient copies of work stations you've selected.

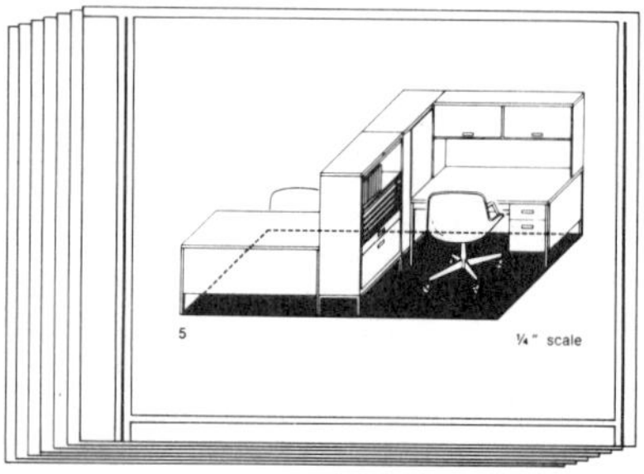


*Figure 21-13.* Instructions for Preparing Three-Dimensional Drawings

Source: *Steelcase Series 9000 Workbook* (Grand Rapids, Mich.: Steelcase, Inc., 1977), pp. 74–75.

5. Rule on the grid sheet the space you'll be laying out.

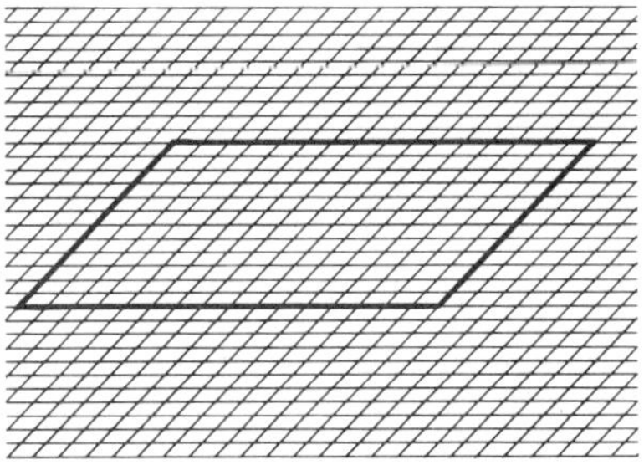

6. Begin with the top of the space and work downwards. Scotch tape or rubber cement each drawing into its proper position. Photocopy the finished product. Color as needed.

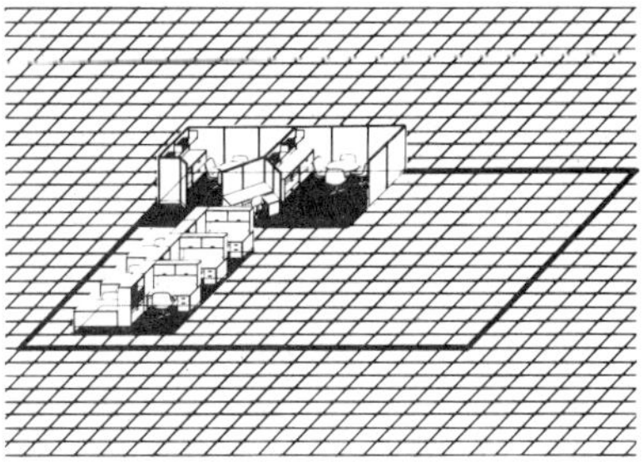

*Figure 21-13, continued.*

ern office furnishings, panels can easily be rearranged and new work stations added without having to tear down walls or make major, expensive changes.

## *Summary*

Most traditional office layouts tend to have personnel located according to the hierarchy of the formal organization chart, and so status is a major factor in deciding where personnel will be located. A more objective approach is to make an office layout analysis.

The five-step administrative systems analysis procedure can be used when planning a new office layout. Work flow is studied by means of the movement diagram, and communication patterns are traced through communication interaction analysis. Layout tools such as floor plans, stencils, templates, models, and drawings aid you in the planning process.

Once information is gathered about the present office layout, the analysis process begins by asking certain key questions. A new layout is developed in accordance with basic office layout principles. Employees are involved in making changes, but full top management support is required.

## *Discussion and Review Questions*

1. Explain the basis on which most traditional offices are planned.
2. Describe how the five-step analysis procedure that you studied in Chapter 19 can be used to analyze office layout.

3. How do office work flow and office communication interaction relate to the layout of an office?
4. In analyzing the present layout of an office, what types of questions should be asked in order to discover the need for possible improvement?
5. Explain how the administrative manager can get changes in layout accepted by office employees.
6. Do you favor the use of private offices for executives and key personnel? Or do you think that they should be either partially or completely eliminated?
7. How should the administrative manager decide how much space should be allocated to the personnel in his or her office?
8. What advantages and disadvantages do you see in using each of the layout tools discussed in the textbook?

## *Application Exercises*

Report as directed by your instructor on the following exercises:

1. Prepare a communication interaction analysis diagram for an office situation (either where you are employed or where you can get approval to conduct the analysis). Limit the number of people involved to a manageable number—not more than ten or twelve.
2. Prepare a movement diagram to show the flow of work in an office setting. Make recommendations for changes that would improve the flow; prepare a second movement diagram to show the proposed changes.
3. Select an office and prepare a detailed layout showing office furnishings, equipment, walls, panels, partitions, doors, windows, and any other pertinent features. (Be sure to obtain permission from the manager.) Use a scale of ¼ inch equals 1 foot. Prepare a short report showing your recommendation for change and reasons for the changes. Prepare a second layout chart with the proposed changes.

## *Case Studies*

1. *Walczak Realty.* Assume that you are the office manager for the rapidly expanding Walczak Realty Co. in Sunnyvale, California. Walczak specializes in custom sales work for exclusive homes. There are 22 people in the office including Mr. Walczak, owner and general manager. Others in the office are 10 sales persons, 1 assistant manager, 3 appraisers, 1 secretary to Mr. Walczak, 1 secretary shared by you and the assistant manager, 4 clerks, and yourself.

You have the assignment of preparing the layout for the new office that the company will move into in two months. The office area is 3,000 square feet of open space in a rectangular shape. In addition, in the center of the office area, there is a 25 by 10-foot area for service facilities such as restrooms, janitors closet, furnace, and hot water heater. All of the rest of the 3,000 square feet is usable office space, located on one floor. All windows are 8 feet above the floor. One entrance, which faces the street, is on the north side of the building on the west end. The other entrance is on the south side in the middle and opens to the parking lot.

You may select any type of office plan that you think is appropriate. You want to provide 200 square feet for Mr. Walczak, 120 square feet each for the assistant manager and yourself, 110 square feet each for the appraisers and the secretaries, 100 square feet each for the clerks and sales persons. Be sure to provide space for expansion, which is anticipated during the next three to six years. Assume that the office force will expand on about the same ratio for the various types of personnel that now exists in the office on a 10 percent growth pattern for each year. For example, with 10 sales persons now, you could expect to add one new sales person each year.

Prepare your layout and a short written report that explains what you did and why you did it.

2. *The Rockford Case.* As director of the systems department at Rockford Insurance Co., you have the responsibility for the development of all systems within the corporation. Recently, your organization has had productivity problems. The time to complete an average systems project has been increasing and deadlines have been missed consistently.

You have been studying the problem for the past month. You have discovered some problems with management techniques and with technical requirements imposed on the systems development process by the corporation. You are taking steps to solve these problems. In response to a questionnaire directed to your systems analysts, you find that, among other things, they feel that the layout of the office is inconveniently arranged. They say that they are not close to people with whom they work, equipment which they use, support personnel in the word-processing center, or supervisors and managers. They dislike being crowded into the "bull pens" with four people.

Note the following facts about the case:

a. All personnel within a team, including the project leader, have frequent contact with each other.
b. Project leaders work closely with the director, the assistant director, and the programmer-manager.
c. The programmer-manager has responsibility for all performance appraisal of all personnel and for all training.
d. The administrative manager works closely with the supervisor of the word-processing center and the assistant director.
e. The director and the assistant director frequently confer with each other and with all members of the department.

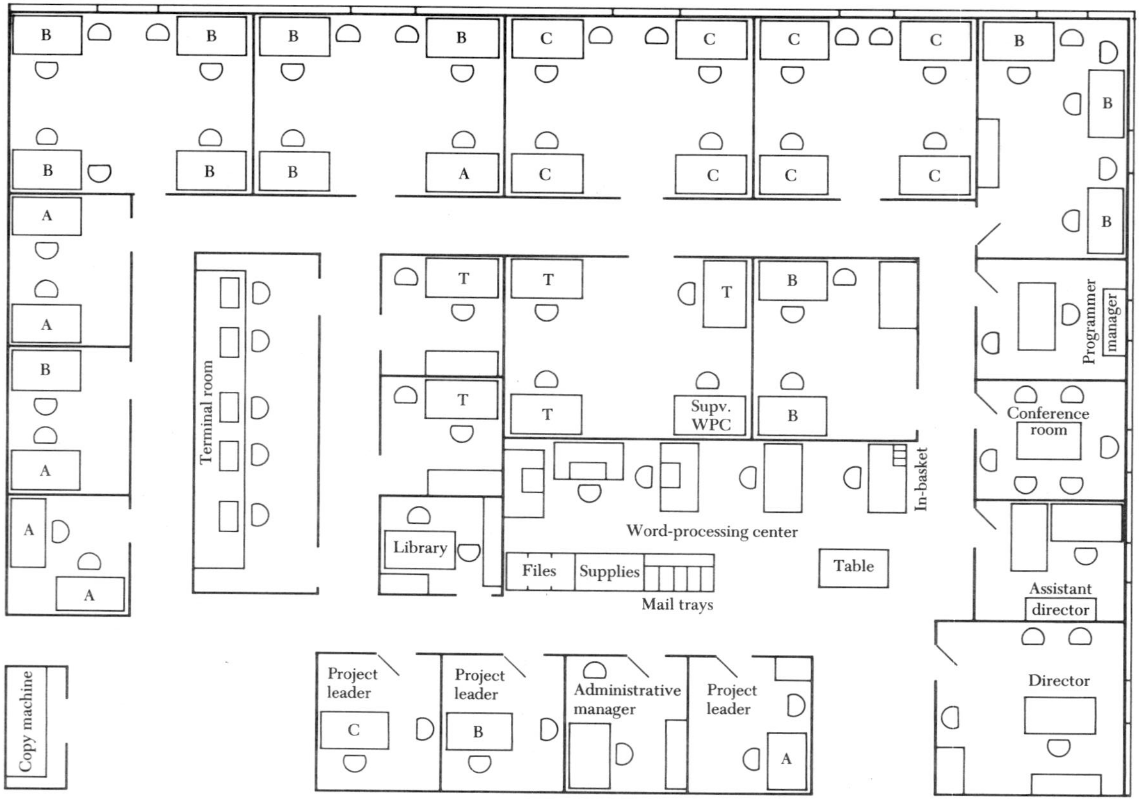


*Figure 21-14.* The Rockford Case — Present Layout of Systems Department

Key: A, B, and C refer to three groups or teams of analysis. T refers to other technical personnel.

f. The technical personnel (T) confer with each other, but rarely with anyone else.
g. All personnel use the word-processing center, terminal room, copy machine, and library frequently. Everyone uses the conference room occasionally.
h. All offices and rooms have partitions that reach the ceiling.
i. A layout of the present office is shown in the attached diagram (Figure 21-14).

Consider the information that you have available about this systems department and develop recommendations that you could give to the director for improving the layout. Prepare a neat, polished layout showing your proposed changes. Be prepared to defend your solution to this problem before the class. Make any reasonable assumptions that are necessary. You may make any changes in the layout that you think are reasonable and beneficial.

# 22

# Records Management and Forms Control

"Let's see now, where did I put that letter from Ajax Insurance? Would it be under 'Ajax' or 'Insurance'? Maybe it's in 'Miscellaneous.' It's got to be here somewhere." Perhaps you have had a similar experience trying to find something that you had misplaced in a file. On a larger scale, misplacing information is very costly to a company. Businesses and other organizations live on information, and they simply cannot afford to have disorganized records management systems. Vital information is critical in the decision-making process, and if that information cannot be located, the entire organization will suffer.

## FORCES THAT INCREASE PAPERWORK

Records management has changed drastically since the beginning of the twentieth century. In fact, the twentieth century could probably go down in history as the age of the paper explosion, because during this time the use of paper has increased by staggering amounts. In 1976, Frank Horton estimated the cost of governmental paperwork carried out by both government and the private sector to be $40 billion ($40,000,000,000) annually.[1] The significance of governmental paper use is further emphasized by the fact that in 1977 the cost of a single copy of all the governmental regulations pertaining only to the Occupational Safety and Health Act was between $4,000 and $6,000. In addition to the impact of government on paper use, other noticeable forces are computers, duplicating and copying machines, expanding businesses and other organizations, and ineffective office managers.

## PURPOSE OF RECORDS MANAGEMENT

The basic purpose of records management is to control all this paper so the proper information is available for decision making. Records management deals with records from creation through storage, maintenance, retrieval, and disposal or permanent retention. The flowchart illustrated in Figure 22-1 shows the steps involved in the records management cycle—the basic phases in the life of a record. The eight steps shown in the figure will be explained throughout this chapter.

Information in records should be at the right place at the right time; for if it cannot be found, it is of no value. Therefore, the main emphasis in records management must be on *finding* information, not on filing and maintaining records. Filing and maintaining records are not important functions in and of themselves, but they derive their importance from the contribution they make to easy and quick retrieval of information. The major factors that contribute to the effectiveness of a filing system are file integrity, retrieval speed, and cost.

*File integrity* refers to the degree to which individual records are where they ought to be.

File integrity can be measured by using an accuracy ratio that is computed by dividing the number of records actually located by the number of records requested. If 2,000 records are requested during a given period of time and 1,961 are found, the accuracy ratio is 0.9805. The accuracy ratio of an organization should never fall below 97 percent.

*Retrieval speed* can be computed simply by recording the time it takes to provide records that are requested.

To determine retrieval speed, you should stamp the line for each record request as it is received and as the request is filled. Then, the lengths of time recorded for a given number of requests are averaged to determine the average retrieval speed. For example, a records department may find that its average retrieval speed is 45 minutes, and measures may be taken to reduce that time.

*Cost* can be subdivided into personnel cost, filing equipment cost, and overhead cost.

More specifically, cost evaluations should consider personnel cost to file, to retrieve, and to maintain files; cost of files, folders, filing and retrieval equipment, and other miscellaneous equipment used in enhancing filing effectiveness; and cost of floor space, lights, heat and air conditioning, fire protection, and theft protection. A records manager may find that a typical five-drawer file is costing the company the following amounts annually:

| | |
|---|---|
| Personnel costs | $400 |
| Supplies and equipment | 106 |
| Overhead | 35 |
| Total | $541 |

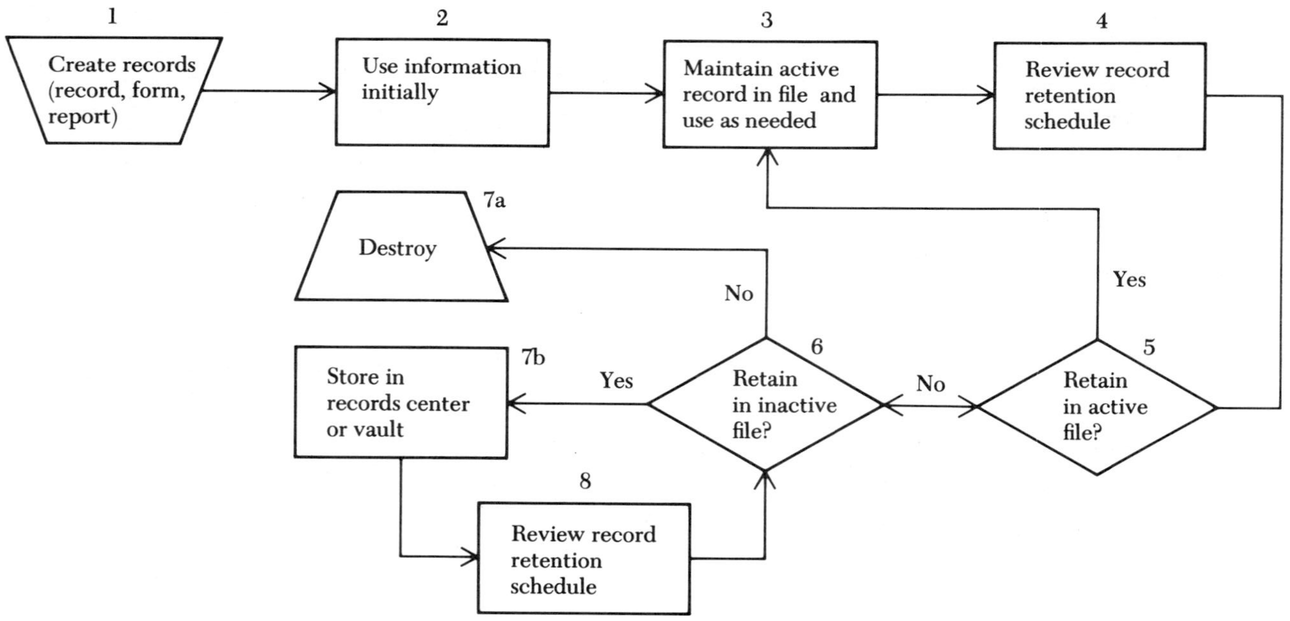


*Figure 22-1.* Records—Creation through Final Disposal

## RECORDS CREATION AND CONTROL

Because the storage and management of records are such expensive and vital functions, every effort possible must be made to streamline records management activities in an organization. A major part of this effort begins when business forms are first designed.

### Business Forms

Business forms make up a major part of all records that are created, used, and retained by most organizations. A form can be defined as any sheet of paper or card with preprinted data and spaces to be filled in. A few of the forms that are found in many businesses are application blanks, orientation checklists, training requests, appraisal forms, personnel action forms, requisitions, purchase orders, invoices, receipts, and inventory forms. A form requesting reference information is shown in Figure 22-2. Forms are used to avoid the unnecessary writing of common repetitive kinds of information and to standardize variable information. Forms are intended to save time, make work easier, and make operations more efficient.

While forms are useful, they also tend to become burdensome when they are used unnecessarily. At times they may become so numerous that they clog the administrative system. Frequently, many forms involve duplication of information and require extra work in maintaining filed forms.

***Methods of Control.*** Control measures are necessary to help combat the unnecessary development of new forms and the inefficiency of existing ones. Several steps are important in accomplishing this objective. First, analyze the forms used by the organization. To conduct the analysis, appoint one or more individuals who are familiar with the organization, its systems, and its needs. Samples of all forms being used by the organization should be collected and compared to reveal (1) information that is being collected on more than one form, (2) useless information that is being collected, and (3) information that is being collected in an inefficient manner. A simple tool that can be used to analyze similar forms is the Forms Analysis Worksheet, illustrated in Figure 22-3. On the worksheet, each form used is listed in a separate column, and in the left column all items of information appearing in each form are listed. A checkmark is then placed in each column opposite the item of information. Several checkmarks next to an item reveal duplication and indicate a need for combining forms.

Next, the forms analysts should determine whether each item of information requested on each form is being used. All employees who use each form should be asked to indicate the items of information they use. After this information is gathered, the analyst can eliminate the items of information that are not used by anyone.

# WRITTEN REQUEST FOR REFERENCE

(CONFIDENTIAL)

Date ____________

NAME ____________ Social Security Number ____________

Has applied to us for employment as ____________ and has stated that he (she) was in your employ from ________ to ________ in the capacity of ____________ . Will you please complete the following form and return it to us in the self addressed envelope at your earliest convenience.

SIGNED ____________
Director of Personnel

Date of Employment ____________ Date of Termination ____________

Position held ____________

Reason for termination ____________

PLEASE CHECK THE APPROPRIATE COLUMN INDICATING YOUR RATING OF THE APPLICANT

| | Excellent | Good | Adequate | Unsatisfactory | Unable to Evaluate |
|---|---|---|---|---|---|
| Technical Ability | | | | | |
| Attendance Record | | | | | |
| Ability to get along with others | | | | | |
| Cooperation | | | | | |
| Appearance | | | | | |
| Ability to take instructions | | | | | |
| Common Sense | | | | | |
| Effective Utilization of time | | | | | |
| | | | | | |

Any injury on the job? ________ If yes, please state date, nature, lost time ____________

Would you re-employ? ________ If no, why ____________

Do you recommend applicant? ____________

Additional Remarks ____________

Date ____________ Signed ____________

Title ____________

*Figure 22-2.* Sample Business Form

*Source:* Parkway General Hospital, North Miami Beach, Fla. Reprinted from *Modern Personnel Forms,* Copyright 1976, Warren, Gorham, and Lamont, Inc., 210 South Street, Boston, Mass. 

**Forms Analysis Worksheet**

| Information contained in forms | Form title or number | | | | |
|---|---|---|---|---|---|
| | Form A | Form B | Form C | Form D | Form E |
| Name | | | | | |
| Customer number | | | | | |
| Address | | | | | |
| Salesman | | | | | |
| Salesman's number | | | | | |
| Stock number | | | | | |
| Other | | | | | |
| | | | | | |

*Figure 22-3.* Forms Analysis Worksheet

Finally, to determine the efficiency of forms, the analyst should see if the forms measure up to accepted forms design guidelines. Significant weaknesses in forms design should be corrected and new forms should be printed. Because forms design guidelines are so critical in both the analysis of existing forms and in the development of new forms, they are explained here in greater detail.

***Guidelines for Designing Forms.*** The following guidelines will enable office workers to design forms that are clear, concise, and attractive:

1. Use standard paper or card size. In a legal office, you would probably have numerous forms of an 8½ × 13-inch size; in a business office, you would have many forms of the 8½ × 11-inch size. Forms to be stored in a card file would probably be 3 × 5 inches or 4 × 6 inches in size.
2. Use a title, a form number, and a date. The title describes the purpose of the form or the information it contains, the form number aids in forms inventory and storage management, and the date reveals the latest revision of the form.

3. Make the lines and spaces compatible with standard typewriters (if the forms are totally or partially typewritten).
   a. Lines should be spaced in 1/6-inch or 1/3-inch increments.
   b. Information requested should be aligned vertically so common tab stops can be used.
   c. Descriptors (the words or phrases that tell what information is to be inserted) should be on line with or just above the typing line, so they are not hidden below the typing line of the typewriter.
4. Use terminology that is understood by all users.
5. Reduce the need for writing or typing as much as possible by using checkmark (√) or cross (×) spaces or boxes and by preprinting all information that does not vary from person to person.
6. Leave writing or typing space equal to the amount of information that is requested. For example, you would not leave two full lines for a birthdate.
7. Finally, and most all-encompassing, design the form with the user in mind. Make sure that all information that is needed is requested by the form, and use continuous forms and multiple forms as needed. Continuous forms are connected and perforated for continuous feeding through a typewriter or computer printer. Multiple forms can be made with carbon paper that is preinserted between the several copies, or they can be made with a specially treated duplicate-copy paper that requires no carbon paper.

The form illustrated in Figure 22-4 violates some of the major principles of forms design. Close examination of this form will reveal the following weaknesses:

If this form were completed on a typewriter, the typist would not be able to see the instruction to put last name first.

The spaces for name and address are crowded and there is excessive room for employee number and telephone number.

Items are not aligned vertically, so tab stops on a typewriter could not be efficiently used.

The abbreviation "DOB" and the term "Annual Personnel Audit" could be confusing.

Lines are varying distances apart, so the horizontal spacing of a typewriter would have to be continually changed.

Circling items may be a bit more awkward than just making an "×" or a checkmark.

This form is not a standard size.

Name: Empl. #

(Last) (First) (Middle)

Address: Phone:

(Street) (City) (State)

Age: DOB:

Marital status: Exempt or nonexempt

(Circle one)

Department: Job title:

Supervisor:

Annual personnel audit:

Comments:

*Figure 22-4.* Example of a Form That Violates Forms Design Principles

"Date of birth" and "age" ask for duplicate information.

The line below supervisor could be omitted.

The form has no title or form number for control and identification purposes.

Figure 22-5 illustrates a number of changes that have been made in the previous form. These improvements should make the form much easier to work with. As you examine the improved form, notice that:

1. It has a title and form number.
2. It fits on a standard 3 × 5 card.
3. You can read the description of the information that is to be typed.
4. The tab stops are standard.
5. The duplication of "date of birth" and "age" has been eliminated.
6. Line spaces correspond to standard typewriter spacing.
7. Specific information can be indicated by checking off the correct box.
8. Confusing or incomplete terminology has been clarified.

Since the cost of using forms is usually far greater than the material cost of the form itself, you will make great savings in efficiency as you utilize effective forms design and control procedures.

**EMPLOYEE PERSONNEL RECORD**

| | | |
|---|---|---|
| Name (Last, first, middle initial) | Empl. no. | Date of birth |
| Address | Tel. no. | Marital status |
| Department | Supervisor | |
| Job title | | |
| Annual personnel audit compiled ☐ 1978 ☐ 1979 ☐ 1980 ☐ 1981 | ☐ Exempt ☐ 1982 ☐ 1983 | ☐ Nonexempt ☐ 1984 |
| Comments | | SF No. 25 |

*Figure 22-5.* Example of an Improved Form That Conforms to Major Principles of Forms Design

## Reports Control

Business reports comprise another segment of materials that are filed in most organizations. Reports are documents that give descriptions or analyses of operational concerns of an organization. The two major purposes of reports are to give information and to solve problems (see example in Figure 22-6). Reports may be submitted on a periodic or a one-time basis, depending on the particular organizational needs and reports' functions. Generally, reports are sent *up* the organization to provide management with information for decision making. A report may be either formal or informal, depending on the purpose of the report and the people who will use it.

In spite of the importance of reports, report-use analyses usually reveal many reports that are not required and that should be discontinued. Reports must be timely, and only necessary information should be reported to people who have a need for it.

One excellent reports control technique is to interview all personnel who receive copies of a particular report and to ask them what need they have for the report, what they do with the report, and what items of information could be eliminated. Another interesting technique is to stop sending out a report to see who complains that they are missing the information. Some reports can be eliminated without anyone ever missing them. A third technique is to create a worksheet like the Forms Analysis Worksheet (Figure 22-3) and to determine whether the same information is being needlessly included in more than one report. After a thorough analysis of report creation and use, you can usually find several reports that can be eliminated, combined, or improved.

```
TO:      Charles E. Borg, V. P. of Administration
FROM:    Larry Johnson, Office Operations Manager
DATE:    June 8, 19XX
SUBJECT: 19XX Convention of the International Word
         Processors Association
```

<u>Conclusion</u>

Last Friday I returned from the 19XX Convention of the International Word Processors Association held in Minneapolis. During this convention, we received some information on the future outlook of the word-processing industry that I thought might be useful to you and to our company.

<u>Past Growth</u>

As you know, word processing has experienced tremendous growth during the past few years. For example in 1975, 211,900 text-editing units were installed. These units accounted for only 20 percent of the potential market, however. Since 1975, many new innovations have expanded the uses of word processing. The use of cathode-ray tubes has allowed for instant text editing. New ideas have been implemented to link word processing with electronic data processing. Telecommunications has also produced ways to send word-processing material across regular telephone lines. These new innovations have created a larger market for word-processing equipment.

<u>Future Outlook</u>

Future predictions given at the convention call for sales in text-editing equipment to grow steadily. Estimates suggest that only 25 percent of the potential market has been penetrated.

*Figure 22-6.* Sample Business Report

## ACTIVE USE AND MAINTENANCE OF INFORMATION

After records, such as reports, forms, and letters, have been created and used, many of them must be stored for future reference. At this point in the life of a record, a filing system becomes important.

### Alphabetic Filing

The backbone of most records storage is an alphabetic system much like that used in your own telephone book. The alphabetic filing system is used primarily with correspondence where the letters are filed by the name of the company that wrote the letter. For example, a letter received from Jacobs Equipment Co. of Alberta, Canada would be filed under "J." Figure 22-7 presents an example of an alphabetically arranged file.

*Figure 22-7.* Sample Alphabetic Filing
*Source:* Oxford Pendaflex Corporation

An alternate alphabetic system is the subject filing system, in which correspondence is filed by subject. With a subject system, Jacobs Equipment Co. correspondence would probably be filed under "Equipment." Still another adaptation of the basic alphabetic system is the geographic system, in which correspondence is filed by the location of the firm that originated the letter. Using a geographic system, you would file Jacobs Equipment Co. correspondence under Alberta, Canada.

In order to make an alphabetic system function efficiently, all who work with the files must follow very specific rules established for alphabetic systems. If these rules are not followed, chaos will result. For example, would you file a letter from Dr. W. H. Carr-Smith under "D" for doctor, under "C" for Carr, or under "S" for Smith? By consulting a rules guide, you would find that the letter should be filed under "C" for Carr. Many people, however, would probably make a different choice unless they checked the rule beforehand. Several good filing books are available to give you good coverage of filing rules.

The major advantages and disadvantages of the alphabetic systems are as follows:

*Advantages*

1. It is a direct system; you can tell what is in a folder simply by reading the caption on the folder tab.
2. It is a logical system; items are filed under terms that are usually thought of by most people.

*Disadvantages*

1. Same and similar names occasionally result in misfiling.
2. Numerous filing rules must be followed exactly; otherwise, misfiling will result.
3. Expansion of files may be more difficult than with numeric systems.

Because of the important advantages offered by alphabetic filing, most organizations make heavy use of this system.

## Numeric Filing

As important and prevalent as alphabetic systems are, many files are based on numeric systems—especially when the records are identified by numbers rather than by names. The most common use of the numeric system is the filing of numbered forms and other types of information that are usually identified by a number. Examples of records that are readily adaptable to numeric filing are social security records, insurance records, invoices, work orders, accounts receivable and accounts payable records, and credit card records. Figure 22-8 shows how a typical numeric file might appear.

In a few cases, such as in an insurance company, it may be advantageous even to file correspondence by a number. In an insurance company, the number used would probably be the policy number; and the company would make an effort to encourage all the people they insure to include the policy number with each letter or insurance claim. If the number is included with the letter, finding the person's file is simple. But if the number is not included, the filing clerk must consult an alphabetic card file that includes a person's name and policy number. After finding the number from the alphabetic card file, the clerk can then go to the numeric file. Thus, numeric filing is sometimes called a two-step filing system. The major advantages and disadvantages of most numeric filing systems are as follows:

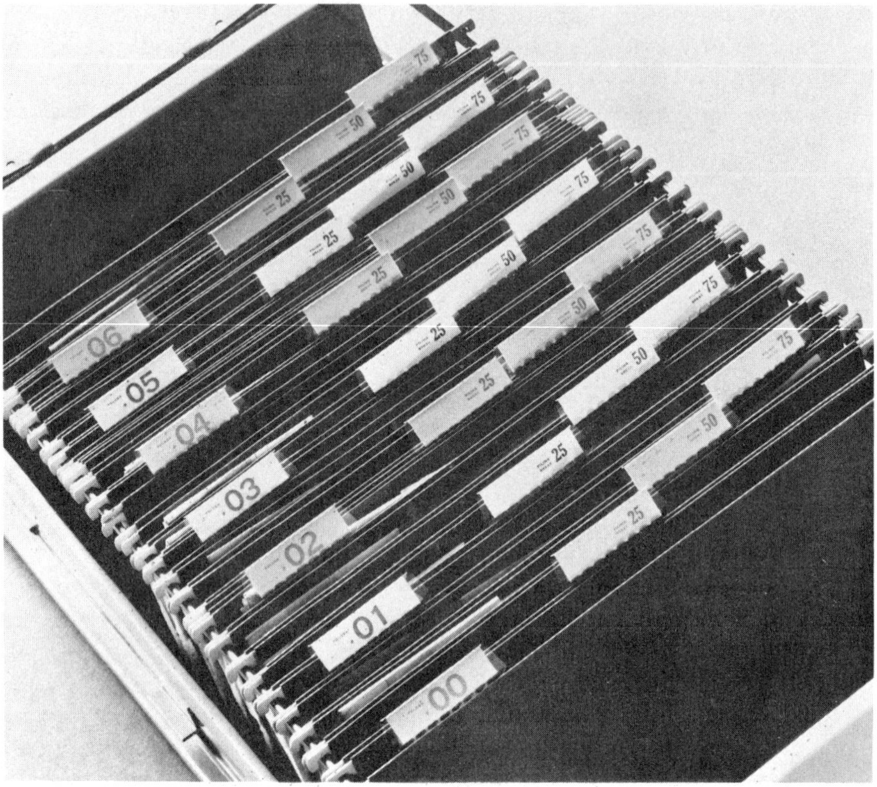

*Figure 22-8.* Sample Numeric Filing
*Source:* Oxford Pendaflex Corporation

*Advantages*

1. Finding and refiling numbered materials are rapid because most file clerks know the sequence of numbers better than they know the sequence of the alphabet.
2. File auditing (checking for misfiled folders) is easy because numbers out of sequence are readily spotted.
3. Files are easily expanded simply by adding new folders to the end of existing files. If your last folder is #10015, you number the next folder #10016.
4. File security is enhanced because a number on a folder does not reveal what is in the folder.

*Disadvantages*

1. Finding certain records sometimes involves two filing systems—thus a two-step filing process is involved.

2. Numeric filing is not a logical system because the number assigned to a folder tells nothing about the contents of the folder. Thus, transposition errors (143 instead of 134) and other copying errors are easily made.
3. The overall cost of a numeric filing system is usually higher than it is with an alphabetical system.

Other adaptations of the basic numeric system have been developed and are valuable in certain situations. These systems generally reflect a numeric adaptation of primarily alphabetic, subject, or geographic information. Consider the insurance folder number 46-622-10989-842. The 46 is a number designating the state in which the insurance agent resides; the 622 is a number assigned to the individual agent; the 10989 is a number reflecting the type of coverage the insured person carries; and the 842 is a number assigned specifically to the insured individual.

### Record Check-Out Methods

Regardless of the filing system used, filing personnel must always be concerned about file integrity—keeping records where they should be so they can be found when needed. Along with misfiled records, unreturned records cause serious records management problems. To fight against missing records, two general approaches are used:

1. *Duplicate-copy method.* When a request is received by the records department, a copy is made and sent to the person needing the record. The original document is refiled so there is no chance of losing it; and after the copy is used, it is destroyed. This method can be used with either regular paper copy or with microfilm records. It is very effective in maintaining file integrity, an important advantage when vital records are involved. Using this method, a manager in a medical services and equipment business might have a need for an order letter sent by a Dr. Newell Crookston. The manager would complete a record request form and submit that form to a records clerk. When the record is located, the clerk would make a copy of the record on a copy machine; and the copy would be taken to the manager who requested it.

2. *Out-card method.* When a request is received by the records department, a check-out card or form is completed that contains information about who has the record, what record is taken, when it was removed, and when it should be returned. This out-card or form is usually inserted into the space of the checked-out record, so that anyone needing the record before it is returned will know of its location. This method eliminates the copy machine cost incurred in the duplicate-copy method, but it results in less file integrity because of unreturned records. Adapting the preceding example of the manager in the medical services and equipment business to the out-card method, you would find that the manager would submit the same type of request to the

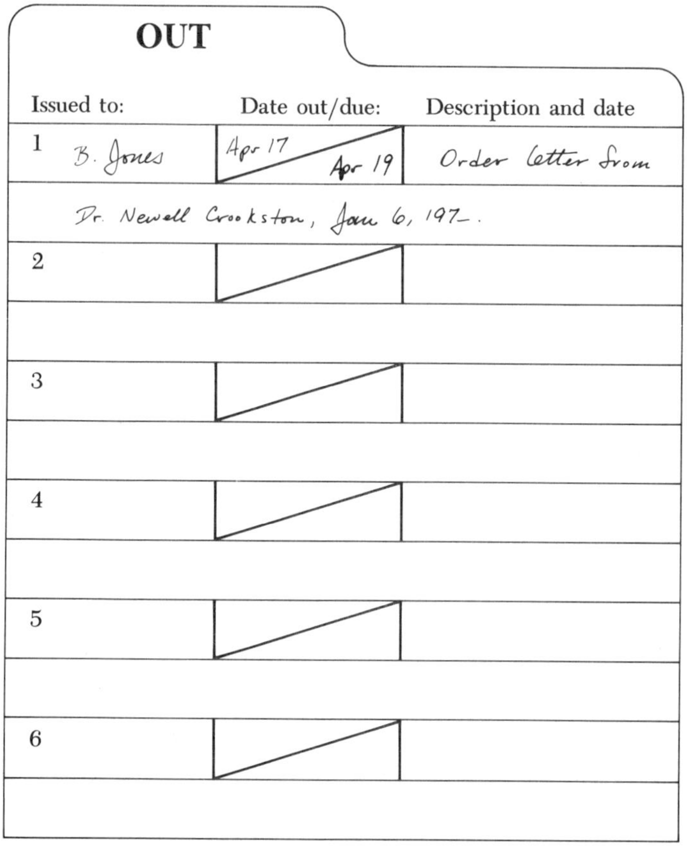

OUT

| Issued to: | Date out/due: | Description and date |
|---|---|---|
| 1 B. Jones | Apr 17 / Apr 19 | Order letter from |
| Dr. Newell Crookston, Jan 6, 197_. | | |
| 2 | | |
| | | |
| 3 | | |
| | | |
| 4 | | |
| | | |
| 5 | | |
| | | |
| 6 | | |
| | | |

*Figure 22-9.* Sample of an Out-Card

records clerk. But instead of making a copy of the letter, the clerk would complete an out-card (shown in Figure 22-9) and give the original copy of the letter to the manager.

## FILING EQUIPMENT

Numerous items of equipment are available for records storage. Storage containers range from special cardboard boxes used in inactive record retention to heavy-duty files designed to protect records against theft or natural disaster. The type of equipment used depends on such factors as records management philosophy, uses of the records being stored, and frequency of record use. We will comment here on four types of filing equipment: vertical files, lateral files, desk-top files, and automated files.

The most common type of filing cabinet is the *vertical file*. This file usually has from two to six drawers stacked on top of each other, but vertical files used in records centers (inactive record storage areas) frequently are stacked clear to the ceiling (see Figure 22-10). Vertical files occupy approximately 2.5 square feet of floor space when the file drawers are closed. In an open position, a vertical file occupies approximately 5 square feet of floor space, and another square foot must be allowed in front of the open drawer for the worker to stand. Since vertical files do not use additional floor space as more file drawers are added, offices should consider using files with at least five drawers.

*Lateral files* are built much the same as vertical files except that with lateral files the drawers pull out from the long side of the file (see Figure 22-11). Although both files require the same number of square feet, the

*Figure 22-10.* Vertical Files in a Typical Records Center

*Source:* STAXONSTEEL Transfer Files. Photo courtesy of Bankers Box/Records Storage System.

drawers of a lateral file require only one linear foot to be fully extended; vertical file drawers require about two and one half linear feet to be fully extended. The unique side-mount characteristic makes the lateral file a wise choice in certain office locations.

A very popular adaptation of the lateral file is called *open-shelf filing*, illustrated in Figure 22-12. Open-shelf filing uses no drawers; the individual folders are placed on their edges with the folder tabs protruding from the side instead of the top, as is the case with vertical and lateral drawer files. Because all folders are exposed, file retrieval is faster with an open-shelf system than with a drawer system. In addition, open-shelf files make better use of vertical space than drawer files do. To find a folder in a drawer file, for example, the file clerk must look *down* into the drawer. Consequently, six-drawer files usually require a step stool when material is retrieved from the top drawers. In an open-shelf file, individual folders can be located and retrieved without the aid of a step stool even when they are two feet above the eye level of the file clerk. Hence, a six-level open-shelf file is usually more feasible than a six-drawer vertical file.

*Action files*, files that contain high-use documents, are found in a variety of circular or rectangular drawer styles (see Figure 22-13). These types of files

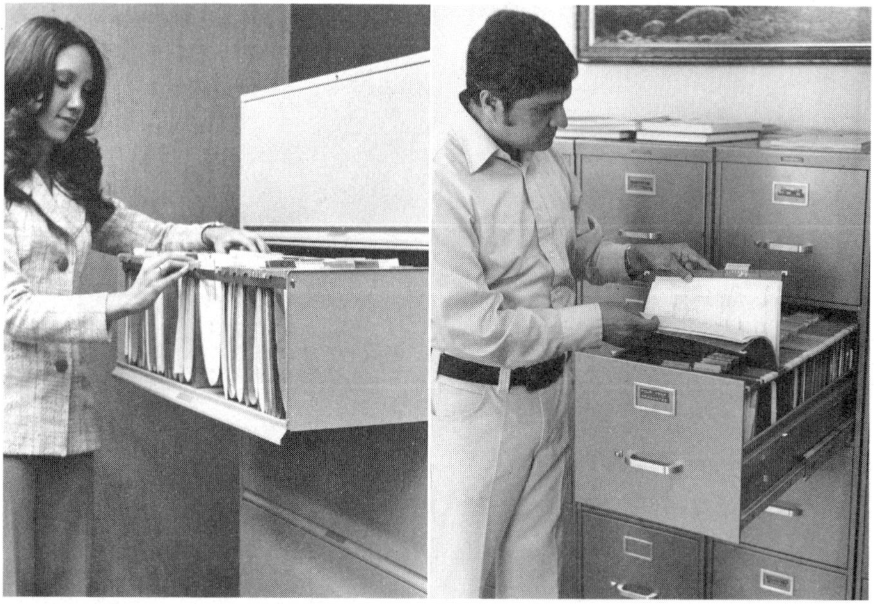

*Figure 22-11.* A Four-Drawer Lateral File and a Four-Drawer Vertical File

*Figure 22-12.* Open-Shelf Filing

*Source:* Advertising Associates, Inc., Minneapolis, Minn.

are built for rapid retrieval and are usually located about thirty inches from the floor so file clerks can sit comfortably to do all the file searches.

The need to store computer tapes, disks, cards, and other computer-related materials has resulted in the introduction of relatively new types of filing equipment. Because of the diverse nature of the various computer items that must be stored, these files are generally constructed as versatile lateral files. Figure 22-14 shows the construction of a typical computer materials file.

*Desk-top files* are used primarily for storing cards. These files are usually of three varieties: vertical card files, visible card files, and wheel (or rotary) card files. *Vertical card files* resemble a vertical drawer file in that they contain cards standing vertically in an alphabetic or numeric arrangement. *Visible card files* are vertical in the sense that they have many thin drawers arranged in a vertical fashion, but the cards in these files lay flat with a small portion of the card exposed to the file clerk. This type of file is also useful for storing microfiche (microfilm cards). Since the exposed part of each card contains the information that identifies the content of the card, the worker can easily find the card that is desired (see Figure 22-15). A *wheel file*, another type of visible card file, stores cards on a wheel that can be easily turned for scanning the entire array of cards (see Figure 22-15).

*Figure 22-13.* Action Files, Built for Rapid Retrieval

*Automated filing* equipment is basically of two types. The first type has a motor drive that revolves all the file drawers or trays past the file clerk. This system includes a keyboard which the operator uses to stop the machine when the appropriate file tray appears. The second type of automated filing equipment involves a mechanical "arm" which moves both laterally and vertically between two tall stacks of files. To activate the arm the file clerk keys in

*Figure 22-14.* Filing Equipment Used to Store a Variety of Computer Materials

*Source:* Wright Line Inc., Worcester, Mass.

information describing the file tray desired. Upon receiving the message, the arm goes to work to find the right file tray and to take it to the worker. Figure 22-16 illustrates one model of the first type of automated filing equipment mentioned; the Sperry Remington Lektriever 110 manufactured by Sperry Univac Office Equipment Division.

## MISCELLANEOUS FILING AIDS

Folders in which documents are stored are of two basic types. The first type sits on its bottom edge on the floor of the file drawer; the second hangs suspended from folder extensions that protrude from the top ends of the folder (see Figure 22-17). Without sufficient support, the first type will sag and

*Figure 22-15.* Example of a Visible Card File and Wheel Card File

buckle; the suspended type, however, has no such problem since it receives support from the metal frame on which it hangs.

To aid file personnel in finding records quickly, filing guides are used. *Guides* are special tabs that guide the worker's eye to the general section of a file that contains the records being sought. Guides are generally of three types: alphabetic, numeric, and color. In an alphabetic file, guides will generally consist of one to three letters such as A, Ba, or Joh. When a worker sees

*Figure 22-16.* Automated Filing Equipment

*Source:* Sperry Univac, Blue Bell, Pa.

the guide "Joh," he/she will automatically know that all files beginning alphabetically after "Joh" are filed behind the "Joh" guide. Numeric guides have numbers instead of letters and are used in numeric filing systems.

Alphabetic and numeric guides are basically of two types—open and closed. The closed variety indicates the range of files between that particular guide and the next guide, but an open guide indicates only the beginning of a new section. Here are some examples of open and closed guides as they might appear in a file drawer:

| *Open Guides* | *Closed Guides* |
|---|---|
| Ba | Ba–Be |
| Bi | Bi–By |
| C | C–Ce |
| Ch | Ch–Cl |
| Co | Co–Cy |
| Da | Da–Do |

Different colors are also used as guides in many files. Color is usually used in conjunction with alphabetic and numeric guides, and different color combinations are frequently used on individual folders to increase the versatility of the color system. For example, if a numeric file ranges from 1000 to 9999, one color combination could be used for the 1000–1999 section, another for the 2000–2999 section, and so forth. Although color adds expense to a filing system, it greatly increases finding and filing speed. It also aids in file auditing—finding folders that are out of sequence.

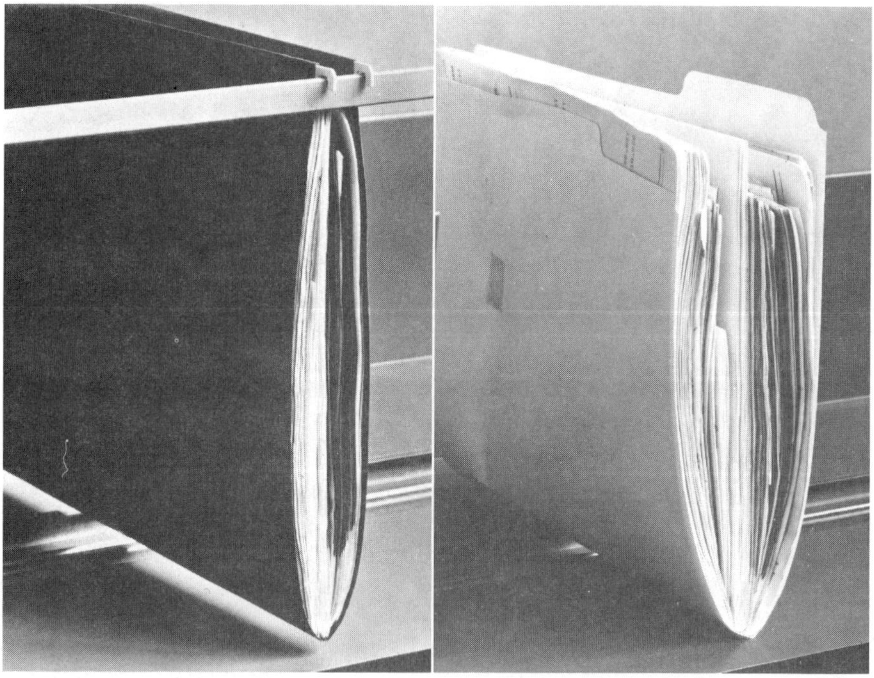

*Figure 22-17.* Two Types of File Folders

*Source:* Oxford Pendaflex Corporation

## CENTRALIZATION VERSUS DECENTRALIZATION OF FILES

Files are usually classified as either centralized or decentralized (also known as departmentalized). Centralized files are usually used in larger organizations that have a large volume of records to be filed and maintained. For example, the division office of a large insurance company might keep all the personal records of the people it insures in a central location in its three-story office building. The advantages of centralized files are as follows:

Elimination of unnecessary duplication of records throughout the organization

Improvement of filing efficiency and effectiveness because better trained personnel are used

Increase in file protection

Decrease in the amount of money spent on filing equipment

Improvement of transfer and disposal of records

Decentralized records are located in individual departments as action files, and the filing work is done by workers who have other responsibilities to perform. For example, records would be located in each of the accounting, marketing, production, administrative services, and personnel departments. The advantages of decentralized filing are that (1) files are close and easily accessible to the department and that (2) confidential materials are kept within the individual departments and are not readily available for others to see.

Some organizations use a *network system* that retains many of the benefits of both extremes. This system involves centralized control with decentralized location. For this system to operate effectively, the administrative manager must make certain that all department filing personnel follow the same procedures and practices, thus maintaining efficiency and effectiveness throughout the organization. An advanced version of the network system involves a central computer that serves as the brain of the system. Files are maintained in decentralized fashion, but the central computer keeps track of the location of all records.

There is no "one right way" to arrange the records of an organization. The wise administrative manager will consider both the needs of the organization and the systems that are available to achieve optimum records management efficiency and effectiveness.

## RECORDS RETENTION

A vital part of any records management program is adequate provision to eliminate useless records from the system. Most records are used only initially and then are seldom referred to later on. In many cases, up to 85 percent of all files are never referred to after they are placed in the file. Most records eventually go into dead files, and the large majority of records that must be retrieved for use are less than two years old.

An organized, systematic approach is required to eliminate deadwood from the files and to ensure that vital information is readily accessible. The tool that is used to perform this function is called the *records retention schedule*. To prepare a retention schedule, several steps are necessary. First, a records inventory must be conducted. A list of all records and their locations is prepared.

Second, decisions must be made as to how long each kind of record should be retained. Some records will be kept permanently if they have legal or historical value. Other records that are not part of these first two categories have varying retention periods such as one year, two years, seven years, or ten years, depending on their administrative value. One good ratio that will help to determine the degree to which files have administrative value is the reference ratio, which is computed by dividing the number of records requested during a given period of time by the total number of records in the file. If a personnel file had 22,500 records in it and 1,823 records were requested during one month, the file would have a reference ratio of 0.081. Whenever the reference ratio falls to 0.05 or less, you should consider destroying some records and transferring others to inactive storage. The decision as to how long specific classes of records should be kept is a complex one and should be made by a team of executives and staff advisers.

Third, these decisions are recorded on the records retention schedule, which is the guideline for retention, transfer, and disposal of records. Figure 22-18 gives suggested retention times for numerous types of records. As a result of applying the records retention schedule in a sampling of organizations, the Association of Records Managers and Administrators (formerly the American Records Management Assoc.) reports that 44 percent of records surveyed remained in the office, 24 percent were disposed of as wastepaper, and 32 percent were transferred to an inactive records center.[2]

When retention schedules are not used, a company continues to add more filing cabinets, thus requiring additional costly space. As the files become more crowded, vital information is increasingly more difficult to find. Obvious cost advantages occur when space and equipment requirements are reduced, and money is saved when information is immediately available to make decisions.

## RECORDS TRANSFER

Records should be transferred to inactive storage according to a well-defined method. One such method is the duplicate file method, which requires two sets of files—one for last year and one for this year. At the end of a prescribed time, all the records in last year's files are transferred to inactive storage. This

# Records Retention Timetable

| LEGEND FOR AUTHORITY TO DISPOSE | LEGEND FOR RETENTION PERIOD |
|---|---|
| AD—Administrative Decision | AC—Dispose After Completion of Job or Contract |
| ASPR—Armed Services Procurement Regulation | AE—Dispose After Expiration |
| CFR—Code of Federal Regulations | AF—After End of Fiscal Year |
| FLSA—Fair Labor Standards Act | AM—After Moving |
| ICC—Interstate Commerce Commission | AS—After Settlement |
| INS—Insurance Company Regulation | AT—Dispose After Termination |
| ISM—Industrial Security Manual, Attachment to DD Form 441 | ATR—After Trip |
| | OBS—Dispose When Obsolete |
| | P—Permanent |
| | SUP—Dispose When Superseded |
| * After Disposed ** Normally | † Govt. R&D Contracts |

| TYPE OF RECORD | RETENTION PERIOD YEARS | AUTHORITY |
|---|---|---|
| **ACCOUNTING & FISCAL** | | |
| Accounts Payable Invoices | 3 | ASPR-STATE, FLSA |
| Accounts Payable Ledger | P | AD |
| Accounts Receivable Ledgers | 5 | AD |
| Authorizations for Accounting | SUP | AD |
| Balance Sheets | P | AD |
| Bank Deposits | 3 | AD |
| Bank Statements | 3 | AD |
| Bonds | P | AD |
| Budgets | 3 | AD |
| Capital Asset Record | 3* | AD |
| Cash Receipt Records | 7 | AD |
| Check Register | P | AD |
| Checks, Dividend | 6 | |
| Checks, Payroll | 2 | FLSA, STATE |
| Checks, Voucher | 3 | FLSA, STATE |
| Cost Accounting Records | 5 | AD |
| Earnings Register | 3 | FLSA, STATE |
| Entertainment Gifts & Gratuities | 3 | AD |
| Estimates, Projections | 7 | AD |
| Expense Reports | 3 | AD |
| Financial Statements, Certified | P | AD |
| Financial Statements, Periodic | 2 | AD |
| General Ledger Records | P | CFR |
| Labor Cost Records | 3 | ASPR, CFR |
| Magnetic Tape and Tab Cards | 1** | |
| Note Register | P | AD |
| Payroll Registers | 3 | FLSA, STATE |
| Petty Cash Records | 3 | AD |
| P & L Statements | P | AD |
| Salesman Commission Reports | 3 | AD |
| Travel Expense Reports | 3 | AD |
| Work Papers, Rough | 2 | AD |
| **ADMINISTRATIVE RECORDS** | | |
| Audit Reports | 10 | AD |
| Audit Work Papers | 3 | AD |
| Classified Documents: Inventories, Reports, Receipts | 10 | AD |
| Correspondence, Executive | P | AD |
| Correspondence, General | 5 | AD |
| Directives from Officers | P | AD |
| Forms Used, File Copies | P | AD |
| Systems and Procedures Records | P | AD |
| Work Papers, Management Projects | P | AD |

*Figure 22-18.* Records Retention Schedule

*Source:* With the permission of Electric Wastebasket Corp., N.Y., N.Y. 10036.

| TYPE OF RECORD | RETENTION PERIOD YEARS | AUTHORITY |
|---|---|---|
| **COMMUNICATIONS** | | |
| Bulletins Explaining Communications | P | AD |
| Messenger Records | 1 | AD |
| Phone Directories | SUP | AD |
| Phone Installation Records | 1 | AD |
| Postage Reports, Stamp Requisitions | 1 AF | AD |
| Postal Records, Registered Mail & Insured Mail Logs & Meter Records | 1 AF | AD, CFR |
| Telecommunications Copies | 1 | AD |
| **CONTRACT ADMINISTRATION** | | |
| Contracts, Negotiated. Bailments, Changes, Specifications, Procedures, Correspondence | P | CFR |
| Customer Reports | P | AD |
| Materials Relating to Distribution Revisions, Forms, and Format of Reports | P | AD |
| Work Papers | OBS | AD |
| **CORPORATE** | | |
| Annual Reports | P | AD |
| Authority to Issue Securities | P | AD |
| Bonds, Surety | 3 AE | AD |
| Capital Stock Ledger | P | AD |
| Charters, Constitutions, Bylaws | P | AD |
| Contracts | 20 AT | AD |
| Corporate Election Records | P | AD |
| Incorporation Records | P | AD |
| Licenses - Federal, State, Local | AT | AD |
| Stock Transfer & Stockholder | P | AD |
| **LEGAL** | | |
| Claims and Litigation Concerning Torts and Breach of Contracts | P | AD |
| Law Records - Federal, State, Local | SUP | AD |
| Patents and Related Material | P | AD |
| Trademark & Copyrights | P | AD |
| **LIBRARY, COMPANY** | | |
| Accession Lists | P | AD |
| Copies of Requests for Materials | 6 mos. | AD |
| Meeting Calendars | P | AD |
| Research Papers, Abstracts, Bibliographies | SUP, 6 mos. AC | AD |
| **MANUFACTURING** | | |
| Bills of Material | 2 | AD, ASPR |
| Drafting Records | P | AD† |
| Drawings | 2 | AD, ASPR |
| Inspection Records | 2 | AD |
| Lab Test Reports | P | AD |
| Memos, Production | AC | AD |
| Product, Tooling, Design, Enginneering Research, Experiment & Specs Records | 20 | STATUE LIMITATIONS |
| Production Reports | 3 | AD |
| Quality Reports | 1 AC | AD |
| Reliability Records | P | AD |
| Stock Issuing Records | 3 AT | AD, ASPR |
| Tool Control | 3 AT | AD, ASPR |
| Work Orders | 3 | AD |
| Work Status Reports | AC | AD |

*Figure 22-18 continued.*

| TYPE OF RECORD | RETENTION PERIOD YEARS | AUTHORITY |
|---|---|---|
| **OFFICE SUPPLIES & SERVICES** | | |
| Inventories | 1 AF | AD |
| Office Equipment Records | 6 AF | AD |
| Requests for: Services | 1 AF | AD |
| Requisitions for Supplies | 1 AF | AD |
| **PERSONNEL** | | |
| Accident Reports, Injury Claims, Settlements | 30 AS | CFR, INS, STATE |
| Applications, Changes & Terminations | 5 | AD, ASPR, CFR |
| Attendance Records | 7 | AD |
| Employee Activity Files | 2 or SUP | AD |
| Employee Contracts | 6 AT | AD |
| Fidelity Bonds | 3 AT | AD |
| Garnishments | 5 | AD |
| Health & Safety Bulletins | P | AD |
| Injury Frequency Charts | P | CFR |
| Insurance Records, Employees | 11 AT | INS |
| Job Descriptions | 2 or SUP | CFR |
| Rating Cards | 2 or SUP | CFR |
| Time Cards | 3 | AD |
| Training Manuals | P | AD |
| Union Agreements | 3 | WALSH-HEALEY ACT |
| **PLANT & PROPERTY RECORDS** | | |
| Depreciation Schedules | P | AD |
| Inventory Records | P | AD |
| Maintenance & Repair, Building | 10 | AD |
| Maintenance & Repair, Machinery | 5 | AD |
| Plant Account Cards, Equipment | P | CFR, AD |
| Property Deeds | P | AD |
| Purchase or Lease Records of Plant Facility | P | AD |
| Space Allocation Records | 1 AT | AD |
| **PRINTING & DUPLICATING** | | |
| Copies Produced, Tech. Pubs., Charts | 1 or OBS | AD |
| Film Reports | 5 | AD |
| Negatives | 5 | AD |
| Photographs | 1 | AD |
| Production Records | 1 AC | AD |
| **PROCUREMENT, PURCHASING** | | |
| Acknowledgements | AC | AD |
| Bids, Awards | 3 AT | CFR |
| Contracts | 3 AT | AD |
| Exception Notices (GAO) | 6 | AD |
| Price Lists | OBS | AD |
| Purchase Orders, Requisitions | 3 AT | CFR |
| Quotations | 1 | AD |
| **PRODUCTS, SERVICES, MARKETING** | | |
| Correspondence | 3 | AD |
| Credit Ratings & Classifications | 7 | AD |
| Development Studies | P | AD |
| Presentations & Proposals | P | AD |
| Price Lists, Catalogs | OBS | AD |
| Prospect Lines | OBS | AD |
| Register of Sales Order | NO VALUE | AD |
| Surveys | P | AD |
| Work Papers, Pertaining to Projects | NO VALUE | AD |

*Figure 22-18 continued.*

| TYPE OF RECORD | RETENTION PERIOD YEARS | AUTHORITY |
|---|---|---|
| **PUBLIC RELATIONS & ADVERTISING** | | |
| Advertising Activity Reports | 5 | AD |
| Community Affairs Records | P | AD |
| Contracts for Advertising | 3 AT | AD |
| Employee Activities & Presentations | P | AD |
| Exhibits, Releases, Handouts | 2 - 4 | AD |
| Internal Publications | P (1 copy) | AD |
| Layouts | 1 | AD |
| Manuscripts | 1 | AD |
| Photos | 1 | AD |
| Public Information Activity | 7 | AD |
| Research Presentations | P | AD |
| Tear-Sheets | 2 | AD |
| **SECURITY** | | |
| Classified Material Violations | P | AD |
| Courier Authorizations | 1 mo. ATR | AD |
| Employee Clearance Lists | SUP | ISM |
| Employee Case Files | 5 | ISM |
| Fire Prevention Program | P | AD |
| Protection - Guards, Badge Lists, Protective Devices | 5 | AD |
| Subcontractor Clearances | 2 AT | AD |
| Visitor Clearance | 2 | ISM |
| **TAXATION** | | |
| Annuity or Deferred Payment Plan | P | CFR |
| Depreciation Schedules | P | CFR |
| Dividend Register | P | CFR |
| Employee Withholding | 4 | CFR |
| Excise Exemption Certificates | 4 | CFR |
| Excise Reports (Manufacturing) | 4 | CFR |
| Excise Reports (Retail) | 4 | CFR |
| Inventory Reports | P | CFR |
| Tax Bills and Statements | P | AD |
| Tax Returns | P | AD |
| **TRAFFIC & TRANSPORTATION** | | |
| Aircraft Operating & Maintenance | P | CFR |
| Bills of Lading, Waybills | 2 | ICC, FLSA |
| Employee Travel | 1 AF | AD |
| Freight Bills | 3 | ICC |
| Freight Claims | 2 | ICC |
| Household Moves | 3 AM | AD |
| Motor Operating & Maintenance | 2 | AD |
| Rates and Tariffs | SUP | AD |
| Receiving Documents | 2 - 10 | AD, CFR |
| Shipping & Related Documents | 2 - 10 | AD, CFR |

*Figure 22-18 continued.*

transfer method is easy to understand and to carry out, but it involves additional equipment costs.

Using this system, a publishing firm would store all its 1977 records in one set of files; then it would store all its 1978 records in another set of files. By July 1, 1978, the company might determine that the reference ratio of the 1977 file was low enough to warrant its transfer, and the 1977 files would all be transferred to inactive storage.

Another transfer method is the periodic transfer method. This method involves a periodic examination of all records in active storage to determine which records should be transferred. This method decreases equipment cost, but it involves much more time than the duplicate file method. When examining records for potential transfer, the examiner has five choices of action that can be taken: (1) destroy the record immediately, (2) retain the record in the active file permanently, (3) transfer the record to inactive files for permanent storage, (4) transfer the record to inactive files for later destruction, or (5) leave the record in active storage for later transfer to inactive storage.

Using the periodic transfer method, a company might decide that during the month of July all records from the previous year should be transferred. Consequently, records clerks would sort through all the active records and remove for transfer all records from the previous year.

## RECORDS CENTERS

Records that are to be transferred from active storage, but which cannot yet be destroyed, should be moved to a records center—usually located in low-cost areas such as basements of office buildings or warehouses located away from the high rental areas of the city. Pacific Mutual Insurance Co. is one such organization that stores its inactive records in the basement of its multistory building. The containers in which inactive records are stored are constructed of very inexpensive materials, and they are stacked to the ceiling to reduce costs even more. A properly located records center can store records at a small fraction of the cost required in active storage areas of the office.

In small offices, the office manager may not have a specially designated records center for storing inactive files. Transferring inactive records from the high-use, high-cost area of the office can be accomplished by placing files in low-cost file containers located in low-traffic areas of the office. The company can also contract with a storage company to store the records or it can rent do-it-yourself storage areas and use them as a records center. Another alternative is to place inactive records in the least convenient drawers of the active file. For example, the top and bottom drawers of a five-drawer file are ideal places for storing inactive records.

Although records in inactive storage are infrequently needed, an efficient numeric or alphabetic storage system should be used to make retrieval of any record as rapid as possible. Such a system is consistent with the major theme of records management—focus on finding, not on filing. Efficient cataloging also makes possible a continuation of efficient records disposal. As records in the records center are kept the length of time specified on the retention schedule, they should be destroyed to keep records space availability at a maximum.

## MICROGRAPHICS

More and more organizations are using microfilming as a major part of their active and inactive records management systems. Microfilming involves the production of special film on which records are reproduced photographically in greatly reduced size. For protection of vital records, two copies of the film are frequently made; one is kept for use within the company and the other is stored in another location as a security copy.

Microfilm is available in several different forms called *microforms*. The most common microforms are roll film, microfiche, and microfilm jackets.

*Roll film* is stored on an open reel or in a cartridge or cassette, as shown in Figure 22-19. Roll film is useful for storing items that are readily stored in some form of sequence. With a standard reduction ratio of 24 : 1, approximately 3,000 microimages of full pages of information can be stored on a single roll of microfilm.

*Figure 22-19.* Roll Film and Microfiche

*Source:* 3M Company, Microfilm Products Division, Saint Paul, Minn.

*Microfiche* is a 4 × 6-inch film card containing microimages in rows and columns (see Figure 22-19). Depending on the reduction ratio, from just a few to several hundred documents can be filmed on a single microfiche. Imagine, this entire book could be filmed on two or three microfiche and be carried in your pocket or purse.

*Microfilm jackets* are made of two plastic sheets that are fused together at regular intervals to form channels into which strips of film are inserted. Microfilm jackets are most useful when related images need to be located together and when periodic updating of the information is necessary.

With recent technology, regular microfiche is now capable of being updated; consequently, microfilm jackets have lost one of the unique advantages over other microforms.

*Computer output microfilm* (COM) is another technological advance in microfilming. With special microfilming equipment, computers are now capable of producing output directly onto microfiche and roll film.

COM eliminates paper cost and saves up to 80 percent of computer output time in addition to offering the space and retrieval time savings of microfilm.

Microfilm is stored in specially designed microfilm files that are compact and easily accessible. Special indexing is used to identify each unit of film and each record on that film. When someone in the organization requests information from the microfilm center, an operator locates the appropriate film unit, places it in a microfilm reader, and quickly finds the individual record needed. Automated roll film readers can find a record in only seconds. In fact, efficient microfilm centers should be able to locate any of their microfilmed records in less than a minute from the time the record is requested. A microfilm retrieval unit is illustrated in Figure 22-20.

In many large businesses, the computer is used as an index for all the microfilmed records. When this arrangement is used, the operator communicates with the computer via a computer terminal located beside the microfilm reader. For example, the operator may request the microfilm code number for the Xerox Corp. The computer searches its memory, locates the Xerox Corp. microfilm number, and displays the number on the operator's terminal—all within a fraction of a second. The operator then uses the number to locate the appropriate file on the microfilm retrieval unit. Microfilm *reader-printers* are capable of producing a *hard copy* (paper reprint) in just a few seconds if the person requesting the information needs an actual copy. Or the operator can easily make a microfilm copy for the requester to read on his or her microfilm reader.

Microfilm must be stored under special atmospheric conditions, although these conditions are not highly restrictive. Under these conditions, microfilm can last as long as regular paper records. The major advantages of microfilm are as follows:

Space savings; up to 98 percent savings over regular paper files.

Retrieval efficiency; records are so small that they can be filed in close proximity to file clerks and are much more accessible.

Improved file integrity; in roll film and microfiche, images cannot be accidentally rearranged once they are photographed; hence, they cannot get out of sequence.

At present, the larger organizations in the U.S. use microfilm systems to the greatest extent, but smaller organizations are becoming a greater part of the market as microfilm service bureaus become more widely available.

Beneficial Standard Life Insurance Co. reported that by implementing a microfilm system they virtually eliminated the thousands of dollars expended each year on file clerks looking for files that had been misplaced or lost. Beneficial also reduced the floor space used by file cabinets from 15,000 to 6,000 square feet while increasing their storage capacity at the same time. They also

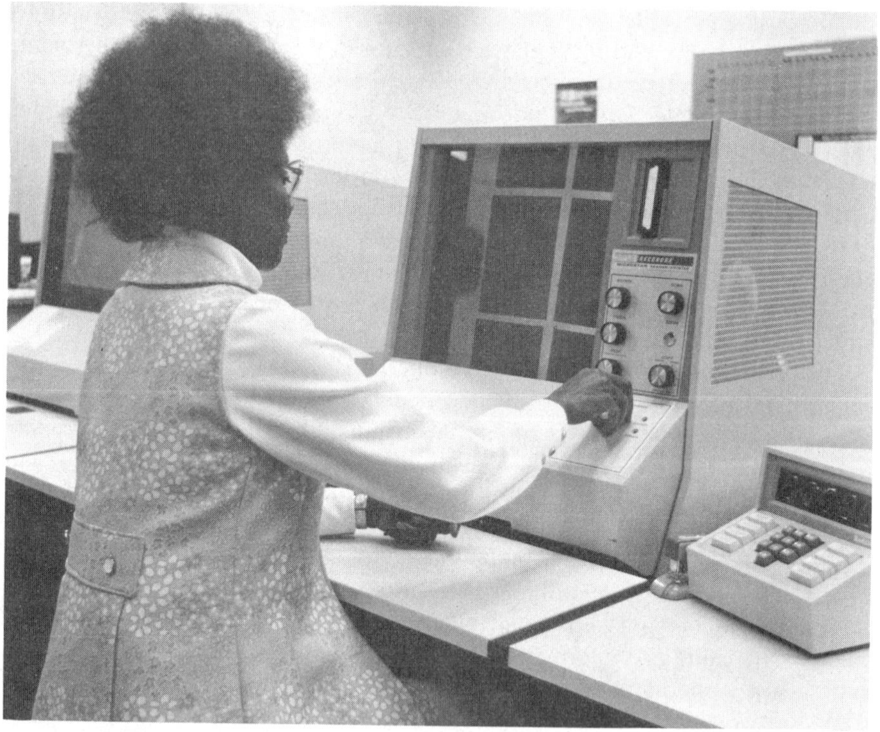

*Figure 22-20.* A Microfilm Retrieval Unit (Reader-Printer)

reduced over 50 percent of their filing staff and eliminated their lost-file problems.[3] Many other companies have reported similar positive results from their adoption of microfilm systems.

## ELECTRONIC RECORDS SYSTEMS

In recent years, more and more files, especially action files, have been computerized. Placed into computers by standard input methods, information can be instantly retrieved via cathode-ray tubes and other types of computer terminals. This wedding of records management and computer technology forms an important part of modern management information systems (MIS's) and makes available to management more timely information for decision-making purposes than has ever been available in the past. Computerized records systems will continue to gain in importance as a records management tool. (Chapter 25 explains the technological aspects of computerized information retrieval.)

## *Summary*

The basic purpose of records is to provide decision-making information. Thus, the focus of records management is on providing information to the right people at the right time. Computers, reprographics services, government regulations, business demands, and ineffective managers tend to perpetuate the paper explosion that has occurred during this century.

Records management deals with records from creation through storage, maintenance, retention, and disposal or permanent retention. Major factors to be considered in records management include file integrity, retrieval speed, and cost.

Forms design and control methods are helpful in improving records management in an organization. Forms control combats excessive development of unnecessary forms. Forms design focuses on proper creation of forms that must be used; properly designed forms result in reduced paper, reduced work, and improved office efficiency. Like forms control programs, reports control efforts also reduce the amount of paper storage requirements.

The most common filing system is alphabetic, although the numeric system is used frequently. Common check-out systems that help maintain file integrity are the duplicate-copy method and the out-card method.

Filing equipment is found in all shapes and sizes to fit every records management need. Vertical files, lateral files, desk-top files, and automated files are major categories of filing equipment. Most files in the past have been vertical, but lateral files are gaining in importance. File folders (standard and suspended) and file guides (alphabetic, numeric, and color) are important filing aids.

Records management is carried out on a centralized or decentralized basis. Centralization results in more control and improved filing methods, while decentralization keeps records in the departments where they are most likely to be used.

Retention schedules are developed to identify appropriate retention, transfer, and disposal of all records. Effective retention schedules will result in both reduced file expansion and improved records retrieval. Records that are transferred from active storage go to record centers—low-cost storage areas that significantly reduce records retention costs.

Microfilm storage of records is being used in increasing numbers of offices. Initially, microfilming can be expensive, but it brings substantial space savings because of its reduced size. Different microform types are roll film, microfiche, and microfilm jackets. Microfilm is created both from photographing actual records and from computer output microfilm (COM), a high-speed process that records computer output directly on to microfilm.

More and more records are being stored in computers, thus making large quantities of valuable information instantly available to managers for decision making.

## *Review and Discussion Questions*

1. Why is the major purpose of records management not that of protecting records?
2. How has government influence increased paperwork in organizations?
3. Why are forms used? Why is forms control necessary?
4. Why is a records retention schedule important?
5. Why is microfilming becoming increasingly popular today?
6. Where does a records center fit in the life cycle of a record?
7. What is *file integrity*? What factors affect file integrity?
8. Why are open-shelf files becoming more popular?
9. What part does color play in filing?
10. What are the advantages of COM? How does COM differ from regular microfilm?

## *Application Exercises*

1. Visit several organizations in your area and observe their records equipment and systems. Ask them about their intentions to use microfilm in the future. Ask them about any special problems they have with their records systems and methods.

2. Obtain a form from your employer, your school, or from some other source. Evaluate the form, make suggestions for its improvement, and design a new form based on your suggestions.
3. Visit a library or a business that uses microfiche storage. Examine the microfiche and look at a sample of it in one of the microfiche readers. Count the number of pages of information stored on several of the microfiche, and determine the average number of pages per card. Then determine how many microfiche cards can be stored in one inch of drawer space. Assume that a vertical file drawer holds 5,000 paper documents, and determine how much space is saved by microfilming a file drawer full of records.
4. Visit the records center of a larger business in your area. Observe the active and inactive record areas of the company. Write a report on the filing equipment found in both areas and describe the location and layout of both areas.

## *Mini-Case*

*Aztek, Inc.* Nancy Dimick was called by Aztek, a small manufacturing firm, to act as a records management consultant. To determine the effectiveness of Aztek's records system, Nancy observed the file workers, examined the filing and retrieval methods, and computed an accuracy ratio and a reference ratio. She also talked with several of the executives to determine the degree of their satisfaction with Aztek's records system.

As a result of Nancy's initial study, she found the following information:

a. The file workers did not consistently follow an established set of filing rules.
b. Both alphabetic and numeric systems were used. The alphabetic system was used primarily for correspondence and the numeric for forms storage.
c. An out-card system was used to keep track of records that were checked out, but an average of 2 percent of records checked out did not come back in on schedule. Approximately 25 percent of these late records were never returned.
d. The accuracy ratio Nancy computed was 92.8.
e. The reference ratio was 3.6.
f. Aztek had been in business for only 10 years, and they had no records center. All their records were in the same location, and new file cabinets were being purchased each year to accommodate the increasing volume of records. Nearly all records were stored in 2- and 4-drawer vertical cabinets.

g. Executives of the firm were generally dissatisfied with the records management program of the firm; 13 out of 14 felt that significant improvement was needed.

If you were Nancy, what would you suggest to the management of Aztek, Inc.?

## *Reference Notes*


1. *The Generalist,* Administrative Management Society, Willow Grove, Pa., January 1977, Vol. 1, No. 5.
2. *Records Management Workshop,* Association of Records Managers and Administrators, Inc., ARMA Publication No. 2, 1962, p. 3.
3. William V. Olsen, "Converting Paper Files to Microfilm," *The Office,* October 1975, pp. 86–88.

# 23

# Communications Services

Communication is the very heart of all management practices. In most cases, businesses that have effective communication systems are successful. And since the administrative manager usually has very direct control over much of an organization's communication network, you should acquire a good working knowledge of both oral and written systems and equipment that comprise the communication services function.

## ORAL COMMUNICATION MEDIA

Telephone systems have become such an important part of today's business world that most business organizations would collapse if their telephones were taken away. Telephone systems exhibit a great degree of sophistication today, and they can be tailored to fit the unique needs of almost any organization. Several of the more popular telephone systems are discussed in this chapter.

### Switchboards (PBX and PABX)

Historically, the most common telephone system in business use is a central switchboard controlled by a company operator. This system, the *private branch exchange* (PBX), consists of a rather large unit with jacks and cords that are plugged in and removed to connect and disconnect callers. Manual systems are still used in some businesses today, but smaller, more streamlined and more efficient units are replacing the large PBX switchboard. Many of the newer units are highly automated and are called *private automatic branch exchanges* (PABX). These units are characterized by desk-top units that use a dial or push button for switching (see Figure 23-1).

PBX and PABX units are centralized telephone systems for handling a company's incoming calls. All the calls coming to the organization from the

*Figure 23-1.* A Desk-Top, Private Automatic Branch Exchange (PABX)

outside must go through the central switchboard. Calls going to the outside from within the organization, however, can be made by dialing a certain digit (usually a "9") and then the regular number; this feature is called *direct outward dialing* (DOD). Calls can be made from one person to another within the organization by dialing the special extension number of the other person.

PBX and PABX systems also feature station hunting, which means that an incoming call will automatically be switched to an open line if one of the organization's other lines is busy. To illustrate, assume that an organization has four telephone lines (trunks) that connect it to outside callers and that these four lines are identified as 2435, 2436, 2437, and 2438. If lines 2435 and 2436 are busy when an incoming call comes to them, the call will automatically be switched to 2437.

More sophisticated PABX systems offer the following additional features:

*Attendant camp-on.* If you are talking on your telephone when another call is made to you, the company operator can press a button which puts the second caller on "hold" (waiting). Then when you finish your call, your telephone automatically rings without operator assistance.

*Indication of camp-on.* When an incoming call is "camped on" your busy line, you hear a tone signal that lets you know another call is waiting.

*Call transfer—individual.* Incoming calls can be transferred by any one in the organization to any other extension without assistance from the operator.

*Attendant controlled conference.* The operator can arrange a conference call for simultaneous communication among several persons from different extensions.

Several other options that help meet an organization's particular needs can be provided by local telephone companies.

**Centrex**

Centrex is a more expensive telephone system than PABX and is generally used only in very large organizations. It offers all the features of the best PABX system plus a decentralized approach for handling incoming calls. When outside callers want to contact you, they do so by dialing a regular seven-digit number that connects them directly to your extension without having to go through a central switchboard. This feature is called *direct inward dialing* (DID). The DID feature saves time in calling, because no switchboard assistance is needed for most calls. This system can automatically record all long-distance calls made by each extension, thus enabling better cost control measures by the organization. Intracompany calls are made the same with Centrex as with PABX systems.

An additional feature that is available on more advanced Centrex systems is *call forwarding.* If you are going to another office and want your incoming calls to be automatically transferred there, you dial a special code plus the telephone number of your destination. This action will automatically transfer all your incoming calls to that number. For example, assume that you are going to attend a meeting with Michael Sommer, of the Data Processing Department. Assuming that his extension is 2293, you would dial 106 (the special code) and then 2293. When you return to your work station you would cancel the call forwarding by dialing 107 (the second special code).

**Special Adaptations**

Other telephone system adaptations are available for more effective telephone communication. Two of the more widely used adaptations are *tie lines* and *WATS.* Tie lines are useful when an organization has a large number of long-distance calls to one or more other organizations. For a set fee, the telephone company will lease an organization one or more telephone lines for making such repetitive calls to each area. For instance, the home office of Kemper Insurance in Long Grove, Illinois, has such an arrangement with its branch office in downtown Chicago. This system results in less work for the telephone company and in lower cost for the individual firm.

WATS (Wide Area Telecommunications Service) is a special adaptation of the tie-line arrangement. When you subscribe to a WATS line, the telephone company divides the country into six geographical areas or bands extending outward from your state (see Figure 23-2). You can then purchase WATS capabilities to include any of these six bands. If you want to have, for example, band 5 included in your calling area, however, you must also purchase bands 1, 2, 3, and 4.

With a WATS system, you specify whether you want inward WATS, outward WATS, or both inward and outward WATS. Inward WATS enables anyone within your purchased bands to call you toll free, while outward WATS enables you to call anyone within your purchased bands without extra charges. Another alternative is that you may purchase either full-time or measured-time WATS. The full-time arrangement is more expensive, but it gives you 240 hours of long-distance calling time per month. With measured-time WATS, you may use up to ten hours of long-distance calling time for a base

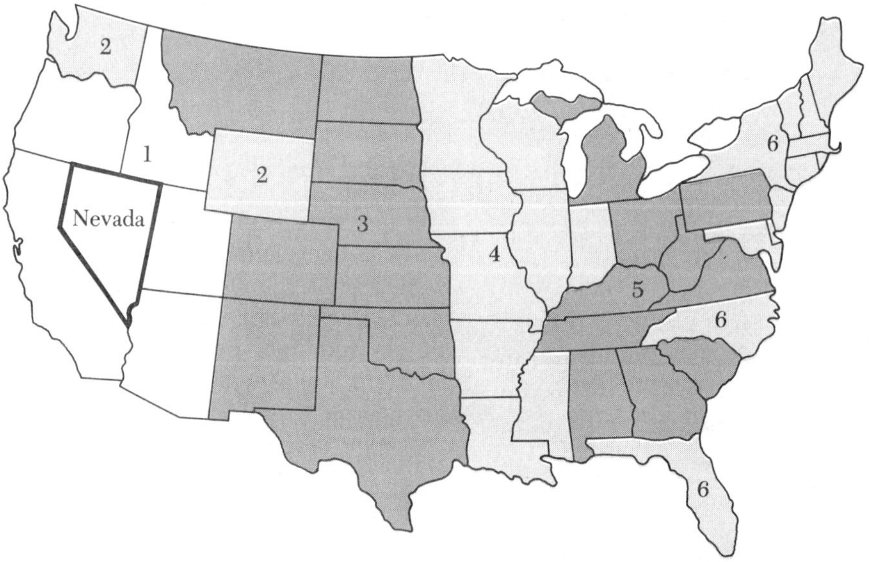


*Figure 23-2.* A WATS Map Indicating the Six Bands Expanding Outward from Nevada

fee. For additional long-distance calls over the ten-hour allotment, you receive extra charges. The difference in cost between measured-time and full-time WATS is usually well over $1,000 a month.

### Supplemental Telephone Equipment

Several items can be obtained to supplement basic telephone equipment. A speakerphone system involves a regular desk telephone along with microphone and loudspeaker units that also sit on the desk (see Figure 23-3). The speakerphone units enable a person to talk and listen on the telephone line without lifting the handset of the telephone although the telephone can function as a regular desk telephone when desired.

Automatic dialing equipment uses a punched card, a magnetic medium, or the central computer of the telephone company to "remember" a limited number of frequently called telephone numbers. When one of these numbers

*Figure 23-3.* A Speakerphone: Microphone and Speaker

must be called, the caller dials an abbreviated number or inserts the appropriate card and the telephone number is dialed automatically.

Many telephone attendants in larger organizations have an intercom paging system which provides greater ability to contact individuals when they are away from their regular work stations. Paging systems usually use a public loudspeaker or a pocket-size unit that receives signals sent by the attendant. These systems may be either one-way or two-way—the two-way system enables the receiver to talk through the intercom and the one-way requires the receiver to contact the attendant by telephone to receive the message.

### Selection of Telephone Systems and Equipment

Before making any changes in your present system, you should conduct a thorough telephone *traffic study* of your organization. Typically, the local telephone company will be happy to provide this service, or you may wish to conduct the study yourself or to have an outside consultant conduct it for you. In this study, you might determine the destination and average number of both local and long-distance calls made each day during a one-month period. You might also discover the time of day during which most telephone calls are made. Then you could determine data transmission needs and telephone dictation needs. Analysis of this information will determine whether your organization needs a basic PBX system or a more elaborate system encompassing such features as inward and outward WATS, tie lines, or Centrex.

By law, the telephone company is required to publish a *tariff* that is open for public inspection. The tariff contains information about the equipment, services, and costs of the local telephone company. By studying your local tariff, you can learn of the different types of systems and services that are available to your organization, and you can do a cost analysis to determine installation, rental, and modification charges that accompany these systems and services.

In addition to the services that are offered by local telephone companies, other companies manufacture telephone equipment that can interconnect with company equipment. Examples of this *interconnect* equipment are automatic dialers, automatic answering equipment, telephone analysis equipment, and actual telephones. Recent legislation has granted much greater freedom to telecommunications businesses, and consumers should analyze the equipment and service offered by these organizations.

The decision-making process described in Chapter 18 should be followed in making telephone and communication equipment decisions. Following the decision and the implementation of the decision, periodic evaluations should be made of your communication system. Attention should be focused on the equipment, on the usage of that equipment, and on changing telecommunication needs of the organization. By conducting periodic evaluations and by keeping current on new developments in telephone technology, you can continue to upgrade the efficiency and effectiveness of your telephone systems.

### Efficient Use of Telephone Equipment

Generally, high telephone cost is accompanied by the following factors: private lines and other extra features and privileges, operator-assisted calls, lengthy telephone calls, daytime calling, and long-distance calls. Therefore, to achieve more efficiency in the use of your telephone equipment, you should focus on these guidelines:

1. Subscribe only to those extra features that are essential to the effectiveness of your company. Eliminate the use of special privileges and equipment that do not result in a proportionate savings or revenue to the organization. For example, you may find that an inward WATS line is not producing sufficient new business to justify retaining that service.
2. Use *direct distance dialing* (DDD) whenever possible. Avoid using the telephone company's operator service unless it is absolutely essential.
3. Encourage employees to keep their telephone calls short. This practice saves on long-distance telephone expense and increases time that can be spent on other activities. The telephone company or other vendors install equipment that will keep an accurate record of the length of all calls made from individual extensions. With this information you can implement a *charge-back* system, wherein individual departments are charged for all long-distance calls they make. A charge-back arrangement encourages department managers to place more controls on their subordinates' calling activities.
4. Use telephone lines during nonbusiness hours whenever feasible. Nighttime and weekend long-distance calls are much less expensive than those made during weekdays from 8 A.M. to 5 P.M. For example, nonvoice transmissions (data and facsimile transmissions from one machine to another via telephone systems) should be sent during nonbusiness hours whenever possible.
5. Evaluate the cost and effectiveness of long-distance calling and business letters. The present cost of an average business letter is over $4, but the use of proper dictation and typing equipment can decrease this figure. Use long-distance calling when time is critical, when the cost of a letter or a personal visit would be more expensive, or when the outcome is very important and the call would be most effective. Many business people dislike writing letters, so they make long-distance calls without considering the cost of calling. Implement a cor-

respondence training program to give employees and managers more self-confidence in letter writing and to acquaint them with efficient dictating methods.

### Telephone Company Service

The telephone company is willing to provide training seminars to teach effective telephone usage. In addition, they publish booklets and provide films that can be used to increase telephone efficiency. These aids will assist you in your efforts to make employees cost conscious and efficiency oriented. Call your local telephone company for materials and services that are available in your area.

Maintenance of equipment is another major function of the telephone company. If you have a problem with any of the telephone equipment that you lease from the telephone company, a single call will usually bring prompt service from a telephone company service representative. If your equipment is leased or purchased from another equipment manufacturer, however, you will need to have a service arrangement with that vendor.

Finally, as was mentioned earlier in the chapter, the telephone company provides consulting services to aid companies in analyzing their telephone traffic. Of course, the telephone company has an ulterior motive in providing this service, but the telephone representatives are well versed in telephone usage analysis and in communication systems problem solving.

## REPROGRAPHICS

Reprographics management results in the effective and efficient utilization of all reproducing, duplicating, and copying processes used in an organization. Today's organizations depend on paper for a large part of their communication and record keeping; therefore, reprographic processes play a major role in the paper flow of any organization. Some people predict a paperless office in the future; but since the office of today relies so heavily on paper, you need a basic understanding of reprographics processes and management.

### Copiers

Copying machines make duplicate copies direct from an original document such as a letter or a report. No special skill is required to operate a copier, and the process is very quick when just a few copies are needed. Xerox, IBM, Savin, and A. B. Dick copiers have been among the leaders in the copier field, and they have been joined in the marketplace by numerous other firms that are competing with their own models. Figure 23-4 shows a modern copier in operation.

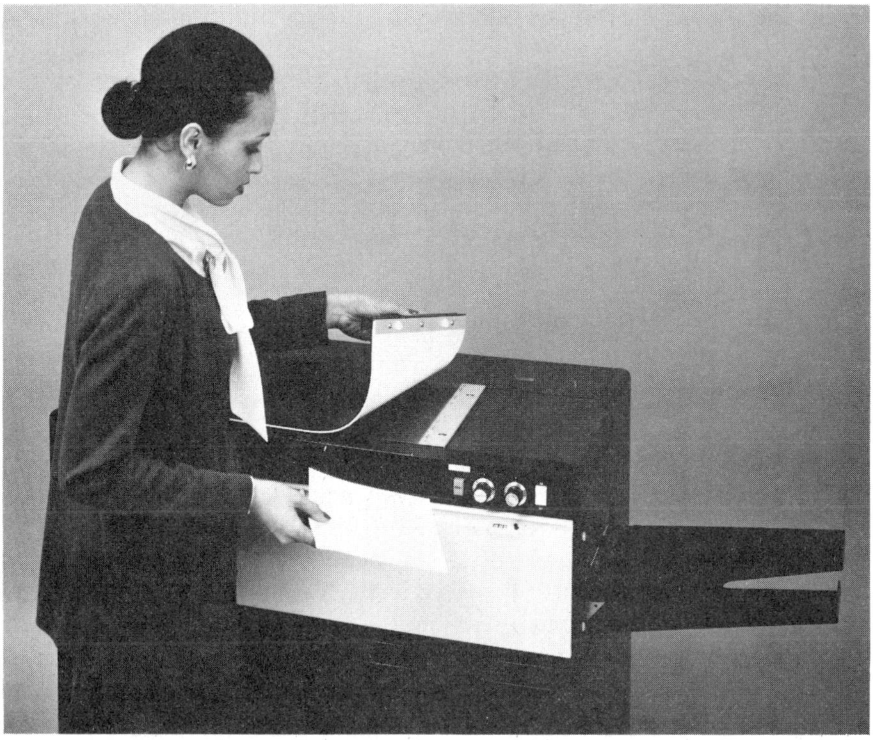

*Figure 23-4.* Modern-Day Copiers Have a Major Impact on Office Reprographics

*Source:* Courtesy of A. B. Dick Company

When copiers first appeared on a large scale in business, very few controls were placed on their usage. Consequently, too many workers in an organization had unlimited access to the copiers, and copying costs rose to unacceptable levels. Some workers would make copies of personal materials without reimbursing the organization, some would make more copies than they actually needed, and some would make copies "just in case" they ever needed them. In an organization requiring an average of 5,000 copies per day, a 20 percent "unnecessary copy" ratio would cost the company over $7,500 each year.

Since those early days of copiers, management has attempted to place more restrictive measures on copiers, but the methods of controlling copy costs differ. One method is to use a centralized location approach. With this system, the copy machine is located in a secretarial pool or in a reprographics center, and all materials are copied by the center personnel. Other methods require the user to insert a special department key or card before the machine will work. With these methods, the attempt is to decrease copy cost and to charge the copying costs to the individuals or departments that are using the copiers. When individuals realize that a charge-back system is in operation, they are more likely to exercise moderation in copier usage. Frequent reminders from managers to their subordinates are also important for copier control.

Some copiers now have the ability to copy in color, to copy both sides of a page, to reduce or enlarge the size of the copy, and to make copies that rival the original document in print quality.

### Duplicating Machines

Three different duplicating processes are common to business: the spirit process, the stencil process, and the offset process.

***Spirit Duplicators.*** The spirit duplication process, also called the liquid, fluid, and ditto process, has been used in business for many years because the spirit duplicator is inexpensive and easy to operate. In addition, spirit masters can simultaneously reproduce in purple, red, green, black, and blue, with purple the most common color. This process produces rather poor quality copies, but the quality is adequate for many intracompany communications.

Spirit duplicators have recently become much less popular because of the ease of operation, easy access, and quality offered by copying machines. Spirit duplicators are manufactured by such companies as A. B. Dick, Ditto, Heyer, Standard Duplicating Machines Corp., Bohn Rex-Rotary, and Copy-Rite Corp. The spirit process is most appropriate under the following conditions:

Copy quality is not important.

Quality paper is not important.

More than 10 but fewer than 300 copies are needed.

Color is wanted without incurring much difficulty.

A spirit duplicator is illustrated in Figure 23-5.

***Stencil Duplicators.*** The stencil or mimeograph process has also been used in business for many years. Its use has been declining recently, however, because of competition from the offset process. Like the spirit duplicator, the stencil machine is inexpensive and easy to operate; but the ink used in the process can be somewhat messy if used carelessly. The reprographic quality of the stencil process is distinctly better than that produced by the spirit process, but it is inferior to that produced by the offset process. Gestetner, A. B. Dick, Heyer, and Speed-O-Print Business Machines Corp. are major manufacturers of stencil duplicators. *The stencil process is most appropriate when copy*

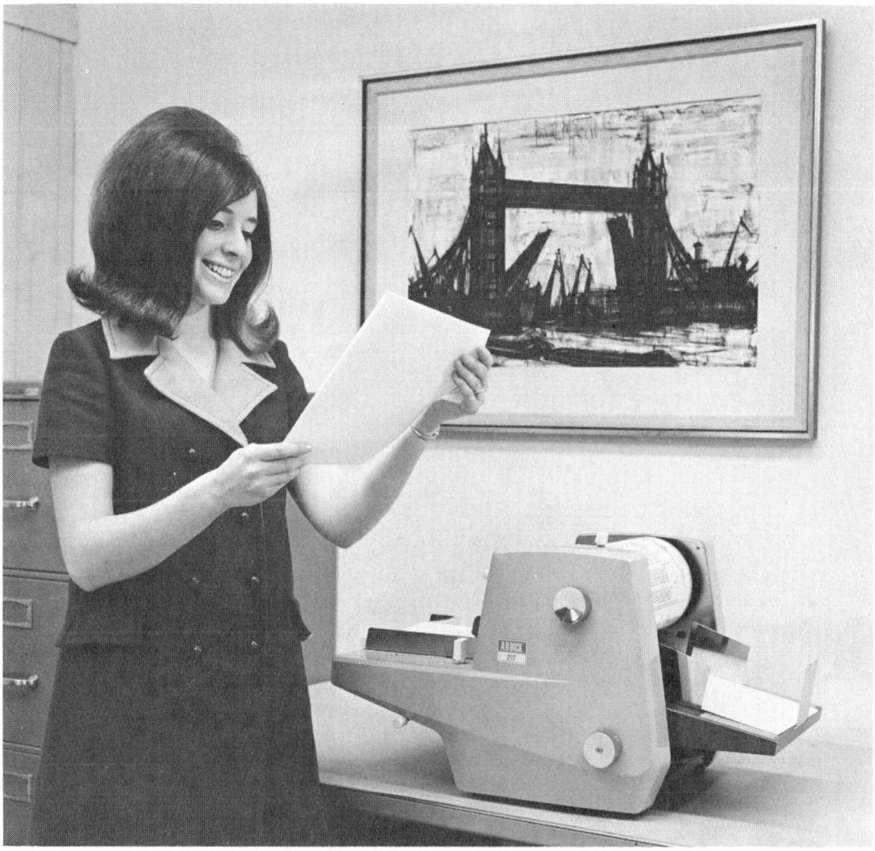

*Figure 23-5.* The Spirit Duplicator Is Effective for Short-Run Jobs
*Source:* Courtesy of A. B. Dick Company

*quality is not a major consideration and when approximately 50 to 5,000 copies are needed.*

***Offset Duplicators.*** In the past, offset machines have been large and bulky and have required special operator skills. While the final product of the process was good, the expense of the equipment and the necessity of a skilled operator made the offset process infeasible for most organizations. Today's offset machine comes in many sizes, from compact table models (see Figure 23-6) to large, versatile floor models. In addition, the machine mechanics have been improved to the point that very little training is required to operate the equipment. The quality of offset duplication is excellent; and with decreased

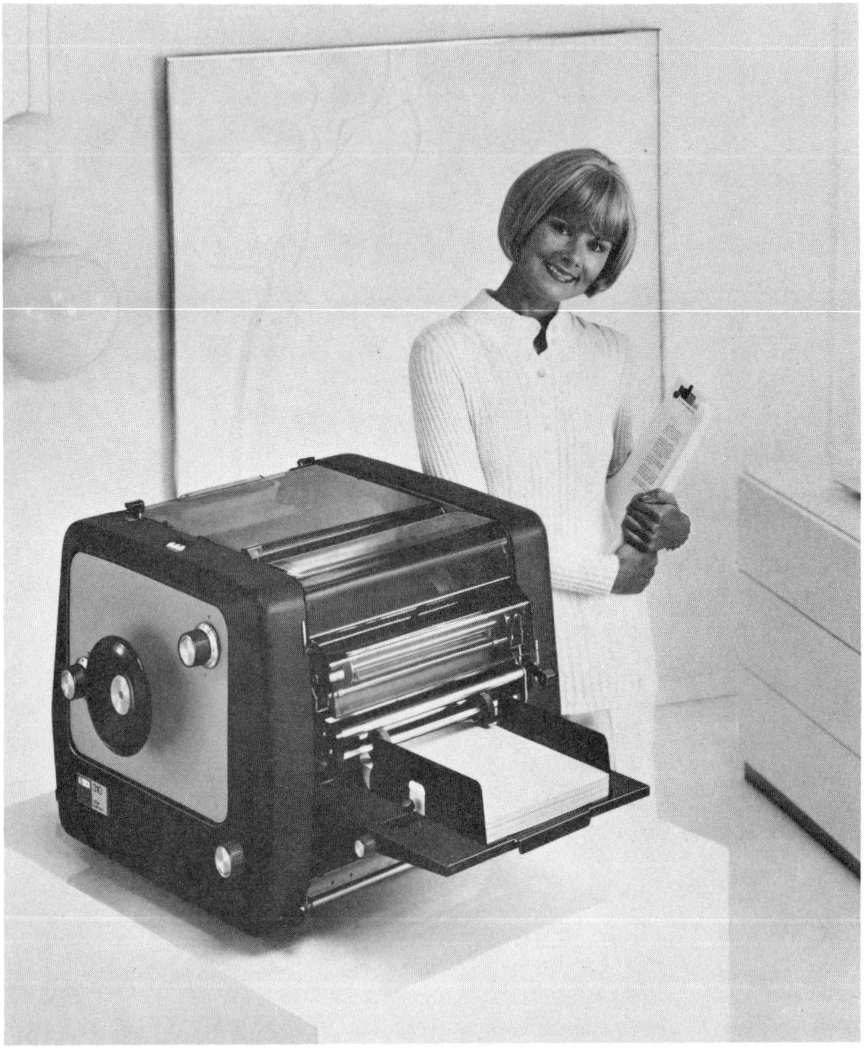

*Figure 23-6.* The Offset Duplicator Is Effective for Medium and Long Runs

*Source:* Courtesy of A. B. Dick Company

machine cost and improved operating efficiency, the offset machine is a very common item in present-day offices.

Addressograph Multigraph, A. B. Dick, and Remington Rand provide much of the offset equipment used in business. *Offset equipment should be used when copy and paper quality are important, when pictures need to be*

**Table 23-1. Basic Characteristics of Three Major Duplicating Processes**

| | *Process** | | |
|---|---|---|---|
| | *Spirit* | *Stencil* | *Offset* |
| Copy quality | 1 | 2 | 3 |
| Paper quality | 1 | 2 | 3 |
| Adaptable to long runs | 1 | 2 | 3 |
| Ease of producing multicolor work | 3 | 1 | 1 |
| Ease of equipment operation | 3 | 3 | 2 |
| Automated master preparation | 3 | 3 | 3 |
| Initial equipment expense | 3 | 2 | 1 |
| Cost per copy | 3 | 3 | 3 |

*Ratings: 3, 2, and 1, with 3 as the highest rating.

*printed, and when medium to long runs are needed.* Automatic self-cleaning, automatic shutoff, multiple-color reproduction, and automatic collating of reproduced work are some of the extras that can be purchased to improve the effectiveness of an offset machine. Since each extra item results in a greater outlay of money, however, you should make sure the extras are really needed before they are purchased. The basic characteristics of these three processes are summarized in Table 23-1.

***Copier-Duplicators.*** Recently, reprographic machines called copier-duplicators have been increasing in popularity in business. Copier-duplicators offer both short-run copy convenience and long-run copy speed. Whereas most copiers can produce from 10 to 30 copies per minute, copier-duplicators can produce several hundred copies per minute. Also, they can automatically print on both sides simultaneously, collate, and staple—all in a single process.

## Reprographics Management

Reprographics may be required to provide two types of materials: (1) planned materials such as reports and brochures and (2) convenience materials such as copies of a letter or magazine report. As much as possible, an organization's planned materials should be prepared by centralized reprographic services. Several distinct advantages occur when a special reprographics department is established:

Economies of scale. Machines have less nonuse time, and the cost of machine investment is spread over a larger number of copies.

Better skilled operators. Operators who do reprographic work full time become highly skilled and efficient and are thereby able to produce higher quality work.

Better control over equipment. Equipment is more easily maintained when it is located in one area; and when the same people work with the same machines all the time, they are better able to sense the need for proper maintenance.

Better administrative control over reprographic personnel. When all workers using the reprographic equipment are located together under one supervisor, the ease of using MBO and other management techniques is significantly enhanced.

In general, the duplication processes should be centralized, but convenience copying on a decentralized basis will still be needed. Even with the decentralized location of these copiers, however, centralized control should still be maintained. Several guidelines should be understood by all who use copiers:

1. Reimburse the company when personal copies are made.
2. Do not use copiers when carbon copies could easily be made during the typing process.
3. Do not use copiers when duplication processes should be used.
4. Do not make extra copies "just in case" you might need them.

To make individual departments and individual employees more cost conscious, charge-back methods should be developed to assess those departments that actually use the services. An individual's name and department should be recorded for each duplication or copying job that is handled, and this detailed information should be summarized and sent to department heads on a periodic basis. Reprographic center personnel can handle this process for duplication work, and a system of keys or cards can accumulate this information for decentralized copiers.

Since large volumes of paper are used in a reprographics center, the center should be provided with sufficient room and storage space. Then an efficient method of managing both new paper and duplicated materials in inventory should be developed. Cost-efficient ordering methods, proper timing for ordering new supplies of paper and for printing new supplies of forms, and effective methods of disseminating duplicated supplies throughout the organization must be established. Too often, reprographic centers incur high costs because of paper misuse and inventory mismanagement. By developing high standards, you can hold the center supervisor accountable for achieving and maintaining these standards. The entire organization will benefit from the reprographic center's efficiency.

## WRITTEN COMMUNICATIONS TRANSMISSION

The transmission of written communications in the United States is big business. The U.S. Postal Service (U.S.P.S.) alone handles nearly 100 billion pieces of mail annually, and individual businesses and other organizations send additional billions of messages internally. One study of a national multiplant business revealed that 80 percent of the company's mail was for internal purposes; only 20 percent went outside the company. Of course, much of the internal mail went among the various plants, but a large percentage stayed within the building in which it was originated. The following section discusses interoffice written messages, and the section dealing with external written communications focuses on written messages that go outside the office.

### Internal Written Communication

Probably the most common method of transporting written communications within an office is for an executive, secretary, or clerk to handcarry the paper from one place to another. This method is very costly because of the amount of time and salary involved. Five other less costly methods are commonly found in offices: messenger service, conveyer system, pneumatic tube system, electronic longhand transmission, and facsimile (Fax). Obviously, messenger service is the oldest form of transmitting written messages; but because of minimum wage requirements, personal messenger service has become rather costly. In addition, personnel turnover, training problems, and motivation difficulties discourage many companies from using messenger service on a large scale. Smaller organizations still use messengers, but these workers are usually employed primarily for other tasks and perform messenger duties only on a part-time basis.

Conveyer systems have been used by some large offices in which large volumes of paper pass from one station to another during the course of business. Conveyers carry papers among various stations on one floor and from one floor to another. Pneumatic tube systems involve a network of tubes through which containers carry documents from one work area to another. The creation of a vacuum pressure inside the tube system enables the containers to travel both horizontally and vertically. Pneumatic tubes and multichannel conveyers have been among the most popular systems used in large offices.

Electronic longhand transmission is a process of sending hand-written messages via electronic circuitry. As the message sender is writing the message on the sending machine, the receiving machine writes the identical message almost instantly. This system works well as a means of requesting records from both active and inactive records areas.

Facsimile transmission or Fax is the process of transmitting images of written documents or graphic displays via telephone lines. Although Fax can travel long distances over telephone systems, its most frequent use has been as an intracompany communication transmission device. Facsimile transmission of one page of information takes from less than a minute to six minutes, depending on the capabilities of the sending and receiving units. A facsimile machine is illustrated in Figure 23-7.

If predictions about a paperless office of the future come to pass, the necessity of transmitting numerous papers among office workers will be significantly lessened. Instead, electronic storage, retrieval, and transmission of information will become very common.

### External Written Communications

Any office depends on fast, reliable communication service with branches of the same organization and with other organizations and people with whom it must interact. External written communications are transmitted between or-

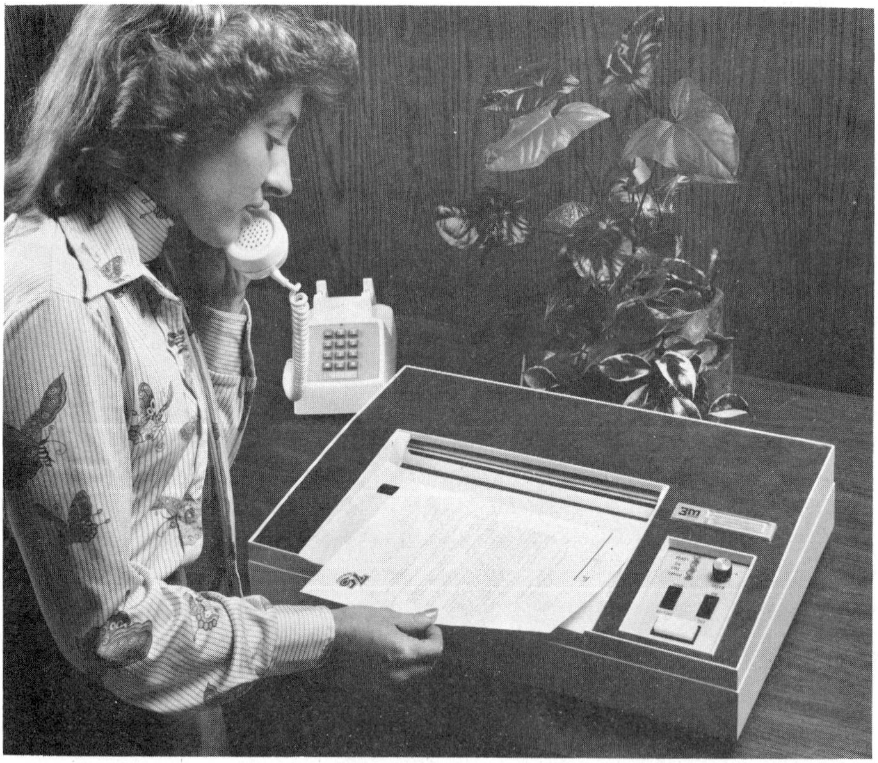


*Figure 23-7.* Facsimile Machines Transmit Graphic and Written Copies via the Telephone Network

*Source:* 3M Company, Saint Paul, Minn.

ganizations by teletypewriters, mailgram service, facsimile machines, mail service, and other services. Facsimile transmission has previously been discussed in the internal written communication section of this chapter and it will not be discussed further here. The other services are discussed below, with mail service receiving greatest treatment because of the large part it plays in the administrative manager's job responsibilities.

***Teletypewriter Communication.*** For many years, Western Union has used teletypewriters for transmitting telegrams from one Western Union office to another. Today, teletypewriters are used also by businesses for written communication transmission. Although all teletypewriter service is operated by Western Union,[1] regular telephone lines are used to transmit messages from one station to another. Two types of teletypewriter machines and services are available.: *Tel*eprinter *Ex*change (Telex—operates at a rate of 66 words per minute) and TWX (operates at a 100-word-per-minute rate); see Figure 23-8. Both services are available for use 24 hours a day, and both can transmit to either TWX or Telex stations.

Telex and TWX machines work much the same as typewriters, but their output is a punched paper tape that contains the message punched in Telex or

*Figure 23-8.* Telex and TWX Machines Transmit Both Alphabetic and Numeric Information via the Telephone Network

*Source:* Western Union Corporation

TWX code. This punched tape is produced before a call to another station is actually made, although on-line typing is possible. Off-line preparation of messages helps to eliminate on-line time waste caused by a person's slow typing speed. Since Telex and TWX machines will transmit and receive without an operator, transmission can be accomplished during after-work hours when telephone rates are less expensive. Compared with long-distance oral telephone calls, Telex or TWX transmission can result in a 75 percent savings. With approximately 100,000 TWX and Telex subscribers in the U.S. and with the economy offered by these services, teletypewriter communication is a very competitive communication channel.

***Mailgrams.*** The U.S.P.S. and Western Union have joined efforts to offer high-speed mailgram service at a very low cost. A mailgram is a written message that is computer routed by zip code and electronically transmitted to a post office near the destination. The mailgram is then delivered the next business day by a U.S. postal carrier. Mailgrams can be submitted to Western Union by TWX, Telex, computer, or live-voice dictation over a telephone anywhere in the forty-eight contiguous states. Although mailgram service is not as fast as teletype service, it is faster than regular business letters.

*Electronic mail* is a term that telecommunication specialists say will become commonplace during the next few years. Electronic mail will feature electronic transmission of much of the mail that is now sent through regular mail channels. By using Telex, TWX, facsimile machines, word processing machines, and other types of telecommunication terminals, businesses can transmit the large majority of their external written communication transactions. Many people predict that private households will eventually have individual terminals that will also permit electronic sending and receiving of written messages.

***Mail Services—Equipment and Handling.*** A well-organized and well-controlled mail center handles mail quickly and can save an organization thousands of dollars each year because of its efficiency. Most large- and medium-sized organizations handle their incoming and outgoing mail on a centralized basis. Centralization of mail handling permits work specialization, automation, and effective managerial control.

*Mailing Equipment.* Because mail handling involves so much routine activity, it is an activity that should be automated as much as possible. Automation reduces job monotony and improves efficiency because high-speed equipment can outperform employees performing the same work manually.

Probably the most important piece of mailing equipment any office can have is the postage meter (see Figure 23-9). The most basic postage meter imprints the proper amount of postage on envelopes and packages. More sophisticated postage meters can feed envelopes into the postage meter, print an advertisement on the envelope, and seal, stack, and count envelopes. Postage meters stop stamp losses, save time and effort spent in licking stamps and envelopes, and alleviate personnel problems.

To determine the amount of postage that should be affixed on an envelope or package, a mailing scale should be used. Mailing scales compute weight in

*Figure 23-9.* A Postage Meter Is Probably the Most Important Piece of Mail-Handling Equipment

fractions of an ounce and include a built-in chart that provides postage rates. Since one of the most frequent causes of high mailing costs is overpayment of postage, a mailing scale is an essential item for a mailing center.

To eliminate misunderstandings between customers and suppliers, stamps that record the date and the time that correspondence is received are frequently used. Electric clocks with automatic time and date stamps are used for this process, thus eliminating human error.

Four other processes, addressing, folding, inserting, and making labels, are very time consuming if a company engages in a great deal of bulk mailing. If bulk mailings are frequently required, an organization should determine the feasibility of procuring the following time-saving items: an addressing machine (for up to 6,000 addresses per hour), a folding machine (for up to 19,000 sheets per hour), an inserting machine (for up to 7,500 envelopes per hour with up to 6 insertions per envelope, see Figure 23-10), and a label-making machine.

Other pieces of equipment that help speed the handling of mail include letter openers, mail-sorting tables, racks and cabinets, and mail-sorting bags. All are designed to streamline the processing of incoming and outgoing mail.

*Handling Incoming Mail.* Incoming mail is generally picked up from the post office by a mail center employee before the regular work day begins. The mail is brought to the mail room where it is time stamped and sorted. Per-

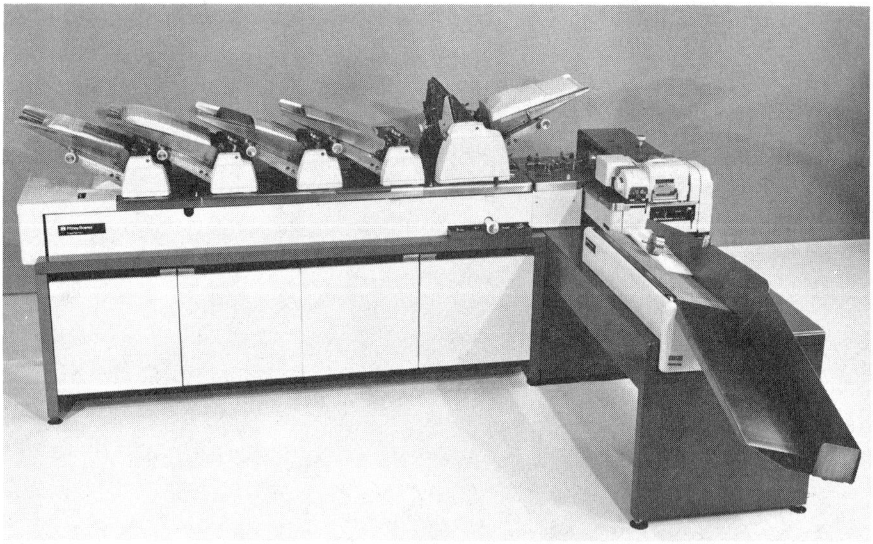

*Figure 23-10.* Inserting Machines Streamline the Process of Stuffing Envelopes

*Source:* Pitney-Bowes, Stamford, Conn.

sonal mail is separated from company mail, and company mail is opened. Any mail that has payments enclosed is placed in a separate pile to be delivered to the cashier. After mail is completely sorted, it is delivered to appropriate individuals and departments throughout the company. Mail is picked up from the post office several more times each day; therefore, this basic process is repeated several times during the day. Companies can decrease sorting time by having different items of mail come to different post office boxes. For example, payments could be sent to one box and new orders could be sent to another. By following this process, a company receives sorting help from post office personnel.

*Handling Outgoing Mail.* Outgoing mail, like incoming mail, is picked up from departments several times each day. Mail should first be weighed on a mailing scale to determine the proper amount of postage required. After the mail is weighed, it is run through the postage meter, which prints the proper amount of postage, seals the envelope, and may print an advertising slogan on the envelope. Mail is then sorted by zip code and bagged accordingly for the post office.

For bulk mailing, this process is somewhat different. The bulk mailing process is likely to involve folding letters and other inserts by a folding machine, addressing the envelopes by an addressing machine, stuffing and sealing envelopes by an inserting machine, and stamping and stacking envelopes by a postage meter.

***Mail Center Management.*** One of the first concerns an administrative manager should have about mail center management is to train mail center employees properly. These employees should understand the following classes of mail:

- First-Class Mail
  - Handwritten and typewritten messages
  - Bills and statements of account
  - Postcards and postal cards
  - Canceled and uncanceled checks
  - Business reply mail
- Second-Class Mail
  - Newspapers and magazines issued at least four times a year
- Third-Class Mail
  - Circulars, booklets, catalogs, and other printed materials such as newsletters and corrected proof sheets with manuscript copy not otherwise required as first-class mail
  - Merchandise, farm and factory products, photographs, keys, and printed drawings
  - All of the above items must weigh less than 16 ounces; otherwise, they are sent as fourth-class mail

Fourth-Class Mail
- Domestic parcels
- Certain catalogs and library materials

The following special services should also be understood.

Special delivery: Means an item of mail is delivered as soon as practicable after it arrives at the addressee's post office.

Certified mail: Provides for a record of delivery to be maintained by the post office from which the item is delivered. An additional fee is charged for a proof-of-delivery receipt.

Registered mail: Provides for a receipt to the customer at the time of mailing and a post office record of the mailing. For an additional fee, a proof of delivery receipt is returned to the mailer.

Insured mail: Insures third- and fourth-class mail against loss or damage.

Business reply mail: Permits a mailer to pay postage for return-requested envelopes. Such envelopes carry the message "No Postage Stamp Necessary If Mailed in the United States."

Collect-on-delivery (C.O.D.): Provides for collection of both the postage and the value of the letter or parcel contents at the point of delivery.[2]

Employees should work to eliminate unnecessary use of special mail services, and they should be trained in the proper use of mail room equipment and in sorting and handling mail properly.

Businesses must also make certain that their envelopes meet U.S.P.S. size requirements. Specifically, envelopes less than 3.5 inches by 5 inches will be subject to a surcharge. In addition, quicker service can be provided for envelopes meeting the U.S.P.S. standards. Since a mail center involves so much repetition, it is a prime candidate for periodic systems analysis. In accordance with the guidelines given in Chapter 19, procedures should be carefully studied to determine those that can be eliminated, combined, improved, or mechanized.

Because the U.S.P.S. grants decreased postage for presorting certain types of mail, the mail room personnel should be alert to ways they can earn this discount.

Mail center personnel should also be aware of the services provided by private firms that compete with the U.S.P.S. in the area of parcel delivery. Firms such as the United Parcel Service can frequently provide service that exceeds that offered by regular mail.

To improve the handling of mail by the postal department, workers should dispatch company mail to the post office as early in the day as possible. Because the large majority of mail arrives at the post office in the afternoon, mail received in the morning will receive more prompt service.

Finally, a system of MBO should be established to ensure that mail personnel understand their job responsibilities, that they are constantly working to upgrade their performance, and that they always have the opportunity to communicate one-to-one with their supervisor.

## *Summary*

The administrative manager usually has very direct control over much of an organization's communication services. One of the major parts of a good communication system is an effective telephone network. PBX and PABX systems are being constantly upgraded to offer the user more features. Centrex is a relatively new telephone system for large companies and features direct inward dialing (DID), a decentralized approach to handling telephone communication. Office employees should be educated in efficient telephone use to decrease telecommunication expenditures.

Reprographics deals with copying and duplicating processes. Liquid, stencil, offset, and copying machines are the most frequently used reprographic processes in business. Effective cost control measures should be implemented to decrease abuse of copying privileges. Duplication services can be improved by centralizing both the location and the control of the equipment and its operation.

Transportation of intracompany written messages is accomplished by messenger service, conveyer systems, pneumatic tubes, electronic longhand transmission, and facsimile transmission. Electronic systems continue to take over more and more of intracompany communication functions.

External written communications are frequently handled by teletypewriter systems such as Telex and TWX. Mailgram service is offered jointly by Western Union and the U.S. Postal Service (U.S.P.S.) to give next-day service on written communications. Fax systems permit electronic transmission of written or graphic materials both within a company and between different companies.

Most external written communication is handled by the U.S.P.S. To the degree possible, mail service should be centralized within an organization. Centralization permits greater utilization of equipment to streamline mail handling and to decrease the monotonous repetition that can be such a problem in a mail center. Effective mail center management should achieve maximum speed at reasonable cost levels.

## *Review and Discussion Questions*

1. What might an organization gain or lose by going from a centralized to a decentralized telephone system?
2. Why is WATS advantageous for both the telephone company and the individual business?

3. How does inward WATS differ from outward WATS? What is the difference between full-time and measured-time WATS?
4. Why is it so important to read the current tariff of the telephone company?
5. How have copiers affected office reprographic systems?
6. Why has so much difficulty been encountered in controlling copier cost?
7. How can an administrative manager improve copier cost control?
8. Why has the offset process become so popular in recent years?
9. What part does the U.S.P.S. play in the mailgram system?
10. What unique telecommunication advantage is offered by Fax?
11. How does a postage meter improve mail efficiency?
12. Why should systems analysis be a regular occurrence in a mail center?

## *Application Exercises*

1. Visit several businesses in your area and examine their telephone systems. Determine whether they use a PBX, PABX, or a Centrex system. Ask them about any plans they have for changing their telephone system in the near future.
2. Invite an executive from your local telephone company to speak to your class about modern telecommunication systems and their outlook for the future. Also have him or her discuss guidelines for efficient telephone usage in an office.
3. Visit the reprographics department of your school and examine the various types of equipment they use. Look for offset equipment, stencil machines, and spirit duplicators. Examine a piece of duplicated copy from each of these machines.
4. Visit the mail center of a large business in your area. Ask the mail center supervisor to show you the equipment used in the center and to explain what each item of equipment does. Also ask about procedures used with incoming and outgoing mail.
5. Determine the most appropriate way to send the following items through the mail (U.S.P.S.):

   A 22-ounce company catalog

   A 2-pound box of glassware that is very breakable

   An important letter that *must* reach a certain company as soon as possible

   A mass-mailing sales campaign with which you want to include a postage-paid envelope

## *Mini-Cases*

1. *Family Mutual Insurance* is a growing insurance company that has its headquarters in Chicago. Major branch offices are located in New York City, Atlanta, and Houston. Family is not well known on the West Coast, but it hopes to continue to expand in that direction more each year. To encourage this movement, Family is planning to advertise on national television in one year. From this advertisement, Family hopes to encourage a relatively high volume of call-in business. At present, the plan is to invite potential customers to call collect, after which a call will be made to the nearest regional office to send an agent to visit the interested persons.

Family presently has financial reports sent from its branch offices at the end of each month, but because of a computer purchase it wants to go to a centralized accounting program involving daily reporting of financial information from branch offices. This move, Family hopes, will permit a reduction in accounting staff located at the branch offices and will give top management more up-to-date information for decision-making purposes. Family now has no telecommunication tie with the branch offices, but it realizes that a system of transmitting data on a daily basis will be needed.

As administrative manager for Family, you would like to do something about the soaring long-distance telephone calls from top management to the management of the various branch offices. Too frequently, person-to-person, operator-assisted calls are made, and efforts to educate top management about less expensive calling methods have shown little change.

You have received permission from top management to do a thorough telecommunication analysis of the organization and to recommend changes that you feel will help the company both now and in the future. Without gathering more information, what would you be inclined to recommend to Family Mutual Insurance?

2. *The WATS Case.* Recently, a member of your staff conducted a survey to determine the telecommunication needs of your organization, located in Los Angeles. Your company manufactures office furniture. The following data have been gathered:

*Incoming Calls*

22,568 calls came into your organization during the month.
18 percent of these were local calls.
64 percent were within a 500-mile radius.
The remaining calls came from farther away than 500 miles (80 percent came from your branch offices located in Denver, Chicago, Dallas, Atlanta, Phoenix, and New York. The calls were relatively evenly distributed among these branches.)

**Table 23-2. A Comparison of Telephone Rates (Approximations)**

| | *Long-distance rates* | | | | | |
|---|---|---|---|---|---|---|
| | WEEKDAY RATE | | EVENING RATE | | NIGHT/WEEKEND RATE | |
| RATES FROM L.A. TO: | FIRST MINUTE | EACH ADD'L. MINUTE | FIRST MINUTE | EACH ADD'L. MINUTE | FIRST MINUTE | EACH ADD'L. MINUTE |
| Phoenix | $0.48 | $0.33 | $0.31 | $0.21 | $0.19 | $0.13 |
| Denver | .51 | .35 | .33 | .23 | .20 | .14 |
| Dallas | .52 | .36 | .33 | .24 | .20 | .15 |
| Chicago | .54 | .38 | .35 | .24 | .21 | .15 |
| Atlanta | .54 | .38 | .35 | .24 | .21 | .15 |
| New York | .56 | .40 | .37 | .25 | .22 | .16 |
| 250-mile radius | .36 | .25 | .24 | .16 | .15 | .10 |
| 500-mile radius | .48 | .33 | .31 | .21 | .19 | .13 |

| | *WATS Rates (monthly charges)*[a] | | | |
|---|---|---|---|---|
| Band | Measured time[b] | Each add'l. hour | Full services | Extra[c] |
| 1 (Phoenix) | $226 | $16.95 | $1,500 | $4.16 |
| 2 (Denver) | 230 | 17.25 | 1,570 | 4.36 |
| 3 (Dallas) | 238 | 17.85 | 1,640 | 4.55 |
| 4 (Chicago) | 242 | 18.15 | 1,660 | 4.61 |
| 5 (Atlanta) | 244 | 18.31 | 1,670 | 4.63 |
| 6 (New York) | 248 | 18.52 | 1,680 | 4.65 |
| Intrastate[d] | 148 | 11.40 | 628 | 1.77 |

[a] Each figure in the table is for one inward or one outward WATS line.

[b] Measured time permits 10 hours worth of calls before additional charges.

[c] Full service permits 240 hours worth of calls or $14,400 worth of calls without additional charges. Extra charges are assessed beyond that time or amount. Each unit of extra charges consists of one hours worth of used time *or* 60 completed calls—whichever is more.

[d] Intrastate calls are not included in any of the bands and must be purchased separately.

*Outgoing Calls*

8,942 calls went out of your building.

46 percent of these were local calls.

14 percent were long-distance in-state calls at an average distance of 250 miles.

18 percent were to states bordering California.

90 percent of the rest went to your six branch offices and were quite evenly distributed.

Average length of in-state and out-of-state long-distance calls was 4 minutes.

Would you recommend that your company subscribe to WATS? If so, what type? Support your recommendation with your analysis. (See Table 23-2 for a comparison of long-distance rates and WATS rates.)

3. *Randex.* You have been hired as a special projects analyst by Randex Corp. and are to examine all paper processing in the company. First, you look at copier usage. After two days' observations, you accumulate the following information.

Three copiers are located on each of the four floors in the building.

Waiting lines are a frequent occurrence at the copiers on the second floor.

Only one copier on the fourth floor is used to any extent.

No control is being placed on copier usage.

Very little carbon paper is being used for correspondence copies.

Without gathering more detailed information, what would you be inclined to recommend in copier management?

## *Reference Notes*

1. Until 1971, Telex was owned by Western Union and TWX was owned by AT & T. In 1971, however, Western Union acquired TWX and now operates both services. Although TWX and Telex use different transmission codes, Western Union has developed a computer interface device that makes the two services compatible.
2. *Mailers Guide*, a booklet published by the U.S. Postal Service, gives additional information about the services offered.

# 24

# Word Processing

---

Ever since commercially successful typewriters were first invented just over a century ago, efforts have been made to make them more efficient. The first big breakthrough came in the first half of the twentieth century when typewriters were made electric. Recently, another major advance has been made, perhaps even more significant than the electric typewriter. This latest innovation has given typewriters a memory and has prompted a new concept in processing written materials. This concept is called word processing.

*Word processing* (WP) is the streamlined production of typewritten materials, generally characterized by the use of machine dictation and transcription along with automatic typewriters with memories.

Word processing focuses both on the modern equipment and on the effective use of the equipment. For without the effective organization of workers, new WP equipment can actually yield less work than an older system. Word processing usually brings together several typists in either a word-processing center or a work group, although some WP equipment is used in a traditional secretary-manager arrangement.

A few of the terms that are commonly associated with word processing are:

*Author* (or word originator): The person who dictates the material that is to be typed.

*Character:* Each letter, special symbol, or number found on a typewriter keyboard.

*Editing:* The correction of errors or the changing of any part of a document.

*Input:* Work that is sent to the WP center, usually in machine-dictated, handwritten, or copy-typed form.

*Operator:* The typist who operates an automatic typewriter.

*Output:* Work that has been typed by the WP personnel.

*Playback:* The typing of material that has been placed in the magnetic memory of a WP typewriter.

*Principal:* A person who receives service from WP or other secretarial personnel.

*Text-editing machines:* Typewriters that have the capability to store, manipulate, edit, and play back written documents.

*Transcription:* The process of changing words from their input form to a typewritten or typewriter memory form.

*Turnaround time:* The period of time from receipt of input to completion of output.

Today's administrative manager needs a good understanding of these terms to make decisions regarding word-processing systems and equipment.

## INPUT

Word-processing centers (or work groups) can receive input in three basic forms: (1) material written in longhand, (2) material that has been previously typed, and (3) material dictated into a magnetic dictating machine. The first method, writing in longhand, is the slowest of the three methods and should be discouraged except for very short messages. The second method is appropriate when previously typed materials must be retyped with only a few changes.

The third method involving machine dictation is the most frequently recommended method of the three. Machine dictation is preferred over traditional shorthand dictation for several reasons:

The machine is always available, whereas the secretary is not.

Machine dictation does not interrupt the secretary; shorthand dictation does.

Portable dictation machines are convenient to take on trips.

Machine dictation involves only one person; shorthand dictation involves two. Therefore, machine dictation is the most cost effective of the three input methods.

Any operator can transcribe machine dictation, but one secretary's shorthand frequently cannot be transcribed by another secretary.

Several different machine dictation arrangements are found in business offices. Probably the oldest form is to have a dictating machine right in the office of the author. With this system the author simply picks up a microphone attached to the dictating unit, dictates the material, replaces the microphone, takes the recorded medium to an operator, and asks a word-processing operator to type the material. With this system, there is always time wasted while the dictated material is hand carried to the WP center.

Many word-processing equipment manufacturers produce portable, battery-powered dictating machines that can be used at home, in the car, on business trips, or anywhere else an author wants to dictate. As with the previous system, the dictated material must then be manually transported back to the WP center.

The most popular system uses an organization's present telephone system. If you have dial telephones with this system, for example, you simply lift the receiver of your telephone and dial a special number to be connected to a dictating machine. By dialing different numbers on your telephone, you direct the dictating machine to perform certain functions for you; touch-tone telephones can also be used with many dictation systems. With most telephone-input systems, dictating from home and long-distance dictation are possible.

Let's listen in as George Palowski dictates a short memorandum on his touch-tone telephone dictation system. George picks up the telephone handset and touches 720. He hears a short tone which signifies that the dictation machine in the WP center is ready to receive his dictation. Therefore, he begins his dictation:

"This is George Palowski. I need to dictate a memo to Betty Darlington, records center supervisor. I need one carbon copy of the memo for my file. The subject of this memo is 'Request for Tour of Records Center.' The body of the memo follows.

"Betty, I received the attached letter from Rand Haas, that's capital H-a-a-s, of General Fidelity Insurance Co., initial capitals on those four words, and he requested information about our conversion to Microfilm in our settled claim files. Would you please accumulate the information and send. . . ." George decides he wants to back up and change the wording slightly, so he touches the 3 on his telephone. The dictation machine backs up about ten words and begins playing back to George—". . . claim files. Would you please accumulate the information . . ."—George touches the 2, which stops the playback and puts the dictation machine in a recording mode. George dictates—". . . requested in Rand's, that's apostrophe s, letter and send it to him. Paragraph. I'd appreciate receiving a carbon copy of your letter. Thanks for your help. End of dictation."

George wants to listen to his first paragraph, so he touches the 3 several times to back up to the desired spot. He listens to the first paragraph and decides it is acceptable. He then touches the 4, which is a fast-forward number. After touching the 4, George listens for a moment and hears ". . . help. End of dictation."

George remembers that Rand was in quite a hurry to get the micrographic data, so he touches the 6, which rings the telephone in the WP center. An operator answers: "Word processing, Darla speaking." George replies, "Darla, this is George Palowski. I just dictated a short memo to Betty Darlington in records, and I need a rush put on it. Think you can handle that for me?" Darla responds, "Sure thing, Mr. Palowski, we'll get to it right away." "Thanks," says George. He then touches the 5 to indicate to the dictating machine that he is finished dictating, and he hangs up his phone.

Another popular dictation input system uses specially installed wiring. With this direct wire system, as it is called, all authors have a special microphone at their individual stations. When they dictate, they use the microphone rather than their telephone (as was the case with the previous system). On each microphone are control buttons that give the authors control over the dictating machines in the WP center. Figure 24-1 shows an author dictating to the WP center from his desk telephone.

*Figure 24-1.* Machine Dictation Is an Effective Input Method for WP Centers

## PROCESSING

After input is received in the WP center, an operator transcribes it. The transcription machine may be separate from the dictation machine that received the original dictation; or, with an endless-loop system, the dictation and transcription processes are built into one machine. The process of transcription involves listening to the dictation, or reading the longhand, and typing it. For example, if a WP center uses dictation machines with magnetic belts, the operator removes the belt from the dictation machine, inserts it into the transcriber, and listens to the dictation on the belt while typing the dictation on the typewriter. The transcriber is controlled by a foot pedal, which permits the operators to vary the machine dictation to correspond with their typing speed.

Typing in a WP center can be accomplished on a variety of typewriters from the most simple to the most sophisticated. Although a few manual typewriters are still used in some offices, electric and automatic typewriters have taken over. With true WP centers, automatic typewriters with some kind of memory system are usually used. An example is the IBM Memory Typewriter, which can store one hundred business letters in its internal memory.

All WP typewriters have a standard alphabetic typewriter keyboard, so an operator's basic typewriting skill is compatible with all models. In addition to the basic keyboard, a number of special command keys that give instruction to the typewriter are usually found. A typical command is "Record," which means to remember the information that is typed on the keyboard.

Information that is typed on the typewriter is accumulated and remembered (stored) in a variety of ways. *Stand-alone WP units* (units that are not connected to a computer) use such storage media as cassette tapes, magnetic cards, magnetic disks (called floppy disks), or internal storage. Minicomputer-based systems (shared-logic systems) usually have one or more terminals (typewriters) connected to the minicomputer. Time-sharing systems have the terminals connected to a large central computer that has virtually unlimited storage capabilities. Use of a minicomputer or large central computer greatly enlarges the storage capacity of a WP system, but it may also add a great amount of cost.

### Display

As WP operators type material into memory, they need to be able to see what they are typing. This visual display of the input is given in one of two ways. First, some WP typewriters type directly onto paper just as standard typewriters do. If operators make an error, they simply backspace and strike the correct character over the incorrect character. This action removes the incorrect character from memory and replaces it with the correct character. Some WP typewriters have a correcting device that will also lift the incorrect charac-

*Figure 24-2.* Paper Display WP Systems Have the Initial Draft of a Document Typed on Paper

*Source:* Courtesy of A. B. Dick Company

ter from the paper, thus enabling operators to insert the correct character both in memory and on the paper. Figure 24-2 illustrates a paper display system.

Second, some typewriters display the input material on a cathode-ray tube (CRT), which looks like a small television screen. When operators make errors in their typing, they backspace and strike the correct character over the incorrect character. This action corrects the error both in the memory and on the CRT screen. A screen display (CRT) system is illustrated in Figure 24-3.

*Figure 24-3.* A Screen Display System Usually Uses a CRT Unit to Show What Material Has Been Stored in the Memory

*Source:* Photo courtesy of Wang Laboratories, Inc., Lowell, Mass.

### Editing

A major aspect of the processing phase of WP is referred to as *text editing.* WP equipment, especially that with CRT screens, gives operators great freedom to alter original input within the WP system. For example, Diana Gudeman works as a word processor in an insurance company. The insurance company must maintain a large number of procedure and policy manuals, and it is Diana's job to update these manuals as changes are made by various departments. Before WP came into being, any changes in the manuals necessitated the complete retyping of the manuals—a tedious and very time-consuming task.

Now Diana has a stand-alone CRT-based WP system and has all the manuals stored on disks. Diana has just received a manual dealing with workman's compensation. The instructions with the job tell Diana to go through the manual and change all references of "workmen's compensation" to "workers' compensation."

Before WP, this job would have taken about three hours. Now, however, Diana just finds the disk that stores the manual, inserts it in the WP machine, and keys in a *global search and replace* message. In other words, she tells the machine to find all the "workmen's compensation" references and to change them to "workers' compensation." The word processor finishes the job by itself—in just 4½ minutes.

As Diana receives work from other people in the organization, she completes it with the same degree of ease. Typing simple commands to her machine will automatically justify the right margin, alter line length or page length, eliminate information and move the text to close the gap created by the omission, add information and move the text to accommodate the new information, and move information from one place in a manual to another. This text editing is all performed internally and appears visually on the screen—before the material is typed in final form on paper.

## OUTPUT

The output of a WP system is produced by playing back the corrected material that is stored in the typewriter or computer memory. Output can be produced through the input typewriter, which serves as both an input and an output (I/O) terminal; or, with CRTs, it is produced through a separate output device, usually referred to as a *printer.*

Playback speed varies according to the type of output device. Earliest word-processing typewriters produced output at 150 words per minute; current stand-alone printers print up to 600 words per minute, and computer-WP printers are capable of printing over 20,000 words per minute. In Figure 24-3 you can see a system that features an input keyboard, a CRT display unit, and a printer. With such a system, an operator can input new material at the same time the printer is producing output. Paper-based systems cannot input and output simultaneously.

When a word-processing job is played out in final form, it is delivered to the author. If the author approves of this copy, it is used according to his or her needs. If the copy is not approved and is changed in any way, however, the copy is sent back to the WP center for correction and subsequent resubmission to the author. A word-processing flowchart is illustrated in Figure 24-4. This flowchart shows the sequence of the WP cycle as follows: (1) "Dictation," the author gives input to the WP center; (2) "Transcription and proofreading," the WP operator records and plays back the material and checks it

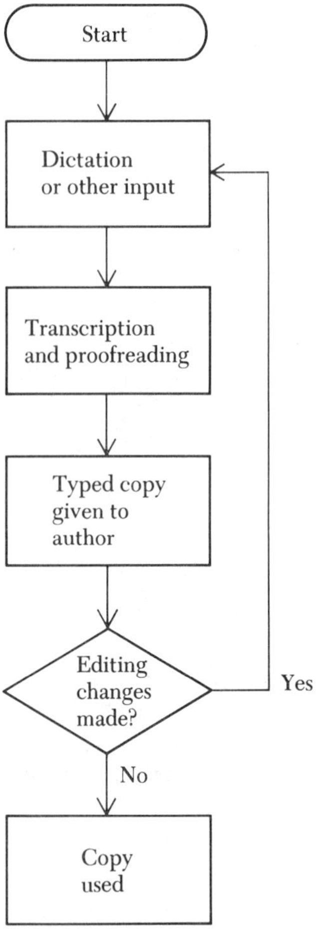


*Figure 24-4.* Word-Processing Flowchart

for correctness; (3) "Typed copy given to author," the author receives a copy of the material; (4) "Editing changes made," the author reads the material to determine whether any changes are needed; and (5) "Copy used," the material is used for whatever purpose the author needs. Steps 2, 3, and 4 may be repeated as needed if the author determines that changes are necessary in the material he or she receives from the WP center.

The modern copying machine is an important output part of the WP center. Copying machines are used when several copies of a document are needed; of course, carbon paper is still a more economical medium for just one or two copies.

## ADMINISTRATIVE SUPPORT TEAM

The typical secretary spends only 20 to 40 percent of a working day in typing activities. The rest of the time is spent performing tasks not requiring typing. Thus, you can see that WP takes care of only a small part of a secretary's work. Someone must continue to perform the tasks that are not WP-oriented.

Associated with most WP centers are administrative support (AS) teams that perform many nontyping services for management. Members of AS teams who specialize in this type of activity become very proficient in providing management assistance. Because of typing and other interruptions, the private secretary is less efficient in performing administrative support functions.

In many organizations, WP has met with resistance because managers realized WP would result in loss of a personal secretary, less prestige, and less "personal touch." The organization of an effective AS team has helped to overcome some of this WP resistance.

WP/AS teams provide secretaries with many opportunities for career growth within an organization. Entry-level responsibilities might focus on such tasks as answering telephones, routing calls, taking messages, copying, filing, and handling mail. A second step up the career ladder might well be in the WP center performing typing operations, which require a much higher level of skill than that required by the first step. The third rung on the ladder might involve working with budgets, supplies, and work schedules and even supervising other secretarial personnel. A fourth step on the career ladder could involve decision-making responsibilities and other tasks frequently performed by administrators.

Joyce Sadlowski currently serves as WP supervisor of Security Bank and Trust Co. To prepare for this position, Joyce has worked for six years in various positions. As a beginning student at Brooklyn Community College, she worked for a year as a receptionist where she handled incoming telephone calls and performed light clerical work. After a year of typewriting training at the community college, Joyce served for a year in the WP center of the college. Joyce then had an opportunity to go to work in the WP center of Security Bank and Trust. The pay was better and she thought she would have more chance for advancement there. After working in Security's WP center for a year and a half, Joyce was asked to serve as a member of the administrative support team. In this capacity, she got to work on many special administrative projects with other AS personnel. She also became acquainted with a number of the company executives. She enjoyed her work and did it well, and she learned a great deal about the company. After two and a half years as an administrative support secretary, the supervisor of the WP center was promoted. The executives of the company had noticed Joyce's abilities and attitude, and she was offered the WP supervisor position. Joyce has found that as long as she continues to do a superior job, she moves ahead in the organization. Those who do only enough to get by are the ones who find themselves in "dead-end" jobs.

## ORGANIZATION OF WP/AS PERSONNEL

The WP/AS personnel can be organized in several different ways ranging from total centralization to total decentralization. In the preceding example, Joyce Sadlowski administers a totally *centralized* center. Because her company is not extremely large, she supervises both WP and AS personnel.

Joyce could organize it differently, however; one way would be to organize by *task*. With this arrangement, the WP/AS personnel would specialize in certain types of jobs. The AS people could be centralized, or they could be decentralized and located in a place appropriate to the performance of their tasks.

Another organizational alternative would be to organize by *principal* with the same WP/AS individuals serving the same business executives on every job. This system is usually organized in a decentralized manner.

Another alternative would be to organize the WP centrally and to decentralize the AS people either by task or by principal. The important thing to remember is that WP/AS services exist to serve the business users, not vice versa. Hence, the needs of the users should dictate the organizational pattern of WP/AS.

## WP/AS MANAGEMENT

According to some personnel specialists, WP is a giant step backward as far as job enrichment is concerned. WP has the potential danger of bringing about the same boredom that accompanies assembly line work in many factories. Boredom is much less a problem with AS personnel, since their work usually involves considerable variety and challenge.

It must be remembered that job enrichment is partly a function of selection procedures and partly a function of work assignment. Since enrichment comes as a result of advancement, achievement, responsibility, and the work itself, the worker and job assignment must be carefully matched so that these features plus reward can be possible. A person who is significantly overqualified for a job will feel little achievement or responsibility if left in the same position for a long period of time. Another person who can experience growth and advancement in the same position, however, will likely be motivated for a relatively long period of time.

For example, a person with good typing and analytical skills and with a desire to work primarily in nontyping tasks will probably become quickly dissatisfied with a lengthy WP assignment. On the other hand, a person with reasonably good typing skills, but limited analytical and interpersonal abilities might be very satisfied for a long period of time in a WP job.

When a person is selected for a WP or AS assignment, he or she should feel needed on the job, be able to advance on the job, and have sufficient challenge on the job to make MBO meaningful. Then, following this matching of person and job, the manager must follow up with effective communication, job enrichment, Theory *Y* supervision, MBO, and other management practices previously explained in this textbook. In a survey that sought to determine what WP operators like and dislike about their positions, Malone obtained the following information:[1]

*What workers like in a word-processing center*

1. A good supervisor
2. Pride in turning out a large volume of work; i.e., own accomplishment
3. Recognition for achievement
4. Pay and opportunity for job enrichment
5. Turning out high-quality work
6. Keeping busy, and a variety of work
7. The people they work with
8. Learning new skills
9. Some responsibility for making basic decisions

*What workers don't like in a word-processing center*

1. Job pressures
2. Overtime requirements (excessive)
3. Being treated like a machine
4. Poor dictation or handwritten copy
5. Unfair allocation of work by supervisors
6. Poor work measurement techniques that do not give credit for all work
7. Private secretaries who are not kept as busy as center operators even though private secretaries sometimes earn more

8. Work not appreciated
9. Inadequate training for job demands; too high expectations

These findings, like those reported in Chapters 4 and 5, suggest that it is human factors and the work itself that will make a WP center successful. Supervision and other factors surrounding the job are the most frequent causes of dissatisfaction and loss of motivation.

Proponents of WP are quick to point out that it provides opportunity for work measurement and subsequent reward for outstanding work. Effective WP supervisors keep a record of the output of each operator, thus making the appraisal process much more objective than has previously been possible with the traditional private secretary. Measurement of output is much more difficult with AS personnel, however. For example, it is much easier to measure 5,000 lines of WP typewriting than to measure such activities as errands completed, copies made, budgets proofread, letters written, and telephones answered. Nevertheless, to the degree possible, performance appraisal should be a part of managing all AS personnel. (Chapter 17 discusses several appraisal methods that can be used very effectively with AS workers.)

Although WP and AS management is a relatively new concern of administrative management, one major conclusion has been borne out very strongly—the success of WP/AS does not depend on the equipment and other electromechanical aspects of the system; it depends on the degree to which the system is sensitive to the needs of people.

## *Summary*

Word processing is the streamlined production of typewritten materials by the use of automated dictation, transcription, and typewriting machines. Input arrives at a WP center in the form of material written in longhand, copy typing, or material dictated onto a magnetic medium—preferably the latter. Magnetic recorded dictation can be transmitted to the WP center by direct wire or telephone input systems, or the magnetic medium may be hand carried if the dictation machine is in the author's office.

After the material is received in the WP center, it is transcribed and stored in the memory of an automatic typewriter. Within the typewriter's memory, the material can be changed to meet the needs of the author. When the material meets the author's approval, it is played out at a high rate of speed. Many newer types of WP equipment are connected to minicomputers or central computers that give the WP machines much greater storage and text-editing capacity.

Whereas typing tasks are performed by WP centers, nontyping tasks are performed by administrative support personnel. WP/AS workers are usually organized either centrally or according to task or principal needs. Managers of WP/AS personnel should follow guidelines suggested throughout this book.

## *Review and Discussion Questions*

1. How does a traditional office differ from a modern office that has a WP/AS center?
2. Why is machine dictation recommended over dictating to a secretary or writing in longhand?
3. What is the major advantage of a WP system that has a separate input and output device?
4. Why has WP been met with resistance from management in so many firms?
5. What is the major advantage of CRT display over a paper display system?
6. Why would a WP operator choose to use carbon paper for two copies of a letter rather than to make the copies on a copy machine?
7. Why do you feel that AS personnel have not been organized centrally like WP personnel have?
8. Why do some personnel managers feel that WP is a giant step backward?
9. What impact has WP had on the setting of work standards in the office?

## *Application Exercises*

1. Visit a WP center in an office near your home or school. Notice the different machines that are used. Talk briefly with the authors, supervisors, and operators who are involved in the center. Make a list of their likes and dislikes about the center. Report your findings in class.
2. Invite a manager who has worked with both the traditional secretary and the WP/AS systems to talk with your class about the transition from the traditional office to the WP/AS office. Prepare a list of questions that you would like this manager to answer and discuss with you.
3. Read an article that pertains to word processing in a current business periodical. In the same periodical, look at all the advertisements that pertain to WP equipment. Write a summary of the article you read and be prepared to present the summary in class.

## *Mini-Case*

*Dillion Research Corp.* installed a WP center in their building six months ago after being persuaded by their administrative manager to do so. Sandy Lizak, the administrative manager, promised top management that WP would save time and personnel expense because work would be done faster and fewer people would be needed for secretarial tasks.

Sandy's manager recently asked her to prepare an analytical report showing the effectiveness and efficiency of the WP changeover and making any further recommendations she thinks are necessary. The research Sandy conducted to complete this report produced the following findings:

Except in three cases, principals have retained their personal secretaries who are performing AS and some typing functions.

Authors are generally pleased with the work produced by the WP center. Eighty-five percent agreed that the WP center work is produced more quickly than it was before WP was installed.

The company has actually experienced an increase of two secretarial personnel since WP was implemented.

WP personnel are receiving lower salaries than their AS counterparts.

Sixty-eight percent of the WP personnel expressed discontent because AS personnel are receiving higher wages but are not expected to work nearly as hard as the WP operators.

Nearly 50 percent of all potential principals use the WP center for producing typewritten materials.

Put yourself in Sandy's place. What problems do you see, and what would you recommend to your manager?

## Reference Note

1. Frank W. Malone, "How to Build Productivity and High Morale," *Modern Office Procedures*, March 1975, pp. 58–59. Reprinted from the March 1975 issue of *Modern Office Procedures* and copyright 1975 by Industrial Publishing Company, Division Pittway Corporation.

# 25

# Data Processing

Data processing is an exciting and challenging type of administrative service because of its close association with computers and technological development. As you will see later on, not all data processing is computerized or even mechanized, but the focus of attention is definitely on computers and automation. Data processing is fun and challenging because of the dynamic nature of computers and because of the potential for achieving new objectives. Understanding the basics of data processing and computers will enhance future career opportunities in administrative management.

Data processing relates to previous areas which have been discussed such as records management and word processing. You will recall from Chapter 22 that the primary purpose of records management is to develop an information system that readily supplies needed information to managers and others. Computer output microfilm (COM) and terminals, important elements in that records management system, are also important parts of data processing.

Word processing also relates directly to data processing in that computers are used in both areas. While the current emphasis in word processing is on magnetic typewriters, computers are likely to be used for word processing more extensively in the future.

## BASIC DATA OPERATIONS

Certain basic operations must be performed on data to create input media, to put data into usable form, and to get data into the hands of the user: (1) raw data collection, (2) input, (3) editing, (4) manipulation, (5) output, (6) storage, and (7) transmittal or communication. These basic operations are described in Table 25-1. These operations are necessary, regardless of what methods are used to process data.

*Information,* in data-processing terms, is data that has been processed into a usable form.

**Table 25-1. Basic Data Operations**

| *Operation* | *Explanation* | *Examples* |
|---|---|---|
| 1. Raw data collection | Collection or capture of data from a business transaction or similar event onto a source document or form | Written customer order<br>Sales slip<br>Survey form<br>Examination answer sheet |
| 2. Input | Movement of data and instructions into the data-processing system | Writing series of numbers to be added<br>Dictating of letter<br>Punching keys on calculator |
| 3. Editing | Verification of accuracy and consistency of data | Verifying punched cards<br>Checking sales figures |
| 4. Manipulation | Arithmetic, logical, and physical handling of data | Multiplying price of shirts times quantity sold<br>Sorting of products sold by salesperson<br>Comparing total invoices against customer's credit limit |
| 5. Output | Results of data-processing system obtained after input is processed | Computer printout<br>Finished letter, memo, or other document<br>Report<br>Form |
| 6. Storage | Retaining data or instruction for further use | Filing of purchase orders<br>Storage of data in computer memory<br>Filming of records on microfiche |
| 7. Transmittal or communication | Movement of data output to users | Mailing of letters<br>Distribution of reports<br>Sending of message by teletype<br>Making phone call to convey information |

Thus, the major purpose of data processing is to process data into information.

### Methods of Processing Data

When people think of data processing, they tend to think of computers. Actually, data have been processed since the early days of civilization, thousands of years before computers as we know them today were invented. Four basic methods may be used to process data:

1. Manual method
2. Mechanically assisted method
3. Tabulating method
4. Computer method

With the manual method, data may be manipulated completely within the mind of an individual, or individuals may use pencil and paper to assist in making calculations and keeping track of data. The mechanically assisted method involves limited use of machinery. For example, you may use an adding machine or a calculator to make computations.

When organizations found that these first two methods were not capable of handling all the data that required processing, new methods were developed. In the late 1800s, the U.S. Census Bureau did not have adequate time to process census data before it was time to have a new census. In response to this need, Herman Hollerith and James Powers invented the punched card and the tabulating system in the 1880s. The punched card tabulating system operates on the principle that holes in cards can represent numbers and letters according to the Hollerith code (see Figure 25-1). Note that numbers have only a single punch in a numbered row. Alphabetic characters (letters)

| Row on card | Numeric or alphabetic character | | | | | | | | | | | | | | | | | | | | | | | | | | | | | | | | | | | |
|---|---|---|---|---|---|---|---|---|---|---|---|---|---|---|---|---|---|---|---|---|---|---|---|---|---|---|---|---|---|---|---|---|---|---|---|---|
| | 0 | 1 | 2 | 3 | 4 | 5 | 6 | 7 | 8 | 9 | A | B | C | D | E | F | G | H | I | J | K | L | M | N | O | P | Q | R | S | T | U | V | W | X | Y | Z |
| 12 | | | | | | | | | | | X | X | X | X | X | X | X | X | X | | | | | | | | | | | | | | | | | |
| 11 | | | | | | | | | | | | | | | | | | | | X | X | X | X | X | X | X | X | X | | | | | | | | |
| 0 | X | | | | | | | | | | | | | | | | | | | | | | | | | | | | X | X | X | X | X | X | X | X |
| 1 | | X | | | | | | | | | X | | | | | | | | | X | | | | | | | | | | | | | | | | |
| 2 | | | X | | | | | | | | | X | | | | | | | | | X | | | | | | | | X | | | | | | | |
| 3 | | | | X | | | | | | | | | X | | | | | | | | | X | | | | | | | | X | | | | | | |
| 4 | | | | | X | | | | | | | | | X | | | | | | | | | X | | | | | | | | X | | | | | |
| 5 | | | | | | X | | | | | | | | | X | | | | | | | | | X | | | | | | | | X | | | | |
| 6 | | | | | | | X | | | | | | | | | X | | | | | | | | | X | | | | | | | | X | | | |
| 7 | | | | | | | | X | | | | | | | | | X | | | | | | | | | X | | | | | | | | X | | |
| 8 | | | | | | | | | X | | | | | | | | | X | | | | | | | | | X | | | | | | | | X | |
| 9 | | | | | | | | | | X | | | | | | | | | X | | | | | | | | | X | | | | | | | | X |

*Figure 25-1.* Hollerith Code

(Each X designates a punched hole. Example: punches in rows 12 and 1 = A.)

have two punches in one column. For example, the letter "C" is designated by a punch in the "12" row plus a punch in the "3" row. Figure 25-2 shows a standard, 80-column IBM card and a smaller, more compact 96-column card. The three basic machines found in a punched card system are the *key punch machine*, *sorter*, and *tabulator* or *accounting machine*. The punched card system helped organizations process data at the rate of hundreds of cards per minute. Recently, this system has been almost totally replaced by computer systems.

The computer is a much faster and economical method of processing data than the tabulating method. The first true electronic computer, the ENIAC, was developed in 1946. The first electronic computer used for commercial purposes was installed in 1954. Computers are basically of two types: digital and analog. *Digital computers* count numbers and are primarily used in business. *Analog computers* measure variables and are primarily used for scientific

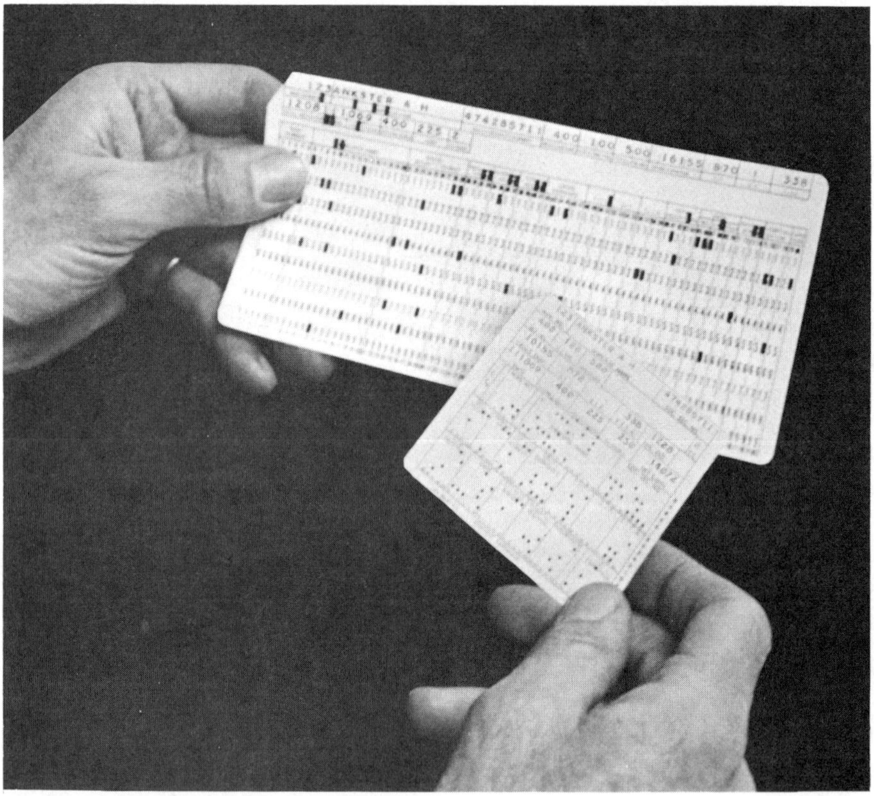

*Figure 25-2.* IBM Punched Cards

*Source:* International Business Machines Corporation

research. This chapter will refer to digital computers because of their relationship to business; an electronic digital computer is shown in Figure 25-3.

## COMPUTERIZED DATA PROCESSING

Any consideration of data processing tends to focus automatically on the computer. In this section, the following topics pertaining to computers will be discussed: important characteristics, development, impact, and applications.

*Figure 25-3.* A Typical Computer Center

*Source:* S. Rothman and C. Mosmann, *Computers and Society,* 2d ed. (Chicago: Science Research Associates, 1976), p. 10.

### Characteristics

The two key features of the computer that set it apart from other forms of data processing are (1) speed and (2) program and data storage capability.

To give you an idea of how fast the computer operates, the following example is given. The problem is calculation of density and velocity of air at mesh points on an aircraft wing section involving eight million calculations. An individual using pencil and paper would take about 15 years to complete this problem. By using a calculator, the problem could be completed in about 80 weeks. The first commercial computer installed in 1954 could solve the problem in 16 minutes; but, in addition, one week would be required to program the computer. The modern computer has been improved in efficiency to the point where the problem can now be completed in about 2 seconds with one day to do the programming.[1]

Computer printers type out reports or listings of information at a rate of up to two thousand lines per minute. Processing time is measured in terms of *nanoseconds*, which are billionths of a second, or on some computers in terms of *pecoseconds*, trillionths of a second. Do you have any concept of how fast a nanosecond is? Perhaps this comparison will help:

A nanosecond is to a second as a second is to 32 years.

A pecosecond is one thousand times faster than a nanosecond.

A pecosecond is to a second as a second is to 32,000 years.

The second major feature of the computer is the program and data storage capability. This concept simply means that the computer stores or holds its own instructions internally to allow it to complete the processing on a problem or a series of problems. All possible combinations of circumstances must be considered and provided for with specific, detailed program instructions. The program flowchart shown in Figure 25-4 shows the instructions for a typical inventory program. The stored program allows the computer to operate, uninterrupted, until the desired results are obtained. Also, the computer holds large quantities of data that are being processed.

For the administrative manager, this program and data storage capability has three primary implications:

1. Storage of large quantities of data. The computer is capable of storing millions of items of data in several types of media in a relatively small amount of space. For example, records providing extensive information on 25,000 people can all be stored on one reel of magnetic tape.
2. Retrieval of data. Without leaving his or her desk, the administrative manager can have access to any part of this large amount of stored data almost instantly by means of a terminal.
3. Storage of complex and varied instructions. The computer can store in one place all of the job instructions and decision criteria used by many people in many different offices.

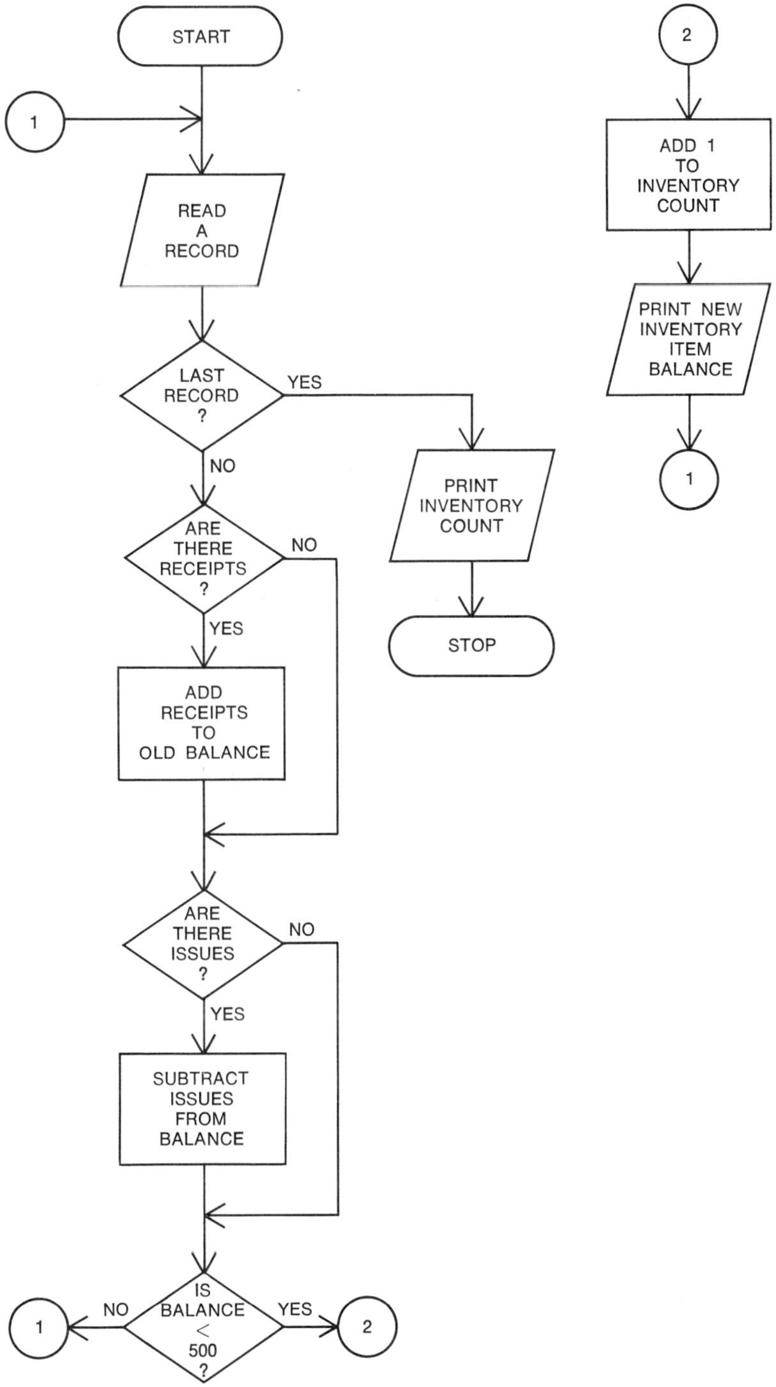


*Figure 25-4.* A Modified Inventory Listing Flowchart

*Source:* Thomas Dock and Edward Essick, *Principles of Business Data Processing*, 2d ed. (Chicago: Science Research Associates, 1974), p. 232.

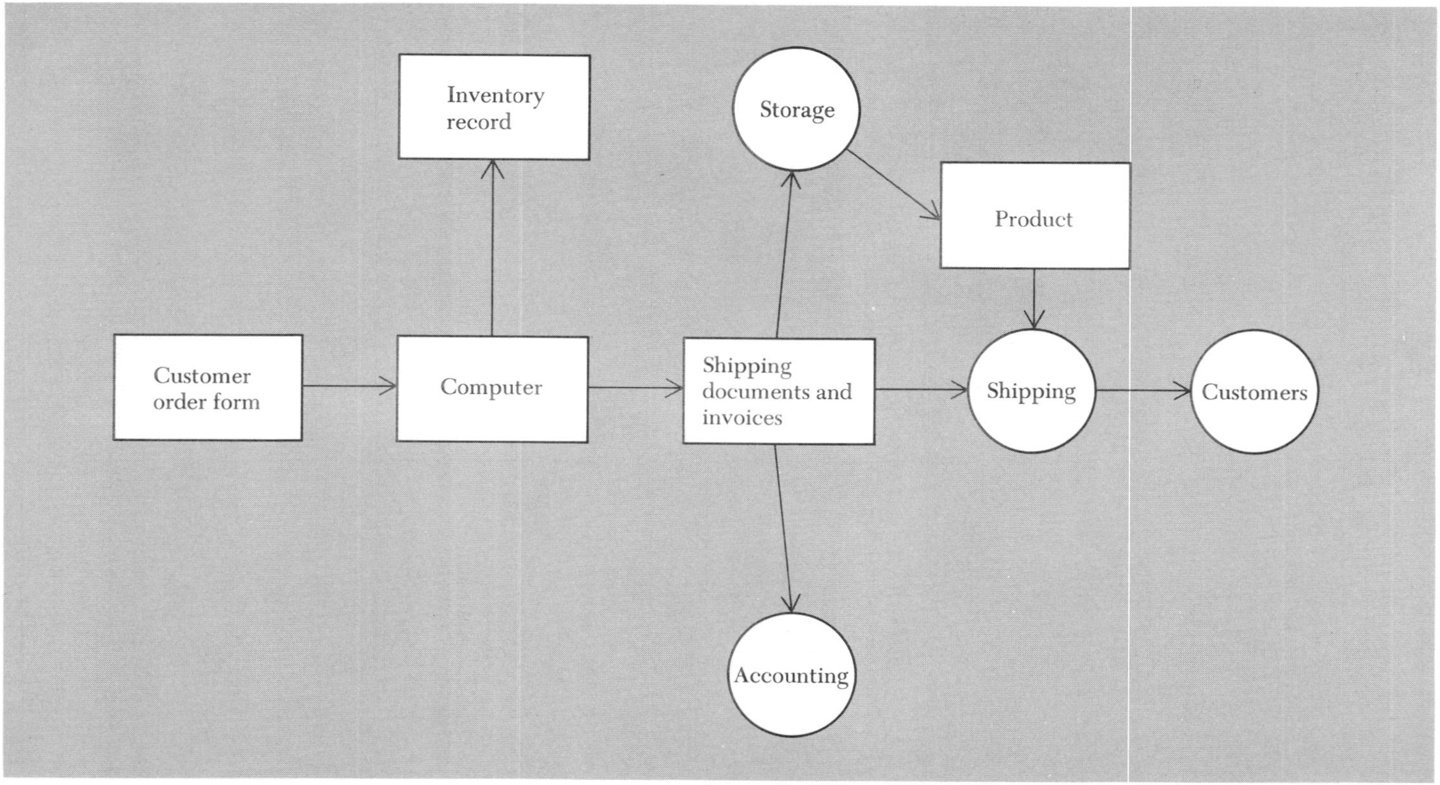


*Figure 25-5.* How the Computer Processes Customer Orders

Figure 25-5 shows how the computer is used to process customer orders. If the customer has ordered two dozen ball-point pens, stock number 45897, at $4.25 per dozen, the computer can perform the following functions:

Calculate price ($8.50)

Add price of other items

Verify accuracy of information

Reduce inventory of pens SN 45897 by 24

Prepare shipping documents (invoices, shipping, notices, and labels) to go to warehouse, shipping section, billing departments, and accounts receivable department (accounting function that keeps track of the amount of money owed to the company)

Post customer accounts with amount owed

### Development

With the advent of computers, the capability of processing data was increased fantastically. The computer industry has developed very rapidly through four generations:

1. *First generation*, 1950–1955. Characterized by the use of vacuum tubes. (Vacuum tubes are relatively large electronic tubes similar to those found in early radio and television sets.)
2. *Second generation*, 1955–1964. Involved use of transistors and diodes that reduced distance and increased speed. (Transistors and diodes are small electronic devices similar to those found in radio and television sets.)
3. *Third generation*, 1964–1969. Introduced microminiaturized circuits that further reduced distances and increased speeds. (Microminiaturized circuits are extremely small electronic devices similar to those found in electronic radar ovens.)
4. *Fourth generation*, 1970–. Involves use of "virtual storage," a method for increasing storage capacity, and microprogramming, which involves the rapid assembly and use of complex processing and control operations.

A development that has had special impact on business is the *minicomputer.* Minicomputers are compact computers that sell for a price of $5,000 to $50,000 and rent for $300 to $1,200 per month. A comparison of prices for various sizes of computers is given in Table 25-2 to help you understand the relationship of the cost of minicomputers to other classes of computers. Their capabilities and storage capacities are naturally limited, but quite often they are well suited to the smaller business. For example, a small business that has used either a manual processing method or a punched card system can readily benefit from the use of minicomputers.

**Table 25-2. Comparison of Computer Prices**

| *Computer* | *Rental cost range ($)* | *Purchase price range ($)* |
|---|---|---|
| Micro | not applicable | 20–500 |
| Mini | 300–1,200 | 5,000–50,000 |
| Small | 1,000–5,000 | 50,000–200,000 |
| Medium | 5,000–20,000 | 200,000–1,000,000 |
| Large | 20,000–250,000 | 1,000,000+ |

Large and small companies are making good use of minicomputers with a concept known as *distributive processing.* A distributive processing network is the linking together of two or more minicomputers with each other or with a large central computer. Each minicomputer has the ability to process data independently and to communicate with other computers in the system. According to Charles Ritley, managing editor of *Modern Office Procedures,* distributive-processing networks have several advantages over large central computers:

1. *Cost.* It may cost less in the long run to purchase several minis outright than to pay a perpetual rental on a large mainframe plus terminals.
2. *Adaptability.* Where different locations have business problems far different from the corporate headquarters, or from other locations, it is easier for each to have its own unique systems than to try to adopt a standard corporate system that all can use. Because of the communications capability, each unique system can still communicate the data that corporate management needs.
3. *Reliability.* Processing power is spread out so that failure of a central computer site will not shut down the entire corporation.
4. *Flexibility.* Minis can be added to the network at will without radical restructuring of the central system.[2]

Another development that has had special impact on small organizations in gaining the advantages of automated data processing is the service center. For a fee, the service center will perform computer services using its own large computer facilities. Large organizations that have their own computers can also use the service center when an overload of work occurs. With this system, the expensive cost of computer operations can be shared by a number of users.

*Time sharing* is another way of spreading the large cost of computers among several users. When an organization or part of an organization that owns or leases a computer is not using it, that organization may choose to allow other users to buy time on the computer. Time sharing allows both the owner and the guest users to reduce their costs.

### Impact of Computers

The computer industry has grown to the point that computers affect the lives of almost everyone. If you will stop to reflect for a few minutes, you will soon realize that almost everything you do is directly or indirectly related to computers. If you go on a shopping trip, for example, you will note that you are driving a car that is dependent upon a computer, to some extent, for design, manufacture, and marketing. The traffic signals may be controlled by a computer. The advertisements you read may have had the printing type set by a computer. The store inventory has been controlled by a computer. The clerk has been paid by a computer. The check you write will be processed by a computer. Even though you may not fully recognize the fact, computers have become an important part of your life. In addition to those areas previously mentioned, computers play an important part in education, space development, medicine, and criminology. Business, industry, and government simply would not be able to operate today without computers.

What impact have computers had on office employment and on office jobs? The answer to this question is that no one really knows definitely. A number of factors in addition to office automation affect the number of clerical workers employed. For example, economic conditions, competition, and increased record keeping and paper work requirements all have an effect. Therefore, one cannot really be certain how much employment shifts are caused by automation and how much by other factors.

Several facts do bear on this question, however. Office automation has been aimed, in addition to other objectives, at reducing the number of low-level clerical functions. On the other hand, according to the *Occupational Outlook Handbook* in 1974, there were 15 million clerical workers. "Employment of clerical workers is expected to increase faster than the average of all occupations through the mid-1980's." The number of clerical workers is expected to increase by one-third for a total of 20 million by 1985. About 1 million job openings will occur each year as a result of death, retirement, and termination in addition to new jobs created.[3] Also, in 1976, for the first time, the white-collar work force constituted more than 50 percent of the total work force.[4] Thus, you can see that office automation has not had much impact on reducing the total number of clerical jobs. Automation may have reduced the number of clerical jobs that would have been necessary had computers not been introduced.

What has happened has been some shifting by employees from clerical occupations to higher level positions such as computer operators, programmers, and systems analysts. In addition, new personnel have been brought in to fill these computer occupations. A study made by the U.S. Department of Labor reviewed 20 companies that had introduced computers and directly affected 2,800 employees. After one year, the employees were affected as follows:

933 (33%) reassigned to new positions in the company

467 (17%) retired or quit

1,391 (50%) remained on old jobs

9 (0.00%) laid off after year of automation.[5]

Perhaps the real impact of office automation is yet to come. Managers are currently becoming aware of the great cost of clerical processing and are starting to look seriously at the possibilities of reducing these costs through office automation. Office employees who are alert to the trends and who are sufficiently flexible to accept new assignments and retraining should have no problem in retaining good employment.

In the long run, many executives feel that computers don't tend to save their organization money, but they do provide increased capability. Organizations are able to do things that simply would not have been possible before the advent of the computer.

Managers have found that they generally spend less time on the controlling function and on routine decision making and more time on planning and leadership. They have to have more technical know-how, but they are not required to store as much business data in their brains. Instead, data are stored in the computer, and on an as-needed basis, the manager can obtain information from the computer.

With the flood of computer information that is becoming available, someone must assume responsibility for managing it and making it usable. Otherwise managers would be inundated. The administrative manager is the logical person to assume this role, and these managers have been affected greatly by computers. If they rise to the challenge, they will become a key link in the organization.

## APPLICATION

Computers can be used as a tool to assist in accomplishing most office activities. For example, the computer prepares routine reports, makes labels, keeps track of inventory, and prepares delivery forms [see Figure 25-6 (a) and (b)]. Since the objective of administrative management is to provide further information to top management for decision-making purposes, it follows that the major role of the computer will be to process information that will eventually be used by management for making decisions. Management cannot possibly use all of the information that the computer is capable of producing. Therefore, the role of the administrative manager is to find ways that the data

# COMPOSITE INVENTORY STOCK STATUS REPORT

| CAT NO | ITEM NUMBER | DESCRIPTION | REORDER POINT | REORDER QUANTITY | OPENING STOCK | VENDOR RECEIPTS | STOCK ORDERS | COMMITTED STOCK | SALES ISSUES | BACK ORDERS | VENDOR RETURNS | STOCK TRANSFERS | CURRENT STOCK |
|---|---|---|---|---|---|---|---|---|---|---|---|---|---|
| DMT | 074132 | RUBBER BAND - #11, 4 LB | 5.500 | 1.000 | 8.627 | 6.000 | 1.000 | 13.671 | 13.671 | | | | 956 |
| GSH | 641039 | CLIPS, PAPER - JUM(100) | 1.000 | 500 | 4.562 | | | 2.051 | 2.051 | | | | 2.511 |
| LMR | 783439 | KIMWIPES - #900L | 4.200 | 1.000 | 9.555 | | 5.000 | 7.452 | 7.452 | | | | 2.103 |
| FGY | 310293 | BOOKEND - METAL, 1 PR | 4.600 | 200 | 5.624 | | 6.000 | 5.024 | 5.024 | | | | 0 |
| HZQ | 803417 | ENVELOPES - MAN., 9X12 | 3.000 | 1.000 | 7.439 | 8.000 | | 11.952 | 6.452 | 5.000 | | | 3.487 |
| MCZ | 452362 | MARKER - RED, GREASE | 2.500 | 500 | 7.828 | | | 3.223 | 3.223 | | | | 4.605 |
| GBN | 283684 | CARDS, FILE - 5X8(100) | 3.000 | 1.000 | 8.403 | | | 6.415 | 6.415 | | | | 1.988 |
| KMR | 673846 | GLUE - RUBBER, 4 OZ | 3.500 | 500 | 6.230 | | 3.000 | 5.033 | 5.033 | | | | 1.197 |
| POC | 415666 | OPENER, LETTER | 3.000 | 200 | 7.015 | | | 3.851 | 3.851 | | | | 3.164 |
| GSB | 724833 | CLIPS, PAPER - #1(100) | 5.000 | 1.000 | 18.415 | | 10.000 | 15.722 | 15.722 | | | 3.010 | 4.703 |
| LLP | 648291 | KIMWIPES - #900S | 5.300 | 1.000 | 12.410 | | 5.000 | 8.732 | 8.732 | | | 3.400 | 3.678 |
| FAE | 783103 | BLOTTER - WHITE, 1 DOZ | 2.500 | 300 | 6.239 | 900 | | 3.039 | 3.039 | | | 374 | 4.474 |
| HMX | 308616 | ENVELOPES - MAN., 6X9 | 5.000 | 1.000 | 16.452 | | 5.000 | 11.674 | 11.674 | | | | 4.778 |
| MCR | 491383 | LEAD - #9030-5H | 5.000 | 1.000 | 10.571 | | 3.000 | 5.782 | 5.782 | | 2.000 | | 2.789 |
| FMX | 341298 | CARDS, FILE - 3X5(100) | 3.000 | 1.000 | 8.403 | 4.000 | | 14.303 | 12.303 | 2.000 | 2.020 | | 3.973 |
| JCC | 417868 | GLUE - WHITE, 3 OZ | 3.000 | 1.000 | 9.871 | | 4.000 | 8.415 | 8.415 | | | | 1.456 |
| NZY | 892303 | NOTEBOOK - COMPOSITION | 300 | 100 | 7.924 | 4.000 | | 6.557 | 6.557 | | | | 4.737 |
| GSA | 892340 | CHALK - YELLOW, 12/BOX | 4.000 | 1.000 | 11.753 | | 5.000 | 10.831 | 10.831 | | | | 922 |
| LLN | 672301 | INK, STAMP PAD - RED | 3.000 | 100 | 4 503 | 1.600 | | 2.782 | 2.782 | | | | 3.321 |
| DTA | 843713 | BINDERS - 3 RING,BLUE | 1.300 | 500 | 4.733 | | 1.000 | 3.452 | 3.452 | | | | 1.281 |
| HMT | 405607 | CORRECTION FLUID | 1.200 | 100 | 3.450 | 500 | 2.000 | 3.513 | 3.413 | 1.000 | | | 437 |
| MBY | 515678 | LEAD - #9030-3H | 5.000 | 1.000 | 12.222 | 4.000 | | 6.430 | 6.430 | | | 3.000 | 12.792 |
| FMA | 309814 | CALENDAR REFILL | 5.000 | 2.000 | 2 749 | 6.000 | | 14.345 | 10.345 | 4.000 | | | 4.404 |
| JBV | 705706 | ERASER - PINK, #101 | 4.600 | 1.000 | 8.293 | | 5.000 | 6.727 | 6.727 | | | 1.200 | 2.766 |
| NSB | 437758 | NOTEBOOK - STENO | 4.200 | 100 | 6.788 | 3.000 | | 4.469 | 4.469 | | | | 5.519 |
| GMY | 642102 | CHALK - WHITE, 12/BOX | 4.000 | 1.000 | 13.455 | 1.000 | 3.000 | 12.456 | 12.456 | | | | 1.999 |
| KSA | 409888 | INK, STAMP PAD - BLK | 4.150 | 300 | 7.063 | | 3.000 | 5.833 | 3.833 | 2.000 | | | 1.230 |
| DPR | 690301 | BINDERS - 3 RING, BLK | 1.300 | 500 | 3.567 | | 2.000 | 3.567 | 3.567 | | | | 0 |
| GYA | 725356 | CLIP BOARD | 500 | 150 | 2.513 | 1.200 | | 1.672 | 1.672 | | | | 2.041 |
| MAB | 717444 | LEAD - #9030-2H | 5.000 | 1.000 | 16.293 | 6.000 | | 14.339 | 12.329 | 2.010 | | | 7.954 |
| FGY | 418328 | CALENDAR BASE | 4.300 | 100 | 8.452 | | 3.700 | 8.284 | 5.284 | 3.000 | | | 168 |
| JBV | 313804 | ERASER, CHALK | 2.500 | 500 | 6.751 | 2.496 | | 5.370 | 4.370 | 1.000 | | | 3.677 |
| NRA | 832747 | MARKER - BLUE, GREASE | 2.500 | 500 | 6.732 | | | 3.017 | 3.017 | | | | 3.715 |
| GMV | 731890 | CEMENT, RUBBER - 4 OZ | 3.500 | 500 | 7.632 | | | 6.232 | 4.732 | 1.500 | | | 1.400 |
| KNX | 458374 | INK, DRAWING - BLK, 1 OZ | 5.200 | 500 | 9.323 | | 7.000 | 9.316 | 9.316 | | | | 7 |
| DMT | 074132 | RUBBER BAND - #11, 4 LB | 5.500 | 1.000 | 8.627 | 6.000 | 1.000 | 13.671 | 13.671 | | | | 956 |

*Figure 25-6.* Routine Computer Reports—Inventory and Deliveries

CUSTOMER DELIVERIES PAGE 4

MEMPHIS REGION
TERRITORY-520
BAXTER

(EQUIV UNITS) PERIOD ENDING 12- 0

| PRODUCT DESCRIPTION | THIS MO | THIS YR CUM | + OR - CUM LY | JAN LY | FEB LY |
|---|---|---|---|---|---|
| TOTAL FRANKENBERRY | 173 | 1,006 | 101 | 90 | 99 |
| COUNT CHOCULA 12 | 240 | 1,427 | 198 | 140 | 132 |
| TOTAL COUNT CHOC | 240 | 1,427 | 198 | 140 | 132 |
| BOO BERRY 12 | 131 | 864 | 256 | 73 | 74 |
| TOTAL BOO*BERRY | 131 | 864 | 256 | 73 | 74 |
| FRUIT BRUTE 12 | 107 | 731 | 66 | 49 | 58 |
| TOTAL FRUIT BRUTE | 107 | 731 | 66 | 49 | 58 |
| TOTAL MONSTERS | 651 | 4,028 | 621 | 352 | 363 |
| LCKY CHRM PRSWT 14 | 255 | 1,580 | 665 | 132 | 173 |
| LCKY CHRM PRESWTND 9 | 210 | 1,059 | 38 | 120 | 82 |
| TOTAL LUCKY CHARMS | 465 | 2,639 | 703 | 252 | 255 |
| TOTAL KABOOM | 0 | 0 | -263 | 0 | 0 |
| GOLDEN GRAHAMS 9 | 0 | 0 | -563 | 147 | 196 |
| GOLDEN GRAHAMS 10 | 231 | 1,729 | 1,729 | 0 | 0 |
| TOTAL GOLDEN GRAHM | 231 | 1,729 | 1,166 | 147 | 196 |
| TOTAL FAMILY | 3,602 | 22,377 | 3,473 | 1,971 | 2,244 |
| GRANOLA BAR H & O | 247 | 506 | 506 | 0 | 0 |
| GRANOLA BAR COCONUT | 158 | 417 | 417 | 0 | 0 |
| TOTAL GRANOLA BAR | 405 | 923 | 923 | 0 | 0 |
| TOTAL BIG G NEWENT | 405 | 923 | 923 | 0 | 0 |
| TOTAL B G DIVISION | 5,537 | 35,438 | 5,833 | 2,991 | 3,570 |
| GMKT PL 10LB | 48 | 423 | -13 | 60 | 51 |
| GMKT SR 10LB | 96 | 672 | 129 | 84 | 71 |
| TOTAL GMKT 10LB | 144 | 1,095 | 116 | 144 | 122 |
| GMKT PL 5LB | 1,132 | 5,154 | 2,734 | 226 | 246 |
| GMKT S.R. 5LB | 1,080 | 6,659 | 3,689 | 469 | 384 |
| GMKT UNBLEACHED 5LB | 128 | 692 | 219 | 24 | 92 |
| TOTAL GMKT 5LB | 2,340 | 12,505 | 6,642 | 719 | 722 |
| GMKT WHOLE WHEAT 5LB | 65 | 449 | 97 | 61 | 78 |
| TOTAL WHOLE WHEAT | 65 | 449 | 97 | 61 | 78 |
| GMKT PL 2LB | 96 | 462 | 66 | 45 | 41 |
| GMKT S.R. 2LB | 41 | 388 | 15 | 42 | 53 |
| TOTAL GMKT 2LB | 137 | 850 | 81 | 87 | 94 |
| TOTAL GMKT PKG | 2,686 | 14,899 | 6,936 | 1,011 | 1,016 |

*Figure 25-6, continued*

can be simplified and summarized into meaningful informational reports. Managers at the top of the organization will need less detailed information than those managers lower in the organization. An illustration showing various levels of information is found in Table 25-3.

The current trend in the computer world is to find ways of making the computer more useful to people by adapting the computer to meet their

**Table 25-3. Organizing Information According to Level of Management**

| *Level of management* | *Level of detail for reports* | *Examples* |
|---|---|---|
| Top | Overall summary for entire organization | Weekly sales by sales district and product |
| Middle | Detailed summary for department | Weekly summary of sales by sales district, product, and customer |
| Supervisory | Operational detail for section | Daily sales transactions by stock numbers, salespersons, and customer |

needs and abilities. The trend is moving away from expecting people to adapt themselves to meet the requirements of the computer. For example, in the past, people have had to learn special languages in order to work with the computer. These languages, known as programming languages, give instructions to the computer that will be understood and acted on by the computer. Programming languages are currently being developed that are similar to ordinary language so that the average person will be able to interact with the computer without first having received specialized training. As this trend develops, the computer will be applied more frequently in all phases of everyone's life. (Chapter 26 will describe in more detail what you can expect in the office of the future.)

## COMPUTER SYSTEMS—HOW THEY WORK

Prior to the computer beginning its operation, a systems person develops a computer system that is designed to meet a need, solve a problem, or achieve an information handling objective. The administrative manager works closely with the systems person to insure that the proper information in a useful form is generated. Based on the system, programs or detailed sets of instructions to the computer are developed by the programmer.

After the business transaction or other event has occurred, data are collected on a source document (a form or report that contains detailed business data). From the source document, input media are prepared. This process is shown in Figure 25-7.

Figure 25-8 gives you the overall framework of the computer system. Notice that after these first two steps of developing the system and preparing input media, the first step directly associated with the computer is insertion of input.

Sales ticket

| Item stock number | Quantity | Price | Cost |
|---|---|---|---|
| 12487 | 4 | .50 | 2.00 |
| 13719 | 2 | 2.50 | 5.00 |
| 27911 | 1 | 4.87 | 4.87 |

Date: 091179
Customer: 4879

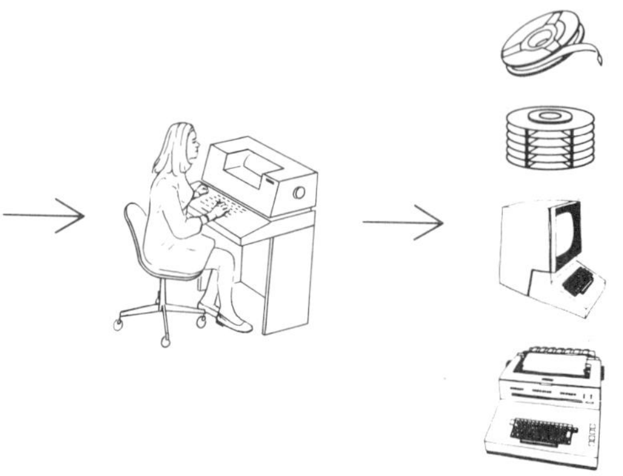

Source document    Data entry    Input media

*Figure 25-7.* Converting Source Document to Input Media for the Computer

**Input**

Input consists of instructions and data that are conveyed by some form of input media such as punched cards, punched paper tape, magnetic tape, and magnetic disks. Punched cards have been the most popular form of input media because they were formerly used with punched card or tabulating systems. In Figure 25-2 you saw a standard punched card and a smaller punched card that has greater capacity than the standard card. Punched cards are read into the computer on a card reader unit, shown in Figure 25-9.

Magnetic forms of media have become popular because of greater speed and capacity than paper cards or tape. Magnetic media are likely to replace punched cards in the future as the most popular form of input media. Data may be entered on magnetic media in two ways: (1) either by a person using a special magnetic data entry machine or (2) data contained in computer storage may be read out onto magnetic media.

Magnetic tape is used extensively as input media. Similar to the tape you use on your own tape recorder, magnetic tape records data as magnetized spots. A magnetic tape drive (a machine used for reading and recording magnetic tape) is illustrated in Figure 25-10. To understand the capacity and speed at which these magnetic tape devices operate, consider the following facts. One reel of tape contains the equivalent of over one million fully punched standard cards. The computer can read this tape at a maximum of one-fifth of a million numbers or letters (characters) per second.

Magnetic disks are also a major type of input media. They look like phonograph records (see Figure 25-11); they are magnetized on both sides and continuously rotate for reading and recording. A disk pack looks like a pot that

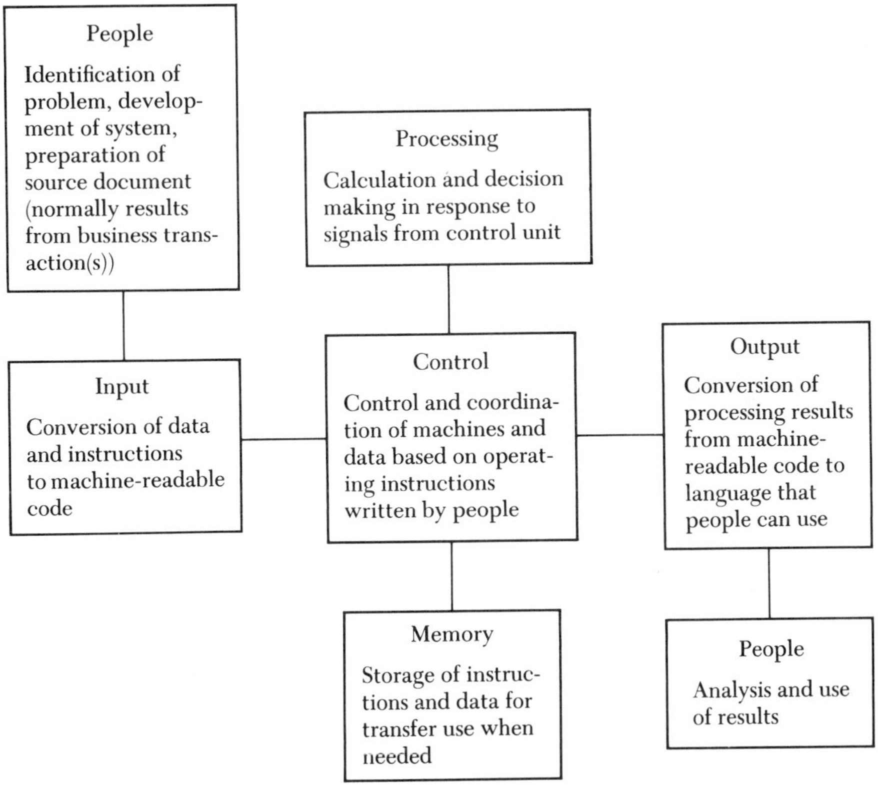


*Figure 25-8.* Framework for a Computer System

contains a set of disks; the pack is interchangeable with other packs. Each disk unit could store 100 million storage characters (alphabetic or numeric symbols) or 62 books that are more than 500 pages in length. Disks also have random access capability.

*Random access* is the ability to go directly to any part of an input-storage device without having to read through previous data to get to that particular item of data.

Magnetic tape, for example, does not have random access. If the tape were recorded in alphabetical order, you would have to read through the entire tape to get to the name of Joe Zabrisky. Magnetic disks are a good example of random access devices. If you wanted to play a specific song on a stereo record, you have random access because you can go directly to the song you want to play. With a tape recorder, you must move through the tape song by song until you come to the one you desire to hear.

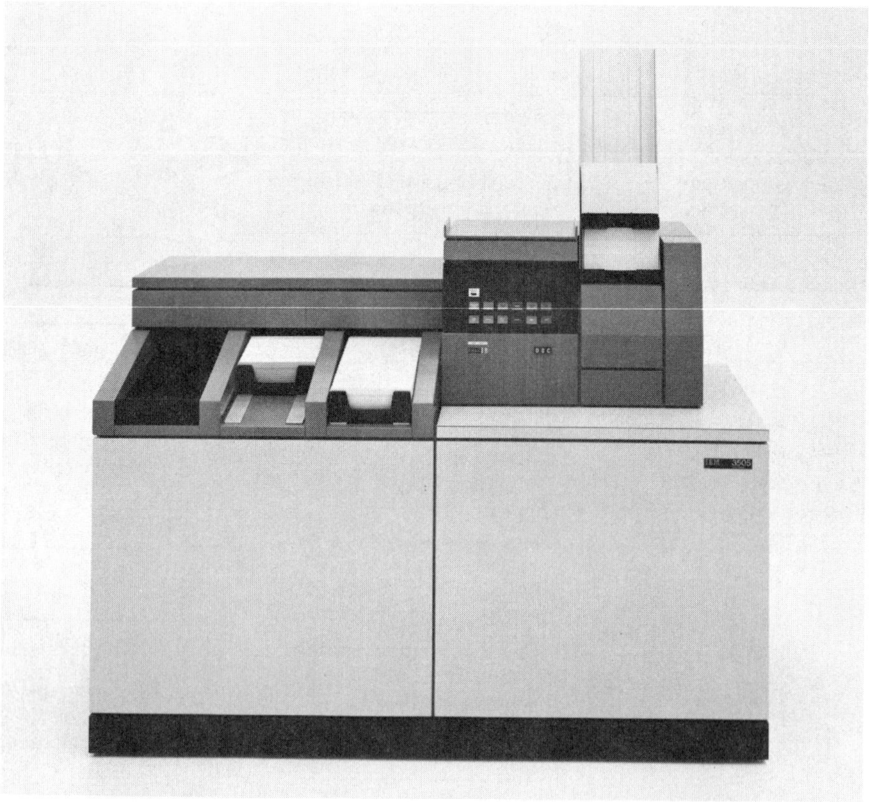

*Figure 25-9.* Card Reader Unit

*Source:* International Business Machines Corporation

The *optical character reader* (OCR) (see Figure 25-12) is a machine that eliminates the need for manual key punching. The OCR can read printed or typed data at the rate of 2,000 letter-size documents per hour onto magnetic tape, which can then be read directly into the computer. This machine is very reliable, but is also costly. Its major advantage is the elimination of the slow process of manually punching the data.

Terminals (see Figure 25-13) are becoming a major means of inputting into the computer. Data and instructions are typed on a keyboard and then the information that is fed into the computer appears in typed form on paper or on a cathode-ray tube (CRT) screen. In addition, instructions are received from the computer.

Let's look at a business example to see how the terminal is used typically. A customer who desires to buy a particular typewriter may call an office supply company to determine if the store has that particular model in stock and, if

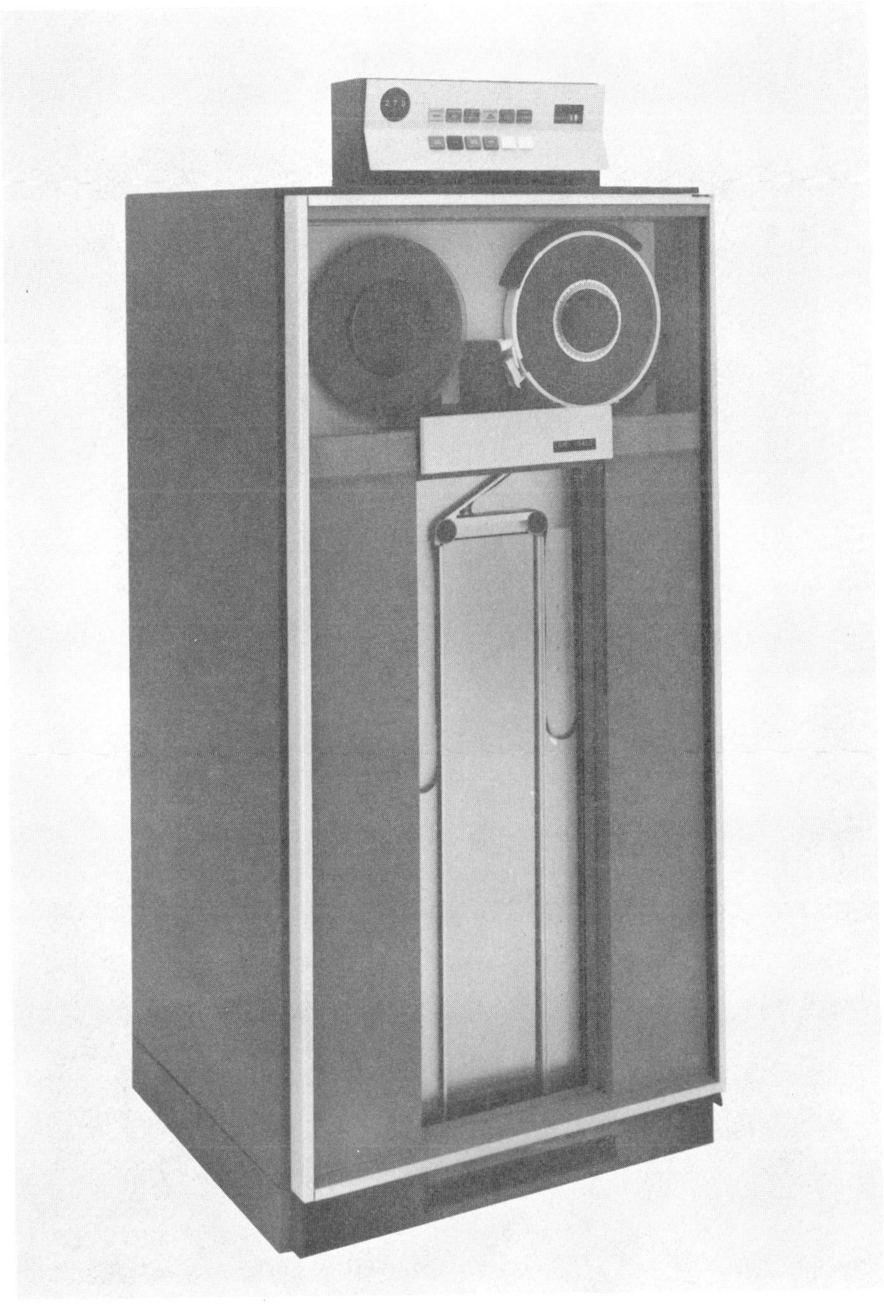

*Figure 25-10.* Magnetic Tape Drive
*Source:* International Business Machines Corporation

*Figure 25-11.* Magnetic Disk Pack
*Source:* International Business Machines Corporation

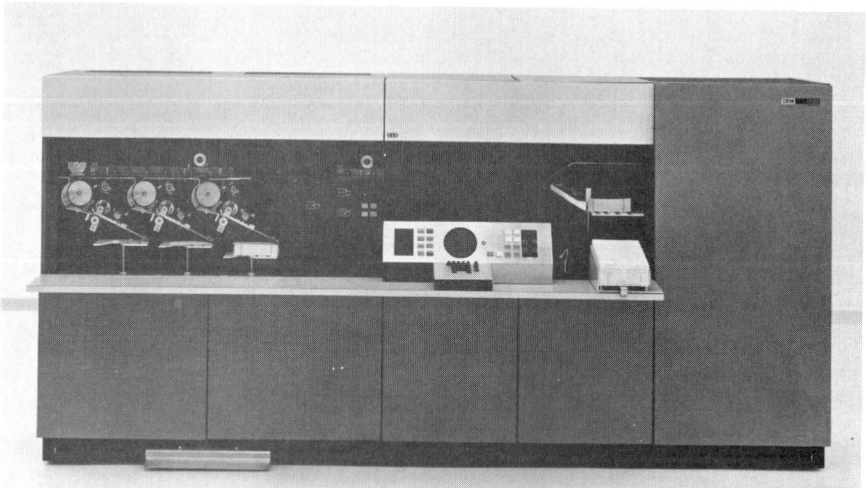

*Figure 25-12.* Optical Character Reader (OCR)
*Source:* International Business Machines Corporation

*Figure 25-13.* Cathode-Ray Tube (CRT) Terminal
*Source:* International Business Machines Corporation

so, what the price is. The clerk keys a special code on that model, number in stock, price, discount, availability if on back order. If the customer has ordered before, his or her credit rating may be displayed. The customer then has a choice of ordering the item over the phone or of going to the store to make the purchase. If the customer decides to order, the clerk obtains the necessary information from the customer about his or her account number, address, and phone number; and quantity, model, color, and other information about the product desired. This information is keyed into the computer via the terminal, and shortly the shipment is on its way to the customer. Let's see how the computer processes information.

**Processing**

Control, memory, and processing are all included in processing. A computer controls its own processing, stores its instructions, and manipulates data under the direction of the user.

The control unit serves as a computer traffic cop. It directs the movement of all data and instructions into, within, and out of the computer. The control unit causes the data to be read into memory, moves data from memory to the processing unit, returns them to storage, and directs the printing of data as output.

The memory or storage unit stores data, instructions, and intermediate results until they are needed for processing or for output. Magnetic core storage is currently the major form of internal storage because access time to this storage is very rapid. Magnetic core storage is a series of doughnut-shaped rings that are charged positively or negatively (see Figure 25-14). Other forms of storage, such as thin film, plated wire, and sheet ferrite, will be used more frequently in the future because they are less costly and easier to manufacture. Other developments such as memory chips will lead toward larger storage capacities and faster processing speeds. *The Wall Street Journal* reports that one electronic chip, one-fourth the size of a postage stamp, can retain all of the information contained on one page of the *Journal*. In the future, molecules may be used to store data, and the contents of the Library of Con-

*Figure 25-14.* Magnetic Core Storage

*Source.* Honeywell Information Systems, Inc.

gress might be stored in an area the size of the head of a pin.[6] External storage devices include: punched cards, punched paper tape, magnetic disk, magnetic tape, magnetic cards, and magnetic drums. Each item of data stored in the computer has an *address* that identifies the storage location.

The processing unit is housed with control and memory in the central processing unit (CPU) (see Figure 25-15). Its functions are to perform addition, subtraction, multiplication, and division operations and to make logical decisions such as determining if one number is equal to, greater than, or less than another number. Also, the data are manipulated internally. Data may be sorted into appropriate categories and common items may be matched. The editing function is used to modify the form or format of the data. All of these functions are performed at very rapid speeds according to a detailed set of instructions known as a program.

A *program* gives step-by-step directions on how the computer will process a particular type of problem. Once the program has been developed, it can be used over and over for similar types of problems, because all possible eventualities have been considered in the program. The computer can do only what it is told to do. It cannot think for itself.

*Figure 25-15.* Central Processing Unit (CPU)
*Source:* International Business Machines Corporation

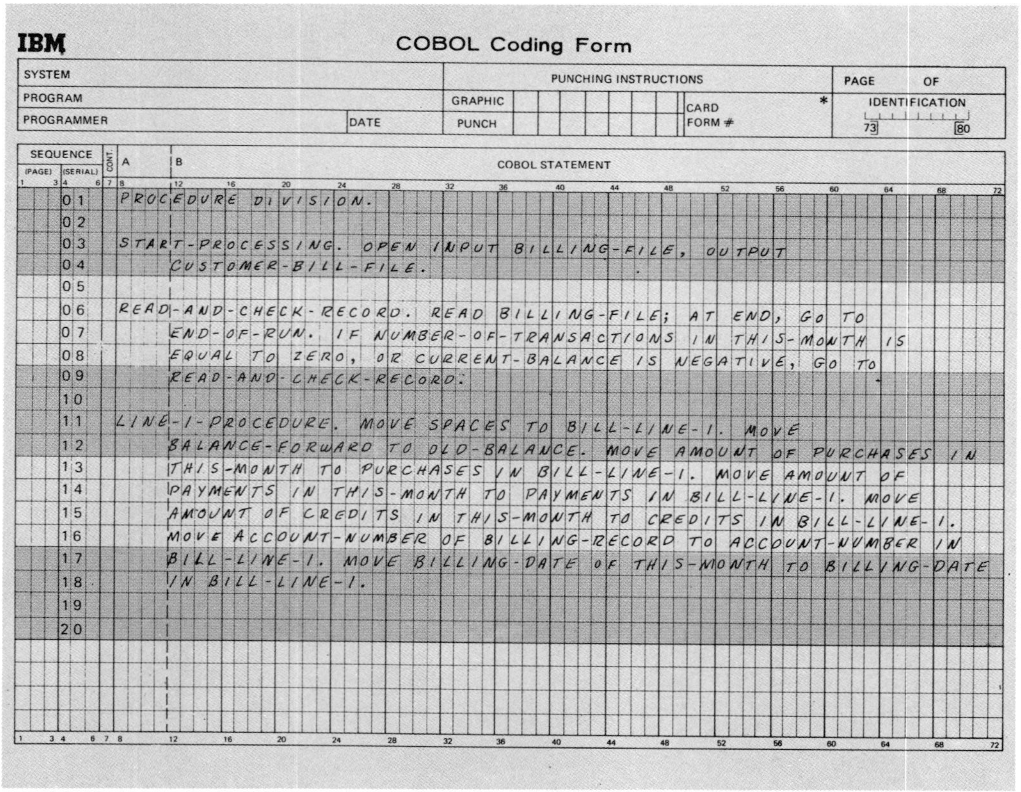


*Figure 25-16.* An Example of a COBOL Program Coding Form

*Source:* International Business Machines Corporation

A *program language* is a defined set of words and symbols that can be converted to machine (binary) language that will be understood by the computer.

The most common programming languages used in business are FORTRAN (formula translation), COBOL (common business oriented language—see Figure 25-16), BASIC (beginner's all-purpose symbolic instruction code).

### Output

The final stage of the computer system is the production of output. Output is processed data that is in a form that can be used by people or by machines for further processing. Reports and listings are types of output. The output used by people may appear in a printed form, on a CRT screen or typewriter terminal, or on microfilm (computer output microfilm, COM). Some sophisticated computers are even able to speak by using a voice response unit. Magnetic tape and disks are common output media used when further machine processing will take place.

High-speed impact printers, as illustrated in Figure 25-17, are capable of producing up to 2,000 lines of output per minute. These impact printers, with typeface and ribbon, function much like a typewriter except they print a full line at one time. A business record with 1,400 pages could be printed in less than 18 minutes. Recently, high-speed printing systems have been developed that are capable of reducing the computer printout page to a standard 8½ by 11-inch size and collating pages into books at speeds up to 18,000 lines per minute. These standard-size pages are more convenient to use.

Because computers are capable of producing so much paper, the problem of what to do with all the reports and records has developed. The computer output microfilm (COM) unit may be the answer; the machine can convert information on magnetic tape directly to microfilm and can film the equivalent of 300–400 pages of computer printout per minute. To give you an idea of what COM is capable of doing, let's look at an example of printing a 1,000-page book on microfilm. COM can print the book onto microfilm in 1½ minutes. By using the microfiche mode, which you are familiar with from Chapter 22, the entire book could be printed on just two microfiche. The reduction ratio for COM is 24 to 1 or 48 to 1.

As you learned earlier when you read about input devices, CRT terminals are very important and are used to obtain information as well as to put it into the computer. Some organizations use the terminals and microfilm extensively and are virtually able to eliminate most of the traditional file systems. When a hard copy of the information is needed, it can be produced and then tossed away after the immediate need is over. An example of the use of a microfilm and terminal system follows, the American Airlines Freight SABRE System.[7]

*Figure 25-17.* High-Speed Printer
*Source:* International Business Machines Corporation

Increased volumes don't necessarily mean increased costs. Quite the contrary. Large systems often justify the use of high technology that permits information handling with more efficiency and lower cost-per-document. American Airlines is a case in point. By automating their freight billing system, they reduced the paperwork in this 2 million document-per-year function by 90 percent, and they're doing it with 30 percent less manpower.

To get the details for our readers, MOP managing editor Chuck Ritley interviewed Wayne Willis, manager of cargo billing at American's Tulsa, Oklahoma, information headquarters. Willis told us: "Our Centralized Cargo Accounts Receivable System is responsible for billing and collecting all money earned by American Airlines for freight hauling. With 150,000 shipments per month, and a minimum of one document per shipment, we were generating a small mountain of paper. Civil Aeronautics Board regulations require that all source documents be kept for 2 years—the equivalent of adding 10 new 5-drawer cabinets per month."

For years, American used a regional office set-up for billing, using 5 offices around the country. These served as information pools for the massive documentation required by shipment. Whenever anything is shipped by air, American must file a document at the sending location, and file another when it arrives at its destination. Copies of both were sent to one of the five regions. Whenever a customer had a question about billing, the documents that detailed the shipment had to be manually pulled from the files at one of these five regional offices. Storage space kept expanding, file access was slowing down, and manpower requirements for handling files grew. Management had decided that the time had come to adopt the same type of advanced technology that American had employed in its passenger reservation system. A team of skilled analysts tackled the project, submitted a final version to top management approval, and—in August of 1975—American closed down its five regional offices and opened the central Tulsa office for business.

A Network in Action

Whenever a shipment leaves an American terminal—whether for a customer or for another airline—a hard copy is still filed for CAB requirements. But, at the same time, a freight agent keys the data into a CRT terminal. This is connected into Freight SABRE, the cargo version of American's well-known SABRE II passenger reservation system. The system responds to the terminal by querying the agent, prompting him to enter all the data that appears on the original hard copy. When the data is all in, and correct, the system stores it in a central file and—at the same time—transmits it to the receiving location, where it is printed out on a teleprinter. When the shipment arrives, the receiving agent keys data into the terminal, which will clear the shipment from the active portion of the files.

Once every two weeks, the SABRE system spins off two magnetic tapes; one contains all receivable transactions, both customers and interline; the other contains only interline billings. Tapes are sent to a COM service bureau, Zytron, Incorporated, which produces one set of microfiche from each tape file. Each individual frame is an electronic reconstruction of the document.

Handling Accounts Receivable

When the A/R fiche arrive at the Tulsa information center, they are sent to the storage-retrieval center. Heart of this vital area are three Bruning 96 automated microfiche retrieval reader/printers. Fully automatic, each Model 96 accepts a special cartridge, which pops into place much like a tape cassette. Each cartridge holds 30 microfiche, and each fiche contains images of 414 air bills—that's 12,400 documents per cartridge.

When the system was first created, an index was constructed on microfiche showing the physical location of each individual air freight bill: cartridge number, fiche number, and frame. This index occupies four separate cartridges, each marked with the first and last air bill numbers referenced on that cartridge. Each time a new batch of fiche arrives, a new index arrives with it. This is the result of a computer run that takes the old index, merges in data on the new batch of fiche, and creates an updated index on COM.

All fiche, index or data, are marked with a reference index number on the top. This is computer generated and shows records personnel what fiche to load in a cartridge. When loading is complete, all fiche and all indexes now agree, and the system is ready for reference.

Each Model 96 is set up as a work station that also includes 4 carousel cartridge holders. Each carousel holds 64 cartridges, putting each operator within arm's length of over 3 million documents.

When a customer or American freight agent calls in with a question regarding billing on a shipment, the 8-digit air freight bill number is sent to the work station. The operator checks the bill number and selects the index cartridge that covers that range of numbers. Inserting the cartridge, she keys in the 8-digit number; within 3 seconds, the Model 96 will flash onto the screen the location of the air bill: cartridge number, fiche, and frame. The operator replaces the index cartridge with the data cartridge, keys in the location, and—within 3 seconds—is looking at the image of the original hard copy. A touch of another key produces as many hard copy prints as are needed. Willis told us: "With this system, we can pull 500 copies per day per operator. With the old system, we peaked out at 175—and we had to re-file the hard copies afterward."

Some computers have an audio response capability: the operator can ask questions through a telephone input device, and through a special audio response unit, the computer can "speak" with a very limited vocabulary in ordinary, human voice.

## DATA COMMUNICATION

Organizations producing large masses of data on their computers find that they must transmit data from one point to another. Particularly, where an organization has many branch offices, data must be gathered and communicated to a central computing facility.

*Figure 25-18.* A Data-Phone
*Source:* Western Electric Co.

*Teletype machines* are used as a major method of data communication. When the typed message is originally prepared, a punched paper tape is prepared simultaneously. The taped message is converted to a series of electronic pulses that are transmitted over telephone lines. The receiving machine decodes the pulse into a typewritten message identical to that typed on the sending machine.

*Data-phones* are a second major method of communication data. Large amounts of data are transmitted over regular telephone lines using the data-phone data set (see Figure 25-18). A phone call is placed either manually or automatically. When ready to transmit, the set is placed in a data mode that enables the business machine terminal to transmit and receive data. To accomplish this process, a data-phone unit receives data in the form of electrical pulses from one of several types of office machines that use punched cards, punched tape, or magnetic tape. The data-phone data set converts these pulses into a tone suitable for transmission. On the other end of the line, data-phone reconverts the tone into electrical pulses that may be fed into a computer or one of several other business machines. Thus, machine talks to machine in machine language.

## OFFICE EFFICIENCY AND THE USE OF COMPUTERS

The computer is a tool that will increase the efficiency and effectiveness of handling administrative activities. As with all administrative services, the technology or hardware, as the computer equipment is called, is important. But as has been stressed throughout this book, people are more important. Just as competent managers help to make their employees more effective, so will competent managers help to make computers more effective.

### Management Functions and the Computer

In administering the computer and its operations, the administrative manager will become involved in the four basic functions of management described in Chapter 1: (1) planning, (2) organizing, (3) controlling, and (4) leading or actuating.

In planning computer operations, management must decide on the objectives to be pursued. Technicians, with the aid of the computer, can help to achieve these goals. Only managers with their overall perspective of the organization are in a position to determine what the objectives should be. As a result of using the computer, the objectives may be modified later on. Computers have tremendous capabilities; managers frequently are challenged to find computer applications that will come near to reaching the potential of the computer.

Proper planning is essential for successful computer operations. Many organizations have been disappointed with results obtained from their computers, but the reasons for failure normally lie in poor planning practices. One company anticipated saving a great amount of money with computers. However, it had not planned on the high cost of developing *software*, which is a collection of programs and routines that makes it possible to use the hardware. Another company relied on the sales representative of a computer manufacturer to decide what the computer should do for the company. The result was that the company was greatly disappointed with the results. The effective manager uses the computer as a tool to get results. The better the planning, the better the results.

As your learned in Chapter 1, "organizing means to arrange or form resources into a complete and functioning whole." The administrative manager is concerned with integrating the computer smoothly into the rest of the organization. All personnel in the organization must understand how the computer fits in and what authority and responsibility each person has in relationship to others. This definition of authority and responsibility is particularly important for managers and computer technicians to understand.

When the first computers were introduced in business, the accounting area normally had responsibility for them because most of the work done on computers was accounting oriented. As more experience is gained with computers, applications throughout the organization are common. Many organizations have set up computer operations in a separate administration unit reporting to top management. From this position computers are better able to serve the entire organization. With the increasing popularity of minicomputers, it is not uncommon for a large organization to have many small computers to process its own work. (For example, one large university owns six computers; one large and one small computer are located in the central computer room; the other small computers are located in the bookstore and the business, mechanical engineering, and chemical engineering buildings.) The question is then raised as to which administrative unit is responsible for the computers. How much responsibility and authority should the computer operations division have over computers housed in various elements of the organization? This issue must be resolved by top management in each organization.

Controlling computer operations involves comparing results with the objectives set up as part of the planning process. Management typically has had difficulty in controlling the computer operations. Part of this difficulty comes from a lack of computer knowledge on the part of managers. Also, there has been a lack of effective communication between computer technicians and managers; computer technicians speak their own language, and it is not understood by others. Both managers and technicians have an obligation to improve this communication process.

Managers should require that computer personnel render an accounting for their area of responsibility. A simple but thorough reporting system should be developed that provides necessary performance information. Computers should be justified on a cost basis as much as possible, but the value of new information not previously available before the computer came into existence should also be considered in this analysis.

To reduce costs, the possibility of using a second and third work shift of computer operations should be considered. These shifts are less costly than the first shift. Another way of reducing computer costs is to rent time on the computer to other organizations.

Finally, consider the leading or actuating function of management. People, not hardware, are the main key to successful computer performance. One of the major difficulties is that computers have developed so rapidly that there is a generation gap between the computer and people. When making the decision to use computers, you would be wise to go relatively slowly. Take time to keep your personnel involved in the steps that lead up to acquiring the computer. Be sure that communication is accurate, complete, and two-way. Employees want to know how the computer will affect them. If management decides that personnel will not be terminated or demoted because of the computer, the policy should be clearly stated and given in writing to all employees. (For an example, see Figure 25-19.) Whenever possible, employees of the company should be given an opportunity to receive training to upgrade their skills and to prepare them for work with the computer. Many people in an organization are capable of developing the required computer skills. Selection of competent computer personnel, whether coming from within or from outside the organization, will be aided if up-to-date job descriptions are available for each position in the computer organization.

Motivational techniques such as job enrichment, MBO, team building, and proper incentives are applicable to working with computer personnel. The jobs of computer personnel vary significantly in terms of responsibility and motivation inherent in the job. For example, the job of systems analyst is very challenging and rewarding by its very nature. On the other hand, jobs such as key puncher, tape librarian, or control clerk may present more difficulty in developing motivated workers. Managers must consider each job and each employee separately and determine what can be done to help all employees become more motivated.

No. 1012

Subject: Termination Because of Automation

The policy of Plunkett Corporation is that no employee shall be terminated or have his/her wages or salary reduced solely because automation has been applied to his/her job.

If the total number of personnel in a department is reduced because of automation, job reductions will be handled by attrition (retirement, death, and voluntary termination) or by transfer to another position within the corporation. In-house company training or college instruction will be provided for those employees who need new skills in order to qualify for new positions. Every reasonable effort will be made to help displaced employees find a new position for which he/she is qualified.

It is anticipated that new positions will be available as computer operators, programmers, and systems analysts. All position announcements will be posted on company bulletin boards in accordance with Policy No. 1002.

Employees who have questions about the status of their employment because of automation are requested to contact their supervisors.

*Figure 25-19.* Policy Statement on the Impact of Computer Installation on Personnel Termination

### Acquiring the Computer

Every organization must make the decision whether it should acquire a computer, obtain computer services from another organization's computer, or process data by some other means. For some organizations, particularly small ones, computers are not needed. Converting to a computer system is a major undertaking and the decision should be thought through carefully and made only after a thorough feasibility study is conducted.

A *feasibility study* is a review of an organization's systems and operations in order to determine if the organization should convert from a manual to a computer system or if the organization should change from an existing computer system. A critical phase of the feasibility study is to review current procedures thoroughly. If procedural improvements are necessary, they should be made before a decision is made to convert to the computer system. Otherwise, you will simply be automating inefficient procedures. This review and improvement of procedures may be the greatest contribution to the organization to come from the feasibility study.

The major question is whether the computer could help solve existing organizational problems as well as provide needed information in a way that would be profitable to the organization. Some of the problems that should be considered are high administrative costs, difficulties and delays in processing orders or providing service to customers, and high-volume clerical procedures.

The feasibility study should review what information is needed by managers in order for them to make effective decisions. Some typical decisions that an administrative manager might make and a listing of information needed for these decisions are shown in Table 25-4. Any system being considered should (1) supply the information needed by management and (2) be cost effective. Cost information on the present system versus a computer system should be obtained.

If the recommendation in the feasibility study is to use computer processing, further decisions must be made. Should the organization lease or buy a computer? Should time be rented on a computer belonging to another organization? Or would it be better to use a computer service bureau? If the decision is made to acquire a computer, you must decide which of several hundred computers would best meet your needs. Another area of concern is how to effect an orderly conversion to the computer system. This conversion is normally a long, expensive process. A typical way of accomplishing the changeover is to run the new system parallel to the old system for a length of time that is adequate to work out most of the "bugs" in the new system.

One final concern is to educate management and others about what the computer is capable of doing. The computer is able to handle or assist with almost any function that can be programmed. It cannot set objectives or make

**Table 25-4. Sample Decisions Made by an Administrative Manager and Types of Information Needed**

| *Decision* | *Information needed* |
|---|---|
| Purchase new typewriters | Replacement policy<br>Service record of old typewriters purchased |
| Trade-in allowance | Cost of new typewriters<br>Amount of trade-in allowance<br>Location of typewriters<br>Equipment budget amount available |
| Authorize trip of staff member to a seminar | Amount of travel budget remaining<br>Amount of travel budget promised to other personnel<br>Cost of proposed trip |
| Purchase office supplies | Amount of supply budget available<br>Quantity of items on hand<br>Quantity of items purchased previous year<br>Cost of supplies by item |

value decisions, but it can help to achieve the objectives. Some typical computer applications to organizational problems are:

- Payroll
- Accounts receivable (money owed by other organizations)
- Accounts payable (money owed to other organizations)
- Order processing
- Purchase order processing
- Inventory
- Production planning and control
- Stock market information
- Income tax preparation
- Check processing (banks)
- Hospital patient records
- Class scheduling and grade processing
- Design
- Law enforcement records
- Meeting scheduling
- Information abstracting and retrieval

Also, simulation is a valuable decision-making tool that can be computerized. Simulation uses a model such as a mathematical formula or a flowchart to show the relationship of various variables and constants. Certain parameters (boundaries), constraints (restrictions), and assumptions are stated. The variables are changed to determine what effect they have on results. Simulation answers "what if" questions.

## *Summary*

Data processing is an essential and dynamic type of administrative service. Data are processed through seven basic operations into a usable form that is known as information. Data can be processed by any one of or a combination of four basic methods: (1) manual, (2) mechanically assisted, (3) tabulating, or (4) computer.

Punched cards, which are the media for tabulating systems, were developed in the 1880s. The first electronic computer was developed in 1946 and has undergone four generations of development since then.

Three unique features of the computer that distinguish it from other means of processing data are its speed, program storage, and data storage capability. By pressing the start button and feeding in instructions and data, you can tell the computer to follow those instructions step-by-step until a final solution is reached.

Computers have had a major impact on almost everyone's life, and they have particularly affected the office where most routine kinds of data processing work have been taken over by the computer. For the most part, people have not been replaced by the computer but rather have been displaced. Given additional training, employees have found themselves upgraded in the organization because of the computer. Managers have found that they spend less time in controlling and routine decision making and more time in planning and leading. Administrative managers must assume the role of managing the flood of information that pours from the computer.

The basic parts of the computer system are (1) input, (2) control, (3) memory, (4) processing, and (5) output. Punched cards have been the most popular input medium but they are rapidly being replaced by magnetic media that have faster access and greater capacities. Some media have random access capability, which means that instant movement to any portion of a record to obtain data is possible. Equipment such as the optical character reader and the terminal have reduced input time and increased flexibility. Magnetic core is currently the most popular memory or storage device. The program is a step-by-step series of instructions that tell the computer exactly how to process a problem. The final result of the computer process is output, which is carried by various media. Computer output microfilm (COM) is quickly gaining popularity as an output medium because of its speed and drastically reduced size as compared with data printed on paper. Data are communicated via data-phones and teletype machines at very rapid rates.

Computers can be applied to all office operations, particularly those that involve the processing of information. The current trend is to adapt computers to meet the needs and abilities of people rather than to ask people to adapt themselves to the computer.

The four basic functions of management—planning, organizing, controlling, and leading or actuating—are applied by the administrative manager in managing computer operations. Managers must learn what the computer is capable of doing and how it can best serve the organization.

## *Review and Discussion Questions*

1. Why are the two key features of the computer vitally important?
2. Briefly explain why the stored program concept is important.
3. List and briefly explain the seven basic data operations.
4. Discuss the four basic methods that may be used to process data.
5. List three types of punched card machines and briefly describe their functions.
6. Briefly explain the difference among the four generations of computers.
7. Explain how the computers affect your life.
8. What impact has the computer had on (a) the job market, (b) the manager's work, and (c) the administrative manager?
9. Explain the difference between *input* and *input media.* Which media are used for input, storage, and output? Point out advantages and disadvantages of each medium.
10. What are the basic functions of (a) control unit, (b) memory unit, (c) processing unit, and (d) output unit?
11. What is the purpose of a computer program? List four common program languages.
12. Explain why random access is important.
13. What are (a) COM, (b) CRT terminals, and (c) data-phones and what are the major advantages of each?
14. How can the computer be applied in the office?
15. Why is the feasibility study important in making the decision to convert to computer operations?

## *Application Exercises*

Report on the following exercises as directed by your instructor:

1. Interview one or more administrative managers to determine their thinking about computers. Ask specific questions such as:
   a. Does your company own or lease a computer?
   b. If so, has the computer met your expectations? If not, why not?
   c. What impact has the computer had on your job as an administrative manager? On your company in general?
   d. How much do you expect your administrative employees to know about computers to effectively perform in your organization?

e. Does your organization use a service center or time sharing plan to reduce equipment costs?
f. Does your organization use a minicomputer in addition to or in place of a medium- or large-scale computer?
g. What have you done as an administrative manager to become familiar with computers and their capabilities?

2. Take a tour of a computer center to see the computer in operation. Identify various parts of the computer and media discussed in the text. Try to bring the textbook learning to life.
3. Read three or four articles of a general nature on data processing. Use the *Business Periodicals Index* to locate your articles. Try to get a feel for current thinking and present developments in the computer world. (Report back as directed by your instructor.)
4. Interview people who are working directly with computers and data processing to get a feel for their viewpoint about data processing and the considerations they feel are most important to them.
5. Take a "quickie course" in a program language that may be offered in your area.
6. Read your newspapers and select articles that reveal how much impact the computer has on your daily life. Report on your findings as directed by your instructor.

## *Case Studies*

1. *Bob Reeves Office Supply.* Bob Reeves is the owner of one of two small office supply companies in Joseph, Missouri. Walt Terry, who owns the other company, is a friendly rival of Bob. Walt's store has a higher volume of sales because it serves most of the commercial businesses. Walt has dealership for several business machine companies, whereas Bob caters to individuals. Sales are adequate to produce a good profit for both companies.

Recently, Walt Terry did a thorough feasibility study and decided to lease a small computer to handle financial and inventory procedures. Bob, hearing about Walt's decision, thinks that he might be wise to get a computer also. He reasons that Walt's store is very much like his own and that the computer would probably save him money. He thinks that Debbie, one of his employees, could probably run the machine because she has worked in a computer center.

Bob comes to you to seek advice, knowing that you have some background in computers and data processing. He urges you to get back to him as soon as possible because he is quite anxious to get started.

2. *American United Insurance Co.* Four years ago, your company decided to switch from punched card tabulating equipment to a medium-scale Standard

Business Machines (S.B.M.) 950-35 Computer. Since getting the machine, many problems have occurred. You have had much downtime (periods when machine is not operating because of machine failure) and very slow maintenance service. You have had to develop much of the software (programs) with your own staff, when you had expected that all software would be supplied by S.B.M. Changeover was very slow and costly. The turnover rate in your computer center has been very high. Your total costs are very high and your productivity below average for the industry. In addition to these problems, you have been getting many complaints from managers throughout your company because of late reports produced by the computer.

Assume you are a management consultant with a specialization in computers; you have been called upon by the vice-president for administration of the American United Insurance Co. to help solve computer problems. What recommendations could you give them to solve current problems and prevent future problems?

## *Reference Notes*

1. Brigham Young University Computer Research Center Information Notes (unpublished).
2. Charles N. Ritley, "Distributed Processing," reprinted from the March 1977 issue of *Modern Office Procedures* and copyrighted 1977 by Penton/IPC, subsidiary of Pittway Corporation, p. 51.
3. *Occupational Outlook Handbook,* U.S. Department of Labor, Bureau of Labor Statistics, 1976–77 Edition, Bulletin 1875, pp. 81, 17.
4. *The U.S. Fact Book* (New York: Grosset & Dunlap, ninety-seventh edition, 1977), p. 372.
5. Stanley Rothman and Charles Mosmann, *Computers and Society,* 2d ed. (Chicago: Science Research Associates, 1976), p. 316.
6. Richard A. Shaffer, "Memory Explosion: New Advances Could Lead to Pocket Computers," *Wall Street Journal,* March 29, 1977, p. 24.
7. "A Giant Step toward the Paperless Office," reprinted from the April 1977 issue of *Modern Office Procedures* and copyrighted 1977 by Penton/IPC, subsidiary of Pittway Corporation, pp. 80–82.

# 26

# A Glimpse of the Office of the Future

Currently, there is strong pressure to automate the office so that it will be less costly to operate and more productive. Ultimately, the objective should be to make executives and their organizations more effective. Let's turn the calendar ahead to 1985 and look in on a typical middle-level manager who will be working in this automated office of the future.

## ALL IN A DAY'S WORK—1985

It's 9:30 A.M. when Malcolm Mid-Level Manager steps off the shuttle bus in front of his suburban office building. He's not late for work—he's just one of millions of office workers around the country who has taken advantage of flexible work hours to set a schedule that matches his personal preferences. Malcolm, not being a morning person, chooses to come a little later than the "normal" 9:00 A.M. starting time.

The headquarters facility of Malcolm's company moved here from the neighboring city five years ago, as part of a total overhaul of operating procedures. Malcolm's firm is highly paperwork oriented, and decided over a decade ago that it would have to adopt some radically different procedures to avoid becoming overwhelmed by its own output. Extensive work flow analysis made it apparent that substantial gains would be achievable through investment in new automated office equipment. Space requirements for this equipment were figured into the design of the new building.

When the elevator opens on the fifth floor, Malcolm is greeted by a vista totally different from what he was accustomed to before. The entire floor is made up of "open landscape" offices, similar to those that started coming into vogue in the 1970s. Only senior executives in this building have permanent offices. Lower-level managers and clerical staff work in quarters made up of movable partitions. Malcolm still has a private office, but it's constructed of modules that can be broken up and moved around to accommodate the changing needs of the organization.

Like many of his co-workers, Malcolm initially feared that the din from all the equipment the company was going to install would prove distracting. Fortunately, by the time this building was outfitted, partitions and sound-deadening systems were vastly improved over those of the mid-1970s. Moreover, the equipment available from office suppliers was much quieter than the clattering, ringing, and buzzing systems that characterized the old offices.

If there's one thing Malcolm misses when he arrives in the morning, it's his secretary's greeting, which, though not always cheerful, at least acknowledged his arrival. Malcolm now obtains secretarial services from a pool shared by several managers in his group. The company has dubbed this pool "the administrative supportive center." Although it's not as personalized as the old way, Malcolm has to admit it's considerably more efficient. If one of the people in the center is unavailable, even for a few minutes, an alternate is there to act without delay.

Administrative support centers are scattered throughout the facility. They supply general office services to a specific management group, but can share work with each other during overload periods. They are a distinct organizational function on a par with personnel, data processing, and similar service departments. In the case of Malcolm's company, they form the largest department in the headquarters facility.

The support team in each center consists of an administrative supervisor, administrative support specialists, information storage/retrieval specialists, communications specialists, and word processing specialists. We'll have an opportunity later on to view how these individuals perform their jobs.

The furniture in these new landscape offices is streamlined and functional. Malcolm's old kneehole desk with drawers on each side has been replaced by an off-the-floor design supported by one of the partitions. Another side of Malcolm's office is devoted to a work table where he can spread out large charts and statistical compilations. A lamp is attached to the partition above this work station to supplement the overall lighting, which is of low intensity so that it generates less heat and makes more efficient use of energy than conventional lighting. The designers like to refer to the individual lamps as "task lighting."

Built into Malcolm's desk itself is a communications control panel, including the company's centralized dictation system. Since Malcolm is one of the managers authorized to access the company's central computer, his communications panel includes a secure card reader, into which he inserts an identification card to gain access. There is also an unobtrusive signaling system to indicate an incoming phone call when Malcolm's phone is in use (either for dictation or conversation), so that he can decide whether to accept the call or push a button to have it automatically diverted to another extension.

One of the first things Malcolm does upon entering his office is to call up [for] his messages. He knows some have come in for him by the signal light on his communications panel. One message was a request for information from a business associate in the Southwest; rather than calling back when Malcolm might be busy and unable to accept the call, he had recorded his request in the memory of an automated verbal communications system. Another of the messages summons Malcolm to a meeting the next afternoon; the message originator recorded the message only once, providing the names of all intended recipients, and it was automatically delivered to each person who was to attend the meeting.

Malcolm decides to refresh his memory on the subject of tomorrow's meeting by reviewing some correspondence. He telephones Francine, the information storage/retrieval specialist at the administrative support center, and asks for the appropriate file to be displayed on his video display screen.

Francine is much more than a retitled file clerk. Unlike her predecessors of a decade ago—typically young, low-paid girls with no more than a high school education and no previous work experience—Francine has three years of college, plus specialized training in the information storage/retrieval field. She earns two to three times as much as those file clerks did.

Francine's job consists of coding information for electronic storage, implementing records retention policies, interacting with the computer to locate and retrieve selected information, and in some cases acting as an experienced librarian to search external data bases offered via time-shared information networks. She is trained to write at least some of the computer programs she needs.

Malcolm used to have his secretary keep a complete set of files in a cabinet outside his office. At first he missed being able to "lay his hands" on the paper, but he has to admit this new system has advantages. Far fewer items, he has noted, are straying from the files since Francine took charge of filing responsibilities for his group. Besides, he can always get hard copies of any particularly important papers he wants to study simply by requesting them from Francine. She orders automatic printouts and delivers them to him. Malcolm still keeps some personal files, but they have shrunk dramatically since the company instituted the facility-wide records retention policies that Francine helps oversee.

As Malcolm is finishing his review of the file, his communication control panel signals another message. He decides to take the call then. This time it's his boss asking what happened to his weekly report. As it would have a decade ago, this entreaty prods Malcolm into action. He picks up the phone and pushes the control button that connects him to the centralized dictation system. He dictates his report and Tillie, a word-processing specialist at the administrative support center, keyboards it to the internal memory system.

Tillie and the other word-processing specialists do most of the routine typing for the company now. They're geared primarily to handling day-to-day correspondence and memoranda; when they get a long or highly complex document, they send it to the facility's centralized word-processing center, which is combined with a duplication and in-house printing/publishing function.

Tillie's typewriter is an automatic one with an electronic keyboard and video display. Her machine is capable of operating in a stand-alone mode with its own computer memories and separate "shared printer" units. For reproducing internal memos and draft documents, Tillie uses the high-speed electrostatic printing unit; for external correspondence, where higher quality output is desired, she orders copies from the ink-jet printers.

The video display terminals that Malcolm and Tillie use are of the gas discharge type. Unlike the eyestraining cathode ray tubes of the 1970s, they're flicker-free.

When Tillie is through keyboarding Malcolm's memo, she signals that it's ready for viewing on his video display. He calls it up and notes a few revisions he wants to make. Since they're minor, he enters them himself. If the memo had been longer or his changes more extensive, he probably would have obtained a hard copy of the draft to work on.

Once corrections are incorporated into the memo, Tillie instructs Cecil, the communications specialist, to notify all addressees that it is available for viewing. Anyone who wants a printout can obtain one from his or her own administrative support center.

The administrative support centers all have convenience copiers, which are tied into the word-processing system. When one of the managers asks for a hard copy of a document he has drafted or received from another person, the automatic typewriter operator merely instructs the system to prepare a copy. The copy machine also, of course, is geared to reproduce individual sheets of paper. Long documents are sent to the centralized processing center for high-speed duplication.

Later in the morning, Malcolm has a meeting with Adelaide, one of the administrative support specialists, to review matters requiring him to make a decision. Adelaide was one of the brightest and most capable secretaries the company had in its old facility and—like many of her peers—was given the opportunity to become an administrative support specialist when the company moved. It was explained to Adelaide that she would no longer be reporting to one manager but would instead be part of an administrative pool. At the same time, her job would be restructured so that she would no longer handle most routine typing, filing, and telephone-handling chores. She was, instead, to take on an increasing share of management tasks so that the managers would have more time to concentrate on key planning and decision making. It was made clear that advancement opportunities would be open to Adelaide and the other administrative specialists elsewhere in the organization.

Most of the administrative support specialists work full time, but a few are there only part [of the] day; they effectively share a job with another individual. Adelaide, a mother with school-age children, has chosen to come in at 9:00 A.M. and leave at 3:00 P.M. For the remainder of the afternoon, her place is taken by Sylvester, a business administration student from the local college; he hopes some practical administrative experience will help him get a spot in the company's management training program when he graduates.

Having cleared up the most pressing items on his agenda, Malcolm is spending the rest of the morning reviewing a monthly report from one of the divisions. Since the document was voluminous with page upon page of computer printout appended, the division recorded it on microfilm for transmittal to the head office. Malcolm has to deal with many such reports, so he has a microfilm reader located by his work table; people who only infrequently need a reader have access to one in the administrative support center.

Malcolm's video display terminal also doubles as an office calculator. He uses it to check on some of the numbers he's poring over. When he spots a suspicious figure, he inserts his identification card into the card reader to call up some records from the data base.

After a noon workout in the company gym, Malcolm has a snack at the health bar and heads back to his office. The rest of the day is set aside to prepare for a big meeting later in the week. Not wishing to have his concentration interrupted, Malcolm presses a button on his communications control panel to indicate that all calls are to be diverted to another extension. At mid-afternoon, he calls the verbal communications center to check on his messages.

One of those messages is a notice that came in earlier from one of the company's overseas divisions. It was transmitted via the company's communicating word-processing system. Several years ago, such notices would have been sent by TELEX; now a word-processing specialist keyboards the message at one facility, and it is transmitted electronically—with no retyping—to any of the company's other locations.

The meeting Malcolm is preparing for is a two-day conference with his counterparts from the divisions. Five years ago these meetings were held semiannually, but now they're quarterly. The increased frequency has come about since the company started using a video conferencing system, rather than having the division managers travel to headquarters for the two days.

On this particular day, Malcolm works late. Even with other personnel taking over much of his day-to-day administrative load, he still finds himself trying to get a head start on the next day's work. At least he's no longer lugging home a briefcase full of paperwork every night.

When the janitorial crew comes on the scene that evening, clean-up goes quickly. Their work takes far less time than it used to when they had to work around or dispose of more paper and when floor-supported furniture interfered with efficient sweeping and cleaning. The company has estimated that it is saving 15% to 20% in clean-up and maintenance time simply as a result of the conversion to a landscaped office concept.[1]

To a person working in a typical office during the late 1970s this picture of the office of the future may appear to be a dream—perhaps even an unrealistic dream. To people fortunate enough to be working in leading-edge organizations such as some research centers, government agencies, or large corporations, much of this picture is already a reality.

Notice at the beginning of this scenario (scene from the office of the future) the reason why it was necessary to investigate the automated office was pointed out. The company was threatened with "becoming overwhelmed by its own output" of paper. Four other major problems found in typical offices:

Cost burden

Time inadequacy

Communication ineffectiveness

Unavailability of information

As these problems are solved, the executive and his/her organization will be more effective.

One of the most difficult parts of the change process is making top management aware of the administrative problem and the need for change. In Malcolm's organization, this top management support was evident, and a work flow analysis was made to determine how to improve office operations. In effect, the systems analysis concepts you studied in Chapter 19 were applied; as a result of the organization's analysis, the decision was made to invest money in automation. In other words, the company decided to spend money on expensive capital equipment (machines such as computers, word processing equipment, electronic mail, and so forth) in order to make their system more efficient and effective.

For purposes of discussion, this example of the office of the future can be divided into three parts: communication and information retrieval, administrative support team, and office environment.

## COMMUNICATION AND INFORMATION RETRIEVAL

The scenario describes the communications control panel built into Malcolm's desk. This device will contain a gas plasma video display screen with audio. The panel will also have a telephone device that will allow Malcolm to send and receive messages and use the computer. Incoming messages—oral or written—will be accepted, stored for later reception, or diverted to someone else. Information about the caller and the subject of the message will be available to Malcolm. He will be able to dictate correspondence or messages and have the information transmitted simultaneously to various locations around the world through an electronic mail system. The information will be received within seconds or hours depending upon its importance.

The article mentioned that video conferencing will probably be used in Malcolm's office. To confer with other executives in distant locations, instead of traveling to see them, Malcolm will confer by using his terminal linked to the terminals of the other executives via a computer in this office of the future. Malcolm will be able to start the conference at any time by presenting information over the terminal system; he will be able to discontinue when he desires and then pick up again later. Other executives can then respond when they have time. Full records of proceedings will be available.

The example implies that much paper will still be processed in 1985. This will probably be true for the average company and for leading-edge organizations in communicating with the public. It is likely that many advanced organizations will eliminate paper in their communications within the organization and with other leading organizations. As well as being more efficient, electronic mail will be less costly.

In the scenario, the process of retrieving and storing information was described. A highly trained information retrieval specialist will be responsible for making sure that Malcolm receives the information that he needs via his terminal. More detail on how this process might operate is presented in a classic article on the office of the future published by *Business Week*. This article describes an experimental office model developed by Xerox Corp.:

> Calling up information from an *electronic file* is incredibly fast, and making changes in the wording of a document displayed on the TV

> screen is very easy. The user moves a hand-held movable controller (called a "mouse") over the desk top, and in response, an electronic pointer moves on the screen to the word or paragraph to be changed. Move the "mouse" left, and the electronic pointer moves left on the screen. Hit a button called "cut", and the word or paragraph disappears. Punch another button labeled "paste" and the paragraph or word is inserted into the text where the pointer is located.[2]

If the executive wants to review materials that have recently arrived, he or she moves the electronic pointer to the in-basket heading (see Figure 26-1); a list of memos and letters that have arrived from other office terminals appears on the screen. The mouse points to any letter that he or she wants to read. By hitting a button on a nearby printer or copier, a "hard copy" is produced or the letter can be filed in the electronic file cabinet.[3] How would you like to work in such an office? The objective is to integrate various types of office equipment such as the terminal, electronic filing cabinet (memory or storage), and copier-printer-facsimile system. An attempt has been made to adapt the terminal to the habits of the managers who will use it.

Other major office equipment manufacturers see the office of the future differently. They see the executive having minimum hardware and using audio devices such as a telephone or a dictation microphone rather than the terminal. This telephone will have a display screen, but the secretary will have the terminal in another room.[4]

Regardless of which of these two approaches predominates, what you probably won't see is very much, if any, paper. The standard file cabinet will be eliminated in favor of electronic storage devices and visual display units. Microfilm is likely to be used for storage of needed documents. Checks are likely to be replaced by an *electronic funds transfer system* (EFTS). EFTS is a system that provides for transfer of funds from one bank account to another by means of a computer transaction. No checks or cash are involved in the transfer of funds. Business letters and memos will bow to direct communication.

*Modern Office Procedures* sees *direct communication* within a company operating like this:

> To send a message, an originator dictates into the plant WP (word processing) center, where the message is transcribed and recorded on a magnetic card. After the originator okays the transcribed message, the WP unit transmits the contents of the card to the CPU (computer central processing unit), which batches and stores messages. When lines are free, the CPU automatically dispatches messages to the intended plants, where they are received on WP card units.[5]

This system speeds up intracompany communication, improves utilization of communication lines, and reduces mailroom requirements. Some companies have this system currently in operation.

*Figure 26-1.* Some Terminals Are Activated by an Electronic Wand as Well as by a Keyboard

*Source:* International Business Machines Corporation

The office of the future will likely be automated. Word processing probably will be the vehicle to lead into total automation. In Malcolm's office both centralized and decentralized word processing was predicted. The *Modern*

*Office Procedures* article suggests that small groups will handle the bulk of the correspondence and a central word-processing center will be used for production of long documents. Very likely, word-processing stations will be linked into networks connected by a sophisticated communication system. The system will be similar to the distributive processing system for data processing described in Chapter 25. Also, data entry for data processing and word-processing keyboarding (rough draft typing on word-processing machines) probably will be combined. Electronic data processing will continue to expand at an increasing rate. At this point, word processing and electronic data processing have started down the road to marriage. What the office of the future will be is likely to be determined by giant office machine companies and the influence they are likely to exert in reducing resistance to change on the part of organization executives.

As improvements are made, more effective methods of handling paperwork will be found. However, gradually, paper will be phased out and completely integrated automation will be introduced. Initial stages of this process have started with the development of magnetic media. Prediction of new technology is uncertain, but one recent development that holds promise for the future is the videodisk.[6] This innovation is a flexible, plastic, chrome-colored disk the size of a long-playing record. The amazing feature of the videodisk is the volume of information it can store. For example, 400,000,000 nine-digit numbers can be stored on just one side of a single disk. This capacity would allow room for more than two recordings of every social security number in the United States on just one side of a disk. Videodisk can also provide full color or black-and-white pictures and stereo or quadraphonic sound.

Several other recent developments are likely to continue. Micrography is increasing in popularity not only as a permanent means of storage, but as an active information retrieval device. The marriage of microfilm and computers has resulted in computer output microfilm (COM) that results in great speed and reduced space requirements. Microfiche provides random access that improves retrieval speeds; recently, microfiche has been developed that can be updated. Malcolm's terminal will probably be used to view microimages; microfilm is particularly appropriate for long documents.

Recently, information retrieval centers providing access to large data banks have come into some use. (A *data bank* is a large depository of information.) Using a remote terminal, a person can request information by using descriptive key words. Abstracts of available information are printed or displayed on the terminal. *Networks of data banks* are likely to be developed that will increase the effectiveness of the office as an information center. Also, information will be real-time. In other words, information and news will be received as it happens. Malcolm will be able to get the latest headlines as the events are occurring.

## ADMINISTRATIVE SUPPORT TEAMS

Thus far, most of the content of this chapter has dealt with automation of equipment. You should remember, however, that the success of any system depends upon the human element. People have been the focus of this book.

In the example, the point was made that Malcolm missed the boss-secretary relationship. The new support system is "not as personalized as the old way," but the approach is "considerably more efficient." This statement is probably true for many organizations. There is no reason why the administrative support system cannot be just as personalized as the traditional one-on-one system. If the group operates as a team, very close relationships can develop.

Effectiveness of the executive and of his/her organization is the goal. If the productivity and effectiveness of clerical personnel are improved but the effectiveness of the executive and his or her organization is left unchanged, the big payoff will have been missed. Mintzberg,[7] in his study of the time usage of executives, found that one-half of their activities lasted for less than 9 minutes. Rather than spending most of his/her time in long-range planning or conceptualizing the future, the manager moves around from one task or problem to another. He/she is often thought of as a "fire fighter" going around putting out little brush fires.

To help the manager become more effective and make better use of his/her time, an effective administrative support team should be organized. This team will consist of a group of specialists who will perform many routine tasks which managers currently perform. The team will consist of administrative assistant(s), correspondence specialist, information specialist, information input specialist, and others as needed. Figure 26-2 shows this team concept. The manager also will serve as a specialist. His/her primary task will be to make key decisions and direct the work of the support team.

This concept of the manager as a specialist who works with a group of other supporting specialists is comparable to the concept of how a surgeon, a dentist, or a scientist operates. The surgeon, for example, is paid to make strategic strokes of the scalpel. The way in which that stroke is made may mean the difference between life and death for the patient. Now you don't expect to find that surgeon also giving medicine, administering anesthesia, taking temperatures, finding surgical instruments, or any one of thousands of other medical and housekeeping tasks. The surgeon is paid a high salary and must make good use of his/her skills.

On the other hand, many business executives don't seem to be able to operate as the surgeon does. For example, if the business executive needs to know the cost of buying new dictation equipment, he/she may call several vendors to get the information rather than ask an assistant to do it. Also the executive may make his/her own copy of a needed paper or walk down the

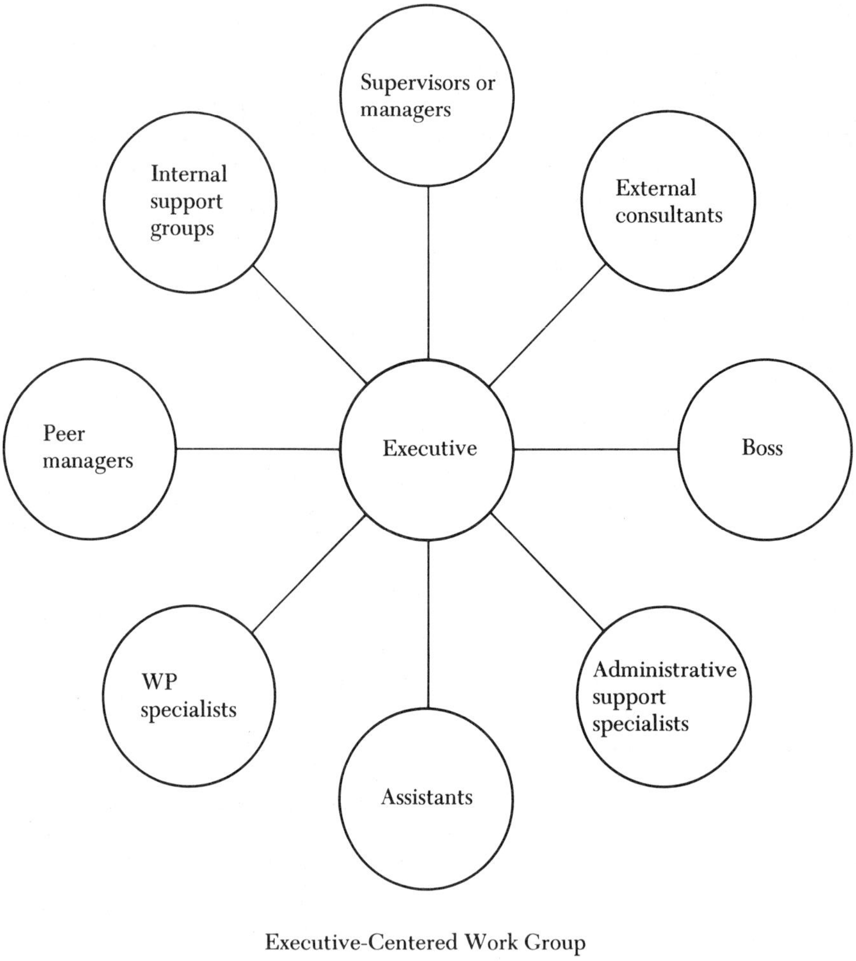


*Figure 26-2.* Administrative Support Team Concept with the Executive as an Integral Part

hall to check on the progress of the development of a new purchasing system. When the secretary is away, the executive may answer the phone and dig in the files for a needed paper. The fact is that many executives spend a large percentage of their time handling trivia. Now some of this may be necessary, but in the office of the future there will have to be a reduction of the executive's time spent on nonessentials. This reduction can be accomplished by more delegation and effective use of the administrative support team.

Several social and organizational issues relate to this discussion of the use of administrative support teams, and one such issue is how much centralization of the administrative support and word-processing functions is desirable. Some large organizations that have gone to complete centralization for word processing and administrative support have been disappointed. The central word-processing center is similar to an assembly line in its effect on employees. One current method is to use a team approach that decentralizes word processing down to the departmental level. Minicomputers, microprocessors and storage units, terminals, and other equipment provide the technology that facilitates decentralization so that management is no longer forced to centralize its organization. Job enrichment tends to move the organization toward decentralization because of the need to provide more responsibility to a greater number of people. Job enrichment responds to a general trend of people desiring a greater amount of self-determination and self-direction.

Another social trend is reflected in the women's liberation movement. Not only do you find a movement toward more equitable pay structures between the sexes but you also find more women starting to move into management.

The administrative management field is an area where women have particularly good opportunities for entry. Many women work as secretaries and gain an excellent understanding of administrative procedures. They also gain an understanding of the business and management concept through their association with their bosses who are managers. Knowledge in these two areas is excellent preparation for advancement into administrative management. Frequently, women are promoted to the position of supervisor of word-processing or filing centers and then enter the ranks of management. A much higher percentage of women managers can be expected if women themselves rise to meet the challenge.

Also, with impetus from EEOC, people of all races, nationalities, and ages are finding good job opportunities in the office and, increasingly, some will work into administrative management positions.

## OFFICE ENVIRONMENT

The third area discussed in the office of the future scenario is the office environment. This topic was discussed under two topics: (1) open landscaping and (2) office furniture.

Under open landscaping several points were made. First, the office furnishings should be modular, that is, parts can be added or taken away depending upon what is needed for a particular situation. Second, changes should be made easily. For example, a right-handed typist who is 5 feet 9 inches may be replaced by a left-handed person who is 5 feet 2 inches. The height of the work surface and the position of the typewriter should be readily changeable. Third, sound-deadening devices and quietly operating equipment should be used to reduce the noise factor. Fourth, office landscaping reduces clean-up and maintenance costs because furnishings hung from partitions are easier to work around.

Under the topic of furniture, three points were discussed. Furniture should be streamlined and functional. Work surfaces and storage areas should be hung from the partitions. Task lighting or lights aimed at specific work surfaces should be used. An artist's conception of how a work station may appear in the future is shown in Figure 26-3.

Another key point relating to the office environment should be stressed. The basic purpose of the office environment should be to help office employees and managers work effectively. The environment also should help individuals to feel more satisfied or, as Fred Herzberg, the authority on motivation and job enrichment, says, less dissatisfied with their jobs.

## *Summary*

In this chapter, you have examined some possibilities for future development of the office. You have seen how technology will improve communication and make information more readily available. At the same time, costs will be reduced. Administrative support teams will help the executive operate more effectively. The office environment will help individuals be more effective and more satisfied with their work.

In the end, the effectiveness of the office depends upon the people who work there, and how effective people are relates to the effectiveness of the manager. The effective administrative manager communicates well with his or her people and treats them as individuals.

## *Review and Discussion Questions*

1. In your own words, describe what you think the office of the future will be like.

*Figure 26-3.* Work Station in an Office of the Future

2. Do you think the office of the future will come about as an evolutionary or revolutionary process? Why?
3. Why is paper likely to be replaced as the primary media of the office?
4. What role will management techniques such as communication, delegation, motivation, and MBO play in the future office which is likely to be highly automated?

## *Application Exercises*

Report on the following exercises as directed by your instructor.

1. Discuss with other people who are likely to be well informed what they think the office of the future will be like. Do some daydreaming yourself about this topic. Let your imagination run wild!
2. Read current periodical articles in magazines and newspapers to keep informed on current developments. Try to integrate these new developments into your concept of the office of the future. Prepare an oral report on your findings to your class.
3. Contact an officer of the nearest chapter of the Administrative Management Society and seek his or her cooperation in sponsoring a panel presentation with "the office of the future" as the topic. Request permission to attend this meeting.
4. Obtain information from the Director of Professionalization, Administrative Management Society, Willow Grove, Pa. 19090, on the Certified Administrative Manager (C.A.M.) designation. Prepare yourself to take the first examination at the earliest opportunity. This step toward professionalization will help you prepare for your office of the future.

## *Reference Notes*

1. Alan Purchase and Carol F. Glover, "Office of the Future," from *Guidelines for Corporate Planning* (Menlo Park, Calif.: SRI International, 1976), pp. 1–4.
2. "The Office of the Future," *Business Week*, June 30, 1975, p. 82.
3. *Ibid.*
4. *Ibid.*, pp. 82–84.
5. WP: Path to the '80s," *Modern Office Procedures*, June 1974, p. 99, copyright 1974 by Industrial Publishing Co., Division Pittway Corporation.
6. Richard Romney, "Videodiscs Expand Communication," *The Daily Universe*, April 11, 1975.
7. Henry Mintzberg, "The Manager's Job: Folklore and Fact," *Harvard Business Review*, July–August 1975.

## *Administrative Manager Profile*

Meet Klaus W. Lukas, work methods manager at American Family Insurance Group at Madison, Wisconsin.

*Background and Experience.* Lukas, a native of Breslau, Germany, graduated from a German technical school and completed some graduate work at the University of Wisconsin, Madison. Prior to joining American Family in 1960, he spent four years in the U.S. Air Force. His first position with American Family was that of claims adjuster. En route to his present position he also performed as services supervisor, systems analyst, and manager of work scheduling systems.

*Company.* American Family was founded October 3, 1927. It had its beginning as Farmers Mutual Automobile Insurance Company of Wisconsin. The company offered low-rate automobile insurance to Wisconsin's farmers. From this humble beginning it grew geographically and in lines of insurance offered to the public. It now operates in eleven midwestern states and offers all lines of insurance.

Presently, American Family is the fifth largest mutual insurance company in the United States, operating out of 19 different regional and branch offices. It has over 2,500 employees and over 3,000 agents. The group's assets are about $400,000,000.

*Job.* In his present position, Lukas, with a staff of seven (six analysts and one clerical), is responsible for administering the group's policies and practices in the functions of records management, work measurement/simplification, micrographics, and word processing. In addition to these administrative duties, it is his responsibility to keep abreast of new developments in technology and methodology. This involves membership in such professional organizations as the Administrative Management Society, the Association of Records Managers and Administrators, the National Micrographics Association, the International Word Processing Association, and several insurance-related organizations. He has presented papers on micrographics and word processing for several of these organizations and has had some of his work published. His duties require him to travel in his quest for continuing professional education and to visit remote regional and branch offices of American Family. Whenever new technology and methodology is introduced, he and his staff act as innovators and sellers of change. The very nature of the phenomenon of change requires that he coordinate his efforts with all levels of the group's management. Almost all employees involved in the group's paper processing are affected by his efforts. In the area of micrographics and word processing he is the group's vendor contact; in this capacity he evaluates equipment and recommends purchasing or leasing arrangements.

To accomplish his objectives, he holds weekly staff meetings in which the flow of information is both "up" and "down." Additionally, he has an "open-door" policy, never being too busy to assist his staff.

*Management Philosophy.* Here are some of Lukas' comments about his own management philosophy and style of leadership:

I am a dedicated worker and expect my staff to be.

I am self-motivated and expect the same from my staff.

I am a firm believer in the principles of management by objectives: (1) I assist each staff member in setting reasonable objectives, (2) I provide guidelines to my staff by which they can accomplish their objectives, (3) I frequently advise and counsel them as to the status of their performance, which provides another opportunity for the exchange of information.

I believe in good communication for the purpose of achieving planned objectives.

I am people-oriented. It is important to me that my staff is successful. In order for them to be successful I believe it to be my obligation to help them.

I make sure that each of my staff, for their particular area of responsibility, is part of the management-planning and decision-making process.

I am honest and open with my staff and expect them to treat me the same.

I pride myself in being fair.

I am a good listener.

I try to expose my staff to the principles of management so as to permit them to grow with the organization.

It gives me great pride whenever one of my staff is chosen for advancement.

# Glossary

The following terms are defined as they are used in context.

### A

**accountability** The obligation that a person has to achieve results.

**accuracy ratio** A figure that reveals the degree of file integrity in a given file.

**action files** Files containing high-use documents; usually located immediately beside the workers who use them.

**active listening** Listening exemplified by the listener's paraphrasing the speaker's message to ensure that understanding is achieved.

**address** A specific computer storage location.

**administrative assistant** A worker who assists a manager with tasks that may be management, secretarial, or clerical in nature.

**administrative costs** The expenses of operating the office and of performing related activities.

**Administrative Management Society (A.M.S.)** A professional organization for administrative managers.

**administrative manager** A manager, usually at the middle level, who has the basic objective of providing information and administrative services to the organization.



**administrative services** Functions as a support service for management; facilitates information flow. Four basic services are records management, administrative systems analysis, data processing, reprographic services, and communication services.

**administrative supervisor** A person who manages or supervises office activities.

**administrative support center** A group of secretaries and typists (administrative support specialists) who perform typing and clerical duties. A more modern and sophisticated term for the "typing pool."

**administrative support team** A team of secretarial personnel who perform primarily nontyping secretarial work.

**administrative systems analysis** Applying a system for making improvements to administrative activities.

**affirmative action officer** An officer in an organization responsible for increasing the employment and promotion of minorities and women in that organization.

**affirmative action program** A program designed to increase the employment and promotion of minorities and women in an organization. (*See* Executive Order 11246.)

**Age Discrimination in Employment Act** A federal act designed to prohibit employers from refusing to hire because of older age.

**analog computers** These computers *measure* rather than count. They are used to act out or simulate situations using numbers, physical phenomena, or nature. (Contrast with *Digital computers.*)

**aptitude tests** Tests that predict a person's future performance.

**assessment center** A technique used to select management candidates; requires the participants to engage in simulated management activities which are then evaluated.

**Association of Records Managers and Administrators** An association established for the advancement of excellence in the management of records.

**attendant camp-on** The capability of a telephone system to "hold" a call when the line of the intended receiver is busy. As soon as the line is free, the telephone rings and the second caller is connected.

**attendant controlled conference** The capability of a telephone system operator to arrange a conference call for simultaneous communication among several persons from different extensions.

**audio interference** Sounds present in a communication setting that compete with messages being transmitted.

**autocratic** A leader who assumes authority for "running the show" without seeking the opinions of his or her followers.

**automatic answering equipment** Special recording equipment that will automatically answer an incoming telephone call, play a prerecorded message to the caller, and provide an opportunity for the caller to record a message.

**automatic dialing equipment** A special telephone adaptation that automatically dials numbers as directed by the user.

## B

**BASIC (Beginner's All-purpose Symbolic Instruction Code)** A programming language specifically designed for instructional purposes and programming using terminals.

**behavior modification** The process of altering a person's behavior by using certain techniques.

**benefits** Nonsalary advantages that accrue to employees because of their affiliation with an organization; for example, insurance benefits and retirement benefits.

**body language** Communication pertaining to gestures and body position.

**bona fide occupational qualification (BFOQ)** A skill, ability, or personal trait that is essential for job success.

**bottom-up approach** A program initiated at the employee level and spread upward and outward throughout the organization.

**bulk mailing** Mailing in volume through the U.S. Postal Service.

**business reply mail** Mail for which the postage has already been paid by the recipient.

## C

**call forwarding** The capability of a telephone system to forward calls automatically from one telephone to another when a special forwarding code is keyed into the system.

**call-transfer** The capability of any individual in an organization to transfer incoming calls to any other extension without assistance from the operator.

**C.A.M.** The Certified Administrative Manager professional designation awarded by the A.M.S. to managers who have met professional criteria.

**card read-punch unit** A machine that reads in or punches out data on punched cards.

**cathode-ray tube (CRT) terminal** A computer or word-processing device used to input data or access information; includes screen and keyboard.

**cause-and-effect relationship** The existence of two aspects of a relationship, one of which causes the other.

**centralized files** The arrangement of nearly all the records of an organization in a central location.

**centralized telephone systems** Telephone systems that route all incoming telephone calls through a central switchboard.

**centrex** A very sophisticated telephone system, designed mainly for large organizations, and offering direct inward dialing.

**certified mail** Mail for which a record of delivery is to be maintained by the post office where the item is delivered.

**chain of command** The line of authority within an organization from an individual through his/her supervisor and on up through various levels to the president or general manager of the organization.

**change agent** A person who initiates and oversees the implementation of change.

**channel** The medium used for transmitting messages.

**character** A letter, number, or special symbol.

**charge-back system** A financial control practice of charging a department for services provided by another department.

**chip** A miniature storage and processing device that is the heart of microcomputers.

**Circle of Confidence** A theory suggesting that feeling good about oneself causes a person to turn outward and to do good things for other people, which in turn reinforces the individual's feeling of self-confidence.

**Circle of Inferiority** A theory that is opposite of the Circle of Confidence. Feeling poorly about oneself causes the person to turn inward and to be seen by others as selfish and uncaring. Negative reactions on the part of other people reinforce the individual's feelings of inferiority.

**Civil Rights Act** A comprehensive act enacted to improve opportunities for people without regard to race, color, national origin, sex, religion, and other factors not related to job success.

**closed questions** Questions designed to obtain specific information without significant elaboration by the interviewee.

**COBOL (Common Business Oriented Language)** A programming language specifically designed to handle masses of input and output found in business.

**collect-on-delivery (C.O.D.) mail** Mail for which the collection of both the postage and the value of the letter or parcel contents is made at the point of delivery.

**COM (computer output microfilm)** Any type of microform produced directly from the computer rather than from a photograph of a paper document.

**commitment** A decision to give total effort to accomplish certain goals or objectives; a dedication to achieve specific results.

**communication** The process of transmitting information from one person to another.

**communication barriers** Those factors that interfere with the achievement of understanding between individuals. These factors are classified as psychological, physiological, or environmental.

**communication climate** The intangible atmosphere that prevails in an organization and that tends to encourage or discourage open communication.

**communication distortion** The loss of meaning that occurs when a message is sent from one person to another.

**communication interaction analysis** A technique designed to determine the communication patterns within the office.

**communication interaction analysis diagram** A chart that shows the interaction (communication) of every person in the office.

**communication patterns** The network of communication lines or flow of communication from one person to another in the organization.

**communication services** Oral and written communication systems used in organizations.

**communication training** Formalized communication training designed to help members of an organization become more effective in their written and oral communications.

**communications control panel** A terminal used by executives and others to help them communicate with other persons inside or outside the organization.

**communications specialists** People who are responsible for preparing external and internal messages and reports.

**compatibility** Technological "fit" between two or more items of equipment.

**competency** An ability to accomplish designated activities.

**computer** An electronic machine that possesses an internal storage capability, a stored program of instructions, and an ability to modify those instructions during processing.

**computer generation** A distinct phase of computer development.

**computer terminal** A typewriter-like device used for entering information into or retrieving information from a computer.

**consultants** Individuals who are experts in a given field and who, for a fee, provide guidance and counsel to companies needing assistance in that field.

**consulting style** A leadership style that calls for participation on the part of employees in the decision-making process.

**contingency approach to management** A variable approach to leadership style selection based on the situation.

**control group** In research, a group that remains constant—no experimental factors are introduced into the group.

**controlled availability** An executive screens calls, interviews, or discussions he will be available for during a business day.

**control unit** An electronic computer traffic cop that directs the movement of all data and instructions into, within, and out of the computer.

**conveyer system** A system involving the use of a moving "track" to take documents from one work area to another in a company.

**cooperative education program** A program that places a student in a business setting for a short-term period to help the student gain real-world experience while still in school.

**copier-duplicator** A relatively new reprographics machine that operates much like a copier but offers high-speed output as well.

**cost-effective systems** Those systems for which costs of purchase and of installation are offset by the savings achieved through the operation of the system during a given period of time.

**CPU (central processing unit)** The part of the computer that performs arithmetic, logic, and other processing functions on input.

**critical incidents list** A list of outstandingly effective or ineffective incidents about the behavior of an employee.

**CRT terminal** See **Cathode-ray tube terminal.**

**cultural conditioning** Learning that is influenced by and reflects differences from one culture to another.

## D

**data** Unprocessed or unorganized facts.

**data bank** A large depository of information.

**data network** A linking of data banks to allow sharing of information.

**data phone** A data communication device that links computers.

**data processing** The operations performed on data to develop and transmit usable information.

**decentralized records** The arrangement of records of an organization in the departments and areas where the records are used.

**delegation** A management technique that involves entrusting work to another person.

**democratic style** A leadership style involving employees in the decision-making process.

**desymbolize** The process of changing perceived words to mental thoughts.

**diagnosis** The process of examining the symptoms accompanying a problem to determine the cause of the problem.

**dictation system** An electronic system designed to allow persons to speak their messages into a recording device (dictation machine) for subsequent typing.

**DID (direct inward dialing)** The capability to make telephone calls from outside a company's telephone system to a telephone inside that system without going through the company's telephone operator.

**digital computers** These computers are based on a binary counting system. That is, they recognize two distinguishable states like "off" or "on," "open" or "closed," "stop" or "go." They are programmed to operate on decimal digits.

**direct communication** Another name for electronic mail.

**direct-wire system** A dictation system that utilizes a special microphone, wired into the word-processing center, for dictation.

**directive interviewing** An interviewing style in which the interviewer takes the lead in directing the content of the interview.

**disk pack** A device, resembling a kitchen kettle, which contains a number of disks.

**distributive processing** The linking together of two or more minicomputers with each other or with a large, central computer to form a decentralized data-processing network.

**DOD (direct outward dialing)** The capability to make telephone calls from within a company's telephone system to a telephone outside that system without going through the company's telephone operator.

**drug and alcohol abuse** The excessive or inappropriate use of drugs or alcohol in a way that interferes with employees' abilities to properly perform their work.

**duplicate-copy method** A method of providing needed records to personnel requesting them; this method involves sending a copy to the person requesting it and retaining the original in the file.

**duplicate-file method** A records-transfer method involving two sets of files, each representing a different period of time. One of the sets of files is transferred when there is minimal activity.

## E

**economies of scale** Cost savings that occur when equipment cost is spread over a larger number of output units.

**EEOC (Equal Employment Opportunity Commission)** A federal commission established to enforce the right to equal employment.

**efficiency experts** People who study work operations to develop the quickest and most efficient methods of accomplishing work.

**EFTS (electronic funds transfer system)** A system that provides for transfer of funds from one bank account to another by means of a computer entry or transaction.

**electronic file** A computer storage device designed to replace the traditional file cabinet.

**electronic longhand transmission** The process of sending handwritten messages via electronic circuitry.

**electronic mail** The electronic transmission of any type of information that traditionally would be sent via regular paper routes. Messages are sent through terminals via a central computer or a computer network.

**employee log method** A record of time and production count kept by employees and used for setting time standards.

**employment agency** An organization that helps people find new employment.

**endless loop system** A dictation system that features an endless magnetic tape on which dictation is recorded. Up to three hours of dictation can be stored on a single endless loop machine.

**environmental factors** Those parts of an individual's surroundings or situation that influence or mold his or her character.

**Equal Pay Act** A federal act passed to ensure that employers provide equal pay for men and women performing similar work.

**ERISA (Employee Retirement Income Security Act)** A federal government act designed (1) to require organizations to communicate clearly their retirement plans and (2) to provide the opportunity for individuals not covered by group pension plans to establish their own individual retirement accounts.

**Executive Order 11246** Amended by Executive Order 11375, this order requires federal contractors to develop and implement written affirmative action programs.

**exit interview** An interview held to determine the reasons why an individual is voluntarily terminating employment.

**experimental group** In research, a group in which an experimental or new factor is introduced.

**external messages** Messages coming into the brain from outside sources.

**extrinsic rewards** Rewards offered as *external* gifts for good performance, such as a bonus or a raise in pay.

## F

**facsimile equipment** Electronic equipment used to transmit and receive via telephone lines any type of information that can be committed to paper; for example, words, tables, and graphs.

**feasibility study** A review of an organization's systems and operations in order to determine if the organization should convert from a manual to a computer system or from an existing computer system to another.

**feedback** Helpful information or reactions given to an individual or a group advising how well an action, a behavior, or a system was performed.

**file auditing** The process of checking for misfiled folders.

**file integrity** The degree to which individual records are filed where they ought to be.

**first-class mail** Mail containing handwritten and typewritten messages, bills and statements of account, cancelled and uncancelled checks; also business reply mail, post cards, and postal cards.

**flexible work hours** A plan that allows the individual worker to set his or her own work schedule to meet individual needs and desires, within limits prescribed by the organization.

**flexigrated** A coined word used to designate an office planning concept that combines the traditional offices, office landscaping, and privacy panel concepts.

**flow diagram** A diagram of the work area showing movement of people or flow of documents through an office.

**flow process chart** A step-by-step description of an office process or method. Visual symbols graphically portray the types of steps involved.

**flowchart** A visual presentation of key steps in a work procedure. Limited narrative description is included.

**forced choice checklist** A list of pairs of behavior characteristics; the appraiser selects one from each pair that is most typical of the behavior of the person being evaluated.

**forms analysis worksheet** An analysis form designed to reveal information that is being collected on more than one form.

**FORTRAN (FORmula TRANslation)** A type of programming language used in science, engineering, and business.

**fourth-class mail** Domestic parcels and certain catalogs and library materials.

**frame of reference** The mental point of view of an individual as he or she perceives environmental cues; a "filter" through which all messages pass.

**full-time WATS** A WATS arrangement that allows the user 240 hours of long-distance calling time per month, after which additional charges are made.

## G

**gas discharge display** A type of visual display terminal that is intended to replace the CRT terminal.

**geographic filing** The arrangement of records in alphabetic order according to some geographical factor of the records.

**gestures** Body movement, generally in the arm and hand areas, that communicates either with or without a verbal message.

**goal-directed activity** Behavior that leads a person toward the attainment of a goal.

**goal or task orientation** A drive or strong desire to get the job accomplished.

**goals** Aims or purposes to be achieved over a long-term period, usually stated in a general way.

**grapevine** An informal communication channel consisting of an indeterminate number of individuals who pass messages from one to another.

**grid sheets** A special type of paper or other material that has horizontal and vertical lines drawn at ¼-inch or ⅛-inch intervals to form many small boxes.

**guides** Special tabs containing file-location information to assist the file worker in searching for records.

## H

**hard copy** Information in paper form.

**hard data** Quantitative or numerical type of data.

**hardware** The machinery part of a computer system.

**Hawthorne studies** A classical series of research studies that demonstrated the importance of human relations in industry and business.

**Herzberg's theory of motivation** An on-the-job approach to motivation that recognizes various motivators and dissatisfiers. The motivators concentrate on the work itself and the responsibility of the job. The dissatisfiers focus on adverse factors in the job situation.

**historical method** A way of determining time standards using production and time records.

**Hollerith code** A system of placing holes in cards to designate alphabetic or numeric characters.

**horizontal job loading** The process of moving responsibility at the same level from one job to another.

**horizontal promotions** Moving an individual to another job neither higher in the organization nor demanding more pay, but offering increased opportunities in the future.

**house organs** Periodic magazine-type publications issued by an organization to its employees or clients.

**hygiene factors** Herzberg's dissatisfiers—factors pertaining to the work situation: company policies and administration, supervision, interpersonal relationships, working conditions, and salaries.

## I

**in-basket exercises** Situations that require the participant to read, evaluate, and take action on a variety of memos, letters, and reports in a hypothetical manager's in-basket.

**incentive wage plan** The payment of money for work units completed beyond the standard for that job.

**indexing rules** Rules used to determine which words shall be used for storing company records.

**indication of camp-on** A tone transmitted to a person who is talking on a telephone line to indicate that a second caller is waiting to talk.

**induction checklist** A list of items that should be covered during employee orientation.

**inferences** Educated guesses that are made to supplement missing facts when one is trying to understand a total situation or concept.

**information** Data that has been processed into a usable form.

**information storage/retrieval specialists** People who find information and maintain information retention systems.

**ink-jet printers** A special printing device that sprays ink into position to form letters and other symbols. Avoids use of traditional typewriter (impact) system.

**input** The introduction of resources into a system, especially the data or instructions entered into a data-processing system by means of input media.

**input media** Materials on which data from source documents is recorded for temporary storage until needed by the computer.

**insured mail** Third- or fourth-class mail that is insured against loss or damage.

**interest tests** Tests that determine occupational areas in which persons have some interest.

**internal messages** Ideas brought into central focus of the brain from some other part of the brain.

**International Word Processing Association** An association created for the promotion of leadership in word processing.

**interpersonal relationship** The interaction of one person with another.

**intracompany communication** Communication, written or spoken, that is sent to someone within the same organization.

**intrinsic rewards** Rewards that arise from *within* an individual, such as feeling proud after a major accomplishment.

## J

**job enlargement** Increasing the scope of a job by adding duties and responsibilities that are usually similar to those previously performed by the individual.

**job enrichment** Structuring or restructuring a job to make work more meaningful for the employee. Usually involves adding decision-making responsibility to the job.

**job promotions** Promotions usually characterized by a change in job title, an increase in pay, and an increase in job responsibilities.

**job responsibilities** Work activities and tasks required in a particular work position.

**job rotation** The practice of training and allowing workers to perform jobs other than their own.

**job structure** The basic activities and tasks assigned to a job that are performed by an employee.

**job tenure** The length of time employees have been with their present employers.

**joining style** A leadership style that relinquishes decision-making authority to employees; the leader becomes a member of the group.

## K

**keypunch machine** A machine used to punch holes in cards according to designated categories.

**key results** Primary objectives that a delegator expects the person doing the delegated assignment to accomplish.

## L

**lateral file** A filing cabinet consisting of file drawers or trays that open from the wide side rather than the end.

**leader** Anyone who inspires other people, causes them to get the task at hand accomplished, and convinces them to do more and better things because they want to.

**leadership style** The approach an individual takes to leadership and management in order to get other people to act.

**leadership traits** The inherent qualities within a person that cause him or her to be effective as a leader.

**leading** The management function of getting people to accomplish specific objectives. It involves selection, orientation, training, motivation, coordination, and supervision.

**long-range planning** The phase of planning that projects ideas into the distant future.

## M

**machine dictation** The process of speaking information into a recording machine (dictation machine) for subsequent playback and typing by an operator.

**magnetic core** An internal computer storage device that consists of a series of doughnut-shaped rings.

**magnetic disk** A storage device resembling a phonograph record that stores data by means of magnetized spots.

**magnetic drum** A storage device in the shape of a cylinder on which magnetized data are recorded.

**magnetic memory** A feature of automated office equipment enabling the equipment to store, or remember, information. Also known as *magnetic medium.*

**magnetic tape** A tape that stores data by means of magnetized spots according to a special code system.

**magnetic tape drive** A machine used for reading and recording magnetic tape.

**magnetized cards** An external storage device in the form of a plastic card that contains data in magnetic form.

**mailgram** A message that is computer routed by zip code and electronically transmitted to a post office near the destination for next-day delivery by the U.S. Postal Service.

**management** The art and science of getting specific results or objectives accomplished through other people.

**management by objectives (MBO)** A management system for determining where an organization is going, deciding how it can get there, and measuring what has been accomplished; provides motivation to individual employees by allowing them to become involved in setting their own work goals.

**management consultants** Professional individuals who, for a fee, come into an organization to help solve a particular problem or to help achieve a particular objective. These individuals are not considered as regular employees, and their affiliation with a company is usually on a part-time or temporary basis.

**management credibility** The degree to which employees in an organization believe in and trust their managers.

**management flowchart** A visual presentation of a work procedure that uses rectangular-shaped symbols and short descriptions of steps.

**management games** Games that simulate management situations and that test a person's ability to plan, organize, and control.

**Management information systems** Modern information systems that provide up-to-date, timely information for management decision making.

**manager** A person who has authority and responsibility for getting specific objectives or results accomplished through other people.

**masking sound** A controlled background noise that is electronically generated and played over a loudspeaker system to drown out the effect of other more distracting noises.

**Maslow's hierarchy of needs** A classification scheme of human needs that suggests a sequence of importance and an order for which needs tend to be satisfied.

**MBO** See **management by objectives.**

**measured-time WATS** A WATS arrangement that allows an organization 10 hours of long-distance calling time per month, after which additional charges are made.

**mental ability tests** Tests designed to measure persons' ability to use their minds to solve problems.

**mental balance** The mental condition present when a person feels good about himself or herself.

**message processing** The process of desymbolizing, interpreting, and storing a message perceived by the brain.

**message transmission** Sending a message by talking, writing, or nonverbal communication.

**microfiche** A 4 × 6-inch microfilm card containing images in rows and columns.

**microfilm** A special photographic film used to contain microimages of information.

**microfilm jacket** A microfiche-sized microform consisting of two plastic sheets that are fused together at regular intervals to form channels into which strips of film are inserted.

**microfilm reader** A microfilm device used for projecting and viewing microfilm images.

**microfilm reader-printer** A microfilm device used for projecting and viewing microfilm images and for printing a paper copy (hard copy) of selected images.

**microfilm service bureaus** Businesses that perform microfilming functions for companies lacking the equipment and capability to perform their own microfilming operation.

**microforms** Different sizes and shapes of microfilm, such as roll film and microfiche.

**micrographics** Technology used to reduce information to microminiature size and to place the information on microfilm.

**micrography** The general field of microfilm and all things directly related to it.

**microminiaturized circuits** A primary component of third-generation computers: ultrasmall electronic devices that are similar to those found in electronic radar ovens.

**middle management** The level of management that serves as a buffer between top and supervisory management levels.

**minicomputer** A small, compact computer that has less capability and a lower price than a large-scale computer.

**model** The person being emulated in a modeling situation. Also, a layout tool that realistically portrays office furnishings and equipment through the use of plastic forms made to scale and shaped in the same pattern as the originals.

**modeling** The process of emulating traits and behaviors observed in others.

**modeling effect** The amount of change observed in the observer after the modeling process.

**moderator** A person who serves as a regulator of oral communication in a group setting.

**modular desk** An office work station comprised of several units that are joined together according to need.

**motion analysis chart** A detailed description of hand and body movements used in accomplishing a task.

**motivation** An internal process that causes a person to act in anticipation of receiving reward and satisfaction.

**motor skills tests** Tests designed to measure applicants' physical and coordination abilities.

**mouse** A hand-held movable pointer device used with display terminals.

**movement** The action that an individual takes to achieve a goal.

**movement diagram** Another name for *flow diagram.*

**multiple forms** Two or more copies of a form fused together to create multiple copies simultaneously as the form is filled out.

**mutual expectations** What two people expect from each other or what they anticipate each of them will do.

## N

**nanosecond** A billionth of a second.

**narrative procedure description** A written statement that describes in a step-by-step form how a procedure is accomplished.

**National Micrographics Association** An association dedicated to the advancement of micrographics and leadership in the microfilm industry.

**network system** Decentralized location of records with centralized control.

**nondirective interviewing** An interviewing style in which the interviewee takes the lead in directing the content of the interview.

**nonverbal communication** Nonword messages such as gestures.

**nonverbal encouragement** The use of nonverbal communication to encourage an interviewee to talk more.

**nonvoice transmissions** Telecommunication transmissions not including the human voice.

**numeric filing** The arrangement of records in numerical order according to numbers assigned to the individual records.

## O

**objective logic** Methodical and critical analysis of a given situation; thought processes not overcome by human bias and emotions.

**objectives** Specific, short-term results to be achieved, usually stated in as precise a manner as possible. Stating objectives in this way helps both worker and supervisor (or student and teacher) to measure the results and to know when an objective has been achieved.

**object language** Information transmitted by the display of objects.

**OCR (optical character reader)** A machine that reads printed or typed data and records them on magnetic media.

**office decor** The furniture and other objects in an office that contribute to an overall mood or feeling in the office.

**office environment** The surroundings in which administrative managers and personnel work.

**office landscaping** An innovative office planning concept that eliminates traditional approaches and focuses on free-flowing communication.

**office layout** A floor plan diagram or model that shows exact locations of various office furnishings and equipment.

**office manager** Another title sometimes used instead of administrative manager. In offices where there are both titles, the office manager normally has less responsibility than the administrative manager.

**office partitions** Dividers, usually five to six feet tall, that separate an office into individual or small-group working areas.

**off-line typing** Typing that is committed to a storage medium, such as a paper tape, before it is transmitted electronically.

**offset duplicator** A duplication process that produces high-quality print but which requires a skilled operator and a larger equipment investment than is required for stencil and spirit duplicators.

**output** The product or results obtained from a system.

**on-line typing** Typing that is transmitted electronically the instant it is keyed into the machine.

**on-the-job training** Training that takes place in an employee's own work station and consists of the performance of actual job duties.

**open questions** Questions designed to encourage the interviewee to talk more and that (1) cannot be answered by a simple "yes" or "no" response, (2) do not disclose your attitudes and biases, and (3) do not lead the interviewees to answer the way you would like.

**open-shelf file** A filing arrangement that uses no drawers but stores folders on an open shelf with tabs protruding from one side of the folders.

**optimum delegation** Delegating jobs that are challenging responsibilities but retaining control over the results.

**optimum level of difficulty** A level of difficulty for goals that is high enough to be challenging but low enough to be attainable.

**oral communication** Voice communication.

**organizational climate** The general feeling within an organization. A good organizational climate means there is an atmosphere of mutual trust and open communication within an organization.

**organizational communications** The entire scope of communication that occurs within an organization, including the flow of information among people and the human relations involved.

**organizational direction.** The pattern of growth or movement an organization takes.

**organizational hierarchy** The structure of an organization, with powerful officers at the top, middle managers next, and supervisors and workers at the bottom.

**organizing** The management function of arranging or forming resources into a complete and functioning whole.

**orientation** Acquainting a new employee with organizational policies and procedures that he/she needs to know to function properly on the job.

**OSHA (Occupational Safety and Health Act)** A federal act designed to improve the degree to which U.S. businesses protect the safety and health of their employees.

**out-card** A card or other type of form used to indicate information about a record that has been checked out.

**output** Computer-processed data used by people or by machines for further processing. The last information product of a system.

**output media** Means used to record output such as reports, business forms, and microfilm.

**overhead cost** Miscellaneous costs (such as the cost of floor space, lights, heat, and air conditioning) that must be considered in addition to the personnel and equipment costs related directly to a given operation.

## P

**PABX (private automatic branch exchange)** An automated telephone call-switching device; it generally features push buttons used to connect callers.

**pace** Rate at which an employee moves or works.

**paging systems** Electronic systems used to contact individuals when they are away from their regular working areas.

**paraphrase** To repeat the gist of another person's comment using your own words.

**past performance method** Another name for the historical method of setting time standards.

**participative management** A managerial practice that involves subordinates in decision making to the maximum degree feasible.

**PBX (private branch exchange)** A telephone call-switching device using jacks and cords to connect and disconnect callers.

**performance appraisal** An evaluation of an employee's work that may or may not involve an interview to inform the employee about his or her job performance.

**performance criteria** Factors on which a person is evaluated.

**performance cycle** The complete process of doing work that starts with the planning, moves to doing the work, and ends with the evaluation of what has taken place.

**periodic transfer method** A records transfer method involving a periodic examination of all records in active storage to determine which records should be transferred.

**permanency** A factor pertaining to the reference life of a message, that is, whether a message is recorded and can be referred to after its original transmission.

**personality tests** Tests that measure a person's major personality traits.

**person-machine chart** A detailed description of the relationship between the work of an employee and one or more machines.

**personnel department** A department that aids in recruiting, screening, and hiring employees and that performs other activities to assist employees in an organization.

**personnel selection** The function of finding, screening, and hiring workers.

**photocomposition unit** A machine that prepares printing plates.

**physiological** A category in Maslow's hierarchy of needs pertaining to body or physical needs.

**physiological barriers** Communication barriers that result from the physical limitations of human beings.

**physiological problem** The inability to perform a certain action because of a physical limitation.

**playback** The typing of material that has

been placed in the magnetic memory of a word-processing typewriter.

**pneumatic tube system** A system involving a network of tubes through which containers carry documents from one work area to another within a company.

**policy** A statement of guidelines used to govern procedure and action within an organization.

**positive reinforcement** Complimenting or supporting desired behavior in an effort to promote a continuation of that behavior.

**predetermined time system method** Standard times to complete basic hand and body motions. Times are derived from numerous stop watch studies.

**President's Committee on Equal Employment Opportunity** A committee established in 1961 to achieve equal employment opportunities in government and in businesses holding government-related contracts.

**printers** An output device capable of printing characters at high speeds onto paper forms.

**privacy panel** An innovative office planning device consisting of free-standing panels placed together to form an enclosure. Work surfaces and filing shelves or cabinets are hung from the panels.

**process chart** A chart that is used to describe work processes.

**processing** The manipulation of resources to form a product or some useful type of output.

**processing time** The amount of time taken by the computer to complete arithmetical or other steps.

**production quota** The amount of work that management expects employees to complete.

**productivity study chart** A record of time spent by employees in major activities.

**profit maximization** The effort to make profits (the amount of money left after expenses and taxes have been paid) as high as possible.

**program** A detailed set of computer instructions.

**program and data storage capability** The ability of a computer to store or hold internally its own instructions and data to be processed.

**programming languages** A special set of symbols and words that are recognized by the computer.

**promotion** The formal granting of a positive advancement to an employee.

**proposal** A recommendation, usually in written form, which proposes a new course of action.

**psychological barriers** Communication barriers that result from faulty reasoning by either the message sender or message receiver.

**punched card** A paper card containing holes that represent letters, numbers, and/or special characters.

**punched tape** A paper tape containing holes that represent data.

**purchasing agent** A worker who has responsibility and authority to make selections for purchase by an organization.

## Q

**quality standard** Management's expectation about the quality of work employees should produce.

**quit rate** The number of people voluntarily terminating their jobs during a given period of time.

## R

**random access** The ability to go directly to any part of an input-storage device without having to scan previous data to get to a particular item of data.

**ranking** Putting in order the names of employees according to ability and performance from high to low.

**rank promotions** Promotions usually characterized by a change in job title and an advancement in pay.

**rating** Making a judgment about ability and performance of an individual according to preset categories or factors of evaluation.

**record request form** A form used to request a record from filing personnel.

**records center** A low-cost area used for storing inactive records.

**records management** A service that deals with developing, maintaining, and disposing of all types of organizational records.

**records retention schedule** A listing of the types of records kept by a company along with the length of time each type of record must be retained.

**rectilinear pattern** Straight rows of desks and other office furnishings.

**reduction ratio** A figure referring to the size of microfilm images; a reduction ratio of 24 times means that the image is one twenty-fourth the size of the original document.

**reference checks** Communications with individuals who know a job applicant for the purpose of learning more about the suitability of the applicant for the work being sought.

**reference initials** Initials placed at the bottom of a business letter by the typist of that letter. The initials are used to determine who typed the letter should that need ever arise.

**reference ratio** A figure indicating the degree to which groups of records are accessed.

**registered mail** Mail for which a receipt is given to the customer at the time of mailing and for which a record of the mailing is provided at the post office.

**reprographics** A technology pertaining to all reproducing, duplicating, and copying processes in an organization.

**resource allocation** Manner in which resources are divided between persons or segments of the organization.

**resource person** A person who provides advisory help and necessary materials to complete a job.

**resources** The people, money, and materials available to the manager that assist in accomplishing specific objectives.

**retrieval speed** The amount of time required to provide records that are requested.

**research and development** The function of a department or an organization devoted to the creation and refinement of new products or services to be sold by the organization.

**reward** Something desirable given as a result of the performance of a certain act.

**role playing** A group interaction situation in which group members act as though they were other individuals.

**roll film** Microfilm that is 16 or 35 millimeters wide, usually 100 feet in length, and stored in rolls.

## S

**safe messages** Messages that will reflect no negative implications on the message sender.

**scientific management** An approach to management that relies on an organized and systematic study of business operations. This approach tends to be cold and unresponsive to individual needs.

**second-class mail** Newspapers and magazines issued at least four times a year.

**selective perception** The mental characteristic of perceiving only a small part of the stimuli that *could* be perceived.

**selective retention** The mental characteristic of remembering only a small part of the stimuli that is perceived by the brain.

**selective transmission** The human tendency to communicate, or transmit, only a small part of the information held in the brain.

**self-acceptance** The degree to which an individual is satisfied with his or her level of achievement and development.

**self-actualization** The process of reaching one's potential.

**self-appraisal** An evaluation made by the individual about his or her own performance.

**self-discipline** Self-control; an individual becomes responsible for his or her own behavior and actions.

**self-evaluation** Another name for self-appraisal.

**self-fulfilling prophecy** The tendency of people to become what they think others expect them to become. Also, visualizing the achievement of a goal in order to bring about the realization of the goal.

**self-generating** A characteristic where individuals are self-motivated: they move on their own without having to be prodded by supervisors. A self-starter.

**selling style** A leadership style wherein the leader persuades others to accept his or her ideas and may resort to manipulation.

**semantics problem** A problem between two or more individuals caused by the individuals' perceiving the meaning of words differently.

**seniority** Individuals' ranks based on the number of months or years they have been in a job.

**serial communication** The passing of a given message through a series of individuals.

**service center** An organization employing its own computer facilities to perform computer services for other organizations on a fee basis.

**shared logic word-processing systems** A word processor system featuring a number of word-processing typewriters (terminals) connected to a minicomputer.

**simulation** A process in which a model of a real situation is acted upon by a computer. Many alternatives are tried so that results of a series of decisions can be predicted.

**Social Security** A federal government program designed to provide financial benefits for retired persons and others needing assistance.

**soft information** Qualitative, verbal type of usable data.

**software** A collection of programs and routines that makes the use of hardware possible.

**space standards** An allotment of office space according to type of job or level of authority.

**spacial communication** Messages that are communicated by the way one uses the space in which he or she lives and works.

**speakerphone** A special telephone adaptation that allows the user to talk and listen on the telephone line without lifting the handset of the telephone.

**special delivery** A service that provides for a mailed item to be delivered as soon as practicable after it arrives at the addressee's post office.

**specimen checklist** A list of critical incidents pertaining to the job of an employee from which the appraiser selects the ones most typical of the person being appraised.

**spirit duplicator** A low-cost duplication process used for short-run jobs not requiring high-quality print.

**stand-alone word processor** A word processor that contains its own memory and processing power without being connected to a host computer. Also known as **stand-alone mode.**

**standard time** The time an employee should take to complete a given amount of work.

**station hunting** The capability of a telephone system to automatically route an incoming call from a busy line to an open line.

**status symbol** Anything that makes a person feel more important because the symbol is socially desirable.

**steering committee** A group of knowledgeable and often high-level people who provide guidance and direction for a given program.

**stencil duplicator** A duplication process utilizing a stencil through which an ink image passes to the paper. This duplicator produces print quality significantly better than that of the spirit process but not as good as the offset process.

**stopwatch method** Another method for setting time standards that uses a stopwatch to determine times taken to accomplish detailed elements of a task.

**stress interviewing** The use of intensive questioning to determine the emotional control of an interviewee.

**subjective feelings** Human feelings arising out of bias or emotions as opposed to those growing out of objective, logical thought.

**suggestion/question boxes** Receptacles used to collect suggestions and questions from employees regarding the operation of the organization.

**supervisory management** The level of management that is in direct contact with employees and is responsible for achieving production goals.

**system** A group of parts or elements that interact to achieve a particular goal. Involves input, processing, and output.

**systems analysis** A detailed investigation of an existing system to develop improvements, or a detailed planning process to define a new system.

## T

**tabulator or accounting machine** A machine that adds, subtracts, and prints reports based on data obtained from punched cards.

**task dimension** A manager's attention to getting the job accomplished. One dimension of leadership style.

**task force** A group of experts organized into a committee for the purpose of solving a major problem or implementing a new program.

**team building** The reorganization of individual workers, now doing only a small part of a total process or unit of work, into a team that is responsible for completing the total process or unit of work. Normally the team is self-regulating.

**telecommunication services** Administrative services established to provide an organization with telephone-related communication capabilities.

**telephone-input dictation system** A dictation system that utilizes a company's regular telephone system for dictation to the word-processing center.

**teletype machine** A data transmittal device that uses punched paper tape and telephone lines.

**teletypewriters** Typewriter-like machines that use punched paper tape to send messages over telecommunication lines. Telex and TWX are the two types of teletypewriters available to users.

**telling style** An autocratic leadership style that places emphasis on the manager's control of the situation.

**terminal** A machine used to obtain information from or insert information into computers or related office equipment.

**termination** The process of ending the employment of an individual for whatever reason.

**text editing** The process of changing information (adding, deleting, rearranging, etc.) in a report, letter, or other written document.

**text editing machines** Typewriters that have the capability to store, manipulate, edit, and play back written documents.

**Theory *X*** A set of assumptions in which people are viewed as being basically lazy. The primary function of management is to control employees and make sure that they do what they are supposed to do.

**Theory *Y*** Another set of assumptions about people that contrasts with Theory *X*. In Theory *Y*, people are viewed as wanting to do their best. Management becomes a supportive function.

**third-class mail** Circulars, booklets, catalogs, and other similar printed materials not otherwise required as first-class mail; merchandise, farm and factory products, photographs, keys, and printed drawings, all of which must weigh less than 16 ounces.

**tie lines** Long-distance telephone lines that are reserved totally for the use of an organization that has leased the lines.

**time analysis** A record of time spent arranged by categories and an analysis of time in order to develop more effective patterns of using time.

**time and motion studies** An analysis of the time required and methods used to complete a unit of work.

**time sharing** An arrangement that allows several organizations or parts of organizations to share time and costs of computer operations.

**top-down approach** An approach to implement a program conceived of by top management and sent down into the organization.

**top management support** Active interest in and promotion of programs by an organization's top managers

**touch-tone telephone system** A telephone system comprised of telephones that require the user to depress or "touch" numbered buttons, rather than "dialing" certain numbers in placing a call.

**trade fairs** Conventions held for companies or individuals having a similar business interest; e.g., word-processing personnel.

**training problem** The existence of a condition caused by insufficiently preparing a worker to perform a job.

**transfer of training** The process of retaining information or skills learned in one situation for application in another situation.

**transistors and diodes** A primary component of second generation computers. They are small electronic devices similar to those found in radio and television sets.

**turnaround time** The time required to complete a given amount of work from start to finish.

**turnover** The rate during a given period at which employees leave an organization and are replaced by newly hired people. Turnover formula:

$$\text{Turnover} = \frac{\text{total number of terminations}}{\text{average annual employment}} \times 100.$$

## V

**vacuum tubes** A primary component of first generation computers. They are relatively large electronic devices similar to those found in early radio and television sets.

**valid test** The quality possessed by a test when it measures what it is designed to measure. Also called *test validity.*

**verbal messages** Word messages, either written or spoken.

**vertical file** A filing cabinet consisting of two or more file drawers stacked on top of each other, with the drawers opening from the narrow side of the file.

**vertical job loading** The process of moving down supervisory and decision-making responsibility to jobs lower in the organization.

**vestibule training** Training that takes place away from an employee's work station and consists of training other than performing real work activities.

**video conferencing** Conferences conducted with the aid of television.

**videodisk** A high-volume information storage device about the size of a phonograph record that is capable of recording sound and pictures as well as words and numbers.

**virtual storage** A method found in fourth-generation computers that increases computer storage capacity.

**visible card files** Card-sized files in which the cards are arranged horizontally on pull-out trays, with a small portion of each card exposed to the user.

**visual distractors** Objects or people that are present in a communication setting and that attract the attention of a person who is or could be receiving another message.

**voice response unit** A terminal that transmits output with a voice-type response.

## W

**wage incentive system** A bonus paid for work completed above a set standard.

**warm-up period** The beginning of an interview during which small talk is engaged in to relax the person being interviewed.

**WATS (Wide Area Telecommunications Service)** A special service provided by the telephone company whereby an organization can pay a set fee for a large volume of either incoming or outgoing long-distance telephone calls. The one fee covers all the calls rather than having a charge for each call.

**wheel file** A card-sized file with the cards extending from the center of the file like spokes in a wheel.

**white sound** Another name for masking sound.

**word-processing center** An organized group of secretarial personnel and automated typing equipment devoted to processing typewritten letters, memos, reports, and other business materials.

**word-processing typewriter** An automatic typewriter that has built-in memory and high-speed typing capabilities.

**work distribution chart** A matrix or table showing time spent on tasks by various employees. Tasks are classified by major activity.

**work flow** The movement of documents being processed in the office.

**work measurement** A program that reports the time taken to accomplish work or the number of units of work completed versus a standard time or number of units.

**work sampling method** A method for setting time standards that involves making observations at random time intervals.

**work simplification** An analysis technique aimed at specializing work to make it more simple and therefore more routine.

**work standards** The time required to complete a given amount of work, or the number of work units that can be completed in a given time period.

# Index